INVITATION
TO
CHRISTIAN
SPIRITUALITY

INVITATION TO CHRISTIAN SPIRITUALITY

An Ecumenical Anthology

Edited by
JOHN R. TYSON

New York   Oxford
OXFORD UNIVERSITY PRESS
1999

Oxford University Press

Oxford   New York
Athens   Auckland   Bangkok   Bogotá   Buenos Aires   Calcutta
Cape Town   Chennai   Dar es Salaam   Delhi   Florence   Hong Kong   Istanbul
Karachi   Kuala Lumpur   Madrid   Melbourne   Mexico City   Mumbai
Nairobi   Paris   São Paulo   Singapore   Taipei   Tokyo   Toronto   Warsaw

and associated companies in
Berlin   Ibadan

Copyright © 1999 by Oxford University Press, Inc.

Published by Oxford University Press, Inc.
198 Madison Avenue, New York, New York 10016

Library of Congress Cataloging-in-Publication Data

Invitation to Christian spirituality : an ecumenical anthology /
edited by John R. Tyson.
   p. cm.
   Includes index.
   ISBN 0-19-510636-9 (alk. paper). — ISBN 0-19-510637-7 (pbk. :
alk. paper)
   1. Spirituality.   I. Tyson, John R.
BV4501.2.I58 1999
248'.09—dc21   98-18227
                                      CIP

1 3 5 7 9 8 6 4 2
Printed in the United States of America
on acid-free paper.

In Memory of My Father
JOHN J. TYSON 1920–1993
Who taught me more about
Christian Spirituality
than either of us realized.

Contents

Contents

Contents

Contents

Contents

Contents

5. CONTEMPORARY SPIRITUALITY 376

Contents

Acknowledgments

There are always many people and publishers to whom "thanks" are due in the production of a literary work, and especially when the work is a comprehensive anthology. First, I want to express my gratitude to friends and colleagues who made formative suggestions for the plan of this *Invitation* or read portions of the manuscript: Ms. Lynn Neal, a former student of mine and current graduate student at the University of North Carolina; Dr. Mary Elizabeth Moore, School of Theology at Claremont, California; Dr. James Pain, Dean of the Graduate School of Drew University, Madison, New Jersey; Dr. William Thompson, at Duquesne University, Pittsburgh; and Dr. Geoffrey Wainwright of the Divinity School, Duke University, Durham, North Carolina, and to Fr. Neil O'Connell, O.F.M. at St. Stephen of Hungry Church, New York. I am also grateful to Mrs. Linda Doezema and Mrs. Eileen Spear, librarians at Williard Houghton Memorial Library, Houghton College, Houghton, New York, for their frequent efforts at locating rare books and arcane editions.

I express my thanks to the following people and publishers for their permission to include their published materials in this collection:

Dr. Rosemary Rader, of Carleton College, Northfield, Minnesota, for the use of "The Martyrdom of Perpetua," from *A Lost Tradition: Women Writers of the Early Church*, translated by Patricia Wilson-Kastner, G. Ronald Kastner, Ann Millin, Rosemary Rader, and Jeremiah Reedy, University Press of America, 1981.

Dr. Patricia Wilson-Kastner, for the use of "Egeria: Account of Her Pilgrimage," from *A Lost Tradition*, University Press of America, 1981.

Dr. Hans J. Hillerbrand, of Duke University, Durham, North Carolina, for the use of Erasmus's "Letter to Paul Voltz," from his *Erasmus and His Age; Selected Letters of Desiderius Erasmus*, Harper & Row, 1970.

Dr. Rosemary Ruether, of Garrett Evangelical Theological Seminary, Evanston, IL, for the use of a selection from her *Disputed Questions on Being a Christian*, Abingdon Press, 1982.

Mr. James Armstrong and Princeton Theological Seminary, Princeton, New Jersey, for the use of quotations from *The Great Shorter Works of Pascal*, by Emile Cailliet and John Blankenagel, Greenwood Press, 1948.

Alba House, for selections from *The Life and Sayings of Saint Catherine of Genoa*, translated by Paul Gavin, 1964.

Augsburg Fortress Press, for selections from *Luther's Works*, Volume 34, edited by Louis Spitz, 1960; *Pia Desideria*, by Philip Jacob Spener, translated by T. G. Tappert, 1964; and *Liturgies of the Western Church*, edited by Bard Thompson, 1961.

Bantam Doubleday Dell Publishing Group, Inc., for selections from *The Autobiography of St. Therese of Lisieux: The Story of a Soul*, translated by John Beevers, 1957; and *The Practice of the Presence of God*, by Brother Lawrence of the Resurrection, translated by John J. Delaney, 1977.

Catholic University Press, for selections from *Basil the Great: Ascetical Works*, translated by Sister Monica Wagner, 1962.

Cassell PLC, for selections from *Crying in the Wilderness*, by Desmond Tutu, 1982; Crossroad Publishing Company, for selections from *Beguine Spirituality*, edited by Fiona Bowie and translated by Oliver Davies, 1990; and *The Practice of Faith*, by Karl Rahner, 1992.

Curtis Brown, Ltd., for selections from *The Seven Story Mountain*, by Thomas Merton, 1975.

William B. Eerdmans Publishing Company, for selections from *Speaking the Truth: Ecumenism, Liberation and Black Theology*, by James H. Cone, 1986; and *Crying in the Wilderness*, by Desmond Tutu, 1982.

Harcourt Brace and Company, for selections from *The Seven Story Mountain*, by Thomas Merton, 1976; and *Surprised by Joy: The Shape of My Early Life*, by C. S. Lewis, 1955.

HarperCollins Publishers, for selections from *Celebration of Discipline: The Path to Spiritual Growth*, by Richard Foster, 1978; *A Gift for God: Prayers and Meditations*, by Mother Teresa, 1975; *Purity of Heart Is to Will One Thing*, by Soren Kierkegaard, translated by Douglas V. Steere, 1966; and the *Screwtape Letters*, by C. S. Lewis, 1982.

Herald Press, for selections from *The Legacy of Michael Sattler*, by John H. Yoder, 1973.

Hodder and Stoughton Publishers, for selections from *Celebration of Discipline: The Path to Spiritual Growth*, by Richard Foster, 1978.

The Howard Thurman Educational Trust, for a selection from *Jesus and the Disinherited*, by Howard Thurman, 1976.

The Institute of Carmelite Studies, for selections from *The Collected Works of St. Teresa of Avila*, Vol. I, translated by Kieran Kavanaugh and Otilio Rodriguez, 1976.

New Directions Publishing Corp., for selections from *New Seeds of Contemplation*, by Thomas Merton, 1972.

Paulist Press, for the use of selections from *Albert and Thomas: Selected Writings*, translated by Simon Tugwell, 1988; *Bartolome' de las Casas, The Only Way to Draw All People to a Living Faith*, translated by Helen Parish and Francis Sullivan, 1992; *Bernard of Clairvaux: Selected Works*, translated by G. R. Evans, 1987; *Bonaventure: The Soul's Journey into God, the Tree of Life, the Life of St. Francis*, translated by Ewert Cousins, 1978; *Ephrem the Syrian*, translated by Kathleen McVey, 1989; *Francis and Clare: The Complete Works*, translated by Regis Armstrong and Ignatius Brady, 1982; *Francis de Sales, Jane de Chantal: Letters of Spiritual Direction*, translated by Peronne Marie Thibert, 1988; *Gregory of Nyssa: The Life of Moses*, translated by Abraham Malherbe and Evertt Ferguson, 1978; *Hildegard of Bingen: Scivias*, translated by Mother Columba Hart and Jane Bishop, 1990; *Ignatius of Loyola: The Spiritual Exercises and Selected Works*, translated by George Ganss, 1991; *Johann Arndt: True Christianity*, translated by Peter Erb, 1979; *John Cassian: Conferences*, translated by Colm Lubheid, 1985; *Julian of Norwich: Showings*, translated by James Walsh, 1978; *Maximus the Confessor: Selected Writings*, translated by George Berthold, 1985; *Meister Eckhart: The Essential Sermons, Commentaries, Treatises, and Defense*, translated by Edmund Colledge and Bernard McGinn, 1981; *Meister Eckhart: Teacher and Preacher*, translated by Bernard McGinn, 1986; *Origen*, translated by Rowan Greer, 1979; and *Pseudo-Dionysius: The Complete Works*, translated by Colm Lubheid, 1987.

Orbis Books, for selections from *We Drink from Our Own Wells: The Spiritual Journey of a People*, by Gustavo Gutierrez, 1984; and *My Soul Looks Back*, by James Cone, 1986.

Penguin Books USA, for a selection from *The Essential Erasmus*, translated by John P. Dolan, 1964.

Putnam Publishing Group, for selections from *Waiting for God*, by Simone Weil, 1979.

SCM Press, Ltd., for selections from *The Cost of Discipleship*, by Dietrich Bonhoeffer, 1959; *The Practice of Faith*, by Karl Rahner, 1992; and *We Drink from Our Own Wells: The Spiritual Journey of a People*, by Gustavo Gutierrez, 1984.

Simon and Schuster, for selections from *A Source Book for Medieval History*, by Oliver J. Thatcher and Edgar H. McNeal, 1905; and *The Cost of Discipleship*, by Dietrich Bonhoeffer, 1959.

The Society for Promoting Christian Knowledge (SPCK), for selections from *Prayer*, by Karl Barth, 1985; and *Beguine Spirituality*, edited by Fiona Bowie and translated by Oliver Davies, 1990.

Westminster John Knox Press, for selections from *Prayer*, by Karl Barth, 1985.

Writers House, Inc., by arrangement with the heirs to the estate of Martin Luther King, Jr. for selections from *Strength to Love*, by Martin Luther King, Jr., 1963; copyright renewed by Coretta Scott King, 1991.

INVITATION
TO
CHRISTIAN
SPIRITUALITY

Introduction

Invitation to Christian Spirituality

NATURE OF CHRISTIAN SPIRITUALITY

"Christian Spirituality" describes the relationship, union, and conformity with God that a Christian experiences through his or her reception of the grace of God, and a corresponding willingness to turn from sin and (to use a Pauline phrase) "to walk according to the Spirit."[1] This relationship with God is made possible because of the life, death, and resurrection of Jesus Christ; hence Fr. George Lane aptly emphasized that "Christian Spirituality is always rooted in the experience of Jesus."[2] Karl Rahner described the experience of Jesus as a unique, unsurpassable, and total event: "This experience in which Jesus becomes for a particular person the event of the unique and qualitatively unsurpassable and irreversible approach of God, is always affected by the totality of its elements as a single entity even if each of the elements is not necessarily immediately present and explicitly and clearly in conscious awareness."[3] This is certainly the witness of the New Testament; the Synoptic writers exemplify discipleship as following Jesus (Mt 4:18ff), the Johannine writings depict it as union with Christ through love

---

[1] As described by St. Paul in Romans 6:1–19, for example, where the apostle urges Christians to be "dead to sin and alive to God in Christ" (v. 11). Because they are "united with Christ" (v. 5), Christians are no longer "slaves to sin," but rather are in the process of being "obedient [to God] from the heart" (v. 17). Cf. Romans 8:1–15, and numerous similar texts. Viewing this process from the standpoint of mysticism, Walter Capps and Wendy Wright point to the "unitive" and "transformative" dimensions of Christian experience. Cf. *Silent Fire* (New York: Harper and Row, 1978), pp. 3–9.

[2] George A. Lane, S.J., *Christian Spirituality: An Historical Sketch* (Chicago: Loyola University Press, 1984), p. v.

[3] Karl Rahner, *The Practice of Faith: A Handbook of Contemporary Spirituality* (New York: Crossroad, 1986), p. 8.

(1 Jn 4:13ff), in St. Paul Christian life is described as a "new life" that is ours through union with Christ's death and resurrection (Rom 6), Hebrews and I Peter depict Christian life as a pilgrimage: "looking to Jesus the pioneer and perfecter of our faith" (Heb 12:2), who has left us "an example that you should follow in his steps" (I Pet 2:21).

The experience of Jesus Christ is an accepting, healing, and purifying experience; it is manifested to Christians by the power of the Holy Spirit.[4] To be united with Christ is to be united with Christ's Spirit (1 Cor 6:17), and conformed to Christ's image (Rom 8:29); thus "life in the Spirit" is synonymous with "life in Christ." This union has as its goal (Grk. *telos*) a renewal and renovation of the person that produces new life and renewed attitudes. It is, as Jesus described it, an "everlasting" (Jn 4:14), and "abundant" life (Jn 10:10). Or as St. Paul wrote: "If anyone is in Christ he is a new creation; the old has passed away, behold the new has come" (2 Cor 5:17). Being "in Christ" creates a desire for conformity between a Christian's life, attitudes, and aspirations and those of Jesus Christ (Phil 2:3–11).[5] Hence, the goal of Christian Spirituality is Christlikeness and a restoration of the image of God (2 Pet 1:4), wherein humans were originally created (Gen 1:26). While Christians differ as to whether this Christlikeness is to be anticipated in this life or in the life to come, all concur that "Christian Spirituality" implies a growth in grace and sanctity; it, therefore, functions as a popular term for the doctrine and practice of sanctification (from the Latin *sanctus*, "holy," and hence "to be made holy").[6]

Relationships, if they are valid and authentic ones, are characterized by a sense of partnership and mutuality. So it is also in the Divine-human relationship. In terms of Christian Spirituality, mutuality means that the grace of God, received through faith in Jesus Christ, must be received and acted upon by the human will. Having been reconciled to God and received into God's fellowship by grace, through faith, we must also apply ourselves to the things of God and the means whereby God works within us. St. Paul described well the Divine and human sides of this cooperative effort when he wrote: "work out your own salvation with fear and trembling; for God is at work in you, both to will and to work for his good pleasure" (Phil 2:12–13). The appropriate response to the gift

---

[4]Cf. John 14–17, where Jesus described the office of the Holy Spirit for his disciples. Salient features included: (1) The Holy Spirit will be "another Counselor" to them, and thereby the physical absence of Jesus would be rectified by the presence of the Holy Spirit (14:15–16). (2) The Spirit will call to mind the things of Christ (14:25–26), will bear witness to Christ (15:26), and will glorify Christ (16:12–16). (3) The Holy Spirit will convince them of sin and righteousness (16:8–12).

[5]Cf. E. Schweizer, "Pneuma," in *The Theological Dictionary of the New Testament*, 10 Vols. edited by Gerhard Friedrich (Grand Rapids, Mich.: Wm. B. Eerdmans, 1968) (hereafter: TDNT), Vol. VI, pp. 332–455, espec. pp. 415-36 on the spirit in Pauline theology. Josef Sudbrack, "Spirituality," in *Sacramentum Mundi*, edited by Karl Rahner et al. (New York: Herder and Herder, 1970), Vol. VI, pp. 148–49, offers an excellent survey of the role of the Holy Spirit in Christian Spirituality.

[6]The title of Donald Alexander's useful book illustrates this correlation quite well: *Christian Spirituality: Five Views of Sanctification* (Downers Grove, Ill.: Inter Varsity Press, 1988).

of grace is to live a life of grace, to "walk according to the Spirit" and not "according to the flesh."[7] Thus, Richard McBrien correctly observed that Christian Spirituality ". . . is the cultivation of a style of life consistent with the Spirit of the Risen Christ within us and with our status as members of the Body of Christ."[8]

There are few shortcuts in the journey from being a sin-dominated person to becoming a spiritually empowered, Christlike person; it is not a journey that is made quickly or easily. It is often a pilgrimage that proceeds steadily and incrementally as a Christian gives himself or herself more and more over to God's will and is correspondingly recreated more and more in God's character and likeness. The path toward godliness leads through participation in the "means of grace" (such as Word and Sacrament) and "spiritual disciplines" (such as prayer, fasting, and Christian service).

It is very difficult to give a precise definition for "Christian Spirituality."[10] The tremendous scope of the concepts and experiences involved in the process of renewal and restoration makes precision difficult. Thus, the concept of spirituality often is found with various descriptions, such as "Augustinian spirituality," "Franciscan spirituality," "Lutheran spirituality," or "Wesleyan spirituality," which point to various historical patterns that mark out the way of Christlikeness and relationship with God. While there is deep and foundational unanimity among Christians as to the goal of Christian Spirituality, there is a remarkable diversity within the Christian tradition when it comes to the question of "how" this pilgrimage should be most meaningfully pursued. This diversity of spiritual traditions within the Christian faith is a veritable smorgasbord of spiritual resources. But this diversity should also remind us, contrary to the phraseology of garment labels, that "one size" does not "fit all." The texts presented in this collection serve as *an invitation* to a great feast, and yet each person's meal involves matters of personal "taste" and selection; each person's pilgrimage toward godliness is distinctly his or her own pilgrimage. These texts are best read as well-proven road signs along the way to holiness; they should *not* be read as recipes that guarantee the desired results.

The term *Christian Spirituality* is a particularly apt one for describing the thrust of this book, partly because it has meaning and significance all across the Christian tradition and partly because it focuses our attention squarely upon the role

---

[7]Cf.Galatians 3:3–6, Romans 8:4–13, for discussions of these phrases.

[8]Richard P. McBrien, *Catholicism*, 2 vols. (Minneapolis: Winston Press, 1980), Vol. II, p. 1057–58.

[9]That the life of Christian spirituality is aptly described as a journey or pilgrimage is readily demonstrated by the titles of various classical works; St. Bonaventure, *The Soul's Journey into God* (c. 1259); St. John of the Cross, *Ascent of Mt. Carmel* (1587); Robert Bellarmine (1542–1621), *The Soul's Ascension to God*; John Bunyan, *The Pilgrim's Progress* (1675), and etc.

[10]Jones, Wainwright, and Yarnold write: " 'Spirituality,' we confess, is a vague word, often used with no clear meaning, or with a wide and vague significance, but we can think of no better single word to describe the subject" (p. xxii). They did, however, manage to write an extensive and very useful "Note" on the meaning of "Spirituality." Cheslyn Jones, Geoffrey Wainwright, and Edward Yarnold, *The Study of Spirituality* (New York: Oxford University Press, 1986), pp. xxiv–vi.

of the Holy Spirit in creating *spirituality* or sanctification.[11] Other terms, like *piety* and *sanctification,* for example, are less insistent about the source of the renewal they seek. But there is also a danger inherent in theological language that stresses spirituality if one understands it against the backdrop of a dualism that seeks to separate the "spiritual" from "physical" realities. St. Paul's injunctions not to live or walk "according to the flesh" but rather to walk "according to the Spirit" were not given to urge us to fly from physicality or the challenges of life in the world; rather they urge Christians to find their motives, aspirations, and bases for action in the Holy Spirit and the things of God and not in fallen, sinful, rebellious, and self-serving attitudes that do not please God. Christian Spirituality does not signal a flight from physical life, or a withdrawal from the challenges of life in the world; rather it describes the processes whereby Christians seek to live holy lives, while in the flesh and while engaging the challenges of this world. It is a call to actualize Jesus's mandate to be "in" but not "of" the world (Jn 17:15–18) and to live by the Pauline injunction: "Do not be conformed to this world, but be transformed by the renewal of your mind, that you may prove what is the will of God, what is good and acceptable and perfect" (Rom 12:2).

THEMES OF CHRISTIAN SPIRITUALITY

This brief survey is not an attempt at a systematic or constructive theology; it is rather an attempt to introduce a few foundational themes that undergird Christian Spirituality. These foundational themes cut across the boundaries that separate Christians into various Christian traditions and in so doing they remind us of the fundamental and organic unity of the enterprise of Christian Spirituality. But these very same foundational themes take on diverse theological nuances and undergird divergent Christian practices within the various spiritual traditions. This diversity is a good and legitimate aspect of the expression of Body of Christ; indeed, we need to hear afresh the diverse and luminous vision of the various saints—the women and men of God—who have grasped God and been grasped by God in transforming ways. This spiritual diversity is a means of our sanctification; walking with Polycarp or Perpetua, with Martin Luther or Martin Luther King may take us beyond our "comfort zone" to a place where spiritual growth occurs. Even historical debates about Christian doctrine (Luther and the Council of Trent) or Christian practice (Antony and Benedict) have the potential of stretching and correcting our perception of the life of faith. Sometimes it takes both stone and steel rubbing against each other to hone our spirituality to a sharper edge. While the saints may not agree, for example, as to the precise theological expla-

---

[11]So profound is the connection between the Holy Spirit and Christian Spirituality, as they are presented in Scripture and Christian tradition, that Josef Sudbrack concluded that the "banality . . . of the word [Spirituality] . . . is only the product of our own time, as also is unfortunately, the enemic unreality which is almost always connected with the word spirituality." Cf. Sudbrack, "Spirituality," p. 149.

nation of justification or the efficacy of the sacraments, they will certainly be concerned to pursue justification (as they understand it) and to meet God in those ways which they believe God has ordained. Hence our focus upon spirituality points us through the various means of grace and models of spirituality to relationship with, adoration of, and conformity with the God and Father of our Lord Jesus Christ—which is the goal and end of Christian Spirituality.

Creation and Redemption

Creation and the physical world, in Christian Spirituality, are not viewed as being evil per se. We must hear afresh the benedictionlike pronouncements that punctuated the Genesis creation account: seven times God declared "it was good."[12] Created physical and material life, in the Judeo-Christian tradition, is *good* life. Quite unlike their dualistic neighbors, the Hebrew ("Old") and Christian ("New") testaments did not associate being finite, physical, or material with being evil. Creation and creaturely life could and did become the *locus* of evil, but they were not—in and of themselves—evil. Hence, the Psalmist exclaimed: "The heavens are telling the glory of God; and the firmament proclaims his handiwork (19:1)." The created world issues a voiceless declaration of the knowledge and character of its Creator (Ps 19:1–4). It was for this reason that St. Paul concluded that all people ought to acknowledge and obey God: "God is plain to them, because God has shown it [truth] to them. Ever since the creation of the world [God's] invisible nature, namely, his eternal power and deity, has been clearly perceived in the things that have been made" (Rom 1:19–20).

Contemplation of nature and the physical world is a tremendous resource for Christian Spirituality. St. Francis of Assisi (1181?–1226) experienced a profound sense of God's presence through the contemplation of the various aspects of nature and physical life, and in naming them "Brother Sun," "Brother Wind," "Sister Water," and "Sister Bodily Death," Francis affirmed his oneness with God through the natural order.[13] And yet there is within Christian Spirituality, as indeed there was in St. Francis himself, a certain ambivalence about material things. In celebrating the goodness of the creation one must not succumb to the temptation to make creation an end in itself. The creation must not be confused with its Creator—that would be tantamount to turning a window of God's presence into a door that leads to idolatry. In Francis's case (and many others), this temptation was averted by embracing apostolic poverty. In his refusal to own anything St. Francis freed himself from being owned by things.

There is also a sort of ambivalence inherent in the biblical account of the creation of man and woman. Man (*Adam*) was "formed of dust from the ground (Heb. *Adamah*)" and God "breathed into his nostrils the breath of life; and man

---

[12]Genesis 1:3,10,12,18,21,25, and 31.

[13]Cf. Francis of Assisi, "The Canticle of Brother Sun," in *Francis and Clare: The Complete Writings*, edited by Regis Armstrong and Ignatius Brady (New York: Paulist Press, 1982), pp. 37–39. Cf. pp. 165–66 below.

became a living being" (Gen 2:7). This process indicates something of humanity's conflicting identities; linked by frailty and creatureliness to the earth ("from dust to dust," Gen 3:19), and yet also linked to God. Scripture esteems human beings as being created in "the image of God" (Gen 1:26; Lat. *imago Dei*). The creation narrative (Gen 2), which describes the creation of man and woman, shows God drawing near to them and bestowing dignity and honor upon them by allowing them to participate in the creative process. Hence, the Psalmist marveled at the unique status that all people, personified in their ancestor Adam, enjoy before God: ". . . thou has made him little less than God, and dost crown him with glory and honor. Thou hast given him dominion over the works of thy hands; thou has put all things under his feet . . ." (Ps 8:5–6).[14]

While there are many theories as to the precise meaning of the affirmation that human beings are created *imago Dei*, several foundational themes derived from it are particularly significant for Christian Spirituality. First, to affirm that human beings are created *imago Dei* speaks of our being created by and for fellowship with God. The human personality was created to mirror or reflect the Divine personality. This means that human life and Divine life are deeply intertwined. There is in the human heart a longing for fellowship with God. The Psalmist epitomized this "thirst" for God when he wrote: "As a hart longs for flowing streams, so longs my soul for Thee, O God. My soul thirsts for God, for the living God" (Ps 42:1–2). This aspect of the *imago Dei* was depicted, in Genesis 2, as the first man and the first woman walked and talked with God in the paradisiacal garden; they cooperated with God in the creation and naming of the animals, which signified humanity's dominion over them.

The interwoven character of human and Divine existence took expression in what St. Augustine (354–430)[15] and John Calvin (1509–64)[16] called "double knowledge" (Lat. *duplex cognitio*). It meant, on the one hand, that "no one can look upon himself without immediately turning his thoughts to the contemplation of God, in whom he lives and moves."[17] And yet conversely, as Calvin wrote, "it is certain that man never achieves a clear knowledge [of himself] unless he has first looked upon God's face, and then descended from contemplating him to scrutinize himself."[18] Consequently, humanity, when alienated from God by sin and forced to live "east of Eden" (Gen 3:24), experienced not only estrangement from God but also a loss of humanity's authentic identity. In Christian Spirituality this aspect of the *imago Dei* takes expression in the unitive dimension of Christian mysticism, through which people like Meister Eckhart (1260–1327), plumbed the

---

[14]Compare Psalm 8:5–6 with Genesis 1:27–31.

[15]R. S. Pine-Coffin, trans., *Saint Augustine: Confessions* (London: Penguin Books, 1961), Bk. I, ch. 1–2,6, pp. 21–25.

[16]John Calvin, *Institutes of the Christian Religion*, edited by John T. McNeill, 2 vols. (Philadelphia: Westminster Press, 1977), Vol. I, p. 40.

[17]Ibid., p. 35.

[18]Ibid., p. 37.

depths of the inner person in search of the created identity and kinship with God. It is also seen in those people like Catherine of Genoa (1447–1510), who through encountering God's love came to a new and deeper understanding of herself and her role in the world.

The homelessness of the human soul, as separated from God, not only has implications for our self-understanding (*duplex cognitio*), but also for our self-acceptance. In their alienation from God—in whose image they are created—humans lose the ability to truly know and love themselves. St. Bernard of Clairvaux (1090–1153) believed that the love of God and neighbor necessitated an appropriate love of self, but only love of God can give a person a genuine love for one's neighbor and one's self. Thus, Bernard discerned four "degrees" of loving God that, upon passing through them, eventually healed the alienation we experience with God, our neighbor, and ourselves.[19] Through the transformation of the human will, the will (or self) finds its true home in God's will, and it subsequently loves God and itself with pure love and holy intention. St. Bernard described it this way: "O holy and chaste love! O sweet and tender affection! O pure and sinless intention of the will—the more pure and sinless in that there is no mixture of self-will in it, the more sweet and tender in that everything it feels is divine. To love in this way is to become like God [Lat. *deificatio*]."[20] The theme of participation in the Divine through the transforming power of Divine love is a profound element in Christian Spirituality. While the terminology is vivid, and perhaps a bit extravagant, it is nonetheless true that—through the transforming power of God's love (1 Jn 3)—Christians become "partakers of the divine nature" (2 Pet 1:40).

Second, humanity's identity, as beings created *imago Dei*, suggests that there is a sense in which we are called to reflect the Divine character. "Be ye holy, as I am holy," is an oft-repeated injunction that undergirds biblical ethics and aspirations.[21] Scripture urges those who love God to reflect God's actions and attitudes (Ex 20: 8–11). Thus, the Ten Commandments that the Lord gave His people were to enable them to be "a kingdom of priests, and a holy nation" (Ex 19:6), and while the second commandment forbade Israel the use of "graven images" (Ex 20: 4–6), the moral image of God was to be reflected in God's people. The recovery of this moral image, as holiness, righteousness and purity of intention, has long been the goal of Christian Spirituality.

Third and finally, the *imago Dei* reminds us of the homelessness of humanity when apart from God. The *imago Dei*, although marred or effaced, continued in humanity after the fall (Gen 9:6), and it serves as a powerful reminder of our

---

[19]G. R. Evans, trans., *Bernard of Clairvaux: Selected Works* (New York: Paulist Press, 1987, "On Loving God," pp 192–95. This text is printed as "Four Degrees of Love," on pp. 148–53.
[20]Ibid., p. 196.
[21]Compare texts like Levitivus 11:44–45 with Jesus's words in Matthew 5:48: "You . . . must be perfect, as your heavenly Father is perfect."

true identity. St. Augustine's "restless heart" described this sense of yearning and contradiction with utter poignancy:

> Man is one of your creatures, Lord, and his instinct is to praise you. He bears about him the mark of death, the sign of his own sin, to remind him that you "thwart the proud" [1 Pet 5:5]. But still, since he is a part of your creation, he wishes to praise you. The thought of you stirs him so deeply that he cannot be content unless he praises you, because you made us for yourself and our hearts find no peace until they rest in you.[22]

The same *imago Dei* that gave Augustine this sense of contradiction, also gave him the longing that sent him in search of the life-giving presence of God.

Yearning for Eden is what sets men and women in pursuit of paradise lost. It reminds us that creation and redemption (re-creation) stand together in one grand sweep of Divine action. The purity and fellowship God granted the first man (Adam), which was subsequently lost through disobedience, is being restored in the Second Adam (Christ).[23] Thus, St. Irenaeus (d. 190) and writers of the ancient Eastern Church, were apt to conceive of salvation as the restitution of the *imago Dei* within. This recapitulation of humanity's original nature also explained the mystery behind the incarnation and coming of Jesus Christ, the God-Man: ". . . our Lord Jesus Christ, Who did, through His transcendent love, become what we are that He might bring us to be what He is Himself."[24] This theme continued in writers like St. Catherine of Siena, whose *Dialogue* (1377) depicts a mystical conversation between the human soul and God:

> How greatly were they indebted to me, then, since I had given them their very existence, creating them in my image and likeness! They owed me glory, but they stole it from me and took it to themselves and my enemies. But with humility I destroyed their pride: I stooped to take on their humanity, rescued them from their slavery to the devil and made them free. And more than this—can you see?—through this union of the divine nature with the human, God was made human and humanity was made God.[25]

Sin and Fallenness

The Bible is replete with expressions for describing human sin, most of which describe sin as "transgression" of God's law, "rebellion" against God's will, or "missing the mark" of God's intention. St. Paul's description (Rom 3:23) epitomized

---

[22]Pine-Coffin, trans., *Saint Augustine*, Bk. I, ch. 1, p. 21.

[23]As in Romans 5:12–21, and I Corinthians 15:20–29.

[24]Irenaeus, "Against Heresies," in *The Ante-Nicene Fathers*, edited by Alexander Roberts and James Donaldson, 10 vols. (Grand Rapids, Mich.: Wm. B. Eerdmans, reprint 1950) (hereafter: TANF), Vol. I, p. 526.

[25]Catherine of Siena, *The Dialogue*, translated by Suzanne Noffke, O.P. (New York: Paulist Press, 1980), p. 53.

these expressions: "All have sinned (Grk. *hamartano*, "missed the mark") and fall short of the glory of God." The Old Testament (OT) description of sin as "crooked-ness" (Heb. *awon*) reminds us that sin is primarily an inner state, a bentness or perversion of the human soul, that issues forth in sinful acts. In this sense "sin" describes a severe curvature of the self (*imago Dei*); a self so turned in upon itself that it cannot turn outward toward God and others. In classical theological terms this aspect of sin is described as "concupiscence" or *hubris* (Lat., "inordinate pride, self-centeredness"). It symbolizes the depth of human alienation from God, and therefore alienation from our true self and from others.

The dynamics of human sin are aptly depicted in the "fall narrative" (Gen 3). The ambiguity of the human predicament, a being made from the dust of the earth and simultaneously created in the image of God, provides the potential for sin. Our contradictory nature tempts us either to rise above our creaturely status to play God, or to sink below our authentic status (*imago Dei*) to live as though there were no God. The first people succumbed to the former temptation, and through a desire to "be like God" (3:5), broke God's commandment not to eat from "the tree of life" (3:2–3). The results of this transgression were manifold: original innocence was lost and they experienced shame.[26] When confronted with their transgression, the man and the woman refused to accept responsibility for their wrong-doing: Adam blamed Eve, Eve blamed the serpent (3:12–14). Their refusal to acknowledge their transgression barred the way to repentance and rec-onciliation with God. Hence, God judged the people guilty of sin and also pro-nounced judgments against them and the serpent (3:14–24). Of particular signif-icance was the way in which sin broke fellowship; the mutuality of the relationship between Adam and Eve would be lost in Eve's longing for Adam and in Adam's will to dominate Eve (Gen 3:16b). The authentic relationship they both enjoyed with God would be lost, and humans would no longer "walk with God in the cool of the morning"; henceforth the law, sacrifices, and mediators would neces-sarily stand between God and humanity. Further, with the transgression death came to the human race (3:19).

St. Paul's Epistle to the Romans drew these themes into a coherent whole. Sin, as he described it, is a universal human condition (Rom 3:9–18,23). It has such power over human nature that sin is said to "reign over" (Rom 5:21, 6:12) or "en-slave" (Rom 6:17,20, 7:14,23) humanity. Fallen humanity is deeply conflicted, caught between the law of life and the law of sin and death (Rom 7:25; 8:2). So deep are the corruption and bondage produced by sin that a person cannot act upon his or her good intentions. The apostle, speaking on behalf of conflicted per-sons, painfully described their plight: ". . . I can will what is right, but I cannot do it. For I do not do the good I want, but the evil I do not want is what I do. Now if I do what I do not want, it is no longer I that do it, but sin which dwells within me" (Rom 7:19–21). St. James (1:8) describes the same sort of person as be-

---

[26]This is symbolized through the discovery of their "nakedness." In Genesis 2:25, Adam and Eve were naked "and were not ashamed." But in 3:9–12, their nakedness—along with their transgression—produces shame and they attempt to hide from God's presence.

ing "double-minded" (Grk, *dipsuchos*, lit. "two souls"); they are a walking civil war waged between good and evil intentions, with each side struggling for dominance. "Death" is Paul's most comprehensive term for describing the debilitating effects of sin; it signifies both physical and spiritual death. Physical death, the apostle noted, came into the world through the sin of Adam.[27] Sin also produces spiritual death through its destructive and enslaving effects upon the human soul, which produce alienation from God. Sin binds us to a pattern of selfishness and rebellion that brings us under God's condemnation and judgment (Rom 6:23). This is a serious matter since it reverses St. Paul's exuberant exclamation, "If God is for us, who can be against us?" and turns it into Martin Luther's (1483–1546) woeful lament: "If God is against us, who can be for us?"[28]

Sin and sinful attitudes are the great foes of Christian Spirituality. No one has stated this more emphatically than St. Augustine. His spiritual pilgrimage and theological conflicts with the Pelagians caused him to see all of humanity deeply corrupted and condemned by their sin.[29] A similar concern sent an Augustinian monk, Martin Luther, in quest of a "gracious God." Liberation, for Luther, came through his realization that the righteousness that justifies us before God was not our "proper" or merited righteousness, but rather the "alien" (Ger. *fremde*) righteousness of Christ which is made ours by faith. This realization broke through Luther's attempts to merit God's forgiveness and the inner conflict (Ger. *Anfechtung*) that had plagued him. His treatise *Christian Freedom* (1520) epitomized the significance of this liberation: ". . . a Christian lives not in himself, but in Christ and in his neighbor. Otherwise he is not a Christian. He lives in Christ through faith, in his neighbor through love. By faith he is caught beyond himself into God. By love he descends beneath himself into his neighbor. Yet he always remains in God and in his love. . . ."[30] Dame Julian of Norwich (1342–c. 1423), in her *Showings*, described the painful "scourge" of sin that robs a person of a true understanding of herself and of the hope of reconciliation with God, but the Holy Spirit can lead that same person to confession and to hope: "Sin is the sharpest scourge . . . which scourge belabours man or woman, and breaks a man and purges him in his own sight so much that at times he thinks himself that he is not fit for anything but as it were to sink into hell, until contrition seizes him by the inspiration of the Holy Spirit and turns bitterness into hope of God's mercy."[31]

Because sin resides in the human will, the mastery and cleansing of the will

---

[27] Compare Romans 5:12, 19 and Genesis 3:19.

[28] In Romans 8:31, the apostle wrote: "If God is for us, who is against us? . . ." Martin Luther (1483–1546), weighed down under a deep awareness of his sin and unworthiness before God, reversed the Pauline phraseology to describe the sense of godforsakenness he felt.

[29] Mary Clark, ed., *Augustine of Hippo* (New York: Paulist Press, 1984), pp. 48–50.

[30] Martin Luther, "The Freedom of a Christian," in *Luther's Works*, Vol. 31, *Career of the Reformer*, pt. I, edited by Harold Grim (Philadelphia: Fortress Press, 1957), p. 371. Selections of this treatise are reprinted below, pp. 213–16.

[31] Edmund Colledge and James Walsh, eds., *Julian of Norwich: Showings* (New York: Paulist Press, 1978), p. 244. Cf. pp. 189–92 below.

has been a prominent theme in Christian Spirituality. Ignatius of Loyola (1491–1556), in his *Spiritual Exercises*, offered a pattern for achieving self-discipline and holiness based on self-examination, meditation, and imitation of Christ. Loyola described these spiritual exercises as ". . . any means of preparing and disposing our soul to rid itself of all its disordered affections, and then, after their removal, of seeking and finding God's will in the ordering of our life for the salvation of our soul."[32]

Justification and Righteousness

Justification (Grk. *dikaioo*) and righteousness (Grk. *dikaiosune*) are inseparably linked by common linguistic roots, and by soteriological significance.[33] The basis of these terms is to be found in OT words for describing a "just" ruler and "right" conduct (from the Heb. SDQ family of words); the root word may come from an ancient term meaning "straight" or "firm," and hence that which is "just" or "right" conforms to a particular norm or standard.[34] These terms sometimes take on legal connotations when used to describe the fair and appropriate decisions of a judge, and hence a person who is righteous (in this sense) is one who has been judged to be in the right (Ex 23:7; Dt 25:1). Since God's will and law (*Torah*) supply the basis and standards of OT life and conduct, "justice" or "righteousness" readily took on religious connotations, describing right relationship with God ("justification") and right conduct ("righteousness") before God. This pattern continued into the New Testament (NT), where "God justifies" the unrighteous (Rom 3:30; Gal 3:8), and our "righteousness" must exceed that of the "scribes and the pharisees" if we are to enter the kingdom of heaven (Mt 5:20).

While all Christians affirm the critical importance of justification, how this process is to be understood and how it relates to righteousness has been a matter of controversy and schism in the church. Two underlying considerations have shaped the development of this doctrine; the one has to do with the character of justification, and the other has to do with the nature of the righteousness involved. Is justification, as Protestants often emphasize, a "declaring righteous?"[35] Or does "justification" describe, as Roman Catholics generally affirm, a process of "mak-

---

[32]George Ganss, S.J., trans., *The Spiritual Exercises of Saint Ignatius: A Translation and Commentary* (Chicago: Loyola University Press, 1992), p. 21.

[33]Gottfried Quell and Gottlob Schrenk, "*dika dikaios, dikaiosuna, dikaio, dikaioma, dikaiosis, dikaiokrisa*," in TDNT, Vol. II, pp. 174–225 offer the definitive treatment of these terms. E. C. Blackman, "Justification, Justify," in George Buttrick, ed., *The Interpreter's Bible*, 4 vols., (Nashville, Tenn.: Abingdon Press, 1962) (hereafter: IDB), Vol. II, pp. 1027–30; P. J. Achtemeir, "Righteousness in the NT," IDB, Vol. IV, pp. 91–99; and P. De. Letter, "Justification," in *The New Catholic Encyclopedia*, 14 vols. (Washington D.C.: Catholic University, 1967), (hereafter: NCE), Vol. III, pp. 77–92, offer comprehensive summaries.

[34]Abraham Cronback, "Righteousness in the OT," IDB, Vol. IV, pp. 80–91.

[35]Norman Snaith, "Justification," in Alan Richardson, ed., *A Theological Word Book of the Bible* (New York: Macmillan, 1950) (hereafter: TWBB), p. 119.

ing just" or righteous.[36] There are many fundamental features common to both approaches: (1) justification is the act of God's grace on our behalf, it is not something we do for ourselves; (2) justification describes a right relationship with God; (3) justification marks the initial stage of Christian life; and (4) from this gracious beginning flows growth in grace or sanctification. But within the context of substantial agreement, significant differences also emerge. Protestants tend to speak of "justification" largely in terms of God's declaring believers justified by faith in Christ. Christian righteousness (in this sense) is not their own, it is Christ's righteousness reckoned to them by grace, through faith. This sort of justification is termed "forensic" because it refers to a person's outward status before God rather than his or her inward life, and this sort of righteousness is called "imputed" because it is the righteousness of another (Christ) applied to our account. Roman Catholics generally describe justification as the process of making just or righteous. This approach emphasizes justification as an "intrinsic" process that begins a transformation of the inner person. As a person responds to God's grace through faith in Jesus Christ, grace comes into that person's life and begins to make him or her new; hence, the righteousness described in this approach is called "imparted" or "infused" because it is actually given to Christians and adheres to their lives. While it may appear that this is distinction without a difference, it has bearing upon our understanding of how God's grace operates in Christian life, as well as what role good works play in our salvation and growth in grace.

An appeal to the teaching of Scripture is instructive in our attempt to understand the character of justification; both approaches find voice in Holy Writ. This tension is as fundamental to the NT as are the writings of St. Paul and St. James. Pauline theology of justification was worked out against the background of serious controversy with the Pharisaic (and indeed Paul's own former) understanding of the concept; that is, Paul's view stood over and against the view of those who imagined that they could establish their own righteousness through moral adherence to the Torah (OT law) and traditions of the Hebrew community of faith. It is for this reason, then, that Paul's teaching, as it is preserved in Galatians and Romans, is decidedly forensic in its emphasis[37]; justification is God's act, on our behalf, which is made ours by faith. Abraham is St. Paul's prime example of one who has been "declared" or "reckoned as righteous" because of his faith (Gal 3:6; Rom 4:3–5). The Romans text is particularly insistent: ". . . what does the Scripture say? 'Abraham believed God, and it was reckoned to him as righteousness' [Gen 15:6]. Now to one who works, his wages are not reckoned as a gift but as his due. And to one who justifies the ungodly, his faith is reckoned as righteousness." It should also be added that Paul's position was not *exclusively* forensic; the righteousness that was "reckoned" to a person by faith in Christ must also be actualized in a life of faithfulness. And so in the life of faith, as well as in Romans and Galatians, the forensic element was followed immediately by the be-

---

[36]Richard McBrien, *Catholicism*, 2 vols. (Minneapolis: Winston Press, 1980), Vol. I, "Glossary," p. xlvii.
[37]Romans 2–6; Galatians 2:11–4.

ginning of a transformation (intrinsic element) of the person who had been "reckoned righteous."[38]

The Pauline emphasis seems even more emphatic when it is laid beside that of St. James. The thrust of James's epistle is aptly summarized in his injunction: "Be doers of the Word, and not hearers only . . ." (Jas 1:22). The author was deeply concerned about the hypocrisy of people who had professed Christian faith and yet were not living Christian lives. So we find James attacking a hypothetical or superficial sort of faith. His declaration that "faith by itself, if it has no works is dead" (Jas 2:17) sounds like direct assault upon Paul's message ". . . that a man is justified by faith apart from works of law" (Rom 3:28). St. James, like St. Paul, turns to father Abraham to illustrate his point: "Was not Abraham our father justified by works, when he offered his son Isaac upon the altar? You see that faith was active along with his works, and faith was completed by works, and the Scripture was fulfilled which says 'Abraham believed God and it was reckoned to him as righteousness' [Jas 2:22–24]."

The apparent controversy between James and Paul is muted, to some degree, by recalling what sort of "faith" James assails; this is not the Pauline forensic-intrinsic model that stresses the priority of God's act in Jesus Christ and the subsequent reality of the transformation of Christian lives by faith in Christ. It is rather a hypothetical or empty faith that mistakenly separates faith and works. James seemed to mouth the faith-claims of his opponents when he retorted: "But some one will say, 'You have faith and I have works . . .'" (Jas 2:18). He also illustrated this sort of faith with his forceful example of the person who dismisses the desperate needs "of a brother or sister" with pious rhetoric: "'Go in peace, be warmed and filled,' without giving them the things needed for the body . . ." (Jas 2:16). It was precisely this sort of faith, one that is estranged from Christian works and is used as an excuse for avoiding them, that was criticized by St. James when he wrote: "So faith by itself, if it has no works, is dead" (2:17).

Tension is not always harmful; sometimes we find ourselves better prepared or a bit more able because we have faced a significant challenge. This theological tension and the apparent controversy between the writings of Paul and James can have very productive results for us *if* we refuse to choose between St. Paul and St. James as though their approaches were mutually exclusive. With Paul we must affirm the absolute priority of God's grace (manifested toward us in the saving death and resurrection of Jesus Christ), which when received by faith is "reckoned to us as righteousness." And with James we must embrace the deeply interwoven character of justification and righteousness; the faith that justifies is a lively faith that is manifested in actual righteousness and good works. We must, as Schrenk suggests, recognize the actual intention of Paul's forensic, law-court imagery.[39] The intention of Paul's declaration that God justifies the ungodly (Lat. *iustificatio iniusti*) is not based in some sort of repeat offender syndrome; God does not pardon wicked people so that they may go on being wicked, nor does God

---

[38]See Romans 5–6, and Galatians 4–6.
[39]Schrenk, "dikaiosune etc.," TDNT, Vol. IV, pp. 204–5.

pardon the ungodly "as if" they were righteous (for they are not). Instead God justifies the ungodly (forensic) so that God can bring them into relationship with Himself and thereby make them righteous (intrinsic). Thus the foremost "church father" of the twentieth century, Karl Barth (1886–1968), reminds us that while justification should be thought of (initially) as God's act in declaring us righteous, that act cannot be separated, in any decisive way, from God's intention to make us righteous: "It is a declaring righteous which can without any reserve be called a making righteous."[40]

The question would emerge again and again whether human works can prepare the way for justification and how much or to what degree the human will is free to cooperate with or initiate the process of conversion (justification). Two historical turning points in the examination of the relationship of faith and works demand particular attention. The first of these occurred in the teaching of St. Augustine and the church's struggle with Pelagianism during his day.[41] Pelagius (c. 350–425) was concerned about human moral action; he posited the belief that Adam's sin affected only Adam, which gave Pelagius an optimistic view of the capacities of the human will. Pelagius's understanding of justification stressed the ability of the human will to apply itself to the things of God and thereby initiate and facilitate the process of justification. Such an approach emphasized the action of the free, human will and seemed to minimize the action of God in justification.[42] Augustine's response took shape in his famous doctrines of the bondage of the human will apart from grace, and predestination, which stressed the priority and continuity of God's grace throughout the whole process of salvation. Pelagius's views were condemned at the Council of Carthage (418), and Augustinian views on the universal fall and the bondage of human sin, as well as the universal necessity of grace, were upheld. St. Augustine's approach stressed the role of Divine grace so thoroughly that he is appropriately called "the Doctor of Grace."[43] His approach also seemed to minimize the role that the human will and human works played in justification and the subsequent development of righteousness.

The Eastern Orthodox Church was not as deeply affected by Pelagianism, and Augustine was not as decisive for the development of Byzantine doctrine as he was for Latin theology. The Eastern Church continued along the routes laid down by Irenaeus and his successors: justification by faith was affirmed, but so was the lively cooperation of the human will in the process of justification. Justification was deemed the beginning of sanctification, and so the Eastern empha-

---

[40] Karl Barth, *Church Dogmatics*, 4 vols., translated by G. W. Bromley and T. F. Torance (Edinburgh: T & T Clark, 1936–75), Vol. IV, 1, p. 95.

[41] George Tavard, *Justification: An Ecumenical Study* (New York: Paulist Press, 1983), p. 20. Tavard's work offers an insightful overview of the development and historical debates surrounding justification. Cf. William Thompson's "The Saints, Justification and Sanctification: An Ecumenical Thought Experiment," forthcoming in *Pro Ecclesia*.

[42] Joanne McWilliam, "Pelagius, Pelagianism," in *Encyclopedia of Early Christianity*, edited by Everett Ferguson (New York: Garland Publishing Co., 1990), pp. 704–8.

[43] P. De Letter, "Justification," in NCE, Vol. III, p. 82.

sis was not so much upon forensic justification, but rather upon sanctification—which was expressed in terms of "being partakes of the divine nature [2 Pet 1:4]."

A second, significant historical turning point emerged as Augustinian theology was moderated by a voluntarism that stemmed from the spirituality of activists and mystics. It gradually became a medieval axiom that "to those who do what is in them God does not deny grace."[44] This approach, prominent especially among the nominalists (William of Occam, c. 1290–1349), affirmed that God's grace is necessary for salvation, but persons of good will can prepare the way for it. Gabriel Biel (c. 1410–95), one of the last great Occamists, represented the apex of this movement away from Augustinian soteriology. Hence, Heiko Oberman observed, "Biel teaches an essentially Pelagian doctrine of justification. . . ."[45]

Young Martin Luther (1483–1545) studied Biel's work at Erfurt University under two of Biel's most able students. Luther's break with Occamism and subsequent break with Roman Catholicism involved a myriad of theological, ecclesiological, and political issues all wound together. While it is difficult to untangle the knots, it is clear that the Lutheran Reformation had its beginnings in Luther's legitimate criticism of Biel's approach to justification. This criticism was emotionally charged with the sense of bondage Luther felt under the Occamist soteriology, and the exuberance that came into Luther's life through his famous "tower experience."[46] But it is also clear, as Fr. George Tavard points out, that Luther's initial criticisms were essentially Augustinian ones: "Luther's doctrine on justification in 1519 was in harmony with the dominant trend of the previous Catholic tradition as this had taken shape under the impact of Augustine. . . ."[47]

Luther's insistent declaration of "the head [Ger. *Haupt*] and chief doctrine"—justification by faith alone—and forceful denunciations of "good works" made it seem that Luther had no place for "proper righteousness" in his theology, although his more carefully nuanced work indicates otherwise.[48] The constructive thrust of Luther's understanding of justification was to be found in his Christocentrism and in his fidelity to Augustinian concepts like the "bondage of the will," as well as in an approach to salvation that preserved the Divine initiative throughout the process.

The Council of Trent (1545–63), which sought to consolidate the energies of the Catholic Reformation and respond to Protestant doctrine, steered a course between the positions of Martin Luther and Gabriel Biel. The Tridentine fathers attacked a Pelagian understanding of justification that stressed "good works" as a

---

[44]*Facienti quod in se est Deus non denegat gratiam.*

[45]Tavard, *Justification*, pp. 45–48. Tavard correctly points out that Occam "rejected Pelagianism in principle, though on a practical level . . . one's free acts contribute to the preparation for grace" (p. 46). Under Occam's successors, like Gabriel Biel, nominalism seemed to veer dangerously close to Pelagianism. Cf. Heiko Oberman, *The Harvest of Medieval Theology* (Durham, N.C.: Labyrinth Press, 1983), p. 196.

[46]See below "The Tower Experience," pp. 212–13.

[47]Tavard, *Justification*, pp. 57–58.

[48]See Luther's sermon "Two Kinds of Righteousness" (1519).

basis for new relationship with God.[49] But Luther also sounded too extreme to the Council, and several of the "Canons on Justification" seem to have been formulated with his doctrine of "justification by faith alone" in mind. Canon IX, for example, defended the concept of cooperation with God's grace, perhaps against Luther's view: "If any one saith, that by faith alone the impious is justified, in such wise as to mean that nothing else is required to cooperate in order to the obtaining of the grace of Justification, and that it is not necessary, that he be prepared and disposed by the movement of his own will: let him be anathema."[50] Playing St. James to Luther's St. Paul, the Tridentine fathers suspected that there was something amiss in the Lutheran doctrine of faith without works: "If any one saith, that justifying faith is nothing else but confidence in the divine mercy which remits sins for Christ's sake; or, that this confidence alone is that whereby we are justified: let him be anathema."[51] The constructive doctrine of Trent affirmed justification by God's grace and by a faith that was not "alone": "Having . . . been thus justified, and made the friends . . . of God [Eph 2:19], advancing 'from virtue to virtue' [Ps 83:8], they are 'renewed,' as the Apostle says, 'day by day' [2 Cor 4:16]; . . . faith co-operating with good works, increase in that justice which they have received through the grace of Christ, and are still further justified. . . ."[52] Thus Trent affirmed that the actual (Luther would say "proper") righteousness of a Christian is based on the previous (Luther would say "alien") righteousness of Christ, which is infused (or imparted) into the Christian for growth in grace through good works: ". . . Jesus Christ himself continually infuses his virtue [Lat. *virtus*; "life, power, vigor"] into the . . . justified—as the head into the members, and the vine into the branches—and this virtue always precedes and accompanies and follows their good works. . . ."[53]

Later Protestants, like John Calvin, the father of the Reformed tradition, embraced Luther's emphasis upon justification by faith alone but also emphasized the role of good works (done after forensic justification) in the process of sanctification. The center of Calvin's approach to salvation was his emphasis upon "union with Christ."[54] In his famous doctrine of the "third use of the law" (Lat. *usus tertius legis*), Calvin offered an important contribution to the clarification of the role of Christian works before and after (forensic) justification.[55] The "third and principal use of the law which pertains more closely to the proper purpose of the law" is not directed to seekers (first use) or the unregenerate (second use), rather it "finds its place among believers in whose hearts the Spirit of God al-

---

[49]Philip Schaff, ed., *The Creeds of Christendom*, 3 vols. (Grand Rapids, Mich.: Baker Book House, 1977, reprint of 1877 edition), Vol. II, p. 110, "On Justification," Canons, I–III.

[50]Ibid., p. 112.

[51]Ibid., Canon XII, p. 113. Cf. Canons XXIV, XXVI, and etc.

[52]Ibid., "Canons and Decrees of the Council of Trent," ch. 10, p. 99.

[53]Ibid., "Trent," ch. 16, p. 108–9.

[54]See the reading entitled "Union with Christ," pp. 233–34 below.

[55]Lewis Ford Battles, ed., *Calvin's Institutes of the Christian Religion*, 2 vols. (Philadelphia: Westminster Press, 1960), Vol. I, pp. 354–62, Institutes Bk. II, ch. 7, para. 12–14.

ready lives and reigns. . . ."[56] The moral law of God provides the faithful with the ". . . best instrument for them to learn more thoroughly each day the nature of the Lord's will to which they aspire, and to confirm them in the understanding of it."[57] For Luther the law and the gospel stood in dialectical opposition: "Hereby we may see the difference between the Law and the Gospel. The Law never bringeth the Holy Ghost, but only teacheth what we ought to do: therefore it justifieth not. But the Gospel bringeth the Holy Ghost, because it teacheth what we ought to receive. Therefore the Law and the Gospel are two quite contrary doctrines."[58] This law-gospel dialectic was especially evident in Luther's *Galatians Commentary* (1535).

Thomas Cranmer (1489–1556), architect of the Anglican tradition, stood closer to Calvin than to Luther on the relationship of faith and works. Anglican Article XII evidenced a willingness to combine justification by faith alone and good works: "Albeit that Good Works, which are the fruits of Faith, and follow after Justification, can not put away our sins, and endure the severity of God's judgement; yet are they pleasing and acceptable to God in Christ, and do spring out necessarily of a true and lively Faith; insomuch that by them a lively Faith may be as evidently known as a tree discerned by the fruit."[59] In a similar way, Methodism, with its roots in eighteenth-century Anglicanism, sought to embrace justification by faith alone and the role of works in cultivating piety. John Wesley (1703–91), the founder of the Methodist movement who had his "Aldersgate experience" while he was listening to one who ". . . was reading Luther's preface to the Epistle to the Romans,"[60] sought to maintain Luther's emphasis upon the forensic character of justification (initial), and along with the Council of Trent, Calvin, Cranmer—and indeed Luther himself—Wesley also sought to maintain a place for works of piety ("means of grace") in the process of sanctification (or making a person "just").[61]

The Presence of God

The first commandment of the Decalogue urges us to acknowledge the uniqueness and sovereignty of God (Ex 20:2–6; Mt 4:10). The apostle Paul considered it to be the creature's duty to honor the Creator and give thanks because God's invisible nature is so profoundly displayed in creation (Rom 1:19–25). The creature longs for the Creator's presence, and yet because of sin we are more apt to cre-

---

[56] Ibid., p. 360.

[57] Ibid.

[58] Philip S. Watson, ed., *Martin Luther: A Commentary on St. Paul's Epistle to the Galatians* (Cambridge & London: James Clarke, 1953), p. 205 (Hereafter: *Luther's Galatians*).

[59] Schaff, ed., *Creeds of Christendom*, Vol. III, "Thirty-Nine Articles of the Church of England," Art. XII, p. 494.

[60] Richard Heitzenrater, general ed., *The Works of John Wesley*, Vol. 18, edited by Reginald Ward and Richard Heitzenrater, *Journals and Diaries*, pt. 1, (Nashville, Tenn.: Abingdon Press, 1988), John Wesley's journal entry for May 24, 1738, pp. 249–50. For the full text of this event cf. pp. 319–20 below.

[61] See Wesley on "The Means of Grace," pp. 325–27 below.

ate gods of convenience than to seek the presence of the Holy God. God's presence is an awesome and mysterious spectacle. As the Psalmist exclaimed: "O LORD my God, thou art very great! Thou art clothed with honor and majesty, who coverest Thyself with light as a garment, who hast stretched out the heavens like a tent . . . who makest the clouds thy chariot, who ridest on the wings of the wind . . ." (Ps 104:1–4). Because of God's holiness and because of human sinfulness, it is—simultaneously—a threatening and enthralling event for a human being to stand in God's presence. Even for someone like Moses—one of the greatest prophets of God and the only one who spoke to God "face to face, as a man speaks with his friend" (Ex 33:11)—to actually see God's face invited certain death (Ex 33:17–23). Spiritual pilgrims who have sought God's presence in prayer, reflection, or visionary experiences have found it to be a comforting and disturbing presence. Rudolph Otto's (1869–1937) seminal work, *The Idea of the Holy* (1923), noted five salient features resident in an experience of God's mysterious presence (*mysterium tremendum*): (1) awfulness or a sense of deep awe; (2) a sense of "overpoweringness" (*majestas*); (3) a sense of urgency; (4) a recognition that one has met the Wholly Other; and (5) a sense of fascination.[62]

A sense of the absence of God, such as occurs in St. John of the Cross's *Dark Night of the Soul* (1587), is an equally awe-filled and overpowering experience since it can lead to a resolute detachment from worldly things that purifies the soul and allows it to wait in darkness for the piercing presence of God. Through "active" and "passive" experiences of Divine absence the soul is purified by God, and is transformed into godlikeness, just as wood is dried and transformed into fire by Divine light: ". . . The soul is purged and prepared for union with the divine light just as the wood is prepared for transformation into the fire . . . by heating and enkindling it from without the fire transforms the wood into itself and makes it as beautiful as itself."[63]

Not only is God's presence an "enkindling" and purifying presence, it is also a nuturing and gracious presence. Hence, Julian of Norwich noted ". . . as truly as God is our Father, so truly is God our Mother."[64] She found the Motherhood of God expressed in three foundational ways: ". . . The first is the foundation of our nature's creation; the second is his taking of our nature, where the motherhood of grace begins; the third is the motherhood at work. And in that, by the same grace, everything is penetrated, in length, and in breadth, in height and in depth without end; and it is all one love."[65]

There is a profound sense in which all of one's life is lived out in God's presence (Lat. *coram Deo*), and this recognition becomes a powerful tool for understanding all of one's life as being consecrated unto God. The Carmelite lay brother

---

[62]Rudolph Otto, *The Idea of the Holy*, translated by John W. Harvey (London: Oxford University Press, 1936), pp. 12–41.

[63]Kieran Kavanaugh, O.C.D., and Otilio Rodriguez, O.C.D. eds., *The Collected Works of St. John of the Cross* (Washington, D.C.: Institute of Carmelite Studies, 1979), "The Dark Night of the Soul," ch. 10, p. 350.

[64]Colledge and Walsh, eds., *Julian of Norwich*, p. 296.

[65]Ibid., p. 297.

Nicholas Herman (1611–91), known as "Brother Lawrence," cultivated and practiced this sort of life, and its character has been preserved for us under the title *Practice of the Presence of God* (1692). Without forsaking the *mysterium tremendum*, Brother Lawrence advocated a style of spirituality that developed a continual sense of being in God's presence, and the practice of returning to God's presence through deliberate acts of prayer. He aspired to a habitual sense of God's presence that penetrated and invigorated all of a Christian's life. Brother Lawrence wrote: "This presence of God . . . if practiced faithfully works secretly in the soul and produces marvelous effects . . . and leads it insensibly to the simple grace, that long sight of God every where present, which is the most holy, the most solid, the easiest, the most efficacious manner of prayer."[66]

While prayer is one of the main avenues into God's presence, it is by no means the only one. The community of faith—reaching all the way back to Passover (Ex 12) with its liturgy and sacred reenactment—has entered God's presence through Word and Sacrament. The Lord's Supper or Mass is one of the means whereby the mysterious presence of God is made tangible and accessible to the worshipping community. Catherine of Genoa (1447–1510) experienced a transforming sense of God's presence as she prepared for her Lenten participation in the Mass; on March 23, 1473, she felt herself overwhelmed by a sense of the love of Christ and her own utter unworthiness. From May 1474 until her death in 1510 Catherine practiced *daily* communion as a way of experiencing the presence of God. Spiritual pilgrims as diverse as St. Bernard of Clairvaux (1090–1153) and Thomas a' Kempis (c. 1380–1471) experienced a tangible sense of the presence of God through meditation upon Holy Scripture. The inner voice and outer Word merged as a' Kempis described "how Christ speaks inwardly to the soul": "'I will hear what the Lord God speaks within me.' Blessed is the soul that hears the Lord speaking within it, and receives comfort from His Word. Blessed are the ears that hear the still, small voice of God, and disregard the whispers of the world. . . ."[67]

Christology

As we noted at the outset, Christian Spirituality is rooted in Jesus Christ; virtually anything that can be said of Christian Spirituality relates—directly or indirectly—to Jesus Christ. Christians esteem Jesus Christ as prophet (revealer), priest (mediator), and king (risen lord); these three "offices" or titles delineated by John Calvin are sometimes used to summarize the far-reaching significance Christ has for Christians.[68] Jesus Christ reveals God, reconciles people to God, and

---

[66]John Delaney, trans., *The Practice of the Presence of God by Brother Lawrence of the Resurrection* (New York: Doubleday, 1977), p. 110. Cf. pp. 314–18 below for selections of Brother Lawrence's work.

[67]Thomas a' Kempis, *The Imitation of Christ,* translated by Leo Sherley-Price (New York: Penguin Books, 1952), p. 91. Cf. pp. 195–203 below.

[68]As in Calvin's *Institutes*, Vol. II, ch. 15, "To Know the Purpose for Which Christ Was Sent by the Father, and What He Conferred Upon Us, We Must Look Above All at Three Things in Him: the Prophetic Office, Kingship, and Priesthood." Battles trans., Vol. I, pp. 494–503.

exercises God's spiritual reign ("kingdom") in the lives of those who belong to God. Christian Spirituality revolves around many Christological axes, and yet several themes stand out among the rest as being of particular importance in the development of spirituality.

The Incarnation. The "incarnation" (Lat. *carno*, "flesh") describes the mystery of the Word (*logos*) of God taking flesh and dwelling among us (Jn 1:1–17); it has always been a focal point of Christian belief and reflection. The incarnation of God's Son speaks volumes about God's will-to-be-known, as well as the Son-sending love God extends toward us. Belief in Jesus Christ as the God-Man was articulated by the church's earliest writers, such as St. Ignatius of Antioch (d. 117?), who sought to keep early Christians from slipping into an erroneous resolution of the tension inherent in the concept. Against gnostics (Docetics)—who claimed that Christ was a spirit who only seemed to have a physical body—Ignatius stressed the true humanity of Jesus[69]; against Judaizers—who saw Jesus as another one of the great prophets sent from God—Ignatius stressed the real divinity of Jesus Christ.[70]

The incarnation is a permanent hedge against the pagan belief that matter and sanctity cannot coexist. The reality of the incarnation is reenacted in the Mass or Eucharist, and in the theology of sanctification. In the incarnation Jesus not only brought deity "down" to us, he began the process of elevating humanity to its proper place and station ("a little lower than God"). Thus, reflecting upon the incarnation, St. Irenaeus (d. 202?) wrote that "Our Lord Jesus Christ . . . became what we are that he might bring us to what He is himself."[71] Catherine of Siena (1347–80) expressed a similar theme in one of her oracles: ". . . through this union of the divine nature with the human, God was made human and humanity was made God."[72] The transforming power of the incarnation has continuing import for Christian Spirituality; the Word not only "took flesh" in the historical event (Jn 1:14), the Word continues to take and transform human "flesh" through the process of sanctification.

This sort of soteriological reflection on the incarnation caused the Eastern (Greek) Church Fathers to embrace *theosis*, the vision of being "partakers of the Divine nature" (2 Pet 1:4), as being constitutive for sanctification. It was a prominent theme in Athanasius's classic work, *On the Incarnation of the Word of God* (c. 320); the Word ". . . was made man that we might be made God [*theopoiethomen*]. . . ."[73] Hence Byzantine theology, in distinction from that of the Latin West, which tended to separate the categories of nature and grace, sees them not as opposites

---

[69] Cyril Richardson, ed., *Early Christian Writers* (New York: Macmillan, 1970), "Letter of Ignatius to the Smrynaens," chs. 1–4, pp. 112–13. Cf. pp. 56–57 below.

[70] Ibid., "To The Philadelphians," chs. 6–9, pp. 109–11.

[71] Irenaeus, "Against Heresies," p. 527.

[72] Catherine of Siena, *The Dialogue*, p. 53.

[73] Philip Schaff and Henry Wace, eds., *A Select Library of Nicene and Post-Nicene Fathers of the Christian Church*, Series Two, Vol. IV, *St. Athanasius: Select Works and Letters*, edited by Archibald Robertson (Grand Rapids: Wm. B. Eerdmans, 1978 reprint), p. 65 (hereafter NPNF).

but in terms of their interrelationship, as avenues whereby humanity participates in the Divine.[74] The *Nativity Hymns* of Ephrem the Syrian (c. 306–73) preserve poignant examples of this kind of reflection upon the incarnation of our Lord:

> The two things You asked [Jn 17],
> we have by Your Birth.
> You put on our visible body;
> let us put on your hidden power.
> Our body became Your garment;
> Your spirit became our robe.
> Blessed is He Who was adorned and adorned us![75]

A similar conception undergirds the Wesleyan conception of sanctification as Christian Perfection.[76] Writing more than a millennium later, Charles Wesley (1707–88) cofounder of Methodism, penned similar lines:

> Let earth and heaven combine,
> Angels and men agree,
> To praise in songs divine
> The incarnate Deity,
> Our God contracted to a span,
> Incomprehensibly made man.
>
> He deigns in flesh to appear,
> Widest extremes to join;
> To bring our vileness near,
> And make us all divine;
> And we the life of God shall know,
> For God is manifest below.[77]

Imitation of Christ. Jesus's life has often been the focus of Christian reflection and as such becomes a model for Christian life. Christ urged His disciples to "follow" Him in the way of self-giving and suffering (Mk 8:34). The servant attitude that Jesus modeled for His disciples throughout His life and perhaps most pro-

---

[74]John Meyendorff, *Byzantine Theology* (New York: Fordham University Press, 1974), p. 138. Meyendorff writes: "This basic proposition explains why the terms 'nature' and 'grace,' when used by Byzantine authors, have a meaning quite different from the Western usage; rather than being in direct opposition, the terms 'nature' and 'grace' express a dynamic, living, and necessary relationship between God and man, different by their *natures*, but in *communion* with each other through God's energy, or grace."

[75]Kathleen E. McVey, ed., *Emphrem the Syrian* (New York: Paulist Press, 1989), pp. 185–86. The "hostages" referred to here may be the body and soul of Christ. Cf. note #497. Several of Ephrem's "Nativity Hymns" are reprinted below, pp. 80–86.

[76]Cf. Albert Outler, *John Wesley* (New York: Oxford University Press, 1964), pp. 30–33; John R. Tyson, *Charles Wesley* (New York: Oxford University Press, 1989), pp. 41–43; and Frank Whaling, *John and Charles Wesley* (New York: Paulist Press, 1981), pp. 7–14.

[77]John Wesley, *A Collection of Hymns for the Use of the People Called Methodists* (London: Wesleyan-Methodist Book Room, 1883), Hymn #685, verses 1 and 4, pp. 626–27.

foundly at the end of His life in the upper room (Jn 13:1–11), was—through "participation in the Spirit" and "the incentive of love"—to be embued upon the Christian's mind (Phil 2:1–11). Christians are urged to "be imitators of God" by walking in love and obedience as Christ did, and by offering themselves "as a fragrant offering and sacrifice to God" (Eph 5:1–5). Nor is Christlike suffering to be shunned, as St. Peter noted, "For to this you have been called, because Christ also suffered for you, leaving you an example that you should follow in his steps" (2 Pet 2:20–25). Imitating the actions and aspirations of Jesus Christ marks out the way to renion with His Father and the cultivation of Christian virtues.

Imitation of Christ is woven deeply into the liturgical life of the church. In baptism Christians imitate and participate sacramentally in Christ's dying and rising (Rom 6; Col 2:12–15); in so doing they put off their old nature and "put on Christ" (Gal 3:37), and live transformed lives "by virtue . . . of the washing of regeneration and renewal in the Holy Spirit" (Ti 3:5). Jesus provided His disciples with a model for their prayers (the "Our Father," Mt 6:5–15). In praying the "Lord's Prayer" Christians align themselves with Christ's proclamation of the Kingdom of God and with Christ's ministry of reconciliation.

It is not surprising that Christians of all eras have sought to pattern their lives after that of Jesus Christ. St. Antony the Hermit (c. 215–356), whose remarkable life was recounted by Athanasius, went into the desert and spent forty years there learning the utter self-surrender to which Christ called Christians.[78] St. Benedict of Nursia (c. 480–550), patriarch of Western monasticism, believed that the imitation of Christ epitomized the Christian life and vocation, and it was the goal he had in view as he drew up his *Rule*:

> . . . the Lord also says in the Gospel, "Everyone who listens to these words of mine and acts on them, will be like a sensible man who built his house on rock; floods rose, gales blew and hurled themselves against that house, and it did not fall; it was founded on the rock." Thus the Lord concludes his reply, and daily expects us to respond through our dutiful actions to his only precepts.[79]

The most famous treatise on this topic, *The Imitation of Christ* (c. 1441), also begins with a citation of the words of Jesus Christ: "'He who follows Me shall not walk in darkness,' says Our Lord [Jn 8:12]. In these words Christ counsels us to follow His life and way if we desire true enlightenment and freedom from all blindness of heart. Let the life of Jesus Christ, then, be our first consideration."[80] For St. Ignatius of Loyola (c. 1491–1556) it seemed more appropriate to begin his *Spiritual Exercises* (1548) with "the consideration and contemplation of sins"; but the second week of exercises attended ". . . to the life of Christ our Lord up

---

[78] Cf. pp. 86–88 for selections from *The Life of Antony*.

[79] Abbot Parry, O.S.B., trans., *The Rule of Saint Benedict* (Leominster, England: Gracewing Books, 1990), p. 3.

[80] a` Kempis, *Imitation of Christ*, p. 27. Cf. pp. 195–203 below.

to and including Palm Sunday; the Third [Week], to the Passion of Christ our Lord. . . ."[81]

In naisant Protestantism, *imatatio Christi* themes found strong expression in the Anabaptist tradition's insistence upon Christian discipleship (Ger. *Nachfolge*, lit. "following after") being construed as a life of radical obedience (*Gehorsam*) to Jesus's commands and conformity to Jesus's life. Thus the early Anabaptist writer Hans Denck wrote, in 1526, that Christ is the only means whereby a person comes before God, but the knowledge of Christ is not a superficial matter: ". . . this Means is Christ, whom none may truly know unless he follow after Him with his life. . . . Whoever does not know Him has Him not and cannot without Him come to the Father. But whoever knows Him and does not testify thereto by his manner of life, God will judge along with others who are perverse. . . ."[82] Imitation of Christ was also a prominent theme in Anabaptist hymnody of the same period (1527):

> He who would follow Christ in life
> Must scorn the world's insult and strife,
> And bear his cross each day.
> For this alone leads to the throne;
> Christ is the only way.
>
> Christ's servants follow him to death,
> And give their body, life, and breath
> On cross and rack and pyre.
> As gold is tried and purified
> They stand the test of fire.
>
> Renouncing all, they choose the cross,
> And claiming it, count all as loss,
> E'en home and child and wife.
> Forsaking gain, forgetting pain,
> They enter into life.[83]

Among Protestants the imitation of Christ became, as it had been among Catholics before them, a structural device for the cultivation of spirituality. *Pia Desideria* (1675), penned by the Pietist patriarch Philip Jacob Spener, advocated the establishment of small groups, "colleges of piety" (Lat. *collegia pietatis*), in which the life and teachings of Christ were embraced as patterns for personal ho-

---

[81]George E. Ganss, SJ, trans., *The Spiritual Exercises of Saint Ignatius* (Chicago: Loyola University Press, 1992), p. 22.

[82]Hans Denck, "Whether God Is the Cause of Evil?," in *Spiritual and Anabaptist Writers*, edited by George H. Williams (Philadelphia: Westminster Press, 1957), p. 108.

[83]Jorg Werner, "Wer Christo jetzt will folgen noch," 1527. Printed in *Ausband, Das ist: Entliche schöne Christliche Lieder* (Germantown: Christoph Saur, 1742). Reprinted in Walter Klassen, ed., *Anabaptism in Outline: Selected Primary Sources* (Scottdale, Pa., 1981), p. 88. The hymn was translated by David Augusburger (1962).

liness.[84] In this venture Spener expressed explicit indebtedness to a' Kempis's *Imitation of Christ*.[85] The modern Lutheran martyr, Dietrich Bonhoeffer (1906–45), looked to the life of Jesus Christ to distinguish between "cheap grace" and "costly grace." "Cheap grace," Bonhoeffer wrote in *The Cost of Discipleship*, "is the preaching of forgiveness without requiring repentance, baptism without church discipline, Communion without confession, absolution without personal confession. Cheap grace is grace without discipleship, grace without the cross, grace without Jesus Christ, living and incarnate."[86] "Costly grace" stands in stark contrast to this: it ". . . is *costly* because it calls us to follow, and it is *grace* because it calls us to follow *Jesus Christ*. It is costly because it costs a man his life, and it is grace because it gives a man the only true life."[87]

The Cross of Christ. The cross is a symbol of the crucifixion of Jesus Christ and the saving significance of that event. In it the NT writers understood Jesus's death as the epitome of his servant-life; the Incarnate God was willing to "humble himself . . . taking the form of a servant . . . and became obedient unto death, even death on a cross" (Phil 2:6–7). At its most foundational level "the cross" was the means whereby God offered forgiveness of sins and reconciliation to humanity (1 Cor 15:3). The cross is a vivid demonstration of the love of God (Jn 3:16). In the broadest sense, "Christ crucified," which is the "word of the cross," summarizes the entire Christian gospel (1 Cor 2:2).

The cross or crucifix has long been an object of Christian reflection and meditation.[88] Reaching back to the words of Jesus, the cross was a metaphor for the costly character of Christian discipleship; as Jesus urged his disciples, "If anyone would come after me, let him deny himself and take up his cross and follow me."[89] So saying, Jesus not only foreshadowed his own death, He also characterized Christian discipleship as a life of self-denial and self-giving. As the early Christians reflected upon the cross of Christ two elements were stressed: the suffering (Heb 2:9; 1 Pet 4:13) and the shame (Heb 12:4; 13:13) involved in such a death. The cross is referred to as "the tree" in several passages,[90] perhaps to solidify the connection between Jesus's death on the cross and the bearing of the ancient curse (Gal 3:13). Because of Jesus's death on the cross the curse of the law (*Torah*), which rested upon all who had not kept the law, was borne away (Gal 3:13; Col 2:14). Because of His voluntary submission to death, as the God-Man, Jesus Christ fulfilled the demands of the moral law on behalf of sinners (Phil 2:8) and won a victory over the powers of darkness, death, and evil (Col 2:1). Thus the cross, which was a dreaded implement of torture and death, became for Christians a short-

---

[84]Philip Jacob Spener, *Pia Desideria*, translated by Theodore Tappert (Philadelphia: Fortress Press, 1964), pp. 89–92.

[85]Peter Erb, ed., *Pietists: Selected Writings* (New York: Paulist Press, 1983), p. 45.

[86]Dietrich Bonhoeffer, *The Cost of Discipleship* (New York: Macmillan, 1963), p. 47.

[87]Ibid., p. 47.

[88]Cf. St. Francis's "Prayer Before the Crucifix," p. 164.

[89]Matthew 16:24 = Mark 10:21 = Luke 9:23.

[90]Acts 5:30, 10:19, 13:9.

hand expression for the saving death of Christ and its reconciling implications for humanity (Col 1:20; 2 Cor 5:19). For this reason, then, the "word of the cross" became a description for the gospel (1 Cor 1:18), and St. Paul indicated that the cross was the foundation of all of his preaching and teaching (1 Cor 2:2). While the "word of the cross" was a scandal to the Greeks (1 Cor 1:23–24), and an offense to the Jews (Gal 5:11), it is to the Christian a demonstration of the love of God toward humanity in Christ Jesus (2 Cor 3:14; 1 Cor 1:24–25). Seen in its theological significance, as it is in the St. John's Gospel, the cross of Christ can be described with the language of praise; Jesus is said to be "lifted up,"[91] or "glorified,"[92] and these are descriptions of Christ's saving death. Apart from the theological understanding of the cross, which the Christians were given by the NT writings and proclamation, the cross was a heinous emblem indeed; but seen from the standpoint of the saving, reconciling, liberating death it signified for Christians, the cross became—literally—"good news" (Grk. *evangelion*).

Just as Christ had His cross, so also have Christians sought to follow the way of the cross (Lat. *via crucis*), which in many instances became a way of self-denial and a way of suffering (Lat. *via dolorosa*). A single-minded consideration of the sufferings ("passion") of Christ on the cross was the pattern of St. Paul, who resolved "to know nothing . . . but Christ and Him crucified" (1 Cor 2:2). The risen Christ, in Whose life we participate by faith and by sacramental union, continues to bear the marks of His passion (Rev 5:6). If it was "fitting" that the Savior would be made "perfect through suffering" (Heb 2:10), then how could those who followed Him aspire to anything less than Christ's way in the world?

For many early Christians, like St. Ignatius (d. 117)—the martyred Bishop of Antioch—taking up "the cross" resulted in emulating the Lord in life as well as in death. Ignatius approached his end without fear; indeed he longed to "imitate the Passion of my God." This triumph over the fear of death was based in Ignatius's belief that his martyrdom marked both the culmination of his discipleship and the way to be with Christ: "Now is the moment I am beginning to be a disciple," he wrote. He was motivated by a "passion for death" that extinguished his desire for worldly things: "For though alive, it is with a passion for death that I am writing to you. My Desire has been crucified and there burns in me no passion for material things. There is living water in me, which speaks and says inside me, 'Come to the Father. . . .'"[93]

Devotion that was based upon the contemplation of and identification with the sufferings of Christ was very much a part of the spirituality of the Middle Ages. Thus, St. Bernard of Clairvaux asked: ". . . what can be so effective a cure for the wound of conscience and so purifying to keenness of mind as steady meditation on the wounds of Christ?"[94] In an age full of decadence and human suf-

---

[91] John 3:14–15, 8:28.

[92] John 7:39, 12:23, 13:31–32.

[93] Cyril Richardson, ed., *Early Christian Fathers* (New York: Macmillan, 1979),"Letters of Ignatius: Romans," p. 105.

[94] Evans, trans., *Bernard of Clairvaux*, pp. 250–51.

fering, sensitive souls, like St. Francis of Assisi (c. 1182–1226), sought to purify their lives and aspirations through contemplation of the suffering of Christ. St. Bonaventure, one of Francis's earliest biographers, recalled: "In all things he wished to be conformed to Christ crucified, who hung on the cross poor, suffering, and naked. . . . He strove to conform himself to Christ and to imitate him perfectly—while living to imitate Christ living, dying to imitate Christ dying, and after death to imitate Christ after death—and he merited to be honored with the imprint of Christ's likeness."[95] The "imprint of Christ's likeness," to which Bonaventure alluded, was the five wounds of Christ—the *stigmata*—which St. Francis received in 1224. Through his conformity to the passion of Christ, St. Francis, like the apostle Paul, bore on his body "the marks of Jesus Christ" (Gal 6:17).

For others, like the mystic and visionary Catherine of Genoa (1447–1510), contemplation of the sufferings of Christ brought an effusion of Divine love into the human soul: "One day there appeared to her inner vision Jesus Christ incarnate crucified, all bloody from head to foot. It seemed that the body rained blood. From within she heard a voice say, 'Do you see this blood? It has been shed for your love, to atone for your sins.' With that she received a wound of love that drew her to Jesus with such trust that it washed away all previous fright, and she took joy in the Lord."[96] The entire "Third Week" of St. Ignatius of Loyola's *Spiritual Exercises* was dedicated to the contemplation of the passion of our Lord Jesus Christ.[97] Protestant hymnody showed similar interest in the sufferings of Christ, and often portrayed the Lord's passion in vivid fashion. In Charles Wesley's famous hymn, "Arise my Soul, Arise" (1742), the wounds of Christ are personified to express their intercessory role as well as their "all-redeeming love"; the Spirit of God responds to the pleading wounds of Christ by speaking forgiveness and acceptance into the penitent's heart:

> He ever lives above,
>   For me to intercede,
> His all-redeeming love,
>   His precious blood, to plead;
> His blood atoned for all our race,
> And sprinkles now the throne of grace.
>
> Five bleeding wounds he bears,
>   Received on Calvary;
> They pour effectual prayers,
>   They strongly speak for me;
> 'Forgive him, O forgive,' they cry,
>   'Nor let that ransomed sinner die!'
>
> The Father hears him pray,
>   His dear Anointed One;

---

[95] Ewert Cousins, ed., *Bonaventure* (New York: Paulist Press, 1978), p. 318, "The Life of Francis."
[96] Serge Hughes, ed., *Catherine of Genoa* (New York: Paulist Press, 1979), p. 118.
[97] Ganss, trans., *The Spiritual Exercises*, pp. 190–217.

He cannot turn away
  The presence of his Son;
His Spirit answers to the blood,
  And tells me I am born of God.[98]

Union with Christ. Indeed, the heart of the Christian religion is union with Christ; union with Christ is both the means and the goal of Christian Spirituality. As James Stewart wrote, "Everything that religion meant for Paul is focused for us in such great words as these: 'I live yet not I, but Christ liveth in me' [Gal 2:20]. 'There is therefore now no condemnation to them which are in Christ Jesus' [Rom 8:1]. 'He that is joined unto the Lord is one spirit' [1 Cor 6:17]."[99] Union with Christ was profoundly expressed in the apostle's preference for the phrase "in Christ." The Synoptic gospels frequently describe the disciples of Jesus Christ as being "with him" (Grk. *meta*), but never "in him" (*en*). In the Pauline corpus the Christian is frequently said to be "in Christ" (*en*) and never said to be "with him" (*meta*).[100] The death and resurrection of Christ stand as a watershed between these two phrases; those who had been "with Christ" in life could be "in Christ" only if they were joined to Christ by faith in His death and resurrection, and by the renewal wrought by the Holy Spirit. Thus, St. Paul urges Christians to be united with Christ in His death,[101] in His burial,[102] and in His resurrection.[103]

As a response to God's grace, imitation of Christ leads to conformity with Christ because—through faith and conversion—Christians have "treasure" ("transcendent power") "in earthen vessels," they have the "life of Jesus" being made "manifested in our mortal flesh" (2 Cor 4:7–12). In union with Christ, Christians no longer live according to the law of "sin and death," they live according to the "law of the Spirit," which brings the life which is in Christ Jesus (Rom 8:2). This life "in Christ" is remarkable for its "newness" (Rom 6:4) and for its "eternal" quality—and as such it is the "end" (*telos*, "goal," or "completion") of our sanctification (Rom 6:22–23). Hence St. Paul concluded: ". . . if any one is in Christ, he is a new creation; the old has passed away, behold the new has come. All this is from God . . ." (2 Cor 5:17–18a). Johann Arndt (1555–1621), author of *True Christianity* (1609) and forerunner of German pietism, illustrated this theme well when he insisted that true Christianity was constituted by transformation of one's life through union with Christ:

A true Christian is known by a Christian life and not by the name "Christian." He who wishes to be a true Christian must endeavor to let one see Christ in

---

[98]Wesley, *Collection of Hymns*, #202, p. 194, verses 2–4.

[99]James S. Stewart, *A Man in Christ: The Vital Element of St. Paul's Religion* (New York: Harper and Brothers, n.d.), p. 155.

[100]Ibid. Steward cites 164 occurrences of "in Christ" language in the Pauline corpus.

[101]Romans 6:7, 7:4, 8:1; Colossians 2:20, 3:8; 2 Corinthians 5:14; Galatans 2:20, 5:24–25; Philippians 3:10; etc.

[102]Romans 6:4; Colossians 2:12.

[103]Romans 6:4, 8:6; Colossians 2:12.

him, in his love, humility, and graciousness, for no one can be a Christian in whom Christ does not live. . . . The spirit of Christ must rule a Christian's life and make him conformed to Christ.[104]

The Holy Spirit

The biblical words, both in Hebrew and in Greek, that describe "the Spirit" of God are connected to "wind, or "breath." The wind is a good word picture for the mysterious and invisible operation of the Holy Spirit; like the wind, the Spirit is better known by the sense and results of its presence than by our ability to see or discern its presence or operations. One may summarize the role of the Holy Spirit in the OT, as George Johnston did: ". . . the Spirit is the Divine Power immanent in human history. . . . It is immanent only because it is essentially transcendent, coming forth out of the supernatural life of God who deals directly with men."[105]

The Synoptic gospels built upon and extended the OT teaching by demonstrating that the Spirit authenticated (Mt 3:16–17) and directed Jesus's ministry (Mt 4:1). The gospel according to John delineated the theological connection between Jesus and the Holy Spirit; the "Spirit of truth," whom Jesus will send upon His ascension, will be "another Counselor" (Grk. *paracletos*, "helper," "advocate,") and will make the ascended Christ present among his disciples (Jn 14:15–24). Gregory Nazianzus (c. 330–90) aptly noted that the Holy Spirit ". . . came after Christ, that a Comforter should not be lacking unto us; but *another* Comforter, that you might acknowledge His co-equality. For 'another' is not said . . . of different kinds, but of things consubstantial."[106] Sending the Holy Spirit is synonymous with sending Christ's peace among his disciples because, as Jesus told them, the Spirit "will teach you all things, and bring to your remembrance all that I have said to you" (Jn 14:26). In a similar way, the "Spirit of truth, who proceeds from the Father," will "bear witness" to Christ (Jn 15:26) and "will convince the world concerning sin and righteousness and judgment . . ." (Jn 16:8). The "Spirit of truth," when he comes, will "guide" the disciples of Jesus "into all truth; for he will not speak on his own authority. . . . He will glorify me [Christ], for he will take what is mine and declare it to you" (Jn 16:14).

It is by the power of the Holy Spirit that Christians confess Jesus as God incarnate (1 Jn 4:4), and confess Him as Lord (1 Cor 12:3). The Spirit aids Christians in their prayers for "adoption" as God's children and for "the redemption of our bodies" (Rom 8:22–27), as well as for the "perseverance" of the saints through the proclamation of the gospel (Eph 6:18). The Spirit creates a sense of belonging to God in the heart of the Christian, which St. Paul characterized as "the spirit of sonship," that cries "Abba, Father!" (Gal 4:6; Rom 8:16); "it is the Spirit himself bearing witness with our spirit that we are children of God . . ." (Rom 15:16).[107]

---

[104]Johann Arndt, *True Christianity*, translated by Peter Erb (New York: Paulist Press, 1979), p. 117.
[105]George Johnston, "Spirit," in TWBB, pp. 236–37.
[106]Gregory Nazianzen, "Orations on Pentecost," in NPNF, Series Two, Vol. VII, p. 383.
[107]1 John 3:19–24, 4:13–5:12.

Christians are said to able to "rejoice" in their sufferings, because suffering produces endurance, Christian character, and hope, because "God's love has been poured into our hearts through the Holy Spirit which has been given to us" (Rom 5:5). The Holy Spirit not only enables us to begin Christian life, by confessing Christ; the Holy Spirit creates Christian life within us by its witness, perseverance, and love.

In a similar way the Holy-Spirit sanctifies Christians by enabling them to "believe in the name of His [God's] Son Jesus, to love another" and to "keep his commandments . . ." (1 Jn 4:23–24). The Spirit bears fruit in the Christian's life by producing love, joy, peace, patience, kindness, goodness, faithfulness, gentleness, and self-control (Gal 5:16–26). To make this connection concrete, Catherine of Siena likened the work of the Holy Spirit to that of a waiter: "The Holy Spirit . . . is the waiter who serves [Christians] my [God's] gifts and graces."[108] It is by the power of the Holy Spirit that Christians are changed into the "likeness" of Christ, "from one degree of glory to another . . . for this comes from the Lord who is the Spirit" (2 Cor 3:18).

The Spirit produces "varieties of gifts" (Grk. charismata) for "varieties of service" in the body of believers. Among these gifts are proclamation, spiritual guidance, and healing (1 Cor 12:4–14). The most abiding of these spiritual gifts are faith, hope and love, "but the greatest of these is love" (1 Cor 13:13). St. Augustine's comment on the phrase "varieties of service" is illuminating; ". . . various duties are harmoniously allotted to the various members. . . . despite these members being different, they rejoice in a common equal health [1 Cor 12:26] all together, not separately, no one with more, another with less."[109] Intercessory prayer (Eph 6:18), and "making melody to the Lord" with "psalms, hymns and spiritual songs" are also attributed to the inspiration of the Holy Spirit (Eph 5:18–20). At various points in the history of the Church the Spirit has also given gifts of prophetic utterance, "speaking in tongues" (glossolalia, 1 Cor 14) and "the working of miracles" (1 Cor 12:10).

As a Christian strains to hear the voice of the Holy Spirit, St. Augustine points us to the interconnection of the Word of God and the Spirit of God. Commenting on John 3, he wrote: "No one sees the Spirit; how do we hear the voice of the Spirit? A Psalm is sung, it is the voice of the Spirit; the Gospel is read, it is the voice of the Spirit; the Word of God is preached, it is the voice of the Spirit. You hear His voice but you know not whence it comes or wither it goes."[110] In a similar way, the "spiritual birth" that Jesus enjoined upon Nicodemus (Jn 3) comes to us through the Word and Sacrament of God.[111] The voice of the Spirit is also heard in the human soul. For John Wesley "The Witness of the Spirit" (1746) ". . . is an inward impression on the soul that I am 'a child of God'; that Jesus Christ hath loved me, and given himself for me; that all my sins are blotted out,

---

[108]Catherine of Siena, *Dialogue*, p. 146.
[109]Clark, ed., *Augustine of Hippo*, p. 413.
[110]Ibid., p. 285.
[111]Ibid.

and I, even I am reconciled to God."[112] This experiential communication between the human spirit and the Spirit of God was precisely the premise of St. Catherine of Siena's *The Dialogue* (1370), and of numerous other significant works.

The Holy Trinity

Jesus's last and great commission to His disciples was ". . . to make disciples of all nations, baptizing them in the name of the Father and of the Son and of the Holy Spirit . . ." (Mt 28:19). So saying the Lord indicated that the making of disciples was indeed a Trinitarian process. This Trinitarian work is also established in the Johannine narrative, since the Spirit "proceeds from the Father" (15:26) at the prayer of the Son (14:16). The Spirit calls to remembrance (14:26) and declares the things of Christ (16:14), which Jesus also described as being the things of the Father, since "All that the Father has is mine; therefore I said that he [the Spirit] will take what is mine and declare it to you" (Jn 16:15). Just as Jesus spoke the words of "the Father who sent me," so also the Holy Spirit, "whom the Father will send in my name . . . will teach you all things, and bring to your remembrance all things that I have said to you" (Jn 14:24–26). St. Augustine, commenting on this same passage, noted: "The whole Trinity, therefore, both speaketh and teacheth; but were it not also brought before us in its individual personality, it would certainly altogether surpass the power of human weakness to comprehend it."[113] Because of this inter-Trinitarian connection, St. Bernard of Clairvaux found all three persons of the Holy Trinity involved in the process of sanctification:

> . . . those whom the Son first humbles by word and example, and upon whom the Spirit afterward pours out love, these the Father receives at length in glory. The Son makes us disciples. The Paraclete comforts us as friends. The Father raises us up as sons. And because not only the Son but also the Father and the Holy Spirit are truly called Truth, it is agreed that one and the same truth . . . works in these three steps. The first teaches us like a master. The second comforts us like a friend or brother. The third embraces us as a father does his son.[114]

The Holy Trinity also builds the church. Ignatius of Antioch (d. 117), reflecting upon the "living stones" imagery of 1 Peter 2:5, viewed the church as a spiritual temple that is being constructed by the Holy Trinity in cooperation with the Christian's faith and love: "Like living stones of God's Temple, ready for a building of God the Father, you are being hoisted up by Jesus Christ, as with a crane

---

[112] Albert Outler ed., *The Works of John Wesley*, Vol. I, *Sermons*, (Nashville, Tenn.: Abingdon Press, 1984), Sermon #10, "The Witness of the Spirit," pt. I, p. 274.

[113] Augustine, *The Works of St. Augustine*, "Homilies on the Gospel of John," Homily LXXVII, in NPNF, Series One, Vol. II, p. 338.

[114] Evans, trans., *Bernard of Clairvaux*, "On Humility and Pride."

(that's the cross!), while the rope you use is the Holy Spirit. Your faith is what lifts you up, while love is the way you ascend to God."[115]

St. Augustine's exploration of the Trinity suggested that there are analogical connections between the nature of the Triune God and the Christian understanding of human nature as being created in the image of the Triune God. His *De Trinitate* ("On the Trinity," c. 416) used the doctrine of the Trinity, which Augustine expounded in books I through VII, to discover and explain human nature (books VIII–X). Employing the concept of "triads" (groups of three elements), borrowed from Neoplatonism, Augustine developed a sort of "trinity of the mind" that was to be understood as "a real image of the Trinity."[116] In the mind's self-knowledge and self-love he found a reflection of the image of the Triune God: ". . . in these three, when the mind knows itself and loves itself, there remains a trinity: mind, love, knowledge; and this trinity is not confounded together by any combining: although they are each severally in themselves and mutually all in all. . . ."[117]

The Communion of Saints

Modern Christians do not feel very comfortable calling themselves "saints." The word conjures up pictures of heroes and heroines of the faith, as depicted by sacred art, with their halos well intact. But the popular conception of the term *saints* will not bear close comparison with Christian teaching. In the Hebrew Bible, "holy" (*Qodesh*) described persons, places, and things that had been separated from normal use, and were set apart or consecrated unto God. The NT uses "saints" (from Lat. *sanctus*) to translate various words for "holy" (Grk. *hagios*). It describes Christians as people who are consecrated unto God, professing Christ and being sanctified by the Holy Spirit; "saints" describes the church and her members from the standpoint of their position (in Christ) and from the standpoint of their potential of being sanctified or made holy by God's grace.[118]

The "communion" in the term *communio sanctorum* means "fellowship" or "sharing" (Grk. *koinonia*).[119] The fellowship or communion that characterizes the Christian church is created by "sharing" in Christ and His benefits. It means "sharing" in God's grace (Phil 1:7), the gospel (1 Cor 9:23), the Holy Spirit (Phil 2:1), and the Eucharistic body and blood of Jesus Christ (1 Cor 10:16–17.) Eucharistic fellowship with Christ unites the many individual members of the church ("though we are many") in "the cup of blessing," and forms them into "one body" (1 Cor 10:16–17). The Johannine narrative focuses our attention on the trans-

---

[115]Richardson, ed., *Early Christian Fathers*, ch. 9, p. 90.

[116]Andrew Louth, "Augustine," in Jones, Wainwright, and Yarnold, eds., *Study of Spirituality*, pp. 141–45.

[117]Augustine, *On the Trinity*, in NPNF, First Series One, Vol. III, p. 128, bk. IX, ch. 5, para. 8.

[118]S. Rankin, "Saints, Holy," in TWBB, pp. 214–16.

[119]F. Hauck, "Koinonia," in TDNT, Vol. III, pp. 804ff.

forming and reconciling power that the "flesh and blood" of Christ have for the individual Christian (Jn 6:52–60),[120] and thereby reminds us that the individuality and uniqueness of the "many members" are also to be affirmed and safeguarded. Because of the depth of this "fellowship" in Christ, Christians are said to share in the glory that is to be revealed (1 Pet 5:1), and to be "partakers" ("sharers") of the Divine nature (2 Pet 1:4).

The sharing *in* and *with* Christ undergirds and empowers fellowship *among* Christians. As Gustavo Gutierrez noted, "the breaking of the bread is at once the point of departure and the point of arrival of true Christian community."[121] *Koinonia*, in this sense, describes the abiding in the company and friendship of Christians (2 Cor 6:14); it is a fellowship based upon a sharing in the life and knowledge of God through the gospel (1 Jn 1:2–3). The Eucharist, perhaps more than any other single event, epitomizes the fellowship *with* Christ that creates *koinonia among* Christians (1 Cor 10:16–17). Hence the earliest Christians ". . . devoted themselves to the apostle's teaching and fellowship, to the breaking of bread [Eucharist], and the prayers" (Acts 2:42). So deeply interwoven were the concepts of "coming together as a church" (1 Cor 11:17) and "coming together to eat" the Lord's Supper (1 Cor 11:33), that the word that stands for "to come together" (Grk. *synaxis*) quickly became a shorthand expression for the gathering of Christians for the Lord's Supper and worship.[122] St. Ignatius of Antioch used it (d. 117), for example, when he urged the Ephesians to "try to gather together more frequently to celebrate God's Eucharist, and to praise him."[123] The *Didache*, (an anonymous Christian instructional treatise of the late first- or early second-century) used *synaxis* to describe the reconciling practices of "every Lord's Day": "On every Lord's Day—his special day—*come together* and break bread and give thanks, first confessing your sins so that your sacrifice may be pure."[124]

The Christian has "fellowship" with Christ in His sufferings (Phil 3:10), and "partnership" in the work of Christ in the world (Phil 1:5). So significant was this fellowship (*koinonia*) among the early Christians that they shared their material possessions (Acts 2:44). They sold their goods and pooled their resources so that they might be able to support each other (Acts 2:45) and give to the less fortunate (Rom 15:26). St. Paul's benediction to the church at Rome, which invoked God's blessing upon them in "steadfastness and encouragement," anticipated that through the manifestation of those blessings they would be "in accord with Christ Jesus," and in living "in such harmony with one another . . . that together you

---

[120]Jesus said, for example, ". . . he who eats my flesh and drinks my blood has eternal life, and I will raise him up at the last day. . . . He who eats my flesh and drinks my blood abides in me, and I in him" (Jn 6:53–56).

[121]Gustavo Gutierrez, *We Drink from Our Own Wells: The Spiritual Journey of a People* (Maryknoll, NY: Orbis Books, 1984), p. 134.

[122]Geoffrey Wainwright, *Doxology: The Praise of God in Worship, Doctrine, and Life* (New York: Oxford University Press, 1980), p. 142.

[123]Richardson, ed., *Early Christian Fathers*, p. 91.

[124]Ibid., with emphasis added. Cf. pp. 57–58 below. See also Maximus the Confessor, "Holy Assembly," pp. 132–37.

may with one voice glorify the God and Father of our Lord Jesus Christ" (Rom 15:5–6). So saying, the apostle indicated that union with Christ, lived harmony among Christians, and the fellowship of Christian worship are inextricably wound together.[125] Christian fellowship and community have long been considered essential to the development of Christian Spirituality. This recognition began in the pattern of the church established in the Day of Pentecost (Acts 2:42–45), as well as in the churches of the Pauline missions, and it continued in the ancient church of the first three centuries. Self-denial and the contemplative life have long been elements of spirituality; in the monastic withdrawal from society early Christians pursued holiness upon avenues that had been traveled by both Jews and Greeks before them. But the growth and wide-spread popularity that monasticism enjoyed in the fourth century and thereafter also reflected something of the changing character of the church.

The countercultural character of the early church—the oppressed and persecuted church of the martyrs—made the church's identity as being "in" but not "of" the world as obvious as it had been painful. The NT church, on these terms, was described as the "assembly" or "summoned" Christians, a community of persons (Grk. *ekklesia*). The church became first tolerated (313 AD) and then supported by the Roman government (324) under Emperor Constantine the Great, and by the end of his reign (337) the Romans had become Christians—at least in a nominal way.

The marriage of church and state, which in Constantine's mind would preserve and enhance both, significantly altered both church and state. It became increasingly difficult for the church to stand apart from popular culture in the Christianized Roman Empire, and as the church grew through the infusion of nominal Christians her task and identity began to undergo significant changes. As the church became more enmeshed in politics it became difficult to maintain her prophetic stance over against the state; as the church was blessed financially and in numerical strength it became increasingly difficult to maintain the *koinonia* that was so much a part of the oppressed fellowship.[126] The church of the houses and catacombs was becoming the church of great cathedrals and imperial endowments, and a few among the saints began to believe that in her acquisition of wealth, property, and popularity the church was losing the path that led to perfection. Christians began to pursue holiness outside the functions of the local congregation, and the monk gradually replaced the martyr as the person who most epitomized the Christian life of radical discipleship.

Christian monasticism initially took shape through the countercultural reaction of solitary individuals who withdrew from the world in pursuit of holiness. The monks sought to live lives of self-denial and utter obedience to God and in this way they marked out both the means and goals of Christian Spirituality. Abba

---

[125]Cf. F. X. Lawlor, "Communion of Saints," in NCE, Vol. IV, pp. 41–43; G. W. H. Lampe, "Communion," in IDB, Vol. I, pp. 664–66.

[126]Cf. H. Richard Niebuhr, *Christ and Culture* (New York: Harper Colophon Books, 1951), for the standard discussion of this "enduring problem" and various models that approach resolutions of it.

Germanus, one of the Desert Fathers, described the means and the goal of the ascetic life in this fashion:

> Everything we do, our every objective, must be undertaken for the sake of . . . purity of heart. This is why we take on loneliness, fasting, vigils, work, nakedness. For this we must practice the reading of the Scripture, together will all the other virtuous activities, and we do so to trap and to hold our hearts free of the harm of every dangerous passion and in order to rise step by step to the high point of love.[127]

The word *monk* came from the Greek *monos,* "alone," and hence "monk" meant "solitary one."[128] *The Life of Saint Antony,* by St. Athanasisus (c. 357), presented the Egyptian hermit as the founder of monasticism. His work popularized monastic ideals in the fourth-century church. The anchorite (Grk. *anchoresis,* "withdrawal") vision of holy solitaries called men and women to a separate life of prayer and contemplation, and it continued to influence the development of Christian Spirituality through the impact of people like Julian of Norwich, but—at least in terms of the sheer number and influence of its adherents—monastic communities superceded the hermit's hut as places of spiritual instruction and formation.

Cenobitic (from the Greek word for "common") monasticism drew more directly upon the koinoina concepts of shared life and fellowship as a basis for monastic life. Pachomius (c. 292–346) is traditionally identified as the founder of communal monasticism with its emphasis upon shared work and shared worship under a common "rule" of conduct and practice. Benedict of Nursia (c. 480–550) authored and popularized one of the most influential of these monastic rules. St. Benedict's rule epitomized Western monasticism up through the Middle Ages; it aims at the perfection of the individual soul through the living of Christian life in community. This life was lived in the rhythmic harmony established by liturgical prayer, manual labor, and *lectio divina* (the meditative study of the Scriptures).[129] Obedience marked out the way to humility, and humility pointed the way to love; love was esteemed as the path to perfection.[130]

Where St. Benedict's ideal of monastic community was separate and self-contained, the mendicant (Lat. *mendicare,* "to beg") traditions established by St. Francis and St. Dominic (1170–1221) extended Christian community more directly into the "secular" world by sending monks penniless into the highways and byways as ambassadors and troubadours of the Risen Christ. Late medieval piety,

---

[127] Colm Luibheid, trans., *John Cassian: Conferences* (New York: Paulist Press, 1985), "Conference One," p. 41.

[128] James E. Goehring, "Monasticism," in *Encyclopedia of Early Christianity,* edited by Everett Ferguson (New York: Garland Publishing Co., p. 1990), pp. 612-19 (hereafter: EEC).

[129] Cf. Lane, *Christian Spirituality,* pp. 19–26, for a brief but useful discussion of "Benedictine Spirituality."

[130] St. Benedict's twelve steps of humility are found on pp. 125–28 below.

as exemplified by the *Devotio Moderna* of the Brethren of the Common Life, sought to popularize monastic spirituality among the laity by establishing houses of spiritual formation that were not based upon a formal rule nor upon vows but upon the "Resolutions and Intentions, but Not Vows" of master Geert Grote (1340–84). While his resolutions were certainly based on those of monasticism, Grote's abhorrence of monastic vows was based on his hope of popularizing monastic values and practices by depicting them as normative Christian virtues instead of constituting a higher standard to be followed only by the spiritually serious person.[131] Grote's vision prepared the way for modern approaches by reminding us that the cultivation of Christian Spirituality is the task of every Christian. These same profound motivations subsequently gave the world spirituality reflected in *The Imitation of Christ*, attributed to Thomas a' Kempis.[132]

Among early Protestants the *communio sanctorum* continued to be a principle for Christian identity and congregational life. The Anabaptist tradition, in particular, sought to recover and manifest the NT *koinonia* as the basis for defining congregational life. This church, in the mind of Peter Riedeman (1506–56) and others, was a "gathered church" of saints who confessed Christ through "believer's baptism" (as opposed to being a territorial or state church); it was a community (Ger. *Gemeinschaft*) of Christians that " . . . only want to be like Christ, to partake of his nature, and diligently to do his will. . . ."[133] Adult believer's baptism, peaceful nonresistance and the community of goods became hallmarks of the Anabaptists' intention to replicate the life and experience of the apostolic church; the results of persecution and martyrdom were deemed the inevitable reactions of a fallen world to true Christian discipleship (Jn 15:18–27).[134]

Pietism emerged within the context of an overly academic Lutheran Church and the pressures of a modern world. Philip Spener, founder of the movement, penned a manifesto for reform that epitomized Pietism: *Pia Desideria: or Heartfelt Desire for a God-Pleasing Reform of the True Evangelical Church, Together with Several Simple Christian Proposals Looking Toward This End* (1675).[135] Spener's idea of instituting small group meetings for the cultivation of holiness (*collegia pietatis*) within the larger context of local congregations was one of his most enduring proposals.[136] It enabled the church to focus more intentionally upon *koinonia* and, like the earlier monastic orders, the *collegia pietatis* used community life to revitalize the life of the church. A similar sort of development lay at the heart of the Wesleyan revival. Drawing upon various resources, chiefly the NT (especially Acts

---

[131]John van Engen, trans., *Devotio Moderna: Basic Writings* (New York: Paulist Press, 1988), pp. 65ff.

[132]Selections from this classical text are carried below on pp. 195–203.

[133]Peter Riedeman, *Account of Our Religion, Doctrine, and Faith* (1542), "Through Whom Is Gathered Together One, Holy Christian Church," in Klaasen, ed., *Anabaptism in Outline*, pp. 111–13.

[134]Cf. John H. Yoder, trans., *The Legacy of Michael Sattler* (Scottdale, Pa: Herald Press, 1973), "The Schleitheim Brotherly Union," and "Congregational Order," pp. 27–45; Riedeman, "Concerning Community of Goods," in Klassen, ed., *Anabaptism in Outline*, pp. 238–40.

[135]Spener, *Pia Desideria.* Selections are reprinted below on pp. 301–6.

[136]Ibid., "Proposals to Correct Conditions," pp. 89–92.

2:42–45)[137] and the Church Fathers,[138] the Wesleys understood Methodism as a restatement of what was best in "Primitive Christianity."[139] Working within the communion of seventeenth-century Anglicanism, Methodism intended to invigorate the contemporary Church through the *koinonia* created by Methodist classes, bands, and societies. By embracing the disciplines and practices of the early Christians they hoped to rekindle Christian experience and vital discipleship within the Anglican communion.[140]

Contemporary Christians, like those embracing the "base-communities" movement in Latin America, continue to evidence the power of the koinonia basis of Christian Spirituality.[141] Gustavo Gutierrez, writing from a Latin American context, finds "the development of the community dimension of faith is a characteristic of Christian life in our day."[142] For Gutierrez, rediscovery of the "community dimension" is crucial for our times because it counteracts several important misconceptions about Christian Spirituality; of these misconceptions two are particularly damaging. First, "Christian Spirituality has long been presented as geared to *minorities*. It seems to be the peculiar possession of a select and to some extent, closed group."[143] And "a second characteristic of the Spirituality in question, and one that is also being challenged today, is its *individualistic bent*. The spiritual journey has often been presented as a cultivation of individualistic values, as a way to personal perfection. . . ."[144] For Christian Spirituality to be powerful in its own context, Gutierrez argued, these perceptions must be overcome in favor of a spirituality that has its basis in community, and in solidarity with the sufferings of Christ and Christ's people. Hence, he concluded, "Spirituality is a community enterprise. It is the passage of a people through the solitude and dangers of the desert, as it carves out its own way in the following of Jesus Christ. This spiritual experience is the well from which we must drink. From it we draw the promise of resurrection."[145]

---

[137]Frank Baker, editor-in-chief, *The Bicentennial Edition of the Works of John Wesley* (Nashville, Tenn.: Abingdon Press, various dates), Vol. II, Sermon 2, "The General Spread of the Gospel," p. 494 (hereafter cited as Works of JW). Works of JW, Vol. IX, "The Character of a Methodist," (1742), p. 41; "A Plain Account of the People Called Methodists," (1749) p. 254. See also John Wesley, *Explanatory Notes Upon the New Testament* (San Francisco: Carlton and Thomas, reprint), p. 281, for Wesley's commentary on Acts 2:42–45.

[138]Ted A. Campbell, *John Wesley and Christian Antiquity* (Nashville, Tenn.: Kingswood Books, 1991).

[139]Charles Wesley's hymn by this title, based on Acts 2:42–45, was a quintessential statement of the nature of the Methodist movement as the Wesleys understood it. Cf. John R. Tyson, ed., *Charles Wesley: A Reader* (New York: Oxford University Press, 1989), pp. 185–88, for the full text of this hymn with interpretive notes.

[140]Cf. Works of JW, Vol. IX, Rupert Davies, ed., *The Methodist Societies*, "The Nature, Design, and General Rules of the United Societies," pp. 67–77, for a survey of the spiritual disciplines practiced by early Methodists.

[141]Rahner, *Practice of Faith*, pp. 167–75.

[142]Gutierrez, *Our Own Wells*, p. 128. Cf. pp. 448–54 for a selection from this document.

[143]Ibid., p. 13.

[144]Ibid., p. 14

[145]Ibid., p. 136.

The transcendent and sacramental unity of Christ and Christians that takes expression in the *communio sanctorum* reminds us that life and death, time and eternity are not barriers to Christian *koinonia*. Indeed, Scripture enjoins us to draw example and encouragement from reflection upon the great deeds of men and women who "died in faith." The writer of the epistle to the Hebrews urged: ". . . since we are surrounded by so great a cloud of witnesses, let us also lay aside every weight and sin which clings so closely to us, and let us run with perseverance the race that is set before us . . ." (Heb 12:1).

Beginning in the third century AD the *church militant* (on earth) began to venerate, pray to, and ask intercession of the saints of the *church triumphant* (in heaven). The Second Vatican Council (1962–65) affirmed the practice of invoking the saints, and described the veneration of the saints as a method of venerating Christ: "Every authentic witness of love, indeed, offered by us to those who are in heaven tends to and terminates in Christ, 'the crown of all the saints,' and through him in God who is wonderful in his saints and is glorified in them."[146] While this is a complex matter,[147] Protestant spirituality, beginning with the Lutheran *Augsburg Confession* (1530), has affirmed the saints as models and examples of Christian faith but has denied their role as intercessors—believing that such practice may detract from the distinctive mediatorial role of Jesus Christ.[148]

Protestants and Catholics alike now find in the *communio sanctorum* a basis and models for examining Christian faith and practice; William Thompson's work *Fire and Light*, for example, surveyed "today's theologians and the saints" and found that Christian theologians from Protestant, Roman Catholic, and Eastern Orthodox traditions have become increasingly willing to consult "the saints" while engaged in the tasks of doing "fundamental, systematic, and practical theology."[149] A similar direction has been signaled in the three-volume *Systematic Theology* by Thomas C. Oden. In the preface to his first volume, *The Living God*, Oden elaborated his ecumenical and consensual approach: "My purpose is . . . to listen single-mindedly for the voice of that deeper, ecumenical consensus that has been gratefully celebrated as received teaching by believers of vastly different cultural

---

[146]Council of Trent, session 25, *De Invocatione . . . Sanctorum*, in *Vatican Council II: The Conciliar Documents and Post Conciliar Documents*, edited by Austin Flannery (Collegeville, Min.: Liturgical Press, 1975), pp. 411–12; cf. 2 Thessalonians 1:10.

[147]Robert Kolb, *For All the Saints: Changing Perceptions of Martyrdom and Sainthood in the Lutheran Reformation* (Macon, Ga.: Mercer University Press, 1987), offers an insightful overview of this development in the Lutheran tradition.

[148]Theodore Tapper, ed., *The Book of Concord* (Philadephia: Fortress Press, 1959), Articles XXI, "The Cult of the Saints," pp. 46–47. The Article affirms: "Our churches teach that the remembrance of saints may be commended to us so that we imitate their faith and good works according to our calling. . . . However, the Scriptures do not teach us to pray to the saints or seek their help, for the only mediator, propitiation, highpriest, and intercessor whom the Scriptures set before us is Christ. . . ."

[149]See William M. Thompson, *Fire and Light: The Saints and Theology* (New York: Paulist Press, 1987), pp. 3–33 for this insightful survey of recent works.

settings—whether African or European, Eastern or Western, sixth or sixteenth century."[150]

The "communion of saints" is an important resource for the cultivation of Christian Spirituality. A portion of the current consensus is based in a willingness to think of the "saints" in a fashion that includes and yet goes beyond the formal process of canonization. Lawrence Cunningham, for example, suggests that ". . . the saint is a person whose life is so centered on a profound religious vision that it is radically different; that difference is so apparent to others for its quality and depth that the sympathetic observer can see the value of the religious vision that has grasped the saint."[151] Karl Rahner and William Thompson pointed in this same direction as they linked the classical saints and mystics to the spirituality of "Every Day Mystics."[152] Viewed in this fashion, Cunningham was correct to point out that consultation of the saints ". . . serves both a paradigmatic and prophetic function" for Christian Spirituality.[153] It is *paradigmatic* because the saints offer us models for pursuing and practicing Christian Spirituality that are road-tested and reliable; it is *prophetic* insofar as the luminous sanctity of the saints' lives carries with it—either implicitly or explicitly—a judgment upon our own lives and values.

The Virgin Mary holds a significant place in the *communio sanctorum*. The gospel narratives, particularly that of St. Luke, accord Mary particular attention among the followers of Jesus. Luke's birth narrative emphasizes Mary's role over that of Joseph (Matthew takes the opposite approach) and includes several significant stories that locate Mary at their center.[154] It is on this basis, then, that Mary is ". . . hailed as pre-eminent and as a wholly unique member of the Church, as its type and outstanding model in faith and charity."[155] And so contemporary Catholic theologian Karl Rahner urges that Mary ". . . must have a place in theology."[156] The Blessed Virgin's place in theology is determined, as Rahner points out, by the fact that ". . . she is the mother of Him on whom salvation is entirely built, because He is God and man in one person."[157] Rahner finds that the theological significance of Mary also points to the potential of our own humanity when yielded unreservedly to God, and Mary reminds us that "each of us is responsi-

---

[150]Thomas C. Oden, *Systematic Theology*, Vol. 1, *The Living God* (San Francisco: Harper and Row, 1987), p. ix.

[151]Lawrence Cunningham, *The Meaning of Saints* (San Francisco: Harper and Row, 1980), p. 83.

[152]Rahner, *Practice of Faith*, pp. 69–70, 73–84; Thompson, *Fire and Light*, "Consulting Every Day Mystics," pp. 178–96.

[153]Cunningham, *Meaning of Saints*, p. 83.

[154]Among these are the annunciation of the conception of Jesus (Lk 1:26–38), Mary's visit to Elizabeth (Lk 1:39–56), the birth of Jesus (Lk 2:1–7), and finding him in the temple (Lk 2:41–52). The role of Mary in these incidents is one of being the Mother of God by giving birth to the Savior (Lk 2:6–7), as well as being the servant of the Lord (1:38), who sings the Lord's praise (Lk 1:46–55). Mary was a witness to Jesus' death (Jn 19:25–27) and was united with the apostles after Christ's resurrection (Acts 1:13–14).

[155]Flannery, ed., *Vatican II: Documents*, p. 441.

[156]Rahner, *Practice of Faith*, p. 162.

[157]Ibid.

ble for the salvation of his brethren, and can intercede for them with prayer and sacrifice and aid. That is why Mary is not only the Mother of our Lord, but our Mother too."[158]

The ancient church, beginning with Ignatius of Antioch (d. 117) placed particular emphasis on the role of Mary in the coming of the Savior, and generally this emphasis was Christological in character since it underscored the true humanity of Jesus Christ. The role of Mary in the economy of salvation was further annunciated by St. Irenaeus of Lyons (c. 115–202); he saw Mary as antitype to Eve, who by her virtue and yieldedness to God undid (recapitulated) the errors of the first woman. The virginity of Mary drew the attention of champions of Christian morality like St. Athanasius (d. 373), and St. Ambrose (d. 397). When the Council of Ephesus (431) declared that Mary is to be esteemed as *Theotokos* (Grk., "God-bearer") by orthodox Christians of both the East and the West, devotion to the cult of Mary began to grow significantly, and greater attention was given to her role as a heavenly intercessor.[159] Protestants, as exemplified by "The Apology of the Augsburg Confession of Faith" (1531), esteemed Mary as being "worthy of the highest honors" but stopped short of the practice of praying to Mary or asking for her intercession.[160]

Devotion to the Blessed Virgin Mary consists of three foundational elements: (1) veneration and reverent recognition of the dignity due Mary as the holy Virgin Mother of God; (2) invocation or the calling upon Mary for her queenly intercession on our behalf; and (3) acts of consecration and dedication that are based in our willingness to imitate her virtues.[161] Richard McBrien has urged Roman Catholics to steer a course between the extremes of *Marian minimalism* and *Marian maximalism*, between which ". . . there is a broad spectrum of legitimate devotional options."[162] Recent Protestant scholarship, like that of the Anglican theologian John Macquarrie, has sought "to see Mary as a reconciling influence of different Christian traditions," and yet as Macquarrie observed, "it would be wrong to ignore the fact that she also raises issues that have been divisive."[163] The role of the Blessed Virgin Mary in Christian Spirituality poses significant issues

---

[158]Ibid., p. 163.

[159]E.R. Carroll, "Mary, Blessed Virgin, Devotion To," in NCE, Vol. IX, pp. 364–69; and Eugene La Verdiere, "Mary," in EEC, pp. 583–87.

[160]Philip Melanchthon, "The Apology of the Augsburg Confession of Faith," in Tappert, ed., *Book of Concord*, Article XXI, pp. 232–33. Melanchthon wrote: Granted that blessed Mary prays for the church, does she receive souls in death, does she overcome death, does she give life? What does Christ do if blessed Mary does all this? Even though she is worthy of the highest honors, she does not want to be put on the same level as Christ but to have her example considered and followed. The fact of the matter is that in popular estimation the blessed Virgin has completely replaced Christ. Men have invoked her, trusted in her mercy, and sought through her to appease Christ, as though he were not a propitiator but only a terrible judge and avenger. . . .

[161]Carroll, "Mary, Blessed Virgin," p. 364.

[162]McBrien, *Catholicism*, Vol. II, pp. 889–95. Especially helpful are McBrien's eleven "theological criteria" for evaluating "various expressions of Marian devotion," pp. 892–93.

[163]John Macquarrie, *Mary for All Christians* (Grand Rapids, Mich.: Wm. B. Eerdmans, 1990), p. 106.

for contemporary Christians; in addition to the historical debates about the place of Mary in liturgy, prayer, and devotion, Mary must also be seen in the context of the spiritual quest of modern women and men who seek to live lives wholly yielded to God.

The role of the *communio sanctorum* in Christian Spirituality is a multifaceted one. The concept is based in the fellowship with Christ and fellowship among Christians that is epitomized in the Eucharistic celebration of Christ's body. It emphasizes the transcendent unity of Christians, "the saints" past and present, that shapes Christian Spirituality through the quality of life engendered by Christian *koinonia* and that takes expression in congregational life, community life, and various forms of devotion. "Such devotions," Edward Yarnold reminds us, "can express a joy and confidence in the way in which God works through human intermediaries; they depend upon the doctrine of the communion of saints, which asserts the interdependence of all Christians, living and dead."[164]

Eschatology

It seems appropriate to consider eschatology last, since the term stems directly from the Greek word for the "last things" (*eschaton*). While many profitable things might be said regarding the theology of "the end," three themes stand out as being of particular significance for Christian Spirituality.

The Kingdom of God. The Kingdom ("reign," or "rule") of God was central to Jesus's proclamation, especially as it was recorded in the synoptic gospels. It was as the herald and bearer of this Kingdom that Jesus began his earthly ministry.[165] Indeed, Jesus's ministry was filled with signs that suggested God's Kingdom had come upon the earth through Jesus's mission. From the darkness of Herod's dungeon, John the Baptist inquired after Jesus: "Are you the one who is to come, or shall we look for another [Mt 11:3]?" Jesus answered by describing his messianic deeds, using the prophetic words of Isaiah: "Go and tell John . . . 'the blind receive their sight, and the lame walk, lepers are cleansed and the deaf hear, and the dead are raised up, and the poor have good news preached to them'" (Mt 11:5). In a similar way, Jesus's ability to "bind the strong man," Satan (Mk 3:27) and to cast out demons (Lk 11:20 = Mt 12:28) was to be understood as a sign of the arrival of the Kingdom of God. It was, however, a rather inauspicious arrival given the dimensions of the OT predictions of the scope and magnitude of the events that would accompany God's visitation at the end of the world.[166] Neither the paradisiacal utopia of Isaiah 11:1–9, nor the terrible judgment of Isaiah 24, were unambiguously evident in the Kingdom Jesus inaugurated. The Kingdom of God seemed more like a grain of mustard seed or a speck of leaven whose

---

[164]Edward Yarnold, "Media of Spirituality," in Jones, Wainwright, and Yarnold, eds., *Study of Spirituality*, p. 43.
[165]Mark 1:14–15; Luke 4:18ff, 7:22; Matthew 4:23.
[166]Isaiah 10:24–27; 27:1; Zephaniah 2:11; Hosea 4:1–2; Micah 6:1ff; Jeremiah 11:21–23, 20:1–6.

small beginnings would eventually produce prodigious results (Mt 13:31–33). It was a powerful in-breaking of God, which met with varied degrees of success depending upon what sort of soil the Kingdom's proclamation was sown (Mt 13:18–23).

There are several provocative tensions inherent in the Kingdom theology.[167] One of these, which became a constant concern in Christian Spirituality, was the struggle between the Kingdom of God and the Kingdom of "this world", "since the world is in the power of the evil one" (1 Jn 5:19). While this was a particularly prominent theme in Johannine literature,[168] it is also present in the Synoptics: "no one can serve God and mammon" (Mt 6:24). The gospel of Mark narrates a persistent record of Jesus's struggle against demonic evil as a witness to the war being waged against this world and its prince by the strong Son of God. The extrabiblical books of Jewish and Christian apocalypticism were especially hostile in their assessment of the viability of life in this fallen world. But the NT apocalypse—as depicted in the canonical book Revelation—presupposes a world that is not so thoroughly corrupt that it cannot be rectified by Divine intervention; hence, we are reminded powerfully that "the Lamb who had been slain" (Rev 5: 6–12) is also the fierce and conquering Lion of Judah (Rev 5:5). In conflict there is also transformation.[169] Christian baptism and conversion are foreshadows of this "new creation" (2 Cor 5:17), and in our Eucharistic fellowship with Christ and Christians we have a foretaste of the renewal and *koinonia* which is yet to come with Christ's return.

In Christian Spirituality the inevitable conflict between this fallen world and the Kingdom of God invigorated the death-denying faith of the martyrs, as well as the "world"-denying life of hermits, monastics, and ascetics who withdrew from culture and the congregational life of the imperial church in search of a purer way to God. As George Florovsky observed, "The desert is to the empire as apocalypse is to history."[170] This "Christ Against Culture" typology[171] spells itself out not only in the Christian Spirituality that is associated with monasticism; it was sounded in Soren Kierkegaard's (1813–55) countercultural tirades against "Christendom," as well as in modern Pentecostalism's *glossolalia* ("tongues") which, as Wainwright observed, "can be understood as a counter-cultural protest against the rationalistic and materialistic language of late Western Christendom."[172] So also, Gutierrez writes urgently of the challenges Christian Spirituality faces in

---

[167]Cf. McBrien, *Catholicism*, Vol. II, pp. 1157–63, for forty-seven points that aptly summarize the place and function of the Kingdom of God in Christian eschatology.

[168]Satan as "ruler of this world," John 12:31, 14:30, 16:11; and 2 Corinthians 4:4 and Revelation.

[169]This is essentially Niebuhr's resolution of the dilemma of *Christ and Culture*. Cf. "Christ as Transformer of Culture," pp. 190–229.

[170]George Florovsky, *Christianity and Culture: Collected Works*, Vol. II (Belmont, Mass.: Norland, 1974), p. 128.

[171]Niebuhr, *Christ and Culture*, pp. 45–83; and Wainwright, "Types of Spirituality, " in Jones, Wainwright, and Yarnold, eds., *Study of Spirituality*, pp. 592–605.

[172]Wainwright, "Types of Spirituality," p. 595.

Latin America, where dehumanizing conditions of poverty and violence create a seemingly irresolvable conflict between Christianity and an exploitative culture.[173]

A second and deeply interrelated tension inherent in the Kingdom of God has to do with its timing. Jesus's ministry inaugurated the Kingdom of God; it has already begun[174] and yet it awaits a future culmination in "the Age to Come."[175] Thus we live, as Karl Barth described it, "between the times," between the Kingdom's coming and its completion. Jesus's Eucharistic words, "I shall not drink again of this fruit of the vine until that day when I drink it new with you in my Father's Kingdom" (Mt 26:29), reflect upon this temporal tension, and that reflection is preserved in eucharistic prayers of contemporary Christian communions.[176]

This tension between "the already" and "the not yet" also characterizes the pilgrimage aspect of Christian Spirituality; it implies that we have begun on a journey toward sanctity, whose end is not in immediate view. Martin Luther's *simul justus et peccator* ("simultaneously righteous and a sinner"), which implies that the tension between nature and grace is irresolvable in this life, reflects this same tension. It focuses Lutheran spirituality upon the reconciling and renewing grace of God, as opposed to human endeavors, and stands as a permanent hedge against those inclinations that might cause us to imagine that we have "arrived" at sanctity, even though—in truth—we are somewhere between the already and the not yet. While it seems inadvisable for Christians to assume that they have "arrived" with respect to their pilgrimage toward holiness, it must also be affirmed that the purifying and right-making Kingdom of God will indeed arrive at the return of Christ and that the Kingdom will bring to completion the reconciliation that was begun in Jesus's first Advent.

Death and Resurrection. Eschatology impinges upon human life not only in the intervention of the Kingdom of God, but also in the fact of death—which casts its shadow across all human life. But death has been robbed of "its sting"[177] by the victory of Jesus Christ over the power of sin and by His resurrection from the grave. The resurrection of Christ is the basis of the Christian's "living hope" (1 Pet 1:3). As St. Paul pointed out, ". . . if Christ has not been raised, then our preaching is in vain and your faith is in vain" (1 Cor 15:14). Alan Richardson aptly concluded, "The resurrection of Christ is God's mightiest act; it has created our faith; and it is . . . an eschatological symbol in history of our ultimate salvation and therefore the ground of our hope (Rom 5:1–5)."[178] The resurrection of Christ in history points to and validates our own hope for resurrection-life with Christ be-

---

[173]Gutierrez, *Our Own Wells*, "How Shall We Sing to the Lord in a Foreign Land," pp. 9–18.

[174]Mark 1:28, 10:15; Luke 4:21, 17:20; Matthew 11:2–6, 12:29.

[175]Matthew 13:36–43, 25:41; Luke 13:28–29.

[176]See for example, "The Great Thanksgiving," *Book of Common Prayer* (New York: Seabury Press, 1979), Holy Eucharist I, p. 341.

[177]1 Corinthians 15:55–56, quoting Isaiah 25:8, and Hosea 13:14: "'Death is swallowed up in victory.'O death, where is thy victory? O death, where is thy sting?'"

[178]Alan Richardson, "Hope," in TWBB, p. 109.

yond history. It was on the basis of such a hope that martyrs like Sts. Ignatius (d. 117) and Perpetua (d. 203) faced horrible deaths, unflinchingly.

Resurrection of the body implies a continuity between this life and the life to come. Our ultimate life with God is not based on saving the soul *from* the body, it is a continuation of our whole self (body and soul) in a new and purified existence before God. St. Paul used the analogy of a seed sown in the soil to describe this continuity between the earthly and heavenly body: "What is sown is perishable, what is raised is imperishable. It is sown in dishonor, it is raised in glory. It is sown in weakness, it is raised in power. It is sown a physical body, it is raised a spiritual body" (1 Cor 15:42–44). The resurrection of the body not only declares that Christian faith opens a door through death to a life with God beyond death, it also affirms a transformation and purification of our humanity so complete that the temporal tension between the "already" and the "not yet" will be dissolved into actual (instead of approximate) holiness. In this sense, then, resurrection of the body has its culmination in the communion of saints as the church militant (on earth) joins the church triumphant (in heaven).

The purifying and renewing effects of the resurrection have long been the object of Christian reflection, and Christians of a mystical bent have sometimes longed for a faith-filled death that would subsequently occasion their resurrection to transformed life in the likeness of God's Son and in the glory of God's presence. St. Paul expressed a sense of this longing when he wrote: "For to me to live is Christ, and to die is gain. . . . My desire is to depart and be with Christ, for that is better" (Phil 1:22–23). Catherine of Siena, in her *Dialogue*, assigned these aspirations to those souls who had arrived at the third and fourth stages of union with God:

> Death gives these souls no difficulty. They long for it. With perfect contempt they have done battle with their bodies. . . . They long for death, and so they say, "Who will free me from my body? I long to be set free from my body and to be with Christ" [Phil 1:23]. And as such as these say along with Paul, "Death for me is in longing, and life in patience."[179]

Charles Wesley, poet laureate of Methodism, expressed similar sentiments in his hymn, "O Death, My Hope Is Full of Thee." In this instance the death of the faithful person was personified as a long and lovely embrace:

> Extend thy arms, and take me in,
> Weary of life, and self, and sin;
>   Be thou my balm, my ease:
> I languish till thy face appears;
> No longer now the king of fears,
>   Thou art all loveliness.[180]

[179]Catherine of Siena, *Dialogue*, #84, p. 154.

[180]G. Osborn, ed., *The Poetical Works of John and Charles Wesley*, 13 vols. (London: Wesleyan Conference, 1869), Vol. III, p. 163.

Reflection upon death and resurrection is not only within the purview of martyrs and mystics. It belongs to all of us since it impinges upon us through the existential reality of our personal *eschaton*. For this reason death and resurrection are enshrined in the church's most ancient affirmations: "I believe . . . in the resurrection of the body and in the life everlasting."[181] Christian liturgy developed funeral rites that stressed the anticipation of "life through death" and enabled the church to live out her great hope.[182] St. Augustine enjoined that contemplation and preparation, for death ". . . alone ought to be the topic of our reflection."[183] The principal result of this reflection should be amendment of life. The author of *The Imitation of Christ* raised an exhortation that was sounded by many other writers and practitioners of Christian Spirituality: "Very soon the end of your life will be at hand; consider therefore, the state of your soul. . . . You should order your every deed and thought, as though today were the day of your death. Had you a good conscience, death would hold no terrors for you; even so, it were better to avoid sin than to escape death."[184] This kind of reflection upon death, which stressed its ethical payload, became particularly prominent in Protestant Spirituality; it was exemplified by sources as diverse as Jeremy Taylor's *Holy Living, Holy Dying* (1650–51), and C. S. Lewis's *The World's Last Night* (1959).

The Parousia. The return (Grk. *parousia*, lit. "appearing") of Jesus Christ marks the culmination of Christian eschatology.[185] If the incarnation of Christ signaled the beginning (*terminus a quo*) of the coming of the Kingdom of God, then the *parousia* of Christ at the end of the age will mark its end (*terminus ad quem*).[186] In the return, the risen Christ will bring the unambiguous rule of God upon the earth. The NT is persistent in its witness to the soon coming of Christ; frequently the event is said to be "at hand."[187] This emphasis was gradually diminished as the church moved further into the Christian centuries and further from the Advent of the Lord.

Adoration and contemplation of the Risen Christ is central to the spirituality of mystics like St. Teresa of Avila (1515–82). Her seminal work, *The Interior Castle* (1588), guides the reader through seven interior "mansions" of the soul. The means of this journey are mental prayer and reflection upon Jesus Christ, and their result is the experience of the presence of Christ within the soul that has

---

[181]This phraseology is present in the Apostles' Creed, the Nicene Creed (325), the Nicene-Constantinopolitan Creed (381), and the Athanasian Creed.

[182]Wainwright, *Doxology*, pp. 444–56, offers an excellent summary under this heading.

[183]St. Augustine, *Letters*, #204.

[184]a' Kempis, *Imitation of Christ*, p. 57, ch. 23, "A Meditation upon Death."

[185]The term *parousia* is used in this fashion in 1 Corinthians 15:23, 16:22; James 5:7ff; 2 Peter 3:4; 1 John 2:28; 1 Thessalonians 1:10, and etc.

[186]J.W. Bowman, "Eschatology of the NT," IDB, II, pp. 139–40.

[187]Romans 12:11–14; Philippians 4:5; Hebrews 1:2, 9:26, 10:25, 37–38; James 5:7–9; 1 Peter 1:5,20, 4:7; 1 John 2:18,22, 4:3; Revelations 22:10,12, 20.

been purged, emptied, and filled with love. For the mystic this presence of Christ is a sort of personal *parousia* that is a foretaste of the life to come.[188]

Adoration of Christ and yearning for His presence is also enacted in the sacramental and liturgical life of the congregation. As Christians approach the Lord's Table we anticipate a foretaste of the *parousia*. In the "Act of Great Thanksgiving"—which frequently follows the rite of Word and Table—many Christians sing the Trisagion, "holy, holy, holy Lord" (Rev 4:8) at the invitation of the liturgist: "And so with your people on earth and all the company of heaven, we praise your name and join their unending hymn. . . ." Through acts of worship and devotion the church anticipates—and to that degree participates in—the return of the Lord Jesus Christ and the reunion of the communion among saints (*communion sanctorum*). The *parousia* has often been the focus of Christian hymnody, and its application to congregational song has been especially powerful when the adoration of the Christ merged with the singers' longing for spiritual wholeness and societal liberation; instances of this intermingling are easily illustrated from the context of Methodism's "working poor" and the African American struggle for freedom.[189]

SPIRITUAL DISCIPLINES

Christian Spirituality is living the life of grace. Scripture offers many helpful metaphors for describing this life; it can be said to be "participation in divine life" (1 Pet 1:4), to be "sonship" or being a child of God (Rom 8:14ff), it is "friendship" with God (Jn 15:14-15), or having the Holy Spirit dwelling within you (Rom 8:9) and having God's love "perfected in us" (1 Jn 4:12–13). In contemporary Western culture it seems that we prefer to speak of powerful, emotive experiences indirectly. Perhaps the most obvious example is the way in which people describe how they came to be in love. In almost every instance a person says he or she "fell in love," implying that it was an experience that was neither foreseen nor planned—rather like falling into a hole. Others will say they were "smitten by cupid" or "bitten by the love bug," suggesting that the event came upon them in a way that was uncharted, unbidden, and out of their own control. This is a fascinating way of speaking, but it is—of course—completely untrue. In most instances

---

[188] Kieran Kavanaugh and Otilio Rodriguez, trans., *Teresa of Avila: The Interior Castle* (New York: Paulist Press, 1979), "Seventh Dwelling Place," pp. 172–95, elaborates Teresa's Christological focus. Cf. Thompson, *Fire and Light*, "Doing Christology with St. Teresa of Avila," pp. 143–64; and J. Mary Luti, *Teresa of Avila's Way* (Collegeville, Min.: Liturgical Press, 1991).

[189] See for example Charles Wesley's popular hymns "Rejoice the Lord Is King" and "Lo, He Comes with Clouds Descending," which continue in contemporary hymnals. Expressions like "The Battle Hymn of the Republic," "My Lord, What a Morning," "I Want to Be Ready," and "In That Great Gett'n Up Morning," were formed in the context of the African American struggle. Cf. James H. Cone, *The Spirituals and the Blues* (Maryknoll, NY: Orbis Books, 1991, second ed.), especially ch. 5, for analysis of the eschatological dimension of African American hymnody.

there is a significant amount of strategy, courtship, and perhaps even games-manship involved in this process. But we prefer to speak of "being in love" as a mystical experience that bursts upon the horizon of our emotions suddenly and without warning. There is something in the emotive quality of the experience that causes us to refrain from tarnishing the mystery by speaking of it in terms of strat-egy or our own intentions; perhaps there is also something in the riskiness of love that urges us to leave an escape hatch open (and one without culpability) should love not last. If we fell in love without intention or consideration, it seems rea-sonable that we could also fall out of love without blame or stigma of failure. This same sort of dilemma in language and conception persists in the popular under-standing of Christian Spirituality. We expect a deep and transformative relation-ship with God to come upon us magically, without planning and preparation, without attending to the means of grace, and without attention to formative dis-ciplines like prayer, scripture study, and self-denial. When this relationship fails to grow beyond the initial stages we are willing to excuse ourselves from culpa-bility since it is by grace, or through the power of the Holy Spirit, that "friend-ship with God" occurs at all.

This popular, and perhaps subconscious, understanding of spiritual life is at utter variance with the classical Christian witness. The Pauline injunction bears repeating: "Work out your own salvation with fear and trembling; for God is at work in you, both to will and to work for his good pleasure" (Phil 2:12). The de-velopment of Christian Spirituality is a cooperative effort, it involves God's work (the gift of grace) and our work (the faithful response); taken together and inter-mingled these two works produce transformation, wholeness, and life with God. This means that for spiritual growth to occur many of us will have to become more intentional about Christian Spirituality and spiritual disciplines. We will have to stop thinking of spirituality as something that comes upon us only un-bidden and in full bloom. Rather, we will have to recognize (in accordance with the NT analogies) that the life of grace is cultivated, nurtured, and grown over the span of a lifetime.

Sacraments and Disciplines. There are many ways of approaching the prac-tice of Christian life. Historic differences have sometimes divided communities of faith, but this same diversity also holds the potential to challenge us to greater growth and understanding. One area of significant diversity among Christians is the role the sacraments play in the process of spiritual formation. Liturgical churches, like the Roman Catholic, Lutheran, Anglican, and Greek Orthodox com-munions, which stress the role of sacraments in Christian life, understand the in-dividualistic expressions of piety (such as prayer, fasting, scripture reading, etc.) as being complementary to the sacramental life of the church and as vehicles for enhancing a person's appreciation of those events. Nonliturgical churches, like independent Baptist congregations, the Salvation Army, or Society of Friends, place more emphasis upon personal religious disciplines like prayer, Bible study, and abstinence (alcohol, tobacco) and less emphasis upon the sacramental life of the worshipping community.

In each case the terminology used to name Christian practices reflects something of the divergent emphases at work. Many commentators, like Geoffrey Wainwright, accord "the means of grace" a significant role in one's spiritual development.[190] This emphasis takes Word—in its various forms (scripture, liturgy, creed, hymn, etc.)—and Sacrament, together with other practices, to describe the formative influences of Christian life. This willingness to take Word, Sacrament, and spiritual disciplines together evidences Wainwright's Wesleyan heritage[191] and distinguishes his approach from those of other contemporary writers like Richard Foster. Foster's helpful book, *Celebration of Discipline* (1978),[192] marks out *The Path to Spiritual Growth* (his subtitle) by offering a compelling examination of the (1) inward, (2) outward, and (3) corporate disciplines that cultivate spiritual growth. The absence of any mention of the role of the sacraments in Foster's work is as telling as Wainwright's inclusion of it. Where Wainwright's spiritual heritage lies in a tradition that emphasizes the role of the sacraments, Foster's association with the Society of Friends suggests that his attention looks an opposite direction. Here, in the divergent emphases of two of the most popular contemporary works on Christian Spirituality (at least among Protestants), we see one of the main watersheds regarding Christian practice exemplified. Obviously, sacraments and personal disciplines are both crucial means for cultivating Christian Spirituality, and most Christians locate themselves at some point between these two opposite ends; yet it is also clear that they will tend to gravitate to either the sacraments or personal disciplines as beginning points for their pilgrimage. Significant growth, however, is to be found in a fruitful synthesis of the liturgical and personal elements of spiritual life.

Prayer and Belief. A second watershed issue has to do with the relationship of prayer and belief. This relationship has been described by the Latin terms *lex orandi* ("the rule of prayer"), *lex credendi* ("the rule of belief"). Roman Catholic Spirituality tends to move from what is considered normative liturgical practice toward theological reflection upon and description of that practice—which creates norms for belief. This emphasis makes the congregational life of the worshipping community the starting point for theological discourse or development. Protestant Spirituality tends to approach the interconnection of prayer and doctrine from the opposite direction, stressing "the primacy of doctrine over liturgy." So we will not be surprised to observe commentators from these respective traditions approaching fundamental questions in Christian faith and practice from opposite directions.[193]

---

[190] Wainwright, *Doxology*, pp. 149–286.

[191] See for example John Wesley's delineation of "the means of grace," in his "Large Minutes" of 1746. Thomas Jackson, ed., *The Works of John Wesley*, 14 vols. (London: Wesleyan Conference, 1872), Vol. VIII, pp. 322–24. Cf. "The Means of Grace," pp. 325–27 below.

[192] Richard Foster, *Celebration of Discipline: The Path to Spiritual Growth* (San Franciso: Harper and Row, 1978; second ed. 1988).

[193] Cf. Wainwright, *Doxology*, pp. 218–83, for an illuminating discussion of these categories and their historical implications for Christian Spirituality.

Sacraments

Most Christians, whether they practice the Catholic seven sacraments or the Protestant two, esteem sacraments as sacred acts that function as "means of grace." To speak of sacramental rites in this fashion does not detract from the singular efficacy of God's grace made manifest toward us through Jesus Christ, but it does remind us that we too have a part to play in our own sanctification. John Lawson described this role well when he wrote: "The Church in general holds that sinful man is helpless to save himself. His sole hope is in the grace of God, and therefore he must always *await the divine initiative*. His action is freely and responsibly to cooperate with the divine grace."[194]

Some kinds of waiting are more effective than others. If, for example, we agreed to meet together for lunch, it would be well for me to remember where and when you promised to arrive—our meeting would be more likely to occur that way! The sacraments are esteemed as "means of grace" in precisely this same way; they are divinely designated places for meeting God. Thus, as Lawson points out, we should use the appointed "means of grace" confidently, because of God's promise to meet us there in reconciling and transforming ways: ". . . there is something which man can do if he sincerely wishes God to exert His initiative and visit him with His grace. He can trustfully and obediently wait upon God at the place and in the way which God has ordained. He can do this expectantly, confident that God will fulfill His promise and make Himself known. The means of grace provide this place and method of waiting."[195] The efficacy of these "means" is to be found in their ability to function as channels of Divine grace. Thus the circumspect Christian must steer between the extremes of trusting in the means as though they were ends in themselves—instead of being *doors to the sacred*[196]—and the other extreme of taking lightly our holy obligation to meet God in God's appointed ways.

Prayer

There are, of course, many approaches to prayer. In Scripture we meet examples of praying according to a set form, such as "the Lord's Prayer,"[197] as well as praying spontaneously as need arises.[198] Thus, there needs to be room in the Christian tradition for the Anglican *Book of Common Prayer* and the Roman Catholic *Missal* as well as for the extemporaneous prayers preferred by many Protestants.

---

[194]John Lawson, *Introduction to Christian Doctrine* (Englewood Cliffs, N.J.: Prentice-Hall, 1967), p. 156. Emphasis added.

[195]Ibid., p. 156.

[196]See Joseph Martos's book by this title for a readable historical survey of the seven Roman Catholic sacraments. *Doors to the Sacred* (Ligouri, Mo.: Triumph Books, 1991, revised ed.).

[197]Matthew 6:9–13; Luke 11:2–4.

[198]Luke 22:39–44.

Jesus taught extensively on prayer.[199] He also modeled an active prayer life.[200] Many Christians interpret the Lord's words, "When you pray, . . . pray then like this . . ." (Mt 6:5–9), as a holy injunction that should be followed. But since prayer is talking with God, we desire to pray out of the fullness of love that child has for parent. Prayer, as Karl Rahner notes, is a dialogue in which our creatureliness is brought before God in an act of utter self-surrender.[201] Christians are enjoined to pray with unquestioning faith (Mk 11:24), and to pray in the name and spirit of Jesus (1 Jn 5:14). Intercessory prayer, or prayer on behalf of others, is an important part of the NT teaching.[202] We are also reminded that as we pray, Christ intercedes for us "at the right hand of the Father" (Rom 8:34) and the Holy Spirit "helps us in our weakness," and "intercedes for us with sighs too deep for words" (Rom 8:26–27).

Classical commentators, like Origen of Alexandria (*On Prayer*, 233) and Abba Isaac of the Desert Fathers, distinguished four resources in prayer: (1) supplication, (2) prayer, (3) pleading, and (4) thanksgiving.[203] Modern commentators often distinguish between prayer and meditation or contemplation. In the most basic sense, prayer is talking to God, whereas meditation is listening for God. In listening, the contemplative hears God speaking, as Thomas Merton (1915–68) described it, "in the depths of our own being: for we ourselves are words of His."[204] Thus for Merton, "Contemplation is this echo. It is a deep resonance in the inmost center of our spirit in which our very life loses its separate voice and resounds with the majesty and the mercy of the Hidden and Living One. He answers Himself in us and this answer is new life, divine creativity, making all things new."[205] Meditation often employs mental or physical images as focal points.

In classical Christian Spirituality, particularly in the Roman Catholic tradition, meditation was often approached by the method of prayer known as *lectio divina*. The first step in this process is *lectio* or "reading" the Scriptures. This is not a textbook sort of reading; it is a meditative reading. It is reading with a listening attitude, and with a willingness to personalize the words so that they are read as though God is speaking directly to the reader. The second step, *meditatio*, uses the imagination to expand and draw upon what was read. This process may combine mental visualization with meditative listening to gain illumination. The third stage, *oratio*, or "prayer of the heart," makes emotion—rather than thought—

---

[199]See Luke 11:5–10, 18:1–14, for Jesus's parables on prayer; Matthew 6:5–7, 11:24, 15:22–28, and etc.
[200]Luke in particular is interested in reporting that Jesus prayed regularly: Luke 3:21, 5:16, 6:12, 9:18,28, 11:1, 22:41–44.
[201]Rahner, *Practice of Faith*, pp. 88–94.
[202]Luke 6:28; John 17:9–26; Romans 15:30; 2 Thessalonians 3:1, etc.
[203]Henry Charwick, ed., *Alexandrian Christianity* (Philadelphia: Westminster Press, 1954), "Origen: On Prayer," pp. 266–74; Luibheid, trans., *John Cassian*, "Conference Nine," pp. 107–110. The material from "Conference Nine" is found on pp. 115–18.
[204]Thomas Merton, *New Seeds of Contemplation* (New York: New Directions, 1961), p. 3.
[205]Ibid.

the vehicle for illumination and transformation. The heart pours itself out in long-ing after God and is filled with love for God. The fourth step, *contemplatio* or "con-templation," is entered through a sense of inward darkness (Divine absence). Out of this darkness comes a piercing awareness of God's presence that is so power-ful that it overwhelms our natural faculties and leaves us only with a loving, awed awareness of God's presence. This presence is so awesome that it causes the con-templative to long for union with God.[206]

Scripture Reading

Scripture reading is significant for Christian Spirituality not only because Scrip-ture is a repository of sacred teaching and practices, but because it is the vehicle whereby the Word of the Lord comes to us. This spiritual function of the Bible caused Geoffrey Wainwright to term it "a kind of sacrament" of the Word of God.[207] The Bible fulfills the three classical roles of a sacrament; it is a physical and external sign (*sacramentum tantum*) of God's word; it communicates to us the reality (God's word) of what it signifies (*sacramentum et res*); and it fulfills the sa-cred purpose (*res sacramenti*) that it signifies.[208]

Clement of Alexandria (c. 150–216) recognized the multifaceted character of Scripture. His *Instructor* (*Paedagogos*, 200) urged Christians to become as little chil-dren, and sit at the feet of the Instructor—Jesus Christ—who teaches His church through the Holy Scriptures.[209] For Martin Luther the presence of the Word of God (in its various forms) was what constituted the church; Luther, therefore, quipped that "the church is a mouth-house" (*ein Mundhaus*) where the Word of God is read, preached, spoken, sung, and prayed.[210] John Calvin's famous "marks of the church" followed similar lines: "Wherever we see the Word of God purely preached and heard, and the sacraments administered according to Christ's in-stitution, it is is not to be doubted, a church of God exists."[211] John Wesley listed "Searching the Scriptures" among his "instituted" means of grace, and he enjoined Christians to (1) reading, (2) meditating upon, and (3) hearing the Scriptures.[212] Not surprisingly, Wesley favored a methodical approach to the Bible: ". . . Read-ing constantly, some part of every day; regularly all the Bible in order; carefully

---

[206]This summary of the *lectio divina* is based on Thelma Hall's fine work, *Too Deep for Words: Redis-covering Lectio Divina* (New York: Paulist Press, 1988). A similar, three-step process is utilized in the Eastern Orthodox tradition. Kallistos T. Ware, *Praying with Orthodox Tradition* (Nashville, Tenn.: Abingdon Press, 1990), offers an excellent summary of this process.
[207]Wainwright, *Doxology*, p. 149–50.
[208]Ibid.
[209]A selection from Clement's work is found on pp. 69–73.
[210]Martin Luther, *Operationes in Psalmos, Luther's Werke, Kritische Gesamtausgabe* (Weimar, 1883), Vol. V, ch. 10, p. 537.
[211]Battles, ed., *Calvin's Institutes*, Vol. II, Bk. IV, ch. 1, para. 9, p. 1023.
[212]Wesley, *Works*, Vol. VIII, p. 322

with the *Notes*[213]; seriously with prayer before and after; fruitfully, immediately practicing what you learn there.__."[214]

Acts of Self-Denial

Jesus's words, "If any man would come after me, let him deny himself and take up his cross and follow me,"[215] mark out the way of Christian discipleship as a way of self-denial. Intentional disciplines of self-denial, like fasting,[216] celibacy,[217] apostolic poverty,[218] or simplicity,[219] have their basis in Jesus's command to deny ourselves as a sign of our discipleship. But we must be clear on the fact that one does not deny oneself food or sexual expression because the body or its functions are evil and therefore need to be punished; acts of self-denial use bodily deprivation to cultivate and exercise the human will. St. Jerome, in his "Letter to Eustochium" (384), connected the self-control developed through fasting with that needed for chastity. Thus Jerome urged his friend to fast, "Not because God, the Creator of the universe and its Lord, takes delight in the rumbling of the intestines, the emptiness of our stomach, or the inflammation of our lungs, but because chastity cannot be preserved otherwise. . . ."[220] In fact, the focus of fasting or other acts of self-denial is not the body per se; rather the focus is upon God. Acts of bodily denial enable us to present ourselves as "living sacrifices" (Rom 12:1), in rational service. David Tripp, in describing fasting, likened acts of self-denial to prayer: "It is praying with the body, affirming the wholeness of the person in spiritual action; it gives emphasis and intensity to prayer. . . ."[221] Since undue attachment to physical and material things can readily divert our attention from God, acts of self-denial help us clarify our focus upon God by removing or minimizing other distractions.

Service

A Christian's pattern of life, as derived from the imitation of Christ and the love of God within, takes expression in selfless acts of service. In mirroring the acts of

---

[213]John Wesley, *Notes Upon the Old and New Testaments*, 4 vols. (Bristol: William Pine, 1765; reprinted by Schmul, 1975).

[214]Wesley, *Works*, Vol. VIII, p. 323.

[215]Matthew 16:24 = Luke 9:23. The Lucan parallel verse adds the word "daily," as if to remind us that cross-bearing is an ongoing and intentional lifestyle.

[216]Mark 8:36; Matthew 4:2ff;6:16–18; 1 Corinthians 9:24ff; 2 Corinthians 6:5, 11:27; Colossians 2:23; Acts 13:2, 14:23.

[217]1 Corinthians 7:32–39.

[218]Luke 6:20, 18:18–30.

[219]Matthew 6:19,21, 19:16–22; Luke 6:30, 12:15,16–22,33; 1 Timothy 6:9.

[220]Charles Mierow, trans., *The Letters of Jerome*, Vol. I (New York: Paulist Press, n.d.), #22, "Letter to Eustochium," p. 143. Cf. pp. 99–100 below.

[221]David Tripp, "Fasting," in *The Westminster Dictionary of Christian Spirituality*, edited by Gordon Wakefield (Philadelphia: Westminster Press, 1983), p. 148.

Jesus Christ, one is brought into closer harmony with His motives and aspirations, and Christ's work in the world is accomplished through our works. We are reminded by Jesus's own words, that "the Son of man came not to be served, but to serve . . ." (Mk 10:45), as well as by those of St. Paul that Jesus Christ ". . . did not count equality with God a thing to be grasped, but emptied himself, taking the form of a servant . . ." (Phil 2:6–7). Jesus modeled service before His disiciples and called them to similar deeds: "If I then, your Lord and Teacher, have washed your feet, you also ought to wash one another's feet. For I have given you an example, that you should do as I have done to you" (Jn 13:14–15). There are many forms of selfless service described in the NT, which are enjoined upon Christians: (1) hospitality (1 Pet 4:9); (2) bearing each other's burdens (Gal 6:2); (3) feeding the hungry, clothing the naked, and visiting the sick and imprisoned (Mt 25:35–40). In the later instance, and many others, Jesus placed a special emphasis on identifying with the outcasts and the needy, and so St. Francis found himself among the poor and destitute and Mother Teresa of Calcutta was found among the outcasts of that city. Mother Teresa's prayer might well be our own: "Make us worthy, Lord, to serve our fellowmen throughout the world who live and die in poverty and hunger. Give them, through our hands, this day their daily bread, and by our understanding love, give peace and joy."[222]

---

[222]Mother Teresa of Calcutta, *A Gift for God: Meditations and Prayers* (New York: Harper and Row, 1968), p. 71.

CHAPTER 1

The Ancient Church

The early Christians faced many pressures that are difficult to imagine today. For most of the first three centuries Christianity was an "underground" religion, persecuted by local and national governments, and misunderstood by Jews and Gentiles alike. Many of the documents that have survived from the earliest period concern themselves with practical issues like who Jesus was and what He was about, how to celebrate the Eucharist, and how to face martyrdom. Apologists tried to explain the nature and character of Christian faith and practice. Church Fathers labored to consolidate the Christian movement through the establishment of the canon of the Scriptures, the creeds of the church, and the structures of religious authority. Martyrs and confessors epitomized radical obedience to Christ, as men and women died horrible deaths rather than burn incense and utter "Caesar is Lord."

As the third century waned and the fourth century dawned, Christianity won toleration, religious freedom, and finally imperial support under Emperor Constantine. In his lifetime the Church went from being persecuted to being privileged. Supported by imperial endowments and formal establishment, Christianity began gaining the imposing status it would enjoy throughout the Middle Ages. But as Christianity gained popularity, property, and prosperity under imperial support, it also lost its countercultural, prophetic posture. In the Imperial Church the monks began to replace the martyrs as those who most epitomized the Christian life of holiness and radical obedience.

Ignatius of Antioch (d. 117?)

Ignatius of Antioch was the second or third Christian bishop in that city. Christian tradition suggests that he may have been a disciple of the apostles of Jesus (Peter and Paul). Toward the end of his ministry Ignatius was arrested for failing to honor the emperor, and was transported to Rome for execution in the "games" of the arena. As he traveled to Rome, chained to ten Roman soldiers, Ignatius penned seven letters to the churches he passed along the way. These letters offer us marvelous insight into the lives of early second-century Christians. They also show us that two major concerns weighted heavily upon Ignatius's mind as he went toward his death; one matter was his own martyrdom. Ignatius wanted to explain his understanding of his impending death. He wrote to the Roman Christians to plead with them not to intervene in a way that might stop his martyrdom.

A second concern was the unity of the church in the face of mounting heresy and schism. Two particular heresies troubled the church of Ignatius's day; the one, called Ebionism, understood Christianity in light of Judaism and viewed Jesus as another one of the great Jewish prophets. The other heresy, Gnosticism, also had a deficient understanding of Jesus Christ.[1] The Gnostics were "docetics," who in conforming Christianity to the Greek dualistic world view believed that Christ only *seemed* to have a human body—he was in fact (according to the docetics) a disembodied spirit. These challenges were similar to the heresies that St. Paul addressed in his Galatians Epistle, and St. John confronted in his First Epistle.[2] In opposing these heresies Ignatius not only defended the apostolic tradition, he also championed the unity of the church.

ON MARTYRDOM[3]

I write to all the churches and impress upon them, that I shall willingly die for God, unless you hinder me. I beg you not to show an unseasonable good-will towards me. Allow me to become food for the wild beasts, through whose instrumentality it will be granted to me to get to God. I am the wheat of God, and let me be ground up by the teeth of the wild beasts, that I may be found the pure bread of Christ. . . . Then I shall be a true disciple of Christ, when the world shall not see so much as my body. Pray Christ for me, that by these instruments I may

---

[1] Gnosticism took its name from the Greek word for knowledge (*gnosis*). It was a diverse and syncretistic religion that sought to merge Christian faith with the presuppositions and world view of pagan antiquity. It stressed that secret, saving knowledge comes only to a few spiritually elite people who embrace a gnostic understanding of God and the world. While Gnosticism sought to include many Christian teachings, it was committed to the dualistic world view of antiquity; it believed that matter (including the human body) was inherently corrupt and that only the spirit was good and worthy of salvation. The incarnation of Jesus Christ was a significant problem for Gnosticism; since the incarnation affirmed that the "Word became flesh," to Gnostic ears this amounted to saying that "God became evil." Hence, many Gnostics adopted a "docetic" (Grk. *dokao*, "to seem") approach to the incarnation. They argued that Christ only seemed to have a genuine human body. Actually, the Gnostic reasoned, his body was made of spirit and not flesh.

[2] Galatians 2,3 and 1 John 2:18–28; 4:1–6.

[3] Roberts and Donaldson, eds., **TANF** Ignatius's *Letter to the Romans*, chs. 4–7, pp. 75–77. The longer and shorter texts have been combined, the vocabulary has been modernized, and word order has been changed at some points.

be found a sacrifice [to God]. I do not give you commands, like Peter and Paul. They were apostles; I am but a condemned man: they were free, while I am, even until now, a servant. But when I suffer, I shall be the freedman of Jesus, and shall rise again emancipated in Him. . . .

. . . Now I begin to be a disciple. And let no one of things visible or invisible, envy me that I should get to Jesus Christ. Let fire and the cross; let the crowds of wild beasts; let tearings, breakings and dislocations of bones; let cutting off of members; let shatterings of the whole body; and let all the dreadful tortures of the devil come upon me; only let me get to Jesus Christ.

All the pleasures of the world, and all the kingdoms of this earth, shall profit me nothing. It is better for me to die in behalf of Jesus Christ, than to reign over all the ends of the earth. "For what shall a man be profited, if he gain the whole world, but lose his own soul [Mt 16:26]?" Him I seek, who died for us; Him I desire, who rose again for our sake. This is the gain which is laid up for me. Pardon me, brethren, do not keep me from living, do not wish to keep me in a state of death; while I desire to belong to God, do not give me over to the world. Allow me to obtain pure light, and when I have gone there I shall indeed be a man of God. Permit me to be an imitator of the passion of my God. . . .

ON UNITY[4]

. . . If any one preaches the Jewish law to you, do not listen to him. For it is better to listen to Christian doctrine from a man who has been circumcised, than to [listen] to Judaism from one uncircumcised. But if either of such persons do not speak of Jesus Christ, they are in my judgment but as tombstones and graves of the dead, upon which are written only the names of men. . . .

For though some would have deceived me according to the flesh, yet the Spirit, as being from God, is not deceived. For "it knows both whence it comes and whither it goes" [Jn 3:8], and the deep secrets of the heart. For, when I was among you, I cried out, with a loud voice—the word is not mine but God's—"Give heed to the bishop, and to the presbytery and deacons." . . . [T]he Spirit proclaimed these words: "Do nothing without the bishop; keep your bodies as the temples of God; love unity; avoid divisions; follow Jesus Christ, even as He followed His Father."

I therefore did what belonged to me, as a man devoted to unity. For where there is division and wrath, God doth not dwell. To all them that repent, the Lord grants forgiveness, if they return to the unity of Christ and communion with the bishop. . . . I exhort you to do nothing out of strife, but according to the doctrine of Christ. When I heard some [people] saying, "If I do not find it in the ancient Scriptures, I will not believe the Gospel"; on my saying to them, "It is written,"

---

[4]Ignatius, "Letter to the Philadelphians," in Roberts and Donaldson, eds., **TANF**, Vol. I, chs. 2–10, pp. 79–85, using the longer and shorter versions, with omissions, and minor editorial emendations for readability.

they answered me, "that remains to be proved." But to me Jesus Christ is the ancient documents; His cross, and death, and resurrection, and the faith which is by Him, are undefiled archives of antiquity, by which I desire, through your prayers, to be justified.

CHRIST AND THE CHURCH[5]

I glorify God, even Jesus Christ, who has given you such wisdom. For I have observed that you are perfected in an immovable faith, as if you were nailed to the cross of our Lord Jesus Christ, both in the flesh and in the spirit, and established in love through the blood of Christ, being fully persuaded with respect to our Lord, that He was truly of the seed of David according to the flesh, and the Son of God according to the will and power of God; that He was truly born of a virgin, was baptized by John, that all righteousness might be fulfilled by Him; and under Pontius Pilate and Herod the tetrarch was truly nailed to the cross for us in His flesh. From whom we also derive our being, from His divinely blessed suffering, that He might set up a standard for all the ages, through His resurrection, to rally all His holy and faithful followers, whether among Jews or Gentiles, in the one body of His church.

Now, He suffered all these things for our sake, that we might be saved. And He suffered [them] truly, even as He also truly raised Himself up, not as certain unbelievers maintain, that He only *seemed* to suffer, as they themselves only seem to be [Christians]. And as they believe, so shall it happen to them, when they shall be divested of their bodies, and be mere evil spirits.

For I know that after His resurrection also He was still possessed of flesh, and I believe that he is to so now. When, for instance, He came to those who were with Peter, He said to them, "Lay hold, handle Me, and see that I am not an incorporeal spirit." For this cause also they despised death, and were found its conquerors. And after His resurrection did He not eat and drink with them, as being possessed of flesh, although spiritually He was united with the Father . . . .

Let no one deceive himself. Both things which are in heaven, and the glorious angels, and rulers, both visible and invisible, if they do not believe in the blood of Christ, shall, in consequence incur condemnation. . . . They abstain from the Eucharist and from prayer because they confess not the Eucharist to be the flesh of our Savior, Jesus Christ, who suffered for our sins, and which the Father of His goodness, raised up again. Those therefore who speak against this gift of God, incur death, in the midst of their disputes. But it would be better for them to treat it with respect, that they also might rise again. It is fitting therefore, that you should avoid such persons, in private or public, but to give heed to the Gospel, in which the Passion has been revealed to us, and the resurrection has been fully proved. But avoid divisions, as the beginning of evils.

---

[5]Ignatius, "Letter to the Smyranaens," in ibid., Vol. I, chs. 1–9, pp. 86–90.

See that all of you imitate the bishop, even as Jesus Christ does the Father, and the presbytery as you would the apostles; and reverence the deacons as being the institution of God. Let no one do anything with the Church without a bishop. Let it be deemed proper Eucharist, which is [administered] either by the bishop or by one to whom He has entrusted it. Wherever the bishop shall appear, there let the multitude [of the people] also be; even as, wherever Jesus Christ is, there is the catholic church. It is not lawful either to baptize or celebrate the love feast, but whatsoever He shall approve of, that is also pleasing to God, so that everything that is done may be secure and valid.

The Didache (c. 130)

This anonymous treatise was sometimes called "The Teaching of the Twelve Apostles." Its Greek title, *Didache*, means "teaching." The treatise was not penned by the apostles, but is "apostolic" in the sense that it represents a summary of the teachings that the church received as being in harmony with what the apostles taught. The treatise in its present form seems to be a combination of two earlier documents, both of which may date from the apostolic era (late first century).

THE LIFE OF THE CHURCH[6]

And concerning baptism, you should baptize in this way: having given instruction in these things, baptize in the name of the Father, and of the Son, and of the Holy Spirit, in running[7] water. But if you do not have running water, then baptize with some other water; and if you cannot baptize in cold, [then] in warm. But if you have neither, pour out water three times upon the head in the name of the Father, Son and Holy Spirit. . . . You shall order the baptized to fast one or two days before the baptism.

But let not your fasts be like those of the hypocrites, for they fast on Mondays and Thursdays.[8] You should fast on Wednesdays and Fridays. Neither should you pray like the hypocrites, but pray as the Lord commanded in His Gospel [Mt 6:9–13]: "Our Father who art in heaven, hallowed be Thy name, Thy Kingdom come. Thy will be done, on earth as it is in heaven. Give us this day our daily bread, and forgive us our debt as we also forgive us our debtors. And bring us not into temptation, but deliver us from evil. For Thine is the power and the glory for ever." Pray this way three times a day.

---

[6]"The Teaching of the Twelve Apostles," in Roberts and Donaldson, eds., **TANF**, Vol. VII, pp. 379–80, with omissions and stylistic emendations.
[7]Literally, "living water."
[8]These are the traditional Jewish days for fasting, hence the "hypocrites" identified here are probably Jews.

Now about the Eucharist,[9] give thanks[10] in this way: First, concerning the cup,[11] [Pray] "We thank Thee, our Father, for the holy vine of David [Is 11:1; Jn 15], Thy servant, which Thou madest known to us through Jesus Thy servant; to Thee be the glory for ever." And about the broken bread [say]: 'We thank Thee, our Father, for the life and knowledge which Thou madest known to us through Jesus Thy servant; to Thee be the glory forever." Even as this broken bread was scattered over the hills, and was gathered together and became one, so let Thy church be gathered together from the ends of the earth into Thy kingdom, for Thine is the glory and the power through Jesus Christ forever." Let no one eat or drink of your Eucharist except that they have been baptized in the name of the Lord. . . . [As] the Lord said, "Do not give dogs what is holy" [Mt 7:6].

After your participation, give thanks in this way: "We thank Thee, holy Father, for Thy holy name which Thou didst cause to dwell in our hearts, and for the knowledge and faith and immortality, which Thou madest known to us through Jesus Thy Servant; to Thee be the glory for ever. Thou, Master almighty, didst create all things for Thy name's sake; Thou gavest food and drink to people for their enjoyment, that they might give thanks to Thee; but to us Thou didst freely give spiritual food and drink and life eternal through Thy Servant. Before all things we thank Thee that Thou are mighty; to Thee be the glory for ever. Remember Lord, Thy church, to deliver it from all evil and to make it perfect through Thy love, and gather it from the four winds [Mt 24:31], sanctified for Thy kingdom which Thou hast prepared for it; for Thine is the power and glory for ever. Let grace[12] come, and let this world pass away [1 Cor 7:31]. Hosanna to the God of David [Mt 21:9,15]! If any one is holy, let him come; if any one is not, let him repent. Maranatha [1 Cor 16:22]. Amen.[13] . . ."

Epistle to Diognetus (c. 130)

This anonymous epistle, which may have been composed by the apologist Quadratus, uses an elegant classical Greek style to explain Christian beliefs and practices to the pagan world. It may constitute the first formal defense of the Christian faith.

---

[9] The Eucharistic prayers offered here are patterned after Jewish prayers of thanksgiving. Cf. Louis Bouyer, *A History of Christian Spirituality*, 3 vols. (Minneapolis: Winston Press, 1960), Vol. I, pp. 175–82, for a thorough examination of the Jewish character of the Didache's Eucharistic prayers.

[10] The word *eucharist* means "to give thanks." The author created a pun that used both meanings of "eucharist."

[11] Compare Matthew 26:26–30. In the gospel Jesus's institution of the Eucharist begins with the bread and then moves to the cup. The Didache's order has reversed the process.

[12] "Grace" is used here as a way of speaking of Jesus Christ, whose saving death and resurrection makes grace available to us.

[13] These phrases may have been prayed as versicles and responses, or they may have been patterned after the Jewish custom of reciting Scripture verses (after the benediction) about the future hope of the community of faith.

The epistle is addressed to a learned reader, Diognetus, in hopes of communicating the truth about Christianity and thereby gaining clemency for Christians under persecution. The identity of Diognetus is unknown. Of particular interest is the epistle's definition of relationship of the church and the world, which is developed through the analogy of the soul's habitation within the human body.

THE CHURCH IN THE WORLD[14]

. . . [T]he Christians cannot be distinguished from other people by country, or language or the customs they observe. For they neither inhabit cities of their own, nor employ a peculiar form of speech, nor lead a life which is marked out by any singularity. The course of conduct which they follow has not been devised by any speculation or deliberation of inquisitive minds; nor do they, like some, proclaim themselves the advocates of any merely human doctrines. But, inhabiting Greek as well as barbarian cities, according to the lot each of them has been cast, and following the customs of their nationality in respect to clothing, food, and the rest of their ordinary conduct, [yet] they display to us their wonderful and confessedly striking method of life.

They dwell in their own countries, but only as aliens [1 Pet 2:11]. As citizens, they share in all things with others, and yet endure all things as foreigners. Every foreign land is to them as their native land, and every land of their birth is as a foreign land to them. They marry, as do all [others]. They beget children, but they do not cast away their offspring.[15] They have a common table, but not a common bed. They are "in the flesh," but they do not "live according to the flesh."[16] They pass their days upon the earth, but they are citizens of heaven [Phil 3:20]. They obey the prescribed laws, and at the same time surpass the laws by their own lives. They love all men, and are persecuted by all. They are unknown and condemned; they are put to death, and [are] restored to life [2 Cor 6:9]. They are poor, yet make many rich [2 Cor 6:10]; they are lacking of all things, and yet they live in abundance of all; they are dishonored, and yet in their very dishonor they are glorified. They are spoken evil of, and yet are justified; they are reviled, and [yet they] bless [2 Cor 4:12]; they are insulted, and [they] repay the insult with honor; they do good, yet are punished as evil-doers. When punished, they rejoice as if by it they are brought to life. They are assailed by the Jews as foreigners, and are persecuted by the Greeks; yet those who hate them are unable to assign any reason for their hatred.[17]

To sum it up . . . What the soul is in the body, that Christians are in the world. The soul is dispersed through all the members of the body, and Christians are

---

[14]"The Epistle to Diognetus," in Roberts and Donaldson, eds., **TANF**, Vol. I, ch. 5–6, pp. 26–27, with omissions and minor linguistic changes.

[15]This may refer to the Greek practice of "exposing" or abandoning unwanted infants.

[16]1Corinthians 10:3, 5:16; Romans 8:4; John 17:13–19, 18:36–37.

[17]This passage is patterned after 2 Corinthians 6:4–10.

scattered through all the cities of the world. The soul dwells in the body, and yet is not of the body, and Christians dwell in the world, but are not "of the world" [Jn 17:11–16]. The invisible soul is guarded by the visible body; in the same way, Christians are indeed to be in the world, but their godliness remains invisible. The flesh hates the soul and wars against [it], though it has suffered no injury, because it is prevented from enjoying its pleasures; the world also hates the Christians, even though it is in no way injured by them, because they reject its pleasures. The soul loves the flesh that hates it, and [also loves] its members; in the same way, Christians love those who hate them. The soul is imprisoned in the body, and yet preserves that very body; while Christians are confined in the world as in a prison, and yet they are preservers of the world. The immortal soul dwells in a mortal dwelling, and Christians dwell as sojourners in corruptible [bodies], looking for an incorruptibility dwelling in the heavens. The soul, when ill provided for with respect to food and drink, becomes better; in like manner, the Christians though they are subjected day by day to punishment, increase more and more. God has assigned them this illustrious position, which it is unlawful for them to forsake.

Vibia Perpetua (c. 181–203)

Vibia Perpetua was a young woman of Carthage, North Africa. She was among the Christian catechumens arrested during the persecutions of Emperor Septimius Severus. Perpetua wrote an account of her imprisonment and the visions she had during that trying period of her life. Her work, sometimes called *passio* or the *Passion of Perpetua*, shows the important role that spiritual experiences played in popular Christian piety. Perpetua and her fellow Christians were martyred in the arena. It is thought that Tertullian wrote the introduction and conclusion to Perpetua's *passio*. The work became a source of encouragement and reflection for the church of North Africa and the Latin-speaking West.

A MARTYR'S VISIONS[18]

. . . A few days later we were imprisoned. I was terrified because never before had I experienced such darkness. What a terrible day! Because of crowded conditions and rough treatment by the soldiers the heat was unbearable. My condition was aggravated by my anxiety for my baby. Then Tertius and Pomponius,

---

[18]"The Martyrdom of Perpetua," in Patricia Wilson-Kastner, G. Ronald Kastner, Ann Millin, Rosemary Rader, and Jeremiah Reedy, trans. *A Lost Tradition: Women Writers of the Early Church* (Lanham, Md.: University Press of America, 1981), pp. 20–29, with omissions. Used by kind permission of Dr. Rosemary Rader, Benedict Distinguished Professor of the History of Christianity, Carleton College, Northfield, Minn.

those kind deacons who were taking care of our needs, paid for us to be moved for a few hours to a better part of the prison where we might refresh ourselves. Leaving the dungeon we all went about our own business. I nursed my child, who was already weak from hunger. In my anxiety for the infant I spoke to my mother about him, tried to console my brother, and asked that they care for my son. I suffered intensely because I sensed their agony on my account. These were trials I had to endure for many days. Then I was granted the privilege of having my son remain with me in prison. Being relieved of my anxiety and concern for the infant, I immediately regained my strength. Suddenly the prison became my palace, and I loved being there rather than any other place. Then my brother said to me, "Dear sister, you already have such a great reputation that you could ask for a vision indicating whether you will be condemned or freed." Since I knew that I could speak with the Lord, whose great favors I had already experienced, I confidently promised to do so. I said I would tell my brother about it the next day. Then I made my request and this is what I saw.

There was a bronze ladder of extraordinary height reaching up to heaven, but it was so narrow that only one person could ascend at a time. Every conceivable kind of iron weapon was attached to the sides of the ladder: swords, lances, hooks, and daggers. If anyone climbed up carelessly or without looking upwards, he/she would be mangled as the flesh adhered to the weapons. Crouching directly beneath the ladder was a monstrous dragon who threatened those climbing up and tried to frighten them from ascent.[19]

Saturus[20] went up first. Because of his concern for us he had given himself up voluntarily after we had been arrested. He had been our source of strength but was not with us at the time of the arrest. When he reached the top of the ladder he turned to me and said, "Perpetua, I'm waiting for you, but be careful not to be bitten by the dragon." I told him that in the name of Jesus Christ the dragon could not harm me. At this the dragon slowly lowered its head as though afraid of me. Using its head as the first step, I began my ascent.

At the summit I saw an immense garden, in the center of which sat a tall, grey-haired man dressed like a shepherd, milking sheep. Standing around him were several thousand white-robed people.[21] As he raised his head he noticed me and said, "Welcome, my child." Then he beckoned me to approach and gave me a small morsel of the cheese he was making. I accepted it with cupped hands and ate it. When all those surrounding us said "Amen," I awoke, still tasting the sweet cheese. I immediately told my brother about the vision, and we both realized that we were to experience the sufferings of martyrdom. From then on we gave up having any hope in this world. . . .

One day as we were eating we were suddenly rushed off for a hearing. We arrived at the forum and the news spread quickly throughout the area near the

---

[19]The dragon is a symbol for Satan in Christian apocalyptic literature. Cf. Revelations 12.

[20]He was one of the catechumens who was arrested with Perpetua.

[21]Revelations 7:14 "There are they who have come out of the great tribulation; they have washed their robes and made them white in the blood of the Lamb."

forum, and a huge crowd gathered. We went up to the prisoners' platform. All the others confessed when they were questioned. When my turn came my father appeared with my son. Dragging me from the step, he begged: "Have pity on your son!" Hilarion, the governor . . . said "Have pity on your father's grey head; have pity on your infant son; offer sacrifice for the emperors' welfare." But I answered, "I will not." Hilarion asked, "Are you a Christian?" And I answered, "I am a Christian." And when my father persisted in his attempts to dissuade me, Hilarion ordered him out, and he was beaten with a rod. My father's injury hurt me as much as if I myself had been beaten, and I grieved because of his pathetic old age. Then the sentence was passed; all of us were condemned to the beasts. We were overjoyed as we went back to the prison cell. Since I was still nursing my child who was ordinarily in the cell with me, I quickly sent the deacon Pomponius to my father's house to ask for the baby, but my father refused to give him up. Then God saw to it that my child no longer needed my nursing, nor were my breasts inflamed. After that I was no longer tortured by anxiety about my child or by pain in my breasts. . . .

On the day that we were kept in chains, I had the following vision: I saw the same place as before, but Dinocrates was clean, well-dressed, looking refreshed. In place of the wound there was a scar, and the fountain which I had seen previously now had its rim lowered to the boy's waist. On the rim, over which water was flowing constantly, there was a golden bowl filled with water. Dinocrates walked up to it and began to drink; the bowl never emptied. And when he was no longer thirsty, he gladly went to play as children do. Then I awoke, knowing that he had been relieved of his suffering. . . .

The day before the battle in the arena, in a vision I saw Pomponius the deacon coming to the prison door and knocking very loudly. I went to open the gate for him. He was dressed in a loosely fitting white robe, wearing richly decorated sandals. He said to me, "Perpetua, come. We're waiting for you!" He took my hand and we began to walk over extremely rocky and winding paths. When we finally arrived short of breath, at the arena, he led me to the center saying "Don't be frightened! I'll be here to help you." He left me and I stared out over a huge crowd which watched me with apprehension. Because I knew that I had to fight with the beasts, I wondered why they hadn't yet been turned loose in the arena. Coming towards me was some type of Egyptian, horrible to look at, accompanied by fighters who were to help defeat me. Some handsome young men came forward to help and encourage me. I was stripped of my clothing, and suddenly I was a man. My assistants began to rub me with oil as was the custom before the contest, while the Egyptian was on the opposite side rolling in the sand. Then a certain man appeared, so tall that he towered above the amphitheater. He wore a loose purple robe with two parallel stripes across the chest; his sandals were richly decorated with gold and silver. He carried a rod like that of an athletic trainer, and a green branch on which were golden apples. He motioned for silence and said: "If this Egyptian wins, he will kill her with the sword; but if she wins, she will receive this branch." Then he withdrew.

We both stepped forward and began to fight with our fists. My opponent kept trying to grab my feet but I repeatedly kicked his face with my heels. I felt myself being lifted up into the air and began to strike at him as one who was no longer earth-bound. But when I saw that we were wasting time, I put my two hands together, linked my fingers and put his head between them. As he fell on his face I stepped on his head [Gen 3:15]. Then the people began to shout and my assistants started singing victory songs. He kissed me and said, "Peace be with you, my daughter." And I triumphantly headed towards the Sanavivarian Gate. Then I woke up realizing that I would be contending not with wild animals but with the devil himself. I knew, however, that I would win. I have recorded the events which occurred up to the day before the final contest. Let anyone who wishes to record the events of the contest itself, do so. . . .

The day of their victory dawned, with joyful countenances they marched from the prison to the arena as though on their way to heaven. If there was any trembling it was from joy, not fear. Perpetua followed with quick step as a true spouse of Christ, the darling of God, her brightly flashing eyes quelling the gaze of the crowd. Felicitas[22] too, joyful because she had safely survived child-birth and was now able to participate in the contest with the wild animals, passed from one shedding of blood to another; from midwife to gladiator, about to be purified after child-birth by a second baptism.[23] As they were led through the gate . . . Perpetua was singing victory psalms as if already crushing the head of the Egyptian. Revocatus, Saturnius and Saturus were warning the spectators, as they came within sight of Hilarion they informed him by nods and gestures: "You condemn us; God condemns you." This so infuriated the crowds that they demanded the scourging of these men in front of the line of gladiators. But the ones punished rejoiced in that they had obtained yet another share in the Lord's suffering. . . .

Tertullian of Carthage (c. 160–220)

Tertullian was a native of Carthage, in North Africa. He was converted to Christianity while studying law in Rome, and he became the first great Christian theologian and apologist who wrote in Latin. His legal training left its imprint upon Tertullian's theology; as a lawyer he had a very clear conception of right and wrong, hence as a theologian he was a strong defender of orthodox Christian teaching and practice and a staunch opponent of heretical deviations from orthodoxy. He stressed the utter contrast between Christianity and Hellenistic culture and its accompanying thought forms. He esteemed the Rule of Faith to be the basis for normative Christianity. His rigorous approach to morality is probably what led Tertullian to join the puritanical sect called Montanism that was gaining strength in North Africa in his day and that was eventually rejected by the Catholic Church.

---

[22]Perpetua's servant girl and fellow catechumen.

[23]Martyrdom was sometimes viewed as a baptism in blood, or as a second baptism.

JERUSALEM AND ATHENS[24]

These are "the doctrines" of men and "of demons" [1 Tim 4:14] produced for itching ears of the spirit of this world's wisdom: this the Lord called "foolishness" [1 Cor 11:14], and "choose the foolish things of the world" to confound even philosophy itself. For philosophy is the material of the world's wisdom, the rash interpreter of the nature and the purposes of God. Indeed heresies are themselves instigated by philosophy. . . .

From philosophy springs those "fables and endless genealogies" [1 Tim 1:4] and "unprofitable questions" [Tit 3:9], and "words which spread like a cancer" [2 Tim 2:17]. From all these, when the apostle would restrain us, he expressly names *philosophy* as that which he would have us be on our guard against. Writing to the Colossians, he says, "See that no one beguiles you through philosophy and vain deceit, after the tradition of men, and contrary to the wisdom of the Holy Spirit" [Col 2:8]. He had been at Athens, and had in his interviews with its philosophers become well acquainted with that human wisdom which pretends to know the truth, while it only corrupts it, and is itself divided into its own manifold heresies, by the variety of its mutually repugnant sects.

What indeed has Athens to do with Jerusalem? What concord is there between the Academy and the Church? What between heretics and Christians? Our instruction comes from "the porch of Solomon" [Acts 3:5], who had himself taught that "the Lord should be sought in simplicity of heart" [Wis 1:1]. Away with all attempts to produce a mottled Christianity of Stoic, Platonic, and dialectic composition! We want no curious disputation after enjoying the gospel! With our faith, we desire no further belief. For this is our victorious faith, that there is nothing which we ought to believe besides.

THE RULE OF FAITH[25]

As for us, although we must still seek, and *that* always, yet where ought our search to be made? Among the heretics, where all things are foreign and opposed to our own verity, and to whom we are forbidden to draw near? . . . No one receives get instruction from that which tends to destruction. No one receives illumination from a quarter where all is darkness. Let our "seeking" therefore be in that which is our own, and from those who are our own, and concerning that which is our own—. . . the Rule of Faith.[26]

Now with regard to this Rule of Faith . . . which prescribes the belief that there is only one God, and that He is none other than the Creator of the world,

---

[24]Tertullian, "On Prescriptions Against Heretics," in Roberts and Donaldson, eds., **TANF**, Vol. I, ch. 7, pp. 246–47.

[25]Ibid., ch. 12–13, pp. 248–49.

[26]The *Regula Fidei*, or "Rule of Faith," was a summary of the apostolic preaching and teaching that epitomized Christian faith and practice.

who produced all things out of nothing through His own Word, first of all sent forth; that this Word is called His Son, *and* under the name of God, was seen "in diverse manners" by the patriarchs, heard at all times in the prophets, at last brought down by the Spirit and Power of the Father into the Virgin Mary, was made flesh in her womb, and, being born of her, went forth as Jesus Christ; thenceforth, He preached the new law and the new promise of the kingdom of heaven, worked miracles; having been crucified, He rose again the third day; then having ascended into the heavens, He sat at the right hand of the Father; sent instead of Himself the Power of the Holy Spirit to lead such as believe; will come with glory to take the saints to the enjoyment of everlasting life and of the heavenly promises, and to condemn the wicked to everlasting fire, after the resurrection of both these classes shall have happened, together with the restoration of their flesh. This Rule, as it will be proved, was taught by Christ, and raises amongst ourselves no other questions than those which heresies introduce, and which make men heretics.

So long, however, as its form exists in its proper order, you may seek and discuss as much as you please, and give full rein to your curiosity, in whatever seems to you to hand in doubt, or to be shrouded in obscurity. . . .

MARRIAGE IS GOOD—CELIBACY IS BETTER[27]

. . . In short, there is no place at all where we read that nuptials are prohibited; of course on the ground that they are "a good thing." What, however, is *better* than this "good," we learn from the apostle, who *permits* marrying indeed, but *prefers* abstinence; the former on account of the insidiousness of temptations, the latter on account of the straits of the times [1 Cor 7]. Now, by looking into the reason thus given for each proposition, it is easily discerned that the ground on which the power of marrying is conceded is *necessity*; but whatever *necessity* grants, she by her very nature depreciates.

In fact, that it is written, "To marry is better than to burn" [1 Cor 7:9], what is the nature of this "good" which is only commended by comparison with "evil," so that the reason why "marrying" is *more* good is merely that "burning" is *less*. No, but how far better is it neither to marry nor to burn? . . .

There are some things which are not to be *desired* merely because they are not *forbidden*, albeit they *are* in a certain sense *forbidden* when other things are preferred to them; for the preference given to the higher things is a dissuasion from the lowest. A thing is not "good" merely because it is not "evil," nor is it "evil" merely because it is not "harmful." Further: that which is fully "good" excels on this ground, that it is not only not harmful, but profitable in the bargain. For you are bound to prefer what is profitable to what is merely not harmful. For the *first* place is what every struggle aims at; the *second* has consolation attaching to it, but

---

[27]Tertullian, "Epistle to His Wife," in Roberts and Donaldson, eds., **TANF**, Vol. IV, p. 40, with omissions and modernization of expression.

not victory. But if we listen to the apostle, forgetting what is behind, let us both strain after what is before,[28] and be followers after the better rewards. Thus, although he does not "cast a snare upon us" [1 Cor 7:35], he points out what tends to utility when he says, "The unmarried woman thinks on the things of the Lord, that both in body and spirit she may be holy; but the married is solicitous how to please her husband" [1 Cor 7:34]. But he no where permits marriage in such a way as not rather to wish us to do our utmost in imitation of his own example [1 Cor 7:8]. Happy the person who shall prove [to be] like Paul!

Irenaeus of Lyon (c. 130–202)

Irenaeus of Lyon was born in Smyrna, where he came to Christian faith under the ministry of Polycarp. Irenaeus served a colony of transplanted eastern Christians who populated the Roman city of Lyon, in the south of France. He came to a leadership role during the persecutions of Emperor Marcus Aurelius. It was as a pastor that Irenaeus became an apologist and theological writer. His *Against Heresies* (c. 180) exposed and refuted Gnostic errors that were undermining the church at such a critical time in her existence. Christian tradition reports that Irenaeus suffered a martyr's death, but that is not certain. Irenaeus's theology of "recapitulation" gave the church one of its first patterns for developing a theology of redemption.

ON RECAPITULATION[29]

Therefore, as I have already said, He [Jesus Christ] caused human nature to cleave to and to become one with God. For unless man had overcome the enemy of humanity, the enemy would not have been legitimately vanquished. And again: unless it had been God·who had freely given salvation, we could never have possessed it securely. And unless man had been joined to God, he could never have become a partaker of incorruptibility. For it was incumbent upon the Mediator between God and humanity, by His relationship to both, to bring both to friendship and concord, and present humanity to God, while He could reveal God to humanity. For in what way could we be partakers of the adoption of sons [and daughters], unless we had received from Him through the Son that fellowship which refers to Himself, unless His Word, having been made flesh, had entered into communion with us? Wherefore also He passed through every stage of life, restoring to all communion with God. . . . For it behoved Him who was to destroy sin, and redeem humanity under the power of death, that He should Him-

---

[28]Tertullian borrowed the phraseology of Philippians 3:13–14 to ask his wife to consider the question of celibacy objectively, and not in the context of their own marriage.

[29]Irenaeus, "Against Heresies," in Roberts and Donaldson, eds., **TANF** Vol. I, Bk. III, chs. 18–19, pp. 448–49, with omissions and stylistic alterations.

self be made that very same thing which he was, that is human; who had been drawn by sin into bondage, but was held by death, so that sin should be destroyed by man, and humanity should go forth from death. For as by the disobedience of one man who was originally molded from virgin soil, the many were made sinners [Rom 5:19], and forfeited life; so was it necessary that, by the obedience of one man, who was originally born from a virgin, many should be justified and receive salvation. Thus, then, was the Word of God made man, as also Moses says: "God, true are His works" [Dt 32:4]. But if not having been made flesh, He did not appear as flesh, His work was not a true one. But what He did appear, that He also was: God recapitulated in Himself the ancient formation of humans, that He might kill sin, deprive death of its power, and vivify humanity; and therefore His works are true. . . . [I]t was for this end that the Word of God was made man, and He who was the Son of God became the Son of man, that man, having been taken into the Word, and receiving the adoption might become the son of God. For by no other means could we have attained to incorruptibility and immortality, unless we had been united to incorruptibility and immortality. But how could we be joined to incorruptibility and immortality unless, first, incorruptibility and immortality had become that which we also are, so that the corruptible might be swallowed up by incorruptibility, and the mortal by immortality, that we might receive the adoption of sons [and daughters]? . . .

For as He became man in order to undergo temptation, so also was He the Word that He might be glorified; the Word remaining quiescent, that He might be capable of being tempted, dishonored, crucified, and of suffering death, but the human nature being swallowed up in [the divine nature] when it conquered, and endured [without surrendering] and performed acts of kindness, and rose again, and was received [into heaven]. He therefore, the Son of God, our Lord, being the Word of the Father, and the Son of man, since He had a generation as to His human nature from Mary—who was descended from mankind, and who was herself a human being—was made the Son of man [Is 7:13]. Wherefore also the Lord Himself gave us a sign, in the depth below, and in the height above, which humanity did not ask for, because we never expected that a virgin could conceive, or that it was possible that one remaining a virgin could bring forth a son, and that what was thus born should be "God with us" [Is 7:14], and descend to those things which are of earth beneath, seeking the sheep which had perished, which was indeed His own peculiar handiwork, and ascend to the height above, offering and commending to His Father that human nature (*hominem*) which had been found, making in His own person the first-fruits of the resurrection humanity;[30] that, as the Head [Eph 4:15] rose from the dead, so also the remaining parts of the body—[namely the body] of everyone who is found in life—when the time is fulfilled of that condemnation which existed by reason of disobedience, may arise, blended together and strengthened through means of joints and knit together by the increase of God [Eph 4:15], each of the members having its own proper and fit position in the body [1 Cor 12]. For there are many mansions in

---

[30]Ephesians 4:4–14 and 1 Corinthians 15.

the Father's house [Jn 14:2], inasmuch as there are also many members in the body [1 Cor 12:14].

INCARNATION, EUCHARIST, AND IMMORTALITY[31]

. . . vain in every respect are they who . . . disallow the salvation of the flesh, and treat with contempt its regeneration, maintaining that it is not capable of incorruption. But if this indeed does not attain salvation, then neither did the Lord redeem us with His blood, nor is the cup of the Eucharist the communion of His blood, nor the bread which we break the communion of His body [1 Cor 10:16]. For blood can only come from veins and flesh, and whatsoever else makes up the substance of man, of [such as] the Word of God was actually made. By His own blood He redeemed us, as also His apostle declares, "In whom we have redemption through His blood, even the remission of sins" [Col 1:14]. And as we are His members, we are also nourished by means of the creation—and He Himself grants the creation to us, for He causes His sun to rise, and sends rain when He wills [Mt 5:45]. He has acknowledged the cup—which is a part of creation—as His own blood, by which he strengthens our blood; and the bread—also a part of the creation—He has established as His own body, from which He gives increase to our bodies.

When, therefore, the mingled cup and the manufactured bread receives the Word of God, and the Eucharist of the blood and the body of Christ is made, from which things the substance of our flesh is increased and supported, how can they affirm that the flesh is incapable of receiving the gift of God, which is life eternal, which [flesh] is nourished from the body and blood of the Lord, and is a member of Him. . . . And just as a cutting from the vine planted in the ground bears fruit in its season, or as a corn of wheat falling into the earth and becoming decomposed, rises with manifold increase by the Spirit of God, who contains all things, and then, through the wisdom of God, serves for the use of men, and having received the Word of God, becomes the Eucharist, which is the body and blood of Christ; so also our bodies, being nourished by it, and deposited in the earth, and suffering decomposition there, shall rise at their appointed time, the Word of God granting them resurrection to the glory of God, even the Father, who freely gives to this mortal immortality, and to this corruptible incorruption [1 Cor 15:53], because the strength of God is made perfect in weakness [1 Cor 12:13], in order that we may never become puffed up, as if we had life from ourselves, and exalted against God, our minds becoming ungrateful; but learning by experience that we possess eternal duration from the excelling power of this Being, not from our own nature, we may neither undervalue that glory which surrounds God as He is, nor be ignorant of our own nature, but that we may know what God can effect, and what benefits humanity receives, and thus never wan-

---

[31]Ibid., Bk. V, ch. 2, p. 528, with omissions and stylistic emendations.

der from the true comprehension of things as they are . . . both with regard to God and with regard to humanity.

Clement of Alexandria (c. 150–216)

Clement of Alexandria was born and reared in Athens, where he acquired an appreciation for Platonic philosophy that he retained even after he became a Christian. From 190 to 202 he served as head of the famous catechetical school of Alexandria, Egypt. When the severe persecutions of Septimius Severus came to Alexandria, Clement was forced to leave his teaching post (c. 202). He spent the balance of his life traveling and teaching in the Christian communities throughout Syria and Asia Minor.

The Instructor (Paedagogos, c. 200) was one of Clement's most significant works. The premise of the book is that Jesus Christ, the Word, is the Christian's unerring guide and instructor in the life of faith. He described Christian life as a life of virtue and transformation through fellowship with the Instructor. For transformation to occur we must come to Christ like little children—with humble and teachable hearts. Baptism marks the beginning of our journey toward perfection; in baptism we are cleansed, and in the Word we are illuminated and nourished by spiritual teaching. Clement urged that the Christian must follow Christ and the Scriptures in all things.[32]

THE INSTRUCTOR[33]

As there are these three things in the case of humanity, habits, actions, and passions;[34] habits are the department appropriated by *hortatory* discourse guide to piety, which, like the ship's keel, is laid beneath for the building up of faith; in which, rejoicing exceedingly, and abjuring our old opinions, through salvation we renew our youth, singing with the hymning prophecy, "How good is God to Israel, to such as are upright in heart" [Ps 73:1]! All actions, again, are the province of *preceptive* discourse; while *persuasive* discourse applies itself to heal the passions. It is, however, the self-same word which rescues a person from the custom of this world in which he has been reared, and trains him up in the one salvation of faith in God.

When, then, the Heavenly guide, the Word, was inviting people to salvation,

---

[32]See E. Glenn Hinson, "The Instructor and Miscellanies," in *Christian Spirituality*, edited by Frank Magill and Ian McGreal (San Francisco: Harper & Row, 1988), pp. 1–6, for an excellent survey and summary of the teachings of Clement and the development of *The Instructor*.

[33]Clement, "The Instructor," in **TANF**, Vol. II, pp. 209–95, with omissions and linguistic emendations.

[34]The word *passions* is used here without sexual connotations; it means "strong desires," or "aspirations."

the appellation of *hortatory* was properly applied to Him: His same word was called rousing . . . . For the whole of piety is hortatory, engendering in the kindred a faculty of reason a yearning after life now and to come. But now, being at once curative and preceptive, following in His own steps, He makes what had been prescribed the subject of persuasion, promising the cure of the passions within us. Let us then designate this Word appropriately by the one name *Instructor.*[35]

The Instructor being practical, not theoretical, His aim is thus to improve the soul, not to teach, and to train it to a virtuous [life], not to an intellectual life. Although this same word is didactic, but not in the present instance. For the word which, in matters of doctrine, explains and reveals, is that whose province it is to teach. But our Instructor being practical, first exhorts to the attainment of right dispositions and character, and then persuades us to the energetic practice of our duties, enjoining on us pure commandments, and exhibiting to such as come after representations of those who formerly wandered in error. Both are of the highest usefulness—that which assumes the form of counselling to obedience, and that which is presented in the form of example; which latter is of two kinds, corresponding to the former duality,—the one having for its purpose that we should choose and imitate the good, and the other that we should reject and turn away from the opposite. Hence accordingly ensues the healing of our passions, in consequence of the assuagements of those examples; the Instructor strengthening our souls, and by His benign commands, as by gentle medicines, guiding the sick to perfect knowledge of the truth.

There is a wide difference between health and knowledge; for the latter is produced by learning, the former by healing. One, who is ill, will not therefore learn any branch of instruction till he [or she] is quite well. For neither to learners nor to the sick is each injunction invariably expressed similarly; but to the former in such a way as to lead to knowledge, and to the latter to health. As, then, for those of us who are diseased in body a physician is required, so also those who are diseased in soul require an instructor[36] to cure our maladies; and then a teacher, to train and guide the soul to all requisite knowledge when it is made able to receive the revelation the Word. Eagerly desiring, then, to perfect us by a gradation conducive to salvation, suited for efficacious discipline, a beautiful arrangement is observed by the all-benevolent Word, who first exhorts, then trains, and finally teaches. . . .

Our Instructor, the Word, . . . cures the unnatural passions of the soul by means of exhortations. For with the highest propriety the help of bodily disease is called the healing art—an art acquired by human skill. But the paternal Word is the only . . . physician of human infirmities, and the holy charmer of the sick soul. . . . But the good Instructor, the Wisdom, the Word of the Father, who made man, cares for the whole nature of His creature; the all-sufficient Physician of humanity, the Savior, heals both body and soul. "Rise up," He said to the paralytic;

---

[35]In the Greek, *paedagogos*; it could also be translated "tutor," "educator."
[36]Pedagogue.

"take up your pallet and go home" [Mk 2:11]; and immediately the ill man received strength. And to the dead He said, "Lazarus, go forth" [Jn 10:43]; and the dead man came forth from his coffin such as he was ere he died, having undergone resurrection. Further, He heals the soul itself by precepts and gifts—by precepts indeed, in course of time, but being liberal in His gifts, He says to us sinners, "Your sins are forgiven" [Mt 9:2]. The Lord ministers all good and all help, both as man and as God: as God, forgiving our sins; and as man, training us not to sin. . . .

Our superintendence in instruction and discipline is the office of the Word, from whom we learn frugality and humility, and all that pertains to love of truth, love of humanity, and love of excellence. And so, in a word, being assimilated to God by a participation in moral excellence, we must not retrograde into carelessness and sloth. But labor, and faint not. Thou shalt be what thou dost not hope, and canst not conjecture. And as there is one mode of training for philosophers, another for orators, and another for athletes; so is there a generous disposition, suitable to the choice that is set upon moral loveliness, resulting from the training of Christ. . . . Thus, therefore, the Word has been called also the Savior, seeing He has found out for people those rational medicines which produce vigor of the senses and salvation; and devotes Himself to watching for the favorable moment, reproving evil, exposing the causes of evil affections, and striking at the roots of irrational lusts, pointing out what we ought to abstain from, and supplying all the antidotes of salvation to those who are diseased. For the greatest and more regal work of God is the salvation of humanity. The sick are vexed at a physician, who gives no advice bearing on their restoration to health. But how shall we not acknowledge the highest gratitude to the divine Instructor, who is not silent, who omits not those threatenings that point towards destruction, but discloses them, and cuts off the impulses that tend to them; and who indoctrinates in those counsels which result in the true way of living? We must confess, therefore, the deepest obligations to Him. For what else do we say is incumbent on rational creatures—I mean people—than the contemplation of the Divine? I say, too, that it is requisite to contemplate human nature, and to live as the truth directs, and to admire the Instructor and His injunctions, as suitable and harmonious to each other. According to which image also we ought, conforming ourselves to the Instructor, and making the Word and our deeds agree, to live a real life.

A HYMN TO CHRIST THE SAVIOR[37]

> Bridle of colts untamed,
> Over our will presiding;
> Wing of unwandering birds,

---

[37]This hymn was composed by Clement and appended to *The Instructor*. A. Cleveland Coxe, trans., in Roberts and Donaldson, eds., **TANF**, Vol. II, 295–96.

Our flight securely guiding.
Rudder of youth unbending,
   Firm against adverse shock;
Shepherd, with wisdom tending
   Lambs of the royal flock;
Thy simple children bring
   In one, that they may sing
In solemn lays
   Their hymns of praise
With guileless lips to Christ the King.

King of saints, almighty Word
   Of the Father's highest Lord;
Wisdom's head and chief;
   Assuagement of all grief;
Lord of all time and space,
   Jesus, Savior of our race;
Shepherd, who dost us keep;
   Husbandman, who tillest,
Bit to restrain us, Rudder
   To guide us as Thou willest;
Of the all-holy flock celestial wing;
   Fisher of men, whom Thou to life dost bring;
From evil sea of sin,
   And billowy strife,
Gathering pure fishes in,
   Caught with sweet bait of life:
Lead us, Shepherd of the sheep,
   Reason-gifted, holy One;
King of youths, whom Thou dost keep,
   So that they pollution shun:
Steps of Christ, celestial Way;
   Word eternal, Age unending;
Life that never can decay;
   Fount of mercy, virtue-sending;
Life august of those who raise
Unto God their hymn of praise,
   Jesus Christ!

Nourished by the milk of heaven,
   To our tender palates given;
Milk of wisdom from the breast
   Of that bride of grace expresst;
By a dewy spirit filled
   From fair Reason's breast distilled;
Let us sucklings join to raise
   With pure lips our hymns of praise
As our grateful offering,
   Clean and pure, to Christ our King.
Let us, with hearts undefiled,
   Celebrate the mighty Child.

> We, Christ-born, the choir of peace;
>> We, the people of His love,
> Let us sing, nor ever cease,
>> To the God of peace above.

Origen of Alexandria (185–251)

Origen of Alexandria was born into a Christian family.[38] As a youth he was edu-cated in Neoplatonism and in the Christian faith, and he remained strongly attached to both. Origen was Clement's most able student, and was his successor (c. 202) at the Alexandrian school. He too was forced to flee Alexandria (c. 233), and settling in Caesarea of Palestine, Origen established a school like the one he left (c. 240). Origen published commentaries on almost every biblical book, and produced a par-allel six-version study Bible, called the *Hexapla*. He also wrote numerous practical and theological treatises. Origen was arrested and tortured during the persecutions under Emperor Decius. Because he continued to confess Christ, even under torture, Origen is remembered in Eastern Church tradition as "the confessor."

Origen's main theological work, *On First Principles* (*De Principis*, c. 230), ev-idenced the synthesis of Christian and Platonic concepts that characterized his thought. In it Origen laid down the "first" or foundational principles upon which Christian faith must be built. *De Principis* also described Origen's allegorical ap-proach to Scripture. Origen's "spiritual reading" of the biblical text provided a methodological foundation upon which later mystics would build. His practical trea-tises like *On Prayer* (c. 233) evidence Origen's concern to integrate Christian faith and Christian life. His *Commentary on the Song of Songs* (c. 240) epitomizes the allegorical hermeneutic that undergirded Origen's practical spirituality.[39] Origen's contemplative style of prayer and spirituality influenced later writers and was sig-nificant for the development of Christian asceticism.

The contemplative tradition, which flowed from Origen and others, can be sum-marized as a three-step process. The first step was called, in the Greek, *apatheia*. While the term is the basis of our English word *apathy*, it loses much in translation. *Apatheia* describes the intentional process of becoming insensitive to material things, especially to the demands and longings of our own bodies. Disciplines of self-denial were used to develop the ability to control one's body, and bring it under submission to holy aspirations and spiritual values. By bringing the body under sub-mission, the ascetic sought to transcend it. The second step was called *anaesthe-sia*, the word from which we get *anaesthetic*. Used in the religious sense the word described a kind of contemplative unconsciousness that comes upon the mind when

---

[38]Rowan Greer, trans., *Origen* (New York: Paulist Press, 1979), offers an excellent introduction to Ori-gen's life and thought on pages 1–41.

[39]Jean Faurot, "Commentary on the Song of Songs," in Magill and McGreal, eds., *Christian Spiritual-ity*, pp. 8–12, offers a solid summary of this aspect of Origen's work.

it is emptied of all distractions. The mind must be emptied if it is to be filled by God, and the mind must be unconscious of itself and its desires if it is to be filled with God's loving will. The third step, *gnosis* or "knowledge," describes the deep oneness with God that comes through mutual understanding. For Origen, this knowledge was not merely a mental thing; it was a product of the purifying infusion of God's love, which transformed and perfected the whole person. Renunciation, asceticism, and contemplation were deemed the means whereby this transformation took place.

INTERPRETING SCRIPTURE[40]

. . . [A]s our modest perception admits, we shall address those who believe the sacred Scriptures were not composed by any human words but were written by the inspiration of the Holy Spirit and were also delivered and entrusted to us by the will of God the Father through His Only Begotten Son Jesus Christ. And we shall try to make clear to them what seems to us the right way of understanding Scripture, observing that rule and discipline[41] which was delivered by Jesus Christ to the apostles and which they delivered in succession to their followers who teach the heavenly Church.

. . . [W]e think that the way that seems to us right for understanding the Scriptures and seeking their meaning is such that we are taught what sort of understanding we should have of it by no less than Scripture itself. We have found in Proverbs some such instruction for the examination of divine Scripture given by Solomon. He says, "For your part describe them to yourself threefold in admonition and knowledge, that you may answer words of truth to those who question you" [Pr 22:20]. Therefore, a person ought to describe threefold in soul the meaning of divine letters, that is, so that the simple may be edified by, so to speak, the body of Scripture; for that is what we call the ordinary and narrative meaning. But if any have begun to make some progress and can contemplate something more fully, they should be edified by the soul of Scripture. And those who are perfect like those concerning whom the Apostle says, "Yet among the perfect we do impart wisdom, although it is not a wisdom of this world or of the rulers of this world, who are doomed to pass away. But we impart a secret and hidden wisdom of God, which God decreed before the ages for our glorification" [1 Cor 2:6–7]. Such people should be edified by that spiritual Law [Rom 7:14] which has a shadow of the good things to come [Heb 10:1] edified by the spirit of Scripture. Thus, just as a human being is said to be made up of body, soul, and spirit, so also is sacred Scripture, which has been granted by God's gracious dispensation for man's salvation. . . .

---

[40]Reprinted from *Origen*, translated by Rowan Greer. Copyright 1979 by The Missionary Society of St. Paul the Apostle in the State of New York. Used by permission of Paulist Press. "On First Principles," Bk. II, chs. 2:2, 2:4, 2:6, and 3:4–5, pp. 180, 182, 184, 192–94.

[41]The Rule of Faith.

. . .[W]e must not ignore the fact that there are certain passages in Scripture in which what we have called the body, that is a logically coherent narrative meaning, is not always to be found, as we shall show in what follows. And there are places where only what we have called the soul and the spirit may be understood. I think this is also indicated in the Gospels, when "six stone jars" are said to be "standing there, for the Jewish rites of purification, each holding two or three measures" [Jn 2:6]. As I have said, this verse in the Gospel seems to refer to those whom the Apostle calls "Jews inwardly"[Rom 2:29], because they are purified by the word of Scripture, sometimes holding "two measures," that is, receiving the meanings of the soul and of the spirit, according to what we have just said, and sometimes holding "three measures," when a reading for edification can keep bodily meaning, which is the narrative meaning. And "six stone jars" are mentioned because they bear a logical relation to those who are placed in this world to be purified. For we read that in six days (which is the perfect number)[42] this world and everything in it were finished.

Now the whole multitude of believers, which believes quite faithfully and simply, is a witness to what great profit lies in the first meaning, which I have called narrative. Nor is much argument needed, since the point is perfectly clear to everyone. And the Apostle Paul has given us a great many examples of that meaning which we have called . . . the soul, as it were, of Scripture, first, for example, the passage in his letter to the Corinthians, "For it is written, you shall not muzzle an ox when it is treading out the grain."[43] He goes on to explain how this commandment should be understood and says, "Is it for oxen that God is concerned? Does He not speak entirely for our sake? It was written for our sake, because the ploughman should plow in hope and the thresher in hope of a share in the crop" [1 Cor 9:9]. Moreover, a great many other sayings like this one, which are interpreted from the Law in this way, bestow the greatest instruction upon those who hear them.

Then, the spiritual explanation refers, for example, to someone who can make clear the heavenly things of which those who are Jews according to the flesh served as copies and shadows [Heb 8:5], and the good things to come of which the Law has a shadow [Heb 10:1], and any similar things found in the holy Scriptures. And the spiritual meaning is involved when it is asked what is that "secret and hidden wisdom of God, which God decreed before the ages for our glorification, which none of the rulers of this world understand"[1 Cor 2:7–8], or in what the Apostle himself observes when he is using certain examples from Exodus or Numbers and says, "Now these things happened to them in a type, but they were written down for us, upon whom the ends of the ages have come" [1 Cor 10: 11]. And he gives us an opportunity of understanding how we can direct our minds to the things of which their experiences were types by saying, "For they drank from the spiritual Rock which followed them, and the Rock was Christ" [1 Cor 10:4] . . . .

---

[42]According to the ancients, six is a "perfect number" because it is the sum of its parts: $1 + 2 + 3$.
[43]1 Corinthians 9:9 = Deuteronomy 25:4.

Now we have brought all these examples in order to show that the aim of the Holy Spirit, who thought it right to give us the divine Scriptures, is not that we might be able to be edified by the letter alone or in all cases, since we often discover that the letter is impossible or insufficient in itself because by it sometimes not only irrationalities but even impossibilities are described. But the aim of the Holy Spirit is that we should understand that there have been woven into the visible narrative truths that, if pondered and understood inwardly, bring forth a law useful to men and worthy of God.

But someone might suspect us of the opinion that no narrative in Scripture actually happened, since we believe that some of them did not happen, or that no commandment of the Law can be established according to the letter, since we have said that some cannot be observed according to the letter [of the law], because either reason or the possibility of the matter does not allow it, or that what is written of the Savior should not be thought fulfilled in a way also perceived by the senses, or that His commandments ought not be preserved according to the letter. Our response, therefore, must be that we judge it evident that in a great many cases the truth of the narrative meaning can and ought to be preserved. . . . Nevertheless, if someone reads with great care, I do not doubt that in a great many cases he will hesitate whether this narrative or that should be thought [to be] true according to the letter or less true, and whether this or that commandment should be observed according to the letter or not. For this reason we must rely on great zeal and effort so that each reader may with all reverence understanding that he is pondering words that are divine and not human and that have been sown into the holy books. Therefore, the understanding that we consider should be observed rightly and logically in interpreting the holy Scriptures is, we think, of this kind. . . .

THE BENEFITS OF PRAYER[44]

. . . I believe that profit often meets and joins the person who prays as he ought or who makes every effort to do so as far as he is able. First, the person who composes his mind for prayer is inevitably profited in some way. Through his very disposition for prayer he adorns himself so as to present himself to God and to speak to Him in person as to someone who looks upon him and is present. For just as various impressions and memories of the various things of which they are the measure defile the thoughts that arise under such impressions, in the same way we must believe that remembering God is profitable. This is because we have put our trust in Him, and because He knows the motions of the secret part of our soul, when it harmonizes itself to please Him as present and watching and over-

---

[44]Reprinted from *Origen*, translated by Rowan Greer. Copyright 1979 by the Missionary Society of St. Paul the Apostle in the State of New York. Used by permission of Paulist Press. "On Prayer," pp. 97–101, with omissions.

taking every mind as the One who tries the hearts and searches out the reins [Ps 7:9]. . . .

. . . The person praying must stretch out "holy hands" by thoroughly purging the passion of "anger" from his soul and harboring no rage against anyone and by forgiving each the sins he has committed against him [1 Tim 2:8]. Next, so that his mind may not be muddied by thoughts from outside, he must forget for the time being everything but the prayer he is praying. . . .

The prophet David also says that the holy person when he prays has many other characteristics. It would not be out of place to set these down, so that what is of greatest profit may become clear to us, even if we only consider the attitude and preparation for prayer of the one who dedicates himself to God. What David says is, "To you have I lifted up my eyes, you who dwell in heaven" [Ps 123:1] and "To you, O God, have I lifted up my soul" [Ps 25:1]. For the eyes of the mind are lifted up from their preoccupation with earthly things, and from their being filled with the impression of material things. And they are so exalted that they peer beyond the created order and arrive at the sheer contemplation of God and at conversing with Him reverently and suitably as He listens. How would things so great fail to profit those eyes that gaze at the glory of the Lord with unveiled face and that are being changed into His likeness from glory to glory? [2 Cor 3:18] . . .

We may suppose that renouncing malice is an act of the greatest virtue, since according to the prophet Jeremiah it sums up the entire Law [Jer 7:22–23]. . . . When we leave behind bearing malice in coming to pray, we keep the Savior's commandment, "If you stand praying, forgive, if you have anything against any one" [Mk 11:25] . . . Even if we were to suppose that no other results besides these will attend our prayers, we should nevertheless have gained what is noblest, since we should have succeeded in understanding how we ought to pray. And it is clear that whoever prays this way will be heard while he is still speaking, since he looks to the power of Him who hears . . . and has cast aside all dissatisfaction with providence before he prays. This is made clear by the verse "If you take away from you the yoke, the pointing of the finger, and the word of grumbling" [Is 58:9]. What this means is that the person who is satisfied with what happens is free from bondage to anything that has taken place and does not point his finger at God, since He has ordered what He will for our training. . . .

Therefore, the person who has been profited by praying in this fashion becomes more ready to be mingled with the Spirit of the Lord . . . . Moreover, through the purification that has been mentioned and through prayer he [or she] will partake of the Word of God, who stands in the midst even of those who do not know Him, who is never absent from prayer, and who prays to the Father with the person whose Mediator He is. For the Son of God is a High Priest who makes offerings for us,[45] and an Advocate with the Father.[46] He prays for those who pray and appeals along with those who appeal. . . . Who that believes in the mouth of Je-

---

[45]Hebrews 2:17, 3:1, 4:14, 5:10, 6:20, 7:26, 8:1, 9:11, 10:10.
[46]John 14:16,26, 15:26, 16:7; 1 John 2:1.

sus that cannot lie would hesitate a moment to be persuaded to pray, when He says, "Ask, and it will be given you . . . for everyone who asks, receives" [Lk 11:9–10]? Indeed, the good Father, when we ask for the living breath, gives Him—and not the stone that His adversary wishes to give to Jesus and His disciples for food—to those who have received "the Spirit of sonship" [Rom 8:15] from the Father. And the Father gives a good gift, raining it down from heaven for those who ask Him [Lk 11:13]. . . .

LIFE AS PRAYER[47]

In addition, I believe that the words of the saints are filled with power, especially when praying with the Spirit they also pray with the mind [1 Cor 14:18]. Then the mind is like light rising from the understanding of the one who prays.[48] It goes forth from his mouth to weaken by the power of God the spiritual poison coming from the opposing powers and entering the governing part of the mind of those who neglect to pray and fail to heed the injunction to "pray constantly" [1 Thes 5:17], which Paul gives in accordance with the exhortations of Jesus. For it goes forth from the soul of the one praying like an arrow shot from the saint by knowledge and reason and faith. And it wounds the spirits hostile to God to destroy and overthrow them when they wish to hurl round us the bonds of sin.

And he prays "constantly" (deeds of virtue or fulfilling the commandments are included as part of prayer) who unites prayer with deeds required and right deeds with prayer. For the only way we can accept the command to "pray constantly" [1 Thes 5:17] as referring to real possibility is by saying that the entire life of the saint taken as a whole is a single great prayer. What is customarily called prayer is, then, a part of this prayer. Now prayer in the ordinary sense ought to be made no less than three times a day. This is evident from the story of Daniel, who prayed three times a day when such great peril had been devised for him [Dan 6:13]. And Peter went up to the housetop about the sixth hour to pray; that is when he saw the sheet descending from heaven let down by four corners [Acts 10:9]. He was offering the middle prayer of the three, the one referred to before him by David, "In the morning may you hear my prayer, in the morning I will offer to you and I will watch" [Ps 5:3]. And the last time of prayer is indicated by "The lifting up of my hands is an evening sacrifice" [Ps 141:2]. Indeed, we do not even complete the night time properly without that prayer of which David speaks when he says, "At midnight I rise to praise you because of your righteous ordinances" [Ps 119:62]. And Paul, as it says in the Acts of the Apostles, prayed "about midnight" with Silas in Philippi and sang a hymn to God so that even the prisoners heard them [Acts 16:25].

Now if Jesus prays and does so not in vain, since He gets what He asks for

---

[47]Reprinted from *Origen*, translated by Rowan Greer. Copyright 1979 by The Missionary Society of St. Paul the Apostle in the State of New York. Used by permission of Paulist Press. Pages 104–5.
[48]Psalms 96:11; Isaiah 58:10; Romans 3:13; James 3:8.

in prayer when He might not have done so apart from prayer, which of us would neglect to pray? . . .

HOW TO PRAY[49]

It does not seem to be out of place after these discussions to finish this treatise on prayer by speaking in an introductory way about the disposition and the posture one ought to have in praying, the place where one ought to pray, the direction in which one ought to look barring any chance circumstance, the suitable and special time for prayer, and anything else similar. The question of disposition must be referred to the soul, that of the posture to the body. Thus, Paul, . . . describes the disposition and says that we must pray "without anger or quarrelling," and he describes the posture by the phrase "lifting holy hands" [1 Tim 2:8]. He seems to me to have taken this from Psalms, where it calls "the lifting up of my hands an evening sacrifice" [Ps 141:2]. Concerning place Paul says, "I desire then that in every place the men should pray" [1 Tim 2:8]. Concerning direction, in the Wisdom of Solomon it says, "To make it known that one must rise before the sun to give you thanks, and must pray to you at the dawning of the light" [Wis 16:28].

Then, it seem to me that the person who is about to come to prayer should withdraw for a little and prepare himself, and so become more attentive and active for the whole of his prayer. He should cast away all temptation and troubling thoughts and remind himself so far as he is able of the Majesty whom he approaches, and that it is impious to approach Him carelessly, sluggishly, and disdainfully; and he should put away all extraneous things. This is how he should come to prayer, stretching out his soul, as it were, instead of his hands, straining his mind toward God instead of his eyes, raising his governing reason from the ground and standing it before the Lord of all instead of standing. All malice toward any one of those who seem to have wronged him, he should put away as far as any one would wish God to put away His malice toward him, if he had wronged and sinned against many of his neighbors or had done anything whatever he was conscious of being against right reason. And although there are a great many different positions for the body, he should not doubt that the position with the hands outstretched and the eyes lifted up is to be preferred before all others, because it bears in prayer the image of characteristics befitting the soul and applies it to the body. I mean this position must be preferred barring any chance circumstance. For under certain circumstances it is allowed to pray properly sometimes sitting down because of some disease of the feet that cannot be disregarded or even lying down because of fever or some such sickness. . . .

And kneeling is necessary when someone is going to speak against their own sins before God, since he is making supplication for their healing and their forgiveness. We must understand that it symbolizes someone who has fallen down

---

[49]Reprinted from *Origen,* translated by Rowan Greer. Copyright 1979 by The Missionary Society of St. Paul the Apostle in the State of New York. Used by permission of Paulist Press. Pages 164–70.

and become obedient, since Paul says, "For this reason I bow my knees before the Father, from whom every family in heaven and on earth is named" [Eph 3:14]. And spiritual kneeling is called this because every single existing creature at the name of Jesus has fallen down before God and humbled himself to Him [Phil 2:10]. . . . Moreover, the verse in the prophet says the same thing, "To me every knee shall bow" [Is 45:23].

Now concerning the place, let it be known that every place is suitable for prayer if a person prays well. For "in every place you offer incense to me . . . says the Lord" [Mal 1:11] and "I desire then that in every place the men should pray" [1 Tim 2:8]. But everyone may have, if I may put it this way, a holy place set aside and chosen in his own house, if possible, for accomplishing his prayers in quiet and without distraction. . . . And a place of prayer, the spot where believers assemble together, is likely to have something gracious to help us, since angelic powers are placed near the throngs of believers, as well as the powers of our Lord and Savior Himself, and the spirits of the saints—I think both of those who have already fallen asleep and clearly of those who are still alive, even though it is not easy to say how. . . .

It seems to me I should go on to discuss the topics of prayer and then bring this treatise to a close. It seems to me there are four topics that need to be sketched out and that I have found them scattered in the Scriptures. Each person should organize his prayer according to these topics. This is what they are: In the beginning and the preface of prayer something having the force of *praise* should be said of God through Christ, who is praised with Him, and by the Holy Spirit, who is hymned with Him. After this each person should place general thanksgivings, bringing forward for *thanksgiving* the benefits given many people and those he has himself received from God. After thanksgiving it seems to me that he ought to blame himself bitterly before God for his own sins and then ask first, for healing that he may be delivered from the habit that brings him to sin and, second, for forgiveness of the sins that have been committed. After *confession*, the fourth topic that seems to me must be added is the *request* for great and heavenly things, both private and general, and concerning his household and his dearest. And, finally, the prayer should be concluded with a *doxology* of God through Christ in the Holy Spirit. . . .

Ephrem the Syrian (c. 306–73)

Ephrem the Syrian was the foremost writer of Syrian Christianity. He was born in Nisibis, and served there as an exegete, deacon, and teacher. But it was as a hymn writer that Ephrem made his most lasting contribution to Christian Spirituality. His many collections of hymns were an important resource in the formation of Christian liturgy and spirituality. In 363 AD Nisibis fell into Persian hands and Ephrem relocated to Edessa, where he established a school of biblical and theological studies as well as a women's choir to sing his many hymns. Ephrem the Syrian died on June 9, 373, while ministering to victims of the plague.

NATIVITY HYMN #8[50]

Of particular interest is Ephrem's tendency to weave the themes of incarnation and salvation together to form a whole fabric. His willingness to look to OT women to establish the role of Mary and to illustrate her superiority to the Hebrew women of faith exemplifies the Christian application of the Hebrew Scriptures. For Christians, Mary sums up and surpasses the role of all previous faithful women and signals the birth of the New Age, which is heralded by the birth of Jesus from her womb—by the power of the Holy Spirit.

1   Blessed is the Messenger who came bearing
a great peace.[51] By the mercy of His Father,
He lowered Himself to us.[52] Our own debts
He did not take up to Him. He reconciled
[His] Lordship with His chattels.[53]

Refrain: *"Glory to Your Dawn, Divine and Human."*

2   Glorious is the Wise One Who allied and joined
Divinity with humanity,
one from the height and the other from the depth.
He mingled the natures like pigments[54]
and an image came into being: the God-man.

3   O Zealous One who saw Adam
who became dust and the accursed serpent
eating him. Reality dwelt
in what had lost its flavor. He made him salt
by which the cursed serpent would be blinded.[55]

4   Blessed is the Compassionate One Who saw, next to paradise,
the lance that barred the way
to the Tree of Life.[56] He came to take up the body
that would be struck so that by the opening in His side
He might break through the way to paradise.[57]

---

[50]Reprinted from *Ephrem the Syrian: Hymns*, translated by Kathleen McVey. Copyright 1989 by The Missionary Society of St. Paul the Apostle in the State of New York. Used by permission of Paulist Press. Pages 119–23. Many of the notes applied throughout the text are the work of McVey, a few are my own.

[51]Or "a great greeting."

[52]Philippians 2:6–11.

[53]Or "bondservants."

[54]That is, the colors for making paint.

[55]This may imply that the evil one (serpent) was fooled by the incarnation of Christ.

[56]Genesis 3:24.

[57]Ephrem saw the "sword" as a symbol of the lance that pierced Jesus side.

5   Glorious is the Compassionate One Who did not use
violence, and without force,
by wisdom He was victorious. He gave a type
to human beings that by power
and wisdom they might conquer discerningly.

6   Blessed is Your flock for You are her gate.[58]
and You are her staff, and You are her Shepherd,[59]
and You are her drink; You [are] her pilot[60]
and You are her overseer. O to the Only-begotten[61]
Who was fruitful and multiplied in all [His] benefits.

7   The farmers who cultivated life
came and worshipped before Him. They prophesied to Him,
bursting into song, "Blessed is the Farmer
by Whom is worked the earth of the heart;
He gathers His grains of wheat into the storehouse of life."[62]

8   The laborers came to give glory
to the offshoot that sprang forth from the root
and the stem of Jesse,[63] the virgin cluster
of a parched vine. "Let us be the vessels
for Your new wine that renews all."[64]

9   "In You may my friend's vineyard that gives sour grapes
find peace. Graft its vines
with Your slips. Let it be laden entirely
with Your blessings. Let its fruit appease
The Lord of the vineyard who threatened him."[65]

10   Carpenters came because of Joseph
to the son of Joseph. "Blessed is your offspring,
the Chief of carpenters, by Whom was drawn
even the Ark.[66] By Him was constructed
the temporal Tabernacle that was [only] for a time.[67]

---

[58]John 10:7–18.

[59]John 10:14.

[60]Or "salt"; the author may be employing a pun to include both meanings.

[61]John 1:14.

[62]Matthew 13:30.

[63]Isaiah 11:10.

[64]Mark 2:22.

[65]Isaiah 5:1–7.

[66]The same Syriac word could describe either the Ark of the Covenant or Noah's ark (Gen 6:14–8:19). See 1 Peter 3:18–22 for a Christological interpretation of Noah's Ark. Ephrem probably intends to blend those two images to speak of a saving, tangible presence of God that comes to us through the incarnation of Jesus Christ.

[67]Exodus 26:1ff, 36:8ff; 40. The Ark of the Covenant and the Tabernacle were visible signs of God's invisible presence among the people.

11   "Confess the name of Your craft,
that You are our pride. May You make the yoke
that is light and easy upon those who bear it.[68]
May You make the measure in which deceit
cannot be, for it is full of truth."

12   "Also may You construct and make a balance[69]
from justice, so that whoever steps
onto it will be judged, and whoever is perfect
will be celebrated on it. O Just One, may You weigh
mercy and sins in it, as a judge."

13   When Sarah sang lullabies to Isaac
as to a servant who bore the image
of the King, his Lord; upon his shoulders
the sign of the cross,[70] also upon his hands
bonds and pains, a symbol of the nails.[71]

14   Rachel cried out to her husband; she said,
"Give me sons!"[72] Blessed is Mary
for without her asking, You dwelt in her womb
chastely, O Gift
Who pours Himself out upon His recipients.

15   Anna with bitter sobs
asked for a child,[73] Sarah,[74] and Rebekah[75]
with vows and words, and even Elizabeth,[76]
again with her prayer [asked] for a long time.
Although they suffered, afterward they were consoled.

16   Blessed is Mary, who without vows
and without prayer, in her virginity
conceived and brought forth the Lord of all
the sons of her companions who were and will be
pure and just men, priests and kings.

17   Who will sing a lullaby to the child of her womb
as Mary [did]? Who will dare

---

[68]Matthew 11:28–30.

[69]The "scales" or balance was a symbol for judgment and justice in the ancient world.

[70]Genesis 22:6, Isaac carrying the wood of his own sacrifice was often seen as a "type" or symbolic representation of Jesus carrying the cross.

[71]Isaac's bound hands (Gen 22:9) were seen as a "type" of the nails that bound Jesus to the cross.

[72]Genesis 30:1.

[73]1 Samuel 1:9–20.

[74]Genesis 16:1ff, 17:15ff, 18:9ff.

[75]Genesis 25:21ff.

[76]Luke 1:5–25.

to call her son, Son of the Maker.
Son of the Creator? Who has ever existed
who called her son, Son of the Most High?[77]

18   Bridegrooms shouted joyfully with [their] brides,
"Blessed is the Babe whose mother was
bride of the Holy One. Blessed [was] the marriage feast
at which You were present: even though its wine
suddenly was depleted, by You it became plentiful again."[78]

19   The children cried out, "Blessed [is] He Who was for us
a brother and companion in the streets.
Blessed is the day that with branches
glorified the Tree of Life
Who inclined His height toward our childishness."[79]

20   Women heard that behold a virgin indeed
would conceive and bring forth.[80] Well-born women hoped
that He would shine forth from them, and elegant women
that He would appear from them. Blessed in Your height
that bent down and shone forth from the poor.[81]

21   Even little girls taken by Him [as brides]
spoke prophetically, "Yours, Lord, let me be,
for I am ugly, to You I am fair,
and if I am lowly, to You I am noble.
The bridal chamber that passes away have I exchanged for You."[82]

22   Since youth is both bold
and talkative, the young girls gathered,
daughters of the Hebrews, wise women,
and the mourners, and with their soft words
changed dirges into prophecy.[83]

---

[77]Luke 1:31–35.

[78]John 2:1–12.

[79]Mark 11:1–11; Matthew 21:15ff. The linguistic similarity between "streets" and "branches" (in the original Syriac), allows Ephrem to move readily from the image of Jesus as a boy in the streets to the branches with which children heralded Jesus's arrival in the streets of Jerusalem.

[80]Isaiah 7:14.

[81]Luke 1:46–55.

[82]The bride-bridegroom analogy was based in an allegorical Song of Solomon, as well as passages like Matthew 9:15, 22:1–22, 25:1–12; Mark 2:19–20; John 3:25–30, and etc.

[83]Jeremiah 9:16–21; Joel 3:1; Acts 2:17. The prophesying of young women was deemed a sign of the presence of the Kingdom of God.

NATIVITY HYMN #15[84]

1   "With You I shall begin, and I trust
that with You I shall end. I shall open my mouth,
and You fill my mouth.[85] I am for You the earth
and You are the farmer. Sow in me Your voice.[86]
You who are the sower of Himself in His mother's womb."

Refrain: *Glory be to You, my Lord, and through You to the Father on the day of Your nativity.*

2   "All the chaste daughters of the Hebrews
and virgin daughters of rulers
are amazed at me. Because of You, a daughter of the poor
is envied. Because of You, a daughter of the weak
is an object of jealousy. Who gave You to me?"

3   "Son of the Rich One, Who despised the womb
of rich women, what drew You
toward the poor? For Joseph is needy,
and I am impoverished. Your merchants
brought gold to a house of the poor."

4   She saw the Magi[87]; her songs increased
at their offerings; "Behold Your worshippers
surround me, and their offerings
encircle me. Blessed be the Babe
Who made His mother the lyre of His melodies."

5   "And since the lyre looks toward its master,
my mouth looks toward You. Let Your will arouse
Your mother's tongue. Since I have learned by You
a new way of conceiving, let my mouth learn by You
a new [way of] giving birth to new glory."

---

[84]Reprinted from *Ephrem the Syrian: Hymns,* translated by Kathleen McVey. Copyright 1989 by The Missionary Society of St. Paul the Apostle in the State of New York. Used by permission of Paulist Press. Pages 145–47. Ephrem placed this hymn in the mouth of Mary, at the moment that Wise Men (Magi) arrive to pay homage to Jesus, her son. McVey points to four foundational themes at work in the hymn: (1) Mary is the instrument of Christ's will, in his role as the Son of God (vs. 1, 4–5); (2) God chose the poor and outcasts of this world as vehicles of his revelation (vs. 2–3); (3) Mary is the mouthpiece of Christ, Who enables her to sing a new song in the midst of slander and oppression (vs. 5–7); and (4) David prophesied the gift of the Magi in his Psalms, and all of the Psalms should be interpreted Christologically (vs. 9–10).

[85]In Psalm 81:10, food is given; in this instance, however, Mary's mouth is filled with the prophetic word.

[86]While the word translated "voice" here is not synonymous with *logos,* or "word," the usage is reminiscent of the "word became flesh and dwelt among us. . . ." John 1:14.

[87]Matthew 2:1–12.

6   "If difficult things for You are not difficult
     but easy, so that the womb conceived You
     without intercourse, and without seed
     the womb gave birth to you, it is easy for the mouth
     to be fruitful and to multiply Your great glory."[88]

7   "Behold, I am slandered and oppressed,
     but I rejoice. My ears are full
     of scorn and disdain, but it is a small matter to me
     how much I shall endure, for a single [word of] consolation from You
     is able to chase away myriads of griefs."

8   "Since I am not despised by You, my Son,
     I am confident, I who am slandered
     have conceived and given birth to the True Judge
     Who will vindicate me. For if Tamar
     was acquitted by Judah,[89] how much more will I be acquitted by You!"

9   "David, Your father, sang a psalm to You
     before You came, that to You would be offered
     gold of Sheba.[90] The psalm
     that he merely sang [now] in reality
     heaps before You myrrh and gold."

10   "The hundred and fifty psalms he sang
     were favored by You since all the words
     of prophecy are in need
     of Your seasoning. For without Your salt
     all wisdom would lose its savor."[91]

Athanasius of Alexandria (c. 296–373)

Athanasius was bishop in Alexandria for forty-five years (328–73). For more than fifty years he was a central figure in the defense of orthodox Christian faith in the face of the Arian heresy.[92] Because of the shifting tides of this struggle, Athanasius

---

[88] Genesis 1:22,28.

[89] Genesis 38:26.

[90] Psalms 72:15.

[91] The phraseology here is dependent upon Matthew 5:13.

[92] Arius (c. 260–336) taught that there was a time when the "Father was, and the Son was not," that is to say that since the Scripture states that the Son was born out of the Father (Jn 1:14) they could not be coeternal; the Father must precede and be distinct from the Son. This caused the Arians to posit that the Son was the first and highest creation of the Father, but that the Son was not divine in the same sense that the Father was divine. This view of the nature of Christ was condemned as heretical at the Council of Nicea (325), and ever thereafter orthodox Christian faith has maintained that the Father and Son are coeternal and equally Divine.

spent nearly sixteen of his years as bishop of Alexandria in exile, and much of this exile was lived out in the Egyptian desert where Athanasius met and studied with the venerable St. Anthony. As a deacon Athanasius had attended the monumental Council of Nicea (325). He had already written one of the most important books ever written on the nature and mission of Jesus Christ, *On the Incarnation of the Word of God* (De *Incarnatio Verbi Dei*, 318).

Athanasius's *Life of Antony* (c. 356) marked the birth of the genre of spiritual biography. St. Antony's holy life became a vehicle for teaching orthodox Christianity and the apostolic vision of holy living. The book popularized monastic ideals and provided a model of spirituality that later Christians (like St. Augustine) sought to emulate.

THE LIFE OF ANTONY[93]

Antony . . . was by descent an Egyptian: his parents were of good family and possessed considerable wealth, and as they were Christians he also was reared in the same Faith. . . . After the death of his father and mother he was left alone with one little sister: his age was about eighteen or twenty, and on him the care of both home and sister rested.

Now it was not six months after the death of his parents, and going according to custom into the Lord's House, he communed with himself and reflected as he walked how the apostles [Mt 4:20] left everything and followed the Saviour; and how they in the Acts [4:35] sold their possessions and brought [the proceeds] and laid them at the apostles' feet for distribution to the poor, and what a great hope was laid up for [such people] in heaven. Pondering over these things he entered the church, and as the Gospel was being read, and he heard the Lord saying to the rich man, "If you would be perfect, go and sell what you possess and give to the poor, and you will have treasure in heaven; and come, follow me" [Mt 19:21]. [To Antony it was] as though God had put him in mind of the saints, and [that] the passage had been read on his account, [he] went out . . . from the church and gave the possessions of his forefather to the villagers . . . . And all the rest that was movable he sold, and having got together much money he gave it to the poor, reserving a little, however, for his sister's sake.

And again as he went into the church, he heard the Lord say in the Gospel, "Do not be anxious about tomorrow" [Mt 6:25], [and] he could stay no longer but went out and gave those things also to the poor. Having committed his sister to [the care of] known and faithful virgins, [he] put her into a convent to be brought up, he henceforth devoted himself . . . to discipline, taking heed to himself and training himself with patience. For there were not yet so many monasteries in Egypt . . . but all who wished to give heed to themselves practiced discipline in solitude near their own village. Now there was then in the next village an old man

---

[93]Athanasius, "Life of Antony," in Philip Schaff and Henry Wace, eds., **NPNF**, Vol. IV (New York: Christian Literature Company, 1893; reprint Grand Rapids, Mich.: Wm. B. Eerdmans, 1972), pp. 195–96.

who had lived the life of a hermit from his youth up. Antony, after he had seen this man, imitated him in piety. And at first he began to abide in places outside the village; then if he heard of a good man anywhere . . . he went forth and sought him, and . . . returned having got from the good man—as it were—supplies for his journey in the way of virtue. So dwelling there at first, he confirmed his purpose . . . to keep all his desire and energy for perfecting his discipline. He worked with his hands, however, having heard, "if anyone will not work, let him not eat" [2 Thes 3:10], and part [of what he made, he spent] for bread, and part he gave to the poor. And he was constant in prayer, knowing that a person ought to pray in secret [Mt 7:7], and unceasingly [1 Thes 5:27]. For he had given such heed to what [he] read that nothing that was written [in Scripture] was lost to him, but he remembered everything, and afterwards his memory served him like books.

Thus conducting himself, Antony was beloved by all. He subjected himself in sincerity to the good men whom he visited, and learned thoroughly where each surpassed him in zeal and discipline. He observed the graciousness of one; the unceasing prayer of another; he took knowledge of another's freedom from anger and another's loving-kindness; he gave heed to one as he watched, to another as he studied; one he admired for his endurance, another for his fasting and sleeping on the ground; the meekness of one and the long-suffering of another he watched with care, while he took note of the piety towards Christ and the mutual love which animated [them] all. Thus filled, he returned to his own place of discipline . . . and henceforth strove to unite [in himself] the qualities of each, and was eager to develop in himself the virtues of all . . . .

Macrina the Younger (327–79)

Macrina the Younger was called "the younger" to distinguish her from her illustrious grandmother (d. 340) known by the same name. She was a devout and learned woman, who established a monastic retreat on the family estate in Pontus. Her example in Christian piety and the monastic life left a lasting imprint upon her two famous brothers, St. Basil the Great and St. Gregory Nyssa. Gregory became her biographer through his publication of *Vita Marina Junioris*. Her only extant theological writing has been preserved in Gregory's *On the Soul and the Resurrection* (380).

ON THE RESURRECTION[94]

. . . First let us get a clear notion as to the scope of this doctrine; in other words, what is the end that Holy Scripture has in view in promulgating it and creating the belief in it. Well, to sketch the outline of so vast a truth and to embrace it in

---

[94]Gregory of Nyssa, "On the Soul and Resurrection," in ibid., Schaff, and Wace, **NPNF**, Vol. V, pp. 464–68, with omissions and linguistic emendations.

a definition, we will say that the Resurrection is *"the reconstitution of our nature in its original form."* But in that form of life, of which God Himself was the Creator, it is reasonable to believe that there was neither age nor infancy nor any of the sufferings arising from our present various infirmities, nor any kind of bodily affliction whatever. It is reasonable, I say, to believe that God was the Creator of none of these things, but that man was a thing divine before his humanity got within reach of the assault of evil; that then, however, with the inroad of evil, all these afflictions also broke in upon him. Accordingly a life that is free from evil is under no necessity whatever of being passed amidst the things that result from evil. It follows that when a man travels through ice he must get his body chilled: or when he walks in a very hot sun that he must get his skin darkened; but if he has kept clear of the one or the other, he escapes these results entirely, both the darkening and the chilling; no one, in fact, when a particular cause was removed, would be justified in looking for the effect of that particular cause. Just so our nature, becoming passional, had to encounter all the necessary results of a life of passion: but when it shall have started back to that state of passionless blessedness, it will no longer encounter the inevitable results of evil tendencies. Seeing, then, that all the infusions of the life of the brute into our nature were not in us before our humanity descended through the touch of evil into passions, most certainly, when we abandon those passions, we shall abandon all their visible results. No one, therefore, will be justified in seeking in that other life for the consequences in us of any passion. Just as if a man, who, clad in a ragged tunic, has divested himself of the garb, feels no more its disgrace upon him, so we too, when we have cast off that dead unsightly tunic made from the skins of brutes and put upon us (for I take the "coats of skins" to mean that conformation belonging to a brute nature with which we were clothed when we became familiar with passionate indulgence), shall, along with the casting off of that tunic, fling from us all the belongings that were round us of that skin of a brute; and such accretions are sexual intercourse, conception, parturition, impurities, suckling, feeding, evacuation, gradual growth to full size, prime of life, old age, disease, and death. If that skin is no longer round us, how can its resulting consequences be left behind within us? . . .

. . . whenever the time come that God shall have brought our nature back to the primal state of man, it will be useless to talk of such things then, and to imagine that objections based on such things can prove God's power to be impeded in arriving at His end. His end is one, and one only; it is this: when the complete whole of our race shall have been perfected from the first man to the last—some having at once in this life been cleansed from evil, others having afterwards in the necessary periods been healed by the Fire, others having in their life here been unconscious equally of good and of evil—to offer to every one of us participation in the blessings which are in Him, which, the Scripture tells us, "eye hath not seen, nor ear heard," nor thought ever reached. But this is nothing else, as I at least understand it, but to be in God Himself; for the Good which is above hearing and eye and heart must be that Good which transcends the universe. But the difference between the virtuous and vicious life led at the present time will be illustrated in this way; viz. the quicker or more tardy participation of each in that promised blessedness. According to the amount of the ingrained wickedness of each will be computed the duration of his cure. This cure consists in the cleansing of his soul. . . .

Further, it seems to me that the words of the Apostle in every respect harmonize with our own conception of what the Resurrection is. They indicate the they very same thing that we have embodied in our own definition of it, wherein we said that the Resurrection is no other thing than *"the reconstitution of our nature in its original form."* For, whereas we learn from Scripture in the account of the first Creation, that first the earth brought forth "the green herb" (as the narrative says), and that then from this plant seed was yielded, from which, when it was shed on the ground, the same form of the original plant again sprang up, the Apostle, it is to be observed, declares that this very same thing happens in the Resurrection also; and so we learn from him the fact, not only that our humanity will then be changed into something nobler, but also that what we have therein to expect is nothing else than that which was at the beginning. In the beginning, we see, it was not an ear rising from a grain, but a grain coming from an ear, and after that, the ear grows round the grain: and so the order indicated in this similitude clearly shows that all that blessed state which arises for us by means of the Resurrection is only a return to our pristine state of grace. We too, in fact, were once in a fashion a full ear; but the burning heat of sin withered us up, and then on our dissolution by death the earth received us: but in the spring of the Resurrection she will reproduce this naked grain of our body in the form of an ear, tall, well-proportioned, and erect, reaching to the heights of heaven, and for blade and beard, resplendent in incorruption, and with all the other godlike marks of Deity which once belonged to him who was created in God's image, and which we hope for hereafter. The first man Adam, that is, was the first ear; but with the arrival of evil human nature was diminished into a mere multitude; and, as happens to the grain on the ear, each individual person was denuded of the beauty of that primal ear, and moldered in the soil: but in the Resurrection we are born again in our original splendour; only instead of that single primitive ear we become the countless myriads of ears in the cornfields.

The virtuous life as contrasted with that of vice is distinguished thus: those who while living have by virtuous conduct exercised husbandry on themselves are at once revealed in all the qualities of a perfect ear, while those whose bare grain (that is the forces of their natural soul) has become through evil habits degenerate, as it were, and hardened by the weather . . . will, though they live again in the Resurrection, experience very great severity from their Judge, because they do not possess the strength to shoot up into the full proportions of an ear, and thereby become that which we were before our earthly fall. The remedy offered by the Overseer of the produce is to collect together the tares and the thorns, which have grown up with the good seed, and into whose bastard life all the secret forces that once nourished its root have passed, so that it not only has had to remain without its nutriment, but has been choked and so rendered unproductive by this unnatural growth. When from the nutritive part within them everything that is the reverse or the counterfeit of it has been picked out, and has been committed to the fire that consumes everything unnatural, and so has disappeared, then in this class also their humanity will thrive and will ripen into fruit-bearing, owing to such husbandry, and some day after long courses of ages will get back again to that universal form which God stamped upon us at the beginning. Blessed are they, indeed, in whom the full beauty of those ears shall be developed directly [as] they are born in the Resurrection. Yet we say this without implying that any merely bodily distinctions will be manifest between those who have lived virtuously and those who have lived viciously in this life, as if we ought to think that one will be imperfect as regards his material frame, while another will win perfection as regards it. The prisoner and the free, here in this present world, are just alike as regards the constitutions of their two bodies; though as regards enjoyment and suffering the gulf is wide between them. In this way, I take it, should we reckon the difference between the good and the bad in that intervening time.

For the perfection of bodies that rise from that sowing of death is, as the Apostle tells us, to consist in incorruption and glory and honour and power; but any diminution in such excellencies does not denote a corresponding bodily mutilation of him who has risen again, but a withdrawal and estrangement from each one of those things which are conceived of as belonging to the good. Seeing, then, that one or the other of these two diametrically opposed ideas, I mean good and evil, must any way attach to us, it is clear that to say a person is not included in the good is a necessary demonstration that he [or she] is included in the evil. But then, in connection with evil, we find no honour, no glory, no incorruption, no power; and so we are forced to dismiss all doubt that a person who has nothing to do with these last-mentioned things must be connected with their opposites, viz. with weakness, with dishonour, with corruption, with everything of that nature, such as we spoke of . . . when we said how many were the passions, sprung from evil, which are so hard for the soul to get rid of, when they have infused themselves into the very substance of its entire nature and become one with it. When such, then, have been purged from it and utterly removed by the healing processes worked out by the Fire, then every one of the things which make up our conception of the good will come to take their place; incorruption, that is, and life, and honour, and grace, and glory, and everything else that we conjecture is to be seen in God, and in His Image, man as he was made.

Basil the Great (c. 330–79)

Basil the Great was born into a Christian family in the town of Annesi, in the region of Cappadocia (Asia Minor). He was the older brother of Macrina and Gregory of Nyssa, as well as being the friend and colleague of Gregory Nazianzen. Nazianzen and Basil had both studied in Athens, but forsaking philosophy in search of true wisdom they went to Egypt to explore monastic life. Basil founded one of (if not) the first cenobitic monasteries, and wrote his famous *Long Rules* (c. 358) as a guide to be employed in the monastic life. The *Long Rules* were set in a question-and-answer format, and through the course of fifty-five questions and replies outlined the theological and pragmatic bases of monastic vocation. Of particular importance was Basil's examination of the holy dispositions that monastic life sought to cultivate and the means whereby those dispositions were to be sought. The *Long Rules* formed the basis of later monastic rules that were used in the Eastern and Western churches.

LIVING IN COMMUNITY[95]

. . . I consider that life passed in company with a number of persons in the same habitation is more advantageous in many respects. My reasons are, first, that no one of us is self-sufficient as regards corporeal necessities, but we require one another's aid in supplying our needs. The foot, to cite an analogy, possesses one kind of power and lacks another, and without co-operation of the other members of the body it finds itself incapable of carrying on its activity independently for any length of time, nor does it have wherewithal to supply what is lacking. Similarly, in the solitary life, what is at hand becomes useless to us and what is wanting cannot be provided, since God, the Creator, decreed that we should require the help of one another. Again, apart from this consideration, the doctrine of the love of Christ does not permit the individual to be concerned solely with his or her own private interests. "Love," says the Apostle, "seeks not her own" [1 Cor 13:5]. But a life passed in solitude is concerned only with the private service of individual needs. This is openly opposed to the law of love which the Apostle fulfilled, who sought not what was profitable to himself but to many that they might be saved [1 Cor 10:33]. Furthermore, a person living in solitary retirement will not readily discern his or her own defects, since they have no one to admonish and correct them with mildness and compassion. In fact, admonition even from an enemy often produces in a prudent person the desire for amendment. But the cure of sin is wrought with understanding by him who loves sincerely; for Holy Scripture says: "for he who loves is diligent to discipline" [Pr 13:24]. Such a one is very difficult to find in solitude, if in one's prior state of life one had not been associated with such a person. The solitary, consequently, experiences the truth of the saying, "Woe to him that is alone, for when he falls, he has none to lift him up" [Ec 4:10]. . . .

Besides, if all we who are united in the one hope of our calling [Eph 4:4] are one body with Christ as our Head, we are also members, one of another [1 Cor 12:12]. If we are not joined together each of us should choose to live in solitude, we would not serve the common good in the ministry according to God's good pleasure, but would be satisfying our own passion for self-gratification. How could we, divided and separated, preserve the status and the mutual service of members or our subordinate relationship to our Head which is Christ? It is im-

---

[95]Reprinted from Sister M. Monica Wagner, trans., *Basil the Great: Ascetical Works* (Washington, D.C.: Catholic University Press, 1962), "The Long Rules," Question 7, pp. 247–52. Used with the kind permission of Catholic University Press.

possible, indeed, to rejoice with him who receives an honor or to sympathize with him who suffers [1 Cor 12:26] when, by reason of their being separated from one another, each person cannot, in all likelihood, be kept informed about the affairs of his neighbor. In addition, since no one has the capacity to receive all spiritual gifts, but the grace of the Spirit is given proportionately to the faith of each [Rom 12:6], when one is living in association with others, the grace privately bestowed on each individual becomes the common possession of his fellows. "To one, indeed, is given the word of wisdom; and to another, the word of knowledge; to another, faith, to another, prophecy, to another, the grace of healing" [2 Cor 2:6] and so on. The person who receives any of these gifts does not possess it for his or her own sake, but rather for the sake of others, so that, in the life passed in community, the operation of the Holy Spirit in the individual is at the same time necessarily transmitted to all. The person who lives alone, consequently, and has, perhaps, one gift renders it ineffectual by leaving it in disuse, since it lies buried within themselves. . . .

Community life offers more blessings than can be fully and easily enumerated. It is more advantageous than the solitary life both for preserving the goods bestowed on us by God and for warding off the external attacks of the Enemy. . . .

Wherein will [the solitary] show his humility, if there is no one with whom he may compare and so confirm his own greater humility? Wherein will he give evidence of his compassion, if he has cut himself off from association with other persons? And how will he exercise himself in long-suffering, if no one contradicts his wishes? If anyone says that the teaching of the Holy Scripture is sufficient for the amendment of his or [her] ways, they resemble a person who learns carpentry without ever actually doing a carpenter's work or a person who is instructed in metal-working but will not reduce theory to practice. To such a person the Apostle would say: "Not the hearers of the law are just before God, but the doers of the law shall be justified" [Rom 2:13]. Consider, further, that the Lord by reason of His excessive love for humanity was not content with merely teaching the word, but, so as to transmit to us clearly and exactly the example of humility in the perfection of love, girded Himself and washed the feet of the disciples [Jn 13:5ff]. Whom, therefore will you wash? To whom will you minister? . . . So it is an area for the combat, a good path of progress, continual discipline, and a practicing of the Lord's commandment, when Christians[96] dwell together in community. This kind of life has as its aim the glory of God according to the commandment of our Lord Jesus Christ, who said: "So let your light shine before men that they may see your good works and glorify your Father who is in heaven" [Mt 5:16]. It maintains also the practice characteristic of the saints, of whom it is recorded in the Acts [of the Apostles]: "And all they that believed were together and had all things in common" [Acts 2:44], and again: "And the multitude of believers had but one heart and one soul; neither did anyone say that any of the

---

[96]Basil wrote "brethren."

things which he possessed was his own, but all things were in common among them" [Acts 4:32].

Gregory of Nyssa (c. 335–95)

Gregory of Nyssa was born into an influential Christian family. Gregory was the younger brother of Basil the Great and of Macrina the Younger. He was bishop of Nyssa, a small town in the province of Cappadocia. He was a staunch opponent of Arians, and played a significant role at the Council of Constantinople (381) that resulted in the triumph of orthodox Christianity over Arianism. Gregory's theology was characterized by monastic and mystical tendencies. As an interpreter of the Bible, Gregory followed the allegorical pattern laid down by Origen before him. This approach is evident in Nyssa's *Life of Moses* (c. 357).

The work is divided into two major sections. The first is a literal account of Moses's life and deeds. The second section is an allegorical exposition of Moses's life that seeks to derive moral and spiritual insight from it. In Gregory's work, Moses's journey through the wilderness and ascent of Mt. Sinai into God's very presence becomes a pattern of the faithful person's pilgrimage toward Christian perfection.

THE PERFECT LIFE[97]

. . . You requested, dear friend, that we trace in outline for you what the perfect life is. . . . The perfection of everything which can be measured by the senses is marked off by certain definite boundaries. Quantity, for example, admits of both continuity and limitation, for every quantitative measure is circumscribed by certain limits proper to itself. The person who looks at a cubit or at the number ten knows that its perfection consists in the fact that it has both a beginning and an end. But in the case of virtue we have learned from the Apostle that the[98] one limit of perfection is the fact that it has no limit. For that divine Apostle, great and lofty in understanding, ever running the course of virtue, never ceased "straining toward those things that are still to come" [Phil 3:13]. Coming to a stop in the race was not safe for him. Why? Because no good has a limit in its own nature but is limited by the presence of its opposite, as life is limited by death and light by darkness. And every good thing generally ends with all those things which are perceived to be contrary to the good.

---

[97] Reprinted from Abraham Malherbe and Everett Ferguson, trans., *Gregory of Nyssa: The Life of Moses*. Copyright 1978 by The Missionary Society of St. Paul the Apostle in the State of New York. Used by permission of Paulist Press. From the Preface, pp. 29–33, with large omissions. Nyssa's writing is replete with allusions to classical philosophy and other sources; for the most part I have omitted notation of these. For full notation see Malherbe and Ferguson's edition. Their book also carries an excellent introduction to the life and thought of Gregory of Nyssa.

[98] The original reads "its" instead of "the."

Just as the end of life is the beginning of death, so also stopping the race of virtue marks the beginning of the race of evil. Thus our statement that grasping perfection with reference to virtue is impossible was not false, for it has been pointed out that what is marked off by boundaries is not virtue. I said that it is impossible for those who pursue the life of virtue to attain perfection. The meaning of this statement will be explained.

The Divine One is himself the Good (in the primary and proper sense of the word), whose very nature is goodness. This He is and He is so named, and is known by this nature. Since, then, it has not been demonstrated that there is any limit to virtue except evil, and since the Divine does not admit of an opposite, we hold the divine nature to be unlimited and infinite. Certainly whoever pursues true virtue participates in nothing other than God, because He is Himself absolute virtue. Since, then, those who know what is good by nature desire participation in it, and since this good has no limit, the participant's desire itself necessarily has no stopping place but stretches out with the limitless.

It is therefore undoubtedly impossible to attain perfection, since, as I have said, perfection is not marked off by limits. The one limit of virtue is the absence of a limit. How then would one arrive at the sought-for boundary when he can find no boundary?

Although on the whole my argument has shown that what is sought for is unattainable, one should not disregard the commandment of the Lord which says, "Therefore be perfect, just as your heavenly Father is perfect" [Mt 5:48]. For in the case of those things which are good by nature, even if persons of understanding were not able to attain to everything, by attaining even a part they could yet gain a great deal. We should show great diligence not to fall away from the perfection which is attainable but to acquire as much as is possible: to that extent let us make progress within the realm of what we seek. For the perfection of human nature consists perhaps in its very growth in goodness.

It seems good to me to make use of Scripture as a counselor in this matter. . . . Let us put forth Moses as our example for life in our treatise. First we shall go through in outline of his life as we have learned it from the divine Scriptures. Then we shall seek out the spiritual understanding which corresponds to the history in order to obtain suggestions of virtue. Through such understanding we may come to the perfect life for humanity. . . .

HARDENING OF PHARAOH'S HEART[99]

Let us not be astonished if the history says that the rod of virtue did these things to the Egyptians, for it also says that the tyrant was hardened by God.[100] Now,

---

[99]Reprinted from Malherbe and Fergusson, trans., *Gregory of Nyssa.* Copyright 1989 by The Missionary Society of St. Paul the Apostle in the State of New York. Used by permission of Paulist Press. Pages 70–74. Cf. Exodus 6–8 and Romans 9:14–18.
[100]Exodus 7:3, 9:12; Romans 9:14–18.

how should he be condemned if he were disposed by divine constraint to be stubborn and obstinate? Somewhere the divine Apostle also expresses the same thought: "Since they refused to see it was rational to acknowledge God, he abandoned them to shameful passions" [Rom 1:26], speaking about those who commit sodomy and those who disgrace themselves by dishonorable and unmentionable profligacy.

But even if what has been said before is so stated by Scripture, and God does in this way entirely give up to dishonorable passions the one who gives himself up to them, still Pharaoh is not hardened by the divine will nor is the frog-like life[101] fashioned by virtue. For if this were to be willed by the divine nature, then certainly any human choice would fall into line in every case, so that no distinction between virtue and vice in life could be observed. People act differently— some live uprightly in virtue while others slide into vice. One would not reasonably attribute these differences in their lives to some divine constraint which lies outside themselves. It lies within each person's power to make this choice. Who it is who is delivered up to shameful affections can be clearly learned from the Apostle: it is the person who does not like to have God in his or her knowledge. God delivers up to passion him whom He does not protect because He is not acknowledged by him. But his failure to acknowledge God becomes the reason why he is pulled down into the passionate and dishonorable life.

It is as if someone who has not seen the sun blames it for causing him to fall into a ditch. Yet we do not hold that the luminary in anger pushes into the ditch someone who does not choose to look at it. Rather, we would interpret this statement in a more reasonable manner: it is the failure to participate in the light that causes the person who does not see to fall into the ditch. In the same way, the thought of the Apostle should be clear, that it is those who do not acknowledge God who are delivered up to shameful affections, and that the Egyptian tyrant is hardened by God not because the divine will places the resistance in the soul of Pharaoh but because the free will through its inclination to evil does not receive the word which softens resistance.

. . . In keeping with this insight of mine, consider the air which is darkened to the Egyptians' eyes by the rod while to the Hebrews' it is illuminated by the sun [Ex 10:21–29]. By this incident the meaning which we have been given is confirmed. It was not some constraining power from above that caused the one to be found in darkness and the other in light, but we people have in ourselves, in our own nature and by our own choice, the causes of light or darkness, since we place ourselves in whichever sphere we wish to be. According to the history, the eyes of the Egyptians were not in darkness because some wall or mountain darkened their view and shadowed the [sun's] rays, but the sun cast its rays upon all equally.

---

[101]The frogs from the plague of Exodus 8:1–15 were a symbol of evil for Gregory. He had earlier written: "The breed of frogs is obviously the destructive off-spring of the evil which is brought to life from the sordid heart of men as though from some slimy mire. The frogs overrun the houses of those who choose to live the Egyptian life [e.g., godless life]. . . ." Malherbe and Ferguson, trans., *Gregory of Nyssa*, op. cit., p. 70.

Whereas the Hebrews delighted in its light, the Egyptians were insensitive to its gift. In a similar manner the enlightened life is proposed to all equally according to their ability. Some continue on in darkness, driven by their evil pursuits to the darkness of wickedness, while others are made radiant by the light of virtue. . . .

What we are describing is like some destructive and bilious humor which arises in the intestines because of a dissipated life. When the physician induces vomiting by his medicines, he does not become the cause of the sickness in the body, but on the contrary it is disorderly eating habits which bring it about; medical knowledge only brought it into the open. In the same way, even if one says that painful retribution comes directly from God upon those who abuse their free will, it would only be reasonable to note that such sufferings have their origin and cause in ourselves. To the one who has lived without sin there is no darkness, no worm, no Gehenna, no fire, nor any other of these fearful names and things, as indeed the history [of Moses] goes on to say that the plagues of Egypt were not meant for the Hebrews. Since then in the same place evil comes to one but not to the other, the difference of free choices distinguishing each from the other, it is evident that nothing evil can come into existence apart from our free choice. . . .

THE SERVANT OF GOD[102]

I think there is no need to prolong the discourse by presenting to the reader the whole life of Moses as an example of virtue. For to anyone straining to the higher life what has been said provides amply for true wisdom. To anyone who shows weakness in toiling for virtue there would be no gain even if many more things should be written. . . . Nevertheless, let us not forget our definition in the *Prologue*. There we affirmed that the perfect life was such that no description of its perfection hinders its progress; the continual development of life to what is better is the soul's way to perfection. We would do well, by bringing our discourse up to the end of Moses's life, to show the certainty of the definition of perfection which we have proposed. . . .

What does the history say about this? That "Moses the servant of Yahweh died as Yahweh decreed, and no one has ever found his grave, his eyes were undimmed, and his face unimpaired" [Dt 34:5–8]. From this we learn that, when one has accomplished such noble actions, he is considered worthy of this sublime name, to be called "servant of Yahweh," which is the same as saying that he is better than all others. For one would not serve God unless he had become superior to everyone in the world. This for him is the end[103] of a virtuous life, an end wrought by the word of God. History speaks of "death," a living death, which is

---

[102]Reprinted from Ferguson and Malherbe, trans., *Gregory of Nyssa*, Copyright 1989 by The Missionary Society of St. Paul the Apostle in the State of New York. Used by permission of Paulist Press. From pp. 133, 135–137.

[103]Gregory employed a theological pun here; "goal," or "termination."

not followed by the grave, or fills the tomb, or brings dimness to the eyes and aging to the person.

What then are we taught through what has been said? To have but one purpose in life; to be called servants of God by virtue of the lives we live. For when you conquer all enemies . . . cross the water, are enlightened by the cloud, . . . make your ascent up the mountain through purity and sanctity; and when you arrive there, you are instructed in the divine mystery by the sound of the trumpets, and in the impenetrable darkness draw near to God by your faith, and there are taught the mysteries of the tabernacle and the dignity of the priesthood.

And when you, as a sculptor, carve in your own heart the divine oracles which you receive from God;[104] and when you destroy the golden idol [Ex 32:1–6] (that is, if you wipe from your life the desire of covetousness); and when you are elevated to such heights that you appear invincible to the magic of Balaam [Nu 22–24] (by "magic" you will perceive the crafty deceit of this life through which people are drugged as though by some philtre of Circe[105] are changed into the form of irrational animals and have their proper nature); and when you come through all these things, and the staff of the priesthood blossoms in you, drawing no moisture at all from the earth but having its own unique power for producing fruit . . . ;[106] when you destroy everything which opposes your worth, as Dathan was swallowed in the earth[107] and Core was consumed by the fire[108]— then you will draw near to the goal.

. . . Since the goal of virtuous life was the very thing we have been seeking, and this goal has been found in what we have said, it is time for you, noble friend, to look to that example and, by transferring to your own life what is contemplated [here] . . . to be known by God and to become His friend [Ex 33:11]. This is true perfection: not to avoid a wicked life because like slaves we servilely fear punishment, nor to do good because we hope for rewards, as if cashing in on the virtuous life by some business-like and contractual arrangement. On the contrary, disregarding all those things for which we hope and which have been reserved by promise, we regard fall from God's friendship as the only thing dreadful and we consider becoming God's friend the only thing worthy of honor and desire. This, as I have said, is the perfection of life. . . .

---

[104]The decalogue and the Word of God speaking through creation are these "oracles."

[105]Circe, an enchantress of Greek and Latin mythology, dwelt on the island of Aea, and transformed into swine all who drank the "philtre" or potion from her cup. Cf. Homer, *Odessy*, X, 212ff; Horace, *Epistles*, I.2, 22–23.

[106]Aaron's rod was interpreted as a sign of "true priesthood"; the miracle of the budding of the rod symbolized sacred ordination. The fruits of "true priesthood" or service were: ". . . a life self-controlled, tough and dried in appearance, but containing on the inside (hidden and invisible) what can be eaten." Malherbe and Ferguson, *Gregory of Nyssa*, op. cit., p. 127. Cf. Numbers 17.

[107]Numbers 16:25–35; cf. Deuteronomy 11:6; Psalms 106:17.

[108]"Core" is the Greek form of Korah, who was destroyed along with Dathan. Numbers 16:31–40, 49.

Jerome of Bethlehem (c. 348–420)

Jerome was born in Dalmatia, northern Italy. Living in Rome he became so enamored with classical learning that he subsequently came to believe that his admiration for pagan literature was sinful. During a serious illness this realization was reinforced through a dramatic religious experience. In a dream, Jerome saw himself standing before God's judgment seat; upon being asked who and what he was, Jerome replied: "I am a Christian." "But He who presided said: 'Thou liest, thou art a follower of Cicero and not of Christ.' For 'where thy treasure is, there thy heart will be also' [Mt 6:21]."[109] This experience was so sobering that Jerome resolved, henceforth, to dedicate his life to the study of the scriptures. As he wrote: "I awoke from my sleep, and that thenceforth I read the books of God with a zeal greater than I had previously given to the books of men."[110] The most influential Latin version of the Bible, the *Vulgate*, comes directly from Jerome's resolution.

Seeking to separate himself from the temptations of the city, Jerome went east to the Holy Land. He spent the last thirty-four years of his life in Bethlehem, living as a monk and studying Scripture. Jerome's writings are noteworthy for the frankness with which the author reports his own personal struggles, and for the spiritual remedies he sought to apply to himself and others. His letters of spiritual counsel popularized monasticism and Christian disciplines such as virginity, fasting, and simplicity.

TO EUSTOCHIUM[111]

... I write to you thus, my Lady Eustochium[112]—I am bound to call you my Lord's bride "lady"—to show you by my opening words that my object is not to praise the virginity which you follow, and of which you have proved the value, or yet to recount the drawbacks of marriage.... My purpose is to show you that you are fleeing from Sodom and should take warning by Lot's wife [Gen 19:26]. There is no flattery ... in these pages. A flatterer's words are fair, but for all that he is an enemy. You need expect no rhetorical flourishes setting you among the angels, and while they extol virginity as blessed, putting the world at your feet.... If ... the apostle [Paul], who was a chosen vessel separated unto the gospel of Christ, by reason of the pricks of the flesh and the allurements of vice controls his body and brings it into subjection ... and yet for all of that, sees another law in his

---

[109]St. Jerome, "Letters and Select Works," in Schaff and Wace, eds., *A Select Library* **NPNF**, Vol. VI, Letter XII, p. 35.

[110]Ibid.

[111]Ibid., Letter XII, "To Eustochium." Pages 23–26, with omissions and minor verbal modifications. The letter was written at Rome, in 384 AD.

[112]Eustochium was the third daughter of Paula, a widow from Rome who subsequently served as the head of the convent that Jerome established in Bethlehem. In this, one of the most famous of his letters, Jerome sought to call Eustochium to the monastic life by lauding its great Christian virtues.

members warring against the law of his mind, and bringing him into captivity to the law of sin [Rom 7:23]; if after nakedness, fasting, hunger, imprisonment, scourging and other torments, he turns back to himself and cries: "Oh, wretched man that I am, who shall deliver me from this body of death" [Rom 7:24]? do you fancy that you ought to lay aside apprehension? See to it that God say not someday of you; "The virgin of Israel is fallen and there is none to raise her up" [Amos 5:2]. I will say it boldly, though God may indeed relieve one who is defiled from the penalty of her sin, but He will not give her a crown. Let us fear lest in us also the prophecy be fulfilled, "Good virgins shall faint" [Amos 8:13]. Notice that it is good virgins who are spoken of, for there are bad ones as well. "Whosoever looked on a woman," the Lord says, "to lust after her hath committed adultery with her already in his heart" [Mt 5:28]. So that virginity may be lost even by a thought. Such are evil virgins, virgins in the flesh, not in the spirit; foolish virgins, who, having no oil, are shut out by the Bridegroom [Mt 25:3–10]. . . .

There are, in the Scriptures, countless Divine answers condemning gluttony and approving simple food. . . . [T]he first man, obeying his belly and not God, was cast down from paradise into this vale of tears; and . . . Satan used hunger to tempt the Lord Himself in the wilderness [Mt 4:2–3]; and . . . the apostle cries: "Meats for the belly and the belly for meats, but God shall destroy both it and them" [1 Cor 6:13]; and . . . he speaks of the self-indulgent as people "whose God is their belly" [Phil 3:19]. Because people invariably worship what they like best. Care must be taken, therefore, that abstinence may bring back to Paradise those whom satiety once drove out.

You will tell me, perhaps, that, high-born as you are, reared in luxury and used to lie softly, you cannot do without wine and dainties, and would find a stricter rule of life unendurable. If so, I can only say: "Live, then, by your own rule, since God's rule is too hard for you." Not that the Creator and Lord of all takes pleasure in a rumbling and empty stomach, or in fevered lungs; but that these are indispensable as means to the preservation of chastity. . . .

PAULA[113]

Paula (347–404) was the saintly mother of Eustochium. A wealthy woman of the Roman nobility, at the age of thirty-three Paula rejected high worldly status to embrace a Christian life of sacrifice, service, and prayer. After living in Rome, where she was a friend and colleague of Jerome, she traveled to Bethlehem where she established several important ministries, including a convent for women, a monastic community for men, and a hospice for the homeless. Upon Paula's death, Jerome wrote her daughter a lengthy letter of consolation that recounted her remarkable life. The letter was written at Rome, in 404 AD.

If all the members of my body were to be converted into tongues, and if each

---

[113]St. Jerome, "Letters and Select Works," in Schaff and Wace, eds., *A Select Library of* **NPNF**, Vol. VI, Letter CVIII, "To Eustochium." Pages 195–211, with omissions and minor linguistic emendations.

of my limbs were to be gifted with a human voice, I could still not do justice to the virtues of the holy and venerable Paula. Noble in family, she was nobler still in holiness; rich formerly in this world's goods, she is now more distinguished by the poverty that she has embraced for Christ. . . . [My words] are indeed, inadequate to [describe] the virtues of one whose praises are sung by the whole world, who is admired by bishops, regretted by bands of virgins, and wept for by crowds of monks and poor. Would you know all her virtues, reader, in short? She has left those dependent on her poor, but not so poor as she was herself. In dealing thus with her relatives . . . she has left her daughter, Eustochium—a virgin consecrated to Christ for whose comfort this sketch is made—far from her noble family and rich only in faith and grace. . . .

I am now free to describe at greater length the virtue which was her peculiar charm . . . . Humility is the first of Christian graces, and her's was so pronounced that one who had never seen her and who on account of her celebrity had desired to see her, would have believed that he saw not her but the lowest of her maids. When she was surrounded by companies of virgins she was always the least remarkable in dress, in speech, in gesture, and gait. From the time that her husband died until she fell asleep herself she never sat at meat with a man, even though she might know him to stand upon the pinnacle of the episcopate. She never entered a [public] bath except when dangerously ill. Even in the severest fever she rested not on an ordinary bed but on the hard ground covered only with a mat of goat's hair; if that can be called rest which made day and night alike a time of almost unbroken prayer. Well did she fulfill the words of the Psalter: "Every night I flood my bed with tears; I drench my couch with my weeping" [Ps 6:6]. Her tears welled forth . . . from fountains, and she lamented her slightest faults as if they were sins of the deepest dye. Constantly did I warn her to spare her eyes and to keep them for the reading of the gospel. But she only said: "I must disfigure that face which contrary to God's commandment I have painted with rouge, white lead, and antimony. I must mortify that body which has been given up to many pleasures. I must make up for my long laughter by constant weeping. I must exchange my soft linen and costly silks for rough goat's hair. I who have pleased my husband and the world in the past, desire now to please Christ."

Were I . . . to select her chastity as a subject of praise, my words would seem superfluous; for even when she was still in the world, she set an example to all the matrons of Rome, and bore herself so admirably that the most slanderous never ventured to couple scandal with her name. No mind could be more considerate than hers, or none kinder towards the lowly. She did not court the powerful; at the same time, if the proud and vainglorious sought her, she did not turn from them with disdain. If she saw a poor man, she supported him; and if she saw a rich one, she urged him to do good. Her generosity alone knew no bounds. Indeed, so anxious was she to turn no needy person away that she borrowed money at interest and often contracted new loans to pay off old ones. . . . I wished her to be more careful in managing her [financial] concerns, but she—with a faith more glowing than mine—clave to the Saviour with her whole heart and poor in spirit [she] followed the Lord in His poverty, giving back to Him what she received, and becoming poor for His sake. She obtained her wish at last and died leaving her daughter overwhelmed with a mass of debt. This Eustochium still owes and indeed cannot hope to pay off by her own exertions; only the mercy of Christ can free her from it. . . .

I shall now describe the order of [Paula's] monastery and the method by which she turned the continence of saintly souls to her own profit. She sowed carnal things that she might reap spiritual things; she gave earthly things that she might receive heavenly things; she forewent things temporal that she might in their stead obtain things eternal. Besides establishing a monastery for men, the charge of which she left to men, she divided into three companies the numerous virgins whom she had gathered out of different provinces . . . . [A]lthough they worked and had their meals separately from each other, these three companies met together for psalm-singing and prayer.

After chanting the Alleluia—the signal by which they were summoned to the Collect[114]—no one was permitted to remain behind. But either first or among the first Paula used to await the arrival of the rest, urging them diligence rather by her own modest example than by motives of fear. At dawn, at the third, sixth, and ninth hours, at evening, and at midnight they recited the psalter each in turn. No sister was allowed to be ignorant of the Psalms, and all had every day to learn a certain portion of the holy Scriptures. Only on the Lord's Day did they proceed to the church beside which they lived, each company following its own mother-superior. Returning home in the same order, they then devoted themselves to their allotted tasks, and made garments either for themselves or else for others.

. . . All the sisters were clothed alike. Linen was not used except for drying the hands. So strictly did Paula separate them from men that she would not allow even eunuchs to approach them, lest she would give occasion to slanderous tongues. . . . When a sister was backward in coming to the recitation of the Psalms or showed herself remiss in her work, Paula used to approach her in different ways. Was she quick-tempered? Paula coaxed her. Was she sluggish? Paula chided her, copying the example of the apostle who said: "What do you wish? Shall I come to you with a rod, or with love in a spirit of gentleness" [1 Cor 4:21]?

Apart from food and clothing she allowed no one to have anything she could call her own, for Paul had said: "if we have food and clothing, with these we shall be content" [1 Tim 6:8]. She was afraid lest the custom of having more should breed covetousness in them, an appetite which no wealth can satisfy, for the more it has the more it requires to satisfy it. When the sisters quarrelled with one another she reconciled them with soothing words. If the younger ones were troubled with fleshly desires, she broke their force by imposing redoubled fasts, for she wished her virgins to be ill in body rather than to suffer in soul. If she noticed any sister too attentive to her dress, she reproved her for her error with knitted brows and severe looks, saying: "a clean body and a clean dress mean an unclean soul. A virgin's lips should never utter an improper or an impure word, for such indicate a lascivious mind and by the outward person the faults of the inward person are made manifest."

---

[114]The opening prayer.

... How shall I describe her kindness and attention towards the sick or the wonderful care and devotion with which she nursed them? Although when others were sick she freely gave them every indulgence, and even allowed them to eat meat, but when she fell ill herself she made no concessions to her own weakness and seemed to unfairly charge in her own case to harshness the kindness which she was always ready to show to others. ...

Be not fearful, Eustochium, you are endowed with a splendid heritage. The Lord is your portion, and to increase your joy your mother has now—after a long martyrdom—won her crown. It is not only the shedding of blood that is accounted a witness, the spotless service of a devout mind is itself a daily martyrdom. Both alike are crowned, with roses and violets in the one case, with lilies in the other ... whether the victory is won in peace or in war, God gives the same reward to those who win it. Like Abraham your mother heard the words: "Go from your country and your kindred and your father's house, to the land that I will show you" [Gen 12:1]; and not only that but [also] the Lord's command given through Jeremiah: "Flee from the midst of Babylon, let every man save his life" [Jer 51:6]! To the day of her death she never returned to Chaldaea, or regretted the "fleshpots of Egypt" [Ex 16:3]. ... Accompanied by her virgin bands she became a fellow citizen of the Saviour, and now that she has ascended from her little Bethlehem to the heavenly realms she can say to the true Naomi: "Your people shall be my people, and your God shall be my God" [Ruth 1:16]. ...

Augustine of Hippo (354–430)

Augustine of Hippo was born in Thargaste, North Africa. He imbibed Christ—as he put it—with "his mother's milk." Monica, his saintly mother, had an enduring effect upon him, but as he became a young man Augustine departed from Christian faith and practice. He went looking for love in all the wrong places and had an illegitimate son to show for his efforts. He sought truth in Manicheanism and in philosophy, and also met with unsatisfying results.

Confessions, his most influential work, is St. Augustine's spiritual autobiography. It charts his pilgrimage away from and subsequently back to Christian faith. Augustine became a bishop and doctor of the Church. He was one of the most able and prolific writers Christianity ever produced. A person who had written *Confessions*, *The City of God*, or *On the Trinity* would have been esteemed as a Christian theologian of the first rank—but Augustine wrote all three of those books and dozens of others besides! Since our interest in St. Augustine lies chiefly in the realm of his spirituality, it is in that direction we turn our attention.[115]

---

[115]Peter Brown's, *Augustine of Hippo* (Berkeley: University of California Press, 1969) is the standard survey of Augustine's life and work. It should be supplemented by more recent scholarship, such as that found in Mary Clark, trans., *Augustine of Hippo: Selected Writings* (New York: Paulist Press, 1984), "The Spirituality of St. Augustine," pp. 1–54.

Confessions (c. 400) is a book that can be read at various levels. On the surface it is the spiritual autobiography of a great saint and teacher of the church. Because of its autobiographical character *Confessions* draws us into the narrative, and countless readers—like Catherine of Sienna—have found their own lives reflected in the narrative of Augustine's journey. In this way it is not merely the story of one person; it is the story of all people, who like the prodigal of Jesus's parable (Lk 15:11–32) are trying to find their way back to the Father. But Augustine's *Confessions* is also about the nature of Christian Spirituality. We read here about the human soul's longing for God, as well as the wantonness of human sin. We read about the significance of Christian conversion, and we learn of the providence of God that (unbeknownst to himself) wooed Augustine to return to the Father's household. The way "home" to God is marked out by confession. The word *confession* (Lat. *confessio*), as Augustine applied it, meant the "accusation of oneself and the praise of God."[116] Hence, the book assumes the form of an extended prayer or conversation with God. In this way, then, *Confessions* is not merely a record of Augustine's pilgrimage, it is the medicine of his own healing and perhaps that of his readers as well.

THE RESTLESS HEART[117]

"Great art thou, O Lord, and greatly to be praised [Ps 145:3]; great is thy power, and infinite is thy wisdom" [6]. And man desires to praise thee, for he is a part of thy creation; he bears his mortality about with him and carries the evidence of his sin and the proof that thou dost "resist the proud" [1 Pet 5:5]. Still he desires to praise thee, this man who is only a small part of thy creation. Thou hast prompted him, that he should delight to praise thee, for thou hast made us for thyself and restless is our heart until it comes to rest in thee. . . .

Who shall bring me to rest in thee? Who will send thee into my heart so to overwhelm it that my sins shall be blotted out and I may embrace thee, my only good? What art thou to me? Have mercy that I may speak. What am I to thee that thou shouldst command me to love thee, and if I do it not, art angry and threatenest vast misery? Is it, then, a trifling sorrow not to love thee? It is not so to me. Tell me, by thy mercy, O Lord, my God, what thou art to me. "Say to my soul, I am your salvation" [Ps 35:3]. So speak that I may hear. Behold, the ears of my heart are before thee, O Lord; open them and "say to my soul, I am your salvation." I will hasten after that voice, and I will lay hold upon thee. Hide not thy face from me. Even if I die, let me see thy face lest I die.

The house of my soul is too narrow for thee to come in to me; let it be enlarged by thee. It is in ruins; do thou restore it. There is much about it which must

---

[116]Brown, *Augustine of Hippo*, cites Augustine's *Sermon*, 67, 2, for this definition of "confession."

[117]Albert C. Outler, trans., *Augustine: Confessions and Enchridion* (Philadelphia: Westminster Press, 1955), Bk. II, chs. 1–2, 4–5, pp. 50–52, 54–56, with omissions. Digitized by Harry Plantinga, planting@cs.pitt.edu, 1993.

offend thy eyes; I confess and know it. But who will cleanse it? Or, to whom shall I cry but to thee? "Cleanse thou me from my secret faults," O Lord, "and keep back thy servant from strange sins" [Ps 19:12–13]. "I believe, and therefore do I speak." [Ps 116:10]. But thou, O Lord, thou knowest. Have I not "confessed my transgressions unto thee," O my God; and hast thou "not put away the iniquity of my heart" [Ps 32:5]? I do not contend in judgment with thee, who art truth itself; and I would not deceive myself, lest my iniquity lie even to itself. I do not, therefore, contend in judgment with thee, for "if thou, Lord, shouldst mark iniquities, O Lord, who shall stand" [Ps 130:3]? . . .

THE SINFUL HEART[118]

I wish now to review in memory my past wickedness and the carnal corruptions of my soul—not because I still love them, but that I may love thee, O my God. For love of thy love I do this, recalling in the bitterness of self-examination my wicked ways, that thou mayest grow sweet to me, thou sweetness without deception! Thou sweetness happy and assured! Thus thou mayest gather me up out of those fragments in which I was torn to pieces, while I turned away from thee, O Unity, and lost myself among "the many."[119] For as I became a youth, I longed to be satisfied with worldly things, and I dared to grow wild in a succession of various and shadowy loves. My form wasted away, and I became corrupt in thy eyes, yet I was still pleasing to my own eyes—and eager to please the eyes of men.

But what was it that delighted me save to love and to be loved? Still I did not keep the moderate way of the love of mind to mind—the bright path of friendship. Instead, the mists of passion steamed up out of the puddly concupiscence of the flesh, and the hot imagination of puberty, and they so obscured and overcast my heart that I was unable to distinguish pure affection from unholy desire. Both boiled confusedly within me, and dragged my unstable youth down over the cliffs of unchaste desires and plunged me into a gulf of infamy. Thy anger had come upon me, and I knew it not. I had been deafened by the clanking of the chains of my mortality, the punishment for my soul"s pride, and I wandered farther from thee, and thou didst permit me to do so. I was tossed to and fro, and wasted, and poured out, and I boiled over in my fornications—and yet thou didst hold thy peace, O my tardy Joy! Thou didst still hold thy peace, and I wandered still farther from thee into more and yet more barren fields of sorrow . . . .

Theft is punished by thy law, O Lord, and by the law written in men's hearts, which not even ingrained wickedness can erase. For what thief will tolerate another thief stealing from him? Even a rich thief will not tolerate a poor thief who is driven to theft by want. Yet I had a desire to commit robbery, and did so, compelled to it by neither hunger nor poverty, but through a contempt for well-

---

[118]Ibid., Bk. II, chs. 1–2, 4, 6–7, 9–10, pp. 50–60, with omissions.
[119]Plato, *Enneads*, I, 6, 9:1–2.

doing and a strong impulse to iniquity. For I pilfered something which I already had in sufficient measure, and of much better quality. I did not desire to enjoy what I stole, but only the theft and the sin itself. There was a pear tree close to our own vineyard, heavily laden with fruit, which was not tempting either for its color or for its flavor. Late one night—having prolonged our games in the streets until then, as our bad habit was—a group of young scoundrels, and I among them, went to shake and rob this tree. We carried off a huge load of pears, not to eat ourselves, but to dump out to the hogs, after barely tasting some of them ourselves. Doing this pleased us all the more because it was forbidden.

Such was my heart, O God, such was my heart—which thou didst pity even in that bottomless pit. Behold, now let my heart confess to thee what it was seeking there, when I was being gratuitously wanton, having no inducement to evil but the evil itself. It was foul, and I loved it. I loved my own undoing. I loved my error—not that for which I erred but the error itself. A depraved soul, falling away from security in thee to destruction in itself, seeking nothing from the shameful deed but shame itself. What was it in you, O theft of mine, that I, poor wretch, doted on—you deed of darkness—in that sixteenth year of my age? Beautiful you were not, for you were a theft. But are you anything at all, so that I could analyze the case with you? Those pears that we stole were fair to the sight because they were thy creation, O Beauty beyond compare, O Creator of all, O thou good God—God the highest good and my true good. Those pears were truly pleasant to the sight, but it was not for them that my miserable soul lusted, for I had an abundance of better pears. I stole those simply that I might steal, for, having stolen them, I threw them away. My sole gratification in them was my own sin, which I was pleased to enjoy; for, if any one of these pears entered my mouth, the only good flavor it had was my sin in eating it.

And now, O Lord my God, I ask what it was in that theft of mine that caused me such delight; for behold it had no beauty of its own—certainly not the sort of beauty that exists in justice and wisdom, nor such as is in the mind, memory, senses, and the animal life of man; nor yet the kind that is the glory and beauty of the stars in their courses; nor the beauty of the earth, or the sea—teeming with spawning life, replacing in birth that which dies and decays. Indeed, it did not have that false and shadowy beauty which attends the deceptions of vice. . . .

By what passion, then, was I animated? It was undoubtedly depraved and a great misfortune for me to feel it. But still, what was it? "Who can understand his errors [Ps 19:2]?" We laughed because our hearts were tickled at the thought of deceiving the owners, who had no idea of what we were doing and would have strenuously objected. Yet, again, why did I find such delight in doing this which I would not have done alone? Is it that no one readily laughs alone? No one does so readily; but still sometimes, when men are by themselves and no one else is about, a fit of laughter will overcome them when something very droll presents itself to their sense or mind. Yet alone I would not have done it—alone I could not have done it at all. Behold, my God, the lively review of my soul's career is laid bare before thee. I would not have committed that theft alone. My pleasure in it was not what I stole but, rather, the act of stealing. Nor would I have enjoyed doing it alone—indeed I would not have done it! O friendship all unfriendly!

You strange seducer of the soul, who hungers for mischief from impulses of mirth and wantonness, who craves another's loss without any desire for one's own profit or revenge—so that, when they say, "Let's go, let's do it," we are ashamed not to be shameless. Who can unravel such a twisted and tangled knottiness? . . . I fell away from thee, O my God, and in my youth I wandered too far from thee, my true support. And I became to myself a wasteland.

"TAKE AND READ"[120]

"O Hope from my youth" [Ps 71:5] where wast thou to me and where hadst thou gone away? For hadst thou not created me and differentiated me from the beasts of the field and the birds of the air, making me wiser than they? And yet I was wandering about in a dark and slippery way, seeking thee outside myself and thus not finding the God of my heart. I had gone down into the depths of the sea and had lost faith, and had despaired of ever finding the truth.

By this time my mother had come to me, having mustered the courage of piety, following over sea and land, secure in thee through all the perils of the journey. For in the dangers of the voyage she comforted the sailors—to whom the inexperienced voyagers, when alarmed, were accustomed to go for comfort—and assured them of a safe arrival because she had been so assured by thee in a vision. She found me in deadly peril through my despair of ever finding the truth. But when I told her that I was now no longer a Manichean, though not yet a Catholic Christian, she did not leap for joy as if this were unexpected; for she had already been reassured about that part of my misery for which she had mourned me as one dead, but also as one who would be raised to [life in] thee. . . . Therefore, her heart was not agitated with any violent exultation when she heard that so great a part of what she daily entreated thee to do had actually already been done—that, though I had not yet grasped the truth, I was rescued from falsehood. Instead, she was fully confident that thou who hadst promised the whole would give her the rest, and thus most calmly, and with a fully confident heart, she replied to me that she believed, in Christ, that before she died she would see me a faithful Catholic. And she said no more than this to me. But to Thee, O Fountain of mercy, she poured out still more frequent prayers and tears that thou wouldst hasten thy aid and enlighten my darkness, and she hurried all the more zealously to the church and hung upon the words of Ambrose [of Milan], praying for "the fountain of water that springs up into everlasting life" [Jn 4:14]. For she loved that man as an angel of God, since she knew that it was by him that I had been brought thus far to that wavering state of agitation I was now in, through which she was fully persuaded I should pass from sickness to health, even though it would be after a still sharper convulsion which physicians call "the crisis."

. . . Ambrose himself I esteemed a happy man, as the world counted happi-

---

[120]Outler, trans., *Confessions*, Bk. VI, chs. 1–3, 5, 11, 12, pp. 113–30, and Bk. VIII, chs. 5–12, pp. 164–65, 173–77, with omissions.

ness, because great personages held him in honor. Only his celibacy appeared to me a painful burden. But what hope he cherished, what struggles he had against the temptations that beset his high station, what solace in adversity, and what savory joys thy bread possessed for the hidden mouth of his heart when feeding on it, I could neither conjecture nor experience. . . . I heard him, indeed, every Lord's Day, "rightly dividing the word of truth" [2 Tim 2:15] among the people. And I became all the more convinced that all those knots of crafty calumnies which those deceivers of ours had knit together against the divine books could be unraveled. . . . I blushed that for so many years I had bayed, not against the Catholic faith, but against the fables of fleshly imagination. For I had been both impious and rash in this, that I had condemned by pronouncement what I ought to have learned by inquiry. . . .

Now when this man of thine, Simplicianus, told me the story of Victorinus, I was eager to imitate him. Indeed, this was Simplicianus' purpose in telling it to me. But when he went on to tell how, in the reign of the Emperor Julian, there was a law passed by which Christians were forbidden to teach literature and rhetoric; and how Victorinus, in ready obedience to the law, chose to abandon his "school of words" rather than thy Word, by which thou makest eloquent the tongues of the dumb—he appeared to me not so much brave as happy, because he had found a reason for giving his time wholly to thee. For this was what I was longing to do; but as yet I was bound by the iron chain of my own will. The enemy held fast my will, and had made of it a chain, and had bound me tight with it. For out of the perverse will came lust, and the service of lust ended in habit, and habit, not resisted, became necessity. By these links, as it were, forged together—which is why I called it "a chain"—a hard bondage held me in slavery. But that new will which had begun to spring up in me freely to worship thee and to enjoy thee, O my God, the only certain Joy, was not able as yet to overcome my former willfulness, made strong by long indulgence. Thus my two wills—the old and the new, the carnal and the spiritual—were in conflict within me; and by their discord they tore my soul apart.

Thus I came to understand from my own experience what I had read, how "the flesh lusts against the Spirit, and the Spirit against the flesh" [Gal 5:17]. I truly lusted both ways, yet more in that which I approved in myself than in that which I disapproved in myself. For in the latter it was not now really I that was involved, because here I was rather an unwilling sufferer than a willing actor. And yet it was through me that habit had become an armed enemy against me, because I had willingly come to be what I unwillingly found myself to be. Who, then, can with any justice speak against it, when just punishment follows the sinner? I had now no longer my accustomed excuse that, as yet, I hesitated to forsake the world and serve thee because my perception of the truth was uncertain. For now it was certain. But, still bound to the earth, I refused to be thy soldier; and was as much afraid of being freed from all entanglements as we ought to fear to be entangled.

Thus with the baggage of the world I was sweetly burdened, as one in slumber, and my musings on thee were like the efforts of those who desire to awake, but who are still overpowered with drowsiness and fall back into deep slumber.

And as no one wishes to sleep forever (for all men rightly count waking better)—yet a man will usually defer shaking off his drowsiness when there is a heavy lethargy in his limbs; and he is glad to sleep on even when his reason disapproves, and the hour for rising has struck—so was I assured that it was much better for me to give myself up to thy love than to go on yielding myself to my own lust. Thy love satisfied and vanquished me; my lust pleased and fettered me. I had no answer to Thy calling to me, "Awake, you who sleep, and arise from the dead, and Christ shall give you light" [Eph 5:14]. On all sides, Thou didst show me that Thy words are true, and I, convicted by the truth, had nothing at all to reply but the drawling and drowsy words: "Presently; see, presently. Leave me alone a little while." But "presently, presently," had no present; and my "leave me alone a little while" went on for a long while. In vain did I "delight in thy law in the inner man" while "another law in my members warred against the law of my mind and brought me into captivity to the law of sin which is in my members." For the law of sin is the tyranny of habit, by which the mind is drawn and held, even against its will. Yet it deserves to be so held because it so willingly falls into the habit. "O wretched man that I am! Who shall deliver me from the body of this death" but thy grace alone, through Jesus Christ our Lord [Rom 7:22–25]? . . .

Thus I was sick and tormented, reproaching myself more bitterly than ever, rolling and writhing in my chain till it should be utterly broken. By now I was held but slightly, but still was held. And thou, O Lord, didst press upon me in my inmost heart with a severe mercy, redoubling the lashes of fear and shame; lest I should again give way and that same slender remaining tie not be broken off, but recover strength and enchain me yet more securely.

I kept saying to myself, "See, let it be done now; let it be done now." And as I said this I all but came to a firm decision. I all but did it—yet I did not quite. Still I did not fall back to my old condition, but stood aside for a moment and drew breath. And I tried again, and lacked only a very little of reaching the resolve—and then somewhat less, and then all but touched and grasped it. Yet I still did not quite reach or touch or grasp the goal, because I hesitated to die to death and to live to life. And the worse way, to which I was habituated, was stronger in me than the better, which I had not tried. And up to the very moment in which I was to become another man, the nearer the moment approached, the greater horror did it strike in me. But it did not strike me back, nor turn me aside, but held me in suspense.

It was, in fact, my old mistresses, trifles of trifles and vanities of vanities, who still enthralled me. They tugged at my fleshly garments and softly whispered: "Are you going to part with us? And from that moment will we never be with you any more? And from that moment will not this and that be forbidden you forever?" What were they suggesting to me in those words "this or that"? What is it they suggested, O my God? Let thy mercy guard the soul of thy servant from the vileness and the shame they did suggest! And now I scarcely heard them, for they were not openly showing themselves and opposing me face to face; but muttering, as it were, behind my back; and furtively plucking at me as I was leaving, trying to make me look back at them. Still they delayed me, so that I hesitated to break loose and shake myself free of them and leap over to the place to which I was being called—for unruly habit kept saying to me, "Do you think you can live without them?"

But now it said this very faintly; for in the direction I had set my face, and yet toward which I still trembled to go, the chaste dignity of continence appeared to me—cheerful but not wanton, modestly alluring me to come and doubt nothing, extending her holy hands, full of a multitude of good examples—to receive and embrace me. There were there so many young men and maidens, a multitude of youth and every age, grave widows and ancient virgins; and continence herself in their midst: not barren, but a fruitful mother of children—her joys—by thee, O Lord, her husband. And she smiled on me with a challenging smile as if to say: "Can you not do what these young men and maidens can? Or can any of them do it of themselves, and not rather in the Lord their God? The Lord their God gave me to them. Why do you stand in your own strength, and so stand not? Cast yourself on him; fear not. He will not flinch and you will not fall. Cast yourself on him without fear, for he will receive and heal you." And I blushed violently, for I still heard the muttering of those "trifles" and hung suspended. Again she seemed to speak: "Stop your ears against those unclean members of yours, that they may be mortified. They tell you of delights, but not according to the law of the Lord thy God." This struggle raging in my heart was nothing but the contest of self against self. And Alypius kept close beside me, and awaited in silence the outcome of my extraordinary agitation.

Now when deep reflection had drawn up out of the secret depths of my soul all my misery and had heaped it up before the sight of my heart, there arose a mighty storm, accompanied by a mighty rain of tears. That I might give way fully to my tears and lamentations, I stole away from Alypius, for it seemed to me that solitude was more appropriate for the business of weeping. I went far enough away that I could feel that even his presence was no restraint upon me. This was the way I felt at the time, and he realized it. I suppose I had said something before I started up and he noticed that the sound of my voice was choked with weeping. And so he stayed alone, where we had been sitting together, greatly astonished. I flung myself down under a fig tree—how I know not—and gave free course to my tears. The streams of my eyes gushed out an acceptable sacrifice to thee. And, not indeed in these words, but to this effect, I cried to thee: "And thou, O Lord, how long? How long, O Lord? Wilt thou be angry forever? Oh, remember not against us our former iniquities" [Ps 6:3]. For I felt that I was still enthralled by them. I sent up these sorrowful cries: "How long, how long? Tomorrow and tomorrow? Why not now? Why not this very hour make an end to my uncleanness?"

I was saying these things and weeping in the most bitter contrition of my heart, when suddenly I heard the voice of a boy or a girl I know not which—coming from the neighboring house, chanting over and over again, "Pick it up, read it; pick it up, read it."[121] Immediately I ceased weeping and began most earnestly to think whether it was usual for children in some kind of game to sing such a song, but I could not remember ever having heard the like. So, damming

---

[121]In Latin: *Tolle, lege; tolle, lege.* A much quoted phrase in subsequent Christian Spirituality.

the torrent of my tears, I got to my feet, for I could not but think that this was a divine command to open the Bible and read the first passage I should light upon. For I had heard how Anthony,[122] accidentally coming into church while the gospel was being read, received the admonition as if what was read had been addressed to him: "Go and sell what you have and give it to the poor, and you shall have treasure in heaven; and come and follow me" [Mt 19:21]. By such an oracle he was forthwith converted to thee.

So I quickly returned to the bench where Alypius was sitting, for there I had put down the apostle's book when I had left there. I snatched it up, opened it, and in silence read the paragraph on which my eyes first fell: "Not in rioting and drunkenness, not in chambering and wantonness, not in strife and envying, but put on the Lord Jesus Christ, and make no provision for the flesh to fulfill the lusts thereof" [Rom 13:13]. I wanted to read no further, nor did I need to. For instantly, as the sentence ended, there was infused in my heart something like the light of full certainty and all the gloom of doubt vanished away.

Closing the book, then, and putting my finger or something else for a mark I began—now with a tranquil countenance—to tell it all to Alypius. And he in turn disclosed to me what had been going on in himself, of which I knew nothing. He asked to see what I had read. I showed him, and he looked on even further than I had read. I had not known what followed. But indeed it was this, "Him that is weak in the faith, receive" [Rom 14:1]. This he applied to himself, and told me so. By these words of warning he was strengthened, and by exercising his good resolution and purpose—all very much in keeping with his character, in which, in these respects, he was always far different from and better than I—he joined me in full commitment without any restless hesitation.

Then we went in to my mother, and told her what happened, to her great joy. We explained to her how it had occurred—and she leaped for joy triumphant; and she blessed Thee, who art "able to do exceedingly abundantly above all that we ask or think" [Eph 3:20]. For she saw that Thou hadst granted her far more than she had ever asked for in all her pitiful and doleful lamentations. For thou didst so convert me to thee that I sought neither a wife nor any other of this world's hopes, but set my feet on that rule of faith which so many years before thou hadst showed her in her dream about me. And so thou didst turn her grief into gladness more plentiful than she had ventured to desire, and dearer and purer than the desire she used to cherish of having grandchildren of my flesh.

THE HEART SET FREE[123]

"O Lord, I am thy servant; I am thy servant and the son of thy handmaid. Thou hast loosed my bonds. I will offer to thee the sacrifice of thanksgiving" [Ps 116:16–17]! Let my heart and my tongue praise thee, and let all my bones say,

---

[122]Cf. selection, "The Life of Antony," pp. 87–88.
[123]Outler, trans., *Confessions*, Bk. IX, chs. 1–4, pp. 178–85, with omissions.

"Lord, who is like unto thee?" Let them say so, and answer thou me and say unto my soul, "I am your salvation" [Ps 35:10].

Who am I, and what is my nature? What evil is there not in me and my deeds; or if not in my deeds, my words; or if not in my words, my will? But thou, O Lord, art good and merciful, and thy right hand didst reach into the depth of my death and didst empty out the abyss of corruption from the bottom of my heart. And this was the result: now I did not will to do what I willed, and began to will to do what Thou didst will.

But where was my free will during all those years and from what deep and secret retreat was it called forth in a single moment, whereby I gave my neck to thy "easy yoke" and my shoulders to thy "light burden," O Christ Jesus, "my Strength and my Redeemer"? How sweet did it suddenly become to me to be without the sweetness of trifles! And it was now a joy to put away what I formerly feared to lose. For thou didst cast them away from me, O true and highest Sweetness. Thou didst cast them away, and in their place Thou didst enter in thyself—sweeter than all pleasure, though not to flesh and blood; brighter than all light, but more veiled than all mystery; more exalted than all honor, though not to them that are exalted in their own eyes. Now was my soul free from the gnawing cares of seeking and getting, of wallowing in the mire and scratching the itch of lust. And I prattled like a child to thee, O Lord my God—my light, my riches, and my salvation. . . .

Thou hadst pierced our heart with [the arrows of] Thy love, and we carried thy words, as it were, thrust through our vitals. The examples of thy servants whom thou hadst changed from black to shining white, and from death to life, crowded into the bosom of our thoughts and burned and consumed our sluggish temper, that we might not topple back into the abyss. And they fired us exceedingly, so that every breath of the deceitful tongue of our detractors might fan the flame and not blow it out. . . .

O my God, how did I cry to thee when I read the Psalms of David, those hymns of faith, those paeans of devotion which leave no room for swelling pride! I was still a novice in Thy true love, a catechumen keeping holiday at the villa, with Alypius, a catechumen like myself. My mother was also with us—in woman's garb, but with a man's faith, with the peacefulness of age and the fullness of motherly love and Christian piety. What cries I used to send up to thee in those songs, and how I was enkindled toward thee by them! I burned to sing them if possible, throughout the whole world, against the pride of the human race. . . . By turns, I trembled with fear and warmed with hope and rejoiced in Thy mercy, O Father. And all these feelings showed forth in my eyes and voice when thy good Spirit turned to us and said, "O sons of men, how long will you be slow of heart, how long will you love vanity, and seek after falsehood" [Ps 4:6]? For I had loved vanity and sought after falsehood. . . .

Nor were the good things I saw now outside me, nor were they to be seen with the eyes of flesh in the light of the earthly sun. For they that have their joys from without sink easily into emptiness and are spilled out on those things that are visible and temporal, and in their starving thoughts they lick their very shadows. If only they would grow weary with their hunger and would say, "Who will show us any good?" And we would answer, and they would hear, "O Lord, the light of thy countenance shines bright upon us" [Ps 4:6]. For we are not that Light that enlightens every man, but we are enlightened by thee, so that we who were formerly in darkness may now be alight in thee. If only they could behold the inner Light Eternal which, now that I had tasted it, I gnashed my teeth because I could not show it to them unless they brought me their heart in their eyes—their roving eyes—and said, "Who will show us any good?" But even there, in the inner chamber of my soul—where I was angry with myself; where I was inwardly pricked, where I had offered my sacrifice, slaying my old man, and hoping in thee with the new resolve of a new life with my trust laid in thee—even there thou hadst begun to grow sweet to me and to "put gladness in my heart" [Ps 4:7]. And thus as I read all this, I cried aloud and felt its inward meaning. . . .

John Cassian (c. 365–435)

John Cassian was probably born in a Latin-speaking community in what is now Romania. While the Roman Empire was falling apart in the west, Cassian traveled to Egypt where he spent several years at the feet of the Desert Fathers. Cassian's most influential work, *Conferences* (c. 420), was a compilation of the wisdom of the Desert Fathers. Set in the form of dialogues among the leading spiritual masters, it popularized the Egyptian ideal of monastic life, and became one of the first practical handbooks for the practice of Christian spirituality. The influence of Cassian's *Conferences* can be traced through later monastic rules, like that of St. Benedict of Nursia, as well as through the impact it had upon Western Christendom as a spiritual handbook.

THE MONK'S GOAL[124]

Everything we do, our every objective, must be undertaken for the sake of this purity of heart. This is why we take on loneliness, fasting, vigils, work, nakedness. For this we must practice the reading of the Scripture, together with all the other virtuous activities, and we do so to trap and to hold our hearts free of the harm of every dangerous passion and in order to rise step by step to the high point of love.

It may be that some good and necessary task prevents us from achieving fully all that we set out to do. Let us not on this account give way to sadness or anger or indignation, since it was precisely to repel these that we would have done what in fact we were compelled to omit. What we gain from fasting does not com-

---

[124]Colm Luibheid, trans., reprinted *John Cassian: Conferences*. Copyright 1985 by The Missionary Society of St. Paul the Apostle in the State of New York. Used by permission of Paulist Press. Pages 41–43, "Conference One," attributed to Abba Moses.

pensate for what we lose through anger. Our profit from scriptural reading in no way equals the damage we cause ourselves by showing contempt for a brother. We must practice fasting, vigils, withdrawal, and the meditation of Scripture as activities which are subordinate to our main objective, purity of heart, that is to say, love, and we must never disturb this principal virtue for the sake of those others. If this virtue remains whole and unharmed within us nothing can injure us, not even if we are forced to omit any of those other subordinate virtues. Nor will it be of any use to have practiced all these latter if there is missing in us that principal objective for the sake of which all else is undertaken.

A worker takes the trouble to get hold of the tools[125] he requires. He does so not simply to have them and not use them. Nor is there any profit for him in merely possessing the tools. What he wants is, with their help, to produce the crafted objective for which these are efficient means. In the same way, fasting, vigils, scriptural meditation, nakedness, and total deprivation do not constitute perfection but are the means to perfection. They are not themselves the end point of a discipline, but an end is attained through them. To practice them will therefore be useless if someone instead of regarding these as means to an end is satisfied to regard them as the highest good. One would possess the tools of a profession without knowing the end where the hoped for fruit is to be found. And so anything which can trouble the purity and the peace of our heart must be avoided as something very dangerous, regardless of how useful and necessary it might actually seem to be. . . .

To cling always to God and to the things of God—this must be our major effort, this must be the road that the heart follows unswervingly. Any diversion, however impressive, must be regarded as secondary, low-grade, and certainly dangerous. Martha and Mary provide a most beautiful scriptural paradigm of this outlook and of this mode of activity [Lk 10:38–42]. In looking after the Lord and His disciples Martha did a very holy service. Mary, however, was intent on the spiritual teaching of Jesus and she stayed by His feet, which she kissed and anointed with the oil of her good faith. And she got more credit from the Lord because she had chosen the better part, one which could not be taken away from her. For while Martha was working hard, responsibly and fully intent on her job, she realized that she could not do all the work herself and she demanded the help of her sister from the Lord. "Does it not bother you that my sister leaves me to do the work alone?" she said. "Tell her to come and help me" [Lk 10:40]. Certainly she summons Mary to a task that is not inconsequential but is a praiseworthy service. Yet what does she hear from the Lord? "Martha, Martha, you are full of worry and are upset over many things where actually it should be over a few or even one thing. Mary has chosen the good part and it will not be taken away from her" [Lk 10:42].

You will note that the Lord establishes as the prime good contemplation, that is, the gaze turned in the direction of the things of God. Hence we say that the other virtues, however useful and good we may say they are, must nevertheless

---

[125]The literal translation is "instruments."

be put on a secondary level, since they are all practiced for the sake of this one. "You are full of worry and are upset over many things when actually it should be over a few or even one." In saying this the Lord locates the primary good not in activity, however praiseworthy, however abundantly fruitful, but in the truly simple and unified contemplation of Himself. He says that not much is needed for perfect blessedness. He means here that type of contemplation which is primarily concerned with the example of a few saints. Contemplating these, someone still on the upward road comes at last to that which is unique, namely the sight of God Himself, which comes with God's help. Having passed beyond the activities and the ministry of holy men he will live solely on the beauty and the knowledge of God. "Mary therefore chose the good part and it will not be taken away from her." But one must look carefully at this. In saying "Mary chose the good part," He was saying nothing about Martha and in no way was He giving the appearance of criticizing her. Still, by praising the one He was saying that the other was a step below her. Again, by saying, "it will not be taken away from her" He was showing that Martha's role could be taken away from her—since the service of the body can only last as long as the human being is there—whereas the zeal of Mary can never end.

ON PRAYER[126]

. . . The whole purpose of the monk and indeed the perfection of his heart amount to this—total and uninterrupted dedication to prayer. He strives for unstirring calm of mind and for never-ending purity, and he does so to the extent that this is possible for human frailty. This is the reason for our tireless and unshaking practice of both physical work and contrition of heart. Indeed, there is a mutual and undivided link between these. For just as the edifice of all the virtues strives upward toward perfect prayer so will all these virtues be neither sturdy nor enduring unless they are drawn firmly together by the crown of prayer. This endless, unstirring calm of prayer that I have mentioned can neither be achieved nor consummated without these virtues. And likewise virtues are the prerequisite foundation of prayer and cannot be effected without it. . . .

Prayer, if it is to be fervent and pure, demands that the following be observed. First, there must be a complete removal of all concern for bodily things. Then not just the worry but even the memory of any business or worldly affair must be banished from within ourselves. Calumny, empty talk, nattering, low-grade clowning—suchlike must be cut out. Anger and the disturbance caused by gloominess are especially to be eradicated. The poisonous tinder of carnal desire and avarice must be pulled out by the roots.

Having completely expelled and sliced away these and similar vices which are so manifest to the human eye, having . . . undertaken to this clearing away

---

[126]Reprinted from Luibheid, trans., *Cassian: Conferences.* Used by permission of Paulist Press. Pages 101–3, 107–16, attributed to Abba Isaac.

which results in purity and in the simplicity of innocence, we have then taken to lay the indestructible foundations of deep humility, foundations which can support that tower rising upward to the skies. Next comes the spiritual edifice of virtue. After that, the soul must be restrained from all meandering, from all slippery wanderings, so that it may rise bit by bit to the contemplation of God and to the gazing upon the realms of the spirit. . . .

The soul may quite sensibly be compared to the finest down and the lightest feather which, if spared the onset and penetration of dampness from without, have a nature so mobile that at the slightest breeze they rise up of themselves to the highest points of the sky. But if they are weighed down by any splash, any dampening of moisture, not only will there be no natural impulse to fly up into the air but the pressure of the absorbed liquid will drag them downward to earth. So too with our soul. If sin and worldly preoccupation have not weighed it down, if dangerous passion has not sullied it, then, lifted up by the natural goodness of its purity, it will rise to the heights on the lightest breath of meditation and, leaving the lowly things, the things of earth, it will travel upward to the heavenly and the invisible. . . .

The apostle notes four types [of prayer].[127] "My advice is that first of all supplication should be offered up for everyone, prayers, pleas, and thanksgiving" [1 Tim 2:1]. Now one may be sure that this division was not foolishly made by the apostle. So we must first inquire what is meant by prayer, by petitions, by intercessions, and by thanksgiving. . . .

The first item to be discussed is the exact meaning of the terms. What is the difference between *prayer, supplication* and *plea*? . . . "My advice is that supplication should be offered up for everyone." A *supplication* is a plea or petition made on account of present and past sin by someone who is moved by contrition to seek pardon.

In *prayers* we offer or promise something to God. The Greek term means "vow." Greek has "I shall offer my vows to the Lord" and in Latin it is "I shall do what I have promised to the Lord" [Ps 118:14], which, according to the sense of the term, may be taken as "I shall make my prayers to the Lord." In Ecclesiastes we read: "If you have made a promise to God do not delay in fulfilling it" [Ec 5:3]. The Greek has "If you are to pray to the Lord, do not delay about it."

This is how each of us must do this. We pray when we renounce this world, when we undertake to die to all the world's deeds and mode of living and to serve the Lord with all our heart's zeal. We pray when we promise to despise worldly glory and earth's riches and to cling to the Lord with contrite hearts and poverty in spirit. We pray when we promise to put on the purest bodily chastity and unswerving patience and the gleam which is the harbinger of death. And if we are brought down by laziness, if we return to our old sinful ways because of not doing at all what we promised, we shall have to answer for our prayers and our commitments and it will be said of us, "Better not to promise than to promise

---

[127]This section on the four types of prayer is heavily dependent upon Origen's "On Prayer," chs. XIV–XV.

and not deliver." As the Greek would have it, "It is better that you do not pray than that, having prayed, you do not as you had undertaken" [Ec 5:4].

Third come *pleas*. We usually make them for others when we ourselves are deeply moved in spirit. We offer them for those dear to us or when we beg for peace in the world or, to borrow the words of the apostle, when we are supplicants "on behalf of all men, on behalf of rulers and on behalf of all those in high places" [1 Tim 2:1–2].

Fourth are *thanksgivings*. Unspeakably moved by the memory of God's past kindnesses, by the vision of what he now grants or by all that He holds out as a future reward to those who love Him, the mind gives thanks. In this perspective richer prayers are often uttered. Looking with purest gaze at the rewards promised to the saints, our spirit is moved by the measureless joy to pour out wordless thanksgiving to God.

These, then, are the four rich sources of prayer. Out of contrition for sin is *supplication* born. *Prayer* comes out of fidelity to promises and the fulfillment of what we have undertaken for the sake of a pure conscience. *Pleading* comes forth from the warmth of our love. *Thanksgiving* is generated by the contemplation of God's goodness and greatness and faithfulness. And all this, as we know, often evokes the most fervent and fiery prayers. Hence all of these types of prayer of which I have been speaking are valuable for all people, and indeed quite necessary. And so one person will now offer supplications, prayer then, later the purest and most zealous pleas. . . .

The Lord Himself deigned to initiate those four types of prayer and He gave us examples of them, so that there was a fulfillment of those words said of Him: "What Jesus began to do and to teach" [Acts 1:1]. He offers a *supplication* when He says: "Father, if possible, let this chalice pass from me" [Mt 26:39]. And there are the words put in his mouth in the Psalm, "My God, my God, look at me. Why have you abandoned me?" [Ps 22:2]. And there are others like this. There is a *prayer* when He says: "I have glorified you on earth and I have finished the work which you gave me to do" [Jn 17:4]. And this: "For their sake I consecrate myself so that they may be consecrated in the truth" [Jn 17:19]. There is *blessing* when He says: "I confess to you, Father, Lord of heaven and of earth, for you have hidden these things from the wise and the prudent and have revealed them to the lowly. Yes, indeed, Father, for this is what has pleased you" [Mt 11:25–26]. A *blessing* there surely is when He says: "Father, I thank you because you have listened to me. Indeed I knew that you always listened to me" [Jn 11:41].

It is clear to us that these types of prayer can be distinguished and also used at different times. However, the Lord also showed by example that they can all be put together in one perfect prayer, as in that prayer which, as we read at the end of the gospel of John, He poured forth in such abundance [Jn 17]. It would take too long to cite the whole text but a careful inquirer can discover for himself that matters are indeed as I have said. The apostle in his letter to the Philippians clearly expresses this same idea though he cites the four types of prayer in a somewhat different order. He shows that they must be offered up out of the one burning zeal. This is what he says: "In your every *prayer* and *supplication* let your *pleas* be included in your *blessings* to God" [Phil 4:6]. What he wanted in particular to teach us was that in our prayers and supplication blessings should be mingled with our pleas.

A state of soul more exalted and more elevated will follow upon these types of prayer. It will be shaped by the contemplation of God alone and by the fire of love, and the mind, melted and cast down into this love, speaks freely and respectfully to God, as though to one's own father. We must be careful to aspire to this state of soul. This is what the beginning of the Lord's prayer tells us when it says "Our Father" [Mt 6:9]. With our own voice we proclaim that the God, the Lord of the universe, is our Father and we thereby assert that we have been called out of the state of servitude and to adoption as sons [and daughters]. . . . It would seem, then, that this prayer, the Our Father, contains the fullness of perfection. It was the Lord Himself who gave it to us as both an example and a rule. It raises up those making use of it to that preeminent situation of which I spoke earlier. It lifts them up to that prayer of fire known to so few. It lifts them up, rather, to that ineffable prayer which rises above all human consciousness, with no voice sounding, no tongue moving, no words uttered. The soul lights up with heavenly illumination and no longer employs constricted, human speech. . . .

CONTINUOUS PRAYER[128]

You were quite right to make the comparison between training in continuous prayer and the teaching of children who at first do not know the alphabet, do not recognize letters, and are unable to write with a sure and firm hand. Models are put before them, carefully drawn in wax. By continually studying them, by practicing every day to reproduce them, they learn at last to write. The same happens with contemplation. You need a model and you keep it constantly before your eyes. You learn either to turn it in a salutary way over and over in your spirit or else, as you use it and meditate upon it, you lift yourself upward to the most sublime sights. And what follows now is the model to teach you, the prayer formula for which you are searching. Every monk who wants to think continuously about God should get accustomed to meditating endlessly on it and to banishing all other thoughts for its sake. But he will not hold on to it unless he breaks completely free from all bodily concerns and cares.

This is something which has been handed on to us by some of the oldest of the Fathers and it is something which we hand on to only a very small number of souls eager to know it: To keep the thought of God always in your mind you must cling totally to this formula for piety: "Come to my help, O God; Lord, hurry to my rescue" [Ps 70:2].

It is not without good reason that this verse has been chosen from the whole of Scripture as a device. It carries within it all the feelings of which human na-

---

[128]Reprinted from Luibheid, trans., *John Cassian: Conferences*. Used by permission of Paulist Press. Pages 132–36, "Conference Ten," attributed to Abba Isaac, "On Prayer."

ture is capable. It can be adapted to every condition and can be usefully deployed against every temptation. It carries within it a cry of help to God in the face of every danger. It expresses the humility of a pious confession. It conveys the watchfulness born of unending worry and fear. It conveys a sense of our frailty, the assurance of being heard, the confidence in help that is always and everywhere present. Someone forever calling out to his protector is indeed very sure of having him close by. This is the voice filled with the ardor of love and of charity. This is the terrified cry of someone who sees the snares of the enemy, the cry of someone besieged day and night and exclaiming that he cannot escape unless his protector comes to the rescue.

This short verse is an indomitable wall for all those struggling against the onslaught of demons. It is an impenetrable breastplate and sturdiest of shields. Whatever the disgust, the anguish, or the gloom in our thoughts, this verse keeps us from despairing of our salvation since it reveals to us the One to whom we call, the One who sees our struggles and who is never far from those who pray to Him. If things go well for us in spirit, if there is joy in our hearts, this verse is a warning to us not to grow proud, not to get puffed up at being in a good condition which, as it demonstrates, cannot be retained without the protection of God for whose continuous and speedy help it prays. This little verse, I am saying, proves to be necessary and useful to each one of us and in all circumstances. For someone who needs help in all things is making clear that he [or she] requires the help of God not simply in hard and sad situations but equally amid fortune and joyful conditions. He knows that God saves us from adversity and makes our joys linger and that in neither situation can human frailty survive without His help. . . .

Our prayer for rescue in bad times and for protection against pride in good times should be founded on this verse. The thought of this verse should be turning unceasingly in your heart. Never cease to recite it in whatever task or service or journey you find yourself. Think upon it as you sleep, as you eat, as you submit to the most basic demands of nature. This heartfelt thought will prove to be a formula of salvation for you. Not only will it protect you against all devilish attack, but it will purify you from the stain of all earthly sin and will lead you on to the contemplation of the unseen and the heavenly and to that fiery urgency of prayer which is indescribable and which is experienced by very few. Sleep should come upon you as you meditate on this verse until as a result of your habit of resorting to its words you get in the habit of repeating them even in your slumbers. This verse should be the first thing to occur to you when you wake up. It should precede all your thoughts as you keep vigil. It should take you over as you rise from your bed and go to kneel. After this it should accompany you in all your works and deeds. It should be at your side all times. Following the precept of Moses, you will think upon it "as you sit at home or walk along your way" [Dt 6:7], as you sleep or when you get up. You will write it upon the threshold and gateway of your mouth, you will place it on the walls of your house and in the inner sanctum of your heart. It will be a continuous prayer, an endless refrain when you bow down in prostration and when you rise up to do all the necessary things of life. . . .

Egeria's Pilgrimage (404–17)[129]

Almost nothing is known about the woman who penned a detailed account of her pilgrimage to Jerusalem in the late fourth or early fifth century. The extent of her travels, the freedom she exercised in her journeys, as well as the deference shown her by clergy suggest that Egeria was a woman of wealth and prominence. These same features indicate that women, at least prominent women, exercised considerable influence in the church of her day. Her writing evidences education, a lively intellect, and a thorough knowledge of Scripture; Egeria was especially adept at comparing contemporary places and events with those of the OT. Her *Pilgrimage* is cast in the form of a travel journal, and addressed as correspondence to Egeria's "sisters"; this may suggest that she was a member of a community of learned and devout women.[130]

Egeria's writing shows her particular interest in describing the forms of Christian worship, liturgy, and instruction that she met in her travels. In the small portion of her *Pilgrimage* offered here she describes the Easter (Paschal) celebration of the Jerusalem church, and thereby illustrates the elements of early Christian worship.

EASTER IN JERUSALEM[131]

When the Paschal season is coming, it is celebrated thus. Just as with us the forty days before Pasch[132] are observed, so here the eight weeks before Easter are observed. This is why eight weeks are kept: because they do not fast on the Lord's days and Sabbaths, except for the one Sabbath which is the vigil of Pasch and on which one must fast. Aside from the day there is no fasting on any Sabbath during the entire year. And so when the eight Lord's days and seven Sabbath's are subtracted from the eight weeks . . . there remain forty-one days on which to fast, which they call here *eortae*, that is, Lent.[133]

Each day of every week, this is what they do: on the Lord's Day at the first cock crow the bishop reads the Gospel passage about the Resurrection with the Church of the Resurrection [lit. *Anastasis*] . . . and they do as is the custom to do on the Lord's Days, in the major church called the Martyrium which is in Golgotha behind the Cross. Similarly, the dismissal having been given from the church they go to the *Anastasis* with hymns. . . . When they have done all this, it

---

[129]The dates ascribed to her document differ somewhat, earlier scholarship—for example—offering 381–88 as the time of its composition (cf. Wilson-Kastner et al., eds., *Lost Tradition*, pp. 71–81, for a thorough discussion of the date and composition of Egeria's *Pilgrimage*). Current scholarly consensus utilizes the dates given above.

[130]Amy Oden, ed., *Her Story: Women's Writings in the History of Christian Thought* (Nashville, Tenn.: Abingdon Press, 1994), p. 74.

[131]Reprinted from Wilson-Kastner et al., eds. *Lost Tradition*, "Egeria: Account of Her Pilgrimage," pp. 114–24, with omissions. Used by permission of Dr. Patricia Wilson-Kastner.

[132]Or "Passover" cf. Exodus 12.

[133]Literally, "quadragesimas."

is eleven o'clock; the Lamp-lighting [lit. *Lucernare*] is recited at its proper hour, as always at the Anastasis and the Cross, as is done at each holy place. . . .

The following is their custom about fasting here during Lent. Some who have eaten something on the Lord's Day after the dismissal, that is, at eleven o'clock or noon, do not eat again for the whole week until the Sabbath after the dismissal at the *Anastasis*. Those are the ones who "keep the week." Having eaten on the morning of the Sabbath, they do not eat in the evening, but on the next day, the Lord's Day, they take breakfast after the dismissal from the church, at eleven o'clock or later, and do not eat again until the next Sabbath. . . . Such is the custom here that all those who are, as they say here *aputactitae*, all men and women, not only on the days of Lent, but during the whole, when they eat, eat only once a day. If there are some of the *aputactitae* who cannot fast the whole week . . . they eat mid-week on Thursday. But one who cannot do this fast two consecutive days during Lent: those who cannot do that eat each evening. No one demands that anyone do anything, but all do as they can. No one is praised who does more, nor is the one who does less blamed. For such is the custom here. This is the food here during Lent: there is no bread, for it is not permitted to them, nor do they taste oil, nor anything which is from trees, but only some water and gruel. . . .

The next day, the Lord's Day, begins the Paschal week, which they call the Great Week. When the rites have been celebrated from cock crow until morning, according to custom in the *Anastasis* and the Cross, on the Lord's Day the people proceed according to custom to the great church which is called the Martyrium because it is behind the Cross, where the Lord suffered, and therefore is a martyr's shrine. When all things are celebrated . . . before the dismissal, the archdeacon calls out first and says: "During the whole week which begins tomorrow, let us come together to the Martyrium, the great church." Then he speaks again and says: "Today at one let us all be prepared to go to the Eleona." . . . Then each one goes home to eat a quick meal, so that by one o'clock all will be ready to go to the church which is called Eleona, which is on Mount Olivet, where is the cave in which the Lord taught.

At one o'clock all of the people go up to Mount Olivet, that is, the Eleona, into the church: the bishop is seated, they sing hymns and antiphonies appropriate to the day and place, as are the readings. And when it is about three o'clock, they go down singing hymns to the Imbomon, which is the place from which the Lord ascended into heaven, and everyone sits down there, for in the bishop's presence all the people are ordered to sit down. . . . There are hymns and antiphons appropriate to the day and place are sung; similarly readings and prayers are interspersed. When it is about one o'clock, that place in the Gospel is read where infants with palms and branches ran to the Lord saying, "Blessed is he who comes in the name of the Lord" [Mt 21:9]. Immediately the bishop rises with all of the people and they all walk from there to the summit of Mount Olivet. For all the people walk before the bishop singing hymns and antiphons, always responding: "Blessed is he who comes in the name of the Lord." And whatever children in this place, even those not able to walk, are carried on their parent's shoulders, all holding branches, some of palm, some of olive; thus the bishop is led in the same way that the Lord once was. And from the height of the mountain all the way to the city, and from there to the Anastasis through the whole city, all go on foot, the matrons as well as the noble men thus lead the bishop, singing responses, going slowly so that the people may not tire. Then by evening they arrive at the Anastasis. When they have arrived there, although it is evening, they nonetheless say the Lucernare, and another prayer is said at the Cross and the people are dismissed. . . .

On Thursday that which is customary is done from cock crow until the morning at the Anastasis. . . . At two o'clock according to custom all the people gather together at the Martyrium. . . . When all the people have gathered, everything which is appointed is done. The Oblation[134] is offered at the Martyrium and the dismissal is made at about four. But before the dismissal, the archdeacon calls out and says: "At the first hour of the night let us all gather at the church which is on the Eleona because great labor awaits us tonight." The dismissal having been given at the Martyrium the people go behind the Cross, and there a hymn is sung, prayer is made, and the bishop offers the Oblation and serves communion to everyone. . . . This dismissal having been given there, they go to the Anastasis, pray, and the catechumens are blessed [after] they have come into Gethsemani, first a suitable prayer is offered, then a hymn is sung, and the place in the Gospel is read where the Lord was arrested. While this passage is being read, there is such moaning and groaning with weeping among the people that they can be heard by all the people of the city.

At that hour they go back to the city on foot, singing hymns; they come to the gate at the hour when people can begin to tell one person from another . . . on this day no one leaves the vigil until day break. Thus the bishop is led from Gethsemani up to the gate and from there through the whole city up to the Cross. But when they have come there before the Cross, it is beginning to be clear daylight. Then they read the place in the Gospel where the Lord is led up to Pilate, and everything is written which Pilate spoke to the Lord or to the Jews [Jn 18:28–19:16; Mt 27]. Afterwards the bishop addresses the people, comforting them, because they have labored the whole night long and they are to work this whole day, encouraging them not to weaken, but to have hope in God, who will for this labor bestow on them an even greater reward. So comforting them as he is able, he addresses them: "Now go again, each one of you to your homes, sit there for a while, and be ready to be back here about eight o'clock, so that from that hour until about noon you may be able to see the holy wood of the Cross, which we believe to be profitable to the salvation of each of us. And from noon on we must again assemble here, that is, before the Cross, that we may devote ourselves to readings and prayers until the night."

After this, the dismissal is given from the Cross before sunrise, and everyone who is full of energy goes to Sion to pray at the column where the Lord was whipped. From there they go back to rest in their homes for a short while, and then are ready. Then the bishop's chair is set up on Golgotha behind the Cross,

---

[134]The Lord's Supper.

which now stands there; the bishop is seated on the chair, and before [it] is placed a table with a linen cloth [upon it]. The deacons stand in a circle around the table . . . and the silver casket decorated with gold is brought in, in which is the holy wood of the Cross. It is opened and taken out, and both the wood of the Cross and title are placed on the table. While it is on the table, the bishop sits and grasps the ends of the holy wood with his hands, and the deacons, who are standing around him, keep watch. Here is why they guard it so. It is the custom that all of the people here come one by one . . . bowing before the table, kissing the holy Cross and moving on. I was told that because someone . . . bit off and stole some of the holy Cross; now it is guarded by the deacons so that it dare not be done by someone again. . . .

When noon comes, they go before the Cross, rain or shine, because the place is outdoors and like a large and very beautiful atrium, between the Cross and the Anastasis. All the people are so crowded there that one cannot even open a door. The bishop's chair is placed before the Cross, and from noon to three nothing is done except that Biblical passages are read. First there are readings from the Psalms, whatever speaks of the Passion, then there are readings from the Acts of the Apostles or from the Epistles, whatever speaks of the Passion of the Lord, then places from the Gospels where the Lord suffers, then readings from the prophets where they speak of the Passion; then they read the Gospels where He foretells the Passion. And so from noon to three either there are readings or hymns so that all the people may be shown that whatever the prophets foretold of the Passion of the Lord is done either in the Gospels or the Apostolic writings. And thus during this three hours the people are taught that nothing happened which was not first foretold and nothing was foretold which was not completed. Prayers are always interspersed, and those prayers are always fitting to the day. At each reading and prayer there is such emotion and weeping by all the people that it is a wonder; for there is not one, old or young, who does not on this day weep for those three hours . . . because the Lord has suffered for us. After this, when it is about the ninth hour, the passage in the Gospel of John is read, where He delivers up His spirit [Jn 19:30]; after that reading a prayer is offered and the dismissal. When the dismissal is given before the Cross, immediately everyone gathers in the great church of the Martyrium and they do there those things they have been doing weekly between three o'clock and evening, when they gather at the Martyrium according to custom.

The dismissal having been given, they go from the Martyrium to the Anastasis. And when they have come there, the passage in the Gospel is read where Joseph asks Pilate for the body of the Lord, that he might place it in a new tomb. After the reading a prayer is offered, the catechumens are blessed and the dismissal is given. . . . [T]hose among the people who wish, or who can, keep vigil; those who cannot, however, do not keep the vigil until dawn. . . . [Through] the whole night hymns and antiphons are sung there until morning. A great crowd keep vigil, some from evening, others from midnight, but all doing what they can.

On the Sabbath, the next day, all is done according to custom at nine o'clock and again at noon; but [at] three . . . the Paschal vigil is prepared in the great church, the Martyrium. The Paschal vigil is observed just as with us, but one thing is done more elaborately; the infants,[135] when they have been baptized and clothed, as soon as they come from the font are first led with the bishop to the Anastasis. The bishop goes within the enclosure of the Anastasis, sings a hymn, and thus returns to the great church, where . . . all the people are keeping watch. Everything is done there which is customary with us, and having offered the Oblation the dismissal is given. After the dismissal of the vigil service they come with hymns to the Anastasis and there again the passage of the resurrection gospel is read, and again the bishop makes the [eucharistic] offering. But all is done quickly for the sake of the people, that they may not be delayed too long. . . .

Benedict of Nursia (c. 480–550)

Benedict of Nursia was born in the small Italian town of Nursia. He went to Rome for his formal education, and experienced religious conversion. St. Benedict was so scandalized by the life-style that was popular in Rome that he withdrew from the city and lived as an ascetic. His fame as a holy man of God spread rapidly, and disciples came to Benedict for instruction. He subsequently established a communal (cenobic) monastery at Monte Casino, about eighty miles south of Rome. His famous *Rule for Monasteries* (c. 525) grew out of that experiment, and through it St. Benedict became one of the most influential spiritual guides of Western Christendom.

The *Rule* comprises of seventy-three articles and a prologue which describe the nature and task of the monastic vocation. The articles are very practical in their thrust. The *Rule* drew upon the earlier resources of Egyptian asceticism, but in contrast to the monasticism of the desert, the Benedictine *Rule* stressed a well-ordered, disciplined life instead of one of rigorous asceticism. Spiritual obedience and humility stand at the core of Benedictine spirituality. The person of faith cultivates humility which allows one to live a life of obedience; obedience to God takes concrete expression in obedience to the Abbot of the monastery, and to the *Rule* of the community. St. Benedict's *Rule* stresses spiritual and physical discipline. It defines the life of the community as one of prayer and work; the monks gathered for corporate prayer seven times a day; these became known as "the canonical hours of prayer."[136] Each brother performed manual labor on behalf of the community as an expression of his spirituality. Since each person embraced apostolic poverty, the corporate life and labor of the community were also necessary for the sustenance of the community.

---

[135]"Infants" is probably used here metaphorically to refer to the newly baptized as "babes in Christ."
[136]These hours, beginning in the early morning, became known as Matins, Lauds, Prime, Terce, Sext, None, Vespers, and Compline.

FOUR KINDS OF MONKS[137]

. . . There are four kinds of monks. The first kind is that of the cenobites [that is, those living in common], those who live in a monastery according to a rule, and under the government of an abbot. The second is that of the anchorites, or hermits, who have learned how to conduct the war against the devil by their long service in the monastery and their association with many brothers, and so, being well trained, have separated themselves from the troop, in order to wage single combat, being able with the aid of God to carry on the fight alone against the sins of the flesh. The third kind (and a most abominable kind it is) is that of the sarabites, who have not been tested and proved by obedience to the rule and by the teaching of experience, as gold is tried in the furnace, and so are soft and pliable like a base metal; who in assuming the tonsure are false to God, because they still serve the world in their lives. They do not congregate in the Master's fold, but dwell apart without a shepherd, by twos and threes, or even alone. Their law is their own desires, since they call that holy which they like, and that unlawful which they do not like. The fourth kind is composed of those who are called *gyrovagi* (wanderers), who spend their whole lives wandering about through different regions and living three or four days at a time in the cells of different monks. They are always wandering about and never remain long in one place, and they are governed by their own appetites and desires. They are in every way worse even than the sarabites. But it is better to pass over in silence than to mention their manner of life. Let us, therefore, leaving these aside, proceed, with the aid of God, to the consideration of the cenobites, the highest type of monks.

TWELVE STEPS OF HUMILITY[138]

. . . Brethren, the holy Scripture saith: "And whosoever shall exalt himself shall be abased; and he that shall humble himself shall be exalted" [Mt 23:12]. . . . Therefore, brethren, if we wish to attain to the highest measure of humility and to that exaltation in heaven which is only to be gained by lowliness on earth, we must raise to heaven by our deeds such a ladder as appeared to Jacob in his dream, whereon he saw angels ascending and descending. For the meaning of that figure is that we ascend by humility of heart and descend by haughtiness. And the ladder is our life here below which God raises to heaven for the lowly of heart. Our body and soul are the two sides of the ladder, in which by deeds consistent with our holy calling we insert steps whereby we may ascend to heaven.

Now the first step of humility is this, to escape destruction by keeping ever before one's eyes the fear of the Lord, to remember always the commands of the

---

[137]Olivia Thatcher and Edgar H. McNeal, eds., *A Source Book for Medieval History* (New York: Charles Scribner's Sons, 1905), ch. 1, of the Rule, pp. 434–35. Reprinted by permission of Scribner, a Division of Simon & Schuster.

[138]Ibid., pp. 442–46. Reprinted by permission of Scribner, a Division of Simon & Schuster.

Lord, for they who scorn him are in danger of hell-fire, and to think of the eternal life that is prepared for them that fear him. So a man should keep himself in every hour from the sins of the heart, of the tongue, of the eyes, of the hands, and of the feet. He should cast aside his own will and the desires of the flesh; he should think that God is looking down on him from heaven all the time, and that his acts are seen by God and reported to him hourly by his angels. For the prophet shows that the Lord is ever present in the midst of our thoughts, when he says: "God trieth the hearts and the reins" [Ps 7:9], and again, "The Lord knoweth the thoughts of men" [Ps 94:11], and again he says: "Thou hast known my thoughts from afar" [Ps 139:2], and "The thoughts of a man are known to thee" [Ps 76:11]. So a zealous brother will strive to keep himself from perverse thoughts by saying to himself: "Then only shall I be guiltless in his sight, if I have kept me from mine iniquity" [Ps 18:23]. And the holy Scriptures teach us in diverse places that we should not do our own will; as where it says: "Turn from thine own will" [Ec 18:30]; and where we ask in the Lord's Prayer that his will be done in us; and where it warns us: "There is a way that seemeth right to a man, but the ends thereof are the ways of death" [Prov 14:12]; and again, concerning the disobedient; "They are corrupt and abominable in their desires" [Ps 14:1]. And we should always remember that God is aware of our fleshly desires; as the prophet says, speaking to the Lord: "All my desire is before thee" [Ps 38:9]. Therefore, we should shun evil desires, for death lieth in the way of the lusts; as the Scripture shows, saying: "Go not after thy lusts" [Ec 18:30]. . . .

The second step of humility is this, that a man should not delight in doing his own will and desires, but should imitate the Lord who said: "I came not to do mine own will, but the will of him that sent me" [Jn 6:38] And again the Scriptures saith: "Lust hath its punishment, but hardship winneth a crown."

The third step of humility is this, that a man be subject to his superior in all obedience for the love of God, imitating the Lord, of whom the apostle says: "He became obedient unto death." [Phil 2:8]

The fourth step of humility is this, that a man endure all the hard and unpleasant things and even undeserved injuries that come in the course of his service, without wearying or withdrawing his neck from the yoke, for the Scripture saith: "He that endureth to the end shall be saved" [Mt 10:22], and again: "Comfort thy heart and endure the Lord" [Ps 27:14]. And yet again the Scripture, showing that the faithful should endure all unpleasant things for the Lord, saith, speaking in the person of those that suffer: "Yea, for thy sake are we killed all the day long; we are counted as sheep for the slaughter" [Ps 44:22]; and again, rejoicing in the sure hope of divine reward: "In all things we are more than conquerors through him that loved us" [Rom 8:37]; and again in another place: "For thou, O God, hast proved us; thou hast tried us as silver is tried; thou broughtest us into the net, thou laidst affliction upon our loins" [Ps 66:10f]; and again to show that we should be subject to a superior: "Thou hast placed men over our heads" [Ps 66:12]. Moreover, the Lord bids us suffer injuries patiently, saying: "Whosoever shall smite thee on the right cheek, turn to him the other also. And if any man will sue thee at the law, and take away thy coat, let him have thy cloak also. And whosoever shall compel thee to go a mile, go with him twain" [Mt 5:39–41]. . . .

The fifth step of humility is this, that a man should not hide the evil thoughts that arise in his heart or the sins which he has committed in secret, but should humbly confess them to his abbot; as the Scripture exhorteth us, saying: "Commit thy way unto the Lord, trust also in him" [Ps 37:5]; and again, "O, give thanks unto the Lord, for he is good; for his mercy endureth forever" [Ps 106:1]; and yet again the prophet saith: "I have acknowledged my sin unto thee, and mine iniquity have I not hid. I said, I will confess my transgressions unto the Lord; and thou forgavest the iniquity of my sin" [Ps 32:5].

The sixth step of humility is this, that the monk should be contented with any lowly or hard condition in which he may be placed, and would always look upon himself as an unworthy laborer, not fitted to do what is intrusted to him; saying to himself in the words of the prophet: "I was reduced to nothing and was ignorant; I was as a beast before thee and I am always with thee [Ps 73: 22f].

The seventh step of humility is this, that he should not only say, but should really believe in his heart that he is the lowest and most worthless of all men, humbling himself and saying with the prophet: "I am a worm and no man; a reproach of men, and despised of all people" [Ps 22:6]; and "I that was exalted am humbled and confounded" [Ps 88:15]; and again: "It is good for me that I have been afflicted, that I might learn thy statutes" [Ps 119:7].

The eighth step of humility is this, that the monk should follow in everything the common rule of the monastery and the examples of his superiors.

The ninth step of humility is this, that the monk should restrain his tongue from speaking, and should keep silent even from questioning, as the Scripture saith: "In a multitude of words there wanteth not sin" [Prov 10:19], and "Let not an evil speaker be established in the earth" [Ps 140:11].

The tenth step of humility is this, that the monk should be not easily provoked to laughter, as it is written: "The fool raiseth his voice in laughter" [Ec 21:23].

The eleventh step of humility is this, that the monk, when he speaks, should do so slowly and without laughter, softly and gravely, using few words and reasonable, and that he should not be loud of voice; as it is written: "A wise man is known for his few words."

The twelfth step of humility is this, that the monk should always be humble and lowly, not only in his heart, but in his bearing as well. Wherever he may be, in divine service, in the oratory, in the garden, on the road, in the fields, whether sitting, walking, or standing, he should always keep his head bowed and his eyes upon the ground. He should always be meditating upon his sins and thinking of the dread day of judgment, saying to himself as did that publican of whom the gospel speaks: "Lord, I am not worthy, I a sinner, so much as to lift mine eyes up to heaven" [Lk 18:13]; and again with the prophet: "I am bowed down and humbled everywhere" [Ps 119:107].

Now when the monk has ascended all these steps of humility, he will arrive at that perfect love of God which casteth out all fear [1 Jn 4:18]. By that love all those commandments which he could not formerly observe without grievous effort and struggle, he will now obey naturally and easily, as if by habit; not in the fear of hell, but in the love of Christ and by his very delight in virtue. And thus the Lord will show the working of his holy Spirit in this his servant, freed from vices and sins.

Pseudo-Dionysius (c. 500)

Pseudo-Dionysius was purported to be Dionysius the Areopagite, converted during St. Paul's ministry in Athens (Acts 17:34) and who subsequently became the first bishop of Athens. While the writings of Dionysius reflect the blend of Christian and Platonic mysticism that might be anticipated from an Athenian, it is clear that the four works attributed to him sprang instead from the pen of an anonymous Syrian monk of the late fifth or early sixth century. Because his writings were not widely considered spurious until the sixteenth century (through the efforts of Desiderius Erasmus), Pseudo-Dionysius was one of the most influential mystical writers of the ancient church. His major works included *The Heavenly Hierarchy, The Ecclesiastical Hierarchy*, and *The Divine Names*; these were introduced and summarized in his *Mystical Theology*. Dionysius divided the spiritual life into three stages: purification (the purgative way), meditation on the Word of God (the illuminative way), and union with God (the unitive way); these three categories came to epitomize the classical expressions of Christian Spirituality.[139]

The popularity of Dionysian spirituality in the middle ages was rooted, in part, in its delicious complexity. It also summarized and extended the Alexandrian synthesis of "Athens and Jerusalem," and thereby represented one strand of the ancient Christian tradition. Dionysius' desire to combine classical (Neoplatonic) and Christian Spirituality was precisely the task which the great medieval theologians had set for themselves in their quest for a unified field of knowledge and faith, and so his mysticism paralleled the popularity of scholasticism. Interest in Dionysian spirituality continued through the works of Meister Eckhart and the Rhineland mystics, but it dwindled in the sixteenth century with the unmasking of the spurious character of their authorship.[140]

MYSTICAL THEOLOGY[141]

Ch. 1: What is the divine darkness?

Trinity! Higher than any being,
any divinity, any goodness!

---

[139]Ricard P. McBrien, *Catholicism*, 2 vols. (Minneapolis: Winston Press, 1980), Vol. II, pp. 1061–62.

[140]The three introductions in Colm Luibheid, trans., *Pseudo-Dionysius: The Complete Works* (New York: Paulist Press, 1987), offer an excellent foundation for reading these works in context.

[141]Reprinted from Luibheid, trans., *Pseudo-Dionysius*. Copyright 1987 by The Missionary Society of St. Paul the Apostle in the State of New York. Used by permission of Paulist Press. Pages 135–41, "Mystical Theology." Most of Luibheid's excellent notes have been omitted here.

Guide of Christians
in the wisdom of heaven!
Lead us up beyond unknowing and light,
up to the fartherest, highest peak
of mystic scripture,
where the mysteries of God's Word
lie simple, absolute and unchangeable
in the brilliant darkness of a hidden silence.
Amid the deepest shadow
they pour overwhelming light
on what is most manifest.
Amid the wholly unsensed and unseen
they completely fill our sightless minds
with treasures beyond all beauty.

For this I pray: Timothy, my friend, my advice to you as you look for a sight of the mysterious things, is to leave behind you everything perceived and understood, everything perceptible and understandable, all that is not and all that is, and, with your understanding laid aside, to strive upward as much as you can toward union with Him who is beyond all being and knowledge. By an undivided and absolute abandonment of yourself and everything, shedding all and freed from all, you will be uplifted to the ray of the divine shadow which is above everything that is.

But see to it that none of this comes to the hearing of the uninformed, that is to say, to those caught up with the things of the world, who imagine that there is nothing beyond instances of individual being and who think that by their own intellectual resources they can have a direct knowledge of Him Who has made the shadows His hiding place [Ps 19:11]. And if initiation into the divine is beyond such people, what is to be said of those others, still more uninformed, who describe the transcendent Cause of all things in terms derived from the lowest orders of being, and who claim that it is in no way superior to the godless, multiformed shapes they themselves have made? What has actually to be said about the Cause of everything is this. Since it is the Cause of all beings, we should posit and ascribe to it all the affirmations we make in regard to beings, and, more appropriately, we should negate all these affirmations, since it surpasses all being. Now we should not conclude that the negations are simply the opposites of the affirmations, but rather that the cause of all is considerably prior to this, beyond privations, beyond every denial, beyond every assertion.

This, at least is what was taught by the blessed Bartholomew.[142] He says that the Word of God is vast and minuscule, that the Gospel is wide-ranging and yet restricted. To me it seems that he is extraordinarily shrewd, for he has grasped that the good cause of all is both eloquent and taciturn, indeed wordless. It has

---

[142]Bartholomew, who is mentioned in Matthew 10:3, Mark 3:18, Luke 6:14, and Acts 1:13, was subsequently the focus of several apocryphal works. Pseudo-Dionysius is probably referring to one of these pseudo-apostolic works attributed to Bartholomew.

neither word nor act of understanding, since it is on a place above all this, and it is made manifest only to those who travel through foul and fair, who pass beyond the summit of every holy ascent, who leave behind them every divine light, every voice, every word from heaven, and who plunge into the darkness where, as scripture proclaims, there dwells the One who is beyond all things. It is not for nothing that the blessed Moses is commanded to submit first to purification and then to depart from those who have not undergone this. When every purification is complete, he hears the many-voiced trumpets. He sees the many lights, pure and with rays streaming abundantly. Then, standing apart from the crowds and accompanied by chosen priests, he pushes ahead to the summit of divine ascents.[143] And yet he does not meet God himself, but contemplates, not Him Who is invisible, but rather where He dwells. This means, I presume, that the holiest and highest of the things perceived with the eye of the body or the mind are but the rationale which presupposes all that lies below the Transcendent One. Through them, however, His unimaginable presence is shown, walking the heights of those holy places to which the mind at least can rise. But then he [Moses] breaks free of them, away from what sees and is seen, and he plunges into the truly mysterious darkness of unknowing. Here, renouncing all that the mind may conceive, wrapped entirely in the intangible and the invisible, he belongs completely to Him who is beyond everything. Here, being neither oneself nor someone else, one is supremely united by a completely unknowing inactivity of all knowledge, and knows beyond the mind by knowing nothing.

Ch. 2: How one should be united, and attribute praises, to the Cause of all things Who is beyond all things.

I pray we could come to this darkness so far above light! If only we lacked sight and knowledge so as to see, so as to know, unseeing and unknowing, that which lies beyond all vision and knowledge. For this would be really to see and to know: to praise the Transcendent One in a transcending way, namely through the denial of all beings. We would be like sculptors who set out to carve a statue. They remove every obstacle to the pure view of the hidden image, and simply by this act of clearing aside they show up the beauty which is hidden.

Now it seems to me that we should praise the denials quite differently than we do the assertions. When we made assertions we began with first things, moved down through intermediate terms until we reached the last things. But now as we climb from the last things up to the most primary, we deny all things so that we may unhiddenly know that unknowing which itself is hidden from all those possessed of knowing amid all beings, so that we may see above being that darkness concealed from all the light among beings.

Ch. 3: What are the affirmative theologies and what are the negative?

In my *Theological Representations*,[144] I have praised the notions which are most appropriate to affirmative theology. I have shown the sense in which the divine

---

[143]This section seems to evidence some familiarity with Gregory of Nyssa's *Life of Moses*. Cf. pp. 94–99.
[144]This treatise is fictitious or lost.

and good nature is said to be one and then triune, how the Fatherhood and Sonship are predicated of it, the meaning of the theology of the Spirit, how these core lights of goodness grew from the incorporeal and indivisible good, and how in this sprouting they have remained inseparable from their co-eternal foundation in it, in themselves, and in each other. I have spoken of how Jesus, Who is above individual being, became a being with a true human nature. Other revelations of scripture were also praised in the *Theological Representations*.

In *The Divine Names* I have shown the sense in which God is described as good, existent, life, wisdom, power, and whatever other things pertain to the conceptual names for God. In my *Symbolic Theology*[145] I have spoken of the images we have of Him, of the forms, figures, and instruments proper to Him, of the places in which He lives and of the ornaments He wears. I have spoken of His anger, grief, and rage, of how He is said to be drunk and hung over, of His oaths and curses, of His sleeping and waking, and indeed of all those images we have of Him, images shaped by the workings of the symbolic representations of God. And I feel sure that you have noticed how these latter come much more abundantly than what went before, since *The Theological Representations* and a discussion of the names appropriate to God are inevitably briefer than what can be said in *The Symbolic Theology*. The fact that the more we take flight upward, the more our words are confined to the ideas we are capable of forming; so that now as we plunge into that darkness which is beyond intellect, we shall find ourselves not simply running short of words but actually speechless and unknowing. In the earlier books my argument traveled downward from the most exalted to the humblest categories, taking in on this downward path an ever-increasing number of ideas which multiplied with every stage of the descent. But my argument now rises from what is below up to the transcendent, and the more it climbs, the more language falters, and when it has passed up and beyond the ascent, it will turn silent completely, since it will finally be at one with Him Who is indescribable.

Now you may wonder why it is that, after starting out from the highest category when our method involved assertions, we begin now from the lowest category when it involves a denial. The reason is this. When we assert what is beyond every assertion, we must then proceed from what is most akin to it, and as we do so we make the affirmation on which everything else depends. But when we deny that which is beyond denial, we have to start by denying those qualities which differ most from the goal we hope to attain. Is it not closer to reality to say that God is life and goodness rather than that He is air or stone? Is it not more accurate to deny that drunkenness and rage can be attributed to Him than to deny that we can apply to Him the terms of speech and thought?

Ch. 4: That the supreme Cause of every perceptible thing is not itself perceptible.

So this is what we say. The Cause of all is above all and is not inexistent, lifeless, speechless, mindless. It is not a material body, and hence has neither shape

---

[145]This treatise is ficticious or lost.

nor form, quality, quantity, or weight. It is not in any place and can neither be seen nor be touched. It is neither perceived nor is it perceptible. It suffers neither disorder nor disturbance and is overwhelmed by no earthly passion. It is not powerless and subject to the disturbances caused by sense perception. It endures no deprivation of light. It passes through no change, decay, division, loss, no ebb and flow, nothing of which the senses may be aware. None of all this can either be identified with it nor attributed to it.

Ch. 5: That the supreme Cause of every conceptual thing is not itself conceptual.

Again, as we climb higher we say this. It is not soul or mind, nor does it possess imagination, conviction, speech, or understanding. Nor is it speech *per se*, understanding *per se*. It is not number or order, greatness or smallness, equality or inequality, similarity or dissimilarity. It is not immovable, moving, or at rest. It has not power, it is not power, nor is it light. It does not live nor is it life. It is not a substance, nor is it eternity or time. It cannot be grasped by the understanding since it is neither knowledge nor truth. It is not kingship. It is not wisdom. It is neither one nor oneness, divinity nor goodness. Nor is it a spirit, in the sense in which we understand that term. It is not sonship or fatherhood and it is nothing known to us or to any other being. It falls neither within the predicate of nonbeing nor of being. Existing beings do not know it as it actually is and it does not know them as they are. There is no speaking of it, nor name nor knowledge of it. Darkness and light, error and truth—it is none of these. It is beyond assertion and denial. We make assertions and denials of what is next to it, but never of it, for it is both beyond every assertion, being perfect and unique cause of all things, and, by virtue of its preeminently simply and absolute nature, free of every limitation, beyond every limitation; it is also beyond every denial.

Maximus the Confessor (580–662)

Maximus the Confessor was probably born in Constantinople. He was a monk and theologian of the Eastern church, who was pushed westward by Persian military advances. Maximus's most influential works, including *Mystagogy*, were written during his residency in monasteries at Carthage, and then Crete. He became involved in the controversies that raged about the relationship of Christ's human and divine wills. Maximus was condemned, tortured, and mutilated in his tongue and right hand, and eventually exiled to Lazica, in Russian Georgia, where he died. He is called "the confessor" because he refused to renounce the orthodox Christian faith.

Mystagogy stands in the mystical tradition that flowed from Origen, Gregory of Nyssa, and others. "Mystagogy" means "initiation into a mystery"; by explaining the Christian mysteries Maximus leads his readers into the depths of Christian experience. His descriptions of the symbolism of Christian worship provide insight into the life and liturgy of the seventh-century church.

THE HOLY ASSEMBLY[146]

What mysteries the enduring grace of the Holy Spirit effects and brings to completion through the rites accomplished in the holy synaxis[147] in the faithful and those gathered in the church out of faith. This, indeed, is why the blessed old man believed that every Christian should be exhorted—and he never failed to this—to frequent God's holy church and never to abandon the holy synaxis accomplished therein because of the holy angels who remain there and who take note each time people enter and present themselves to God, and they make supplication for them; likewise because of the grace of the Holy Spirit which is always invisibly present, but in a special way at the time of the holy synaxis. This grace transforms and changes each person who is found there and in fact remolds him in proportion to what is more divine in him and leads him to what is revealed through the mysteries which are celebrated, even if he does not himself feel this because he is still among those who are children in Christ, unable to see either into the depths of the reality or the grace operating in it, which is revealed through each of the divine symbols of salvation being accomplished, and which proceeds according to the order and progression from preliminaries to the end of everything.

Thus we see effected in the first entrance [or processional] the rejection of unbelief, the increase of faith, the lessening of vice, the bestowal of virtue, the disappearance of ignorance, and the development of knowledge. By the hearing of the divine words there is effected the firm and unchangeable habits and dispositions of the realities just mentioned, that is, of faith, virtue, and knowledge. Through the divine chants which follow there is effected the deliberate consent of the soul to virtue as well as the spiritual delight and enjoyment that these arouse in it. By the sacred reading of the holy Gospel there is brought about the end of earthly thinking as of the world of sense. Then by the closing of the doors which follows there is effected the passage and transfer of the soul in its disposition from this corruptible world to the intelligible world, whereby having closed its senses like doors it renders them cleansed of the idols of sin. By the entrance into the holy mysteries we see the more perfect and mystical and new teaching and knowledge of God's dispensation towards us. By the divine kiss there is seen the identity of concord and oneness and love of all with everyone and of each one with himself first and then with God. By the profession of the symbol of faith[148] there is seen fitting thanks for the marvelous ways of our salvation. By the Trisagion there comes about the union with the holy angels and elevation to the same honor, as well as the ceaseless and harmonious persistency in the sanctifying glorifica-

---

[146]Reprinted from George Berthold, trans., *Maximus the Confessor: Selected Writings.* Copyright 1985, by The Missionary Society of St. Paul the Apostle in the State of New York. Used by permission of Paulist Press. Pages 206–13, "Mystagogy," ch. 24, with omissions.

[147]"Synaxis" stems from the Greek word for "to come together." In Eastern church tradition it becomes a shorthand expression for the assembly of the communion of saints for worship, liturgy, eucharist, and other doxological expressions.

[148]That is the creed.

tion of God. By the prayer through which we are made worthy to call God our Father we receive the truest adoption in the grace of the Holy Spirit. By the "One is holy" and what follows, we have the grace and familiarity which unites us to God Himself. By holy communion of the spotless and life-giving mysteries we are given fellowship and identity with Him by participation in likeness, by which a human is deemed worthy from humanity to become God. For we believe that in this present life we already have a share in these gifts of the Holy Spirit through the love that is in faith, and in the future age after we have kept the command-ments to the best of our ability we believe that we shall have a share in them in very truth in their concrete reality according to the steadfast hope of our faith and the solid and unchangeable promise to which God has committed himself. Then we shall pass from the grace which is in faith to the grace of vision, when our God and Savior Jesus Christ will indeed transform us into himself by taking away from us the marks of corruption and will bestow on us the original mysteries which have been represented for us through sensible symbols here below. To make it easier to remember, if you wish, let us recapitulate thus the meaning of what has been said by running over it briefly.

Thus the holy church, as we said, is the figure and image of God inasmuch as through it He effects in His infinite power and wisdom an unconfused unity from the various essences of beings, attaching them to himself as a Creator at their highest point, and this operates according to the grace of faith for the faithful, joining them all to each other in one form according to a single grace and calling of faith, the active and virtuous ones in a single identity of will, the contempla-tive and gnostic ones in an unbroken and undivided concord as well. It is a fig-ure of both the spiritual and sensible world, with the sanctuary as symbol of the intelligible world and the nave as symbol of the world of sense.

It is as well an image of a person inasmuch as it represents the soul by the sanctuary and suggests the body by the nave. Also it is a figure and image of the soul considered in itself because by the sanctuary it bears the glory of the con-templative element and by the nave the ornament of the active part. The first en-trance of the holy synaxis which is celebrated in the church signifies in general the first appearance of Christ our God, and in particular the conversion of those who are being led by Him and with Him from unbelief to faith and from vice to virtue and also from ignorance to knowledge. The readings which take place af-ter it signify in general the divine wishes and intentions in accordance with which everyone should conform and conduct himself, and in particular the teaching and progress in the faith of those who are believers, and the firm disposition of virtue of those who are active in accordance with which, by submitting themselves to the divine law of the commandments, they set themselves bravely and unshak-enly against the devil's wiles and escape his adversary works; finally it signifies the contemplative habits of those who have knowledge, in accordance with which, by bringing together as much as possible the spiritual principles of sensible real-ities and Providence in what concerns them, they are borne without error to the truth.

The divine melodies of the chants indicate the divine delight and enjoyment which comes about in the souls of all. By it they are mystically strengthened in forgetting their past labors for virtue and are renewed in the vigorous desire of the divine and wholesome benefits still to be attained.

The holy Gospel is in general a symbol of the fulfillment of this world; in particular it indicates the complete disappearance of the ancient error in those who have believed; in the active, the mortification and the end of the law and thinking according to the flesh; and in those who have knowledge, the gathering and ascent from the numerous and various principles toward the most comprehensive principle, once the most detailed and varied natural contemplation has been reached and crossed.

The descent of the bishop from the throne and the dismissal of the catechumens signifies in general the second coming from heaven of our great God and Savior Jesus Christ and the separation of sinners from the saints and the just retribution rendered to each. In particular it means the perfect assurance of believers in faith which is produced by the Word of God becomes invisibly present to them, whereby every thought which still limps in some way regarding faith is dismissed from them as are the catechumens. Thus for the active ones there results perfect detachment by which every passionate and unenlightened thought departs from the soul, and for those with knowledge the comprehensive science of whatever is known by which all images of material things are chased away from the soul.

The closing of the doors and the entrance into the holy mysteries and the divine kiss and the recitation of the symbol of faith [the creed] mean in general the passing away of sensible things and the appearance of spiritual realities and the new teaching of the divine mystery involving us and the future concord, unanimity, love, and identity of everyone with each other and with God, as well as the thanksgiving for the manner of our salvation. In a particular way it means the progress of the faithful from simple faith to learning in dogmas, initiation, accord, and piety. The closing of the doors indicates the first thing, the entrance into the holy actions the second, the kiss the third, the recitation of the creed the fourth. For those at the active stage it means the transfer from activity to contemplation of those who have closed their senses and who have become outside the flesh and the world by the rejection of activities for their own sake, and the ascent from the mode of the commandments to their principle, and the connatural kinship and union of these commandments in their proper principles with the power of the soul and the habit which is adapted to theological thanksgiving. For those who have knowledge, it involves the passing of natural contemplation to the simple understanding according to which they no longer pursue the divine and ineffable Word by sensation or anything that appears and the union with the soul of its powers and the simplicity which takes in under one form by the intellect the principle of Providence.

The unceasing and sanctifying doxology by the holy angels in the Trisagion signifies, in general, the equality in the way of life and conduct and the harmony in the divine praising which will take place in the age to come by both heavenly and earthly powers, when the human body now rendered immortal by the resurrection will no longer weigh down the soul by corruption and will not itself be weighed down but will take on, by the change into incorruption, potency, and aptitude to receive God's coming. In particular it signifies, for the faithful, the theological rivalry with the angels in faith; for the active ones, it symbolizes the splendor of life equal to the angels, so far as this is possible for humans, and the persistence in the theological hymnology; for those who have knowledge, endless thoughts, hymns, and movements concerning the Godhead which are equal to the angels, so far as humanly possible.

The blessed invocation of the great God and Father and the acclamation of the "One is holy" and what follows and the partaking of the holy and life-giving mysteries signify the adoption and union, as well as the familiarity and divine likeness and deification which will come about through the goodness of our God in every way on all the worthy, whereby God himself will be "all in all" alike to those who are saved as a pattern of beauty resplendent as a cause in those who are resplendent along with Him in grace by virtue and knowledge.

He used to call faithful, virtuous, and knowing the beginners, the proficient, and the perfect, that is, slaves, mercenaries, and sons, the three classes of the saved. The slaves are the faithful who execute the Lord's commandments out of fear of threats and who willingly work for those who are obeyed. Mercenaries are those who out of a desire for promised benefits bear with patience "the burden and heat of the day," that is, the affliction innate in and yoked to the present life from the condemnation of our first parents, and the temptations from it on behalf of virtue, and who by free choice of will wisely exchange life for life, the present one for the future. Finally, sons are the ones who out of neither fear of threats nor desire of promised things but rather out of character and habit of the voluntary inclination and disposition of the soul toward the good never become separated from God, as that son who whom it was said, "Son, you are always with me, and everything I have is yours" [Lk 15:31]. They have become as much as possible by deification in grace what God is and is believed by nature and by cause.

Let us, then, not stray from the holy Church of God which comprehends in the sacred order of the divine symbols which are celebrated, such great mysteries of our salvation. Through them, in making each of us who conducts himself worthily as best he can in Christ, it brings to light the grace of adoption which was given through holy baptism in the Holy Spirit and which makes us perfect in Christ. Instead, let us with all our strength and zeal render ourselves worthy of the divine gifts in pleasing God by good works. . . . [P]utting aside the old person which is corrupted by the lusts of illusion with his past deeds and lusts, let us walk in a manner worthy of God who has called us to His kingdom and His glory, having clothed ourselves with heartfelt compassion, with kindness, humility, meekness, and patience, bearing with one another in love and forgiving one another if one has a complaint against the other just as Christ has forgiven us, and over all these let us clothe ourselves with love and peace, the bond of perfection, to which we have been called in one body, in short, the new person who is constantly renewed in full Divine promises with a good hope and to be filled "with the knowledge of His will in all wisdom and spiritual understanding . . ." [Col 1:9f].

John of Damascus (c. 674–749)

John of Damascus was born in Damascus, Syria. His father and grandfather before him had been ministers, and St. John followed in their way first by taking up pastoral work, and then by entering the monastery of St. Saba, near Jerusalem. He wrote treatises that defended the Orthodox faith against Nestorians, and other heretical movements. Among his main works were *On the Divine Images*, *Fount of Knowledge*, and *The Orthodox Faith*; the latter became one of the standard expressions of Eastern Orthodox theology. St. John was especially significant because of his ability to summarize, expound, and transmit Byzantine spirituality.

ON GOD[149]

"No one has seen God at any time; the Only-begotten Son, which is in the bosom of the Father, He has declared Him" [Jn 1:18]. The Deity, therefore, is ineffable and incomprehensible. "For no one knows the Father, except the Son, nor the Son except the Father" [Mt 11:27]. And the Holy Spirit, too, so knows the things of God as the spirit of a person knows the things that are in that person [1 Cor 2:11]. Moreover, after the first and blessed nature no one, not of humans only, but even of supermundane powers, and the Cherubim, I say, and Seraphim themselves, has ever known God, except to whom He revealed Himself.

God, however, did not leave us in absolute ignorance. For the knowledge of God's existence has been implanted by Him in all by nature. This creation, too, and its maintenance, and its government, proclaim the majesty of the Divine nature. Moreover, by the Law and the Prophets in former times, and afterwards by His Only-begotten Son, our Lord and God and Savior Jesus Christ, He disclosed to us the knowledge of Himself as that was possible for us. All things, therefore, that have been delivered to us by Law and Prophets and Apostles and Evangelists we receive, and know, and honor, seeking for nothing beyond these. For God, being good, is the cause of all good, subject neither to envy nor to any passion. . . . As knowing all things, therefore, and providing for what is profitable for each, He revealed that which it was to our profit to know; but what we were unable to be He kept secret. With these things let us be satisfied, and let us abide by them, not removing everlasting boundaries, not overpassing the Divine tradition.

. . . It is necessary, therefore, that anyone who wishes to speak or hear of God should understand clearly that alike in the doctrine of Deity and in that of the incarnation, neither are all things unutterable; nor all things unknowable nor all knowable. But the knowable belongs to one order, and the utterable to another; just as it is one thing to speak and another to know. Many of the things relating

---

[149]John of Damascus, "Exposition of the Orthodox Faith," in **NPNF**, Vol. IX, ch. 1, p. 1, with omissions and minor linguistic changes.

to God, therefore, cannot be put into fitting terms, but on things above us we cannot do else than express ourselves according to our limited capacity. . . .

THE INCARNATION OF CHRIST[150]

. . . The angel of the Lord was sent to the holy Virgin, who was descended from David's line. "For it is evident that our Lord sprang out of Judah, of which tribe no one turned his attention to the altar" [Heb 7:14]. . . . And bearing glad tidings to her, [the angel] said, "Hail thou highly favored one, the Lord is with thee" [Lk 1:28]. And she was troubled at his word, and the angel said to her, "Fear not, Mary, for you have found favor with God, and shall bring forth a Son and shall call His name Jesus" [Lk 1:30–31]; for He shall save His people from their sins. Hence it comes that [the name] Jesus has the interpretation "Savior." And when she asked in her perplexity, "How can this be, seeing I know not a man?" [Lk 1:34]," the angel again answered her, "The Holy Spirit shall come upon you, and the power of the Highest shall overshadow you. Therefore also that holy thing which shall be born of you, shall be called the Son of God" [Lk 1:35]. And she said to him, "Behold the handmaiden of the Lord: be it unto me according to Thy word."

So then, after the assent of the Holy Virgin, the Holy Spirit descended on her . . . purifying her, and granting her power to receive the divinity of the Word, and likewise power to bring forth. And then was she overshadowed by enhypostatic Wisdom and the Power of the most high God, the Son of God Who is of like essence with the Father as of Divine seed, and from her holy and most pure blood He formed flesh animated with the spirit of reason and thought, the firstfruits of our compound nature; not by procreation but by creation through the Holy Spirit: not developing the fashion of the body by gradual additions but by perfecting it at once, He Himself, the very Word of God, standing to the flesh in the relation of subsistence. For the divine Word was not made one with flesh that had an independent preexistence, but taking up His abode in the womb of the holy Virgin . . . . So that He is at once flesh, and at the same time flesh of God and the Word, likewise flesh animated, possessing both reason and thought. Wherefore we speak not of man as having become God, but of God as having become Man. . . .

CONCERNING IMAGES[151]

. . . [S]ince some find fault with us for worshipping and honoring the image of our Savior and honoring the image of our Lady, and those, too, of the rest of the saints and servants of Christ, let them remember that in the beginning God cre-

---

[150] Ibid., Bk. III, ch. 2, p. 46.
[151] Ibid., Bk. IV, ch. 16, p. 38, with omissions.

ated man after His own image [Gen 1:26]. On what grounds, then, do we show reverence to each other unless because we are made after God's image? For as Basil, that much-versed expounder of divine things, says, the honor given to the image passes over to the prototype.[152] Now a prototype is that which is imaged, from which the derivative is obtained. Why was it that the Mosaic people honored . . . the tabernacle which bore an image and type of heavenly things, or rather of the whole creation? God indeed said to Moses, "Look that you make them after their pattern which was shown you on the mountain" [Ex 33:20]. The Cherubim, too, which overshadow the mercy seat, are they not the work of human hands [Ex 25:18]? What, further, is the celebrated temple at Jerusalem? Is it not hand-made and fashioned by skilled people? . . .

But besides this who can make an imitation of the invisible, incorporeal, uncircumscribed, formless God? Therefore to give form to the Deity is the height of folly and impiety. And hence it is that in the Old Testament the use of images was not common. But after God in His bowels of pity became in truth man for our salvation, not as He was seen by Abraham in the semblance of a man, nor as He was seen by the prophets, but in being truly man, and after He lived upon earth and dwelt among humanity, worked miracles, suffered, was crucified, rose again and was taken back to Heaven, since all these things actually took place and were seen by people, they were written for the remembrance and instruction of us who were not alive at that time in order that though we saw not, we may still, hearing and believing, obtain the blessing of the Lord. But seeing that not every one has a knowledge of letters nor time for reading, the Fathers gave their sanction to depicting these events on images as being acts of great heroism, in order that they should form a concise memorial of them. Often, doubtless, when we have not the Lord's passion in mind, and see the image of Christ's crucifixion, His saving passion is brought back to remembrance, and we fall down and worship not the material but that which is imaged; just as we do not worship the material of which the Gospels are made, nor the material of the Cross, but that which these typify. For wherein does the cross, that typifies the Lord, differ from a cross that does not do so? It is just the same also in the case of the Mother of the Lord. For the honor which we give to her is referred to Him Who was made of her incarnate. And similarly also the brave acts of holy men [and women] stir us up to be brave and to emulate and imitate their valor and to glorify God. For as we said, the honor that is given to the best of the fellow-servants is a proof of good-will towards our common Lady, and the honor rendered to the image passes over to the prototype. But this is an unwritten tradition, just as is also the worshipping towards the East and the worship of the Cross, and very many other similar things. . . .

---

[152]St. Basil the Great, *De Spiritus Sancto*, ch. 18.

CHAPTER 2

The Medieval Era

By the end of the era of the ancient church, Christianity in the East had reached fixed liturgical and theological forms that would endure into the modern era. In the Latin-speaking West, however, significant new developments lay ahead. The Church had weathered the stormy demise of the Roman Empire and had linked its earthly stability to the Christianized Carolingian Empire of the Franks under Charlemagne (800) and his descendants. In the cloisters, cathedral schools, and newly established universities, Christian learning and spirituality flourished, whether or not the same could always be said for the state of spirituality in culture at large. The Church emerged from the first millennium with renewed vigor. It was the dominant force in the formation of Western culture; so comprehensive were the Church's claims and influence that people spoke of "Christendom" to describe the ideal of a unified Western Europe under her leadership.

It was, as one popular treatment styled it, "the age of belief."[1] The greatest scholars of the Western world were theologians. They believed that religion offered solutions to life's most pressing problems; that Christian faith and life offered a point of integration and synthesis from which all knowledge and all reality could be understood in a comprehensive way. In short, the period of consolidation had passed. Having secured her foundations, the Church now turned inward to plumb the depths of her spiritual resources, and it also turned outward toward new horizons of experience and learning.

The Middle Ages was a very complex and vital period for Christian Spirituality. It seems possible, however, to summarize the dynamism of the era by pointing to three particular approaches to spirituality; the emergence of the mendicants, the scholastics, and the mystics signaled the spiritual vitality of the age.

---

[1]Anne Fremantle, *The Age of Belief* (New York: Meridian Books, 1984).

Louis Bouyer draws attention to a significant "crisis in monasticism" that occurred in the Middle Ages (1095–1145).[2] The crisis stemmed, in part, from the popularity and growth of Benedictine monasticism. With growth had come prosperity, and with prosperity had come a conflict between the ascetic ideal of being separated *from* the world and the challenges abbots of monastic orders faced when they wound up managing significant portions *of* the world. This tension brought reform within the established monastic traditions, such as that of Bernard of Clairvaux, whose efforts established the Cistercians within the Benedictine movement. Others, like Dominic (1170–1221) and Francis, established orders that stressed apostolic poverty as a fundamental and formative virtue. Dominican and Franciscan monks were "mendicants" (Lat. *mendicans*, "to beg") who, like the apostles of old, went into the world "without gold, silver or copper" [Mt 10:9]. The Dominicans described themselves as an Order of Preachers (O.P.), and devoted themselves to study and proclamation. The Franciscans described themselves as the Order of Friars Minor (O.F.M.)—"the lessor brothers"—as a sign of their service among the poor and outcasts. At the end of the Middle Ages, lay fellowships, like the Brethren of the Common Life and the Beguines, sought to popularize the spirituality and practices of revitalized monasticism among the laity.

Scholasticism is a summary term for describing the intellectual tone of the times. It had its roots in an academic renaissance that was spurred on by renewed interest in the resources of classical and Christian antiquity. It is defined in various ways. "Scholasticism" can describe the theological method derived from Aristotle's logic; it can describe the penchant for systematization that dominated the doctrine of the era; or it can describe the deductive-allegorical approach to Scripture that undergirded much of the theology of the period.[3] The spirituality that flowed from scholasticism, as epitomized by Anselm, was intellectually satisfying because of its philosophical and psychological depth. This was also a synthetic and inclusive spirituality, exemplified by Thomas Aquinas, that drew upon the best of the Christian past and shaped it into a new and more coherent whole.

Mysticism was not a new development, but it burst upon the landscape of the Middle Ages with renewed vigor. The resurgence of monasticism and the vitality of scholasticism contributed to the flowering of mysticism. Mystics were often members of the new or renewed religious orders. They frequently quoted or paraphrased the fathers and mothers of the ancient church, along with the Scriptures. But what set the mystics apart was their willingness to emphasize personal, immediate religious experience as a spiritual resource. The mystical way, because of its stress upon personal encounter with God, brought an exciting and intensely personal dimension to Christian Spirituality. There was also a (potentially) anarchic dimension to mysticism, since a person's religious experience—while often mediated by the channels of the church and Christian tradition—could also supersede other means of grace. Not surprisingly, a few of the mystics, like Meister Eckhart, came under sus-

---

[2]Louis Bouyer, Jean Leclercq, and Francois Vanderbroucke, *A History of Christian Spirituality*, Vol. II, *The Spirituality of the Middle Ages* (Minneapolis: Winston Press, 1968), p. 127ff.
[3]Ibid., pp. 223–26.

picion because of the idiosyncratic character of their teaching. Religious experience was also a great leveler of status and privilege in the church; through it the uneducated daughter of a poor family, like Catherine of Siena, could become a great teacher and spiritual leader.

Two distinct approaches to Christian mysticism emerged in this era. The one, teutonic or Rhineland mysticism, epitomized by Meister Eckhart, was sometimes called theosophic mysticism; it emphasized the inward pilgrimage of the human soul toward the Divine spark or presence at the ontological basis of our created nature. The second route, called Latin or Christocentric mysticism, exemplified by Catherine of Siena, looked outward to the acts and aspirations of Jesus Christ to find a basis for inner renewal that brought oneness with God.

Anselm of Canterbury (c. 1033–1109)

Anselm of Canterbury was born in Aosta, in northern Italy.[4] His formative years were spent in the Abbey of Bec, in Normandy, under the tutelage of Lanfranc. Anselm succeeded Lanfranc as Abbot of Bec (1078), and Archbishop of Canterbury (1093). A skilled philosopher and theologian, Anselm is considered the "father of scholasticism." His *Proslogian* and *Monologian* epitomized the rational exposition and defense of the faith that came to characterize scholastic methodology. Like St. Augustine before him, St. Anselm believed that faith preceded reason in the process of understanding; hence, his approach has often been summarized by the phrase *Credo ut intelligantum* ("I believe in order that I might know.")

Anselm's chief contribution to Christian Spirituality were his *Prayers and Meditations* (c. 1080) which he composed during his residency at Bec. Written in Latin poetic form, Anselm's prayers became important models for the development of personal prayer. They were not intended for congregational worship, but for the reflection of the solitary soul and the searching heart. Anselm's spirituality, both in its concerns and its articulation, is heavily dependent upon the *Confessions* of St. Augustine.

THE DIGNITY OF THE HUMAN ESTATE[5]

Our creation to the Image and Likeness of God. Awake, my soul, awake; bestir thy energies, arouse thy apprehension; banish the sluggishness of thy deadly sloth, and take to thee solicitude for thy salvation. Be the rambling of unprofitable fancies put to flight; let indolence retire, and diligence be retained. Apply thyself to

---

[4]G. R. Evans, *Anselm* (Wilton, Conn.: Morehouse Publishing, 1989), offers a brief but reliable examination of Anselm's life and thought.

[5]Reprinted from M.R., trans., *St. Anselm's Book of Meditations and Prayers* (London: Burns and Oats, 1872), "First Meditation," pp. 1–4.

sacred studies, and fix thy thoughts on the blessings that are of God. Leave temporal things behind, and make for the eternal. . . .

It was assuredly a noble purpose which He formed for the dignity of thy state, when, creating and ordering the universal frame of the visible and the invisible creation, He determined to make man; for He determined to lavish richer honours on man's nature than on all other creations in the universe. Behold thy lofty origin, and bethink thee of the due of love thou owest thy Creator. "Let Us make man," said God, "to Our Image and Likeness" [Gen 1:26]. If thou awakest not at this word, O my soul; if thou art not all aflame with love of Him for His so ineffable graciousness of condescension towards thee; if thine inmost marrow burns not with longings after Him, what shall I say? Asleep shall I call thee? Or must I rather think thee dead? Consider diligently, therefore, what it is to have been created to God's Image and God's Likeness; thou hast in this thought the sweet earnest of a pious meditation in which thy musings may have full play. . . .

God's Likeness, then, may be attained by us in this way; if, musing on Him as the Good, we study to be good; if, owning Him the Just, we strive to be just; if, contemplating Him the Merciful, we make endeavours after mercy.

But how to His Image? Listen. God ever remembers Himself, understands Himself, loves Himself. If thou, therefore, after thy poor fashion, art unweariedly mindful of God, if thou understandest God, if thou lovest God, thou wilt then be man "to His Image"; for thou wilt be striving to do that which God doest eternally. Tis the duty of man to bend his whole being to this task; that task of remembering, of understanding, and of loving the Highest Good. To this idea should every thought and every turn and folding of thy heart be moulded, chased, and formed; to be mindful of God, to understand Him, and to love Him; and thus savingly exhibit and display of thine origin in that thou wast created to the Image of the God. . . .

THE SINNER'S HOPE[6]

Breathe again, sinner, breathe again; do not despair; trust in Him thou fearest. Fly home to Him from Whom thou hast fled away; cry cravingly to Him Whom thou hast so proudly provoked. Jesus, Jesus; for the sake of this Thy Name, deal with me according to this Name. Jesus, Jesus; forget Thy proud provoker, and bend Thine eye upon the poor invoker of Thy Name, the Name so sweet, the Name so dear, the Name so full of comfort to a sinner, and so full of blessed hope. For what is Jesus but Saviour? Therefore, Jesus, for Thine own self's sake be a Jesus to me; Thou who formedst me, that I perish not; who redeemest me, that Thou condemn me not; who createdst me by Thy goodness, that Thy handiwork perish not by my iniquity. Recognise and own, Benignest, what is Thine; take away what is another's. Jesus, Jesus, [have] mercy on me, while the day of mercy lasts,

---

[6]Ibid., pp. 42–43.

that Thou damn me not in the day of judgment. For shall I go down into eternal corruption? "For the dead shall not praise Thee, O Lord, nor any of them that go down to hell" [Ps 113:17]. If Thou fold me in the wide, wide Bosom of Thy mercy, that Bosom will be none the less wide on my account. Therefore admit me, O most desired Jesus, admit me into the number of Thine elect; that with them I may praise Thee, and enjoy Thee, and make my boast in Thee amongst all who love Thy Name; who with the Father and the Holy Ghost reignest gloriously throughout unending ages. Amen.

CUR DEUS HOMO?[7]

Christian soul, soul raised from sad death, soul redeemed from miserable slavery and set free by the Blood of God, raise thy thoughts; bethink thee of thy revival from the dead, and ponder well the history of thy redemption and thy liberation. Consider where is the virtue of thy salvation, and what it is. Employ thyself in musing on it, delight thyself in contemplating it; shake off thy sloth, do violence to thy heart, bend thy whole mind to it; taste the goodness of thy Redeemer, break forth in fires of love to thy Saviour. Bite the honeycomb of the words that tell of it, suck their savour pleasant above honey, swallow their health-giving sweetness. Think, and so bite them; understand, and so suck them; love and rejoice, and so swallow them. Gladden thyself by biting, exult in sucking, fill thee to the full with joy by swallowing. Where and what is the virtue and the strength of thy salvation? Christ, Christ assuredly has raised thee up again; He, the good Samaritan, has healed thee; He, the good friend, has redeemed thee with His life, and set thee free. Christ, I say, Christ is He. And so the virtue of thy salvation is the virtue of Christ. And where is it; where is this His virtue? Of a truth, "horns are in His Hands, there is His strength hid" [Hab 3:4]. Yes, horns are in His Hands, for those Hands are fastened to the arms of the Cross. But O, what strength is there in such weakness? What grandeur in such humility? What worship in such contempt? But because in weakness, therefore it is a hidden thing; because in humility, it is veiled; because in contempt, it is concealed and covered up. O hidden strength! that Man fixed to a Cross should transfix the eternal death that oppressed the race of man; that Man bound to a tree should unbind the world which had been fast bound by perpetual death! O veiled omnipotence! that Man condemned with thieves should save men condemned with demons. O virtue concealed and covered up! that one Soul given up to torment should extricate innumerable souls from hell; should as man undergo the death of the body and destroy the death of souls. . . .

　　. . . For man is not restored to that for which he was created if he be not ad-

---

[7]Ibid., pp. 136–45. The Latin title of this meditation, "Why Did God Become Man?," was also the title of Anselm's most famous apologetic work; both works follow the same line of theological argumentation.

vanced to a likeness with the angels, in whom is no sin; which cannot possibly come to pass unless he have received remission of all his sins; and this is not effected without the preliminary of a perfect satisfaction, that satisfaction being of necessity such that the sinner, or some one in the sinner's behalf, offer to God something which is not due by way of debt, and which is of greater value than all that is not God. For if to sin is to dishonour God—and man ought not to commit sin even though the inevitable consequences were that all which is not God should perish—immutable truth and right reason of course require that he who sins should offer to God, by way of restitution for the honour taken from Him, something of greater worth than is that for which he ought not to have dishonoured Him [than all that is outside God]. And, since human nature had not this to give, nor yet could possibly be reconciled without payment of the satisfaction due; lest the justice of God should thus leave sin in God's kingdom—sin, a thing so repugnant to order of that kingdom—the goodness of God intervened, and the Son of God assumed [human nature] into His own Person, so that, in that Person, Man might be God, and thus possess what should not only transcend every existence which is not God, but also the whole sum of the debt which sinners owe; and since He owed nothing for Himself, should pay this in behalf of mankind at large, who had not wherewithal to pay what was due from them. For God-Man's life is of higher price than all that is not God, and transcends in worth all the debt which sinners owe by way of satisfaction. For if the putting Him to death surpasses all other sins, no matter what their heinousness or what their number, which can possibly be imagined outside of and away from the Person of God, it is clear that His life is greater as a good than all the sins outside of and away from the Person of God can ever be as evils. This His life God-Man, since death was not a thing He owed by way of debt, inasmuch as He was not a sinner, offered spontaneously, of His own treasure, to the honour of the Father; He offered it in permitting it, for His justice' sake, to be taken away from Him, that thus He might offer an example to all mankind that the justice of God is not to be foregone by them even on account of death, the death which is in their case a debt that they must needs of necessity pay some day. . . . Thus, then, Human Nature offered to God in that Man spontaneously and not as of debt that which was its own; so as to redeem itself in others, in whom it had not wherewith to pay what was required by way of debt. In all this the Divine Nature suffered no humiliation, but the Human was exalted; nor was the former in any way detracted from, but the latter was mercifully aided. . . .

Thus He, Man, redeems mankind, inasmuch as that which He has of His own will offered to God is reckoned as covering the debt which was owing from them. By which payment man is not only and merely once redeemed from his faults, but how often soever he returns to God with worthy repentance, he is received; a repentance, however, be it well borne in mind, which is not promised unconditionally and absolutely to the sinner. And since this payment was effected on the Cross, our Christ has by the Cross redeemed us. Those, then, who chose to approach with worthy disposition to this grace are saved; whilst those who despise it, since they pay not what is due from them, are justly damned.

MARY, QUEEN OF HEAVEN[8]

But amongst all the dwellers in heaven, be thine, O Mary, the richest and the fullest joy; thine, Virgin among virgins supereminent, Rose of celestial sweetness, bright Star above the brightest of all the primeval lights of Divine illumination. Rejoice with supreme and singular joy above all others; for the very Child whom thou didst bring to a human birth and didst nurse at thy breasts, that Child thou adorest, true and living God, together with angels and all the whole company of the citizens of heaven. Rejoice, O happy Mother, for Whom thou sawest hanging on the wood of the cross, thou now seest reigning in heaven with great glory; thou seest all the grandeurs of heaven, of earth, of hell, bowed down before His royal state, and all the might of His enemies crushed in the dust. All joy, all joy of joys is thine, thou plentitude of holiness, thou blessed Jerusalem, our Mother, who art above. Keep joyful holiday, sweet Mother, joyful and unending in peaceful vision of thy Jesus, the Author of thy immunity from sin.

THE ANNUNCIATION[9]

When, therefore, your mind has been purged from tumultuous thoughts by that practical exercise of virtues, then turn your cleansed eyes back to the past, and first of all enter with blessed Mary into her chamber, and unroll the sacred books in which are foretold a virgin's maternity and the birth of Christ. Then wait, expecting the arrival of the angel, that you may see him enter, and hear him salute her: that then, transported with ecstasy and wonder, you may with the greeting angel greet Mary, thy dearest Queen, saying with heart and voice, "Hail, Mary, full of grace; the Lord is with thee" [Lk 1:27]! Say it over and over again, and ask yourself what this fullness of grace may be, whence all the whole world has gathered grace; what may be the meaning of "the Word made Flesh." O muse, and wonder that the Lord who fills earth and heaven is shut up in that, a maiden's womb, whom the Father has sanctified, the Son taken for His mother, the Holy Ghost overshadowed. O dearest Queen, with what draughts of sweetness wast thou filled, with what fires of love wast thou inflamed, when in thy soul and in thy flesh thou didst own the Presence of so great a Majesty, He of thy flesh taking Flesh to Himself, and after the model of thy sacred limbs clothing Himself with limbs, wherein dwelt corporally all the fullness of the Godhead. And all this, virgin, in your behalf, that you might love the Virgin whom you have taken as a pattern for imitation, and the Virgin's Son, to whom you are espoused.

---

[8]Ibid., pp. 176–77.
[9]Ibid., pp. 199–200.

THE MIND AROUSED TO CONTEMPLATE GOD[10]

And now, poor mortal, avoid for a little while earthly employments, hide thee for a time from thy conflicting thoughts, throw aside thy burdensome cares, and postpone to another time all wearisome distractions. Retire for a little space to God, and rest thee for a while in Him. Enter into the closet of thy heart; shut out all except God, and what may help thee in thy quest of Him, and with closed door seek Him. And then say, O my whole heart, say at once to God, "I seek Thy Face; Thy Face, O Lord, will I seek."

Now, therefore, O Lord my God, teach Thou my heart where and how to seek Thee; when and how to find Thee. If Thou art not here, O Lord, whither shall I go to seek Thee? But if Thou art everywhere, why do I not see Thee here? No; for in truth Thou inhabitest the inapproachable light. But where is the inapproachable light? Or how shall I approach the inapproachable? Or who will lead me into it, that I may see Thee in it? And then, what are the tokens by which I am to seek Thee, what the aspect by which I am to know Thee? O Lord my God, I have never seen Thee, and I know not what Thou art like. . . .

O Lord, Thou art my God and my Lord, and I have never seen Thee. Thou hast made and remade me, and all the blessings that I have are of Thy giving; and as yet I do not know Thee. I was created to behold Thee, and as yet I have not attained to the object of my creation. O sad estate of man! for man has foregone that for which he was created. O hard, O cruel lot! What, alas, did he lose, and what did he find? What went, and what remained? He lost the beatitude for which he was created, and he found the misery for which he was never made; that went without which no happiness is, and that remained which of itself is merest misery. And then he ate the bread of sorrows, and knew it not.

Ah, the general anguish of mankind, the universal wailing of the sons of Adam! Our first father had bread to the full, and we cry out for hunger. He abounded, and we are beggars: he so happy in having, so sad in foregoing; we so unhappy in our need, so miserable in our craving! And yet we remain empty. Why did he not keep and guard, when he might have done it so easily, what we lack so grievously? Why, why did he so block out the light, and cover us up in darkness? Why did he filch away our life, and bring in death instead? O woebegone we! whence are we banished, whither are we driven? Whence hurled headlong, whither fallen low? From our home, to exile; from God and the vision of God, to self and its blindness; from the joys of immortality, to the horror and the bitterness of death. Miserable change! From how great good to how great ill!

Sad loss, sad grief, sad everything! But woe is me, poor me, one of the poor sons of Eve banished from their God. What have I endeavoured, what achieved? Whither did I tend, and what have I reached? To what did I aspire, and where am I now sighing, "I sought for peace, and there is no good; and for the time of healing, and behold trouble" [Jer 14:19].

---

[10]Ibid., pp. 281–86.

I reached forth to God, and I stumbled on self. I sought rest in my secret place, and "I met with trouble and sorrow" [Ps 104:3] in my inmost parts. I wished to return in the joy of my soul, and lo, I am forced "to roar with the groaning of my heart" [Ps 37:9]. Happiness was the goal of my hope, and lo, sigh is crowded upon sigh. And Thou, O Lord, how long? "How long, O Lord, wilt Thou forget me unto the end? how long dost Thou turn away Thy face from me" [Ps 12:1]? When wilt Thou look on me and hear me? When wilt Thou lighten mine eyes and show me Thy Face? When wilt Thou restore Thyself to me?

Look on me, O Lord, and hear me, and enlighten me, and show me Thyself. Restore Thyself to me, that it may be well with me; Thou, without whom it goes ill with me. Direct, O Lord, my labours and my endeavours unto Thee, for without Thee I am nothing worth. Thou invitest me; help me, O Lord, I pray Thee, that I sigh not from despair, but breathe again and hope. O Lord, I pray Thee, for it is soured by its lonesomeness, sweeten my heart with Thy consolations. O Lord, I pray Thee, for I have begun to seek Thee hungering, let me not go away empty; I have drawn near famished with want, let me not depart unsatisfied. I have come, a beggar to the Rich, a wretched to the All-merciful; let me not turn back despised and without an alms. And even if I sigh before I can eat, give me something to eat after I have sighed.

O Lord, I am bowed down low, and cannot look up; raise me, that I may lift mine eyes on high. "My iniquities are gone over my head" [Ps 37:5] and overwhelm me, "and as a heavy burden" they press me sore. Rescue me, unburden me; "let not the pit shut her mouth upon me" [Ps 68:16]. Be it mine to see Thy light from afar, even from the depth. Teach me to seek Thee; and when I seek, show Thyself; for I can neither seek Thee unless Thou teach me, nor find Thee unless Thou show Thyself to me. Let me seek Thee by desiring, and desire Thee in seeking; let me find Thee by loving, and love Thee in finding. I confess to Thee, O Lord, and I give Thee thanks that Thou hast created me in Thine image, so as ever mindfully to muse on Thee and love Thee. But if the image is so defaced by the wear and waste of evil habits, and so befouled with the smoke and stain of sins, that it cannot do that for which it was created unless Thou remake and readorn it. I do not essay to sound Thy depths, O Lord, for I no way match my understanding to such an effort; but I do long in some sort to understand that truth of Thine which my heart believes and loves; for I seek not to understand that I may believe, but I believe that I may understand.

Bernard of Clairvaux (1090–1153)

Bernard of Clairvaux was born in a pious and aristocratic home at Fontaines, about two miles from Dijon, France. Even from his boyhood Bernard had been deeply religious, so it was not entirely surprising that he became a monk at the abbey of Citeaux in 1112. What was more surprising, but also characteristic of St. Bernard, was the fact that he persuaded about thirty of his friends to join the Benedictine Order with him. Bernard is considered to be a founder of the Cistercian Order that emerged from Citeaux, and one of the great reformers of Benedictine spirituality. In 1115 he was sent to Clairvaux to establish a monastery along the lines of Citeaux. Bernard served as head of that house until his death. No fewer than 900 monks joined the community at Clairvaux, under St. Bernard's guidance. He personally instigated the founding of sixty-four new Cistercian houses. Because of his spiritual insight and influence, his contemporaries called St. Bernard "the conscience of Europe."

As a theologian Bernard stood in the Augustinian tradition. Like Anselm before him, St. Bernard believed it was necessary to grasp religious truth by faith before one could probe its meaning. His personal mysticism caused Bernard to look from the mind (as in Anselm) to religious experience for certitude. His theology was deeply concerned about the reality of humans being created in the image of God, and the unity that remains between humans and their Creator. Bernard found this most powerfully expressed and experienced in terms of love (Lat. *caritas*). His interior theology was often phrased in the language of romantic love and courtship. Bernard understood the love song of the Hebrew Scriptures, *Canticles*, as a vivid description of the soul's relationship with God; his sermons on Song of Songs were among his most influential works. His main treatise on spiritual instruction, *On Loving God (c. 1126)*, explored the same theme. Bernard's piety was Christocentric; as an exegete and mystic he stood closer to the style of Origen than to that of St. Augustine.

FOUR DEGREES OF LOVE[11]

First Degree: When One Loves Self for One's Own Sake

. . . because nature has become rather frail and weak, people are driven by necessity to serve nature first. This results in bodily love, by which a person loves himself for his own sake. He does not yet know anything but himself, as it is written, "First came what is animal, then what is spiritual" [1 Cor 15:46]. This love is not imposed by rule but is innate in nature. For who hates his own flesh [Eph 5:29]? But if that same love begins to get out of proportion and headstrong, as often happens, and it ceases to be satisfied to run in the narrow channel of its needs, but floods out on all sides into the fields of pleasure, then the overflow can be stopped at once by the commandment "You shall love your neighbor as yourself" [Mt 22:39].

It is wholly right that he [or she] who is your fellow in nature [2 Pet 1:4] should not be cut off from you in grace, especially in that grace which is innate in nature. If a person feels it [is] a heavy burden to help his brothers in their need and to share in their pleasures, let him keep his desires in check all by himself if

---

[11]Reprinted from G. R. Evans, trans., *Bernard of Clairvaux: Selected Works.* Copyright 1987 by The Missionary Society of St. Paul the Apostle in the State of New York. Used by permission of Paulist Press. Pages 192–96, with omissions.

he does not want to fall into sin. He can indulge himself as much as he likes as long as he remembers to show an equal tolerance to his neighbor. O man, the laws of life and discipline impose restraint [Sir 45:6] to prevent you chasing after your desires until you perish [Sir 18:30], and to save you from making of nature's good things a way to serve the soul's enemy through lust.

Is it not much more right and honest to share nature's goods with your fellow man, that is, your neighbor, than with an enemy? If you take the advice of Wisdom and turn away from your pleasures [Sir 18:30] and make yourself content with food and clothing as the Apostle teaches [1 Tim 6:8], soon you will find that your love is not impeded by carnal desires which fight against the soul [1 Pet 2:11]. I think you will find it a burden to share with your fellow man what you withhold from the enemy of your soul. Then will your love be sober and just, when you do not deny your brother what he needs from the pleasures you have denied yourself. It is in this way that bodily love is shared, when it is extended to the community. . . .

But to love one's neighbor with perfect love is necessary to be prompted by God. How can you love your neighbor with purity if you do not love him in God? But he who does not love God cannot love in God. You must love God, so that in Him you can love your neighbor too [Mk 12:30–31]. God therefore brings about your love for Him, just as He causes other goods. This is how He does it: He who made nature also protects it. For it was so created that it needs its Creator as its Protector, so that what could not have come into existence without Him cannot continue in existence without Him. So that no rational creature might be in ignorance of this fact and (dreadful thought) claim for him [or her] self the gifts of the Creator, the same Creator willed by a high and saving counsel that humans should endure tribulation; then when people fail and God comes to their aid and sets them free, they will honor God as He deserves. For this is what He says: "Call upon me in the day of tribulation. I will deliver you, and you shall honor me" [Ps 50:15]. And so in that way it comes about that man who is a bodily animal [1 Cor 2:14], and does not know how to love anything but himself, begins to love God for his own benefit, because he learns from frequent experience that in God he can do everything which is good for him [Phil 4:13], and that without Him he can do nothing [Jn 15:5].

Second Degree: When One Loves God for One's Own Good

Man therefore loves God, but as yet he loves Him for his own sake, not for God's. Nevertheless the wise person ought to know what he can do by himself and what he can do only with God's help; then you will avoid hurting him who keeps you from harm.

If a person has a great many tribulations and as a result he [or she] frequently turns to God and frequently experiences God's liberation, surely even he [or she] had a breast of iron or a heart of stone [Ezek 11:19], he [or she] must soften toward the generosity of the Redeemer and love God not only for his own benefit, but for Himself?

Third Degree: When One Loves God for God's Sake

Humanity's frequent needs make it necessary for us to call upon God often, and to taste by frequent contact, and to discover by tasting how sweet the Lord is [Ps 34:9]. It is in this way that the taste of His own sweetness leads us to love God in purity more than our need alone would prompt us to do. The Samaritans set us an example when they said to the woman who told them the Lord was there, "Now we believe, not because of your words, but because we have heard Him for ourselves and we know that truly He is the Savior of the world" [Jn 4:42]. In the same way, I urge, let us follow their example and rightly say to our flesh, "Now we love God not because he meets your needs; but we have tasted and we know how sweet the Lord is" [Ps 34:9].

There is a need of the flesh which speaks out, and the body tells by its actions of the kindness it has experienced. And so it will not be difficult for the person who has had that experience to keep the commandment to love his [or her] neighbor [Mk 12:31]. He truly loves God, and therefore he loves what is God's. He loves chastely, and to the chaste it is no burden to keep the commandments; the heart grows purer in the obedience of love, as it is written [1 Pet 1:22]. Such a person loves justly and willingly keeps the just law.

This love is acceptable because it is given freely. It is chaste because it is not made up of words or talk, but of truth and action [1 Jn 3:18]. It is just because it gives back what it has received. For he who loves in this way loves as he is loved. He loves, seeking in return not what is his own [1 Cor 13:5], but what is Jesus Christ's, just as He has sought not His own but our good, or rather, our very selves [2 Cor 12:14]. He who says, "We trust in the Lord for He is good" [Ps 118:1] loves in this way. He who trusts in the Lord not because He is good to him, but simply because He is good truly loves God for God's sake and not for his [or her] own. He of whom it is said, "He will praise you when you do Him favors" [Ps 49:19] does not love in this way. That is the third degree of love, in which, God is already loved for His own sake.

Fourth Degree: When One Loves Oneself for the Sake of God

Happy is the one who has been found worthy to attain to the fourth degree, where a person loves him [or her] self only for God's sake. "O God, your justice is like the mountains of God" [Ps 36:7]. That love is a mountain, and a high mountain of God. Truly, "a rich and fertile mountain" [Ps 67:16]. "Who will climb the mountain of the Lord" [Ps 23:3]? "Who will give me wings like a dove, and I shall fly there and rest" [Ps 55:7]? That place was made a place of peace and it has its dwelling-place in Sion [Ps 76:3]. "Alas for me, my exile has been prolonged!" [Ps 120:5]. When will flesh and blood [Mt 16:17], this vessel of clay [2 Cor 4:7], this earthly dwelling [Wis 9:15], grasp this? When will it experience this kind of love, so that the mind, drunk with Divine love and forgetting itself, making itself like a broken vessel [Ps 30:13], throws itself wholly on God and, clinging to God [1 Cor 6:17], becomes one with Him in spirit and says, "My body and my heart have fainted, O God of my heart; God, my part in eternity" [Ps 73:26]? I should call Him blessed and holy to whom it is given to experience even for a single instant something which is rare indeed in this life. To lose yourself as though you did not exist and to have no sense of yourself, to be emptied out of yourself [Phil 2:7] and almost annihilated, belongs to heavenly not to a human love.

And indeed any mortal is rapt for a moment or is, so to speak, admitted for a moment to this union, at once the world presses itself on him [Gal 1:4], the day's wickedness troubles him, the mortal body weighs him down, bodily needs distract him, he fails because of the weakness of his corruption and—more powerfully than these—brotherly love calls him back. Alas, he is forced to come back to himself, to fall again into his affairs, and to cry out wretchedly, "Lord, I endure violence; fight back for me" [Is 38:14], and "Unhappy man that I am, who will free me from the body of this death" [Rom 7:24]?

But since Scripture says that God made everything for himself [Prov 16:4] there will be a time when He will cause everything to conform to its Maker and be in harmony with Him. In the meantime, we must make this our desire; that as God Himself willed that everything should be for Himself, so we, too, will that nothing, not even ourselves, may be or have been except for Him, that is according to His will, not ours. The satisfaction of our needs will not bring us happiness, not chance delights, as does the sight of His will being fulfilled in us and in everything which concerns us. That is what we ask every day in prayer when we say, "Your will be done, on earth as it is in heaven" [Mt 6:10]. O holy and chaste love! O sweet and tender affection! O pure and sinless intention of the will—the more pure and sinless in that there is no mixture of self-will in it, the more sweet and tender in that everything it feels is divine.

To love in this way is to become like God. As a drop of water seems to disappear completely in a quantity of wine, taking the wine's flavor and color; as red-hot iron becomes indistinguishable from the glow of fire and its own original form disappears; as air suffused with the light of the sun seems transformed into the brightness of the light, as if it were itself light rather than merely lit up; so, in those who are holy, it is necessary for human affection to dissolve in some ineffable way, and be poured into the will of God. How will God be all in all [1 Cor 15:26] if anything of man remain in man? The substance remains, but in another form, with another glory, another power.

When will this be? Who will see this? Who will possess it? "When shall I come and when shall I appear in God's presence" [Ps 42:3]? O Lord my God, "My heart said to you, 'My face has sought you. Lord, I will seek your face' [Ps 27:8]." Shall I see your holy temple [Ps 27:4]?

I think that cannot be until I do as I am bid. "Love the Lord your God with all your heart and with all your soul and with all your strength" [Mk 12:30]. Then the mind will not have to think of the body. The soul will no longer have to give the body life and feeling, and its power will be set free of these ties and strengthened by the power of God. For it is impossible to draw together all that is in you and turn toward the face of God as long as the care of the weak and miserable body demands one's attention. So it is in a spiritual and immortal body, a perfect body, beautiful and at peace and subject to the spirit in all things, that the soul hopes to attain the fourth degree of love, or rather, to be caught up to it; for it lies in God's power to give to whom He will. It is not to be obtained by human effort. That, I say, is when a person will easily reach the fourth degree; when no entanglements of the flesh hold him back and no troubles will disturb him, as he hurries with great speed and eagerness to the joy of the Lord [Mt 25:21,25].

But do we not think that the holy martyrs received this grace while they were still in their victorious bodies—at least in part? They were so moved within by the great force of their love that they were able to expose their bodies to outward torments and think nothing of them. The sensation of outward pain could do no more than whisper across the surface of their tranquility; it could not disturb it. But what of those who are already free of the body? We believe that they are wholly immersed in that sea of eternal life and bright eternity. . . .

Hildegard of Bingen (1098–1179)

Hildegard of Bingen was the precocious daughter of a noble family. Since she was their tenth child, her parents offered her "as a tithe" to the church. At eight years of age, Hildegard began serving in the hermitage of Dame Jutta in the Benedictine monastery of St. Disibod, in Germany. Hildegard took vows as a nun in 1113, at the age of fifteen. In 1136, upon the death of Jutta, she became superior of the monastery. She subsequently established a new community at Rupertsberg (1150) and served as its abbess.

St. Hildegard evidenced an extraordinary array of achievements. She has been heralded as the most significant woman author and musical composer of the period.[12] Her theological trilogy was cast in visionary imagery reminiscent of the Old Testament prophets. Her *magna opus*, *Scitio vias Domini* (1151), which took ten years to complete, comprised twenty-six visions along with their theological interpretation. She composed seventy-seven songs, as well as a morality play entitled *Ordo Virtum* ("The Ritual of the Virtues"), which is still performed today. Her interests also included medicine and the physical sciences, and were evidenced in Hildegard's *Book of Medicine*.

Her spirituality was fired by a dramatic visionary call from God, which Hildegard received in 1141; but she had sensed in herself "wonderfully the power and mystery of secret and admirable visions" from the age of five.[13] She understood her prophetic ministry as being the direct response to this remarkable call from God: ". . . I spoke and wrote these things not by the invention of my heart or that of any other person, but as by the secret mysteries of God I heard and received them in

---

[12]Cf. Harvey Egan, *An Anthology of Christian Mysticism* (Collegeville, Min.: Liturgical Press, 1991), p. 197.

[13]Columba Hart and Jane Bishop, trans., *Hildegard of Bingen: Scivas* (Mahwah, N.J.: Paulist Press, 1990). Copyright 1990, by The Missionary Society of St. Paul the Apostle in the State of New York. Used by permission of Paulist Press. Page 60, "The Declaration."

the heavenly places. And . . . I heard a voice from Heaven saying to me, 'Cry out therefore, and write thus!'"[14]

Although her theology was cast in the somewhat unconventional form of visions and the interpretation of visions, its content was conventional, and it won the warm approval of Pope Eugenius III and St. Bernard of Clairvaux. St. Hildegard and her work are perhaps best understood from the standpoint of her role as a prophet and reformer. She was a prophet of OT intensity, who directed her call to repentance to clergy and laity alike. As a reformer, she stood in the Gregorian tradition, stressing both clerical purity and spiritual power.[15]

GOD ENTHRONED[16]

I saw a great mountain of the color of iron, and enthroned on it One of such great glory that it blinded my sight. On each side of him there extended a soft shadow, like a swing of wondrous breadth and length. Before him, at the foot of the mountain, stood an image full of eyes on all sides, in which, because of those eyes, I could discern no human form. In front of this image stood another, a child wearing a tunic of subdued color but white shoes. upon whose head such glory descended from the One enthroned upon that mountain that I could not look at its face. But from the One who sat enthroned upon that mountain many living sparks sprang forth, which flew very sweetly around the images. Also, I perceived in this mountain many little windows, in which appeared human heads, some of subdued colors and some white.

And behold, He who was enthroned upon that mountain cried out in a strong, loud voice saying, "O human, who are fragile dust of the earth and ashes of ashes! Cry out and speak of the origin of pure salvation until those people are instructed, who, though they see the inmost contents of the Scriptures, do not wish to tell them or preach them, because they are lukewarm and sluggish in serving God's justice. Unlock for them the enclosure of mysteries that they, timid as they are, conceal in a hidden and fruitless field. Burst forth into a fountain of abundance and overflow with mystical knowledge, until they who now think you contemptible because of Eve's transgression are stirred up by the flood of your irrigation. For you have received your profound insight not from humans, but from the lofty and tremendous Judge on high, where this calmness will shine strongly with glorious light among the shining ones.

"Arise therefore, cry out and tell what is shown to you by the strong power of God's help, for He Who rules every creature in might and kindness floods those who fear Him and serve Him in sweet love and humility with the glory of heavenly enlightenment and leads those who persevere in the way of justice to the joys of the Eternal Vision."

---

[14]Ibid., p. 61.

[15]Frances and Joseph Gies, *Women in the Middle Ages* (New York: Harper, 1978), pp. 63–97, offer an excellent overview of the life and times of St. Hildegard.

[16]Reprinted from Hart and Bishop, trans., *Hildegard of Bingen.* Used by permission of Paulist Press. Pages 67–69, "Vision One: God Enthroned Shows Himself to Hildegard."

1. The strength and stability of God's eternal Kingdom

    As you see, therefore, *the great mountain the color of iron*, symbolizes the strength and stability of the eternal Kingdom of God, which no fluctuation of mutability can destroy; and *the One enthroned upon it of such great glory that it blinds your sight* is the One in the kingdom of beatitude Who rules the whole world with celestial divinity in the brilliance of unfading serenity, but is incomprehensible to human minds. But that *on each side of him there extends a soft shadow like a wing of wonderful breadth and length* shows that both in admonition and in punishment ineffable justice displays sweet and gentle protection and perseveres in true equity.

2. Concerning the fear of the Lord

    And before him at the foot of the mountain stands an image full of eyes on all sides. For the Fear of the Lord stands in God's presence with humility and gazes on the Kingdom of God, surrounded by the clarity of a good and just intention, exercising her zeal and stability among humans. And thus *you can discern no human form in her on account of those eyes.* For by the acute sight of her contemplation she counters all forgetfulness of God's justice, which people often feel in their mental tedium, so no inquiry by weak mortals eludes her vigilance.

3. Concerning those who are poor in spirit

    And so before this image appears another image, that of a child, wearing a tunic of subdued color but white shoes. For when the Fear of the Lord leads, they who are poor in spirit follow; for the Fear of the Lord holds fast in humble devotion to the blessedness of poverty of spirit, which does not seek boasting or elation of heart, but loves simplicity and sobriety of mind, attributing its just works not to itself but to God in pale subjection, wearing, as it were, a tunic of subdued color and faithfully following the serene footsteps of the Son of God. *Upon her head descends such glory from the One enthroned upon that mountain that you cannot look at her face;* because He Who rules every created being imparts the power and strength of this blessedness by the great clarity of His visitation, and weak, mortal thought cannot grasp His purpose, since He Who possesses celestial riches submitted himself humbly to poverty.

4. They who fear God and love poverty of spirit are the guardians of virtues

    But from the One Who is enthroned upon that mountain many living sparks go forth, which fly about those images with great sweetness. This means that many exceedingly strong virtues come forth from Almighty God, darting fire in divine glory; these ardently embrace and captivate those who truly fear God and who faithfully love poverty of spirit, surrounding them with their help and protection.

5. The aims of human acts cannot be hidden from God's knowledge

    Wherefore in this mountain you see many little windows, in which appear human heads, some of subdued color and some white. For in the most high and profound and perspicuous knowledge of God the aims of human acts cannot be concealed or hidden. Most often they display both lukewarmness and purity, since people now slumber in guilt, weary in their hearts and in their deeds, and now awaken and keep watch in honor. Solomon bears witness to this for Me, saying:

6. Solomon on this subject

"The slothful hand has brought about poverty, but the hand of the industrious man prepares riches" [Prov 10:4]; which means, a person makes himself weak and poor when he will not work justice, or avoid wickedness, or pay a debt, remaining idle in the face of the wonders of the works of beatitude. But one who does strong works of salvation, running in the way of truth, obtains the upwelling fountain of glory, by which he prepares himself most precious riches on earth and in Heaven.

Therefore, whoever has knowledge in the Holy Spirit and wings of faith, let this one not ignore My admonition but taste it, embrace it and receive it in his soul.

THE LAST DAYS AND THE FALL OF THE ANTICHRIST[17]

Then I looked to the North, and behold! five beasts stood there. One was like a dog, fiery but not burning; another was like a yellow lion; another was like a pale horse; another like a black pig; and the last like a gray wolf. And they were facing the West. And in the West, before those beasts, a hill with five peaks appeared; and from the mouth of each beast one rope stretched to one of the peaks of the hill. All the ropes were black except the one that came from the mouth of the wolf, which was partly black and partly white. And lo, in the East I saw again that youth whom I had first seen on the corner of the wall of the building where the shining and stone parts came together, clad in a purple tunic. I saw him on the same corner, but now I could see him from the waist down. And from the waist down to the place that denotes the male he glowed like the dawn, and there a harp was lying with its strings across his body; and from there to the width of two fingers above his heel he was in shadow, but from there down to the bottom of the feet he was whiter than milk. And I saw again the figure of a woman whom I had previously seen in front of the altar that stands before the eyes of God; she stood in the same place, but now I saw her from the waist down. And from her waist to the place that denotes the female, she had various scaly blemishes; and in that latter place was a black and monstrous head. It had fiery eyes, and ears like an ass', and nostrils and mouth like a lion's; it opened wide its jowls and terribly clashed its horrible iron-colored teeth. . . . And behold, there came suddenly a thunderbolt, which struck that head with such great force that it fell from the mountain and yielded up its spirit in death. And a reeking cloud enveloped the whole mountain, which wrapped the head in such filth that the people who stood by were thrown into the greatest terror. And that cloud remained around the mountain for a while longer. The people who stood there, perceiving this, were shaken with great fear, and said to one another: "Alas, alas! What is this? What do you think this was? Alas, wretches that we

---

[17]Ibid. Used by permission of Paulist Press. Pages 493–511, "Vision Eleven."

are! Who will help us, and who will deliver us? For we know not how we were deceived. O Almighty God, have mercy on us! Let us return, let us return; let us hasten to the covenant of Christ's Gospel; for ah, ah, ah! we have been bitterly deceived!" And lo, the feet of the figure of the woman glowed white, shining with a splendor greater than the sun's. And I heard the voice from Heaven saying to me:

1. The five ferocious epochs of temporal rule

    All things that are on earth hasten to their end, and the world droops toward its end, oppressed by the weakening of its forces and its many tribulations and calamities. But the Bride of My Son, very troubled for her children both by the forerunners of the son of perdition and by the destroyer himself, will never be crushed, no matter how much they attack her. But at the end of time she will rise up stronger than ever, and become more beautiful and more glorious; and so she will move sweetly and delightfully to the embraces of her Beloved. And this is mystically signified by the vision you are seeing. For *you look to the North, and behold! five beasts stand there.* These are the five ferocious epochs of temporal rule, brought about by the desires of the flesh from which the taint of sin is never absent, and they savagely rage against each other. . . .

7. The five peaks and the five ropes

    And in the West, before those beasts, a hill with five peaks appears; for in these peaks is symbolized the power of carnal desire. *And from the mouth of each beast one rope stretches to one of the peaks of the hill;* for each of those powers will extend throughout the period in question. *All the ropes are black except for the one that comes from the mouth of the wolf, which is partly black and partly white.* For the length of the ropes indicates how far people are willing to go in their stubborn pleasures; but though the one that symbolizes greed is partly black and puts forth many evils, yet some will come from that direction who are white with justice. And these latter will hasten to resist the son of perdition by ardent wonders, as My servant Job indicates about the righteous doer of justice, when he says

8. Words of Job

    "The innocent shall be raised up against the hypocrite, and the just shall hold to his path; and to clean hands he shall add strength" [Job 17:8–9]. Which is to say:

    One who is innocent of bloody deeds, murder and fornication and the like, will be aroused like a burning coal against one who deceives in his works. How? This latter speaks of honey but deals in poison, and calls a man friend but stifles him like an enemy; he speaks sweet words but has malice within him, and talks blandly to his friend and then slays him from ambush. But one who has a rod with which to drive away vile brutes from himself walks in the light of the shining sun on the righteous path of his heart; he is raised up in the sight of God as a bright spark and a clear light and a flaming torch. And so, bearing himself the strongest and purest works, he puts them on like a breastplate and a sharp sword, and drives away vice and wins virtue.

9. The Church will shine in her justice until the time of Antichrist

And therefore, *in the East you see again that youth whom you first saw on the corner of the wall of the building where the shining and stone parts come together, clad in a purple tunic, now standing on the same corner.* For here is the Sunrise of Justice, the Son of Man, manifest to you to confirm the truth afresh through His mysteries and miracles; still presiding over the union of reflective knowledge and human deeds, having shed His blood by the will and goodness of the Father for the salvation of the world. So *now you can see him from the waist down;* for now you see Him in the strength of His members who are His elect, and He will flourish as Bridegroom of the Church, with many obscure signs and wonders, until their number is complete. *And from the waist down to the place that denotes the male he glows like the dawn;* for until the time of the son of perdition, who will pretend to be the man of strength, His faithful members will be perfected in fortitude and He will be splendid in the justice of His righteous worshippers. *So, in the same place, a harp is lying with its strings across his body;* which signifies the joyful songs of those who will suffer dire torments in the persecution that the son of iniquity will inflict upon the chosen, torturing their bodies so much that they are released from them and pass over into rest.

10. The Church's faith will be in doubt until the witness of Enoch and Elijah

And from there to the width of two fingers above his heel he is in shadow. For, from the time of the persecution the faithful will suffer from the son of the Devil until the testimony of the two witnesses, Enoch and Elijah, who spurned the earthly and worked toward heavenly desires, faith in the doctrines of the Church will be in doubt. People will say to each other with great sadness, "What is this they say about Jesus? Is it true or not?" . . .

13. When justice grows cold the Church will undergo suffering and persecution

And you see again the figure of a woman whom you previously saw in front of the altar that stands before the eyes of God, standing in the same place. For the Bride of the Son of God is shown to you again, to reveal the truth, always present to the pure prayers of the saints and, as was said before, offering them up devotedly to the eyes of Heaven. *But now you see her from the waist down;* for you see her in full dignity as the Church, replete with the full number of her children, in the mysteries and wonders by which she has saved so many. *And from her waist to the place that denotes female, she has various scaly blemishes.* This is to say that, though she is now flourishing worthily and laudably in her children, before the time in which the son of perdition will try to perfect the trick he played on the first woman, the Church will be harshly reproached for many vices, fornication, and murder and rapine. How? Because those who should love her will violently persecute her. . . .

18. Why God now utters new mysteries by the mouth of an unlearned person

But now the Catholic faith wavers among the nations and the Gospel limps among the people; and the mighty books in which the excelling doctors had summed up knowledge with great care go unread from shameful apathy, and the food of life, which is the divine Scriptures, cools to tepidity. For this reason, I now speak through a person who is not eloquent in the Scriptures or taught by an earthly teacher; I Who Am speak through her of new secrets and mystical truths, heretofore hidden in books, like one who mixes clay and then shapes it to any form he wishes.

19. God's warning to the learned not to spurn these words but exalt them

O fruitful and rewarding teachers! Redeem your souls and loudly proclaim these words, and do not disbelieve them; for if you spurn them, you condemn not them but Me Who am Truth. For you should nurture My people under My law, and care for them until the time for their supervision is past, and all cares and labors cease. But from now on the predestined epoch is approaching, and you are hastening toward the time when the son of perdition will appear. Grow therefore in vigor and fortitude, My elect! Be on your guard, lest you fall into the snare of death; raise the victorious banner of these words, and crush upon the son of iniquity. For those who forerun and follow the son of perdition whom you call Antichrist are in the way of error; but as for you, follow the footsteps of Him Who taught you the way of truth, when He appeared with humility and not with pride in the world in the body. . . .

40. When the Antichrist is dead the Church will shine to recall the erring

And lo, the feet of the figure of the woman glow white, shining with a splendor greater than the sun's. This is to say that when the son of perdition is laid prostrate, as was said, and many of those who had erred return to the truth, the Bride of My Son, standing on a strong foundation, will manifest purity of faith and the beauty that surpasses all the beauty of the glories of earth. . . .

Bonaventure (1221–74)

Giovanni Fidanza was born in Tuscany, in central Italy, at Bagnorea. He attended the University of Paris, where he entered the Franciscan Order (1242). St. Bonaventure taught theology at the University of Paris, and was made minister general (head) of the Franciscans (1257). He subsequently served as Bishop of Albano (1273). In 1274 he was elevated to the cardinalate and played a prominent role in the second Council of Lyons. He died during the council and was buried at Lyons.

So significant was St. Bonaventure's role in the development of the Franciscans that he is regarded as a second founder of the movement. Bonaventure was St. Francis's most prominent biographer, and his *Life of St. Francis* (1266) became the standard text of the Order and one of the most popular books of the Middle Ages. *The Mind's Road to God* (c. 1259) was Bonaventure's most representative original work. It too began on a biographical note, reflecting upon Francis's vision of the six-winged Seraph. The six wings corresponded to the six stages of illumination by which the human soul ascends toward God. Within these six stages are three modes of human understanding: reflecting upon the natural world, considering our natural powers, and receiving illumination through Christ our Mediator. Each of these three modes offered a twofold understanding, since God is seen *through* them, and *in* them.[18]

"REPAIR MY HOUSE"[19]

Up to this time . . . Francis was ignorant of God's plan for him. He was distracted by the external affairs of his father's business and drawn down toward earthly things by the corruption of human nature. As a result, he had not yet learned how to contemplate the things of heaven nor had he acquired a taste of the things of God. Since "affliction can enlighten our spiritual awareness" [Is 28:19], "the hand of the Lord came upon him" [Ezek 1:3], "and the right hand of God effected a change in him" [Ps 77:11]. God afflicted his body with a prolonged illness in order to prepare his soul for the anointing of the Holy Spirit. After his strength was restored, when he had dressed as usual in his fine clothes, he met a certain knight who was of noble birth, but poor and badly clothed. Moved to compassion for his poverty, Francis took off his own garments and clothed the man on the spot. At one and the same time he fulfilled the two-fold duty of covering over the embarrassment of a noble knight and relieving the poverty of a poor man.

The following night, when he had fallen asleep, God in His goodness showed him a large and splendid palace full of military weapons emblazoned with the insignia of Christ's cross. Thus God vividly indicated that the compassion he had exhibited toward the poor knight for love of the supreme King would be repaid with an incomparable reward. And so when Francis asked to whom these belonged, he received an answer from heaven that all these things were for him and his knights. When he awoke in the morning, he judged the strange vision to be an indication that he would have great prosperity; for he had no experience in interpreting Divine mysteries nor did he know how to pass through visible images to grasp the invisible truth beyond. Therefore, still ignorant of God's plan, he decided to join a certain count in Apulia, hoping in his service to obtain the glory of knighthood, as his vision seemed to foretell.

He set out on his journey shortly afterwards; but when he had gone as far as the next town, he heard during the night the Lord address him in a familiar way, saying: "Francis, who can do more for you, a lord or a servant, a rich man or a poor man?" When Francis replied that a lord and a rich man could do more, he was at once asked: "Why, then, are you abandoning the Lord for a servant and the rich God for a poor man?" And Francis replied: "Lord, what will you have me do" [Acts 9:6]? And the Lord answered him: "'Return to your own land' [Gen

---

[18]Ian McGreal, "The Mind's Road to God," in *Christian Spirituality*, edited by Frank Magill and Ian McGreal (San Francisco: Harper & Row, 1988), pp. 122–27; Ewert Cousins, trans., *Bonaventure: The Soul's Journey into God, the Tree of Life, the Life of St. Francis* (New York: Paulist Press, 1978), "Introduction," pp. 18–37.

[19]Reprinted from Cousins, trans., *Bonaventure*. Copyright 1978, by The Missionary Society of St. Paul the Apostle in the State of New York. Used by kind permission of Paulist Press. Pages 187–94, "The Life of St. Francis," with omissions.

32:9], because the vision which you have seen foretells a spiritual outcome which will be accomplished in you not by human but by divine planning." In the morning, then, he returned in haste to Assisi, joyous and free of care; already a model of obedience, he awaited the Lord's will.

From that time on he withdrew from the bustle of public business and devoutly begged God in His goodness to show him what he should do. The flame of heavenly desire was fanned in him by his frequent prayer, and his desire for his heavenly home led him to despise as nothing all earthly things. He realized that he had found "a hidden treasure," and like the wise merchant he planned "to sell all he had" and to buy "the pearl he had found" [Mt 13:44–46]. Nevertheless, how he should do this, he did not yet know; but it was being suggested to him inwardly that to be a spiritual merchant he must be going with contempt for the world and to be a knight of Christ one must begin with victory over one's self.

One day while he was riding on horseback through the plain that lies below the town of Assisi, he came upon a leper. This unforeseen encounter struck him with horror. But he recalled his resolution to be perfect and remembered that he must first conquer himself if he wanted to become a knight of Christ. He slipped off his horse and ran to kiss the man. When the leper put out his hand as if to receive some alms, Francis gave him the money and a kiss. Immediately mounting his horse, Francis looked all around; but although the open plain stretched clear in all directions, he could not see the leper anywhere. Filled with wonder and joy, he began devoutly to sing God's praises, resolving from this always to strive to do greater things in the future.

After that he began to seek out solitary places, well suited for sorrow; and there he prayed incessantly with "unutterable groaning" [Rom 8:26]. After long and urgent prayer, he merited to be heard by the Lord. One day while he was praying in such a secluded spot and became totally absorbed in God through his extreme fervor, Jesus Christ appeared to him fastened to the cross. Francis' soul melted at the sight, and the memory of Christ's passion was so impressed on the innermost recesses of his heart that from that hour, whenever Christ's crucifixion came to his mind, he could scarcely contain his tears and sighs, as he later revealed to his companions when he was approaching the end of his life. Through this the man of God understood as addressed to himself the Gospel text: "If you wish to come after me, deny yourself and take up your cross and follow me" [Mt 16:24]. . . .

One day when Francis went out to meditate in the fields, he walked beside the church of San Damiano which was threatening to collapse because of extreme age. Inspired by the Spirit, he went inside to pray. Prostrate before an image of the Crucified, he was filled with no little consolation as he prayed. While his tear-filled eyes were gazing at the Lord's cross, he heard with his bodily ears a voice coming from the cross, telling him three times: "Francis, go and repair my house, which you see, is falling completely into ruin."

Trembling with fear, Francis was amazed at the sound of the astonishing voice, since he was alone in the church; and as he received in his heart the power of the divine words, he fell into a state of ecstacy. Returning finally to his senses, he prepared to obey, gathering himself together to carry out the command of repairing the church materially, although the intention of the words referred to that Church which Christ had purchased with His own blood, as the Holy Spirit taught him and as he himself later disclosed to the friars.

He rose then, made the sign of the cross, and taking some cloth to sell, hurried off to the town called Foligno. There he sold all he had brought with him, and, lucky merchant that he was, even sold the horse he was riding. Returning to Assisi he reverently entered the church which he had been commanded to repair. When he found the poor priest there, he greeted him with fitting reverence, offered him money for the repairs on the church, and for the poor, and humbly requested that the priest allow him to stay with him for a short time. The priest agreed to his staying there but would not accept the money out of fear of his parents. True despiser of money that he was, Francis threw it on a window sill, valuing it no more than if it were dust.

When his father learned that the servant of God was staying with this priest, he was greatly disturbed and ran to the place. But Francis, upon hearing about the threats of those who were pursuing him and having a premonition that they were approaching, wished [not] to "give place to wrath" [Rom 12:19] and hid himself—being still untrained as an athlete of Christ—in a secret pit. There he remained in hiding for some days, imploring the Lord incessantly with a flood of tears to "deliver him from the hands of those who were persecuting his soul" [Ps 31:16], and in His kindness to bring to realization the pious desires he had inspired. He was then filled with excessive joy and began to accuse himself of cowardice. He cast aside his fear, left the pit and took the road to the town of Assisi. When the townspeople saw his unkempt face and his changed mentality, they thought that he had gone out of his senses. They threw filth from the streets and stones at him, shouting insults at him, as if he were insane and out of his mind. But the Lord's servant passed through it as if he were deaf to it all, unbroken and unchanged by any of these insults. When his father heard the shouting, he ran to him at once not to save him but to destroy him. Casting aside all compassion, he dragged him home, tormenting him first with words, then with blows and chains. But this made Francis all the more eager and stronger to carry out what he had begun, as he recalled the words of the Gospel: "Blessed are they who suffer persecution for justice" sake, for theirs is the kingdom of heaven" [Mt 5:10]. . . .

Thereupon his carnally minded father led this child of grace, now stripped of his money, before the bishop of the town. He wanted to have Francis renounce into his hands his family possessions and return everything he had. A true lover of poverty, Francis showed himself eager to comply; he went before the bishop without delaying or hesitating. He did not wait for any words nor did he speak any, but immediately took off his clothes and gave them back to his father. Then it was discovered that the man of God had a hairshirt next to his skin under his fine clothes. Moreover, drunk with remarkable fervor, he even took off his underwear, stripping himself completely naked before all. He said to his father: "Until now I have called you father here on earth, but now I can say without reservation, 'Our Father who art in heaven' [Mt 6:9], since I have placed all my treasure and all my hope in him." When the bishop saw this, he was amazed at such intense fervor in the man of God. He immediately stood up and in tears drew Francis into his arms, covering him with the mantle he was wearing, like the pious and good man he was. He bade his servants give Francis something to cover his body. they brought him a poor, cheap cloak of a farmer who worked for the bishop. Francis accepted it gratefully and with his own hand marked a cross on it with a piece of chalk, thus designating it as the covering of a crucified man and a half-naked beggar.

> Thus the servant of the Most High King
> was left naked
> so that he might follow
> his naked crucified Lord, whom he loved.
> Thus the cross strengthened him
> to entrust his soul
> to the wood of salvation
> that would save him from the shipwreck of the world.

Released now from the chains of all earthly desires, this despiser of the world left town and in a carefree mood sought out a hidden place of solitude where alone and in silence he could hear the secrets God would convey to him. . . . Francis, the man of God, was making his way through a certain forest, merrily singing praises to the Lord in the French language . . . .

Francis (c. 1181?–1226) and Clare (c. 1193–1254) of Assisi

Francis Bernadone was born in the home of a wealthy merchant family in northern Italy. It was an era of economic explosion and his father was a very successful cloth merchant. Francis, however, evidenced greater proclivities at fun and frolic than the family business. Serving several years in the army of Assisi (1202–4), the experience of being a prisoner of war—for a year—and being racked with disease, sent Francis home to Assisi a more religious and reflective young man.

In 1207 St. Francis experienced a conversion and call to Christian service that radically altered the course of his life. In response to the call of Christ and in reaction to the decadence of his day, Francis embraced apostolic poverty and a mendicant life-style as the most obvious way to imitate Christ and proclaim the Kingdom of God. Gradually a group of men embraced St. Francis's way of life and lived in community together. They marked the beginning of the Friars Minor (*Fratres Minores*) "the lowly brothers" who cherished humility and obedience as being among their chief virtues.

Clare di Favarone was the third child of another wealthy family of Assisi. She was a dedicated woman even before to her conversion, which occurred through her hearing the preaching of St. Francis (1210?). She resolved at that point to embrace a Franciscan approach to Christian life, but her parents opposed that direction and sought instead to have her married. By Palm Sunday, 1212, however, she embarked on the path toward "Gospel Perfection," and entered the Benedictine monastery of San Paolo. St. Clare subsequently established a Franciscan work at the first of the chapels which St. Francis restored. As like-minded women joined her in that work, the "Poor Ladies of Assisi" or "Poor Clares" were formed.

Franciscan spirituality, as it was exemplified by Francis and Clare, stressed four key elements: first, total submission to Christ, which took expression in a willingness to embrace Matthew 10:7–10 as the rule that defined Christian life as a life of apostolic poverty and service. Second, an understanding of Christian life as a life of prayer; where other monks seemed to separate prayer from their daily tasks, Francis insisted that all of life was to be understood as prayer. Third, Francis and Clare recognized that Christian discipleship takes expression through self-denial and a willingness to suffer with and for Christ. And fourth, St. Francis cultivated an acute appreciation for the revelation and encounter with God through nature—in all its forms.[20] "The Admonitions," sometimes called "The Franciscan Sermon on the Mount," is (perhaps) the source that most epitomizes Francis's spiritual vision.

ST. FRANCIS'S PRAYER BEFORE THE CRUCIFIX[21]

Most High,
glorious God,
enlighten the darkness of my heart
and give me, Lord,
a correct faith,
a certain hope,
a perfect charity,
sense and knowledge,
so that I may carry out Your bold and true command.

AN UNTITLED PRAYER[22]

Almighty, eternal and merciful God,
grant us in our misery [the grace]
to do for You alone
what we know You want us to do,
and always
to desire what pleases You.

---

[20]John R. H. Moorman, "The Franciscans," in *The Study of Spirituality*, edited by Cheslyn Jones, Geoffrey Wainwright, and Edward Yarnold (New York: Oxford University Press, 1986), pp. 301–8.

[21]Reprinted from Regis Armstrong and Ignatius Brady, trans., *Francis and Clare: The Complete Works*. Copyright 1982, The Missionary Society of St. Paul the Apostle in the State of New York. Used by permission of Paulist Press. Page 103. This prayer seems to be connected with Francis's experience at San Dominano.

[22]Ibid. Used by permission of Paulist Press. Page 61, "A Letter to the Entire Order," closing prayer.

Thus,
inwardly cleansed,
interiorly enlightened,
and inflamed by the fire of the Holy Spirit,
may we be able to follow
in the footsteps of Your beloved Son,
our Lord Jesus Christ.

And,
by Your grace alone,
may we make our way to You,
Most High,
Who live and rule
in perfect Trinity and simple Unity,
and are glorified
God all-powerful
forever and ever.
Amen.

THE CANTICLE OF BROTHER SUN[23]

Most High, all-powerful, good Lord
  Yours are the praises, the glory, the honor, and all blessing.
To you alone, Most High, do they belong,
  and no one is worthy to mention Your name.

Praised be You, my Lord, with all your creatures,
  especially brother Sun,
Who is the day and through whom You give us light.
And he is beautiful and radiant with great splendor;
  and bears a likeness of You, Most High One.

Praised be You, my Lord, through Sister Moon and the stars;
  in heaven You formed them clear and precious and beautiful.
Praised be You, my Lord, through brother Wind,
  and through the air, cloudy and serene, and every kind of
weather, through which You give sustenance to Your creatures.

Praised be You, my Lord, through Sister Water,
  which is very useful and humble and precious and chaste.
Praised be You, my Lord, through Brother Fire,
  through whom You light the night
and he is beautiful and playful, and robust, and strong.

Praised be You, my Lord, through our Sister Mother Earth,
  who sustains and governs us,
and who produces varied fruits with colored flowers and herbs.

Praised be You, my Lord, through those who give pardon for Your
  love, and bear infirmity and tribulation.

---

[23]Ibid. Used by permission of Paulist Press. Pages 37–39.

Blessed are those who endure in peace
    for by You, Most High, they shall be crowned.

Praised be You, my Lord, through our Sister Bodily Death,
    from whom no living person can escape.
Woe to those who die in mortal sin.
    Blessed are those whom death will find in Your most holy will,
    for second death shall do them no harm.

Praise and bless my Lord and give Him thanks
    and serve Him with great humility.

ST. CLARE'S LETTER TO AGNES OF PRAGUE[24]

. . . As I hear of Your holy conduct and irreproachable life, which is known not only to me but to the entire world as well, I greatly rejoice and exult in the Lord. I am not alone in rejoicing at such great news, but [I am joined by] all who serve and seek to serve Jesus Christ. For, though you, more than others, could have enjoyed the magnificence and honor and dignity of the world and could have been married to the illustrious Caesar[25] with splendor befitting You and His Excellency. You have rejected all these things and have chosen with Your whole heart and soul a life of holy poverty and destitution. Thus You took a spouse of a more noble lineage, Who will keep Your virginity ever unspotted and unsullied, the Lord Jesus Christ:

When You have loved [Him], You shall be chaste; when you
have touched [Him], You shall become pure; when you have
accepted [Him], You shall be a virgin.
Whose power is stronger,
Whose generosity is more abundant,
Whose appearance more beautiful,
Whose love more tender,
Whose courtesy more gracious.
In Whose embrace You are already caught up;
Who has adorned Your breast with precious stones
    And has placed priceless pearls in Your ears
    and has surrounded You with sparkling gems
    as though blossoms of springtime
    and placed on Your head a golden crown
    as a sign [to all] of Your holiness.

---

[24]Ibid. Used by permission of Paulist Press. Pages 190–93, with omissions. Agnes of Prague (1203–82) was the daughter of King Ottakar of Bohemia and Queen Constance of Hungary. She became acquainted with the Friars Minor in 1232, when several brothers came to Prague on a preaching tour. She had soon built a church, a friary, and a hospital dedicated to St. Francis and his ideals. In 1234, St. Agnes herself entered the monastery, where she remained for fifty-four years, working in the hospital. She and St. Clare of Assisi were kindred spirits, and carried on a correspondence of mutual encouragement.

[25]Perhaps Emperor Frederick II.

Therefore, most beloved sister, or should I say, Lady, worthy of great respect: because You are "the spouse" and "the mother" and "the sister" of my Lord Jesus Christ,[26] and have been adorned resplendently with the sign of inviolable virginity and most holy poverty: Be strengthened in the holy service which You have undertaken out of an ardent desire for the Poor Crucified, Who for the sake of all of us took upon Himself the passion of the cross and delivered us from the power of the Prince of Darkness to whom we were enslaved because of the disobedience of our first parent, and so reconciled us to God the Father [2 Cor 5:18].

> O blessed poverty,
>> who bestows eternal riches on those who love and embrace her!
> O holy poverty,
>> to those who possess and desire you
>> God promises the Kingdom of Heaven
>> and offers, indeed, eternal glory and blessed life!
> O God-centered poverty,
>> whom the Lord Jesus Christ
>> Who ruled and now rules heaven and earth,
>> Who spoke and things were made, [Ps 33:9, 149:5]
>> condescended to embrace before all else!

"The foxes have dens," He says, "and the birds of the air have nests, but the Son of Man," Christ, "has nowhere to lay His head" [Mt 8:20], but "bowing His head, gave up His spirit" [Jn 19:30].

If so great and good a Lord, then, on coming into the Virgin's womb, chose to appear despised, needy, and poor in this world, so that people who were in utter poverty and want and in absolute need of heavenly nourishment might become rich [2 Cor 8:9] in Him by possessing the Kingdom of Heaven, "then rejoice and be glad" [Hab 3:18]! Be filled with a remarkable happiness and a spiritual joy! Contempt of the world has pleased you more than [its] honors, poverty more than earthly riches, and You have sought to store up greater treasures in heaven rather than on earth, "where rust does not consume nor moth destroy nor thieves break in and steal" [Mt 6:20]. Your reward then, is "very great in heaven" [Mt 5:12]! And You have truly merited to be called "a sister, spouse, and mother" of the Son of the Father of the Most High and of the glorious Virgin.

You know, I am sure, that the Kingdom of Heaven is promised and given by the Lord only to the poor [Mt 5:3]: for he who loves temporal things loses the fruit of love. Such a person cannot serve God and Mammon, for either the one is loved and the other hated, or the one is served and the other despised [Mt 6:24]. . . .

Again, [you know] that it is easier for a camel to pass through the eye of a needle than for a rich man to enter the Kingdom of Heaven [Mt 19:24]. Therefore, You have cast aside Your garments, that is, earthly riches, so that You might not

---

[26]2 Corinthians 11:2; Matthew 12:50.

be overcome by the one fighting against You, [and] that You might enter the Kingdom of Heaven "through the straight path and the narrow gate" [Mt 7:13–14].

> What a great laudable exchange:
> > to leave the things of time for those of eternity,
> > to choose the things of heaven for the goods of earth,
> > to receive the hundred-fold in place of one,
> > and to possess a blessed and eternal life. [Mt 19:29]

Because of this I have resolved, as best I can, to beg Your excellency and Your holiness by my humble prayers in the mercy of Christ, to be strengthened in His holy service, and to progress from good to better, from virtue to virtue [Ps 84:8], so that He Whom You serve with the total desire of Your soul may bestow on You the reward for which You long.

Mechthild of Magdeburg (c. 1212–97)

Mechthild of Magdeburg was born in the archbishopric of Magdeburg, Germany. Her literary style reflects a familiarity with contemporary culture and chivalry that suggests her parents were nobles. At the age of twelve she began having visions, and at some point her Dominican confessor, Heinrich of Halle, convinced her to begin to write her visions down. Mechthild's principal work, *The Flowing Light of the Godhead* (1265?), was a compilation of her visions, recorded over the middle decades of her life.

In 1230 Mechthild left the home of her parents and went to the city of Magdeburg, where she joined a community of Beguines.[27] The Beguines were a lay women's movement, made up of pious women who desired to live communal lives of prayer and Christian service. The Beguines were not "religious" in the formal sense; they took no official vows. They did not belong to an approved religious order, and did not adhere to a particular monastic rule. They practiced communal life, prayer, celibacy, humanitarian service, and manual labor as aspects of their Christian vocation. Since the Beguines took no formal vows, they could live and work in the world, and—if they left the community—marry. The movement provided important opportunities for self-expression, personal development, and economic support for single women when these aspects where not available to them in society.

Around the year 1270, Mechthild entered the Cisterian convent of Helfta, where Abbess Gertrude of Hackeborn had established a women's community famous for its scholarship and piety. Mechthild remained at Helfta for the rest of her life, and may have completed the final sections of *The Flowing Light* there.

---

[27]See Fiona Bowie's excellent introduction in Oliver Davies, trans., *Beguine Spirituality* (New York: Crossroad, 1990), pp. 3–34, for an insightful treatment of the Beguines and their spirituality.

Mechthild's spirituality explores the soul's relationship with God. Her visions were cast in a poetic form reminiscent of the medieval *Minnesang* (songs of courtly love); what had been a sensual, secular genre became in her hands a medium for describing God's courtship of the human soul. Since it was written by a woman, for a community of women, *The Flowing Light of the Godhead* employs feminine language and images to depict God and the soul.

CONVERSATION OF LOVE AND THE QUEEN[28]

> The soul drew close to love,
> Greeted her reverently
> And said: God greet you, Lady Love!

LOVE: May God reward you, dear Queen.

SOUL: Lady Love, you are most perfect.

LOVE: O Queen, that is why I rule all things. . . .

SOUL: Lady Love, you have taken from me all that I ever possessed on earth.

LOVE: But Lady Queen, what a blessed exchange!

SOUL: Lady Love, you took from me my childhood.

LOVE: Lady Queen, in return I give you heavenly freedom.

SOUL: Lady Love, you took from me all my youth.

LOVE: Lady Queen, in return I gave you many holy virtues.

SOUL: Lady Love, you took from me my family and my friends.

LOVE: O dear! What a pitiful lament, Lady Queen.

SOUL: Lady Love, you took from me worldly honours, worldly wealth and the whole world.

LOVE: Lady Queen, I shall make good your loss with the Holy Spirit in a single hour, according to your wish.

SOUL: Lady Love, you overwhelmed me so completely that my body writhed in a strange sickness.

LOVE: Lady Queen, in return I gave you sublime knowledge and profound thoughts.

SOUL: Lady Love, you have consumed all my flesh and blood.

LOVE: Lady Queen, you have been purified and drawn up to God.

SOUL: Lady Love, you are a thief; you must give me yet more in return.

LOVE: Lady Queen, then take me myself!

SOUL: Lady Love, now you have repaid me with a hundredfold on earth.

LOVE: Lady Queen, now you may ask that God and all His riches be given you.

---

[28]Reprinted from Davies, *Beguine Spirituality*. Used by kind permission of Crossroad Publishing Company. Pages 53–54.

HOW THE SOUL SPEAKS TO GOD[29]

> Lord, you are my lover,
> My longing,
> My flowing stream,
> My sun,
> And I am your reflection.

HOW GOD ANSWERS THE SOUL[30]

> It is my nature that makes me love you often,
> For I am love itself.
>
> It is my longing that makes me love you intensely,
> For I yearn to be loved from the heart.
>
> It is my eternity that makes me love you long,
> For I have no end.

YOU SHOULD ASK GOD TO LOVE YOU LONG, OFTEN AND INTENSELY SO THAT YOU MAY BE PURE, BEAUTIFUL, AND HOLY[31]

> O Lord,
> Love me intensely,
> Love me often and long!
> For the more often you love me, the purer I become.
> The more intensely you love me, the more beautiful I become.
> The longer you love me, the holier I become.

HOW GOD COMES TO THE SOUL[32]

> I descend on my love
> As dew on a flower.

---

[29]Ibid. Used by permission of Crossroad Publishing Company. Page 55.
[30]Ibid. Used by permission of Crossroad Publishing Company. Page 56.
[31]Ibid. Used by permission of Crossroad Publishing Company. Page 57.
[32]Ibid. Used by permission of Crossroad Publishing Company. Page 58.

HOW A FREE SOUL SPEAKS TO GOD WITH LOVE[33]

Lord, because I am beneath all creatures, you have raised me up above all things to yourself. And, Lord, because I have no earthly treasure, neither do I have an earthly heart. Since you, Lord, are my treasure, you are also my heart and my sole good.

HOW THE BRIDE WHO IS UNITED WITH GOD SPURNS THE CONSOLATION OF ALL OTHER CREATURES[34]

I cannot endure a single consolation
But my beloved.
I love my earthly friends
As companions in eternity
And I love my enemies
With a painful and holy longing
For their blessedness.
In all things God has a sufficiency
But in the touching of my soul.

THE POWER OF LOVE[35]

Love penetrates the senses and storms the soul with all its power. When love grows in the soul, then it rises up with great longing to God and flowingly expands to receive the miracle that breaks in upon it. Love melts through the soul and into the senses. And so the body too gains its part and conforms in all ways to love.

THE LOVE OF GOD[36]

Ah, dear love of God, always embrace this soul of mine.
For it pains me above all things
When I am separated from you.
Ah, love, do not allow me to grow cool
For all my works are dead

---

[33]Ibid. Used by permission of Crossroad Publishing Company. Page 68.
[34]Ibid. Used by permission of Crossroad Publishing Company. Page 69.
[35]Ibid. Used by permission of Crossroad Publishing Company. Page 71.
[36]Ibid. Used by permission of Crossroad Publishing Company. Page 75.

When I can feel you no longer.
O love, you sweeten both suffering and need;
You teach and console the true children of God.

Thomas Aquinas (1225–74)

Thomas Aquinas was born near Naples and received his early education at the famous Benedictine monastery at Monte Casino. He attended the University of Naples where he studied Scripture, Aristotle, and the *Sentences* of Peter Lombard; during this same period (1224) St. Thomas entered the Dominican Order. After studying in Paris, Aquinas went to the University of Cologne where he studied under the most notable scholar of the day, the Dominican Albertus Magnus (c. 1200–80). Magnus was hailed as *Doctor Universalis*—"the universal doctor"—because of the scope of his wisdom. In his ability to integrate theology, philosophy, and the natural world into a unified system of thought, the student eventually eclipsed his teacher. Thomas Aquinas returned to the University of Paris, completed his doctorate, and embarked upon a career of preaching, teaching, and writing that would make him one of the most influential figures of his age, and of all time.

Preaching, teaching, and study were the hallmarks of Dominican vocation, and St. Thomas lived out this calling. His most famous work was his summation of theology, *Summa Theologica*—which he began in 1256 and had not entirely completed before his death. *Summa Theologica* is encyclopedic in its scope. It begins with a consideration of the nature of Christian doctrine, and moves through more than 500 questions and replies toward "The Resurrection and Last Things."

St. Thomas's writings on prayer represent well the development of Dominican spirituality.[37] Prayer for Thomas is a rational expression of our willingness to submit ourselves to God's will; in one sense, prayer "ought to be continuous" because it expresses "the constancy of our desire." But in another sense, "prayer . . . as a specific activity, cannot be persistent because we have to devote ourselves to other works."[38] There is also a pragmatism in St. Thomas that was missing in those who stressed seclusion and cultivation of purity and were not as committed to the task of saving and shaping souls in the world.

In the selections that follow, Aquinas's lengthy considerations of biblical and patristic evidence concerning the question at hand (both pro and con) have been omitted so that we can examine more directly the constructive teaching of St. Thomas himself.

---

[37]Cf. Simon Tugwell, "The Dominicans," in Jones, Wainwright, and Yarnold, eds., *Study of Spirituality*, pp. 296–300.

[38]*Summa Theologica*, II, I, Question 83, Ar. XIV.

ON PRAYER[39]

Question I. *Is Prayer an act of our appetitive power?*[40]

Prayer appears to be an act of our appetitive power . . . . On the other hand: (a) Isadore says, "Praying (*orare*) is the same thing as talking." And talking is a matter of the intellect. So prayer is not an act of our appetitive power, but of our intellectual power.

Reply: As Cassiodorus says on Psalm 38, prayer (*oratio*) is so called as being the mouth's reason (*oris ratio*). Now the difference between speculative and practical reason is that speculative reason simply grasps things, whereas practical reason causes things as well as grasping them. And there are two ways in which one thing causes another. It may be a full-fledged cause of something, in that it makes it inevitable that that particular thing will result, but for this to happen the effect must be entirely within the power of that cause. Or one thing may cause another in a less complete way in the sense that it just prepares the way for something, when the effect is not totally within the power of the cause. So reason also can be the cause of things in two ways. In some cases it makes it necessary for something to result: it is in this way that it belongs to reason not only to give orders to our own lower powers and to our bodily limbs, but also to other people who are subject to us; this is done by giving orders. In other cases reason can only try to induce something to happen, preparing the way, as it were, for something to happen; in this way reason asks for something to be done by people who are not subject to us, whether they be our equals or superiors. But both giving orders and asking or entreating imply a certain arranging of things, a planning to bring about something by using certain means, so that they are the concern of reason, since arranging things is a rational activity. This is why the philosopher [Aristotle] says that "reason entreats us toward what is best." And in this sense that we are here discussing *oratio*, as meaning an entreaty or petition in line with Augustine's comment that "prayer is a kind of petition." And Damascene[41] also says that "prayer is a petition made to God for things that are fitting." Thus it is clear that prayer (oratio in the sense presently under discussion) is an act of our reason. In reply to the points raised above:

1. The Lord said to hear the desire of the poor either inasmuch as it is desire that prompts their petition, since petition is a kind of presentation of desire, or in order to show how quickly He hears, inasmuch as God hears the poor before

---

[39]Reprinted from Simon Tugwell, trans., *Albert and Thomas: Selected Writings.* Copyright 1988, by The Missionary Society of St. Paul the Apostle in the State of New York. Used by permission of Paulist Press. Pages 476–89, with omissions; cited from *Summa Theologica,* II, II, Question 83. I am indebted to Tugwell's notes, a few of which are cited throughout.

[40]By "appetitive power" Aquinas is asking whether prayer is a matter of our desire or a matter of reason. p. 476, n. 1.

[41]St. John of Damascus (c. 674–749) was the foremost theologian of the Eastern Orthodox Church. His works *The Fount of Knowledge* and *The Orthodox Faith* remain as standards of the Orthodox tradition. He contributed greatly to worship, liturgy, and spirituality in the Eastern Church.

they formulate their prayer, while it is still only a desire in their hearts. "Before they call, I will hear them" [Is 65:24].

2. As we have already said, the will activates the reason to move toward its own goal, so there is nothing to stop an act of reason, instigated by the will, aiming at the goal of charity, namely union with God. And there are two senses in which prayer, moved by charity in the will, aims at God: with reference to the object of petition, inasmuch as the chief thing we should ask for in prayer is that we may be united with God, as it says in Psalm 26 [27]:4, "One thing I have asked for from the Lord and this is what I will seek, to dwell in the Lord's house all the days of my life." Secondly, with reference to the person praying, a petitioner has to approach the person to whom the petition is to be made; if we are asking another human being for something, this means approaching him physically, but to ask God for something we have to approach him in our minds. So Dionysius, in the same passage, says that "when we call upon God in our prayers, we are present to Him with our minds unveiled." And in this sense Damascene says that prayer is "an ascent of the mind to God."

3. The three activities listed all belong to speculative reason; but practical reason has the further role of causing something either by giving orders or by petition, as we have already said.

Question II. *Is it appropriate to pray?* . . .
Reply: Among the ancients there were three different kinds of mistake made about prayer. Some people maintained that human affairs are not governed by Divine providence, and it follows from this view that it is futile to pray and indeed to worship God at all. Of them it says, "You have said, 'Anyone who serves God is a fool.'" [Mal 3:14]

Secondly, there is the opinion of those who maintained that everything comes about by necessity, including human affairs, either because of the unchangingness of God's providence or because of the absolute control of the stars or because of the way in which causes are linked together. This view leaves us no room for prayer to be useful.

Thirdly, there is the opinion that human affairs are governed by Divine providence and that they do not come about by necessity; but then people went on to say that the arrangements of God's providence could be altered and that God's providence is changed by prayers and other features of Divine worship.

All these views have been rejected. So what we have to do now is find some way of indicating the usefulness of prayer which neither makes out that human affairs, in being governed by Divine providence, are all subject to necessity nor supposes that God's plan can be changed.

We can shed light on the problem by bearing in mind that Divine providence does not merely arrange what effects are to occur; it also arranges the causes of these effects and the relationship between them. And among other causes, some things are caused by human acts. So human being have to do certain things, not so as to change God's plan by their acts, but in order to bring about certain effects by their acts, according to the pattern planned by God. . . . Similarly, in the case of prayer we do not pray in order to change God's plan, but in order to obtain by our prayers those things which God planned to bring about by means of prayers, in order, as Gregory[42] says, that our prayers should entitle us to receive what almighty God planned from all eternity to give us.

In reply to the points raised above:

1. We do not have to present our prayers to God in order to disclose to Him our needs and desires, but in order to make ourselves realize that we need to have recourse to His help in these matters.

2. As we have already said, our prayer is not designed to change what God has already planned.

3. God gives us many things out of sheer generosity, without being asked. The reason why He wants to give us some things in response to our petitions is that it is profitable for us to acquire a certain confidence in running to Him and to recognize that He is the source of all that is good for us. So Chrysostom says, "Consider what a joy is granted you, what glory is bestowed upon you, that you can speak with God in your prayers, that you can engage in conversation with Christ, and plead for whatever you want, whatever you desire."[43] . . .

Question V. *Should we ask God for particular things when we pray?* . . .
Reply: As Maximus Valerius tells us, "Socrates thought we should ask nothing more from the immortal gods except that they would grant us good things, because they know what is good for each individual, whereas we often ask for things it would be better for us not to obtain."[44] In some ways this view is correct, at least so far as those things are concerned which can turn out badly and which we can use badly or well, such as wealth which, as he goes on to say, "has been a disaster for many people, and honors which have ruined people, and kingdoms which we often see coming to a wretched end, and splendid marriages which sometimes completely destroy families." But there are some things which we cannot use badly, things which cannot turn out badly: the things by which we are made blessed or by which we earn beatitude. The saints ask for these things unconditionally when they pray: "Show us your face and we shall be saved" [Ps

---

[42]Pope Gregory I (ca. 540–604), or "Gregory the Great." He was Bishop of Rome (590–604), and served as a civil official, monk, writer, and ecclesiastical leader. His most influential works were *Pastoral Rule* and *Dialogues*. Aquinas is paraphrasing *Dialogues* I.8.

[43]St. John Chrysostom (c. 347–407) was Archbishop of Constantinople from 398 till just before his death. He was reputed to be the greatest preacher, and was an influential pastor and liturgist in the Eastern Church. His *On the Priesthood* as well as his many sermons and commentaries were very influential across the Christian Church. The quotation given by Aquinas cannot be identified from extant sources.

[44]Valerius Maximus, *Facta et Dicta Memorabilia*, VII, 2.6.1.

80:4], or "Lead me in the way of your commandments" [Ps 119:35]. In reply to the points raised above:

1. Although of ourselves we do not know what we ought to pray for, the Spirit, as the same text [Rom 8:26] says, helps our weakness by inspiring us with holy desires so making us plead rightly. This is why the Lord says that the true worshipper must worship "in spirit and truth" [Jn 4:23].

2. When we pray for things in prayer which are relevant to our salvation, then we are conforming our wills to the will of God, of which it says that "he wills everyone to be saved" [1 Tim 2:4].

3. God invites us to good, but we move to accept it, not by taking bodily steps, but by pious desires and devout prayers.

Question VI. *Should we ask God for temporal things in prayer?* . . .
Reply: As Augustine says, it is lawful to pray for what is lawful to desire.[45] And it is lawful to desire temporal things, not as an end in themselves or as our primary object, but as supports which help us on our way toward beatitude, inasmuch as they serve to sustain our bodily life and play an instrumental role in our virtuous deeds, as the philosopher [Aristotle] also says. Therefore it is legitimate to pray for temporal things. And this is what Augustine says. "If you want enough to live off and no more, there is nothing wrong in that; and you do not want it for its own sake, but for your bodily health and to secure circumstances that suit your position, so that you will not be out of place among the people you have to live with. If you have these things, you should pray to keep them, and if you do not have them, you should pray to get them."[46] In reply to the points raise above:

1. Temporal things are to be sought, not as our primary object, but in second place. So Augustine says, "In saying that the former (the Kingdom of God) should be sought first, He indicated that the latter (temporal goods) should be sought afterward—meaning that they come afterward in rank, not in time. The former is sought as a good, the latter only as something we need."[47]

2. What is forbidden is not absolutely any concern about temporal things, but an exaggerated concern for them, outside the proper context, as explained above.

3. When our mind turns to temporal things in order to rest in them, then it does remain weighted down in them. But when it turns to them with a view to attaining beatitude, far from being weighed down by them it rather raises them up.

---

[45]This is not, literally, a quotation from St. Augustine; it comes from Thomas himself (IV, *Sent.* d. 15, q.4a, 4b), but the sentiments are certainly in keeping with Augustine's point of view.
[46]The quotation is from Augustine's *Epistles*, 130.6.12–7.13.
[47]*De Sermone Domini*, II, 16.53.

4. By the sheer fact that we are not asking for temporal things as if they were what we primarily wanted, but only in view of something else, what we are asking for is that God will grant them to us only in so far as they help our salvation. . . .

Meister Eckhart (c. 1260–1327)

Meister Eckhart was born in Thuringia, Germany. He entered the Dominican Order in Erfurt, earned his master's degree at the University of Paris, and thereafter was accorded the title "Meister" (Master) Eckhart. True to the Dominican tradition, Eckhart was a prolific preacher and he raised up a school of mystics ("The Rhineland Mystics") after his own distinctive pattern. His sermons and treatises on spirituality were very influential.

Eckhart's mysticism was very eclectic. He drew upon Dionysius and Augustine, as well as more contemporary figures like Aquinas, and wove them into a fabric that was distinctively one of his own making. His approach was strongly influenced by Neoplatonism, as Eckhart sought to find God within the human soul. Eckhart was a pilgrim of the inner self. He sought, through various practices and reflections, to detach the soul from temporal things and affections, so that in stillness and silence, and in grace and love, the human soul could find union with God.

While Meister Eckhart was a devout Christian and churchman, certain aspects of his teaching were deemed heretical and were subsequently condemned. Modern commentators suspect that it was probably the distinctive character of Eckhart's teaching, as well as his association with more radical groups (like the Beghards and Beguines), more than the content of his doctrine that brought about Eckhart's condemnation.[48] The pantheistic and ontological emphases of his thought make it sound unguarded and perhaps heretical; these same elements also give his theology a tone that sounds strangely contemporary.

ETERNAL GENERATION OF THE SON[49]

. . . What is life? God's being is my life. If my life is God's being, then God's existence must be my existence and God's is-ness is my is-ness, neither less nor more.[50] . . .

---

[48]Cf. Bernard McGinn, trans., *Meister Eckhart: Teacher and Preacher* (New York: Paulist Press, 1986), pp. 2–40; Edmund Colledge and Bernard McGinn, trans., *Meister Eckhart: The Essential Sermons, Commentaries, Treatises, and Defense* (New York: Paulist Press, 1981), pp. 5–61; and Gary Sattler, "The Sermons and Treatises of Meister Eckhart," in Magill and McGreal, eds., *Christian Spirituality*, pp. 132–38, for useful contemporary introductions to Eckhart's life and thought.

[49]Reprinted from Colledge and McGinn, *Meister Eckhart*. Copyright 1981 by The Missionary Society of St. Paul the Apostle in the State of New York. Used by permission of Paulist Press. "Sermon VI," on "The just will live for ever," (Wis 5:16), pp. 185–189, with omissions.

[50]The word translated "is-ness" is *Isticheit* in the German. It is, perhaps, one that Eckhart invented himself. Cf. Ibid., p. 187, n. 8.

The Father gives birth to His Son in eternity, equal to himself. "The Word was with God, and God was the Word" [Jn 1:1]; it [the Word] was the same in the same nature. Yet I say more: He has given birth to Him in my soul. Not only is the soul with Him, and He equal to it, but He is in it, and the Father gives His Son birth in the soul in the same way He gives Him [the Son] birth in eternity, and not otherwise. He must do it whether He likes it or not. The Father gives birth to His Son without ceasing; and I say more: He gives me birth, me, His Son and the same Son. I say more: He gives birth only to me, his Son, but he gives birth to me as Himself and Himself as me and to me as His being and nature. In the innermost source, there I spring out in the Holy Spirit, where there is one life and one being and one work. Everything God performs is one; therefore He gives me, his Son, birth without any distinction. My fleshly father is not actually my father except in one little portion of his nature, and I am separated from him; he may be dead and I alive. Therefore the heavenly Father is truly my Father, for I am his Son and have everything that I have from Him, and I am the same Son and not a different one. Because the Father performs one work, therefore His work is me, His Only-Begotten Son without any difference.

"We shall be completely transformed and changed into God" [2 Cor 3:18]. See a comparison. In the same way, when in the sacrament bread is changed into the Body of our Lord, however many pieces of bread there were, they still become one Body. . . . What is changed into something else becomes one with it. I am so changed into Him that He produces His being in me as one, not just similar. By the living God, this is true! There is no distinction. . . .

Once I said here, and what I said is true: If a person obtains or accepts something from outside himself, he [or she] is in this wrong. One should not accept or esteem God as being outside oneself, but as one's own and as what is within one; nor should one serve or labor for any recompense, not for God or for His honor or for anything that is outside oneself, but only for that which one's own being and one's own life is within one. Some simple people think that they will see God as if He were standing there and they here. It is not so. God and I, we are one. I accept God into me in knowing; I go into God in loving. There are some who say that blessedness consists not in knowing but in willing. They are wrong; for if it consisted only in the will, it would not be one. Working and becoming are one. If a carpenter does not work, nothing becomes of the house. If the axe is not doing anything, nothing is becoming anything. In this working God and I are one; He is working and I am becoming. The fire changes anything into itself that is put into it and this takes on the fire's own nature. The wood does not change the fire into itself, but the fire changes the wood into itself. So are we changed into God, that we shall know Him as He is [1 Jn 3:2]. Saint Paul says: "So shall we come to know Him, I knowing Him just as He knows me" [1 Cor 13:12], neither less nor more, perfectly equal. "The just will live forever, and their reward is with God," perfectly equal. That we may love justice, for its own sake and for God, without asking return, may God help us to this. Amen.

GOD IS LOVE[51]

"God is love." [1 Jn 4:8] . . . "God is love" first because love is common to all, excluding no one. From this joint possession two things follow. First, God is common: He is every being and the whole existence of all things ("in him, through him, and from him" [Rom 11:36]). God is all the best that can be thought or desired by each and every person—and more so! But the whole of what can be desired by all people in relation to the word "more" is really nothing. Hence the axiom "God is the opposite of nothing by means of the mediation of being." Secondly, note that whatever is common insofar as it is common is God, and whatever is not common insofar as it is not common is not God, but is created. Every creature is something finite, limited, distinct, and proper, and thus it is already not love. God with his total self is a common love.

Second, God is and is said to be love principally because He is the One whom everything that can love loves and seeks. Again He alone is the One who is loved and sought by all and in all. Also, everything that exists and can exist subsists in seeking and loving Him. Again, it is He in whom everything that is unpleasant, contrary, sad, or nonexistent is sweet and beautiful. Without Him anything pleasant is disagreeable and nonexistent. Furthermore, God is love because He is totally lovable and totally love.

In the third place, God is love because He loves totally. On God's love toward us note first how much He loves us who loves us totally with His whole being; second, how He loves us with the very same love by which He loves and cherishes Himself, His coeternal Son and the Holy Spirit. Third, it follows that He loves us with the same glory in mind by which He loves Himself, as the texts say: "that you may eat and drink at my table in my kingdom" [Lk 22:30], and "where I am there also shall my servant be" [Jn 12:26]. Fourth, the love with which He loves us is the Holy Spirit Himself. Fifth, Hugh [of St. Victor] says He loves us "as if He had forgotten everything else," or almost everything else.[52] Sixth, He loves us in such a way that it is as if His blessedness depended on it. "I have loved you with an everlasting love" [Jer 31:3], and "My delight is to be with the sons of men" [Pr 8:31]. Seventh, He loved us when we were still His enemies, and so He gave us Himself before His gifts, as if He could not wait for preparations and arrangements [to be made]. Eighth, He gives Himself and everything He has. Nothing created gives its own, nor the whole of it, nor itself.

In the ninth place declare that God's nature, existence, and life consist in sharing Himself and giving Himself totally. "The First is rich in itself." He is absolutely the Absolute. Hence, according to Dionysius, He gives himself without thinking about His love, but as the sun shines forth.[53]

---

[51]Reprinted from McGinn, trans. *Meister Eckhart.* Used by permission of Paulist Press. "Sermon VI," pp. 212–15, with omissions.
[52]Hugh of St. Victor, *Soliloquy on the Earnest Money of the Soul.*
[53]Pseudo-Dionysius, *Divine Names,* 4.1.

On the basis of what has been said three points can be made. First, do not thank God because He loves us—He must do so! But I thank God because He is so good that He must love. Second, note that the soul itself is the noble substance that God, who possesses and [virtually] precontains everything, loves in such a way. Third, note that the soul is within God and God within the soul, and that God, Who loves nothing outside Himself, unlike or different from Himself, loves it in this way. Again, remember not to pray to God to pour the light of His grace upon us or anything like that, but to pray that we may be worthy to receive it, because God either always gives or never, either to all or to none. . . .

THE SOUL AND GOD[54]

The words that I have spoken in Latin[55] are from the epistle, and one can apply them to a holy confessor. In German the words mean: "He was found to be just within his day. He pleased God well in his days." Justice he found from within. My body is more in my soul than my soul is in my body. My body and my soul are more in God than they are in themselves. And this is justice: the cause of all things in truth. As St. Augustine says, "God is nearer to the soul than it is to itself." It is true: The closeness of God and the soul admits no difference [between them]. The same knowledge in which God knows himself is the knowledge of every detached spirit and nothing else. The soul receives its being immediately from God. For this reason God is nearer to the soul than it is to itself, and God is in the ground of the soul with all His divinity. . . .

I once said in a convent: The true image of the soul emerges when it has been formed and fashioned out of nothing that is not God Himself. The soul has two eyes, one inward and one outward. The inward eye of the soul is the one that sees into being and takes its being from God without anything else mediating. This is its proper function. The outward eye of the soul is the one that is turned toward all creatures, taking note of them by means of images in the manner of a [spiritual] faculty. The person who is turned in on himself so that he knows God by his own taste and in his own ground is freed of all created things and is enclosed in himself as in a veritable fortress of truth. I once said that our Lord came to his disciples behind locked doors on the day of Easter. It is the same with the person who has been freed of all otherness and all createdness. God does not come to this person. He is there already as being. . . .

Now [the text] says: "He was found within." That is within which dwells in the ground of the soul, in the innermost of the soul, in the intellect; it does not go out nor look upon any [external] thing. Here all powers of the soul are equally noble. Here within he was found just. That is just which is the same in happiness and sorrow, in bitterness and sweetness, and whom no object hinders from be-

---

[54]Reprinted from McGinn, trans. *Meister Eckhart*. Used by permission of Paulist Press. "Sermon 10," pp. 261–66, with omissions.

[55]*In diebus suis placuit deo et inventus est iustus*, The Wisdom of Jesus the Son of Sirach 44:16–17.

coming one in justice. The just man is one with God. Like loves like. Love loves always what is like it. Hence God loves the just man like himself. So that we find ourselves within on the day and in the time of intellect, in the day of wisdom, in the day of justice, and in the day of happiness, may we receive the help of the Father, the Son, and the Holy Spirit. Amen.

ON DETACHMENT[56]

I have read many writings both by the pagan teachers and by the prophets and in the Old and the New Law, and I have inquired, carefully and most industriously, to find which is the greatest and best virtue with which a person can most completely and closely conform oneself to God, with which one can by grace become that which God is by nature, and with which one can come most of all to resemble that image which he was in God, and between which and God there was no distinction before ever God made created things. And as I scrutinize all these writings . . . I find no other virtue better than pure detachment from all things; because all other virtues have some regard for created things, but detachment is free from all created things. That is why our Lord said to Martha: "One thing is necessary" [Lk 10:42], which is as much as to say: "Martha, whoever wants to be free of care and to be pure must have one thing, and that is detachment." . . .

Now you may ask what detachment is since it is in itself so excellent. Here you should know that true detachment is nothing else than for the spirit to stand as immovable against whatever may chance to it of joy and sorrow, honor, shame and disgrace, as a mountain of lead stands before a little breath of wind. This immovable detachment brings a person into the greatest equality with God, and it is from his detachment that one has His purity and His simplicity, and His unchangeablity. And if a person is to be equal with God, insofar as a creature can have equality with God, that must happen through detachment. It then draws a person into purity, and from purity into simplicity, and from simplicity into unchangeability, and these things produce an equality between God and the person; and the equality must come about in grace, for it is grace that draws a person away from all temporal things, and makes him pure of all transient things. And you must know that to be empty of all created things is to be full of God, and to be full of created things is to be empty of God. . . .

But now I ask: "What is the prayer of a heart that has detachment?" And to answer it I say that purity in detachment does not know how to pray, because if someone prays he asks God to get something for him, or he asks God to take something away from him. But a heart in detachment asks for nothing, nor has it anything of which it would gladly be free. So it is free of all prayer, and its prayer is nothing else than for uniformity with God. That is all its prayer consists

---

[56]Reprinted from Colledge and McGinn, trans., *Meister Eckhart*. Used by permission of Paulist Press. Pages 285–94, with omissions.

in. To illustrate this meaning we may consider what Saint Dionysius said about Saint Paul's words, when he said: "There are many of you racing for the crown, but it will be given only to one" [1 Cor 9:24]. All the powers of the soul are racing for the crown, but it will be given only to the soul's being—and Dionysius says: "The race is nothing but a turning away from all created things and a uniting oneself with that which is uncreated."[57] And as the soul attains this, it loses its name and it draws God into itself, so that in itself it becomes nothing, as the sun draws up the red dawn into itself so that it becomes nothing. Nothing else will bring man to this except pure detachment. And we can also apply this to what Augustine says: "The soul has a secret entry into the divine nature when all things become nothing to it."[58] This entry here on this earth is nothing else than pure detachment. . . . Now a heart that has pure detachment is free of all created things, and so it is wholly submitted to God, and so it achieves the highest uniformity with God, and is most susceptible to the divine inflowing. This is what Saint Paul means when he said: "Put on Christ" [Rom 13:14]. He means through uniformity with Christ, and this putting-on cannot happen except through uniformity with Christ. And you must know that when Christ became man, it was not just a human being He put on Himself; He put on human nature. Therefore, do you too go out of all things, and then there will be only what Christ accepted and put on, and so you will have put on Christ. . . . So detachment is the best of all, for it purifies the soul and cleanses the conscience and enkindles the heart and awakens the spirit and stimulates our longings and shows us where God is and separates us from created things and unites itself with God. . . .

Catherine of Siena (1347–80)

Catherine of Siena was born in Siena, Italy. The youngest of twenty-five children of an uneducated cloth-dyer, she is one of two Roman Catholic women esteemed as a "Doctor of the Church" because of the luster of her life and spiritual teaching. She evidenced religious fervor from her youth, and this took serious manifestation, at the age of thirteen, when she refused to participate in a marriage arranged by her family, and turned instead toward a religious life.

Overcoming nearly three years of parental opposition, St. Catherine became a lay worker (tertiary) of the Dominican Order (c. 1365), and thereby embarked upon her vocation as an ascetic, mystical teacher, and social activist. She was active in ministry to the many refugees from plagues and regional wars. Because of her holy life and spiritual insight, a "family" soon gathered around Catherine (c. 1370), to participate in her work and to receive her teaching. On several instances she became a witness for peace, in the midst of war. St. Catherine also labored for rec-

---

[57]Pseudo-Dionysius, *Divine Names*, 4.9.
[58]This quotation does not actually come from Augustine's published works.

onciliation within the Church as she traveled to Avignon, France, to persuade the Pontiff (Gregory XI) to return the Holy See to Rome.

Her most famous work, *The Dialogue* (c. 1378), is—as the title suggests—an extended conversation between her soul and God. It is, as Guiliana Cavallini termed it, "a great tapestry"[59] of spiritual teaching and experience, and it is a tapestry that is not easily unraveled or treated piecemeal. *The Dialogue* seeks to induce as well as describe spiritual experience. St. Catherine asks petitions and questions of God and God replies to these in extended oracles spoken in first-person form.

PROLOGUE[60]

How a soul, elevated by desire of the honor of God, and of the salvation of her neighbors, exercising herself in humble prayer, after she had seen the union of the soul, through love, with God, asked of God four requests.

The soul, who is lifted by a very great and yearning desire for the honor of God and the salvation of souls, begins by exercising herself, for a certain space of time, in the ordinary virtues, remaining in the cell of self-knowledge, in order to know better the goodness of God towards her. This she does because knowledge must precede love, and only when she has attained love, can she strive to follow and to clothe herself with the truth. But, in no way, does the creature receive such a taste of the truth, or so brilliant a light therefrom, as by means of humble and continuous prayer, founded on knowledge of herself and of God; because prayer, exercising her in the above way, unites with God the soul that follows the footprints of Christ Crucified, and thus, by desire and affection, and union of love, makes her another Himself. Christ would seem to have meant this, when He said: "To him who will love Me and will observe My commandment, will I manifest Myself; and he shall be one thing with Me and I with him." In several places we find similar words, by which we can see that it is, indeed, through the effect of love, that the soul becomes another Himself. That this may be seen more clearly, I will mention what I remember having heard from a handmaid of God, namely, that, when she was lifted up in prayer, with great elevation of mind, God was not wont to conceal, from the eye of her intellect, the love which He had for His servants, but rather to manifest it; and, that among other things, He used to say: "Open the eye of your intellect, and gaze into Me, and you shall see the beauty of My rational creature. And look at those creatures who, among the beauties which I have given to the soul, creating her in My image and similitude, are clothed with the nuptial garment (that is, the garment of love), adorned with many virtues, by which they are united with Me through love. And yet I tell you, if you should ask Me, who these are, I should reply" (said the sweet and amorous Word

[59] Catherine of Siena, *The Dialogue*, translated by Suzanne Noffke, O.P. (New York: Paulist Press, 1980); Guiliana Cavallini, "Preface," p. xi. Cf. Noffke's fine "Introduction," pp. 1–22.

[60] Catherine of Siena, *Dialogue of the Soul*, from the Christian Classics Ethereal Library, http://ccel.wheaton.edu. pdf version

of God) "they are another Myself, inasmuch as they have lost and denied their own will, and are clothed with Mine, are united to Mine, are conformed to Mine." It is therefore true, indeed, that the soul unites herself with God by the affection of love.

So, that soul, wishing to know and follow the truth more manfully, and lifting her desires first for herself—for she considered that a soul could not be of use, whether in doctrine, example, or prayer, to her neighbor, if she did not first profit herself, that is, if she did not acquire virtue in herself—addressed four requests to the Supreme and Eternal Father. The first was for herself; the second for the reformation of the Holy Church; the third a general prayer for the whole world, and in particular for the peace of Christians who rebel, with much lewdness and persecution, against the Holy Church; in the fourth and last, she besought the Divine Providence to provide for things in general, and in particular, for a certain case with which she was concerned.

THE WAY OF PERFECTION[61]

. . . Then, the Eternal Truth seized and drew more strongly to Himself her desire, doing as He did in the Old Testament, for when the sacrifice was offered to God, a fire descended and drew to Him the sacrifice that was acceptable to Him; so did the sweet Truth to that soul, in sending down the fire of the clemency of the Holy Spirit, seizing the sacrifice of desire that she made of herself, saying: "Do you not know, dear daughter, that all the sufferings, which the soul endures, or can endure, in this life, are insufficient to punish one smallest fault, because the offense, being done to Me, who am the Infinite Good, calls for an infinite satisfaction?

"However, I wish that you should know, that not all the pains that are given to men in this life are given as punishments, but as corrections, in order to chastise a son when he offends; though it is true that both the guilt and the penalty can be expiated by the desire of the soul, that is, by true contrition, not through the finite pain endured, but through the infinite desire; because God, who is infinite, wishes for infinite love and infinite grief. Infinite grief I wish from My creature in two ways: in one way, through her sorrow for her own sins, which she has committed against Me her Creator; in the other way, through her sorrow for the sins which she sees her neighbors commit against Me. Of such as these, inasmuch as they have infinite desire, that is, are joined to Me by an affection of love, and therefore grieve when they offend Me, or see Me offended, their every pain, whether spiritual or corporeal, from wherever it may come, receives infinite merit, and satisfies for a guilt which deserved an infinite penalty, although their works are finite and done in finite time; but, inasmuch as they possess the virtue of desire, and sustain their suffering with desire, and contrition, and infinite displea-

---

[61]Ibid.

sure against their guilt, their pain is held worthy. Paul explained this when he said: If I had the tongues of angels, and if I knew the things of the future and gave my body to be burned, and have not love, it would be worth nothing to me. The glorious Apostle thus shows that finite works are not valid, either as punishment or recompense, without the condiment of the affection of love."

THE WAY GOD MANIFESTS HIMSELF TO THE SOUL[62]

. . . "Do you know how I manifest Myself to the soul who loves Me in truth, and follows the doctrine of My sweet and amorous Word? In many is My virtue manifested in the soul in proportion to her desire, but I make three special manifestations. The first manifestation of My virtue, that is to say, of My love and charity in the soul, is made through the Word of My Son, and shown in the Blood, which He spilled with such fire of love. Now this charity is manifested in two ways; first, in general, to ordinary people, that is to those who live in the ordinary grace of God. It is manifested to them by the many and diverse benefits which they receive from Me. The second mode of manifestation, which is developed from the first, is peculiar to those who have become My friends in the way mentioned above, and is known through a sentiment of the soul, by which they taste, know, prove, and feel it. This second manifestation, however, is in men themselves; they manifesting Me, through the affection of their love. For though I am no Acceptor of creatures, I am an Acceptor of holy desires, and Myself in the soul in that precise degree of perfection which she seeks in Me. Sometimes I manifest Myself (and this is also a part of the second manifestation) by endowing men with the spirit of prophecy, showing them the things of the future. This I do in many and diverse ways, according as I see need in the soul herself and in other creatures. At other times the third manifestation takes place. I then form in the mind the presence of the Truth, My only-begotten Son, in many ways, according to the will and the desire of the soul. Sometimes she seeks Me in prayer, wishing to know My power, and I satisfy her by causing her to taste and see My virtue. Sometimes she seeks Me in the wisdom of My Son, and I satisfy her by placing His wisdom before the eye of her intellect, sometimes in the clemency of the Holy Spirit and then My Goodness causes her to taste the fire of Divine charity, and to conceive the true and royal virtues, which are founded on the pure love of her neighbor."

PERFECT LOVE[63]

"It now remains to be told you how it can be seen that souls have arrived at perfect love. This is seen by the same sign that was given to the holy disciples after

---

[62]Ibid.
[63]Ibid.

they had received the Holy Spirit, when they came forth from the house, and fear-lessly announced the doctrine of My Word, My only-begotten Son, not fearing pain, but rather glorying therein. They did not mind going before the tyrants of the world, to announce to them the truth, for the glory and praise of My Name. So the soul, who has awaited Me in self-knowledge as I have told you, receives Me, on My return to her, with the fire of charity, in which charity, while still re-maining in the house with perseverance, she conceives the virtues by affection of love, participating in My power; with which power and virtues she overrules and conquers her own sensitive passions, and through which charity she participates in the wisdom of My Son, in which she sees and knows, with the eye of her in-tellect, My Truth and the deceptions of spiritual self-love, that is, the imperfect love of her own consolations, as has been said, and she knows also the malice and deceit of the devil, which he practices on those souls who are bound by that imperfect love. She therefore arises, with hatred of that imperfection and with love of perfection, and, through this charity, which is of the Holy Spirit, she par-ticipates in His will, fortifying her own to be willing to suffer pain, and, coming out of the house through My Name, she brings forth the virtues on her neighbor. Not that by coming out to bring forth the virtues, I mean that she issues out of the House of Self-Knowledge, but that, in the time of the neighbor's necessity she loses that fear of being deprived of her own consolations, and so issues forth to give birth to those virtues which she has conceived through affection of love. The souls, who have thus come forth, have reached the fourth state, that is, from the third state, which is a perfect state, in which they taste charity and give birth to it on their neighbors, they have arrived at the fourth state, which is one of per-fect union with Me. The two last-mentioned states are united, that is to say, one cannot be without the other, for there cannot be love of Me, without love of the neighbor, nor love of the neighbor without love of Me."

CONCLUSION[64]

"I have now, oh dearest and best beloved daughter, satisfied from the beginning to the end your desire concerning obedience. If you remember well, you made four petitions of Me with anxious desire, or rather I caused you to make them in order to increase the fire of My love in your soul: one for yourself, which I have satisfied, illuminating you with My Truth, and showing you how you may know this truth which you desired to know; explaining to you how you might come to the knowledge of it through the knowledge of yourself and Me, through the light of faith.

"The second request you made of Me was that I should do mercy to the world. In the third you prayed for the mystical body of the holy Church, that I would remove darkness and persecutions from it, punishing its iniquities at [your] own desire in your person. As to this I explained that no penalty inflicted in finite time

---

[64]Ibid.

can satisfy for a sin committed against Me, the Infinite Good, unless it is united with the desire of the soul and contrition of the heart. How this is to be done I have explained to you. I have also told you that I wish to do mercy to the world, proving to you that mercy is My special attribute, for through the mercy and the inestimable love which I had for man, I sent to the earth the Word, My only-begotten Son, whom, that you might understand things quite clearly, I represented to you under the figure of a Bridge, reaching from earth to heaven, through the union of My divinity with your human nature.

"I also showed you, to give you further light concerning My truth, how this Bridge is built on three steps; that is, on the three powers of the soul. These three steps I also represented to you, as you know, under figures of your body—the feet, the side, and the mouth—by which I also figured three states of soul—the imperfect state, the perfect state, and the most perfect state, in which the soul arrives at the excellence of unitive love. I have shown you clearly in each state the means of cutting away imperfection and reaching perfection, and how the soul may know by which road she is walking and of the hidden delusions of the devil and of spiritual self-love. Speaking of these three states I have also spoken of the three judgments which My clemency delivers—one in this life, the second at death on those who die in mortal sin without hope, of whom I told you that they went under the Bridge by the Devil's road, when I spoke to you of their wretchedness. And the third is that of the last and universal judgment. And I who told you somewhat of the suffering of the damned and the glory of the blessed, when all shall have reassumed their bodies given by Me, also promised you, and now again I repeat my promise, that through the long endurance of My servants I will reform My spouse. Wherefore I invite you to endure, Myself lamenting with you over her iniquities. And I have shown you the excellence of the ministers I have given her, and the reverence in which I wish seculars to hold them, showing you the reason why their reverence towards My ministers should not diminish on account of the sins of the latter, and how displeasing to me is such diminution of reverence; and of the virtue of those who live like angels. And while speaking to you on this subject, I also touched on the excellence of the sacraments. And further wishing you to know of the states of tears and whence they proceed, I spoke to you on the subject and told you that all tears issue from the fountain of the heart, and pointed out their causes to you in order.

"I told you not only of the four states of tears, but also of the fifth, which germinates death. I have also answered your fourth request, that I would provide for the particular case of an individual; I have provided as you know. Further than this, I have explained My providence to you, in general and in particular, showing you how everything is made by divine providence, from the first beginning of the world until the end, giving you and permitting everything to happen to you, both tribulations and consolations temporal and spiritual, and every circumstance of your life for your good, in order that you may be sanctified in Me, and My Truth be fulfilled in you, which truth is that I created you in order to possess eternal life, and manifested this with the blood of My only-begotten Son, the Word.

"I have also in My last words fulfilled your desire and My promise to speak of the perfection of obedience and the imperfection of disobedience; and how obedience can be obtained and how destroyed. I have shown it to you as a universal key, and so it is. I have also spoken to you of particular obedience, and of the perfect and imperfect, and of those in religion, and of those in the world, explaining the condition of each distinctly to you, and of the peace given by obedience, and the war of disobedience, and how the disobedient man is deceived, showing you how death came into the world by the disobedience of Adam, and how I, the Eternal Father, supreme and eternal Truth, give you this conclusion of the whole matter, that in the obedience of the only-begotten Word, My Son, you have life, and as from that first old man you contracted the infection of death, so all of you who will take the key of obedience have contracted the infection of the life of the new Man, sweet Jesus, of whom I made a Bridge, the road to Heaven being broken. And now I urge you and My other servants to grief, for by your grief and humble and continual prayer I will do mercy to the world. Die to the world and hasten along this way of truth, so as not to be taken prisoner if you go slowly. I demand this of you now more than at first, for now I have manifested to you My Truth. Beware that you never leave the cell of self-knowledge, but in this cell preserve and spend the treasure which I have given you, which is a doctrine of truth founded upon the living stone, sweet Christ Jesus, clothed in light which scatters darkness, with which doctrine clothe yourself, My best beloved and sweetest daughter, in the truth."

Julian of Norwich (1342–c. 1423)

Julian of Norwich was an unknown anchoress (a holy solitary) who lived in a monastic cell attached to the parish church in Conisford, Norwich, England. Apart from the autobiographical information given in her writings, almost nothing is known about her life. She began receiving visionary revelations or "Showings" on May 13, 1373, and recorded these in a small book called *The Showings* or *Revelations of Divine Love* (Shorter Text, c. 1393). Toward the end of her life, Julian was given particular insight and understanding about the meaning of her sixteen visions, and out of that renewed reflection she produced an extended version of the *Showings* (Longer Text).

Julian's spirituality is a remarkable synthesis of classical Christian themes and images that were derived from her experiences. Of particular interest is the profound Christological and Trinitarian reflection that dominates Julian's spirituality as well as her use of feminine metaphors for contemplating the nature and works of God.[65]

---

[65]James Walsh, S.J., trans., *Julian of Norwich: Showings* (New York: Paulist Press, 1978), pp. 17–119, offers an excellent introduction to Dame Julian's life and spirituality. Cf. Nancy Hardesty, "Revelations of Divine Love," in Magill and McGreal, eds., *Christian Spirituality*, pp. 118–85.

THE FIRST VISION[66]

Here is a vision shown by the goodness of God to a devout woman, and her name is Julian, who is a recluse at Norwich and still alive, A.D. 1413, in which vision are very many words of comfort, greatly moving for all those who desire to be Christ's lovers.

I desired three graces by the gift of God. The first was to have recollection of Christ's Passion. The second was a bodily sickness, and the third was to have, of God's gift, three wounds. As to the first, it came to my mind with devotion; it seemed to me that I had great feeling for the Passion of Christ, but still I desire to have more by the grace of God. I thought that I wished that I had been at that time with Mary Magdalene and with the others who were Christ's lovers, so that I might have seen with my own eyes our Lord's Passion which He suffered for me, so that I might have suffered with Him as others did who loved Him . . . . My intention was, because of that revelation, to have had truer recollection of Christ's Passion. As to the second grace, there came to my mind with contrition— a free gift from God which I did not seek—a desire of my will to have by God's gift a bodily sickness, and I wished it to be so severe that it might seem mortal, so that I should in that sickness receive all the rites which Holy Church had to give me, whilst I myself should believe that I was dying, and everyone who saw me would think the same, for I wanted no comfort from any human, earthly life. In this sickness, I wanted to have every kind of pain, bodily and spiritual, which I should have if I were dying, every fear and assault from devils, and every other kind of pain except the departure of the spirit, for I hope that this would be profitable me when I should die, because I desired soon to be with my God. . . . As to the third, I heard a man of Holy Church tell the story of St. Cecilia, and from his explanation I understood that she received three wounds in the neck from a sword, through which she suffered death. Moved by this, I conceived a great desire, and prayed our Lord God that He would grant me in the course of my life three wounds, that is, the wound of contrition, the wound of compassion, and the wound of longing with my will for God. . . .

And when I was thirty and a half years old, God sent me a bodily sickness in which I lay for three days and three nights; and on the fourth night I received all the rites of Holy Church, and did not expect to live until day. But after this I suffered on for two days and two nights, and on the third night I often thought I was on the point of death; and those who were around me also thought this. . . .

So I lasted until day, and by then my body was dead from the middle downwards, it felt to me. Then I was moved to ask to be lifted up and supported, with clothes held to my head, so that my heart might be more free to be at God's will,

[66]Reprinted from Walsh, trans., *Julian of Norwich.* Copyright 1978, by The Missionary Society of St. Paul the Apostle in the State of New York. Used by permission of Paulist Press. Chapters 1–5, Shorter Text, pages 125–33, with omissions.

and so that I could think of Him whilst my life would last; and those who were with me sent for the parson, my curate, to be present at my end. He came with a little boy, and brought a cross; and by that time my eyes were fixed, and I could not speak. The parson set the cross before my face and said: "Daughter, I have brought you the image of your Savior. Look at it and take comfort from it, in reverence of Him Who died for you and me." It seemed to me that I was well as I was, for my eyes were set upwards towards heaven, where I trusted that I was going; but nevertheless I agreed to fix my eyes on the face of the crucifix if I could, so as to hold out longer until my end came, for it seemed to me that I could hold out longer with my eyes set in front of me rather than upwards. . . .

After that I felt as if the upper part of my body were beginning to die. My hands fell down on either side, and I was so weak that my head lolled to one side. The greatest pain that I felt was my shortness of breath and the ebbing of my life. Then truly I believed that I was at the point of death. And suddenly in that moment all my pain left me, and I was sound, particularly in the upper part of my body, as ever I was before or have been since. I was astonished by this change, for it seemed to me that it was by God's secret doing and not natural; and even so, in this case which I felt, I had no more confidence that I should live, nor was the ease complete, for I thought that I would rather have been delivered of this world, because that was what my heart longed for.

And suddenly it came into my mind that I ought to wish for the second wound, that our Lord, of His gift and of His grace, would fill my body full with recollection and feeling of His blessed Passion, as I had prayed before, for I wished that His pains might be my pains, with compassion which would lead to longing for God. . . . I desired to suffer with Him, living in my mortal body, as God would give me grace. And at this, suddenly I saw the red blood trickling down from under the crown, all hot, flowing freely and copiously, a living stream, just as it seemed to me that it was at the time when the crown of thorns was thrust down upon His blessed head. Just so did He, both God and man, suffer for me. I perceived, truly and powerfully, that it was Himself who showed this to me, without any intermediary; and then I said: "Blessed be the Lord!" This I said with a reverent intention and in a loud voice, and I was greatly astonished by this wonder and marvel, that He would so humbly be with a sinful creatures living in this wretched flesh. I accepted it that at that time our Lord Jesus wanted, out of His courteous love, to show me comfort before my temptations began; for it seemed to me that I might well be tempted by devils, by God's permission and with His protection, before I died. With this sight of His blessed Passion and with His divinity, of which I speak as I understand, I saw that this was strength enough for me, yes, and for all living creatures who will be protected from all the devils of hell and from all their spiritual enemies.

And at the same time as I saw this corporal sight, our Lord showed me a spiritual sight of His familiar love. I saw that He is to us everything which is good and comforting for our help. He is our clothing, for He is that love which wraps and enfolds us, embraces us and guides us, surrounds us for His love, which is so tender that He may never desert us. And so in this sight I saw truly that He is everything which is good, as I understand.

And in this He showed me something small, no bigger than a hazelnut, lying in the palm of my hand, and I perceived that it was as round as any ball. I looked at it and thought: What can this be? And I was given this general answer: It is everything which is made. I was amazed that it could last, for I thought that it was so little that it could suddenly fall into nothing. And I was answered in my understanding: It lasts and always will, because God loves it; and thus everything has being through the love of God.

In this little thing I saw three properties. The first is that God made it, the second is that He loves it, the third is that God preserves it. But what is that to me? It is that God is the Creator and the lover and the protector. For until I am substantially united to Him, I can never have love or rest or true happiness; until, that is, I am so attached to Him that there can be no created thing between my God and me. And who will do this deed? Truly, He Himself, by His mercy and His grace, for He has made me for this and has blessedly restored me.

In this God brought our Lady to my understanding. I saw her spiritually in her bodily likeness, a simple, humble maiden, young in years, of the stature which she had when she conceived. Also God showed me part of the wisdom and truth of her soul, and in this I understood the reverent contemplation with which she beheld her God, marvelling with great reverence that He was willing to be born of her who was a simple creature created by Him. And this wisdom and truth, this knowledge of her Creator's greatness and of her own created littleness, made her say meekly to the angel Gabriel: Behold me here, God's handmaiden. In this sight I saw truly that she is greater, more worthy and more fulfilled, than everything else which God has created, and which is inferior to her. Above her is no created thing, except the blessed humanity of Christ. This little thing which is created and is inferior to our Lady, St. Mary—God showed it to me as if it had been a hazelnut—seemed to me as if it could have perished because it is so little.

In this blessed revelation God showed me three nothings, of which nothings this is the first that was shown to me. Even man and woman who wishes to live contemplatively needs to know of this, so that it may be pleasing to them to despise as nothing everything created, so as to have the love of uncreated God. For this is the reason why those who deliberately occupy themselves with earthly business, constantly seeking worldly well-being, have not God's rest in their souls; for they love and seek their rest in this thing which is so little and in which there is no rest, and do not know God who is almighty, all wise and all good, for He is true rest. God wishes to be known, and it pleases Him that we should rest in Him; for all things which are beneath Him are not sufficient for us. And this is the reason why no soul has rest until it has despised as nothing all which is created. When the soul has become nothing for love, so as to have Him Who is all that is good, then is it able to receive spiritual rest.

And during the time that our Lord showed me this spiritual vision which I have now described, I saw the bodily vision of the copious bleeding of the head persist, and as long as I saw it I said, many times: Blessed be the Lord! In this first revelation of our Lord I saw in my understanding six things. The first is the tokens of His blessed Passion, and the plentiful shedding of His precious blood. The second is the virgin who is His beloved mother. The third is the blessed divinity, that always was and is and ever shall be, almighty, all wisdom and all love. The fourth is everything which He has made; it is great and lovely and bountiful and good. But the reason why it seemed to my eyes so little was because I saw it in the presence of Him who is the Creator. For to a soul who sees the Creator of all things, all that is created seems very little. The fifth is that He has made everything which is made for love, and through the same love is it preserved, and always will be without end, as has been said already. The sixth is that God is everything which is good, and the goodness which everything has is God.

This everything God showed me in the first vision, and He gave me space and time to contemplate it. And then the bodily vision ceased, and the spiritual vision persisted in my understanding, and I waited with reverent fear, rejoicing in what I saw and wishing, as much as I dared, to see more, if that were God's will, or to see for a longer time what I had already seen. . . .

THREE PROPERTIES OF THE TRINITY[67]

God the blessed Trinity, who is everlasting being, just as He is eternal from without beginning, just so was it in His eternal purpose to create human nature, which fair nature was first prepared for His own Son, the second person; and when He wished, by full agreement, of the whole Trinity He created us all once. And in our creating He joined and united us to Himself, and through this union we are kept as pure and as noble as we were created. By the power of that same precious union we love our Creator and delight in him, praise him and thank him and endlessly rejoice in him. And this is the work which is constantly performed in every soul which will be saved, and this is the godly will mentioned before.

And so in our making, God almighty is our loving Father, and God all wisdom is our loving Mother, with the love and goodness of the Holy Spirit, which is all one God, one Lord. And in the joining and the union He is our very true spouse and we His beloved wife and His fair maiden, with which wife He was never displeased; for He says: "I love you and you love, and our love will never divide in two."

I contemplated the work of all the blessed Trinity, in which contemplation I saw and understood these three properties: the property of the fatherhood, and the property of the motherhood, and the property of the lordship in one God. In our almighty Father we have our protection and our bliss, as regards our natural substance, which is ours by our creation from without beginning; and in the second person, in knowledge and wisdom we have our perfection, as regards our sensuality, our restoration and our salvation, for He is our Mother, Brother, and Savior; and in our good Lord the Holy Spirit we have our reward and our gift for our living and our labor, endlessly surpassing all that we desire in His marvelous courtesy, out of His great plentiful grace. For all our life consists of three:

---

[67]Ibid. Used by kind permission of Paulist Press. Ch. 58, Longer Text, pp. 295–99, with omissions.

In the first we have our being, and in the second we have our increasing, and in the third we have our fulfillment. The first is nature, the second is mercy, the third is grace.

As to the first, I saw and understood that the high might of the Trinity is our Father, and the deep wisdom of the Trinity is our Mother, and the great love of the Trinity is our Lord; and all these we have in nature and in our substantial creation. And furthermore I saw that the second person, Who is our Mother, substantially the same beloved person, has now become our Mother sensually, because we are double by God's creating, that is to say substantial and sensual. Our substance is the higher part, which we have in our Father, God almighty; and the second person of the Trinity is our Mother in nature in our substantial creation, in whom we are founded and rooted, and He is our Mother of mercy in taking our sensuality. And so our Mother is working on us in various ways, in whom our parts are kept undivided; for in our Mother Christ we profit and increase, and in mercy He reforms and restores us, and by the power of His Passion, His death and His Resurrection He unites us to our substance. So our Mother works in mercy on all His beloved children who are docile and obedient to Him, and grace works with mercy, and especially in two properties, as it was shown, which working belongs to the third person, the Holy Spirit. He works, rewarding and giving. Rewarding is a gift for our confidence which the Lord makes to those who have labored; and giving is a courteous act which He does freely, by grace, fulfilling and surpassing all that creatures deserve.

Thus in our Father, God almighty, we have our being, and in our Mother of mercy we have our reforming and our restoring, in whom our parts are united and all made perfectly human,[68] and through the rewards and the gifts of grace of the Holy Spirit we are fulfilled. And our substance is in our Father, God almighty, and our substance is in our Mother, God all wisdom, and our substance is in our Lord God, the Holy Spirit, all goodness, for our substance is whole in each person of the Trinity, who is one God. And our sensuality is only in the second person, Christ Jesus, in Whom is the Father and the Holy Spirit; and in Him and by Him we are powerfully taken out of hell and out of the wretchedness on earth, and gloriously brought up into heaven, and blessedly united to our substance, increased in riches, and nobility by all the power of Christ and by the grace and operation of the Holy Spirit.

OUR TRUE MOTHER[69]

. . . Jesus Christ, who opposes good to evil, is our true Mother. We have our being from Him, where the foundation of motherhood begins, with all the sweet protection of love which endlessly follows.

---

[68]The published edition reads: "perfect man."
[69]Reprinted from Walsh, trans., *Julian of Norwich.* Used by kind permission of Paulist Press. chs. 55–56, Longer Text, pp. 295–99, with omissions.

As truly as God is our Father, so truly is God our Mother, and He revealed that in everything, and especially in these sweet words where He says; I am He; that is to say: I am He, the power and goodness of fatherhood; I am He, the wisdom and lovingness of motherhood; I am He, the light and grace which is all blessed love; I am He, the Trinity; I am He the unity; I am He, the great supreme goodness of every kind of thing; I am He who makes you to love; I am He who makes you to long; I am He, the endless fulfilling of all true desires. For where the soul is highest, noblest, most honourable, still it is lowest, meekest, and mildest.

And from this foundation in substance we have all the powers of our sensuality by the gift of nature, and by the help and the furthering of mercy and grace, without which we cannot profit. Our great Father, almighty God, who is being, knows us and loved us before time began. Out of this knowledge, in His most wonderful deep love, by the prescient eternal counsel of all the blessed Trinity, He wanted the second person to become our Mother, our brother and our saviour. From this it follows that as truly as God is our Father, so truly is God our Mother. Our Father wills, our Mother works, our good Lord the Holy Spirit confirms. And therefore it is our part to love God in whom we have our being, reverently thanking and praising Him for our creation, mightily praying to our Mother for mercy and pity, and to our Lord the Holy Spirit for help and grace. For in these three we is all our life: nature, mercy, and grace, of which we have mildness, patience and pity, and hatred of sin and wickedness; for the virtues must of themselves hate sin and wickedness.

And so Jesus is our true Mother in nature by our first creation, and He is our true Mother in grace by His taking our created nature. All the lovely works and all the sweet loving offices of beloved motherhood are appropriated to the second person, for in Him we have this godly will, whole and safe forever, both in nature and in grace, from His own goodness proper to Him.

I understand three ways of contemplating motherhood in God. The first is the foundation of our nature's creation; the second is His taking of our nature, where the motherhood of grace begins; the third is the motherhood at work. And in that, by the same grace, everything is penetrated, in length and in breadth, in height and in depth without end; and it is all one.

But now I should say a little more about this penetration, as I understood our Lord to mean: How we are brought back by the motherhood of mercy and grace into our natural place, in which we were created by the motherhood of love, a mother's love which never leaves us.

Our Mother in nature, our Mother in grace, because He wanted altogether to become our Mother in all things, made the foundation of His work most humbly and most mildly in the maiden's womb. And he revealed that in the first revelation, when He brought that meek maiden before the eye of my understanding in the simple stature which she had when she conceived; that is to say that our great God, the supreme wisdom of all things, arrayed and prepared Himself in this humble place, all ready in our poor flesh, Himself to do the service and the office of motherhood in everything. The mother's service is nearest, readiest and surest: nearest because it is most natural, readiest because it is most loving, and surest because it is truest. No one ever might or could perform this office fully, except only Him. We know that all our mothers bear us for pain and for death. O, what is that? But our true Mother Jesus, He alone bears us for joy and for endless life, blessed may He be. So He carries us within Him in love and travail, until the full time when He wanted to suffer the sharpest thorns and cruel pains that ever were or will be, and at the last He died. And when He had finished, and had borne us so for bliss, still all this could not satisfy His wonderful love. And he revealed this in these great surpassing words of love: "If I could suffer more, I would suffer more." He could not die any more, but He did not want to cease working; therefore He must needs nourish us, for the precious love of motherhood has made Him our debtor.

The mother can give her child to suck of her milk, but our precious Mother Jesus can feed us with Himself, and does, most courteously and most tenderly, with the blessed sacrament [Eucharist], which is the precious food of true life; and with all the sweet sacraments He sustains us most mercifully and graciously, and so He meant in these blessed words, where he said: "I am He Whom Holy Church preaches and teaches to you. That is to say: All the health and the life of the sacraments, all the power and the grace of my word, all the goodness which is ordained in Holy Church for you, I am He." . . .

This fair lovely word "mother" is so sweet and so kind in itself that it cannot truly be said of anyone or to anyone except of Him and to Him Who is the true Mother of life and of all things. To the property of motherhood belong nature, love, wisdom and knowledge, and this is God. For though it may be so that our bodily bringing to birth is only little, humble and simple in comparison with our spiritual bringing to birth, still it is He who does it in the creatures by whom it is done. The kind, loving mother who knows and sees the need of her child guards it very tenderly, as the nature and condition of motherhood will have. And always as the child grows in age and in stature, she acts differently, but she does not change her love. And when it is even older, she allows it to be chastised to destroy its faults, so as to make the child receive virtues and grace. This work, with everything which is lovely and good, our Lord performs in those by whom it is done. So He is our Mother in nature by the operation of grace in the lower part, for love of the higher part. And He wants us to know it, for He wants to have all our love attached to Him; and in this I saw that every debt which we owe by God's command to fatherhood and motherhood is fulfilled in truly loving God, which blessed love Christ works in us. And this was revealed in everything, and especially in the great bounteous words when He says: "I am He whom you love."

Thomas a' Kempis (1380–1471)

Thomas Hammerken was born at a place called Kempen, near Dusseldorf, Germany. He left home at the age of thirteen and traveled to Deventer, in the Netherlands, where Geert Groote had established the Brethren of the Common Life (1376).

In 1406 Thomas professed a call to religious life, and in 1413 he entered the priesthood.

The spirituality of the Brethren was strongly Christocentric. They intended (as the title of their most significant work indicates) to imitate Christ; to live in Christ and to have Christ live in them. To this end, the reverent reading of Holy Scripture—especially the gospels—formed a critical portion of their regiment. Their interest in the Word had an ethical edge to it, since the Brethren were studying Christ and the Bible to cultivate moral sanctity. And, finally, imitation of Christ affected the inner person, and the New Devout were concerned about the "training of the heart" so that one's fallen nature might be subdued and purged out and replaced by a renewing, affectionate devotion to Christ.[70]

Scholars have debated whether Thomas a' Kempis actually wrote *The Imitation of Christ*, though there is ample evidence to suggest that he did.[71] But Thomas probably did not create the teaching contained in the book; it is more likely that he compiled, organized, and set the Deventer devotional tradition into a fixed form. There seems to be a strong correlation between the authorship of the book and Thomas's work as "Master of the Novices," a post he held from 1425 till his death.

The Imitation comprises of four subsections (or "Books"): (1) Counsels on the Spiritual Life, (2) Counsel on the Inner Life, (3) On Inward Consolation, and (4) On the Blessed Sacrament. Each section is made up of a series of short meditations that lead the novice deeper and deeper into union with Christ. Unity with Christ was to be realized not only through contemplation, but also through inward and outward imitation of Christ, as well as sacramental oneness with him.

THE IMITATION OF CHRIST[72]

"He who follows Me, walks not in darkness," [Jn 8:12] says the Lord. By these words of Christ we are advised to imitate His life and habits, if we wish to be truly enlightened and free from all blindness of heart. Let our chief effort, therefore, be to study the life of Jesus Christ.

The teaching of Christ is more excellent than all the advice of the saints, and he who has His spirit will find in it a hidden manna. Now, there are many who hear the Gospel often but care little for it because they have not the spirit of Christ [Rom 8:9].

Yet whoever wishes to understand fully the words of Christ must try to pattern his whole life on that of Christ. What good does it do to speak learnedly

---

[70]John Van Egen, trans., *Devotion Moderna* (New York: Paulist Press, 1988), "Introduction," pp. 5–63, offers an excellent summary of the spirituality of the movement.

[71]Leo Sherley-Price, trans., *Thomas a` Kempis: Imitation of Christ* (London: Penguin Books, 1952), pp. 23–25, "The Authorship."

[72]Reprinted from Thomas a` Kempis, *The Imitation of Christ*, Bk. I, ch. 1, from the Christian Classics Ethereal Library, http://ccel.wheaton.edu, digitized by Harry Plantinga.

about the Trinity if, lacking humility, you displease the Trinity? Indeed it is not learning that makes a man holy and just, but a virtuous life makes him pleasing to God. I would rather feel contrition than know how to define it. For what would it profit us to know the whole Bible by heart and the principles of all the philosophers if we live without grace and the love of God? Vanity of vanities and all is vanity [Ec 1:2], except to love God and serve Him alone. This is the greatest wisdom—to seek the kingdom of heaven through contempt of the world.

It is vanity, therefore, to seek and trust in riches that perish. It is vanity also to court honor and to be puffed up with pride. It is vanity to follow the lusts of the body and to desire things for which severe punishment later must come. It is vanity to wish for long life and to care little about a well-spent life. It is vanity to be concerned with the present only and not to make provision for things to come. It is vanity to love what passes quickly and not to look ahead where eternal joy abides.

Often recall the proverb: "The eye is not satisfied with seeing nor the ear filled with hearing" [Ec 1:8]. Try, moreover, to turn your heart from the love of things visible and bring yourself to things invisible. For they who follow their own evil passions stain their consciences and lose the grace of God.

PURITY OF MIND AND UNITY OF PURPOSE[73]

A man is raised up from the earth by two wings—simplicity and purity. There must be simplicity in his intention and purity in his desires. Simplicity leads to God, purity embraces and enjoys Him. If your heart is free from ill-ordered affection, no good deed will be difficult for you. If you aim at and seek after nothing but the pleasure of God and the welfare of your neighbor, you will enjoy freedom within.

If your heart were right, then every created thing would be a mirror of life for you and a book of holy teaching, for there is no creature so small and worthless that it does not show forth the goodness of God. If inwardly you were good and pure, you would see all things clearly and understand them rightly, for a pure heart penetrates to heaven and hell, and as a man is within, so he judges what is without. If there be joy in the world, the pure of heart certainly possess it; and if there be anguish and affliction anywhere, an evil conscience knows it too well.

As iron cast into fire loses its rust and becomes glowing white, so he who turns completely to God is stripped of his sluggishness and changed into a new man. When a man begins to grow lax, he fears a little toil and welcomes external comfort, but when he begins perfectly to conquer himself and to walk bravely in the ways of God, then he thinks those things less difficult which he thought so hard before.

---

[73]Ibid., Bk. I, ch. 4.

THE INTERIOR LIFE[74]

"The kingdom of God is within you," [Lk 17:21] says the Lord. Turn, then, to God with all your heart. Forsake this wretched world and your soul shall find rest. Learn to despise external things, to devote yourself to those that are within, and you will see the kingdom of God come unto you, that kingdom which is peace and joy in the Holy Spirit [Joel 2:12], gifts not given to the impious. Christ will come to you offering His consolation, if you prepare a fit dwelling for Him in your heart, whose beauty and glory, wherein He takes delight, are all from within. His visits with the inward man are frequent, His communion sweet and full of consolation, His peace great, and His intimacy wonderful indeed.

Therefore, faithful soul, prepare your heart for this Bridegroom that He may come and dwell within you; He Himself says: "If any one love Me, he will keep My word, and My Father will love him, and We will come to him, and will make Our abode with him" [Jn 14:25]. Give place, then, to Christ, but deny entrance to all others, for when you have Christ you are rich and He is sufficient for you. He will provide for you. He will supply your every want, so that you need not trust in frail, changeable men. Christ remains forever, standing firmly with us to the end.

Do not place much confidence in weak and mortal man, helpful and friendly though he be; and do not grieve too much if he sometimes opposes and contradicts you. Those who are with us today may be against us tomorrow, and vice versa, for men change with the wind. Place all your trust in God [1 Pet 5:7]; let Him be your fear and your love. He will answer for you; He will do what is best for you.

You have here no lasting home [Heb 13:14] . You are a stranger and a pilgrim wherever you may be, and you shall have no rest until you are wholly united with Christ. Why do you look about here when this is not the place of your repose? Dwell rather upon heaven and give but a passing glance to all earthly things. They all pass away, and you together with them. Take care, then, that you do not cling to them lest you be entrapped and perish. Fix your mind on the Most High, and pray unceasingly to Christ.

If you do not know how to meditate on heavenly things, direct your thoughts to Christ's passion and willingly behold His sacred wounds. If you turn devoutly to the wounds and precious stigmata of Christ, you will find great comfort in suffering, you will mind but little the scorn of men, and you will easily bear their slanderous talk. When Christ was in the world, He was despised by men; in the hour of need He was forsaken by acquaintances and left by friends to the depths of scorn. He was willing to suffer and to be despised; do you dare to complain of anything? He had enemies and defamers; do you want everyone to be your friend, your benefactor? How can your patience be rewarded if no adversity test it? How can you be a friend of Christ if you are not willing to suffer any hardship? Suffer with Christ and for Christ if you wish to reign with Him.

---

[74]Ibid., Bk. II, ch. 1.

Had you but once entered into perfect communion with Jesus or tasted a little of His ardent love, you would care nothing at all for your own comfort or discomfort but would rejoice in the reproach you suffer; for love of Him makes a man despise himself. A man who is a lover of Jesus and of truth, a truly interior man who is free from uncontrolled affections, can turn to God at will and rise above himself to enjoy spiritual peace.

He who tastes life as it really is, not as men say or think it is, is indeed wise with the wisdom of God rather than of men. He who learns to live the interior life and to take little account of outward things, does not seek special places or times to perform devout exercises. A spiritual man quickly recollects himself because he has never wasted his attention upon externals. No outside work, no business that cannot wait stands in his way. He adjusts himself to things as they happen. He whose disposition is well ordered cares nothing about the strange, perverse behavior of others, for a man is upset and distracted only in proportion as he engrosses himself in externals.

If all were well with you, therefore, and if you were purified from all sin, everything would tend to your good and be to your profit [Rom 8:28]. But because you are as yet neither entirely dead to self nor free from all earthly affection, there is much that often displeases and disturbs you. Nothing so mars and defiles the heart of man as impure attachment to created things. But if you refuse external consolation, you will be able to contemplate heavenly things and often to experience interior joy.

FRIENDSHIP WITH JESUS[75]

When Jesus is near, all is well and nothing seems difficult. When He is absent, all is hard. When Jesus does not speak within, all other comfort is empty, but if He says only a word, it brings great consolation. Did not Mary Magdalen rise at once from her weeping when Martha said to her: "The Master is come, and calleth for thee" [Jn 11:28]? Happy is the hour when Jesus calls one from tears to joy of spirit. How dry and hard you are without Jesus! How foolish and vain if you desire anything but Him! Is it not a greater loss than losing the whole world [Mt 16:26]?

For what, without Jesus, can the world give you? Life without Him is a relentless hell, but living with Him is a sweet paradise. If Jesus be with you, no enemy can harm you. He who finds Jesus finds a rare treasure [Mt 13:44], indeed, a good above every good, whereas he who loses Him loses more than the whole world. The man who lives without Jesus is the poorest of the poor, whereas no one is so rich as the man who lives in His grace.

It is a great art to know how to converse with Jesus, and great wisdom to know how to keep Him. Be humble and peaceful, and Jesus will be with you. Be devout and calm, and He will remain with you. You may quickly drive Him away and lose His grace, if you turn back to the outside world. And, if you drive Him

---

[75]Ibid., Bk. II, ch. 8.

away and lose Him, to whom will you go and whom will you then seek as a friend? You cannot live well without a friend, and if Jesus be not your friend above all else, you will be very sad and desolate. Thus, you are acting foolishly if you trust or rejoice in any other.

Choose the opposition of the whole world rather than offend Jesus. Of all those who are dear to you, let Him be your special love. Let all things be loved for the sake of Jesus, but Jesus for His own sake. Jesus Christ must be loved alone with a special love for He alone, of all friends, is good and faithful. For Him and in Him you must love friends and foes alike, and pray to Him that all may know and love Him [Phil 2:12]. Never desire special praise or love, for that belongs to God alone Who has no equal. Never wish that anyone's affection be centered in you, nor let yourself be taken up with the love of anyone, but let Jesus be in you and in every good man.

Be pure and free within, unentangled with any creature. You must bring to God a clean and open heart if you wish to attend and see how sweet the Lord is. Truly you will never attain this happiness unless His grace prepares you and draws you on so that you may forsake all things to be united with Him alone. When the grace of God comes to a man he can do all things, but when it leaves him he becomes poor and weak, abandoned, as it were, to affliction. Yet, in this condition he should not become dejected or despair. On the contrary, he should calmly await the will of God and bear whatever befalls him in praise of Jesus Christ, for after winter comes summer, after night, the day, and after the storm, a great calm.

THE ROYAL ROAD OF THE CROSS[76]

To many the saying, "Deny thyself, take up thy cross and follow Me" [Mt 16:24], seems hard, but it will be much harder to hear that final word: "Depart from Me, ye cursed, into everlasting fire" [Mt 25:41]. Those who hear the word of the cross and follow it willingly now, need not fear that they will hear of eternal damnation on the day of judgment. This sign of the cross will be in the heavens when the Lord comes to judge. Then all the servants of the cross, who during life made themselves one with the Crucified, will draw near with great trust to Christ, the judge.

Why, then, do you fear to take up the cross when through it you can win a kingdom? In the cross is salvation, in the cross is life, in the cross is protection from enemies, in the cross is infusion of heavenly sweetness, in the cross is strength of mind, in the cross is joy of spirit, in the cross is highest virtue, in the cross is perfect holiness. There is no salvation of soul nor hope of everlasting life but in the cross. Take up your cross, therefore, and follow Jesus [Lk 14:27], and you shall enter eternal life. He Himself opened the way before you in carrying His cross, and upon it He died for you, that you, too, might take up your cross and long to

---

[76]Ibid., Bk. II, ch. 12.

die upon it. If you die with Him, you shall also live with Him, and if you share His suffering, you shall also share His glory [2 Cor 1:5].

Behold, in the cross is everything, and upon your dying on the cross everything depends. There is no other way to life and to true inward peace than the way of the holy cross and daily mortification. Go where you will, seek what you will, you will not find a higher way, nor a less exalted but safer way, than the way of the holy cross. Arrange and order everything to suit your will and judgment, and still you will find that some suffering must always be borne, willingly or unwillingly, and thus you will always find the cross. Either you will experience bodily pain or you will undergo tribulation of spirit in your soul.

At times you will be forsaken by God, at times troubled by those about you and, what is worse, you will often grow weary of yourself. You cannot escape, you cannot be relieved by any remedy or comfort but must bear with it as long as God wills. For He wishes you to learn to bear trial without consolation, to submit yourself wholly to Him that you may become more humble through suffering. No one understands the passion of Christ so thoroughly or heartily as the man whose lot it is to suffer the like himself. The cross, therefore, is always ready; it awaits you everywhere. No matter where you may go, you cannot escape it, for wherever you go you take yourself with you and shall always find yourself. Turn where you will—above, below, without, or within—you will find a cross in everything, and everywhere you must have patience if you would have peace within and merit an eternal crown.

If you carry the cross willingly, it will carry and lead you to the desired goal where indeed there shall be no more suffering, but here there shall be. If you carry it unwillingly, you create a burden for yourself and increase the load, though still you have to bear it. If you cast away one cross, you will find another and perhaps a heavier one. Do you expect to escape what no mortal man can ever avoid? Which of the saints was without a cross or trial on this earth? Not even Jesus Christ, our Lord, Whose every hour on earth knew the pain of His passion. "It behooveth Christ to suffer, and to rise again from the dead and so enter into his glory" [Lk 24:26]. How is it that you look for another way than this, the royal way of the holy cross? The whole life of Christ was a cross and a martyrdom, and do you seek rest and enjoyment for yourself? You deceive yourself, you are mistaken if you seek anything but to suffer, for this mortal life is full of miseries and marked with crosses on all sides. Indeed, the more spiritual progress a person makes, so much heavier will he frequently find the cross, because as his love increases, the pain of his exile also increases. . . .

To carry the cross, to love the cross, to chastise the body and bring it to subjection, to flee honors, to endure contempt gladly, to despise self and wish to be despised, to suffer any adversity and loss, to desire no prosperous days on earth—this is not man's way. If you rely upon yourself, you can do none of these things, but if you trust in the Lord, strength will be given you from heaven and the world and the flesh will be made subject to your word. You will not even fear your enemy, the devil, if you are armed with faith and signed with the cross of Christ. Set yourself, then, like a good and faithful servant of Christ, to bear bravely the cross of your Lord, Who out of love was crucified for you. Be ready to suffer many adversities and many kinds of trouble in this miserable life, for troublesome and miserable life will always be, no matter where you are; and so you will find it wherever you may hide. Thus it must be; and there is no way to evade the trials and sorrows of life but to bear them.

Drink the chalice of the Lord [Mt 20:23] with affection if you wish to be His friend and to have part with Him. Leave consolation to God; let Him do as most pleases Him. On your part, be ready to bear sufferings and consider them the greatest consolation, for even though you alone were to undergo them all, the sufferings of this life are not worthy to be compared with the glory to come.

When you shall have come to the point where suffering is sweet and acceptable for the sake of Christ, then consider yourself fortunate, for you have found paradise on earth. But as long as suffering irks you and you seek to escape, so long will you be unfortunate, and the tribulation you seek to evade will follow you everywhere. If you put your mind to the things you ought to consider, that is, to suffering and death, you would soon be in a better state and would find peace. . . .

With good reason, then, ought you to be willing to suffer a little for Christ since many suffer much more for the world. Realize that you must lead a dying life; the more a man dies to himself, the more he begins to live unto God. No man is fit to enjoy heaven unless he has resigned himself to suffer hardship for Christ. Nothing is more acceptable to God, nothing more helpful for you on this earth than to suffer willingly for Christ. If you had to make a choice, you ought to wish rather to suffer for Christ than to enjoy many consolations, for thus you would be more like Christ and more like all the saints. Our merit and progress consist not in many pleasures and comforts but rather in enduring great afflictions and sufferings.

If, indeed, there were anything better or more useful for man's salvation than suffering, Christ would have shown it by word and example. But He clearly exhorts the disciples who follow Him and all who wish to follow Him to carry the cross, saying: "If any man will come after Me, let him deny himself, and take up his cross daily, and follow Me" [Lk 9:23]. When, therefore, we have read and searched all that has been written, let this be the final conclusion—that through much suffering we must enter into the kingdom of God.

UNION WITH CHRIST IN HIS SUPPER[77]

The Disciple: Let it be granted me to find You alone, O Christ, to open to You my whole heart, to enjoy You as my soul desires, to be disturbed by no one, to be moved and troubled by no creature, that You may speak to me and I to You alone, as a lover speaks to his loved one, and friend converses with friend. I pray for this, I desire this, that I may be completely united to You and may withdraw

---

[77]Ibid., Bk. IV, ch. 13.

my heart from all created things, learning to relish the celestial and the eternal through Holy Communion and the frequent celebration of Mass.

Ah Lord God, when shall I be completely united to You and absorbed by You, with self utterly forgotten? You in me and I in You? Grant that we may remain so together. You in truth are my Beloved, chosen from thousands, in Whom my soul is happy to dwell all the days of her life. You are in truth my pledge of peace, in Whom is the greatest peace and true rest, without Whom there is toil and sorrow and infinite misery.

You truly are the hidden God. Your counsel is not with the wicked, and Your conversation is rather with the humble and the simple. O how kind is Your spirit, Lord, Who in order to show Your sweetness toward Your children, deign to feed them with the sweetest of bread, bread come down from heaven! Surely there is no other people so fortunate as to have their god near them, as You, our God, are present everywhere to the faithful, to whom You give Yourself to be eaten and enjoyed for their daily solace and the raising of their hearts to heaven.

Indeed, what other nation is so renowned as the Christian peoples? What creature under heaven is so favored as the devout soul to whom God comes, to feed her with His glorious Flesh? O unspeakable grace! O wonderful condescension! O love beyond measure, singularly bestowed upon man!

What return shall I make to the Lord for this love, this grace so boundless? There is nothing I can give more pleasing than to offer my heart completely to my God, uniting it closely with His. Then shall all my inner self be glad when my soul is perfectly united with God. Then will He say to me: "If you will be with Me, I will be with you." And I will answer Him: "Deign, O Lord, to remain with me. I will gladly be with You. This is my one desire, that my heart may be united with You."

CHAPTER 3

The Reformation Era

The Age of Reform was a pivotal period in the development of Christian Spirituality. Drawing upon resources and patterns already well established in the Middle Ages, Christians of the waning fifteenth century and dawning of the sixteenth drew upon and extended those earlier patterns in ways that gave them new potency and diversity.[1] While it is possible to see this multiplicity of religious expression as a sign of the waning of the Middle Ages, because it marks an end of the homogeneity of the old order,[2] the explosion of Christian piety that shook the sixteenth century is more aptly understood as an indication of steadily growing religious interest and excitement; Bernd Moeller, for example, suggests "one dare . . . call the late fifteenth century in Germany one of the most churchly-minded and devout periods of the Middle Ages."[3]

While it drew upon a great variety of sources, this religious exuberance must also be seen in the context of even larger social and cultural transformations. The known world was expanding at a staggering rate. The Age of Reform was also the Age of Exploration; as Hernando Cortes (1485–1547) plundered the halls of Montezuma, another Spanish adventurer named Inigo Lopez de Recalde—who would become Ignatius of Loyola—contemplated the premature end of his career as warrior because of the terrible wound he suffered in the battle of Pampeluna (1521). That these two worlds often overlapped is evidenced by the life and work of

---

[1] Richard Kieckhefer, "Major Currents in Late Medieval Devotion," in *Christian Spirituality: High Middle Ages and Reformation*, edited by Jill Raitt (New York: Crossroad, 1988), pp. 75–108. Cf. Steven Ozment, ed., *The Reformation in Medieval Perspective* (Chicago: Quadrangle Books, 1971).

[2] Johan Huizinga, *The Waning of the Middle Ages* (Garden City, N.Y.: Doubleday, 1956).

[3] Bernd Moeller, "Piety in Germany around 1550," in Ozment, ed., *Reformation*, p. 60.

Batholome de las Casas (1474–1566), who championed and defended the rights of Native Americans.

Explorations of the inner worlds of the spirit and intellect were also well under way. The Renaissance, which was born in fourteenth-century Florence, had gradually spilled over the Alps to northern Europe, and it created an international interest in classical culture, language, and art. Ironically this "new learning" stressed a return to the ancient sources (*ad fonts*) to find the foundations for new ideas, and patterns for art. What began as a celebration of the culture and literature of ancient Greece and Rome soon became (and especially so in the "Northern Renaissance" and Spain) an exploration of the literature of the Bible and the writings of the ancient Church. As it moved from pagan toward patristic sources, the Renaissance retained an optimism about the ability and capacity of humanity, but instead of finding patterns for art and literature it found patterns of piety. Reformers of the Protestant (John Calvin) and Roman Catholic (Desiderius Erasmus) traditions were deeply influenced by the new learning. The Renaissance gave the church renewed access to sacred texts as well as the linguistic tools to explore them.

The old land-based economic system, rooted in feudalism and the manorial system, gradually gave way to a money-based economy and a resurgence in trade. With increased trade and technological advances came a more diversified economy, and the emergence of crafts, guilds, and merchants signaled the dawning of a new day. Where large tracts of land created wealth under the old system, access to trade, resources, and skilled labor created wealth under the new system. Trading cities began to replace feudal manors and monasteries as focal points of life and industry, and feudal principalities gradually gave way to rising national states. In a similar way, new ideas and trends in Christian thought and practice seemed intent upon remaking the religious landscape of the Middle Ages. Religious unity, one of the ideals of the old order, seemed permanently shattered through the emergence of Protestantism; 1521 saw Ignatius of Loyola's conversion as well as Martin Luther's excommunication.

As the world changed around them, reformers (both Catholic and Protestant) of the early sixteenth century sought to reconfigure Christian faith and life in ways that corresponded to new challenges. One fundamental shift discernible among the reformers (and one that stands upon the shoulders of late medieval mysticism and nominalism) was an enhanced sense of individualism. Reformation-era spirituality was strongly shaped by the lives and personalities of charismatic individuals. The first half of the sixteenth century gave rise to Lutheran, Reformed (Calvinist), Anabaptist (Michael Sattler), Anglican (Thomas Cranmer), and Jesuit (Ignatian) spirituality. Martin Luther's "bound conscience," John Calvin's "teachable mind," and Ignatius of Loyola's "exercises" of the will all have in common the basic assumption that Christian Spirituality has a powerfully personal aspect. As a corollary to this assumption came a second—that Christian Spirituality was for all persons—clergy and lay, "religious" and "secular," and so the reformers sought to engender and cultivate the spiritual life of the laity.

Catherine of Genoa (1447–1510)

Catherine Fieschi was born into a wealthy, aristocratic family. She possessed the intelligence and beauty and the sort of social connections that should have brought her success and happiness. But she was depressed and withdrawn. At the age of thirteen Catherine received a strong and decisive call to enter a religious life. She presented herself at the Augustinian convent of Santa Maria delle Grazie, but was refused admission on account of her youth.

The untimely death of her father, in 1461, caused Catherine's life to take a rather different direction. According to the custom of the age, her future was placed in the hands of her oldest brother, Giacomo, who was determined to marry her into one of the leading families of Genoa. Arrangements went ahead more or less without Catherine's consent. She was married to Giuliano Adorno on January 14, 1463, with her uncle, Bishop Napolone Fieschi, officiating.

What followed then for Catherine was a decade of loneliness, depression, and seclusion. Her husband was crude, lewd, and unfaithful. His misdeeds and mistresses only deepened her depression. On March 22, 1743, during her Lenten confession, and in the midst of personal turmoil, Catherine was visited by a deep and overwhelming experience of God's love and a poignant realization of her own sinfulness. A prayer of gratitude came to her mind: "O Love, was it possible that you have called me with so much love, and have revealed to me in a moment what no tongue could describe?"

St. Catherine's subsequent years were marked with visionary like experiences and inward impressions on her soul that gradually transformed her life through an effusion of Divine love. Her spirituality stressed the purifying effects of God's love. It also took expression through her leadership in a hospital for incurably ill people, and through the formation of a holy club that gave birth to the Oratory of Divine Love—one of the great renewal movements of the Catholic Reformation.

CONVERTED IN A REMARKABLE MANNER[4]

. . . Catherine of Genoa was born in the year 1447, the daughter of Jacopo Fieschi and Francesca di Negro, both of very noble family. Her father was Viceroy of Naples and died while still holding that office; among her ancestors were two popes, Innocent IV and Adrian V. Though high-born, elegant and attractive looking, Catherine began from an early age to feel scorn for the pride of the nobles and their luxurious mode of life. In her room there was a picture of Christ taken down from the Cross, and every time she entered and her glance fell on it, she felt an overwhelming grief and love at the thought of the bitter suffering that God had taken on Himself for love of us. She lived in great simplicity without mixing

---

[4]Reprinted from Paul Gavin, trans., *The Life and Sayings of Catherine of Genoa* (Staten Island: Alba House, 1964), pp. 22–27, 29–30, 33–34, 38–40. Used by kind permission of Alba House.

with others; she was well instructed in her religion and greatly zealous to acquire virtue.

At about the age of thirteen she had a strong wish to enter the religious life. She tried by all means possible with the help of her confessor to gain admittance into the Convent of Santa Maria delle Grazie, in which her sister was already a nun. However, she was refused on account of her age, and this caused her great sorrow.

When she was about sixteen, her family married her to Giuliano Adorno, a gentleman of noble Genoese family. In spite of her repugnance she consented from a spirit of obedience, but in order to prevent her from setting her love on the world and flesh, God permitted she should be given a husband whose character was the very opposite of her own. A man of strange and wayward nature and dissolute ways, he made her suffer so much that for ten years her life was a very unhappy one, and squandered all her fortune until they were on the verge of poverty. However, she was obedient to him and forbearing, but the strain of living with him undermined her health and caused her to pine away with melancholy. The life she led was like a hermit's, shut up as she was all alone in her house, without any contact with the world, and going out only to attend Mass, but she bore it all without complaint.

At the end of these ten years Catherine was called by God and suddenly converted in a remarkable manner. For three months previous to her conversion she was filled with great sadness and profound disgust with life, which led her to avoid all company and mope in solitude; so deep was her melancholy that she became insufferable to herself, not knowing what it was she really wanted. For five years she had sought distraction in the pleasures and vanities of the world, as a compensation for her wretchedness during the early years of her married life, but this had the effect of only increasing her distress instead of lessening it. . . .

. . . [S]he was persuaded by the sister of hers who was a nun to go and see the chaplain of her convent. She had no desire to go to confession, but her sister had said to her: "At least go and talk to him, for he is a good priest," and in fact he was a saintly man. She had hardly knelt down before him when her heart was suddenly pierced by an immense love of God, with such a clear awareness of her own miseries and sins and of God's goodness, that she was ready to swoon. The feeling produced in her a change of heart that purified her and drew her wholly away from the follies of the world. She was almost beside herself and cried out in her heart with burning love: "No more world! No more sin!" At that moment she felt that, if she had possessed a thousand worlds, she would have spurned them all.

While she thus knelt, incapable of speech and almost senseless, her confessor did not notice anything amiss. He was called away on some matter, and when he returned shortly afterwards, she recovered herself so far as to be able to murmur: "Father, if you don't mind, I would like to leave this confession for another time." Rising to her feet, she left him and returned home, all on fire and pierced to the heart by the love that God had inwardly shown her. As if beside herself, she chose out the most private room there was, and there gave vent to her burning tears and sighs. The only prayer she could think of to say was: "O Love, is it possible that you have called me with so much love and have revealed to me in one moment what no tongue can describe?" In the following days the only sounds that came from her were deep sighs, and so keen was the sorrow she felt for the sins she had committed against God's goodness that if she had not been sustained by a super-human power, her heart would have burst and she would have surely died.

Christ appeared to her in spirit with His Cross on His shoulder, dripping with blood. The whole house seemed to her to be full of streams of His blood, and she saw that it had all been shed for love alone. Horror of sin and disgust at herself made her cry out: "O Lord, if it is necessary, I am ready to confess my sins in public." A few days after this she made a general confession with such con-trition and compunction as to pierce her soul. Though God had already pardoned all her sins, consuming them in the fire of His love at the very moment He had struck her heart with it, yet He wished her to satisfy the claims of justice and led her along the path of satisfaction for sin. This period of contrition and illumina-tion lasted some fourteen months, after which the memory of her former life was withdrawn from her mind and she never again saw even a shadow of her past sins, as if they had been cast into the depths of the sea. . . .

The first four years after her conversion she performed great penances until all her senses were mortified. At first, when she felt a natural desire for some-thing she would refuse it, and she would do anything that she felt to be dis-agreeable. She would wear rough haircloth, eat no meat or anything appetizing, and never fruit either fresh or dried. When her relations visited her she would not converse with them except about what was strictly necessary, though she was by nature courteous and affable, and as to anything else, she paid heed neither to herself nor to them. She acted thus for the purpose of self-conquest, and if any-one was surprised at it, she took no notice. . . .

After these four years she was given a mind so clear, free and filled with God that nothing else ever entered it. At sermon or Mass she was so absorbed in this interior feeling that she neither heard nor saw what was being said or done around her. Yet it was strange that, with all her interior absorption, God never allowed her to be negligent. She would come back to herself whenever it was necessary, such as to answer a question addressed to her, and no one ever had to complain of her. Sometimes she was so far transported that she would have to hide herself, as she would lose the use of her senses and appear dead.

She would be found lying on the ground with her face in her hands, beside herself with joy, and unable to hear however loudly she was called. At other times she would walk quickly up and down for no apparent reason. She would remain as though dead for six hours, but on being called to attend to some matter, how-ever trifling it might seem, she would rise instantly to see to it. When she came out of her hiding-place her face would be so flushed that she looked like a cherub, and she seemed to have on her lips the words of the Apostle, "Who shall sepa-rate me from the love of God?" [Rom 8:35] . . .

In the period immediately following her conversion she gave herself actively to good works, by going round to seek out the poor in the city. She was engaged to do this by the *Donne della Misericordia*, a pious association of Genoese ladies for the care of the poor. They supplied her with money and food for them, and she was greatly zealous in carrying out all that was laid on her; bringing help to the sick and the poor to the best of her ability. She would clean the most nauseating filth, and if she felt her stomach heaving, she would put some of it in her mouth to overcome her squeamishness. She would take home clothes full of vermin or ordure to wash and bring back clean. She gave all her care to this kind of work, and it was remarkable that with so much touching of dirt, she never had any on herself. She served the sick with fervent devotion, both as regards their souls, reminding them of spiritual things, and their bodies, never hesitating before the most loathsome disease or foul-smelling breath.

Later she entered the Hospital of Genoa and was appointed Matron in complete charge. She devoted herself to her task in such a way that her zeal never interfered with her feeling for her Dear Lord, nor her feeling with any of her duties. It was extraordinary how a person so occupied in exterior matters could at the same time be so filled with interior joy, and one so immersed in the fire of divine love could always be so conscious and unforgetful of what had to be done.

She remained many a time in company with her many spiritual friends, discoursing of divine love, in such a way that they felt as though in Paradise, both collectively, and each one in his own particular way. How delightful were these conversations! He who spoke and he who listened, each one fed on spiritual food of a delicious kind; and because the time flew so quickly, they could never attain satiety, but, all on fire within them, they would remain there, unable at last to speak, unable to depart, as though in ecstasy. . . .

PURE LOVE[5]

Love is God Himself, infused by His immense goodness into our hearts and ever on the watch for what is useful to us. Benign and gentle in all and to all, Love gives up its own will, and takes as its will God's will, to which it submits in everything. Then God with His incomparable love enkindles, purifies, enlightens and so fortifies this will that it fears nothing but sin, because this alone displeases God. Rather than commit the slightest sin it would endure the most fearful torment and suffering imaginable.

• • •

Divine love is our own true love. It separates us from the world and from ourselves, and joins us to God. When divine love is poured into our hearts, what else can matter to us in this world or the next? Death would be a relief to it, and you cannot frighten it with hell, for it fears nothing except losing the thing loved, which can only be lost by sin.

• • •

---

[5]Ibid., "Sayings," pp. 65–68. Used by kind permission of Alba House.

If Love took any account of suffering, it would not be love of God, but self-love.

• • •

I see clearly that God loves all creatures He has created with pure love, and there is nothing He hates but sin, so that it is impossible to measure or imagine His aversion to it. He loves His creatures with such perfection that there never was and never will be a mind that can understand the tiniest spark of it. If God wished a soul to be able to understand it, He would first have to make the body immortal, for in its own nature it could never understand it.

THE THREE RULES OF LOVE[6]

Her Love once said within her mind: Observe these three rules. Never say "I will," or "I will not." Never say "my" but always "our." Never excuse yourself, but be always ready to accuse yourself.

He said to her another time: When you say the "Our Father," take for your foundation "Thy will be done." In the "Hail Mary" take "Jesus"; let Him be ever fixed in your heart and he will be your guide and shield in the course of life in all your needs. In Holy Scripture take "Love," with which you will ever go straightly, exactly, lightly, attentively, swiftly, enlightenedly, without error, without guide, and without the means of other creatures, since Love is sufficient for itself to do all things without fear or weariness, so that martyrdom itself appears a joy.

• • •

"You command me to love my neighbor, and yet I cannot love anything but you, or admit any other admixture with you. How then shall I act." And she received the interior answer: "Whoever loves Me, loves all that I love."

• • •

I see all good is in one place only, in God. All else that is good and exists below Him is good by participation. But pure and full Love cannot desire anything from God, however good it may be, that has the name of participation, because it wants God all whole, pure and great as He is. If even the smallest particle were lacking, it could not be content but would think it were in hell. That is why I say that I want no created love, a love that can be savored, understood and enjoyed. I want no love that comes through the intellect, memory or will. Pure Love passes above all these and transcends them, saying, "I shall not be satisfied until I am

---

[6]Ibid., pp. 68–71. Used by kind permission of Alba House.

locked and enclosed in the divine breast where all created forms are lost, and so lost become divine."

Martin Luther (1483–1546)

Martin Luther, the inaugurator of the Protestant Reformation, was born the son of a miner in Eisleben, Germany. He was well educated, despite his family's modest means, because his father intended Martin to have a career as a lawyer. He attended school at Magdeburg (1497) under the direction of the Brethren of the Common Life, and the "modernist" (nominalist) University of Erfurt (1501). After having begun studying law, and against the strong objections of his father, Luther entered the Augustinian monastery at Erfurt in July of 1505. A gifted scholar, Luther earned a doctor's degree in theology (1512) and became Professor of Biblical Literature at Wittenberg.

Luther had a tender conscience, and no amount of attention to the spiritual remedies offered by monasticism gave him a personal sense of God's acceptance. As he worked harder and harder at being holy, Martin felt more and more despondent and distant from God. A subsequent encounter with God, through the text of St. Paul's Epistle to the Romans—his "Tower Experience" as Luther called it—caused him to recognize that justification is a matter of faith, and that he had previously misapprehended the nature of Christian righteousness as consisting principally in good works.

It is not insignificant that Luther mentions St. Paul and St. Augustine in his description of what happened to him in the tower; while appreciating the romantic mysticism of St. Bernard and St. Bonaventure, as well as the teutonic mysticism of Meister Eckhart and John Tauler, Luther's spirituality was chiefly shaped by Pauline and Augustinian theology. The goal of human life is union with God, but this union is hindered by original sin—which is manifested in our persistence in seeking our own way instead of seeking God. The great chasm between God and sinful humanity is spanned by God's grace; grace is not to be received in striving for self-justification but rather in self-resignation and self-emptying. When one dies to self, one can rise in Christ. Justification occurs when the righteousness of Christ, which Luther termed "alien (fremd) righteousness," becomes ours by faith. As Luther declared in his "Sermon on Two Kinds of Righteousness," "Through faith in Christ, therefore, Christ's righteousness becomes our righteousness and all that He has becomes ours; rather He Himself becomes ours."[7]

Many of Luther's writings explored the relationship of faith and works in the living of a Christian life. His celebration of the constancy of God's faithfulness, over against the assaults of conscience and trials of this world, is powerfully expressed

---

[7]Harold Grimm, ed., *Luther's Works*, Vol. 31 (Philadelphia: Fortress Press, 1957), "Sermon on Two Kinds of Righteousness" (1519), pp. 297–302.

in Martin Luther's most famous hymn ("A Mighty Fortress Is Our God"). Lutheran spirituality stresses—as Gerald Forde phrased it—"the art of getting used to justification."[8] Luther's liberating encounter with the justifying power of the gospel is enshrined in Lutheran liturgies and hymns. His distrust of good works, evidenced below in "Christian Liberty," gave Lutheranism an emphasis upon freedom and spontaneity in the Christian's living out his or her justification by faith. Martin Luther's Augustinian roots gave him a robust appreciation for the depth of human sin, and hence even Christian life was viewed as a struggle against "the world, the flesh, and the devil." God is the Christian's mighty fortress (feste Berg) in the midst of this tumultuous life. By prayer and faithful attention to the Word and Spirit of God Christians are more than conquerors over the assaults of the evil one.[9]

THE TOWER EXPERIENCE[10]

. . . I had already during that year returned to interpret the Psalter anew. I had confidence in the fact that I was more skillful, after I had lectured in the university on St. Paul's epistles to the Romans, to the Galatians, and the one to the Hebrews. I had indeed been captivated with an extraordinary ardor for understanding Paul in the Epistle to the Romans. But up till then it was not the cold blood about the heart,[11] but a single word in Chapter 1 [:17], "In it the righteousness of God is revealed," that had stood in my way. For I hated that word "righteousness of God," which, according to the use and custom of all the teachers, I had been taught to understand philosophically regarding the formal or active righteousness, as they called it, with which God is righteous and punishes the unrighteous sinner.

Though I lived as a monk without reproach, I felt that I was a sinner before God with an extremely disturbed conscience. I could not believe that He was placated by my satisfaction. I did not love, yes, I hated the righteous God who punishes sinners, and secretly, if not blasphemously, certainly murmuring greatly, I was angry with God, and said, "As if, indeed, it is not enough, that miserable sinners, eternally lost through original sin, are crushed by every kind of calamity by the law of the decalogue, without having God add pain to pain by the gospel and also by the gospel threatening us with His righteousness and wrath!" Thus I raged

---

[8]Donald Alexander, ed., *Christian Spirituality: Five Views of Sanctification* (Downers Grove: Inter Varsity Press, 1988), p. 13.

[9]Cf.Frank Senn, "Lutheran Spirituality," in *Protestant Spiritual Traditions*, edited by Frank Senn (New York: Paulist Press, 1986), pp. 9–55; D. H. Tripp, "Luther," in *The Study of Spirituality*, edited by Cheslyn Jones, Geoffrey Wainwright, and Edward Yarnold (New York: Oxford University Press, 1986), pp. 342–46; and Marc Lienhard, "Luther and the Beginnings of the Reformation," in Riatt, ed., *Christian Spirituality*, pp. 268–300.

[10]Reprinted from Louis Spitz, ed., *Luther's Works*, Vol. 34. Copyright 1960 Muhlenberg Press. Used by kind permission of Augsburg Fortress Press. Pages 336–38, "The Preface to the Complete Edition of Luther's Latin Works" (1545).

[11]Alluding to Virgil, *Georgics*, 2.

with a fierce and troubled conscience. Nevertheless, I beat importunately upon Paul at that place, most ardently desiring to know what St. Paul wanted.

At last, by the mercy of God, meditating day and night, I gave heed to the context of the words, namely, "In it the righteousness of God is revealed, as it is written, "He who through faith is righteous shall live" [Rom 1:17]. There I began to understand that the righteousness of God is that by which the righteous lives by a gift of God, namely by faith. And this is the meaning; the righteousness of God is revealed by the gospel, namely, the passive righteousness with which merciful God justifies us by faith, as it is written, "He who through faith is righteous shall live." Here I felt that I was altogether born again and had entered paradise itself through open gates. There a totally other face of the entire Scripture showed itself to me. Thereupon I ran through the Scriptures from memory, I also found in other terms an analogy, as, the work of God, that is, what God does in us, the power of God, with which He makes us strong, the wisdom of God, with which He makes us wise, the strength of God, the salvation of God, the glory of God.

And I extolled my sweetest word with a love as great as the hatred with which I had before hated the word "righteousness of God." Thus that place in Paul was for me truly the gate to paradise. Later I read Augustine's *The Spirit and the Letter*, where contrary to hope I found that he, too, interpreted God's righteousness in a similar way, as the righteousness with which God clothes us when he justifies us. Although this was heretofore said imperfectly and he did not explain all things concerning imputation clearly, it nevertheless was pleasing that God's righteousness with which we are justified was taught. Armed more fully with these thoughts, I began a second time to interpret the Psalter. . . .

CHRISTIAN LIBERTY[12]

Christian faith has appeared to many [to be] an easy thing; nay, not a few even reckon it among the social virtues, as it were; and this they do, because they have not made proof of it experimentally, and have never tasted of what efficacy it is. For it is not possible for any one to write well about it, or to understand well what is rightly written, who has not at some time tasted of its spirit, under the pressure of tribulation. While he who has tasted of it, even to a very small extent, can never write, speak, think, or hear about it sufficiently. For it is a living fountain, springing up unto eternal life, as Christ calls it in the 4th chapter of St. John.

Now, though I cannot boast of my abundance, and though I know how poorly I am furnished, yet I hope that, after having been vexed by various temptations, I have attained some little drop of faith, and that I can speak of this matter. . . . That I may open, then, an easier way for the uneducated—for these alone I am

---

[12]Reprinted from Henry Wace and C. A. Bucheim, trans., *First Principles of the Reformation by Dr. Martin Luther*, Vol. I (London: J. Murray, 1883), pp. 104–37, with omissions and minor linguistic emendations.

trying to serve—I first lay down these two propositions, concerning spiritual liberty and servitude.

A Christian is the most free lord of all, and subject to none; a Christian is the most dutiful servant of all, and subject to every one.

Although these statements appear contradictory, yet, when they are found to agree together, they will be highly serviceable to my purpose. They are both the statements of Paul himself, who says: "Though I be free from all men, yet have I made myself servant unto all" (1 Cor. ix. 19), and: "Owe no man anything, but to love one another." (Rom. xiii. 8.) Now love is by its own nature dutiful and obedient to the beloved object. Thus even Christ, though Lord of all things, was yet made of a woman; made under the law; at once free and servant; at once in the form of God and in the form of a servant [Phil 2:7ff]. . . .

But you ask how it can be the fact that faith alone justifies, and affords without works so great a treasure of good things, when so many works, ceremonies, and laws are prescribed to us in the Scriptures. I answer: before all things bear in mind what I have said, that faith alone without works justifies, sets free, and saves. . . . From all this it is easy to understand why faith has such great power, and why no good works, nor even all good works put together, can compare with it; since no work can cleave to the word of God, or be in the soul. Faith alone and the word reign in it; and such as is the word, such is the soul made by it; just as iron exposed to fire glows like fire, on account of its union with the fire. It is clear then that to a Christian . . . his faith suffices for everything, and that he has no need of works, neither has he need of the law; and, if he has no need of the law, he is certainly free from the law, and the saying is true: "The law is not made for a righteous man." (1 Tim. I.9.) This is that Christian liberty, our faith, the effect of which is, not that we should be careless or lead a bad life, but that no one should need the law or works for justification and salvation.

Let us consider this as the first virtue of faith; and let us look also to the second. This also is an office of faith, that it honours with the utmost veneration and the highest reputation him in whom it believes, inasmuch as it holds him to be truthful and worthy of belief. . . .

The third incomparable grace of faith is this, that it unites the soul to Christ, as the wife to the husband; by which mystery, as the Apostle teaches, Christ and the soul are made one flesh. Now if they are one flesh, and if a true marriage— nay, by far the most perfect of all marriages—is accomplished between them . . . then it follows that all they have become is theirs in common, as well good things as evil things; so that whatsoever Christ possesses, that the believing soul may take to itself and boast of as its own, and whatever belongs to the soul, that Christ claims as His. . . . Thus the believing soul, by the pledge of its faith in Christ, becomes free from all sin, fearless of death, safe from hell, and endowed with the eternal righteousness, life, and salvation of its husband Christ. Thus he presents to himself a glorious bride, without spot or wrinkle, cleansing her with the washing of water by the word; that is, by faith in the word of life, righteousness, and salvation. . . .

Although, as I have said, inwardly, and according to the spirit, a man is amply enough justified by faith, having all that he requires to have, except that this very faith and abundance ought to increase from day to day, even till the future life; still he remains in this mortal life upon earth, in which it is necessary that he should rule his own body. . . . Here then works begin; here he must not take his ease; here he must give heed to exercise his body by fasts, watchings, labour, and other moderate discipline, so that it may be subdued to the spirit, and obey and conform itself to the inner man and faith, and not rebel against them nor hinder them, as is its nature to do if it is not kept under. For the inner man, being conformed to God, and created after the image of God through faith, rejoices and delights itself in Christ, in whom such blessings have been conferred on it; and hence has only this task before it, to serve God with joy and for nought in free love. . . .

True then are these two sayings: Good works do not make a good person, but a good person does good works. Bad works do not make a bad person, but a bad person does bad works. Thus it is always necessary that the substance or person should be good before any good works can be done, and that good works should follow and proceed from a good person. As Christ says: "A good tree cannot bring forth evil fruit, neither can a corrupt tree bring forth good fruit." (Matt. vii. 18.) Now it is clear that the fruit does not bear the tree, nor does the tree grow on the fruit; but, on the contrary, the trees bear the fruit and the fruit grows on the trees. . . .

So too no good work can profit an unbeliever to justification and salvation; and on the other hand no evil work makes him an evil and condemned person, but that unbelief, which makes the person and the tree bad, makes his works evil and condemned. Wherefore, when any man is made good or bad, this does not arise from his works, but from his faith or unbelief, as the wise man says: "The beginning of sin is to fall away from God"; that is, not to believe. Paul says: "He that cometh to God must believe" (Heb. xi. 6); and Christ says the same thing: "Either make the tree good, and his fruit good; or else make the tree corrupt, and his fruit corrupt." (Matt. xii. 33.) As much as to say: He who wishes to have good fruit, will begin with the tree, and plant a good one; even so he who wishes to do good works must begin, not by working, but by believing, since it is this which makes the person good. For nothing makes the person good but faith, nor bad but unbelief. . . . We do not then reject good works; nay, we embrace them and teach them in the highest degree. It is not on their own account that we condemn them, but on account of this impious addition to them, and the perverse notion of seeking justification by them.

. . . [W]e will speak also of those works which we perform towards our neighbor. For one does not live for oneself alone in this mortal body, in order to work on its account, but also for all people on earth; nay, we live only for others and not for ourselves. For it is to this end that we bring our own body into subjection, that we may be able to serve others more sincerely and more freely; as Paul says: "None of us liveth to himself, and no man dieth to himself. For whether we live, we live unto the Lord; and whether we die, we die unto the Lord." (Rom. XIV. 7, 8.) Thus it is impossible that we should take our ease in this life, and not work for the good of our neighbours; since we must needs speak, act, and converse among men; just as Christ was made in the likeness of men, and found in fashion as a man, and had His conversation among men. Yet a Christian has need of none of these things for justification and salvation, but in all his works he ought to entertain this view, and look only to this object, that he may serve and be useful to others in all that he does; having nothing before his eyes but the necessities and the advantage of his neighbour. . . .

Here is the truly Christian life; here is faith really working by love; when a person applies himself [or herself] with joy and love to the works of that freest servitude, in which one serves others voluntarily and for nought; himself abundantly satisfied in the fulness and riches of our own faith. . . . Thus from faith flow forth love and joy in the Lord, and from love a cheerful, willing, free spirit, disposed to serve our neighbour voluntarily, without taking any account of gratitude or ingratitude, praise or blame, gain or loss. Its object is not to lay people under obligations, nor does it distinguish between friends and enemies, or look to gratitude or ingratitude, but most freely and willingly spends itself and its goods, whether it loses them through ingratitude, or gains good will. For thus did its Father, distributing all things to all people abundantly and freely; making His sun to rise upon the just and the unjust. Thus too the child does and endures nothing, except from the free joy with which it delights through Christ in God, the giver of such great gifts. . . .

We conclude therefore that a Christian . . . does not live in himself, but in Christ and in his neighbour, or else is no Christian; in Christ by faith, in his neighbour by love. By faith he is carried upwards above himself to God, and by love he sinks back below himself to his neighbour, still always abiding in God and His love, as Christ says: "Verily I say unto you, hereafter he shall see heaven open, and the angels of God ascending and descending upon the Son of man." (John I. 51.)

Thus much concerning liberty, which, as you see, is a true and spiritual liberty, making our hearts free from all sins, laws and commandments; as Paul says: "The law is not made for a righteous man" (1 Tim. I. 9); and one which surpasses every other and outward liberty, as far as heaven is above earth. May Christ make us to understand and preserve this liberty. . . .

It is not from works that we are set free by the faith of Christ, but from the belief in works, that is, from foolishly presuming to seek justification through works. Faith redeems our consciences, makes them upright and preserves them, since by it we recognise the truth that justification does not depend on our works, although good works neither can nor ought to be wanting to it; just as we cannot exist without food and drink and all the functions of this mortal body. Still it is not on them that our justification is based, but on faith; and yet they ought not on that account to be despised or neglected. Thus in this world we are compelled by the needs of this bodily life; but we are not hereby justified. . . . Thus our doings, life, and being, in works and ceremonies, are done from the necessities of this life, and with the motive of governing our bodies; but yet we are not justified by these things, but by the faith of the Son of God. . . .

Desiderius Erasmus (c. 1466–1536)

Desiderius Erasmus was born in Rotterdam, the illegitimate son of a local priest. When his mother died, the care of Desiderius and his sister passed into the hands of trustees, who rapidly squandered their meager inheritance. The pain and poverty of his early life became a prod for educational excellence. Erasmus attended the Deventor school of the Brethren of the Common life (1475–84), and then entered the Augustinian monastery at Steyn (1486–92) perhaps because he could study for free among the monks. In 1492 he was ordained a priest and entered the service of the Bishop of Cambrary as a private secretary; the Bishop enabled Erasmus to attend the University of Paris (1495–99), but he did not complete the doctor's degree. The balance of his career was spent as a scholarly vagrant, "chasing bread" as he termed it, seeking patronage as he traveled to the citadels of Renaissance learning on the continent and to England to study the sources of classical and Christian antiquity.

Erasmus epitomized the desire of the Christian humanists to drink deeply at the fonts of classical learning. And by the end of his career, he was universally esteemed as the most educated man in Europe. His most lasting contribution was the production of the *Greek Testament* (1516), which paved the way for the vernacular versions of Protestants like Luther (German) and William Tyndal (English).

As a reformer, Erasmus was very much a Christian humanist. He was deeply distressed about the ethical abuses that abounded in the church of his day, and he also hated dispute and separation. Hence he refused to leave Roman Catholicism. His program for reform was one that was rooted in the New Testament. He firmly believed that the Church could reform herself if she embraced "the simple philosophy of Jesus" and eschewed the diatribes and broadsides that were so much a part of late medieval theology. As an ethicist, Erasmus attacked the abuses of the Church as one who loved her deeply, and his satirical *In Praise of Folly* was one of the most read books of the day. His *Enchridion* (1504) epitomized Erasmus's desire to return Christian reflection to the life and teachings of Jesus, and in that concern it is possible to discern echoes of a` Kempis and the Brethren of the Common Life.

TO PAUL VOLTZ[13]

A great part of holiness consists in desiring with all one's heart to become holy; I do not feel that we should look down on a person striving for such a goal even if the attempt sometimes falls short of success. This challenge should be faced in every man's life; frequently renewed efforts at length beget a happy issue. For

---

[13]Reprinted from Hans Hillerbrand, ed., *Erasmus and His Age: Selected Letters of Desiderius Erasmus* (New York: Harper & Row, 1970), pp. 125–28, with omissions. The letter was dated August 14, 1518, and was subsequently published as the preface to Erasmus's *Enchridion*. Used by kind permission of Dr. Hans J. Hillerbrand, Department of Religion, Duke University, Durham, N.C.

whoever has carefully conned the map has completed much of a journey along a confusing route. Therefore I am not at all upset by the taunts of certain people who spurn this little book as being not very learned and maintain that it could have been written by any novice, since it fails to treat of Scotistic questions, as though without these nothing at all would be scholarly. It may not be very profound, if only it inspires. It may not train men for combat at the Sorbonne, if only it does train them for Christian tranquility. It may not be useful for a theological disputation, if only it is of use for theological living. What would I achieve by discussing what everybody discusses? Who in these times does not engage in theological questions? What other purpose is there for examinations in the schools? There are almost as many commentaries on the books of the *Sentences* as there are names of theologians. . . . [L]et those mighty volumes be the occupation of mighty professors, though they should be few in number. At the same time, we must remember the unlettered masses, for whom Christ died. The most important part of Christian piety is taught by him who inflames men with a love for it. A wise king, in educating his son for true wisdom, spends much more time on motivation than on information, as if the love of wisdom were almost the attainment of it. Doctors and lawyers have the shameful practice of deliberately making their profession very difficult so that their profits may be more lucrative and their renown also more extensive among the uninitiated; but far more shameful would such a practice be in the case of the philosophy of Christ. Rather, our efforts should be in the opposite direction: to make this philosophy as uncomplicated as possible and intelligible to all. We should not strive to appear learned, but to win over as many as possible to the Christian way of life. . . .

I am well aware that every font and vein of Christian wisdom is stored up in the Gospels and the apostolic writings. However, a work written in a foreign tongue, in a style that is often confusing, with involved metaphors and figures of speech, is so difficult that even we professionals often have to struggle and strain before we can understand it. So, in my opinion, it would be most helpful to assign such a task to men as holy as they are learned, men who could draw the complete philosophy of Christ from the pure sources of the evangelists and the apostles and from the most approved interpreters, and then reduce it to a summary statement in a manner that is simple but learned, brief but clear. Dogmas of faith would be handled in as few paragraphs as possible. Directives for daily life would be spelled out in equally few words, but in such a way that the Turks, for example, would understand that Christ's yoke is mild and agreeable, not burdensome, and that they have found a father, not a tyrant; a shepherd, not a robber; and that they are called to salvation, not dragged into slavery. They too are human beings; they do not have iron or adamant in their breasts. They can be softened, they can be won over by kindnesses, which tame even wild beasts. And the most efficacious means is the Christian truth. But to whomever the Pope decides to entrust this responsibility, by the same token he will order them not to swerve from Christ their model, and to disregard the passions or lusts of men.

Some such work, poor though it was, I had in mind when I published the first edition of my *Enchiridion*. I could see that the rank and file of Christians had been led astray not only by inordinate desires but also by false views. I considered that a large number of those who professed to be shepherds and teachers were using to their own advantage the privileges they have in the name of Christ. . . . In the deep darkness of our age, amidst its great confusion, with all the conflicting views of men, what better refuge have we than that truly sacred anchor, the gospel teachings? What truly pious person does not sigh as he views this modern era, by far the most corrupt ever? When did tyranny, when did greed ever enjoy a wider sway, and with greater impunity? When was more attention ever given to ceremonial observances? When did wickedness ever flourish with greater license? When has charity grown so cold? Is anything presented, read, heard, decided except what smacks of ambition and profit? O unhappy generation, has Christ not left us some traces of His teaching and of His spirit?

Do not infect that heavenly philosophy of Christ with human decrees. Let Christ remain what He is, namely the center, while various circles surround Him. Do not remove the target from its position. Those who are nearest to Christ—priests, bishops, cardinals, popes, and those whose duty it is to follow the Lamb wherever he goes—let them have a thorough grasp of what is the absolutely pure center, and then, as much as possible, transmit that spirit to those next to them. Let the second circle contain the secular princes whose arms and laws in their own way do service to Christ—whether in just wars they overcome the enemy and safeguard the public order, or by legitimate punishments they restrain criminals. . . .

In the third circle let us gather together the common people; true, they form the grossest part of our series of circles, but even so they do belong to Christ's body. For the eyes are not the only members of this body. So are the legs, the feet, the genitals. A kindly consideration must be shown to them so that they may always be encouraged, as far as possible, to the things that Christ prefers. For in this body, he who was once a foot, can become an eye.

THE WEAPONS OF CHRISTIAN WARFARE[14]

I think we can truthfully say that nothing is more important in military training than a thorough knowledge of the weapons to be employed and the nature of the enemy to be encountered. I would add to this that the need for preparedness, of having the weapons close at hand, is also of the utmost importance. In ordinary warfare it is customary that leave of absence or actual retirement to winter quarters brings about a cessation of hostilities from time to time. This is certainly not the case in the kind of warfare we are describing. We can never permit ourselves to be even a finger's length from our weapons. Since our enemy is incessant in his attacks, we must be constantly on the battle line, constantly in a state of preparedness. As a matter of fact, our enemy, when he appears peaceful, when he

---

[14]Reprinted from John P. Dolan, trans., *The Essential Erasmus*. Translation copyright (c) 1964 by John P. Dolan. Used by permission of Dutton Signet, a division of Penguin Books USA Inc. Pages 34–40, with omissions.

feigns flight or a truce, can at that very moment be assumed to be preparing for an attack. He is most dangerous when he appears peaceful, and it is during his violent attacks that we can actually feel most secure. It is for this reason that our primary concern must be to keep the mind armed. Our enemies are armed for no other purpose than to destroy us; surely we should not be ashamed to take up arms so as not to perish.

   We will speak about Christian armor more in detail when we treat that subject later on. Meanwhile I would like to point out briefly two weapons that we should prepare to use in combating the chief vices. These weapons are prayer and knowledge. St. Paul clearly expresses the desire that men be continually armed when he commands us to pray without ceasing. Pure prayer directed to heaven is able to subdue passion, for it is, as it were, a citadel inaccessible to the enemy. Knowledge, or learning, fortifies the mind with salutary precepts and keeps virtue ever before us. These two are inseparable, the former imploring but the latter suggesting what should be prayed for. St. James tells us that we should pray always for faith and hope, seeking the things of salvation in Jesus' name. We may recall that Christ asked the sons of Zebedee if they really knew what they were praying for. We must always emphasize the dual necessity of both prayer and knowledge. In your flight from sin imitate Aaron as a model of prayer and Moses as an example of knowledge of the law. Neither allow your knowledge to lessen nor your prayer to become sterile.

   . . . Try to let this be a practice with you: When the enemy assaults you and the other vices give you trouble, lift up your mind to heaven and in your faith do not fail to raise up your hands also. Perhaps the best remedy in this matter is to be continually occupied with works of piety so that you will revert, not to worldly affairs, but to Christ.

   You must believe me when I say that there is really no attack from the enemy, no temptation so violent, that a sincere resort to Holy Writ will not easily get rid of it. There is no misfortune so sad that a reading of the Scriptures does not render bearable. Therefore, if you will but dedicate yourself entirely to the study of the Scriptures, if you meditate day and night on the divine law, nothing will ever terrorize you and you will be prepared against any attack of the enemy. I might also add that a sensible reading of the pagan poets and philosophers is a good preparation for Christian life. . . .

   We must forge a handy weapon, an *enchridion*, a dagger, that you can always carry with you. You must be on guard when you eat or sleep, even when you travel in the course of worldly concerns and perhaps become weary of bearing this righteous armor. Never allow yourself to be totally disarmed, even for a moment, lest your wily foe oppress you. Do not be ashamed to carry this little sword with you. For it is neither a hardship to bear nor useless in defending yourself. Though it is a small weapon, it will enable you, if you use it skillfully, to withstand the enemy's tumultuous assaults quite easily and avoid a deadly wound. Now is the time for us to teach ourselves a kind of "manual of arms." I promise that, if you diligently train yourself in it, our sovereign Lord, Jesus Christ, will transfer you, rejoicing and victorious, form this garrison to the city of Jerusalem, where there is neither tumult nor war at all, but everlasting peace and perfect tranquility. Meanwhile, all hope of safety should be placed in your arms and your armor. . . .

GENERAL RULES FOR LIVING A CHRISTIAN LIFE[15]

First Rule: Now since faith is the only gateway to Christ, the first rule I would lay down is that we ought to place great reliance on the Scriptures. This belief should not be, as is the case with most Christians, something cold, careless, and calculated, but rather should come from a fullness of heart. Be convinced that there is not a single item contained in Holy Writ that does not pertain to your salvation. . . .

Second Rule: If our first rule demands that we doubt nothing in the divine promises, the second is that we act upon these promises without delay and hesitation. With resolute purpose we must be prepared to undergo loss of everything—property, life itself—for Christ's sake. The kingdom of heaven does not belong to the lazy; it suffers violence, and "the violent bear it away." As you advance on the path to perfection, you must determine not to turn back. Neither the affection of your loved ones, the allurements of the world, nor the cares of domestic life should stand in your way. Whenever you cannot disentangle yourself from the affairs and business of the world, you must knife your way through them. The fleshpots of Egypt must be forsaken once and for all. . . .

Third Rule: I feel that fear is one of the real obstacles to the pursuit of virtue. This pursuit seems difficult because it involves relinquishing so many things we have come to love and because it demands incessant struggle against those three really formidable elements, the flesh, the devil, and the world. With that in mind I would like to propose a third rule. We must analyze these unfounded fears; when we do, we will find that they are not as bad as they appear. Even if we rescind from the notion of reward, the way of Christ is the most sensible and logical one to follow. . . .

Fourth Rule: In order to help you expedite this decision I am going to lay down a fourth rule: Make Christ the only goal of your life. Dedicate to Him all your enthusiasm, all your effort, your leisure as well as your business. And don't look upon Christ as a mere word, an empty expression, but rather as charity, simplicity, patience, and purity—in short, in terms of everything He has taught us. Consider as the devil, on the other hand, anything that deters us from Christ and His teaching. "When your eye is single, your whole body will be filled with light [Mt 6:22]." Direct your gaze toward Christ alone to the extent that you love nothing, or desire nothing, unless it be either Christ or because of Christ. . . .

Tenth Rule: Here are some suggestions for handling temptation: Make a violent effort to put sinful thoughts out of your mind. Turn around and spit, as it were, in the face of the tempter. Or fasten your attention on some holy task and

---

[15]Ibid. Used by permission of Dutton Signet, a division of Penguin Books USA Inc. Pages 53–83, with omissions.

apply all your powers of concentration to it. Or pray with all your might. You might have some particularly stirring passages from the Bible ready to use to encourage yourself in time of particularly painful mental agony.

Eleventh Rule: You have two dangers to face: one is giving in; the other is becoming proud after a temptation has been conquered. To be always safe from temptation, remember that Christ will help His followers do all things, because He says to them, "Have confidence; I have overcome the world." After temptation has passed you, or while you are performing some worthy task, give all the credit to God's kindness. If you allow yourself to feel that you have done this on your own ability and merit, your mind, the inner shrine, will become filled with prideful pleasure. Keep yourself in check by remembering St. Paul's words: "What do you have that you did not receive? And if you received, why do you boast, as if you had not received it?" . . .

Seventeenth Rule: Each temptation has its own appropriate remedy. There is, however, one remedy that can be applied to any and all temptations, and that is the Cross, which is the example for those who fall, the refuge of those who toil, and the weapon for those in the fray. This is the one weapon you should use against the devil. The people have the Passion read to them and adore the image of the Cross. They strengthen themselves by hanging crosses about themselves and by keeping parts of the true Cross about their homes. They work themselves into veritable agonies as they meditate on Christ's Passion and cry tears of compassion for Him. This is all well and good for the ignorant. The true value of the Cross, however, is in profiting from its many examples. You cannot say that a person loves Christ if he does not follow His example.

If you want to meditate successfully on the Cross, you must have a plan of action, realizing that you are fighting a life and death battle. . . . You must match the various parts of the Passion with the particular vices you are afflicted with and want to be rid of. There is no temptation or vice for which Christ did not furnish a remedy on the Cross. For example, when ambition pushes you to want to be great in the eyes of men, think, my suffering brother, of how great Christ is, and to what extent He lowered Himself to atone for your sins. When envy fills your mind, remember how gently and sincerely He poured Himself out for our benefit. He was good to the very worst of us. When gluttony is the problem, think of how He drank vinegar and gall. When lust tempts you, remember how Christ lived. All His life He denied Himself these pleasures and suffered discomfort, punishment, and misfortune. He will assist you, too, when anger burns inside of you. Think of how He stood like a lamb, silent before His shearers. . . .

Michael Sattler (c. 1490–1527)

Born at Stauffen in Breisgau, Germany, Michael Sattler entered St. Peter's Benedictine monastery near Freiburg, where Sattler distinguished himself in learning and in service. By the early 1520s he came into contact with Protestant ideas; by March of 1525 he had left the monastery, left the Roman Catholic Church, married, and become one of the leaders of the Anabaptist movement that had begun in Zurich only two months before. He was present at the Zurich Disputations (Nov. 6–8, 1525), after which he was imprisoned and subsequently exiled from the city on November 18.

Sattler continued his reformatory work in southern Germany; visiting Strassburg (1526) and beginning a church in Hob. Through his efforts, Anabaptist pastors gathered at Schleitheim and drafted *Seven Articles*, alternately called the *Schleitheim Confession* (1527), that characterized the movement. The document epitomized the distinctive practices and perspectives of Anabaptist spirituality. Since they viewed infant baptism as no baptism at all, the founders of the movement were rebaptized as adults when they came to personal faith in Christ; hence they were called *Ana* (Lat. "again") baptists. In terms of theological doctrines, the Anabaptists were in basic agreement with classical Christianity, but they viewed various practices of contemporary Roman Catholics and Protestants to be "abominations" to the word and will of God. In their view, the other sixteenth-century reformations did not go far enough in removing these abuses. Hence the Anabaptists became "radical" reformers, intent upon instituting the pure Christianity of the New Testament and the primitive church of the book of Acts.[16]

During his return from Schleitheim to Hob, Sattler was arrested by the Roman Catholic authorities of Rottenburg. Documents found on his person identified Michael Sattler as an Anabaptist, and therefore as a heretic. After a brief trial, he and several others were found guilty of heresy and were executed on May 20, 1527. His martyrdom was recorded in the *Martyr's Mirror*, and the account of his death gave courage and encouragement to those who came after him. A hymn, attributed to Sattler, evidences the connection between Christian discipleship and persecution that was so much a part of the life and faith of early Anabaptists.

THE SCHLEITHEIM CONFESSION[17]

The articles we have dealt with, and in which we have been united are these: baptism, ban, the breaking of bread, separation from abomination, shepherds in the congregation, the sword, the oath.

I. Notice concerning baptism. Baptism shall be given to all those who have been taught repentance and the amendment of life and [who] believe truly that their sins are taken away through Christ, and to all those who desire to walk in the resurrection of Jesus Christ and be buried with Him in death, so that they might rise with Him; to all those who with such an understanding themselves desire and request it from us; hereby is excluded all infant baptism, the greatest and first abomination of the Pope. For this you have the reasons

---

[16]George H. Williams, *The Radical Reformation* (Philadelphia: Westminster Press, 1975), remains the standard treatment of this movement.

[17]Used by permission of Herald Press, Scottdale, Pa., from *The Legacy of Michael Sattler*, by John H. Yoder, 1973. Pages 36–43. Many of Yoder's extensive notes have been omitted.

and the testimony of the writings and the practice of the apostles. We wish simply yet resolutely and with assurance to hold to the same.

II. We have been united as follows concerning the ban. The ban shall be employed with all those who have given themselves over to the Lord, to walk after [Him] in His commandments; those who have been baptized into the one body of Christ, and let themselves be called brothers or sisters, and still somehow slip and fall into error and sin, being inadvertently overtaken. The same [shall] be warned twice privately and the third time be publicly admonished before the entire congregation according to the command of Christ (Mt 18). . . .

III. Concerning the breaking of bread, we have become one and agree thus: all those who desire to break the one bread in remembrance of the broken body of Christ and all those who wish to drink of one drink in remembrance of the shed blood of Christ, they must beforehand be united in the one body of Christ, that is the congregation of God, whose head is Christ, and that by baptism. For Paul indicates [1 Cor 10:21], we cannot be partakers at the same time of the table of the Lord and the table of devils. . . . So it shall and must be, that whoever does not share the calling of the one God to one faith, to one baptism, to one spirit, to one body together with all the children of God, may not be made one loaf together with them, as must be true if one wishes truly to break bread according to the command of Christ.

IV. We have been united concerning the separation that shall take place from the evil and the wickedness which the devil has planted in the world, simply in this; that we have no fellowship with them, and do not run with them in the confusion of their abominations. So it is; since all who have not entered into the obedience of faith and have not united themselves with God so that they will to do His will, are a great abomination before God, therefore nothing else can or really will grow or spring forth from them than abominable things. . . . To us, then, the commandment of the Lord is also obvious, whereby He orders us to be and to become separated from the evil one, and thus He will be our God and we shall be His sons and daughters [2 Cor 6:17]. . . .

From all this we should learn that everything which has not been united with our God in Christ is nothing but an abomination which we should shun. By this are meant all popish and repopish works and idolatry, gatherings, church attendance, winehouses, guarantees and commitments of unbelief, and other things of the kind, which the world regards highly, and yet which are carnal or flatly counter to the command of God, after the pattern of all the iniquity which is in the world. From all this we shall be separated and have no part with such, for they are nothing but abominations, which cause us to be hated before our Christ Jesus, who has freed us from the servitude of the flesh and fitted us for the service of God and the Spirit whom He has given us. Thereby shall also fall away from us the diabolical weapons of violence—such as sword, armor, and the like, and all their use to protect friends or against enemies—by virtue of the word of Christ: "You shall not resist evil" [Mt 5:39].

V. We have been united as follows concerning shepherds in the church of God. The shepherd in the church shall be a person according to the rule of Paul [1 Tim 3:7], fully and completely, who has a good report of those who are outside the faith. The office of such a person shall be to read and exhort and teach, warn, admonish, or ban in the congregation, and properly to preside among the sisters and brothers in prayer, and in the breaking of bread, and in all things to take care of the body of Christ, that it may be built up and honored through us, and the mouth of the mocker be stopped. . . .

VI. We have been united as follows concerning the sword. The sword is an or-dering of God outside the perfection of Christ. It punishes and kills the wicked, and guards and protects the good. In the law the sword is estab-lished over the wicked for punishment and for death, and the secular rulers are established to wield the same. But within the perfection of Christ only the ban is used for the admonition and exclusion of the one who has sinned, without the death of the flesh, simply the warning and the command to sin no more.

Now many, who do not understand Christ's will for us, will ask: whether a Christian may or should use the sword against the wicked for the protec-tion and defense of the good, or for the sake of love. The answer is unani-mously revealed: Christ teaches and commands us to learn from Him, for He is meek and lowly of heart and thus we shall find rest for our souls [Mt 11:29]. . . .

VII. We have been united as follows concerning the oath. The oath is a confir-mation among those who are quarreling or making promises. In the law it is commanded that it should be done only in the name of God, truthfully and not falsely. Christ, who teaches the perfection of the law, forbids His [followers] all swearing, whether true or false; neither by heaven nor by earth, neither by Jerusalem nor by our head; and that for the reason which He goes on to give: "For you cannot make one hair white or black." You see, thereby all swearing is forbidden. We cannot perform what is promised in swearing, for we are not able to change the smallest part of ourselves [Mt 5:34–36]. . . . Christ taught us similarly when He says, "Your speech shall be yea, yea; and nay, nay; for what is more than that comes of evil" [Mt 5:37]. . . . Christ is simply yea and nay, and all those who seek Him simply will understand His Word. Amen.

THE MARTYRDOM OF MICHAEL SATTLER[18]

. . . Michael Sattler requested that he might be able to consult with his brothers and sisters; this was granted to him. When he had spoken with them only a short time, he took the floor and answered fearlessly thus: "Concerning the articles

---

[18]Ibid. Used by permission of Herald Press, Scottdale, Pa. Pages 69–75.

which have to do with me, my brothers and sisters, hear the following brief statement:

1. We do not admit that we have acted counter to the imperial mandate; for it says that one should not adhere to the Lutheran doctrine and seduction, but only to the gospel and the Word of God; this we have held to. Counter to the gospel and the Word of God I do not know that I have done anything; in witness thereto I appeal to the words of Christ.

2. That the real body of Christ the Lord is not in the sacrament, we admit: for Scripture says: "Christ has ascended to heaven and sits at the right hand of His heavenly Father, whence He shall come to judge the living and the dead."[19] It follows therefrom, since He is in heaven and not in the bread, that He cannot be eaten bodily.

3. Regarding baptism we say: infant baptism is not useful toward salvation, for it stands written, that "we live only by faith [Rom 1:17?]." Further: "He who believes and is baptized, will be saved" [Mk 16:16]. Peter says in 1 Peter 3[21] "which also now saves you in baptism, which thereby signifies not the laying off of filth of the flesh but the covenant of a good conscience with God through the resurrection of Christ."

4. We have not rejected oil, for it is a creature of God. What God has made is good and not to be rejected. But what pope, bishop, monks, and priests have wanted to do to improve on it, this we think nothing of. For the pope has never made anything good. What the epistle of James [5:14] speaks of is not the pope's oil.

5. We have not dishonored the Mother of God and the saints; rather the Mother of Christ is to be praised above all women because to her was given the grace that she could give birth to the Savior of the whole world. That she, however, is a mediatrix and advocate, the Scripture knows nothing of; for she must like us await judgment. Paul says to Timothy [1 Tim 2:5] that Christ is our mediator and advocate before God. Concerning saints, we say that we who live and believe are the saints. I testify to this with the epistle of Paul to the Romans, Corinthians, Ephesians, and elsewhere: he always writes: "To the beloved saints." Therefore we, who believe, are the saints. Those who have died in the faith we call the "blessed."

6. We hold that one should not swear allegiance to government for the Lord says in Matthew 5[37]: "You should swear no oath, but your speech shall be yea, yea, nay, nay."

7. When God called me to testify to His Word, and I read Paul, I considered the unchristian and dangerous estate in which I had been, in view of the pomp,

---

[19]This is not from the Bible, but from the Apostles Creed.

usury, and great fornication of the monks and priests. I therefore obeyed and took a wife according to the command of God. Paul was prophesying well on the subject to Timothy: "In the last days it shall come to pass that they will forbid marriage and food, which God has created that they might be enjoyed with thanksgiving" [1 Tim 4:3].

8. If the Turk comes, he should not be resisted, for it stands written: "thou shalt not kill." We should not defend ourselves against the Turks or our other persecutors, but with fervent prayer should implore God that He might be our defense and our resistance. As to me saying that if waging war were proper I would rather take the so-called Christians who persecute, take captive, and kill true Christians, than against the Turks, this was for the following reason: the Turk is a genuine Turk and knows nothing of the Christian faith. He is a Turk according to the flesh. But you claim to be Christians, boast of Christ, and still persecute the faithful witnesses of Christ. Thus you are Turks according to the Spirit.

To conclude: you servants of God, I admonish you to consider whereto you have been established by God to punish evil, to defend and protect the just. Since, then, we have done nothing counter to God and the gospel, consider therefore what you are doing. You should also ask, and you will find, that I and my brothers and sisters have not acted against any government in words or deeds.

Therefore, you servants of God, in case you might not have heard or read the Word of God, would you send for the most learned [people] and for the godly books of the Bible, in whatever language they might be, and let them discuss the same with us in the Word of God. If they show us with Holy Scripture that we are in error and wrong, we will gladly retract and recant, and will gladly suffer condemnation and the punishment for our offense. But if we cannot be proved in error, I hope to God that you will repent and let yourselves be taught.

After this speech most of the judges laughed and shook their heads. The City clerk (*Stadtschreiber*) of Ensisheim spoke: "O yes, you disreputable, desperate, and mischievous monk, you think we should debate with you? Sure enough, the hangman will debate with you, you can believe me." . . . [Sattler] spoke: "You servants of God, I have not been sent to defend the Word of God in court. We are sent to testify thereto. Therefore we cannot consent to any legal process, for we have no such command from God. If, however, we have not been able to be justly convinced, we are ready to suffer, all for our faith in Christ Jesus our Saviour . . . unless we should be convinced otherwise with Scripture." . . .

Whereafter the judges arose, went into another room, and remained there perhaps an hour and a half to reach their verdict. . . . When the judges returned to the room the verdict was read, as follows: "In the matter of the prosecutor of the imperial majesty versus Michael Sattler, it has been found that Michael Sattler should be given into the hands of the hangman, who shall lead him to the square and cut off his tongue, then chain him to a wagon, there tear his body twice with red hot tongs, and again when he is brought before the gate, five more times. When this is done to be burned to powder as a heretic.

. . . Afterward[20] he was led back to prison until the third day, but first of all into a room where he spoke thus to the Prosecutor: "*Schultheiss,* you know that you and your fellow judges have condemned me contrary to justice and without proof, therefore look out, and repent, for if not, you and they will be eternally condemned before the judgment of God to eternal fire."

Whereafter on May 20 he was led to the marketplace and the judgment which had been pronounced was executed against him. After cutting off his tongue he was chained to the cart and according to the verdict torn with red hot tongs; then burnt in fire. Nevertheless, at first in the square and then again at the place of execution he prayed to God for his persecutors and also encouraged others to pray for them and finally spoke thus: "Almighty eternal God, Thou who art the way and the truth, since I will testify this day to the truth and seal it with my blood." He also exhorted the Prosecutor as he had spoken before, he was answered, that he should busy himself with God. When he had commended his spirit to God he was thrown on the frame into the fire, and immediately the bands on his hands opened and he gave the agreed sign with both hands; thus he longsufferingly died. . . .

CHRIST'S DISCIPLES[21]

1. When Christ with His teaching true
   Had gathered a little flock
   He said that each with patience
   Must daily follow Him bearing his cross.

2. And said: You, my beloved disciples,
   Must be ever courageous
   Must love nothing on earth more than Me
   And must follow My teaching.

3. The world will lie in wait for you
   And bring you much mockery and dishonor;
   Will drive you away and outlaw you
   As if Satan were in you.

4. When then you are blasphemed and defamed
   For My sake persecuted and beaten

---

[20]This portion of the account comes from the report of Klaus von Graveneck. He was a Protestant Swabian nobleman, who was present at the trial because of feudal obligation.

[21]This hymn is attributed to Michael Sattler. Reprinted from the Amish *Ausbund,* "Als Christus mit sein'r Wahren Lehr," No. 7, p. 46. Used by permission of Herald Press, Scottdale, Pa., from *The Legacy of Michael Sattler* by John H. Yoder, 1973. Pages 141–45.

Rejoice; for behold your reward
Is prepared for you at heaven's throne.

5.   Behold Me: I am the Son of God
And have always done the right.
I am certainly the best of all
Still they finally killed Me.

6.   Because the world calls Me an evil spirit
And malicious seducer of the people
And contradicts My truth
Neither will it go easy with you.

7.   Yet fear not such a man
Who can kill only the body
But far more fear the faithful God
Whose it is to condemn both.

8.   He it is who tests you as gold
And yet is loving to you as His children.
As long as you abide in My teaching
I will nevermore forsake you.

9.   For I am yours and you are Mine
Thus where I am there shall you be,
And he who abuses you touches My eye,
Woe to the same on that day.

10.   Your misery, fear, anxiety, distress, and pain
Will be great joy to you there
And this shame a praise and honor,
Yes, before the whole host of heaven.

11.   The apostles accepted this
And taught the same to everyman;
He who would follow after the Lord,
That he would count on as much.

12.   O Christ, help Thou Thy people
Which follows Thee in all faithfulness,
That though through Thy bitter death
It may be redeemed from all distress.

13.   Praise to Thee, God, on Thy throne
And also to Thy beloved Son
And to the Holy Ghost as well.
May He yet draw many to His kingdom.

John (Jean) Calvin (1509–64)

John Calvin was born in the shadow of the ancient cathedral of Noyon, sixty miles northeast of Paris. Calvin was destined for the study of theology. His father, Garard, was a solicitor at the Bishop's court, and he was able to have his twelve-year-old son appointed as a chaplain to one of the altars in the cathedral. Supported by that benefice, John embarked upon his educational career in Paris, enrolling at the university in 1521. Humanism had settled into Paris more than a decade before Calvin, and the work of Jacques Lefevre and William Bude made it one of the citadels of the new study of biblical literature and languages.

In 1528 Calvin's career took a decisive detour. His father—who had reputedly embezzled funds from the bishop's coffers—was dismissed from his position at the ecclesiastical court and excommunicated. Under intense parental pressure and his own disillusionment, John entered the University of Orleans, where he studied law with an intensity that rewarded him with a stomach ulcer. But the study of law brought little satisfaction. When his father died in 1531, he returned to Paris and stepped back into his life as a Christian humanist. During this period John experienced a "sudden" conversion by which his "obstinate" mind was brought to a more "teachable frame." It was characteristic of Calvin that he would describe his conversion, in the only instance that he writes of it, in intellectual terms.

Calvin's new perspective was dangerous in November of 1533, as steps were taken to suppress Protestant ideas in Paris. He fled the city, and by the providence of God (through seemingly indirect steps) was led to embark upon his career as a Protestant reformer, in Geneva, then in Strassburg, and finally back in Geneva again. In 1536 he published the first edition of what would become his most famous work, *The Institutes of the Christian Religion*; its six slim chapters would be multiplied many times over prior to the emergence of the definitive edition of the *Institutes* in 1559.

It has been rightly written that *unio mystica* ("mystical union with Christ") is the heart of Calvin's spirituality,[22] and certainly that assessment sets him in the mainstream of Christian Spirituality. Perhaps the more distinctive element in Calvin's spirituality, particularly compared with that of other Protestants, was his willingness to employ specific "means" and structures that helped produce piety and realize mystical union with Christ. This development seems to have its basis in Calvin's tendency to view the (ideal) Christian life as an orderly and harmo-

---

[22] Sinclair B. Ferguson, "The Reformed View," in Alexander, ed., *Christian Spirituality*, pp. 47–76; Howard G. Hageman, "Reformed Spirituality," in Senn, ed., *Protestant Spiritual Traditions* pp. 60–62; and Wilhelm Niesel, *Reformed Symbolics* (Edinburgh: Oliver & Boyd, 1962), pp. 182–92. Lucien Richard's delineation of the roots of Calvin's spirituality traces it back through the French Christian humanists Jean Gerson and to the Brethren of the Common Life. Richard stressed *pietas* ("piety") as his foundational theme. Cf. Lucien Joseph Richard, *The Spirituality of John Calvin* (Atlanta: John Knox, 1974).

nious life. As he wrote, for example, "The object of regeneration . . . is to manifest in the life of believers a harmony and agreement between God's righteousness and their obedience, and thus to confirm the adoption that they have received as sons." He returned to the law, at just the point that Martin Luther eschewed it—its relevancy for regulating a Christian's life (*Inst.* VII. 1.) Hence, "orderly" became one of Calvin's favorite descriptions for Christian life, and his church orders and *Ecclesiastical Ordinances* (1541) employ church discipline (a process that could culminate in excommunication) as a way of regulating and ordering the community of faith.

MY MIND BECAME TEACHABLE[23]

. . . When I was as yet a very little boy, my father had destined me for the study of theology. But afterwards, when he considered [that] the legal profession commonly raised those who followed it to wealth, this prospect induced him suddenly to change his purpose. Thus it came to pass, that I was withdrawn from the study of philosophy, and was put to the study of law. To this pursuit I endeavoured faithfully to apply myself, in obedience to the will of my father; but God, by the secret guidance of His providence, at length gave a different direction to my course. And first, since I was too obstinately devoted to the superstitions of Popery to be easily extricated from so profound an abyss of mire, God by a sudden conversion subdued and brought my mind to a teachable frame, which was more hardened in such matters than might have been expected from one at my early period of life. Having thus received some taste and knowledge of true godliness, I was immediately inflamed with so intense a desire to make progress therein, that although I did not altogether leave off other studies, I yet pursued them with less ardour.

I was quite surprised to find that before a year had elapsed, all who had any desire after purer doctrine were continually coming to me to learn, although I myself was as yet but a mere novice. . . . Being of a disposition somewhat unpolished and bashful, which led me always to love the shade and retirement, I then began to seek some secluded corner where I might be withdrawn from the public view; but so far from being able to accomplish the object of my desire, all my retreats were like public schools. In short, whilst my one great object was to live in seclusion without being known, God so led me through different turnings and changes, that He never permitted me to rest in any place, until, in spite of my natural disposition, he brought me forth to public notice. . . .

---

[23]Reprinted from James Anderson, trans., *Commentary on the Book of Psalms by John Calvin* (Grand Rapids, Mich.: Wm. B. Eerdmans, 1949), Vol. I, xl–xlviii, with omissions. Calvin originally published his *Psalms* in 1557.

KNOWLEDGE OF GOD—KNOWLEDGE OF OURSELVES[24]

True and substantial wisdom principally consists of two parts, the knowledge of God, and the knowledge of ourselves. But while these two branches of knowledge are so intimately connected, which of them precedes and produces the other, is not easy to discover. For, in the first place, no man can take a survey of himself but he must immediately turn to the contemplation of God, in whom he "lives and moves" [Acts 17:28], since it is evident that the talents which we possess are not from ourselves, and that our very existence is nothing but a subsistence in God alone. These boundaries, distilling to us by drops from heaven, form, as it were, so many streams conducting us to the fountain-head. Our poverty conduces to a clearer display of the infinite fulness of God. Especially, the miserable ruin into which we have been plunged by the defection of the first man, compels us to raise our eyes towards heaven, not only as hungry and famished, to seek thence a supply for our wants, but aroused with fear, to learn humility. For since man is subject to a world of miseries, and has been spoiled of his divine array, this melancholy exposure discovers an immense mass of deformity; every one, therefore, must be so impressed with a consciousness of his own infelicity, as to arrive at some knowledge of God. Thus a sense of our ignorance, vanity, poverty, infirmity, depravity, and corruption, leads us to perceive and acknowledge that in the Lord alone are to be found true wisdom, solid strength, perfect goodness, and unspotted righteousness; and so, by our imperfections, we are excited to a consideration of the perfections of God. Nor can we really aspire toward Him, till we have begun to be displeased with ourselves. For who would not gladly rest satisfied with himself? Where is the person not actually absorbed in self-contemplation, while he remains unacquainted with his true situation, or content with his own endowments, and ignorant or forgetful of his own misery? The knowledge of ourselves, therefore, is not only an incitement to seek after God, but likewise a considerable assistance towards finding Him.

On the other hand, it is plain that no one can arrive at the true knowledge of himself [or herself], without having first contemplated the divine character, and then descended to the consideration of their own. For, such is the native pride of us all, we invariably esteem ourselves righteous, innocent, wise, and holy, till we are convinced, by clear proofs, of our unrighteousness, turpitude, folly, and impurity. But we are never thus convinced, while we confine our attention to ourselves, and regard not the Lord, who is the only standard by which this judgment ought to be formed. Because, from our natural proneness to hypocrisy, any vain appearance of righteousness abundantly contents us instead of the reality; and, every thing within and around us being exceedingly defiled, we are delighted with what is least so, as extremely pure, while we confine our reflections within the limits of human corruption. . . . Indeed, the senses of our bodies may assist

---

[24]Reprinted from John Allen, trans. *Institutes of the Christian Religion by John Calvin*, 2 vols. (Philadelphia: Presbyterian Board of Education, 1813), Vol. I, Bk. I, ch. 1, pp. 46–48, with minor linguistic changes.

us in discovering how grossly we err in estimating the powers of the soul. For if at noon-day we look either on the ground, or at any surrounding objects, we conclude our vision to be very strong and piercing; but when we raise our eyes and steadily look at the sun, they are at once dazzled and confounded with such a blaze of brightness, and we are constrained to confess, that our sight, so piercing in viewing terrestrial things, when directed to the sun, is dimness itself. Thus also it happens in the consideration of our spiritual endowments. For as long as our views are bounded by the earth, perfectly content with our own righteousness, wisdom, and strength, we fondly flatter ourselves, and fancy we are little less than demigods. But, if we once elevate our thoughts to God, and consider His nature, and the consummate perfection of His righteousness, wisdom, and strength, to which we ought to be conformed,—what before charmed us in ourselves under the false pretext of righteousness, will soon be loathed as the greatest iniquity; what strangely deceived us under the title of wisdom, will be despised as extreme folly; and what wore the appearance of strength, will be proved to be most wretched impotence. So very remote from the divine purity is what seems in us the highest perfection. . . . [T]hough the knowledge of God and the knowledge of ourselves be intimately connected, the proper order of instruction requires us first to treat of the former, and then to proceed to the discussion of the latter.

UNION WITH CHRIST[25]

We are now to examine how we obtain the enjoyment of those blessings which the Father has conferred on His only begotten Son, not for his own private use, but to enrich these poor and needy. And first it must be remarked, that as long as there is a separation between Christ and us, all that He suffered and performed for the salvation of mankind is useless and unavailing to us. To communicate to us what He received from His father, He must, therefore, become ours, and dwell within us. On this account He is called our "Head," and "the first-born among many brethren"; and we, on the other hand, are said to be "grafted into him," and to "put him on"; for, as I have observed, whatever He possesses is nothing to us, till we are united to Him. But though it be true that we obtain this by faith, yet, since we see that the communication of Christ, offered in the gospel, is not promiscuously embraced by all, reason itself teaches us to proceed further, and to inquire into the secret energy of the Spirit, by which we are introduced to the enjoyment of Christ and all His benefits. . . .

For as "there are three that bear record in heaven, the Father, the Word, and the Spirit," so also "there are three on earth, the spirit, the water, and the blood" [1 Jn 5:7–8]. . . . This passage suggests to us, that our souls are purified by the secret ablution of the Spirit, that the effusion of that sacred blood may not be in vain. For the same reason also Paul, when speaking of purification and justifica-

---

[25]Ibid., Vol. I, Bk. III, ch. 1–4, pp. 484–86.

tion, says, we enjoy both "in the name of the Lord Jesus, and by the Spirit of our God" [1 Cor 6:11]. The sum of all this is this—that the Holy Spirit is the bond by which Christ efficaciously unites us to Himself. . . . It has, indeed, already been clearly stated, that till our minds are fixed on the Spirit, Christ remains of no value to us; because we look at Him as an object of cold speculation without us, and therefore at a great distance from us. But we know that He benefits none but those who have Him as their "Head," and "elder brother," and how have "put him on" [Eph 4:15]. This same union alone renders His advent in the character of a Saviour available to us. We learn from the same truth from that sacred marriage, by which we are made flesh of His flesh and bone of His bone, and therefore one with Him [Eph 5:30]. It is only by the Spirit that He unites himself with us; and by the grace and power of the same Spirit we are made His members; that He may keep us under himself, and we may mutually enjoy him. But faith, being His most principal work, is the object principally referred to in the most frequent expressions of his power and operation; because it is the only medium by which He leads us into the light of the gospel . . . .

THREE OFFICES OF THE LAW[26]

. . . By the word *law*, I intend, not only the decalogue, which prescribes the rule of a pious and righteous life, but the form of religion delivered from God by the hands of Moses. . . . [F]or the better elucidation of the subject, let us state in a compendious order, the office and use of what is called the moral law. It is contained, as far as I understand it, in these three points. The first is, that while it discovers the righteousness of God, that is, the only righteousness which is acceptable to God, it warns every one of his own unrighteousness, places it beyond all doubt, convicts, and condemns him. For it is necessary that man, blinded and inebriated with self-love, should thus be driven into a knowledge of himself, and a confession of his own imbecility and impurity. . . .

The second office of the law is, to cause those who, unless constrained, feel no concern for justice and rectitude, when they hear its terrible sanctions, to be at least restrained by a fear of its penalties. And they are restrained, not because it internally influences or affects their minds, but because, being chained, as it were, they refrain from external acts, and repress their depravity within them, which otherwise they would have wantonly discharged. This makes them neither better nor more righteous in the Divine view. . . . [T]his constrained and extorted righteousness is necessary to the community, whose public tranquility is provided for by God in this instance, while He prevents all things being involved in confusion, which would certainly be the case, if all men were permitted to pursue their own inclinations. . . .

---

[26]Ibid., Vol. I, Bk. II, ch. 7, pp. 313–24.

The third use of the law, which is the principal one, and which is more nearly connected with the proper end of it, relates to the faithful, in whose hearts the Spirit of God already lives and reigns. For although the law is inscribed and engraved on their hearts by the finger of God—that is, although they are so excited and animated by the direction of the Spirit, that they desire to obey God—yet they derive a twofold advantage from the law. For they find it an excellent instrument to give them, from day to day, a better and more certain understanding of the Divine will to which they aspire, and to confirm them in the knowledge of it. As, though a servant be already influenced by the strongest desire of gaining the approbation of his master, yet it is necessary for him carefully to inquire and observe the orders of his master, in order to conform to them. Nor let any one of us exempt ourselves from this necessity; for no one has already acquired so much wisdom, that he [or she] could not by the daily instruction of the law make new advances into a purer knowledge of the Divine will. In the next place, as we need not only instruction, but also exhortation, the servant of God will derive this further advantage from the law; by frequent meditation on it we will be excited to obedience, we will be confirmed in it, and restrained from the slippery path of transgression. . . .

Bartholome de las Casas (1474–1566)

Bartholome de las Casas was born in Seville, Spain, but his heritage linked him to "the new world." He was the son of a merchant who had accompanied Columbus on his second voyage. Bartholome ventured to Hispaniola in 1502, where he was ordained as a priest. The savage exploitation and oppression of native people, which he met in the Caribbean, caused las Casas to denounce the abuses of Spanish colonialism and take up the defense of the Indians. His various attempts at reforming the colonial system met with very meager results, and—in part due to his disillusionment with pursuing secular means—he joined the Dominican Order (1523). After a lengthy period of retreat and study, he returned to the new world to undertake missionary work in Nicaragua and Guatemala.

Returning to Spain in 1540, he pushed for comprehensive reform of the colonial process. His efforts culminated in new laws of 1542–43, which prohibited Indian slavery and were intended to gradually dissolve the *encomienda* system. While these laws epitomized las Casas's appellation, "Defender of the Indians," they met with very limited success in the Spanish colonies, where they were strongly opposed. Indeed, when he returned to America, in 1544, as Bishop of Chiapa, las Casas was not able to fully implement the new laws even in his own diocese.

In 1547 las Casas returned to Spain, to take up the pen in defense of Native Americans. Through three major writings he made his most lasting contribution to the cause of the Indians. His *Apologetica historia* (1550) not only elaborated a theological basis for viewing the rights and dignity of native people, but also carried a large amount of the author's first-hand observations of the significant intellectual and religious capacities of American Indians. The *Apologetica*, directed against the arguments of Juan Gines de Sepulveda—who taught that the Spaniards may even wage war against the Indians in order to convert them—sought to undercut the moral and theological foundations used to justify Spanish colonialism. The more basic issue, for las Casas, was the humanity of the Indians and the Spaniards' own profession of Christian faith: "The Indians are our brothers, and Christ has given his life for them. Why then, do we persecute them with such inhuman savagery when they do not deserve such treatment?"[27] He campaigned against the colonial practice of forced conversion, since it was repugnant to the gospel and contrary to the commands of Christ. In *The Only Way to Draw All People to a Living Faith* (1534), las Casas looked to the example of Jesus Christ and the apostles for a model of the way people should be evangelized. His *Historia de las Indias* (History of the Indies) did much to popularize the plight of the Indians and raise sentiments against their inhumane and unjust treatment.

CONVERSION TO SENSITIVITY[28]

Diego Velasquez and the group of Spaniards with him left the port of Xagua to go and found a settlement of Spaniards in the province, where they established the town called Sancti Espiritus. Apart from Bartolome' de las Casas, there was not a single cleric or friar on the whole island [of Cuba], except for one in the town of Baracoa. The feast of Pentecost was coming up. So he agreed to leave his home on the Arimao River (accent on the penult) a league from Xagua where his holdings were and go say mass and preach for them on that feast. Las Casas looked over the previous sermons he had preached to them on that feast and his other sermons for that season. He began to meditate on some passages of Sacred Scripture. If my memory serves me, the first and most important was from Ecclesiasticus 34:18ff:

> Unclean is the offering sacrificed by an oppressor. [Such] mockeries of the unjust are not pleasing [to God]. The Lord is pleased only by those who keep to the way of truth and justice. The Most High does not accept the gifts of unjust people, He does not look well upon their offerings. Their sins will not be expiated by repeat sacrifices. *The one whose sacrifice comes from the goods of the poor*

---

[27]Lewis Hanke, *All Mankind Is One: A Study of the Disputation Between Bartolome de Las Casas and Juan Gines de Sepulveda in 1550 on the Intellectual and Religious Capacity of the American Indians* (DeKalb: Northern Illinois University, 1974), p. 76.

[28]Reprinted from Helen Rand Parish and Francis Patrick Sullivan, *Bartolome' de las Casas: The Only Way.* Copyright (c) 1992, by The Missionary Society of St. Paul the Apostle in the State of New York. Used by permission of Paulist Press. Pages 187–89. The selection is taken from las Casas's *Historia de las Indias.*

is like one who kills his neighbor. The one who sheds blood and the one who defrauds the laborer are kin and kind.

He began to reflect on the misery, the forced labor the Indians had to undergo. He was helped in this by what he had heard and experienced on the island of Hispaniola, by what the Dominicans preached continually—no one could, in good conscience, hold the Indians in encomienda, and those friars would not confess and absolve any [one] who so held them—a preaching Las Casas had refused to accept. One time he wanted to confess to a religious of St. Dominic who happened to be in the vicinity. Las Casas held Indians on the island of Hispaniola, as indifferent and blind about it as he was on the island of Cuba. The religious refused him confession. Las Casas asked him why. He gave the reason. Las Casas objected with frivolous arguments and empty explanations, seemingly sound, provoking the religious to respond, "Padre, I think the truth has many enemies and the lie has many friends." Then Las Casas offered him the respect due his dignity and reputation because the religious was a revered and learned man, much more so than the padre, but he took no heed of the confessor's counsel to let his Indians go. Yet it helped him greatly to recall his quarrel later, and also the confession he made to the religious, so as to think more about the road of ignorance and danger he was on, holding Indians as others did, confessing without scruple those who held or wanted to hold Indians, though he did not do so for long. But he had heard many confessions on that island of Hispaniola, from people who were in the same mortal sin.

He spent some days thinking about the situation, each day getting surer and surer from what he read concerning what was legal and what was actual, measuring the one by the other, until he came to the same truth by himself. Everything in these Indies that was done to the Indians was tyrannical and unjust. Everything he read to firm up his judgment he found favorable, and he used to say strongly that from the very moment he began to dispel the darkness of that ignorance, he never read a book in Latin or Spanish—a countless number over the span of forty-two years—where he didn't find some argument or authority to prove or support the justice of those Indian peoples, and to condemn the injustices done to them, the evils, the injuries.

He then made a decision to preach his conclusion. But since his holding Indians meant holding a contradiction of his own preaching, he determined to give them up so as to be free to condemn allotments, the whole system of forced labor, as unjust and tyrannical, and to hand his Indians back to Governor Diego Velasquez. They were better off under the padre's control, to be sure. He had treated them with greater respect, would be even more respectful in the future. He knew that giving them up meant they would be handed over to someone who would brutalize them, work them to death, as someone did ultimately. Granted, he would give them a treatment as good as a father would give his children. Yet, since he would preach that no one could in good conscience hold Indians, he could never escape people mocking back at him, "You hold Indians nonetheless. Why not release them? You say holding them is tyranny!" So he decided to give them up completely.

WINNING THE MIND AND THE WILL[29]

One way, one way only, of teaching a living faith, to everyone, everywhere, always, was set by Divine Providence: the way that wins the mind with reasons, that wins the will with gentleness, with invitation. It has to fit all people on earth, no distinction made for sect, for error, even for evil.

Many proofs support this thesis: proofs from reason, from the practice of the patriarchs, from the once-and-for-all way of preaching willed by Christ, from the practice of the apostles, and the procedures they ordered, from the teachings of Church Doctors, the ancient Church customs, the long list of Church degrees.

First from reason, a crucial proof. One, only one way is characteristic of Divine Wisdom in its care for creatures, in its leading of them to fulfill their natural purposes—a gentle, coaxing, gracious way. . . . So Divine Wisdom leads the rational creature, the human, to fulfill its natural purpose in a gentle, coaxing, gracious way. But it is a teaching of the faith that people be called to, be led to a living faith under the universal command as it is stated in Matthew 28:19–20: "Go teach all nations, baptizing them in the name of the Father, and of the Son, and of the Holy Spirit, teaching them to obey all that I have commanded you." And Paul to the Romans (10:17): "Faith comes from hearing, hearing from the word of Christ." Therefore the way of teaching people has to be a gentle, coaxing gracious way. It wins the mind with reasons, it wins the will with graciousness. So, one way, one way only, of teaching a living faith, to everyone, everywhere, always, was set by Divine Providence, a way that wins the mind with reasons, that wins the will with gentleness, with invitation. . . .

In a certain sense, creatures are not just led to fulfill their purposes, they do so of themselves, as if the movement originates within. For this reason Wisdom 8:1 says that Divine Wisdom "reaches the whole of creation with its power." That is, it runs all things perfectly. . . . So each creature moves toward what Divine Wisdom wants for it by means of a nature divinity gives it, according to the learning built into nature. It is the goodness in God from which all natures flow . . . so every creature has in it a power to want goodness due to the imprint of the Creator upon it.[30] Goodness means fulfillment because each thing's activity is normed by its goal, the activity being one perfection, the fulfillment being a second. We call something good and virtuous when it acts harmoniously with itself, and thus with the goal set for it by God, in God's own way. And so, in creation, there is a certain circularity; goodness going out, goodness coming back.

---

[29]Ibid., Used by permission of Paulist Press. Pages 68–69, "The Only Way to Draw All People to a Living Faith."
[30]This is a paraphrase from Pseudo-Dionysius, "De divinis nominibus."

THE WAY OF CHRIST[31]

. . . We can add a germane saying from Matthew 11:29–30: "Come to me all you who labor and are sorely burdened and I will refresh you. Take my yoke upon you and learn of me, for I am meek and humble of heart, and you shall find rest for your souls. My yoke is easy, my burden is light." It all means: learn from me that you also may be meek and humble of heart.

This is the way, the form of preaching Christ's law, of drawing people to a living faith, to Christianity. It is what Christ Himself, Son of God, Wisdom of the Father, fashioned and prescribed for His apostles, His disciples, and their successors, the method He first used and they kept to with consummate tact in their approach to everyone. Now to see that this way, this form of preaching a living faith wins the mind with reasons, wins the will gently, by attraction, by graciousness. First off, because Christ, when He said preach that the Kingdom of God is near, meant preach repentance for the remission of sins. That God is near, meant preach repentance for the remission of sins. That was the theme of His sermon in Matthew 4:17, "Jesus began to preach and say, 'Repent, the Kingdom of Heaven is near.'" Also in Mark 6:12 the description is of apostles setting out preaching that people should repent, so that by repentance they would be brought near to the kingdom of heaven. . . .

. . . We have listed above all the reasons for winning the mind. The point is self-evident. So the way, the form Christ gave His apostles and disciples for preaching His message, the way He willed, was to win the mind.

Next, that this way wins the will with gentleness, draws it, invites it, is clear also. It is so precious it makes people greet one another first, in the cities and towns and households they enter, before any other ritual. People are accustomed in their first words to each other, especially to strangers, to use a polite greeting, so that the start of speech between them is a good wish. If anyone does not greet others politely, people think him an ill-mannered clod. So a greeting is a necessity, almost, between people, the customary start of a relationship. It is why Christ ordered His apostles to be first in greeting others. It is more generous to offer a respect before receiving one. Paul says in Romans 12:10, "Out do one another in showing honor." . . .

Christ commanded a special greeting, used the words, "Peace to this house!" . . . The apostles preached peace first—a value so wanted, so palatable, so loved and lovable by those people who lived in city, town, and household that it's clear they could only attract such people! And render them gracious and kind enough to welcome the apostle and shelter them generously and warmly and listen to their teaching willingly. . . .

It is now clear that the way Christ wanted for preaching the gospel, and

---

[31]Reprinted from Parish and Sullivan, *Bartolome' de las Casas.* Used by permission of Paulist Press. Pages 69–78.

willed for His apostles and their successors, was to win the mind with reasons and win the will with motives, gently, graciously. After the Lord taught His apostles and disciples the form and fashion for their behavior toward the city, the town, the household that took them in, willingly, even graciously, He then gave them a norm they should act on toward those who were resistant. "Whoever is unreceptive, who does not listen to your words, leave the house, the town, shake its dust off your feet. I tell you solemnly it will go easier for Sodom and Gomorrah on judgment day than for that town" (Mt 10:14).

What is clear is that Christ gave His apostles permission and power to preach the gospel to those willing to hear it, and that only! Not power to punish the unwilling by any force, pressure, or harshness. He granted no power to apostle or preacher of the faith to force the unwilling to listen, no power to punish even those who drove the apostles out of town. He decreed punishment in eternity, not in time: "Whoever is unreceptive, and does not listen to your words, leave the place." He did not say, "Confront them! Preach to them willy nilly! If they persist tenaciously in trying to drive you out, do not hesitate to use human punishment!" He said: "Shake the dust off your feet. I tell you solemnly it will go easier for Sodom and Gomorrah on judgment day than for that town." As if He said flatly: "I reserve the punishment for such rejection to myself. I do not grant it to you!" . . . So this is the pattern: Christ did not give human beings the power to inflict earthly punishment on those who refused to listen to the faith being preached or on those who refused to welcome or want the preachers of that faith— it was an eternal punishment payable in the life hereafter. He reserved to Himself the punishment of both types. . . .

Thomas Cranmer (1489–1556)

Thomas Cranmer, the architect of Anglicanism and first Protestant Archbishop of Canterbury, was born at Aslocton, in Nottinghamshire, England. He was educated at Jesus College, Cambridge, and was ordained to the priesthood in 1523. He remained at the university as preacher and lecturer in theology. In 1529 Cranmer came to public prominence by suggesting that the thorny question of King Henry VIII's divorce from Catherine of Aragon should be referred to the English universities. This solution to Henry's dilemma brought Cranmer to the King's attention and in 1533 he was appointed Archbishop of Canterbury.

As Archbishop of Canterbury, Cranmer played a leading role in working out the Anglican synthesis or "middle way" (*via media*) between Protestant and Roman Catholic spirituality. His influence was felt in the founding documents of the Church of England; the most enduring of these, however, were the First (1549) and Second (1552) Edwardian Prayer Books, and the Anglican Articles of Religion (1553). The Prayer Books (later called *Book of Common Prayer*) shaped the liturgical and devotional life of the Church of England, just as the Articles became the standard expression of Anglican theology. Cranmer also authored several of the most important sermons that were included in a collection of *Standard Homilies* that served as models for Sunday sermons and norms of Anglican faith and practice. When the Roman Catholic Queen, Mary I, succeeded her Protestant brother Edward in 1553, Cranmer was arrested and subsequently burned at the stake at Oxford.

The genius of Cranmer's work is to be seen in his ability to combine Catholic liturgical forms and spiritual disciplines with Protestant theological insights—in a way that captures much of the vitality of both traditions. Anglicans, perhaps more than other Protestants, feel themselves linked to the Patristic past, and understand themselves as being in continuity with the ancient, universal ("catholic") church. Yet, the Anglican Articles, as well as the *Standard Homilies*, evidence a debt to the Protestant reformers, and react (to some degree) against Roman Catholic teaching. Because of the theological tensions and historical context of its inception, Anglicanism carved out its own distinctive niche between those two great religious traditions.

PRAYER FOR THE WHOLE STATE OF CHRIST'S CHURCH[32]

Almighty and everliving God, which by Thy holy Apostle hast taught us to make prayers and supplications, and to give thanks for all men; we humbly beseech Thee most mercifully to accept our alms and to receive these our prayers which we offer unto Thy divine majesty; beseeching Thee to inspire continually, the universal church with the Spirit of truth, unity and concorde; and grant that all they that do confess Thy holy name, may agree in the truth of Thy holy word, and live in unity and Godly love. We beseech Thee also to save and defend all Christian kings, Princes, and governors, and especially thy servant, Edward our King, that under him we may be Godly and quietly governed; and grant unto his whole counsel, and to all that be put in authority under him, that they may truly and indifferently minister justice, to the punishment of wickedness and vice, and to the maintenance of God's true religion and virtue. Give grace, O heavenly Father, to all Bishops, pastors, and curates, that they may both by their life and doctrine set forth Thy true and lively word, and rightly and duely administer Thy holy Sacraments; and to all Thy people give Thy heavenly grace, and especially to this congregation here present, that with meek heart and due reverence, they may hear and receive Thy holy word, truly serving Thee in holiness, and righteousness all the days of their life. And we most humbly beseech Thee of Thy goodness, O Lord, to comfort and succor all them which in this transitory life be in trouble, sorrow, need, sickness, or any other adversity; Grant this O father, for Jesus Christ's sake, our only mediator and advocate. Amen.

---

[32]Reprinted from Bard Thompson, *Liturgies of the Western Church*. Copyright (c) Bard Thompson. Used by permission of Augsburg Fortress. Pages 273–74, from the *First Edwardian Prayer Book* (1549), the spelling has been modernized.

PRAYER OF GENERAL CONFESSION[33]

Almighty God, father of our Lord Jesus Christ, maker of all things, Judge of all men, we acknowledge and bewail our manifold sins and wickednesses, which we from time to time most grievously have committed, by thought, word, and deed, against Thy divine Majesty; provoking most justly Thy wrath and indignation against us; we do earnestly repent, and be heartily sorry for these our misdoings; the remembrance of them is grievous unto us, the burden of them is intolerable; have mercy upon us, have mercy upon us most merciful Father, for Thy Son our Lord Jesus Christ's sake: forgive us all that is past, and grant that we may ever hereafter, serve and please Thee, in newness of life, to the honor and glory of Thy name: Through Jesus Christ our Lord, Amen.

PRAYER OF HUMBLE ACCESS[34]

We do not come to this Thy table, O merciful Lord, trusting in our own right-eousness, but in Thy manifold and great mercies; we be not worthy so much as to gather up the crumbs under Thy table, but thou art the same Lord, whose prop-erty is always to have mercy: grant us therefore, gracious Lord, so to eat the flesh of Thy dear Son Jesus Christ and to drink his blood, that our sinful bodies may be made clean by His body, and our souls washed through His most precious blood, and that we may evermore dwell in Him, and He in us. Amen.

A TRUE AND LIVELY FAITH[35]

The first entry unto God, good Christian people, is through faith, whereby . . . we be justified before God. And lest any man should be deceived for lack of right understanding thereof, it is diligently to be noted, that faith is taken in the scrip-ture two manner of ways. There is one faith, which in scripture is called a dead faith, which bringeth forth no good works, but is idle, barren, and unfruitful. And this faith by the holy apostle St. James is compared to the faith of devils, which believe God to be true and just, and tremble for fear; yet they do nothing well, but all evil. And such a manner of faith have the wicked and naughty Christian people, "which confess God," as St. Paul saith, "in their mouth, but deny him in their deeds, being abominable, and without the right faith, and in all good works reprovable" [Tit 1:16]. . . . [A]lthough it may be said that such a person hath a faith and belief to the words of God, yet it is not *properly* said that he believeth in God, or hath such faith and trust in God, whereby he may surely look for grace,

---

[33]Ibid. Used by permission of Augsburg Fortress. Page 278, from the *First Edwardian Prayer Book* (1549).
[34]Ibid. Used by permission of Ausburg Fortress. Page 280, from the *First Edwardian Prayer Book* (1549).
[35]Reprinted from John Edmund Cox, ed., *Miscellaneous Writings and Letters of Thomas Cranmer* (Cambridge: Cambridge University Press, 1846), pp. 134–41, with omissions.

mercy, and eternal life at God's hand, but rather for indignation and punishment, according to the merits of his wicked life. . . . This dead faith therefore is not that sure and substantial faith, which saveth sinners.

Another faith there is in scripture, which is not, as the foresaid faith, idle, unfruitful, and dead, but "worketh by charity," as St Paul declareth (Gal. 5[6]); which, as the other vain faith is called a dead faith, so may this be called a quick or lively faith. And this is not only the common belief of the Articles of our faith, but it is also a sure trust and confidence of the mercy of God through our Lord Jesus Christ, and a steadfast hope of all good things to be received at God's hand; and that, although we through infirmity, or temptation of our ghostly enemy, do fall from him by sin, yet if we return again unto him by true repentance, that he will forgive and forget our offences for his Son's sake, our Saviour Jesus Christ, and will make us inheritors with him of his everlasting kingdom; and that in the mean time, until that kingdom come, He will be our protector and defender in all perils and dangers . . . evermore He will be a loving father unto us, correcting us for our sin, but not withdrawing his mercy finally from us, if we trust in him, and commit ourselves wholly to him, hang only upon him, and call upon him, ready to obey and serve him. This is the true, lively, and unfeigned Christian faith, and is not in the mouth and outward profession only, but it liveth and stirreth inwardly in the heart. And this faith is not without hope and trust in God, nor without the love of God and of our neighbours, nor without the fear of God, nor without the desire to hear God's word, and to follow the same, in eschewing evil and doing gladly all good works. . . .

Of this faith three things are specially to be noted. First, that this faith doth not lie dead in the heart, but is lively and fruitful in bringing forth good works. Second, that without it can no good works be done, that shall be acceptable and pleasant to God. Third, what manner of good works they be that this faith doth bring forth.

For the first, as the light cannot be hid, but will shew forth itself at one place or other; so a true faith cannot be kept secret, but, when occasion is offered, it will break out, and shew itself by good works. And as the living body of a man ever exerciseth such things as belongeth to a natural and living body . . . even so the soul, that hath a lively faith in it, will be doing alway[s] some good work, which shall declare that it is living, and will not be unoccupied. . . . For the very sure and lively christian faith is, not only to believe all things of God which are contained in holy scripture; but also is an earnest trust and confidence in God, that He doth regard us, and that He is careful over us, as the father is of the child, whom He doth love, and that He will be merciful unto us for His only Son's sake, and that we have our Saviour Christ our perpetual advocate and priest, in whose only merits, oblation, and suffering, we do trust that our offences be continually washed and purged, whensoever we, repenting truly, do return to him with our whole heart, steadfastly determining with ourselves, through His grace, to obey and serve Him in keeping His commandments, and never to turn back again to sin. Such is the true faith that the scripture doth so much commend; the which, when it seeth and considereth what God hath done for us, is also moved, through continual assistance of the Spirit of God, to serve and please Him, to keep His favour, to fear His displeasure, continue His obedient children, shewing thankfulness again by observing his commandments, and that freely, for true love chiefly, and not for dread of punishment or love of temporal reward; considering how clearly, without our deservings, we have received His mercy and pardon freely. . . .

. . . You have heard in the second part of this sermon, that no one should think that he [or she] hath that lively faith which scripture commandeth, when he [or she] liveth not obediently to God's laws. For all good works spring out of that faith. And also it hath been declared unto you by examples, that faith maketh men steadfast, quiet, and patient in all affliction. . . .

Deceive not yourselves therefore, thinking that you have faith in God, or that you love God, or do trust in Him, or do fear Him, when you live in sin; for then your ungodly and sinful life declareth the contrary, whatsoever ye say or think. It pertaineth to a Christian man to have this true Christian faith, and to try himself whether he hath it or no, and to know what belongeth to it, and how it doth work in him. . . . Christ Himself speaketh of this matter, and saith: "The tree is known by the fruit" [Lk 6:44]. Therefore let us do good works, and thereby declare our faith to be the lively Christian faith. Let us by such virtues as ought to spring out of faith shew our election to be sure and stable, as St. Peter teacheth: "Endeavour yourselves to make your calling and election certain by good works" [2 Pet 1:10]. . . . For true faith doth ever bring forth good works, as St. James saith: "Shew me thy faith by thy deeds" [2:18]. Thy deeds and works must be an open testimonial of thy faith: otherwise thy faith, being without good works, is but the devils' faith, the faith of the wicked, a phantasy of faith, and not a true christian faith.

. . . Therefore, as you profess the name of Christ, good Christian people, let no such phantasy and imagination of faith at any time beguile you; but be sure of your faith, try it by your living, look upon the fruits that cometh of it, mark the increase of love and charity by it towards God and your neighbour, and so shall you perceive it to be a true lively faith. If you feel and perceive such a faith in you, rejoice in it, and be diligent to maintain it, and keep it still in you; let it be daily increasing, and more and more be well working, and so shall you be sure that you shall please God by this faith; and at the length, as other faithful men have done before, so shall you, when His will is, come to him, and receive "the end and final reward of your faith," as St. Peter nameth it, "the salvation of your souls" [1 Pet 1:9]; the which God grant us, that hath promised the same unto his faithful! To whom be all honour and glory, world without end. Amen.

Ignatius of Loyola (1491–1556)

Inigo Lopez de Recalde was born in the Guipuzcoa province, a picturesque and mountainous region in the north of Spain. His parents were nobles, and he grew to manhood in their castle, steeped in chivalry and tales of daring do. While engaged in a military campaign against the French, in 1521, he was seriously wounded. The reading and reflection that accompanied his lengthy convalescence led to a dramatic conversion. Out of this experience came the resolve to bring all of his life under the dominion of Christ, most especially his inner life of attitudes and thoughts. As he developed an approach for cultivating and refining Christlike attitudes, Ignatius laid the foundations for his most famous literary work, *Spiritual Exercises* (written in 1522, published in 1548).

Ignatian spirituality is characterized by a rigorous and formative approach that stresses discipline (physical and mental), and continued self-examination. The essence of Christianity is understood as imitation of Christ. Prayer, meditation, and reflection upon the life, death, and resurrection of Jesus Christ are aids to developing conformity to the image of Christ. His interest in the "discernment of spirits" connected the cultivation of Christian character with a person's decision-making processes. The Jesuit Order founded by Ignatius (1540) epitomized his understanding of Christian Spirituality. The Jeusits took his *Spiritual Exercises* as their rule for spiritual life. Its popularity and use in the Order gradually turned *Spiritual Exercises* into a textbook for renewal that was appreciated throughout the church.[36]

A SOLDIER FOR CHRIST[37]

Up to the age of twenty-six he was a man given to the vanities of the world; and what he enjoyed most was warlike sport, with a great and foolish desire to win fame. And so, whilst in a fortress that the French were attacking, when all were of the view that they should surrender, with their lives safe-guarded—for they saw clearly that they could not offer resistance—he gave so many reasons to the commander that he actually persuaded him to resist, even against this view of all the officers, who drew courage from his spirit and determination.

When the day came on which the bombardment was expected, he confessed to one of these companions in arms. And after the bombardment had lasted a good while, a shot struck him on one leg, shattering it completely; and as the cannon ball passed between both legs, the other [leg] also was badly damaged. So with his fall those in the fortress soon surrendered to the French, who on taking possession of it treated the wounded men very well—treated him with courtesy and kindness. And after he had been in Pamplona for twelve or fifteen days, they took him home in a litter. Here he felt quite unwell. All the doctors and surgeons who were summoned from many places decided that the leg ought to be broken again and the bones reset, saying that because they had been badly set the other time, or had got broken on the road, they were out of place, and this way he could

---

[36]Michael Ivens, "Ignatius Loyola," in Jones, Wainwright, and Yarnold, eds., *Study of Spirituality*, pp. 357–62; William Leonard, "The Spiritual Exercises of St. Ignatius Loyola," in *Christian Spirituality*, edited by Frank Magill and Ian McGreal (San Francisco: Harper & Row, 1988), pp. 232–37.

[37]Reprinted from George Ganss, trans., *Ignatius of Loyola: The Spiritual Exercises and Selected Works.* Copyright (c) 1991, by The Missionary Society of St. Paul the Apostle in the State of New York. Used by kind permission of Paulist Press. Pages 68–81.

not mend. And once again this butchery was gone through. During it, as in all the others he underwent before or after, he never said a word nor showed any sign of pain other than to clench his fists tightly.

Yet he kept getting worse, not being able to eat, and with the other symptoms that usually point to death. When St. John's day came, because the doctors were far from confident about his health, he was advised to confess. He received the sacraments on the eve of St. Peter and St. Paul. The doctors said that if he did not feel any improvement by midnight, he could be taken for dead. It happened that this sick man was devoted to St. Peter, so Our Lord deigned that he should begin to get better that very midnight. His improvement proceeded so well that some days later it was judged that he was out of danger of death.

And his bones having knit together, one bone below the knee was left riding on another, which made the leg shorter. The bone protruded so much that it was an ugly business. He could not bear such a thing because he was set on a worldly career and thought that this would deform him; he asked the surgeons if it could be cut away. They said it could indeed be cut away, but that the pain would be greater than all that he had suffered, because it was already healed and it would take a while to cut it. And yet he chose on his own to make himself a martyr, though his elder brother was shocked and said that he himself would not dare suffer such pain; but the wounded man bore it with his wonted endurance.

After the flesh and excess bone were cut away remedial measures were taken that the leg might not be so short. Ointment was often applied, and it was stretched continually with instruments that tortured him for many days. But Our Lord kept giving him health, and he felt so well that he was quite fit except that he could not stand easily on his leg and had perforce to stay in bed. As he was much given to reading worldly books of fiction, commonly labeled chivalry, when he felt better he asked to be given some of them to pass the time. But in that house none of those that he usually read could be found, so they gave him a life of Christ and a book of the lives of the saints in Castilian.

As he read them over many times, he became rather fond of what he found written there. But, interrupting his reading, he sometimes stopped to think about the things he had read and at other times about the things of the world that he used to think of before. Of the many foolish ideas that occurred to him, one had taken such a hold on his heart that he was absorbed in thinking about it for two and three and four hours without realizing it. He imagined what he would do in the service of a certain lady; the means he would take so he could go to the place where she lived; the quips—the words he would address to her; the feats of arms he would perform in her service. He became so infatuated with this that he did not consider how impossible of attainment it would be, because the lady was not of ordinary nobility; not a countess nor a duchess; but her station was higher than any of these.

Nevertheless Our Lord assisted him, by causing these thoughts to be followed by others which arose from the things he read. For in reading the life of Our Lord and of the saints, he stopped to think, reasoning within himself, "What if I should do what St. Francis did, and what St. Dominic did?" Thus he pondered over many things that he found good, always proposing to himself what was difficult and burdensome; and as he so proposed, it seemed easy for him to accomplish it. But he did no more than argue within himself, saying, "St. Dominic did this, therefore I have to do it; St. Francis did this, therefore I have to do it." These thoughts also lasted a good while; then, other things coming in between, the worldly ones mentioned above returned, and he also stayed long with them. This succession of such diverse thoughts lasted for quite some time, and he always dwelt at length on the thought that turned up, either of the worldly exploits he wished to perform or of these others of God that came to his imagination, until he tired of it and put it aside and turned to other matters.

Yet there was this difference. When he was thinking of those things of the world he took much delight in them, but afterwards, when he was tired and put them aside, he found himself dry and dissatisfied. But when he thought of going to Jerusalem barefoot, and of eating nothing but plain vegetables and of practicing all the other rigors that he saw in the saints, not only was he consoled when he had these thoughts, but even after putting them aside he remained satisfied and joyful.

He did not notice this, however; nor did he stop to ponder the distinction until the time when his eyes were opened a little, and he began to marvel at the difference and to reflect upon it, realizing from experience that some thoughts left him sad and others joyful. Little by little he came to recognize the difference between the spirits that were stirring, one from the devil, the other from God. This was his first reflection on the things of God; and later, when he composed the *Exercises*, this was his starting point in clarifying the matter of diversity of spirits.

From this lesson he derived not a little light, and he began to think more earnestly about his past life and about the great need he had to do penance for it. At this point the desire to imitate the saints came to him, though he gave no thought to details, only promising with God's grace to do as they had done. But the one thing he wanted to do was to go to Jerusalem as soon as he recovered, as mentioned above, with as much of disciplines and fasts as generous spirit, fired with God, would want to perform.

And so he began to forget the previous thoughts with these holy desires he had, and they were confirmed by spiritual experience in this manner. One night while he was awake he saw clearly an image of Our Lady with the holy Child Jesus. From this sight he received for a considerable time very great consolation, and he was left with such loathing for his whole past life and especially for the things of the flesh that it seemed to him that his spirit was rid of all the images that had been painted on it. Thus from that hour until August '53 when this was written, he never gave the slightest consent to the things of the flesh. For this reason it may be considered the work of God, although he did not dare to claim it nor said more than to affirm the above. But his brother as well as all the rest of the household came to know from his exterior the change that had been wrought inwardly in his soul.

. . . [H]e persevered in his reading and his good resolutions, and all his time of conversation with members of the household he spent on the things of God; thus he benefited their souls. As he very much liked those books, the idea came to him to note down briefly some of the more essential things from the life of

Christ and the saints. So he set himself very diligently to write a book (because he was now beginning to be up and about the house a bit) with red ink for the words of Christ, blue ink for those of Our Lady, on polished and lined paper, in a good hand because he was a very fine penman. This had nearly 300 pages, all written quarto size. Part of the time he spent in writing and part in prayer. The greatest consolation he experienced was gazing at the sky and the stars, which he often did and for long, because he thus felt within himself a very great impulse to serve Our Lord. He often thought about his intention and wished he were now wholly well so he could be on his way. . . .

Until this time he had remained always in nearly the same interior state of very steady joy. without having any knowledge of interior things of the spirit. The days while that vision lasted or somewhat before it began (for it lasted many days), a forceful thought came to trouble him by pointing out the hardships of his life, like a voice within his soul, "How will you be able to endure this life for the seventy years you have to live?" Sensing that it was from the enemy, he answered interiorly with great vehemence, "Wretch! Can you promise me an hour of life?" So he overcame the temptation and remained at peace. This was the first temptation that came to him after what is mentioned above. It happened when he was entering a church where he heard High Mass each day and Vespers and Compline, all sung, finding in this great comfort. Usually he read the Passion at Mass, always retaining his serenity.

. . . At this time he still conversed occasionally with spiritual persons who had regard for him and wanted to talk to him, because even though he had no knowledge of spiritual matters, yet in his speech he revealed great fervor and eagerness to go forward in God's service. At that time there was at Manresa a woman of great age, with a long record also as a servant of God, and known as such in many parts of Spain, so much so that the Catholic King had summoned her once to communicate something. One day this woman, speaking to the new soldier of Christ, said to him, "Oh! May my Lord Jesus Christ deign to appear to you some day." But he was startled at this, taking the matter quite literally, "How would Jesus Christ appear to me?" He persevered steadily in his usual confession and communion each Sunday. . . .

This happened one Sunday after he had received Communion; he persevered the whole week without putting anything into his mouth, not ceasing to do his usual exercises, even going to divine office and saying his prayers on his knees, even at midnight, and the like. But when the next Sunday came and he had to go to confession, since he used to tell his confessor in great detail what he had done, he also told him how he had eaten nothing during that week. His confessor ordered him to break the fast; and though he still felt strong, he nevertheless obeyed his confessor. And that day and the next he felt free from scruples. But on the third day, which was Tuesday, while at prayer he began to remember his sins; and so, as in a process of threading, he went on thinking of sin after sin from his past and felt he was obliged to confess them again. But after these thoughts, disgust for the life he led came over him, with impulses to give it up.

In this way the Lord deigned that he awake, as from sleep. As he now had some experience of the diversity of spirits from the lessons God had given him, he began to examine the means by which that spirit had come. He thus decided with great lucidity not to confess anything from the past anymore; and so from that day forward he remained free of those scruples and held it for certain that Our Lord had mercifully deigned to deliver him.

. . . God treated him at this time just as a schoolmaster treats a child whom he is teaching. Whether this was because of his lack of education and of brains, or because he had no one to teach him, or because of the strong desire God himself had given him to serve him, he believed without doubt and has always believed that God treated him in this way. Indeed, if he were to doubt this, he would think he offended his Divine Majesty. Something of this can be seen from the five following points.

FIRST. He had great devotion to the Most Holy Trinity, and so each day he prayed to the three Persons separately. But as he also prayed to the Most Holy Trinity, the thought came to him: Why did he say four prayers to the Trinity? But this thought gave him little or no difficulty, being hardly important. One day while saying the Office of Our Lady on the steps of the same monastery, his understanding began to be elevated so that he saw the Most Holy Trinity in the form of three musical keys. This brought on so many tears and so much sobbing that he could not control himself. That morning, while going in a procession that set out from there, he could not hold back his tears until dinner time; nor after eating could he stop talking about the Most Holy Trinity, using many comparisons in great variety and with much joy and consolation. As a result, the effect has remained with him throughout his life of experiencing great devotion while praying to the Most Holy Trinity.

SECOND. Once, the manner in which God had created the world was presented to his understanding with great spiritual joy. He seemed to see something white, from which some rays were coming, and God made light from this. . . .

THIRD. At Manresa too, where he stayed almost a year, after he began to be consoled by God and saw the fruit which he bore in dealing with souls. . . . One day in this town while he was hearing Mass in the church of the monastery mentioned above, at the elevation of the Body of the Lord, he saw with interior eyes something like white rays coming from above. Although he cannot explain this very well after so long a time, nevertheless, what he saw with his understanding was how Jesus Christ our Lord was there in that Most Holy Sacrament.

FOURTH. Often and for a long time, while at prayer, he saw with interior eyes the humanity of Christ. The form that appeared to him was like a white body, neither very large nor very small, but he did not see any distinction of members. He saw it . . . many times. . . . He has also seen Our Lady in a similar form, without distinguishing parts. These things he saw strengthened him then and always gave him such strength in his faith that he has often thought to himself: If there were no Scriptures to teach us these matters of faith, he would be resolved to die for them, solely because of what he has seen.

FIFTH. Once he was going out of devotion to a church situated a little more than a mile from Manresa. . . . As he went along occupied with his devotions, he sat down for a little while with his face toward the river, which ran down below. While he was seated there, the eyes of his understanding began to be opened; not that he saw any vision, but he understood and learnt many things, both spiritual and matters of faith and of scholarship, and this with so great an enlightenment that everything seemed new to him. This left his understanding so very enlightened that he felt as if he were another man with another mind. . . .

SPIRITUAL EXERCISES[38]

Introductory Explanations[39]

The First Explanation. By the term Spiritual Exercises we mean every method of examination of conscience, meditation, contemplation, vocal or mental prayer, and other spiritual activities, such as will be mentioned later. For, just as taking a walk, traveling on foot, and running are physical exercises, so is the name of spiritual exercise given to any means of preparing and disposing our soul to rid itself of all its disordered affections and then, after their removal, of seeking and finding God's will in the ordering of our life for the salvation of our soul.

The Second. The person who gives to another the method and procedure for meditating or contemplating should accurately narrate the history contained in the contemplation or meditation, going over the points with only a brief or summary explanation. For in this way the person who is contemplating, by taking this history as the authentic foundation, and by going over it and reasoning about it for oneself, can thus discover something that will bring better understanding or a more personalized concept of the history—either through one's own reasoning or to the extent that the understanding is enlightened by God's grace. This brings more spiritual relish and spiritual fruit than if the one giving the Exercises had lengthily explained and amplified the meaning of the history. For, what fills and satisfies the soul consists, not in knowing much, but in our understanding the realities profoundly and in savoring them interiorly.

The Third. In all the following Spiritual Exercises we use the acts of the intellect in reasoning and of the will in eliciting act of the affections. In regard to the affective acts which spring from the will we should note that when we are conversing with God our Lord or His saints vocally or mentally, greater reverence is demanded of us than when we are using the intellect to understand.

The Fourth. Four Weeks are taken for the following Exercises, corresponding to the four parts into which they are divided. That is, the First Week is devoted to the consideration and contemplation of sins; the Second Week, to the life of Christ our Lord up to and including Palm Sunday; the Third Week, to the Pas-

---

[38]Ibid. Used by kind permission of Paulist Press. Pages 121–35.
[39]The full text offers twenty of these "Explanations."

sion of Christ our Lord; and the Fourth, to the Resurrection and Ascension. To this are appended Three Methods of Praying. . . .

Making The General Examination of Conscience[40]

The First Point is to give thanks to God our Lord for the benefits I have received from Him. *The second* is to ask grace to know my sins and rid myself of them. *The third* is to ask an account of my soul from the hour of rising to the present examen, hour by hour or period by period; first as to thoughts, then words, then deeds. . . . *The fourth* is to ask pardon of God our Lord for my faults. *The fifth* is to resolve, with His grace, to amend them. Close with an Our Father.

THE FIRST EXERCISE[41]

The Preparatory Prayer is to ask God our Lord for the grace that all my intentions, actions, and operations may be ordered purely to the service and praise of His Divine Majesty.

The First Prelude is a composition made by imagining the place. Here we should take notice of the following. When a contemplation or meditation is about something that can be gazed upon, for example, a contemplation of Christ our Lord, who is visible, the composition consists of seeing in imagination the physical place where that which I want to contemplate is taking place. By physical place I mean, for instance, a temple or mountain where Jesus Christ or our Lady happens to be, in accordance with the topic I desire to contemplate. When a contemplation or meditation is about something abstract and invisible, as in the present case about the sins, the composition will be to see in imagination and to consider my soul imprisoned in this corruptible body, and my whole compound self as an exile in this valley [of tears] among brute animals. I mean, my whole self as composed of soul and body.

The Second Prelude is to ask God our Lord for what I want and desire. What I ask for should be in accordance with the subject matter. For example, in contemplation on the Resurrection, I will ask for joy with Christ in joy; in a contemplation on the Passion, I will ask for pain, tears, and suffering with Christ suffering. In the present meditation it will be to ask for shame and confusion about myself, when I see how many people have been damned for committing a single mortal sin, and how many times I have deserved eternal damnation for my many sins.

---

[40]The original heading was "A Method for Making the General Examination of Conscience."
[41]Reprinted from Ganss, trans., *Ignatius of Loyola.* Used by kind permission of Paulist Press. Pages 136–38, "The First Exercise Is a Meditation by Using the Three Powers of the Soul about The First, Second, and Third Sins."

NOTE. All the contemplations or meditations ought to be preceded by this same preparatory prayer, which is never changed, and also by the two preludes, which are sometimes changed in accordance with the subject matter.

The First Point will be to use my memory, by going over the first sin, that of the angels; next, to use my understanding, by reasoning about it; and then my will. My aim in remembering and reasoning about all these matters is to bring myself to greater shame and confusion, by comparing the one sin of the angels with all my own sins. For one sin they went to hell; then how often have I deserved hell for my many sins!

In other words, I will call to memory the sin of the angels: How they were created in grace and then, not wanting to better themselves by using their freedom to reverence and obey their Creator and Lord, they fell into pride, were changed from grace to malice, and were hurled from heaven into hell. Next I will use my intellect to ruminate about this in greater detail, and then move myself to deeper affections by means of my will.

The Second Point will be meditated in the same way. That is, I will apply the three faculties to the sin of Adam and Eve. I will recall to memory how they did long penance for their sin, and the enormous corruption it brought to the human race, with so many people going to hell.

Again in other words, I will call to memory the second sin, that of our first parents: How Adam was created in the plain of Damascus and placed in the earthly paradise; and how Eve was created from his rib; how they were forbidden to eat of the tree of knowledge, but did eat, and thus sinned; and then, clothed in garments of skin and expelled from paradise, they lived out their whole lives in great hardship and penance, deprived of the original justice which they had lost.

Next, I will use my intellect to reason about this in greater detail, and then use the will, as is described just above.

The Third Point will likewise be to use the same method on the third sin, the particular sin of anyone who has gone to hell because of one mortal sin; and further, of innumerable other persons who went there for fewer sins than I have committed. That is, about this third particular sin too I will follow the same procedure as above. I will call to memory the gravity and malice of the sin against my Creator and Lord; then I will use my intellect to reason about it—how by sinning and acting against the Infinite Goodness the person has been justly condemned forever. Then I will finish by using the will, as was described above.

Colloquy. Imagine Christ our Lord suspended on the cross before you, and converse with him in a colloquy: How is it that he, although he is the Creator, has come to make himself a human being? How is it that he has passed from eternal life to death here in time, and to die in this way for my sins?

In a similar way, reflect on yourself and ask: What have I done for Christ? What am I doing for Christ? What ought I to do for Christ? In this way too, gazing on him in so pitiful a state as he hangs on the cross, speak out whatever comes to your mind. A colloquy is made, properly speaking, in the way one friend speaks to another, or a servant to one in authority—now begging a favor, now accusing oneself of some misdeed, now telling one's concerns and asking counsel about them. Close with an Our Father. . . .

RULES FOR THE DISCERNMENT OF SPIRITS[42]

The First Rule. In the case of persons who are going from one mortal sin to another, the enemy ordinarily proposes to them apparent pleasures. He makes them imagine delights and pleasures of the senses, in order to hold them fast and plunge them deeper in their sins and vices. But with persons of this type the good spirit uses a contrary procedure. Through their habitual sound judgment on problems of morality he stings their consciences with remorse.

The Second. In the case of persons who are earnestly purging away their sins, and who are progressing from good to better in the service of God our Lord, the procedure used is the opposite of that described in the First Rule. For in this case it is characteristic of the evil spirit to cause gnawing anxiety, to sadden, and to set up obstacles. In this way he unsettles them by false reasons aimed at preventing their progress. But with persons of this type it is characteristic of the good spirit to stir up courage and strength, consolations, tears, inspirations, and tranquility. He makes things easier and eliminates all obstacles, so that the persons may move forward in doing good.

The Third, about spiritual consolation. By [this kind of] consolation I mean that which occurs when some interior motion is caused within the soul through which it comes to be inflamed with love of its Creator and Lord. As a result it can love no created thing on the face of the earth in itself, but only the Creator of them all. Similarly, this consolation is experienced when the soul sheds tears which move it to love for its Lord—whether they are tears of grief for its own sins, or about the Passion of Christ our Lord, or about other matters directly ordered to his service and praise. Finally, under the word consolation I include every increase in hope, faith, and charity, and every interior joy which calls and attracts one toward heavenly things and to the salvation of one's soul, by bringing it tranquility and peace in its Creator and Lord.

The Fourth, about spiritual desolation. By [this kind of] desolation I mean everything which is the contrary of what was described in the Third Rule; for example, darkness of soul, turmoil within it, an impulsive motion toward low and earthly things, or disquiet from various agitations and temptations. These move one toward lack of faith and leave one without hope and without love. One is completely listless, tepid, and unhappy, and feels separated from our Creator and Lord. For just as consolation is contrary to desolation, so too the thoughts which arise from consolation are likewise contrary to those which spring from desolation.

The Fifth. During a time of desolation one should never make a change. Instead, one should remain firm and constant in the proposals and in a decision in

---

[42]Ibid. Used by permission of Paulist Press. Pages 201–05.

which one was on the day before the desolation, or in a decision in which one was during a previous time of consolation. For just as the good spirit is chiefly the one who guides and counsels us in time of consolation, so it is the evil spirit who does this in time of desolation. By following his counsels we can never find the way to a right decision.

The Sixth. It is taken for granted that in time of desolation we ought not to change our former plans. But it is very helpful to make vigorous changes in ourselves as counterattack against the desolation, for example, by insisting more on prayer, meditation, earnest self-examination, and some suitable way of doing penance.

The Seventh. When we are in desolation we should think that the Lord has left us in order to test us, by leaving us to our own natural powers so that we may prove ourselves by resisting the various agitations and temptations of the enemy. For we can do this with God's help, which always remains available, even if we do not clearly perceive it. Indeed, even though the Lord has withdrawn from us His abundant fervor, augmented love, and intensive grace, He still supplies sufficient grace for our eternal salvation. . . .

The Ninth. There are three main reasons for the desolation we experience. The first is that we ourselves are tepid, lazy, or negligent in our spiritual exercises. Thus the spiritual consolation leaves us because of our own faults. The second reason is that the desolation serves to test how much we are worth, that is, how far we will go in the service and praise of God, even without much compensation by way of consolation and increased graces. The third reason is to give us a true recognition and understanding, in order to make us perceive interiorly that we cannot by ourselves bring on or retain increased devotion, intense love, tears, or any other spiritual consolation; and further, that all these are a gift and grace from God our Lord. . . .

The Thirteenth. Similarly the enemy acts like a false lover, insofar as he tries to remain secret and undetected. For such a scoundrel, speaking with evil intent and trying to seduce the daughter of a good father or the wife of a good husband, wants his words and solicitations to remain secret. But he is deeply displeased when the daughter reveals his deceitful words and evil design to her father, or the wife to her husband. For he easily infers that he cannot succeed in the design he began. In a similar manner, when the enemy of human nature turns his wiles and persuasions upon an upright person, he intends and desires them to be received and kept in secrecy. But when the person reveals them to his or her good confessor or some other spiritual person who understands the enemy's deceits and malice, he is grievously disappointed. For he quickly sees that he cannot succeed in the malicious project he began, because his manifest deceptions have been detected.

The Fourteenth. To use still another comparison, the enemy acts like a military commander who is attempting to conquer and plunder his objective. The captain and leader of an army on campaign sets up his camp, studies the strength and structure of a fortress, and then attacks at its weakest point. In the same way, the enemy of human nature prowls around and from every side probes all our theological, cardinal, and moral virtues. Then at the point where he finds us weakest and most in need in regard to our eternal salvation, there he attacks and tries to take us.

Teresa of Avila (1515–82)

Teresa de Cependa y Ahumada was born to a wealthy merchant family in Avila, Spain. In 1536 she went against the wishes of her family and secretly entered the Carmelite Order. At the age of twenty-one she entered the Carmelite convent in her native town.

In 1538 she began an extended illness in which she suffered fainting fits, heart problems, and eventually periods of paralysis. A severe cataleptic fit left her unconscious and paralyzed for four days; she was so deadlike that a grave was dug for her. It was through the intercession of St. Joseph, Teresa believed, that she recovered consciousness, and gradually also her health. Her remarkable recovery and the spiritual experiences associated with it left her with a prompting to write *The Book of Her Life* (1562).

In her fortieth year she began the apostolic work of reforming the Carmelite Order, through championing an enhanced spiritual climate and higher levels of observance. The result of her efforts was the founding of the "Discalaced" (shoeless) Carmelites, as a renewed and invigorated part of the order. St. Teresa personally founded fourteen convents of the movement in Spain.

On May 28, 1577, Teresa received an inner urging to write what would become her most famous literary work, *The Interior Castle* (1588). The central concept, which fit well with her own culture and world of castles, was probably drawn from Jesus's saying to His disciples, "in my Father's house are many mansions, and I go there to prepare a place for you. . . ." She used the metaphor of the castle to describe the character of Christian spiritual life; it is an *interior* castle. This castle is made up of seven dwelling places, and the goal of devotion is to proceed through the outer dwelling places into that interior castle where God Himself dwells. Mental prayer is the gateway that takes one into this castle. The work divides into two parts. The first part describes three dwelling places that can be achieved through human efforts at putting off imperfection and applying oneself to the helps of God's grace. The second part of the book describes four dwelling places that can only be reached passively through mental prayer or the prayer of Quiet. There was a place in her spirituality for Mary and Martha (see below), but the final stages of this spiritual pilgrimage were made passively.

St. Teresa's spirituality is Christocentric. She considered Christ to be the bridegroom of the soul, and sought to find that living union (spiritual marriage) with Christ that brought with it a corresponding transformation into Christlikeness. Through this divine friendship with Christ a person becomes perfected or divinitized.

GOD TOOK PITY ON ME[43]

... [My] soul ... was tired; and, in spite of its desire, my wretched habits would not allow it rest. It happened to me that one day entering the oratory I saw a statue they had borrowed for a certain feast to be celebrated in the house. It represented the much wounded Christ and was very devotional so that beholding it I was utterly distressed in seeing Him that way, for it well represented what He suffered for us. I felt so keenly aware of how poorly I thanked Him for those wounds that, it seems to me, my heart broke. Beseeching Him to strengthen me once and for all that I might not offend Him, I threw myself down before Him with the greatest outpouring of tears. . . .

This was my method of prayer I then used: since I could not reflect discursively with the intellect, I strove to picture Christ within me, and it did me greater good—in my opinion—to picture Him in those scenes where I saw Him more alone. It seemed to me that being alone and afflicted, as a person in need, He had to accept me. I had many simple thoughts like those.

The scene of His prayer in the garden, especially, was a comfort to me; I strove to be His companion there. If I could, I thought of the sweat and agony He had undergone in that place. I desired to wipe away the sweat He so painfully experienced, but I recall that I never dared to actually do it, since my sins appeared to me so serious. I remained with Him as long as my thoughts allowed me to, for there were many distractions that tormented me. Most nights, for many years before going to bed when I commended myself to God in preparation for sleep, I always pondered for a little while this episode of the prayer in the garden. I did this even before I was a nun since I was told that one gains many indulgences by doing so. I believe my soul gained a great deal through this custom because I began to practice prayer without knowing what it was; and the custom became so habitual that I did not abandon it, just as I did not fail to make the sign of the cross before sleeping. . . .

At this time they gave me *The Confessions of St. Augustine*. It seems the Lord ordained this, because I had not tried to procure a copy, nor had I ever seen one. I am very fond of St. Augustine, because the convent where I stayed as a lay person belonged to his order; and also because he had been a sinner, for I found great consolation in sinners whom, after having been sinners, the Lord brought back to Himself. . . . As I began to read the *Confessions*, it seemed to me I saw myself in them. I began to commend myself very much to this glorious saint. When I came to the passage where he speaks about his conversion and read how he heard that voice in the garden, it only seemed to me, according to what I felt in my

---

[43]Reprinted from Kieran Kavanaugh and Otilio Rodriguez, trans., *The Collected Works of St. Teresa of Avila*, Vol. I. Copyright (c) 1976 by Washington Province of Discalaced Carmelites, ICS Publications, 2131 Lincoln Road, N.E. Washington, D.C. 20002. "The Book of Her Life," ch. 9, pp. 70–73. Used with the kind permission of ICS Publications.

heart, that it was I the Lord called. I remained for a long time totally dissolved in tears and feeling within myself utter distress and weariness. Oh, how a soul suffers, God help me, by losing the freedom it should have in being itself; and what torments it undergoes! I marvel now at how I could have lived in such great affliction. May God be praised who gave me the life to rise up from a death so deadly.

It seemed to me my soul gained great strength from the Divine Majesty and that He must have heard my cries and taken pity on so many tears. The inclination to spend more time with Him began to grow. I started to shun the occasions of sin, because when they were avoided I then returned to loving His Majesty. In my opinion, I clearly understood that I loved Him; but I did not understand as I should have what true love of God consists in.

It doesn't seem to me I was yet finished preparing myself to desire to serve Him when His Majesty began to favor me again. Apparently, what others strive for with great labor, the Lord gains for me only through my desire to receive it, for He was now, in these later years, giving me delights and favors. I did not beseech Him to give me tenderness of devotion, never would I have dared to do that. I only begged Him to pardon my great sins and to give me the grace not to offend Him. Since I saw that my sins were so great, I would never have had the boldness to desire favors or delights. Clearly, it seems, He took pity on me and showed great mercy in admitting me before Him and bringing me into His presence, for I saw that if He Himself had not accomplished this, I would not have come. . . .

MENTAL PRAYER[44]

The good that one who practices prayer possesses has been written of by many saints and holy men; I mean mental prayer—glory be to God for this good! If it were not for this good, even though I have little humility, I should not be so proud as to dare speak about mental prayer. . . . For mental prayer in my opinion is nothing else than an intimate sharing between friends; it means taking time frequently to be alone with Him who we know loves us. In order that love be true and the friendship endure, the wills of the friends must be in accord. The will of the Lord, it is already known, cannot be at fault; our will is vicious, sensual, and ungrateful. And if you do not yet love Him as He loves you because You have not reached the degree of conformity with His will, you will endure this pain of spending a long while with one who is so different from you when you see how much it benefits you to possess His friendship and how much He loves you. . . .

---

[44]Ibid., Vol. I, "Life," ch. 8, para. 5, p. 67. Used with the kind permission of ICS publications.

THE PRAYER OF UNION[45]

. . . With regard to the nature of union, I do not think I can say any thing further; but when the soul to which God grants these favours prepares itself for them, there are many things to be said concerning what the Lord works in it. Some of these I shall say now, and I shall describe that soul's state. In order the better to explain this, I will make use of a comparison which is suitable for the purpose; and which will also show us how, although this work is performed by the Lord, and we can do nothing to make His Majesty grant us this favour, we can do a great deal to prepare ourselves for it.

You will have heard of the wonderful way in which silk is made—a way which no one could invent but God—and how it comes from a kind of seed which looks like tiny peppercorns (I have never seen this, but only heard of it, so if it is incorrect in any way the fault is not mine). When the warm weather comes, and the mulberry-trees begin to show leaf, this seed starts to take life; until it has this sustenance, on which it feeds, it is as dead. The silkworms feed on the mulberry-leaves until they are full-grown, when people put down twigs, upon which, with their tiny mouths, they start spinning silk, making themselves very tight little co-coons, in which they bury themselves. Then, finally, the worm, which was large and ugly, comes right out of the cocoon a beautiful white butterfly. . . .

The silkworm is like the soul which takes life when, through the heat which comes from the Holy Spirit, it begins to utilize the general help which God gives to us all, and to make use of the remedies which He left in His Church—such as frequent confessions, good books and sermons, for these are the remedies for a soul dead in negligences and sins and frequently plunged into temptation. The soul begins to live and nourishes itself on this food, and on good meditations, un-til it is full grown—and this is what concerns me now: the rest is of little impor-tance. . . .

Here, then, daughters, you see what we can do, with God's favour. May His Majesty Himself be our Mansion as He is in this Prayer of Union which, as it were, we ourselves spin. When I say He will be our Mansion, and we can con-struct it for ourselves and hide ourselves in it, I seem to be suggesting that we can subtract from God, or add to Him. But of course we cannot possibly do that! We can neither subtract from, nor add to, God, but we can subtract from, and add to, ourselves, just as these little silkworms do. And, before we have finished do-ing all that we can in that respect, God will take this tiny achievement of ours, which is nothing at all, unite it with His greatness and give it such worth that its reward will be the Lord Himself. And as it is He Whom it has cost the most, so His Majesty will unite our small trials with the great trials which He suffered, and make both of them into one.

On, then, my daughters! Let us hasten to perform this task and spin this co-

---

[45]Teresa of Avila, *The Interior Castle*, Mansion V, ch. 2. Translated and edited by E. Allison Peers, from the *critical edition* of P. Silverio de Santa Teresa, C.D (1959). This document (last modified March 8, 1996) is from the Christian Classics Ethereal Library, http://ccel.wheaton.edu.

coon. Let us renounce our self-love and self-will, and our attachment to earthly things. Let us practise penance, prayer, mortification, obedience, and all the other good works that you know of. Let us do what we have been taught; and we have been instructed about what our duty is. Let the silkworm die—let it die, as in fact it does when it has completed the work which it was created to do. Then we shall see God and shall ourselves be as completely hidden in His greatness as is this little worm in its cocoon. Note that, when I speak of seeing God, I am referring to the way in which, as I have said, He allows Himself to be apprehended in this kind of union.

And now let us see what becomes of this silkworm, for all that I have been saying about it is leading up to this. When it is in this state of prayer, and quite dead to the world, it comes out a little white butterfly. Oh, greatness of God, that a soul should come out like this after being hidden in the greatness of God, and closely united with Him, for so short a time—never, I think, for as long as half an hour! I tell you truly, the very soul does not know itself. For think of the difference between an ugly worm and a white butterfly; it is just the same here. The soul cannot think how it can have merited such a blessing—whence such a blessing could have come to it, I meant to say, for it knows quite well that it has not merited it at all. It finds itself so anxious to praise the Lord that it would gladly be consumed and die a thousand deaths for His sake. Then it finds itself longing to suffer great trials and unable to do otherwise. It has the most vehement desires for penance, for solitude, and for all to know God. And hence, when it sees God being offended, it becomes greatly distressed. . . .

SPIRITUAL MARRIAGE[46]

. . . Let us now come to treat of the Divine and Spiritual Marriage, although this great Favour cannot be fulfilled perfectly in us during our lifetime, for if we were to withdraw ourselves from God this great blessing would be lost. When granting this favour for the first time, His Majesty is pleased to reveal Himself to the soul through an imaginary vision of His most sacred Humanity, so that it may clearly understand what is taking place and not be ignorant of the fact that it is receiving so sovereign a gift. To other people the experience will come in a different way. To the person of whom we have been speaking the Lord revealed Himself one day, when she had just received Communion, in great splendour and beauty and majesty, as He did after His resurrection, and told her that it was time she took upon her His affairs as if they were her own and that He would take her affairs upon Himself; and He added other words which are easier to understand than to repeat. . . .

. . . But what passes in the union of the Spiritual Marriage is very different. The Lord appears in the centre of the soul, not through an imaginary, but through an intellectual vision (although this is a subtler one than that already mentioned),

---

[46]Ibid., Mansion VII, ch. 2.

just as He appeared to the Apostles, without entering through the door, when He said to them: "Pax vobis." This instantaneous communication of God to the soul is so great a secret and so sublime a favour, and such delight is felt by the soul, that I do not know with what to compare it, beyond saying that the Lord is pleased to manifest to the soul at that moment the glory that is in Heaven, in a sublimer manner than is possible through any vision or spiritual consolation. It is impossible to say more than that, as far as one can understand, the soul (I mean the spirit of this soul) is made one with God, Who, being likewise a Spirit, has been pleased to reveal the love that He has for us by showing to certain persons the extent of that love, so that we may praise His greatness. For He has been pleased to unite Himself with His creature in such a way that they have become like two who cannot be separated from one another: even so He will not separate Himself from her.

The Spiritual Betrothal is different: here the two persons are frequently separated, as is the case with union, for, although by union is meant the joining of two things into one, each of the two, as is a matter of common observation, can be separated and remain a thing by itself. This favour of the Lord passes quickly and afterwards the soul is deprived of that companionship—I mean so far as it can understand. In this other favour of the Lord it is not so: the soul remains all the time in that centre with its God. We might say that union is as if the ends of two wax candles were joined so that the light they give is one: the wicks and the wax and the light are all one, yet afterwards the one candle can be perfectly well separated from the other and the candles become two again, or the wick may be withdrawn from the wax. But here it is like rain falling from the heavens into a river or a spring; there is nothing but water there and it is impossible to divide or separate the water belonging to the river from that which fell from the heavens. Or it is as if a tiny streamlet enters the sea, from which it will find no way of separating itself, or as if in a room there were two large windows through which the light streamed in: it enters in different places but it all becomes one.

Perhaps when St. Paul says: "He who is joined to God becomes one spirit with Him" [1 Cor 6:17], he is referring to this sovereign Marriage, which presupposes the entrance of His Majesty into the soul by union. And he also says: "For me to live is Christ, and to die is gain" [Phil 1:21]. This, I think, the soul may say here, for it is here that the little butterfly to which we have referred dies, and with the greatest joy, because Christ is now its life. . . .

MARY AND MARTHA[47]

. . . This, my sisters, I should like us to strive to attain: we should desire and engage in prayer, not for our enjoyment, but for the sake of acquiring this strength which fits us for service. Let us not try to walk along an untrodden path, or at the best we shall waste our time: it would certainly be a novel idea to think of re-

---

[47]Ibid., Mansion VII, ch. 4.

ceiving these favours from God through any other means than those used by Him and by all His saints. Let us not even consider such a thing: believe me, Martha and Mary must work together when they offer the Lord lodging, and must have Him ever with them, and they must not entertain Him badly and give Him nothing to eat. And how can Mary give Him anything, seated as she is at His feet, unless her sister helps her? His food consists in our bringing Him souls, in every possible way, so that they may be saved and may praise Him for ever.

You will reply to me by making two observations. The first, that Mary was said to have chosen the better part—and she had already done the work of Martha and shown her love for the Lord by washing His feet and wiping them with her hair [Lk 7:37–38]. And do you think it would be a trifling mortification to a woman in her position to go through those streets—perhaps alone, for her fervour was such that she cared nothing how she went—to enter a house that she had never entered before and then to have to put up with uncharitable talk from the Pharisee and from very many other people, all of which she was forced to endure? What a sight it must have been in the town to see such a woman as she had been making this change in her life! Such wicked people as we know the Jews to have been would only need to see that she was friendly with the Lord, Whom they so bitterly hated, to call to mind the life which she had lived and to realize that she now wanted to become holy, for she would of course at once have changed her style of dress and everything else. Think how we gossip about people far less notorious than she and then imagine what she must have suffered. I assure you, sisters, that that better part came to her only after sore trials and great mortification—even to see her Master so much hated must have been an intolerable trial to her. And how many such trials did she not endure later, after the Lord's death! I think myself that the reason she was not granted martyrdom was that she had already undergone it through witnessing the Lord's death. The later years of her life, too, during which she was absent from Him, would have been years of terrible torment; so she was not always enjoying the delights of contemplation at the Lord's feet.

The other thing you may say is that you are unable to lead souls to God, and have no means of doing so; that you would gladly do this, but, being unable to teach and preach like the Apostles, you do not know how. That is an objection which I have often answered in writing, though I am not sure if I have done so in discussing this Castle. But, as it is a thing which I think must occur to you, in view of the desires which the Lord implants in you, I will not omit to speak of it here. I told you elsewhere that the devil sometimes puts ambitious desires into our hearts, so that, instead of setting our hand to the work which lies nearest to us, and thus serving Our Lord in ways within our power, we may rest content with having desired the impossible. Apart from praying for people, by which you can do a great deal for them, do not try to help everybody, but limit yourselves to your own companions; your work will then be all the more effective because you have the greater obligation to do it. Do you imagine it is a small advantage that you should have so much humility and mortification, and should be the servants of all and show such great charity towards all, and such fervent love for the Lord that it resembles a fire kindling all their souls, while you constantly awaken their zeal by your other virtues? This would indeed be a great service to the Lord and one very pleasing to Him. By your doing things which you really can do, His Majesty will know that you would like to do many more, and thus He will reward you exactly as if you had won many souls for Him.

"But we shall not be converting anyone," you will say, "for all our sisters are good already." What has that to do with it? If they become still better, their praises will be more pleasing to the Lord, and their prayers of greater value to their neighbours. In a word, my sisters, I will end by saying that we must not build towers without foundations, and that the Lord does not look so much at the magnitude of anything we do as at the love with which we do it. If we accomplish what we can, His Majesty will see to it that we become able to do more each day. We must not begin by growing weary; but during the whole of this short life, which for any one of you may be shorter than you think, we must offer the Lord whatever interior and exterior sacrifice we are able to give Him, and His Majesty will unite it with that which He offered to the Father for us upon the Cross, so that it may have the value won for it by our will, even though our actions in themselves may be trivial. . . .

John of the Cross (1542–91)

John of the Cross was born Juan de la Cruz in Hontiveros, Avila, Spain. His ancestors were wealthy silk merchants, but his father (Gonzalo) spurned wealth and social station to marry a poor weaver named Catalina Alvarez. The family disowned Gonzalo, and he and Catalina raised their three sons on modest means. When Juan was three years old his father died, which plunged Catalina and her children into poverty and hunger. Juan worked in a hospital for seven years, while attending a Jesuit school nearby. He received his advanced education at the University of Salamanca and the Carmelite College of San Andres (1564-68).

In 1563 he joined the Carmelite Order and was ordained a priest (1567)—taking the name "John of the Cross." Soon thereafter he became a friend and colleague of Teresa of Avila, and they worked together for reform of the Carmelite Order. They shared a desire to return to the earlier rigor and contemplative life of the order and organized many Discalaced (shoeless) Carmelite monasteries. Not all members of the Order were sympathetic to these reforms and in 1578, John was kidnapped and imprisoned for nine months by a faction of the Carmelites that resisted reform. So significant were his reforming efforts that John of the Cross, along with Teresa of Avila, is considered cofounder of the Discalaced Carmelites.

St. John's mysticism, like that of St. Teresa, begins with human experience; both had a robust anthropology and theology of the cross.[48] John stressed the need to empty and purify the soul through contemplation and the mortification of creaturely desires (*via negativa* or apophatic mysticism), as a basis for union with God. In de-

---

[48]Cf. E. W. Trueman Dicken, "Teresa of Jesus and John of the Cross," in Jones, Wainwright, and Yarnold, eds. *Study of Spirituality*, pp. 363–78, for an extensive examination of their mysticism.

tachment from creaturely things ("dark night of the soul"), the soul is purified. Active and passive steps of reflection and discipline are essential to this purification, which leads to illumination and ultimately to union with God (the unitive way).

Taken together, his writings, *The Ascent of Mount Carmel* and *The Dark Night of the Soul* (c. 1587), describe this process of purifying the soul: (1) the active purgation of the senses (*Ascent*, Bk I), (2) passive purgation of the senses (*Dark Night*, Bk. I), (3) active purgation of the spirit (*Ascent*, Bks. II and III), and (4) passive purgation of the spirit (Dark Night, Bk. II). As the soul is purged through "darkness" she is transformed by Divine Light and conformed to the will of God.[49] Other important works by St. John include *The Spiritual Canticle* (1578) and *Living Flame of Love* (1585).

DARK NIGHT OF THE SOUL[50]

The reason for which it is necessary for the soul, in order to attain to Divine union with God, to pass through this dark night of mortification of the desires and denial of pleasures in all things, is because all the affections which it has for creatures are pure darkness in the eyes of God, and, when the soul is clothed in these affections, it has no capacity for being enlightened and possessed by the pure and simple light of God, if it first cast them not from it; for light cannot agree with darkness; since, as Saint John says: "The darkness could not receive the light" [Jn. 1:5].

2. The reason is that two contraries (even as philosophy teaches us) cannot co-exist in one person; and that darkness, which is affection set upon the creatures, and light, which is God, are contrary to each other, and have no likeness or accord between one another, even as Saint Paul taught the Corinthians, saying: . . . "What communion can there be between light and darkness [2 Cor 6:14]?" Hence it is that the light of Divine union cannot dwell in the soul if these affections first flee not away from it.

3. In order that we may the better prove what has been said, it must be known that the affection and attachment which the soul has for creatures renders the soul like to these creatures; and, the greater is its affection, the closer is the equality and likeness between them; for love creates a likeness between that which loves and that which is loved. For which reason David, speaking of those who set their affections upon idols, said thus: ". . . Let them that set their heart upon them be like to them." And thus, he that loves a creature becomes as low as that creature, and, in some ways, lower; for love not only makes the lover

---

[49]Mary Giles, "Ascent of Mount Carmel and Dark Night of the Soul," in Magill and McGreal, eds., *Christian Spirituality*, pp. 242–47.

[50]John of the Cross, *Ascent of Mount Carmel*, Bk. I, ch. 4, translated by E. Allison Peers. Document from the Christian Classics Ethereal Library, http://ccel.wheaton.edu.

equal to the object of his love, but even subjects him to it. Hence in the same way it comes to pass that the soul that loves anything else becomes incapable of pure union with God and transformation in Him. For the low estate of the creature is much less capable of union with the high estate of the Creator than is darkness with light. . . .

And even as he that is in darkness comprehends not the light, so the soul that sets its affection upon creatures will be unable to comprehend God; and, until it be purged, it will neither be able to possess Him here below, through pure transformation of love, nor yonder in clear vision. . . .

TWO KINDS OF DARKNESS[51]

1. This night, which, as we say, is contemplation, produces in spiritual persons two kinds of darkness or purgation, corresponding to the two parts of man's nature—namely, the sensual and the spiritual. And thus the one night or purgation will be sensual, wherein the soul is purged according to sense, which is subdued to the spirit; and the other is a night or purgation which is spiritual, wherein the soul is purged and stripped according to the spirit, and subdued and made ready for the union of love with God. . . .

2. The first purgation or night is bitter and terrible to sense, as we shall now show. The second bears no comparison with it, for it is horrible and awful to the spirit, as we shall show presently. . . .

3. Since, then, the conduct of these beginners upon the way of God is ignoble, and has much to do with their love of self and their own inclinations, as has been explained above, God desires to lead them farther. He seeks to bring them out of that ignoble kind of love to a higher degree of love for Him, to free them from the ignoble exercises of sense and meditation (wherewith, as we have said, they go seeking God so unworthily and in so many ways that are unbefitting), and to lead them to a kind of spiritual exercise wherein they can commune with Him more abundantly and are freed more completely from imperfections. For they have now had practice for some time in the way of virtue and have persevered in meditation and prayer, whereby, through the sweetness and pleasure that they have found therein, they have lost their love of the things of the world and have gained some degree of spiritual strength in God; this has enabled them to some extent to refrain from creaturely desires, so that for God's sake they are now able to suffer a light burden and a little aridity without turning back to a time which they found more pleasant. When they are going about these spiritual exercises with the greatest delight and pleasure, and when they believe that the sun of Divine favour is shining most brightly

---

[51]John of the Cross, *Dark Night of the Soul*, Bk. I, ch. 8, translated by E. Allison Peers, from the critical edition of P. Silverio de Santa Teresa (1959). Document from the Christian Classics Ethereal Library, http://ccel.wheaton.edu.

upon them, God turns all this light of theirs into darkness, and shuts against them the door and the source of the sweet spiritual water which they were tasting in God whensoever and for as long as they desired. (For, as they were weak and tender, there was no door closed to them, as Saint John says in the Apocalypse, iii, 8.) And thus He leaves them so completely in the dark that they know not whither to go with their sensible imagination and meditation; for they cannot advance a step in meditation, as they were wont to do afore time, their inward senses being submerged in this night, and left with such dryness that not only do they experience no pleasure and consolation in the spiritual things and good exercises wherein they were wont to find their delights and pleasures, but instead, on the contrary, they find insipidity and bitterness in the said things. For, as I have said, God now sees that they have grown a little, and are becoming strong enough to lay aside their swaddling clothes and be taken from the gentle breast; so He sets them down from His arms and teaches them to walk on their own feet; which they feel to be very strange, for everything seems to be going wrong with them. . . .

5. With regard to this way of purgation of the senses, since it is so common, we might here adduce a great number of quotations from Divine Scripture, where many passages relating to it are continually found, particularly in the Psalms and the Prophets. However, I do not wish to spend time upon these, for he who knows not how to look for them there will find the common experience of this purgation to be sufficient.

THE NIGHT OF THE SPIRIT[52]

2. Wherefore, in this night following, both parts of the soul are purged together, and it is for this end that it is well to have passed through the corrections of the first night, and the period of tranquillity which proceeds from it, in order that, sense being united with spirit, both may be purged after a certain manner and may then suffer with greater fortitude. For very great fortitude is needful for so violent and severe a purgation, since, if the weakness of the lower part has not first been corrected and fortitude has not been gained from God through the sweet and delectable communion which the soul has afterwards enjoyed with Him, its nature will not have the strength or the disposition to bear it.

3. Therefore, since these proficients are still at a very low stage of progress, and follow their own nature closely in the intercourse and dealings which they have with God, because the gold of their spirit is not yet purified and refined, they still think of God as little children, and speak of God as little children, and feel and experience God as little children, even as Saint Paul says, because they

---

[52]Ibid., Bk. II, chs. 3 and 4.

have not reached perfection, which is the union of the soul with God. In the state of union, however, they will work great things in the spirit, even as grown men, and their works and faculties will then be Divine rather than human, as will afterwards be said. To this end God is pleased to strip them of this old man and clothe them with the new man, who is created according to God, as the Apostle says, in the newness of sense. He strips their faculties, affections and feelings, both spiritual and sensual, both outward and inward, leaving the understanding dark, the will dry, the memory empty and the affections in the deepest affliction, bitterness and constraint, taking from the soul the pleasure and experience of spiritual blessings which it had aforetime, in order to make of this privation one of the principles which are requisite in the spirit so that there may be introduced into it and united with it the spiritual form of the spirit, which is the union of love. All this the Lord works in the soul by means of a pure and dark contemplation, as the soul explains in the first stanza. This, although we originally interpreted it with reference to the first night of sense, is principally understood by the soul of this second night of the spirit, since this is the principal part of the purification of the soul. And thus we shall set it down and expound it here again in this sense. . . .

> On a dark night,
> Kindled in love with yearnings
> Oh, happy chance!
> I went forth without being observed,
> My house being now at rest.

1. Interpreting this stanza now with reference to purgation, contemplation or detachment or poverty of spirit, which here are almost one and the same thing, we can expound it after this manner and make the soul speak thus: In poverty, and without protection or support in all the apprehensions of my soul—is, in the darkness of my understanding and the constraint of my will, in affliction and anguish with respect to memory, remaining in the dark in pure faith, which is dark night for the said natural faculties, the will alone being touched by grief and afflictions and yearnings for the love of God—I went forth from myself— that is, from my low manner of understanding, from my weak mode of loving and from my poor and limited manner of experiencing God, without being hindered therein by sensuality or the devil.

2. This was a great happiness and a good chance for me; for, when the faculties had been perfectly annihilated and calmed, together with the passions, desires and affections of my soul, wherewith I had experienced and tasted God after a lowly manner, I went forth from my own human dealings and operations to the operations and dealings of God. That is to say, my understanding went forth from itself, turning from the human and natural to the Divine; for, when it is united with God by means of this purgation, its understanding no longer comes through its natural light and vigour, but through the Divine Wisdom wherewith it has become united. And my will went forth from itself, becoming Divine; for, being united with Divine love, it no longer loves with its nat-

ural strength after a lowly manner, but with strength and purity from the Holy Spirit; and thus the will, which is now near to God, acts not after a human manner, and similarly the memory has become transformed into eternal apprehensions of glory. And finally, by means of this night and purgation of the old man, all the energies and affections of the soul are wholly renewed into a Divine temper and Divine delight. . . .

UNION WITH GOD[53]

3. In order, then, to understand what is meant by this union whereof we are treating, it must be known that God dwells and is present substantially in every soul, even in that of the greatest sinner in the world. And this kind of union is ever wrought between God and all the creatures, for in it He is preserving their being: if union of this kind were to fail them, they would at once become annihilated and would cease to be. And so, when we speak of union of the soul with God, we speak not of this substantial union which is continually being wrought, but of the union and transformation of the soul with God, which is not being wrought continually, but only when there is produced that likeness that comes from love; we shall therefore term his the union of likeness, even as that other union is called substantial or essential. The former is natural, the latter supernatural. And the latter comes to pass when the two wills— namely that of the soul and that of God—are conformed together in one, and there is naught in the one that repugnant to the other. And thus, when the soul rids itself totally of that which is repugnant to the Divine will and conforms not with it, it is transformed in God through love.

4. This is to be understood of that which is repugnant, not only in action, but likewise in habit, so that not only must the voluntary acts of imperfection cease, but the habits of any such imperfections must be annihilated. . . .

    Wherefore, although it is true that, as we have said, God is ever in the soul, giving it, and through His presence conserving within it, its natural being, yet He does not always communicate supernatural being to it. For this is communicated only by love and grace, which not all souls possess; and all those that possess it have it not in the same degree; for some have attained more degrees of love and others fewer. Wherefore God communicates Himself most to that soul that has progressed farthest in love; namely, that has its will in closest conformity with the will of God. And the soul that has attained complete conformity and likeness of will is totally united and transformed in God supernaturally. Wherefore, as has already been explained, the more completely a soul is wrapped up in the creatures and in its own abilities, by habit and affection, the less preparation it has for such union; for it gives not God a complete opportunity to transform it supernaturally. The soul, then, needs only

---

[53]John of the Cross, *Ascent of Mount Carmel*, Bk. II, ch. 5, with omissions.

to strip itself of these natural dissimilarities and contrarieties, so that God, Who is communicating Himself naturally to it, according to the course of nature, may communicate Himself to it supernaturally, by means of grace.

5. And it is this that Saint John desired to explain when he said: . . . As though he had said: He gave power to be sons of God—that is, to be transformed in God—only to those who are born, not of blood—that is, not of natural constitution and temperament—neither of the will of the flesh—that is, of the free will of natural capacity and ability—still less of the will of man—wherein is included every way and manner of judging and comprehending with the understanding [Jn 1:13]. He gave power to none of these to become sons of God, but only to those that are born of God—that is, to those who, being born again through grace, and dying first of all to everything that is of the old man, are raised above themselves to the supernatural, and receive from God this rebirth and adoption, which transcends all that can be imagined. For, as Saint John himself says elsewhere: . . . "He that is not born again in the Holy Spirit will not be able to see this kingdom of God" [Jn 3:5], which is the state of perfection; and to be born again in the Holy Spirit in this life is to have a soul most like to God in purity, having in itself no admixture of imperfection, so that pure transformation can be wrought in it through participation of union, albeit not essentially. . . .

7. In thus allowing God to work in it, the soul (having rid itself of every mist and stain of the creatures, which consists in having its will perfectly united with that of God, for to love is to labour to detach and strip itself for God's sake of all that is not God) is at once illumined and transformed in God, and God communicates to it His supernatural Being, in such wise that it appears to be God Himself, and has all that God Himself has. And this union comes to pass when God grants the soul this supernatural favour, that all the things of God and the soul are one in participant transformation; and the soul seems to be God rather than a soul, and is indeed God by participation; although it is true that its natural being, though thus transformed, is as distinct from the Being of God as it was before, even as the window has likewise a nature distinct from that of the ray, though the ray gives it brightness.

8. This makes it clearer that the preparation of the soul for this union, as we said, is not that it should understand or perceive or feel or imagine anything, concerning either God or aught else, but that it should have purity and love—that is, perfect resignation and detachment from everything for God's sake alone; and, as there can be no perfect transformation if there be not perfect purity, and as the enlightenment, illumination and union of the soul with God will be according to the proportion of its purity, in greater or in less degree; yet the soul will not be perfect, as I say, if it be not wholly and perfectly bright and clean. . . .

CHAPTER 4

≈

Modern Spirituality

As the Reformation era gave way to the Enlightenment, faith and reason seemed to be at odds with one another. With the passing of the last vestiges of the medieval world, faith seemed less relevant to human life in the age of reason and science. The Christian Spirituality of the early modern period paralleled the gradual emergence of nation-states and national cultural identities; it was categorized by the emergence of regional schools of religious expression. Hence, the designation of "The Spanish School" (Ignatius of Loyola, John of the Cross, and Teresa of Avila), "The Italian School" (Catherine of Genoa), "The French School" (Francis de Sales, Francis Fenelon),[1] and "The English School" or "Caroline Divines" (Jeremy Taylor and George Herbert) made significant and distinctive contributions to their regions and the period.

"Modernity" also brought with it a new set of values that were in one sense linked to the failures and discoveries of previous ages, and yet were in another sense contradictory to the fundamental impulses of Christian Spirituality. The confident individualism of the reformers merged with the Enlightenment's optimistic assessment of human talents and abilities to produce an ethos that stressed the exercise of human reason, and a corresponding apprehension about matters of faith. Exciting new developments in science validated an unbounded confidence in the human intellect. Gradually the dark curtain of religious superstition was pushed back in favor of scientific explanations for the operations of the world of nature. Nature seemed more and more like a wonderfully intricate machine, and less like a creaturely reflection of its almighty Creator. Scientific "objectivity" replaced mystery and wonder as a constitutive component for understanding the natural order.

Along with its general optimism about human reason and abilities, modernism brought with it a profound sense of progress and development. "New" would grad-

---

[1] Cf. William Thompson, ed., *Berullie and the French School* (New York: Paulist Press, 1989).

ually come to imply "better," and things seemed—almost inevitably—to be getting better. Progressives had little patience for traditionalism, and the conservators of the old order. Hence, religious strife and civil war in England gave rise to Puritanism, and laid the foundations for Evangelicalism. Similar social conditions in Germany gave rise to Pietism.

As scientific objectivity analyzed the world known by empiricism, religious faith was increasingly relegated to the realm of personal experience and ethical motivations. Not surprisingly, then, writers of the period are frequently found to be concerned with a spirituality of the heart, yet their approaches to the cultivation of inner life are inseparably linked with challenges of living a Christian life in a rapidly changing world. With colonialism and expansionism came war, the evils of slavery and social decay; with rapid industrialization came the exploitation of immigrants, the poor, women and children, and urban ghettos. Modern culture seemed to have an easy conscience about its social failings, hence many spiritual writers of the era drew a direct connection between inner renewal and social reform.

Writers and practitioners of Christian Spirituality in the modern era were deeply affected by its cultural ethos. They were most profoundly advocates of a spirituality of the heart, and yet they could not be blind to the societal issues that pressed down upon them. Christian philosophers like Blaise Pascal and Søren Kierkegaard explored the relationship between faith and reason. The Pietists (Philip Jacob Spener) and Methodists (John and Charles Wesley) sought to cultivate holiness of heart and life among the laity through small groups that gave them religious identity and spiritual support in the face of the challenges of the modern world. Advocates of practical Christianity, like Hannah More, challenged the modern optimism about human nature and Deism's claim that rational religion made traditional devotional practices irrelevant.

At the close of the period, revivalist models of soteriology and Christian practice—which had in earlier periods provided an impetus for personal renewal and societal change—seemed increasingly irrelevant in the face of the staggering social problems faced by a modern, urban, industrial, multicultural society. Horace Bushnell offered a model for conversion, based on the concept of Christian nurture, that held an implicit criticism of the notion of instantaneous conversion and provided an impetus for revitalizing the understanding and function of the church. In a similar way, Walter Rauschenbusch's emphasis upon the Social Gospel offered a criticism of revivalism's tendency to stress the individual and personal aspects of the gospel at the expense of its social and collective dimensions. In so doing, the Social Gospel provided a new basis for Christian social reform, which stressed that all Christians must work together for good if, indeed, the Kingdom of God was going to be visited upon the earth.

Johann Arndt (1555–1621)

Johann Arndt, born the son of a German Lutheran pastor in Edderitz, Anhalt, Germany, evidenced a profound interest in religious matters. Following studies at Helmstedt, Wittenberg, Strassburg, and Basel, Arndt entered the Lutheran ministry in 1583. Through his studies Arndt had been deeply influenced by the writings of the medieval mystics (especially Bernard of Clairvaux and John Tauler), as well as by the formative spirituality of *The Imitation of Christ.*

Arndt frequently found himself at odds with the rather rationalistic and doctrinaire expressions of Christianity that seemed to dominate the church of his day. He was forced to move from one church to another because of his dissenting views. Finally, in 1609, he became general superintendent of the Luneburg Church at Celle, a position he held until his death.

While adhering to the theological content of the doctrines and creeds of the Lutheran Church, Arndt stressed that right doctrine alone was insufficient. In his view true Christianity was union with Christ through the transformation and purification of the inner person. Arndt's work is frequently identified as the formative influence behind the German Pietism that subsequently took expression through the efforts of Philip Jacob Spener (1635–1705) and August Herman Francke (1663–1727). Arndt's principal work, *True Christianity,* has been appropriately described as "*the* handbook of the mainline pietists."[2] Not only did Arndt point Pietism back to its Reformation roots, in Martin Luther, but he also directed the way back *through* Luther to the Christ-centered mysticism of the Middle Ages (exemplified by Bernard of Clairvaux and Thomas a' Kempis). Arndt's spirituality is noteworthy for his stress upon the "new birth" (a theme that will become increasingly significant in subsequent writers), for his emphasis upon the humanity of Jesus Christ as providing a pattern for Christian practice, and for his willingness to see sanctification as a foretaste of the life to come.[3]

TRUE CHRISTIANITY[4]

. . . Many think that theology is a mere science, or rhetoric, whereas it is a living experience and practice. Everyone now endeavors to be eminent and distinguished in the world, but no one is willing to learn to be pious. Everyone now seeks out men of great learning, from whom one may learn the arts, languages, and wisdom, but no one is willing to learn, from our only teacher, Jesus Christ, meekness and sincere humility, although His holy, living example is the proper rule and directive for our life. Indeed, [He is] the highest wisdom and knowledge, so that we can clearly say "The Pure life of Christ can give us all things."[5] Everyone wishes very much to be a servant of Christ, but no one wishes to be His follower. Yet He says in John 12:26, "*If any man serves me, he must follow me.*" Hence,

---

[2]David W. Lotz, "Continental Pietism," in *The Study of Spirituality,* edited by Cheslyn Jones, Geoffrey Wainwright, and Edward Yarnold (New York: Oxford University Press, 1986), p. 450.

[3]Jean H. Faurot, "Four Books on True Christianity," in *Christian Spirituality,* edited by Frank N. Magill and Ian McGreal (San Francisco: Harper & Row, 1988), pp. 261–66.

[4]Reprinted from Peter Erb, trans., *Johann Arndt: True Christianity.* Copyright (c) 1979, by The Missionary Society of St. Paul the Apostle in the State of New York. Used by permission of Paulist Press. From Arndt's "Foreword to the Christian Reader," pp. 21–23, with omissions.

[5]Latin: *Omnia nos Christi vita docere potest.*

a true servant and lover of Christ must be Christ's follower. He who loves Christ will also love the example of His holy life, His humility, meekness, patience, suffering, shame, and contempt, even if the flesh suffers pain. And although we cannot, in our present weakness, perfectly imitate the holy and noble life of Christ . . . nevertheless, we ought to love it, and yearn to imitate it, for thus we live in Christ, and Christ lives in us, as John in the first Epistle 2:6 says: *"He who says he abides in Him ought to walk in the same way in which He walked."* . . . No one can love Christ who does not follow the example of His holy life. There are many men in this world who are ashamed of the holy example of Christ, namely of His humility and lowliness, that is, they are ashamed of the Lord Jesus Christ. Of them the Lord says, in Mark 8:38: *"Whoever is ashamed of me and of my words in this adulterous generation, of him also shall the Son of man be ashamed when He comes."* Christians now desire an imposing, magnificent, rich Christ, conformed to the world, but no one wishes to receive or to confess and to follow the poor, meek, humble and despised Christ. He will, therefore, say: *"I never knew you; you were not willing to know me in my humility, and therefore I do not know you in your pride"* (Mt. 7:23). . . .

Now, to this end, dear Christian, this book will serve as a guide [showing you] not only how you may, through faith in Christ, obtain the forgiveness of your sins, but also how you may properly use the grace of God to lead a holy life, and how you may demonstrate and adorn your faith by a Christian way of life. True Christianity consists, not in words or in external show, but in living faith, from which arise righteous fruits, and all manner of Christian virtues, as from Christ Himself. Since faith is hidden from human eyes and is invisible, it must be manifested by its fruits inasmuch as faith creates from Christ all that is good, righteous, and holy. . . .

THE NEW BIRTH[6]

. . . The new birth is a work of God the Holy Spirit, by which a man is made a child of grace and blessedness from a child wrath and damnation, and from a sinner a righteous man through faith, word, and sacrament by which our heart, thoughts, mind, understanding, will, and affections are made holy, renewed, and enlightened as a new creature in and according to Jesus Christ. The new birth contains two chief aspects in itself: justification and sanctification or renewal (Tit. 3:5). . . .

Note how we are newborn out of Christ. Just as the old birth in a fleshly manner was continued from Adam, so the new birth in a spiritual manner is contin-

---

[6]Reprinted from Erb, trans., *Johann Arndt.* Used by permission of Paulist Press. Pages 37–40, with omissions.

ued from Christ and this occurs through the Word of God. The Word of God is the seed of the new birth. . . . This Word awakens faith and faith clings to this Word and grasps in the Word Jesus Christ together with the Holy Spirit. Through the Holy Spirit's power and activity, man is newborn. The new birth occurs first through the Holy Spirit (Jn. 3:4). This is what the Lord calls "to be born of the Spirit." Secondly, it occurs through faith (1 Jn. 5:1). In the third place it occurs through holy baptism (Jn. 3:5). On this, note the following:

Out of Adam and from Adam man inherited the greatest evil as sin, curse, wrath, death, the Devil, hell, and damnation. These are the fruits of the old birth. Out of Christ, however, man inherited the highest good through faith, namely, righteousness, grace, blessing, life, and eternal blessedness. Out of Adam, man has a carnal spirit and inherited the dominion and tyranny of the evil spirit; out of Christ, however, man inherited the Holy Spirit with His gifts and a consolatory government. Whatever kind of spirit a man has, such a birth, quality, and characteristic he has in himself as the Lord says in Luke 9:55: "*Do you not know what manner of spirit you are of?*" Out of Adam man has received a proud, arrogant, haughty spirit through the fleshy birth. If he wishes to be born again, he must receive through faith out of Christ a humble, lowly, simple spirit. The Lord calls this in John 3:6, "to be born of the Spirit." Out of Adam man has inherited a faithless, unthankful soul opposed to God; out of Christ he must receive through faith a faithful, thankful soul giving thanks to God. Out of Adam man has received a disobedient, haughty, loose spirit; out of Christ he must receive an obedient, moral, kind spirit through faith. Out of Adam man inherited a wrathful, antagonistic, vengeful, murdering spirit by his fleshly birth; out of Christ he must inherit a loving, merciful, long-suffering spirit through faith. Out of Adam man received a covetous, unmerciful, self-oriented, thieving spirit; out of Christ he must receive a merciful, mild, helpful spirit through faith. Out of Adam man inherited an unchaste, unclean, intemperate spirit; out of Christ he must receive a pure, chaste, and temperate spirit. Out of Adam man received a lying, false, slandering spirit; out of Christ he must receive a true, upright, consistent spirit. Out of Adam man has received a bestial, earthly, animal spirit; out of Christ he must receive a heavenly, divine spirit.

For this reason, Christ had to become man and be grasped by the Holy Spirit, become sanctified with the Holy Spirit beyond all measure. "*For indeed, the spirit of the Lord rested upon Him, the spirit of wisdom and understanding, the spirit of counsel and might, the spirit of knowledge and the fear of the Lord*" (Is. 11:2) so that in Him and through Him human nature might be renewed and we in Him, out of Him, and through Him might be born again and become new creatures so that we might inherit from Him the spirit of wisdom and of understanding for the spirit of foolishness, the spirit of knowledge for our inherited blindness, the spirit of the fear of God for the spirit of opposition to God. This is the new life and the new birth in us. . . .

The new birth arises and springs from the wellspring of the suffering, death, and resurrection of Christ (1 Pet. 1:3). We have been born anew to the living hope through the resurrection of Jesus Christ. As a result, the holy apostles always laid as the foundation for repentance and the new life, the holy suffering of Christ (Rom. 6:3; 1 Pet. 1:18–19). Peter gives the reason why we should live in holy life, namely, because we were purchased with so great a price (1 Pet. 2:25). Our Lord Christ made a similar statement in Luke 24:47: *"Thus it is written, that the Christ should suffer and on the third day rise from the dead, and that repentance and forgiveness of sins should be preached in His name to all nations."* Thus we hear that the Lord Himself indicated that both things, preaching and repentance, were living streams flowing from the well of His suffering, death, and resurrection.

The suffering of Christ is, therefore, two things—namely, a payment for all our sins and a renewal of man through faith and true repentance. Both belonging to man's renewal. They are the fear and the power of [the] suffering of Christ, which work in us renewal and sanctification (1 Cor. 1:30), and thus the new birth arises from Christ in us. As a means to it, holy baptism is ordered by which we are baptized in the death of Christ so that we might die with Christ to our sins by the power of His death and once again arise from our sins through the power of His resurrection.

George Herbert (1593–1633)

George Herbert was the younger son of a noble English family. He was born at the Castle of Montgomery, in Wales, and was educated at Westminster School and Trinity College, Cambridge. After a brief period of service at the court of King James I, he entered the ministry in 1626. He was ordained priest in 1630, and served effectively as rector of a small parish in Bremerton, near Salisbury in Wiltshire, until his untimely death.

Herbert's hymns and poems epitomize Anglican spirituality of the period, and were significant contributions to the life of the Church. His most influential work, *A Priest to the Temple: or the Country Parson* was published posthumously in 1652. *The Temple* (1633) was not only an important resource for personal devotion, it also provided the church with an important pastoral model and a device for pastoral teaching. *The Temple* provided subsequent hymnologists with a ready resource; several of its poems (like "The Call") were transformed into hymns that continue to be used in Christian worship.

The Temple was a collection of religious poems, written over the course of the author's life and ministry. Since they are poems of and for the church, they were collected into an order that mirrored the structure of a church building and Christian worship. Beginning with "The Porch" Herbert leads us into the church, and through the church's tools and resources of worship. In a second section, the author examines the spiritual virtues that are cultivated by Christian worship. The collection concludes with "The Church Militant," a long, poetic treatment of the history of the church that celebrates the saving presence of God in human history.

THE ALTAR[7]

A Broken Altar, Lord, thy servant rears,
Made of a heart, and cemented with tears:
Whose parts are as thy hand did frame;
No workmans tool hath touch'd the same.
A Heart alone
Is such a stone,
As nothing but
Thy pow'r doth cut.
Wherefore each part
Of my hard heart
Meets in this frame,
To praise thy name.
That if I chance to hold my peace,
These stones to praise thee may not cease.
O let thy blessed S a c r i f i c e be mine,
And sanctifie this A l t a r to be thine.

REDEMPTION[8]

Having been tenant long to a rich lord
Not thriving, I resolved to be bold,
And make a suit unto him, to afford
A new small-rented lease, and cancell th'old.

In heaven at his manour I him sought:
They told me there, that he was lately gone
About some land, which he had dearly bought
Long since on earth, to take possession.

I straight return'd, and knowing his great birth,
Sought him accordingly in great resorts;
In cities, theatres, gardens, parks, and courts;
At length I heard a ragged noise and mirth

Of theeves and murders: there I him espied,
Who straight, *Your suit is granted*, said,
and died.

---

[7]Reprinted from George Herbert, *The Temple (with Notes and Introduction by Edgar Gibson)* (New York: Frederick A. Stokes Co., n.d.), No. 3, p. 25.
[8]Ibid., No. 10, p. 44.

HOLY BAPTISME[9]

Since, Lord, to thee
A narrow way and little gate
Is all the passage, on my infancie
Thou didst lay hold, and antedate
My faith in me.
O let me still

Write thee great God, and me a child;
Let me be soft and supple to thy will,
Small to my self, to others milde,
Behither[10] ill.

Although by stealth
My flesh get on, yet let her sister
My soul bid nothing, but preserve her wealth:
The growth of flesh is but a blister;
Childhood is health.

PRAYER[11]

Prayer the Churches banquet, Angels age,
Gods breath in man returning to his birth,
The soul in paraphrase, heart in pilgrimage,
The Christian plummet sounding heav'n and earth;

Engine against th'Almightie, sinners towre,
Reversed thunder, Christ-side-piercing spear,
The six-daies-world transposing in an houre,
A kind of tune, which all things heare and fear;

Softnesse, and peace, and joy, and love, and blisse,
Exalted Manna, gladness of the best,
Heaven in ordinarie, man well drest,
The milkie way, the bird of Paradise,

Church-bels beyond the starres heard, the souls bloud,
The land of spices; something understood.

THE HOLY COMMUNION[12]

Not rich furniture, or fine aray,
Nor in a wedge of gold,
Thou, who from me wast sold,
To me dost not thy self convey;

---

[9]Ibid., No. 15, p. 51.
[10]That is, "beyond" ill.
[11]Herbert, *The Temple*, No. 21, pp. 60–61.
[12]Ibid., No. 22, pp. 61–63.

For so thou should'st without me still have been,
        Leaving within me sinne:

But by the way of nourishment and strength
            Thou creep'st into my breast;
            Making thy way my rest,
        And thy small quantities my length;
Which spread their forces into every part,
            Meeting sinnes force and art.

Yet can these not get over to my soul,
            Leaping the wall that parts
            Our souls and fleshly hearts;
    But as th'outworks, they may controll
My rebel-flesh, and carrying thy name.
            Affright both sinne and shame.

Onely thy grace, which with these elements comes,
            Knoweth the ready way,
            And hath the privie key,
    Op'ning the souls most subtile rooms;
While those to spirits refin'd, at doore attend
            Dispatches from their friend.

Give me my captive soul, or take
            My bodies also thither,
Another lift like this will make
            Them both to be together.

Before that sinne turn'd flesh to stone,
            And all our lump to leaven;
A fervent sigh might well have blown
            Our innocent earth to heaven.

For sure when Adam did not know
            To sinne, or sinne to smother;
He might to heav'n from Paradise go,
            As from one room t'another.

Thou hast restor'd us to this case
            By this thy heav'nly bloud;
Which I can go to, when I please,
            And leave th' earth to their food.

LOVE I[13]

    Immortal Love, authour of this great frame,
Sprung from that beautie which can never fade;
    How hath man parcel'd out thy glorious name,
        And thrown it on that dust which thou hast made.

---

[13]Ibid., No. 24, pp. 64–65.

While mortall love doth all the title gain!
   Which siding with invention, they together
Bear all the sway, possessing heart and brain,
   (Thy workmanship) and give thee share in neither.

Wit fancies beautie, beautie raiseth wit:
   The world is theirs; they two play out the game,
Thou standing by: and though thy glorious name
   Wrought our deliverance from th'infernall pit,

      Who sing thy praise? onely a skarf or glove
      Doth warm our hands, and make them write of love.

LOVE II[14]

Immortall Heat, O let thy greater flame
   Attract the lesser to it: let those fires,
   Which shall consume the world, first make it tame;
And kindle in our hearts such true desires,

As may consume our lusts, and make thee way.
   Then shall our hearts pant thee; then shall our brain
   All her invention on thine Altar lay,
And there in hymnes send back thy fire again:

Our eies shall see thee, which before saw dust;
   Dust blown by wit, till that they both were blinde:
Thou shalt recover all thy goods in kinde,
   Who wert disseized by usurping lust:

      All knees shall bow to thee; all wit shall rise,
      And praise him who did make and mend our eies.

THE HOLY SCRIPTURES I[15]

Oh Book! infinite sweetness! let my heart
   Suck ev'ry letter, and a hony gain,
   Precious for any grief in any part;
To cleare the breast, to mollife all pain.

Thou art all health, health thriving, till it make
   A full eternitie; thou art a masse
   Of strange delights, where we may wish and take,
Ladies, look here; this is the thankfull glasse,

That mends the lookers eyes; this is the well
   That washes what it shows. Who can indeare
   Thy praise too much? thou art heav'ns Lidger[16] here,
Working against the states of death and hell.

---

[14]Ibid., p. 65.
[15]Ibid., No. 29, pp. 70–72.
[16]"Ambassador."

Thou art joyes handsell: heav'n lies flat in thee,
Subject to ev'ry mounters bended knee.

THE HOLY SCRIPTURES II

Oh that I knew how all thy lights combine,
And the configurations of their glorie!
Seeing not onely how each verse doth shine,
But all the constellations of the storie.

This verse marks that, and both do make a motion
Unto a third, that ten leaves off doth lie:
Then as dispersed herbs do watch a potion,
These three make up some Christians destinie:

Such are thy secrets, which my life makes good,
And comments on thee: for in ev'ry thing
Thy words do finde me out, and parallels bring,
And in another make me understood.

Starres are poore books, and oftentimes do misse:
This book of starres light to eternall blisse.

CHURCH LOCK AND KEY[17]

I know it is my sinne, which locks thine eares,
And bindes thy hands;
Out-crying my requests, drowning my tears;
Or else the chilnesse of my faint demands.

But as cold hands are angrie with the fire,
And mend it still;
So I do lay the want of my desire,
Not on my sinnes, or coldnesse, but thy will.

Yet heare, O God, onely for his bloods sake
Which pleads for me:
For though sinnes plead too, yet like stones they make
His bloods sweet current much more loud be.

AFFLICTION[18]

My heart did heave, and there came forth, *O God!*
By that I knew that thou wast in the grief,
To guide and govern it to my relief,
Making a scepter of the rod:
Hadst thou not had thy part,
Sure the unruly sigh had broke my heart.

---

[17]Herbert, *The Temple*, pp. 82–83. A manuscript version entitles this same poem "Prayer."
[18]Ibid., No. 48, p. 92.

But since thy breath gave me both life and shape,
      Thou knowst my tallies; and when there's assign'd
So much breath to a sigh, what's then behind?
      Or, if some yeares with it escape,
          The sigh then onely is
A gale to bring me sooner to my blisse.

Thy life on earth was grief, and thou art still
Constant unto it, making it to be
A point of honour, now to grieve in me,
      And in thy members suffer ill.
          They who lament one crosse,
Thou dying dayly, praise thee to thy losse.

CONSCIENCE[19]

      Peace, pratler, do not lowre:
Not a fair look, but thou dost call it foul:
Not a sweet dish, but thou dost call it sowre:
      Musick to thee doth howl.
    By listning to thy chatting fears
    I have both lost mine eyes and eares.

      Pratler, no more I say:
My thoughts must work, but like a noiselesse sphere;
Harmonious peace must rock them all the day:
      No room for pratlers there,
    If thou persistest, I will tell thee,
    That I have physick to expell thee.

      And the receit shall be
My Saviours blood; when ever at his board
I do but taste it, straight it cleanseth me,
      And leaves thee not a word;
    No, not a tooth or nail to scratch,
    And at my actions carp, or catch.

      Yet if thou talkest still,
Besides my physick, know there's some for thee;
Some wood and nails to make a staffe or bill
      For those that trouble me:
    The bloudie cross of my deare Lord
    Is both my physick and my sword.

---

[19]Ibid., No. 80, pp. 132–33.

HOPE[20]

I gave to Hope a watch of mine: but he
  An anchor gave to me.
Then an old prayer-book I did present:
  And he an optick sent.
With that I gave a viall full of tears:
  But he a few green eares:
Ah Loyterer! I'le no more, no more I'le bring:
  I did expect a ring.

THE CALL[21]

Come, my Way, my Truth, my Life:
  Such a Way, as gives us breath:
Such a Truth, as ends all strife:
And such a Life, as killeth death.

Come, my Light, my Feast, my Strength:
Such a Light, as shows a feast:
Such a Feast, as mends in length:
Such a Strength, as makes his guest.

Come, my Joy, my Love, my Heart:
Such a Joy, as none can move:
Such a Love, as none can part:
Such a Heart, as joynes in love.

THE 23 PSALM[22]

The God of love my shepherd is,
  And he that doth me feed:
While he is mine, and I am his,
  What can I want or need?

He leads me to the tender grasse,
  Where I both feed and rest;
Then to the streams that gently passe:
  In both I have the best.

---

[20]Ibid., No. 93, p. 153.
[21]Ibid., No. 125, p. 196.
[22]Ibid., No. 144, p. 215.

> Or if I stray, he doth convert
> > And bring my minde in frame:
> And all this not for my desert,
> > But for his holy name.
>
> Yea, in deaths shadie black abode
> > Well may I walk, not fear:
> For thou art with me; and thy rod
> > To guide, thy staffe to bear.
>
> Nay, thou dost make me sit and dine,
> > Ev'n in my enemies sight:
> My head with oyl, my cup with wine
> > Runnes over day and night.
>
> Surely thy sweet and wondrous love
> > Shall measure all my dayes;
> And as it never shall remove,
> > So neither shall my praise.

Francis de Sales (1567–1622)

Francis de Sales was born at Thoren, Savoy, France, and was educated at the Jesuit College of Clermont in Paris. He also studied law at the University of Padua, but his strong interest in theology and the religious life drew him into the service of the Church instead. He was ordained a priest in 1593. He was active in missionary work and ecclesiastical reform. As Elisabeth Stropp noted: "Francis' life and all his varied apostolic work formed an unbroken unity. He gave himself completely to the work of converting souls in the spirit of the reforms . . . laid down by the Council of Trent."[23] In 1610, together with Madame de Chantal (1572–1641), de Sales founded the Order of the Visitation of Mary. He was canonized in 1665, and in 1677 was made a Doctor of the Church.

Francis's spirituality was shaped by the Christian humanism he encountered in Italy and France. Like Erasmus before him, Francis was an apostle of "devout" Christian humanism, which—unlike its Renaissance counterpart—recognized the reality of human sin and corruption and still managed to celebrate the glories of humanity as well as the glorious potential that humans are offered through the redemption of Jesus Christ. In de Sales's hands, rigorous ideals like absolute commitment to Jesus Christ and the pursuit of Christian perfection received a humane and credible explication that made these goals—which had too frequently been reserved for monks and mystics—seem accessible to all Christians.

---

[23]Elisabeth Stropp, "François de Sales," in Jones, Wainwright, and Yarnold, eds., *The Study of Spirituality*, p. 381.

TO MADAME BRULART ON CHRISTIAN PERFECTION[24]

Madam, . . . You have a great desire for Christian perfection; this is the most generous desire you could have. Nurture it and help it to grow every day. The means of attaining perfection vary according to the diversity of callings: religious, widows, and married persons—all must seek this perfection, but not all by the same means. For you, Madam, who are married, the means is to unite yourself closely to God and to your neighbor, as well as to all that concerns them.

The principal means of uniting yourself to God are the sacraments and prayer. As to the sacraments, you should not let a month go by without receiving communion; and after a while, depending on the progress you will have made in the service of God and following the counsel of your spiritual guides, you should communicate more often. But as to confession, I advise you to go even more frequently, especially if you have fallen into some imperfection which troubles your conscience, as often happens at the beginning of the spiritual life. Still, if you cannot conveniently get to confession, then contrition and repentance will do.

As for prayer, you should apply yourself to it frequently, especially to meditation, for which, it seems to me, you are well suited. So every day spend a short hour in prayer in the morning before going out, or else before supper; be careful not to make your prayer either after dinner or after supper, for that would be harmful to your health. To help yourself pray well, you might prepare beforehand the point on which you are to meditate so that, as you begin your prayer, you have your subject matter ready. And for this purpose you may read authors who have written on the life and death of our Lord . . . from these choose the meditation you want to make, read it attentively so as to remember it at the time of prayer when you will have nothing more to do than to recall the points . . . .

Besides that, often pray spontaneously to our Lord, whenever you can, and in whatever setting, always seeing God in your heart and your heart in God. Enjoy Grenada's books on prayer and meditation, for there are none that can teach you better or move you more powerfully than these.[25] I should like you not to let a day go by without giving half an hour or an hour to spiritual reading, for that could be like a sermon for you. These are the principal means of uniting yourself to God.

The ways by which we can unite ourselves to our neighbor are very numerous; but I will mention only a few of them. Since God wants us to love and cherish others, we must see our neighbor in Him. This is the counsel of St. Paul who orders servants to serve God in their masters and their masters in God [Eph 6:5–7]. We must practice this love of our neighbor and express it outwardly; and even if

---

[24]Reprinted from Peronne Marie Thilbert, trans., *Francis de Sales, Jane de Chantal: Letters of Spiritual Direction.* Copyright (c) 1988, by The Missionary Society of St. Paul the Apostle in the State of New York. Used by permission of Paulist Press. Pages 102–7.

[25]Louis of Grenada (1504–88) was a Spanish Dominican whose meditations were often recommended by Francis de Sales.

at first we seem to do so reluctantly, we must not give up on that account, for this feeling of aversion will, in the end, be conquered by the habit and good dispositions that result from repeated acts. We must bring this intention to our prayer and meditation; having begged God for His love, we must ask Him also to grant us love of others, especially of those persons we have no inclination to love.

I advise you to take the trouble now and then to visit hospitals, to comfort the sick, and to have compassion for their infirmities, letting these touch your heart; and pray for the sick even as you give them whatever help you can. But in all this, be very careful that your husband, your servants, and your relatives be not inconvenienced by overly long visits to church, by too lengthy withdrawals to pray and noticeable neglect of your household responsibilities or, as sometimes happens, by your trying to control the actions of others, or showing too much disdain for gatherings where the rules of devotion are not precisely observed. In all these instances charity must prevail and enlighten us so that we yield to the wishes of our neighbor in whatever is not contrary to the commandments of God.

You must not only be devout and love devotion, but you must render it loveable and pleasing. Now you will make it loveable if you render it useful and pleasing. The sick will love your devotion if they receive care and comfort from it; your family will love it if they see you more attentive to their well-being, more gentle in handling affairs, more kind in correcting, and so on; your husband will love it if he sees that as your devotion increases, you become more warm and affectionate toward him; your relatives and friends will love if they see you more free, supportive of others, and yielding to them in matters that are not contrary to God's will. In short, we must, as far as possible, make our devotion attractive.

I am sending you a little paper I have written about Christian perfection, which I would like you to pass on to Madame du Puits d' Orbe. Receive it in good part, as also this letter, which comes from a heart that is totally devoted to your spiritual good and which has no greater desire than to see the work of God accomplished in you perfectly.

I beg you to remember me in your prayers and communions, and I assure you that I shall always remember you in mine and shall ever be, Madam, your very affectionate servant in Jesus Christ.

MEMO ON CHRISTIAN PERFECTION

Everyone is obliged to strive for the perfection of Christian life, because our Lord commands that we be perfect and St. Paul says the same.[26] Perfection of Christian life consists in conforming our wills to that of our good God, who is the sovereign standard and norm for all actions. So in order to acquire perfection we must always consider and recognize what God's will is in everything that con-

---

[26]Matthew 5:48 and 2 Corinthians 13:11, which in the Latin Vulgate version reads, *"perfecti estote."*

cerns us, so that we can flee what He wants us to avoid and accomplish what He wants us to do.

There are some matters in which it is clear what God will is, as in what concerns the commandments or the duties of one's vocation. That is why we must always seek to carry out well what God expects of all Christians, as well as what our own vocation requires of us in particular. Anyone who does not do this much with care can possess nothing but a fraudulent devotion.

There are still other matters about which there is no doubt whether God wills them, such as trials, illnesses and chronic conditions. That is why we should accept them with a good heart, and conform our will to that of God who permits them. Anyone who can arrive at the point of not only supporting them patiently but even of willing them, that person can be said to have acquired a great conformity. Thus, the death of relatives, various losses, illnesses, dryness or distractions in prayer—these give us opportunities to grow in perfection.

But we must go further and see this will not only in great afflictions but even in little reversals and minor inconveniences that we will always meet with in this unhappy life. In this regard many people make a mistake because they prepare themselves only for major afflictions and remain totally without defense, strength or resistance when it comes to small ones. Actually, it would be more understandable to be less prepared for major afflictions which happen but rarely, and to be prepared for the little ones which come up every day and at every moment. I will give you an example of what I mean: I prepare myself to suffer death patiently—which can happen to me but once—and I do not prepare myself at all to put up with the inconveniences I encounter from the moods of those I am with, or the pressing spiritual demands which my work brings me and which arise a hundred times a day. And that is what makes me imperfect.

There are many other things I am not obliged to do either by the general commandments of God or by the duties of my own vocation, and with these it is necessary to consider carefully in liberty of spirit what would tend to the greatest glory of God, because that is what God wills. I said "in liberty of spirit" because this should be done without pressure of anxiety, but by a simple glance at the good which our action can produce, such as, for example, to make a short pilgrimage, to go on to confession, to visit a sick person, to give a small sum for the love of God. If it is not a matter of great importance, then we should not invest a great concern in it, but after a little thought we must decide. And if afterward the action or the decision doesn't seem good, and it looks as if I had made a mistake, I should in no way blame or bother myself about it, but rather humble myself and laugh at myself.

But if it is a matter of importance, like changing one's profession, making final vows, undertaking a long voyage, or giving a great sum of money to charity—after having thought about it for a while, we must confer with the spiritual persons to whom we look for direction, and go along with their advice with simplicity, for God will assist them to direct us rightly. And if through their fault the decision is not the best in itself, that won't prevent it from being the most useful and meritorious for you, for God will render it fruitful. . . .

Jeremy Taylor (1613–67)

Jeremy Taylor was born the fourth of six children, in Cambridge, England. His father and his father's father before him had been church wardens at Holy Trinity Church, where Jeremy Taylor was baptized.[27] He attended Gaius College, Cambridge. Taylor's significant ability and staunch Anglicanism brought him to the attention of Archbishop William Laud, and through Laud's influence he secured a fellowship at All Soul's College, Oxford. He was subsequently appointed rector at Uppingham, a post he held till 1642.

The times in which Jeremy Taylor found himself were filled with turmoil and extraordinary changes. The new learning of the English Enlightenment, epitomized by the empiricism of Francis Bacon (1561–1626), repudiated the metaphysics of Aristotle and the medieval edifice that had been erected upon that foundation. England was thrown into civil war as the royalists of House of Lords and the parliamentarians in House of Commons struggled for political dominance. The struggle had ecclesiastical overtones, since the Anglican bishops sat in the House of Lords and the Puritans were in the process of taking control over the House of Commons. Archbishop William Laud, who had sought to keep Puritanism in check, was martyred for his efforts in 1645. The divine right of the king came to a sudden end as the Puritans in parliament seized the government and subsequently beheaded Charles I (1649).

Taylor's career and literary works were affected by this tumultuous context. He was deprived of his position at Uppingham as the Puritans took control of parliament. The next year he spent as a chaplain in the Royalist cause, and the subsequent year (1644) as a prisoner of war. He eventually settled at Garden Grove, Wales, where he served as the chaplain to Lord and Lady Carbery. Taylor's most influential works, *The Rule and Experience of Holy Living* (1650) and *The Rule and Experience of Holy Dying* (1651), were aids to self-examination and improvement, written in the decade of seclusion he spent at Garden Grove. The latter work was written at the request of Lady Carbery, who was at that time embarking upon the illness that would claim her life.

Jeremy Taylor relocated to Ireland in 1658, serving an English church parish at Lisburn and Portmore, near Dublin. After the restoration of the monarchy and Anglicanism in England (1660), he continued to work in Ireland, where he was named Vice Chancellor of the University of Dublin and Bishop of Down and Connor in Ulster.

The spirituality reflected in *Holy Living* and *Holy Dying* aims at the ideal of the Caroline divines; "true piety with sound learning."[28] Taylor's work evidences

---

[27]Cf. Thomas K. Carroll's fine introduction in his *Jeremy Taylor: Selected Works* (New York: Paulist Press, 1990).

[28]Martin Thornton, "The Caroline Divines and the Cambridge Platonists," in Jones, Wainwright, and Yarnold, eds., *Study of Spirituality*, pp. 431–37 offers an excellent overview of the spirituality of the Caroline divines. Cf. Jean H. Faurot, "The Rule and Exercises of Holy Living and Holy Dying," in Magill and McGreal, eds., *Christian Spirituality*, pp. 309–14.

the practical and pastoral side of the Caroline tradition. The Caroline quest for an orderly Christian life extends to the life of prayer where "the monastic ethos lives on, [even though] the monasteries are gone."[29] Taylor's penchant for holy rules epitomizes the Caroline concern for order—amidst very disorderly times—and links his work with earlier, formative classics like *Spiritual Exercises* and *Imitation of Christ.* It also anticipated the methodical approach to holiness, for which Methodists (like John and Charles Wesley), would become famous. The Wesleys frequently expressed their indebtedness to Taylor's work. Particularly noteworthy in this regard was Bishop Taylor's insistence that holiness—while being expressed in Christian duties like worship and prayer—embraced a person's entire life and understood it from the standpoint of one's vocation. *Holy Living* "is comprised in responsibilities to one's own person, one's fellow human beings, and to God."[30]

PURITY OF INTENTION[31]

That we should intend and design God's glory in every action we do, whether it be natural or chosen, is expressed by St. Paul, "Whether ye eat or drink, do all to the glory of God" [1 Cor 10:21]. Which rule when we observe, every action of nature becomes religious, and every meal is an act of worship, and shall have its reward in its proportion, as well as an act of prayer. Blessed be that goodness and grace of God, which, out of infinite desire to glorify and save mankind, would make the very works of nature capable of becoming acts of virtue, that all our life-time we may do Him service.

This grace is so excellent, that it sanctifies the most common action of our life; and yet so necessary, that, without it, the very best actions of our devotion are imperfect and vicious. For he that prays out of custom, or gives alms for praise, or fasts to be accounted religious, is but a pharisee in his devotion, and a beggar in his alms, and a hypocrite in his fast. But a holy end sacrifices all these and all other actions, which can be made holy, and gives distinctions to them, and procures acceptance. . . .

Holy intention is to the actions of a person that which the soul is to the body, or form to its matter or the root to the tree, or the sun to the world, or the fountain to a river, or the base to a pillar; for, without these, the body is a dead trunk, the matter is sluggish, the tree is a block, the world is darkness, the river is quickly dry, the pillar rushes into flatness and a ruin; and the action is sinful, or unprofitable and vain. The poor farmer, that gave a dish of cold water to Artaxerxes, was rewarded with a golden goblet; and he that gives the same to a disciple in the name of a disciple, shall have a crown: but if he gives water in despite, when

---

[29]Thornton, "The Caroline Divines," p. 433.
[30]Faurot, "Holy Living and Holy Dying," p. 310.
[31]Reprinted from Jeremy Taylor, *Holy Living and Dying With Prayers: Containing the Complete Duty of A Christian* (Philadelphia: Thomas Wardle, 1835), sec. 2, pp. 16–22.

the disciple needs wine or a cordial, his reward shall be, to want water to cool his tongue. But this duty must be reduced to rules:

Rules For Our Intentions

1. In every action reflect upon the end: and in your undertaking it, consider why you do it, and what you propound to yourself for a reward, and to your action as its end.

2. Begin every action in the name of the Father, of the Son, and of the Holy Ghost: the meaning of which is, (i) That we be careful, that we do not the action without the permission or warrant of God. (ii) That we design it to the glory of God, if not in the direct action, yet at least in its consequence; if not in the particular, yet at least in the whole order of things and accidents. (iii) That it may be so blessed, that what you intend for innocent and holy standing of men, be turned into evil, or made the occasion of sin.

3. Let every action of concernment be begun with prayer, that God would not only bless the action, but sanctify your purpose: and make an oblation of the action to God: holy and well intended actions being the best oblations and presents we can make to God; and, when God is entitled to them, he will the rather keep the fire upon the altar bright and shining. . . .

8. If any temptation to spoil your purpose happens in a religious duty, do not presently omit the action, but rather strive to rectify your intention, and to mortify the temptation. St. Bernard taught us this rule: for when the Devil, observing him to preach excellently and to do much benefit to his hearers, tempted him to vain glory, hoping that the good man, to avoid that, would cease preaching, gave this answer only: "I neither began for thee, neither for thee will I make an end."

9. In all actions, which are of long continuance, deliberation, and abode, let your holy and pious intention be actual; that is, that it be, by a special prayer or action, by a peculiar act of resignation or oblation, given to God; but in smaller actions, and little things and indifferent, fail not to secure a pious habitual intention; that is, that it be included within your general care, that no action have an ill end; and that it be comprehended in your general prayers, whereby you offer yourself and all you do, to God's glory.

10. Call not every temporal end, a defiling of thy intention, but only, (i) when it contradicts any of the ends of God; or (ii) when it is principally intended in an action of religion. For sometimes a temporal end is part of our duty; and such are all the actions of our calling, whether our employment be religious or civil. We are commanded to provide for our family; but if the minister of divine offices shall take upon him that holy calling for covetous or ambitious ends, or shall not design the glory of God principally and especially, he hath polluted his hands and his heart; and the fire of the altar is quenched, or it sends forth nothing but the smoke of mushrooms or unpleasant gums. And

it is a great unworthiness to prefer the interest of a creature before the ends of God, the Almighty Creator.

But because many cases may happen, in which a person's heart may deceive him, and he may not well know what is his own spirit; therefore, by these following signs, we shall best make a judgment, whether our intentions be pure, and our purposes holy.

Signs of Purity of Intention

1. It is probable our hearts are right with God, and our intentions innocent and pious, if we set upon actions of religion or civil life with an affection proportionate to the quality of the work; that we act our temporal affairs with a desire no greater than our necessity; and that in actions of religion, we be zealous, active, and operative, so far as prudence will permit; but in all cases, that we value a religious design before a temporal, when otherwise they are in equal order to the several ends: that is, that whatsoever is necessary in order to our soul's health be higher esteemed, than what is for bodily; and the necessities, the indispensable necessities, of the spirit, be served before the needs of nature, when they are required in their several circumstances; or plainer yet, when we choose any temporal inconvenience, rather than commit a sin, and when we choose to do a duty, rather than to get gain. . . .

2. It is likely our hearts are pure, and our intentions spotless, when we are not solicitous of the opinion and censures of men; but only that what we do be our duty and accepted of God. For our eyes will certainly be fixed there, from whence we expect our reward: and if we desire, that God should approve us, it is a sign we do his work, and expect him our paymaster.

3. He that does as well, in private, between God and his own soul, as in public, in pulpits, in theatres, and market places, hath given himself a good testimony, that his purposes are full of honesty, nobleness, and integrity. . . .

4. It is well, also, when we are not solicitous or troubled concerning the effect and event of all our actions; but that being first by prayer recommended to Him, is left at His dispose: for then, in case the event be not answerable to our desires, or to the efficacy of the instrument, we have nothing left to rest in, but the honesty of our purposes; which it is the more likely we have secured, by how much more we are indifferent concerning the success. . . .

6. He that despises the world, and all its appendant vanities, is the best judge, and the most secured of his intentions; because he is the farthest removed from a temptation. Every degree of mortification is a testimony of the purity of our purposes; and in what degree we despise sensual pleasure, or secular honours, or worldly reputation, in the same degree we shall conclude our heart right to religion and spiritual designs.

7. When we are not solicitous concerning the instruments and means of our actions; but use those means, which God hath laid before us, with resignation, indifference, and thankfulness; it is a good sign, that we are rather intent upon the end of God's glory, than our own conveniency, or temporal satisfaction. He that is indifferent whether he serve God in riches or in poverty, is rather a seeker of God than of himself; and he that will throw away a good book because it is not curiously gilded, is more curious to please his eye, than to inform his understanding. . . .

When our intentions are thus balanced, regulated, and discerned, we may consider; 1. That this exercise is of so universal efficacy in the whole course of a holy life, that it is like the soul of every holy action, and must be provided for in every undertaking; and is, of itself alone, sufficient to make all natural and indifferent actions to be adopted into the family of religion.

2. That there are some actions, which are usually reckoned as parts of our religion, which yet, of themselves, are so relative and imperfect, that, without the purity of intention, they are degenerate: and unless they be directed and proceed on to those purposes, which God designed them to, they return into the family of common, secular, or sinful actions. Thus, alms are for the charity, fasting for temperance, prayer is for religion, humiliation is for humility, austerity or sufferance is in order to the virtue of patience; and when these actions fail of their several ends, or are not directed to their own purposes, alms are mispent, fasting is an impertinent trouble, prayer is but lip-labour, humiliation is but hypocrisy, sufferance is but vexation; for such were the alms of the pharisee, the fast of Jezebel, the prayer of Judah reproved by the prophet Isaiah, the humiliation of Ahab, the martyrdom of heretics; in which nothing is given to God, but the body, or the forms of religion; but the soul and the power of godliness is wholly wanting.

3. We are to consider, that no intention can satisfy an unholy or unlawful action. . . . [W]hen a person does evil, that good may come of it, or good to an evil purpose, that person does like him who rolls himself in thorns, that he may sleep easily; he roasts himself in the fire, that he may quench his thirst with his own sweat; he turns his face to the east, that he may go to bed with the sun. I end this with the saying of a wise heathen: "He is to be called evil, that is good only for his own sake. Regard not, how full hands you bring to God, but how pure. . . .

A Prayer for Holy Intention in the Beginning and Pursuit of Any Considerable Action, as Study, Preaching Etc.[32]

O eternal God, who hast made all things for man, and man for thy glory, sanctify my body and soul, my thoughts and my intentions, my words and actions, that whatsoever I shall think, or speak, or do, may be by me designed to the glorification of thy name; and by thy blessing it may be effective and successful in the work

---

[32]Ibid., p. 46.

of God, according as it can be capable. Lord turn my necessities into virtue; the works of nature into the works of grace, by making them orderly, regular, temperate, subordinate, and profitable to ends beyond their own proper efficacy: and let no pride or self-seeking, no covetousness or revenge, no impure mixture or unhandsome purposes, no little ends and low imaginations, pollute my spirit, and unhallow my words and actions: but let my body be a servant of my spirit, and both body and spirit servants of Jesus; that doing all things for thy glory here, I may be partaker of thy glory hereafter; through Jesus Christ our Lord. Amen.

HOLY DYING[33]

1. He that would die well, must always look for death, every day knocking at the gates of the grave: and then the gates of the grave shall never prevail upon him to do him mischief. This was the advice of all the wise and good men of the world, who, especially in the days and periods of their joy and festival egressions, chose to throw some ashes into their chalices, some sober remembrances of their fatal period. . . .

2. "He that would die well, must, all the days of his life, lay up against the day of death;" not only by the general provisions of holiness and a pious life indefinitely, but provisions proper to the necessities of that great day of expense, in which a person is to throw his last cast for an eternity of joys or sorrows; ever remembering, that this alone, well performed, is not enough to pass us into Paradise; but that alone, done foolishly, is enough to send us to hell; and the want of either a holy life or death makes a man to fall short of the mighty price of our high calling. In order to this rule, we are to consider what special graces we shall then need to exercise, and by the proper arts of the spirit, by a heap of proportioned arguments, by prayers and a great treasure of devotion laid up in heaven, provide beforehand a reserve of strength and mercy. Men in the course of their lives walk lazily and incuriously, as if they had both their feet in one shoe; and when they are passively revolved to the time of their dissolutions, they have no mercies in store, no patience, no faith, no charity to God, or despite of the world, being without gust or appetite for the land of their inheritance, which Christ with so much pain and blood had purchased for them. When we come to die indeed, we shall be very much put to it to stand firm upon the two feet of a Christian, faith and patience. When we ourselves are to use the articles, to turn our former discourses into present practice, and to feel what we never felt before, we shall find it to be quite another thing, to be willing presently to quit this life and all our present possessions for the hopes of a thing, which we were never suffered to see, and such a thing, of which we may fail so many ways, and of which if we fail any way, we are miserable for ever. Then we shall find, how much we have need to have secured the Spirit of God and the grace of faith, by an habitual, perfect, unmov-

---

[33]Ibid., ch. 2, sec. 1, pp. 42–46.

able resolution. . . . [I]n the distribution of our time God seems to be strait-handed, and gives it to us, not as nature gives us rivers, enough to drown us, but drop by drop, minute after minute, so that we never can have two minutes together, but he takes away one when he gives us another. This should teach us to value our time, since God so values it, and by his so small distribution of it, tells us it is the most precious thing we have. Since therefore, in the day of our death, we can have still but the same little portion of this precious time, let us in every minute of our life, I mean, in every discernible portion, lay up such a stock of reason and good works, that they may convey a value to the imperfect and shorter actions of our death-bed; while God rewards the piety of our lives by his gracious acceptation and benediction upon the actions preparatory to our death-bed.

3. He that desires to die well and happily, above all things, must be careful that he do[es] not live a soft, a delicate, and a voluptuous life; but a life severe, holy, and under the discipline of the cross, under the conduct of prudence and observation, a life of warfare and sober counsels, labour, and watchfulness. No man wants cause of tears and a daily sorrow. Let every man consider what he feels, and acknowledge his misery; let him confess his sin, and chastise it; let him bear his cross patiently, and his persecutions nobly, and his repentances willingly and constantly; let him pity the evils of all the world, and bear his share of the calamities of his brother; let him long and sigh for the joys of heaven; let him tremble and fear, because he hath deserved the pains of hell; let him commute his eternal ear with a temporal suffering, preventing God's judgment by passing one of his own; let him groan for the labours of his pilgrimage, and the dangers of his warfare; and by that time he hath summed up all these labours, and duties, and contingencies, all the proper causes, instruments, and acts of sorrow, he will find, that for a secular joy and wantonness of spirit there are not left many void spaces of his life. It was St. James's advice, "Be afflicted, and mourn, and weep; let your laughter be turned into mourning, and your joy into weeping [4:9];" and Bonaventure, in the *Life of Christ*, reports that the holy Virgin-mother said to St. Elizabeth, that grace does not descend into the soul of a person but by prayer and affliction. Certain it is, that a mourning spirit and an afflicted body are great instruments of reconciling God to a sinner, and they always dwell at the gates of atonement and restitution. . . .

Blaise Pascal (1623–62)

Blaise Pascal was born at Clermont-Ferrand, France, but his family relocated to Paris so that their children could receive a more adequate education. Seemingly in response to their efforts, Pascal distinguished himself in mathematics, science, philosophy, and religion. As a mathematician he made significant contributions to the development of probability theory. As a scientist he conducted landmark experiments with vacuum and atmospheric pressure; he also invented a calculating machine. In the era of the French Enlightenment, Pascal was indeed a "Renaissance man" whose talents overflowed many of the boundaries we customarily place upon professional expertise.

In 1654 Blaise Pascal had a serious accident, which nearly cost him his life and resulted in his conversion to vital Christian faith. Pascal's spirituality, as it developed following his conversion, centered upon the person of Christ. As a philosopher, Pascal found himself attracted to the sovereign God of the Jansenist sect, and he wrote nineteen *Lettres Provinciales* (under a pseudonym) defending this variety of Roman Catholic Calvinism against its Jesuit critics. The Jansenist cause understood itself as an attempt to recover genuine Augustinian soteriology, in the face of what it considered to be the Church's official semi-Pelagian position. The foundational document of Jansenism was the *Augustinus* (1640), Jansen's magna opus of 1,300 pages, which sought to reestablish Augustinian theology in post-Tridentine Catholicism.[34]

Pascal's most influential religious work, and the basis upon which he is to be considered a spiritual writer, was called *Pensées* (1670) or *Thoughts*. It amounted to a collection of elegantly written reflections, which he had intended to develop into a full-scale defense of the Christian faith. While death claimed Blaise Pascal before his apologetic work could be finished, his *Thoughts* adequately point out the direction he would have us follow. His spirituality is an interesting combination of the logic of the professional mathematician and the mysticism of a man who had a personal encounter with Christ in 1654. Pascal's famous "wager" draws upon his studies in probability to urge the reader to risk his or her life in Christian faith— probability says there is much to gain if Christianity is true, and very little has been lost if it is not. Like de Sales, Pascal gloried in the classical understanding of humanity (fallen, but created in the image of God), which he sets over and against the estimates advocated by the Age of Reason. In a similar way, Paschal the logician affirmed the goodness of human reason and then went on to show reason's inadequacies when it comes to knowing the central verities of Christian faith.

PASCAL'S MEMORIAL[35]

> In the year of Grace, 1654,
> On Monday, 23rd of November, Feast of St. Clement, Pope and Martyr,
> > and of others in the Martyrology,
> > Vigil of Saint Chrysogonus, Martyr, and others,
> > From about half past ten in the evening until about half past twelve,

---

[34]Elfrieda Dubois, "Jansenism," in Jones, Wainwright, and Yarnold, eds., *Study of Spirituality*, pp. 396–405. Five propositions, drawn from Jansen's the *Augustinus*, are often used to summarize the Jansenist position: (1) Some of God's commandments are impossible to just men. (2) In the state of fallen nature no resistance is ever made to interior grace. (3) For merit and demerit man does not need freedom from necessity, but only freedom from compulsion. (4) Semi-Pelagians were heretical because they held that the human will could resist grace or correspond to it. (5) It is semi-Pelagian to say that Christ died for all." Ibid., pp. 401–2).

[35]Reprinted from Emile Cailliet and John C. Blankenagel, trans., *The Great Shorter Works of Pascal* (Westport, Conn.: Greenwood Press, 1948), pp. 117–18. Used with the kind permission of Princeton Theological Seminary.

FIRE

God of Abraham, God of Isaac, God of Jacob,
> not of the philosophers and scholars.

Certitude. Certitude. Feeling. Joy. Peace.

God of Jesus Christ

Deum meum et Deum vestrum.

> ["Thy God shall be my God," Jn 20:17],

Forgetfulness of the world and of everything, except God.

> He is to be found only by the ways taught in the Gospel.

> Greatness of the human soul.

> "Righteous Father, the world hath not known Thee, but I have
> > known Thee."

Joy, joy, joy, tears of joy.

I have separated myself from Him

Derelinquerunt me fontem aquae vivae.

> ["They have forsaken Me, the fountain of living waters," Jer 2:13].

> "My God, wilt Thou leave me?" [Mt 27:46]

> Let me not be separated from Him eternally.

"This is the eternal life, that they might know Thee, the only true God, and the one whom
Thou has sent, Jesus Christ." [Jn 17:3]

> Jesus Christ.

> Jesus Christ.

> I have separated myself from Him: I have fled from Him, denied Him,
> crucified Him.

> Let me never be separated from Him.

> We keep hold of Him only by the ways taught in the Gospel.

> Renunciation, total and sweet.

> Total submission to Jesus Christ and to my director.

> Eternally in joy for a day's training on earth.

> *Non obliviscar sermones tuos.*

["I will not forget Thy words," Ps 118:16]

> Amen.

THE CONVERSION OF SINNERS[36]

The first thing which God inspires in the soul which He truly deigns to touch is an understanding and a quite extraordinary insight by means of which the soul considers things and itself in an entirely new manner. This new light brings fear to the soul and an agitation which disturbs the repose which it found in the things that delighted it.

The soul can no longer tranquilly enjoy the things which charmed it. Constant scruples assail it in this enjoyment and because of this introspection it no longer finds the accustomed sweetness in the things to which it abandoned itself

---

[36]Ibid. pp. 118–120. Used with the kind permission of Princeton Theological Seminary.

freely with an overflowing heart. But the soul finds even more bitterness in the practice of holiness than in the vanities of the world. On the one hand, the presence of visible things touches it more than the hope of things unseen; on the other hand the stability of things unseen touches more than the vanity of visible things. And thus the presence of the one and the stability of the other contend for its affection; the vanity of the one and the absence of the other arouse its aversion. Consequently discord and confusion are born in it. . . .

The soul considers perishable things as perishing and even as already perished. In the definite prospect of the annihilation of all that it loves, it is frightened by this consideration, when it sees every moment snatch away the enjoyment of its endowment; when that which is dearest to it slips away every moment, and when finally a certain day will come when it will find itself destitute of all the things on which it had set its hopes. And so it understands perfectly that since its heart is attached only to fragile and vain things, the soul must find itself alone and abandoned on leaving this life, since it has not taken care to unite itself with a good which is genuine, which exists independently, and which may sustain it during and after this life.

As a result, the soul begins to regard as nothing all that must return to nothingness, the sky, the earth, its mind, its body, its relatives, its friends, its enemies, its goods, its poverty, disgrace, prosperity, honor, ignominy, esteem, scorn, authority, indigence, health, illness, and life itself; in short, everything which is less enduring than the soul is incapable of satisfying the design of this soul which seriously seeks to establish itself in a felicity as enduring as it is itself.

It begins to wonder at the blindness in which it has lived; and when it considers on the one hand how long it has lived without such reflections and how people live in this manner, and on the other hand how certain it is that the soul, being immortal, can never find its happiness among perishable things which are taken from it at least in death, it then enters into a holy state of confusion and of wonder which bring it to a wholly salutary agitation.

For it considers that no matter how great may be the number of those who grow old in the maxims of this world, no matter what authority may reside in this multitude of examples of those who see their happiness in the world, nevertheless this is certain: If the things of this world afforded substantial pleasure—which is recognized as false through an infinite number of deadening and continual experiences, it is inevitable that the loss of these things or that death will ultimately deprive us of these things. As a result, since the soul has amassed treasures of temporal goods of whatever kind they may be, either gold or science or reputation, it is inevitable that it will ultimately find itself denuded of all the objects of its happiness. And so, even if they were capable of satisfying it, they will be unable to satisfy it forever; moreover, if this means producing genuine happiness, it does not offer a very enduring happiness, since it must be limited by the course of this life.

Thus through a holy humility which again elevates God above vain-glory the soul begins to rise above the generality of men, it condemns their conduct, it detests their maxims, it mourns their blindness, it inclines to seek the true good; it understands that it must have these two qualities, the one, which endures as long as it does and which can be taken from it only by its consent, and the other, than which there is nothing more lovable.

It sees that in the love which it had for the world it found this second quality in its blindness, for it recognized nothing more lovable; but since it does not see the first, it knows that it is not the sovereign good. Hence the soul seeks this elsewhere, and knowing by an utterly pure light that this is not in the things which are in it, nor outside it, nor in front of it (hence nothing in it, nothing at its sides), it begins to seek this above it.

This elevation is so eminent and so transcendent that it does not stop at the sky (this has nothing that would satisfy it), nor above the sky, nor with the angels, nor with the most perfect beings. It penetrates all creatures, and the heart can stop beating only when it has surrendered itself at the very throne of God where it begins to find its repose and this good which is such that there is nothing more lovable, and which can be taken from it only by its own consent.

For although it does not feel these charms with which God rewards habitual piety, it nevertheless understands that creatures cannot be more lovable than their Creator; its reason, aided by the light of grace, teaches it that there is nothing more lovable than God and that He can be taken only from those who reject Him, since to possess Him is to desire Him, and to refuse Him is to lose Him.

Thus it rejoices at having found a good which cannot be taken from it so long as it desires this good, and which is transcended by nothing. And amid these new reflections it comes to see the greatness of its Creator both in humiliations and deep adoration. In consequence it annihilates itself, and, unable to form a low enough idea of itself, nor to conceive one high enough of its sovereign, it makes new efforts to humble itself to the very depth of nothingness, while considering God in the boundlessness which it multiplies incessantly. Finally, in this conception which exhausts its powers, it adores Him in silence, it considers itself as His vile and useless creature, and by this reiterated respect it adores Him and blesses Him and would like to bless and adore Him forever. Then it recognizes the grace He has bestowed upon it by manifesting His infinite majesty to so feeble a worm; and, after a firm resolve to be eternally grateful for this, it blushes at having preferred so much vanity to this divine Master; in a spirit of contrition and of penitence it has recourse to His pity so as to stop His wrath whose effect it seems appalling. . . .

It raises ardent prayers to God to obtain from His mercy that, having deigned to reveal Himself, He may be pleased to guide the soul and make known the means of coming to God. For since it is to God that the soul aspires, it aspires also to come to Him only by the means which come from God Himself, because it desires God alone to be its path, its object, and its ultimate end. As a result of these prayers, it begins to act and seeks among those . . . It is resolved to conform to His will for the rest of its life; but since its natural weakness, together with the habit it has of sinning wherever it has lived, have reduced it to the impossibility of attaining such happiness, it implores of His mercy the means of coming to Him, of attaching itself to Him and of adhering to Him eternally. . . .

Thus the soul recognizes that as a creature it must adore God, as a debtor it must render Him thanks, being culpable it must make amends, and being needy it must implore Him.

HUMAN NATURE[37]

Man is but a reed, the weakest in nature, but he is a thinking reed. It is not necessary that the entire universe arm itself to crush him. A breath of air, a drop of water, suffices to kill him. But were the universe to crush him, man would still be more noble than that which kills him, because he knows that he dies; and the universe knows nothing of the advantage it has over him.

Our whole dignity consists, then, in thought. Our elevation must be derived from this, not from space and duration, which we cannot fill. Let us endeavor, then, to think well—this is the principle of ethics.

• • •

Let man now rightly estimate himself. Let him love himself, for he has in him a nature capable of good; but let him not love for this reason what is base therein. Let him despise himself, since this capacity is void; but let him not, on this account, despise the natural capacity itself. Let him hate himself, let him love himself: he has in himself the capacity of knowing truth, and of being happy; but he has no truth, either constant or satisfying.

I would therefore bring man to desire to find truth, to be ready, and free from passions, to follow it wherever he shall find it, knowing how much his knowledge is obscured by the passions; I would indeed that he hated in himself the concupiscence that determines him of itself, in order that it should not blind him in making his choice, and arrest him when he has chosen.

THE HEART HAS ITS REASONS[38]

The heart has its reasons, which the reason knows nothing about; we know it in a thousand things. I say that the heart loves the universal Being naturally, and it loves itself naturally, according to its inclination; and it hardens itself against the one or the other at its choice. You have rejected the one and preserved the other: is it through reason that you love? It is the heart that feels God, and not the reason. This is faith: God sensible to the heart, not to the reason.

The heart has its order; the mind has its own order, which is by principles and demonstrations; the heart has another. We do not prove that we ought to be loved by making a systematic exposition of the causes of love: this would be ridiculous.

---

[37]Blaise Pascal, *Pensees*, translated by W.F. Trotter, #347. Document is from the Christian Classics Etherial Library, http://ccel.wheaton.edu.
[38]Ibid., #277, #283.

Jesus Christ, and St. Paul have the order of charity, not of the mind; for they wished to warn, not to instruct. St. Augustine the same. This order consists, principally, in a digression on each point that has a relation to the end, so as to show it always.

THE WAGER[39]

Infinite, nothing—Our soul is thrown into the body, wherein it finds number, time, dimension. It reasons thereon, and calls this nature, necessity, and cannot believe any thing else.

Unity joined to the infinite augments it is nothing any more than a foot added to an infinite measure. The finite is annihilated in the presence of the infinite, and becomes a pure nothing. Thus our mind before God; thus our justice before the divine justice.

There is not so great a disproportion between our justice and God's, as between unity and infinity. The justice of God must be great as his mercy: now, the justice toward the reprobates is not so great, and ought to shock us less, than the mercy toward the elect.

We know that there is an infinite, and know not its nature. As we know that it is false that numbers are finite, then it is true that there is an infinite in number: but we know not what it is. It is not true that it is even, it is not true that it is odd; for, in adding unity to it, it does not change its nature; yet it is a number, and every number is odd or even: it is true that this is understood of all finite numbers.

Thus we may easily know that there is a God without knowing what he is. We know, then, the existence and the nature of the finite, because we are finite and extended as it is. We know the existence of the infinite, and know not its nature, because it has extent like us, but it has no limits like us.

But we know neither the existence nor the nature of God, because he has neither extent nor limits.

But by faith we know his existence; by glory we shall know his nature. Now, I have already shown that we may easily know the existence of a thing without knowing its nature.

Let us speak now according to the light of nature. If there is a God he is infinitely incomprehensible, since, having neither parts nor limits, he has no proportion to us; we are then, incapable of knowing either what he is, or whether he is. This being true, who will dare to undertake to resolve this question? It is not we, who have no proportion to him.

Who, then, shall blame, as not being able to give a reason for their belief, those Christians, men who profess a religion for which they can give no reason? They declare, in exposing it to the world, that it is a folly, *stultitiam* [1 Cor 1:18];

---

[39] Ibid., #233, #239, #240.

and then you complain that they do not prove it! If they proved it, they would not keep their word: it is in lacking proofs, that they do not lack sense. Yes; but though this may excuse those who offer it such, and take away the blame for producing it without reason, this does not excuse those who receive it. Let us examine this point then, and say: God is, or he is not. But to which side shall we incline? Reason cannot decide it at all. There is an infinite chaos that separates us. A game is being played, at the extremity of this infinite distance, in which heads or tails must come up. Which will you take? By reason you can wager on neither; by reason you can hinder neither from winning.[40]

Do not then, charge with falsehood those who have made a choice; for you know nothing about it.—No: but I blame them for having made, not this choice, but a choice; for, although he who takes heads, and the other, are in the same fault, they are both in fault: the proper way is not to wager.

Yes, but you must wager: this is not voluntary, you are embarked. Which will you take then? Let us see. Since a choice must be made, let us see which interests you the least. You have two things to lose, the true and the good; and two things to stake, your reason and your will, your knowledge and your beatitude; and your nature has two things to shun, error and misery. Your reason is not more wounded, since a choice must necessarily be made, in choosing one rather than the other. Here is a point eliminated; but your beatitude? Let us weigh the gain and the loss, in taking heads that God exists. Let us weigh these two cases: if you gain, you gain all; if you lose, you lose nothing. Wager then that he is without hesitation.—This is admirable: yes, it is necessary to wager; but perhaps I wager too much.—Let us see. Since there is equal hazard of gaining or losing, if you had to gain but two lives for one, still you might wager. But if there were three to gain, it would be requisite to play (since you are under the necessity of playing), and you would be imprudent, when you are forced to play, not to hazard your life in order to gain three in a play where there is equal hazard of loss and gain. But there is an eternity of life and happiness. And this being true, even were there an infinity of chances, only one of which might be for you, you would still be right in wagering one in order to have two, and you would act foolishly, being obliged to play, to refuse to play one life against three in a game where among an infinity of chances there is one for you, if there was an infinity of life infinitely happy to gain. But there is here an infinity of life happy to gain, a chance of gain against a finite number of chances of loss, and what you play is finite. This is quite settled: wherever the infinite is, and where there is not an infinity of chances of loss against the chance of gain, there is nothing to balance, we must give all. And thus, when we are forced to play, we must renounce reason in order to keep life rather than to hazard it for the infinite gain, as ready to come as the loss of nothingness.

For there is no use in saying that it is uncertain whether we shall gain, and that it is certain that we hazard; and that the infinite distance between the cer-

---

[40]The wager Pascal has in mind here is the toss of a coin: "Heads, I win; tails, you lose."

tainty of what we risk, and the uncertainty of what we shall gain, raises the finite good which we risk with certainty, to an equality with the infinite which is uncertain. It is not so: every player hazards with certainty to gain with uncertainty, and nevertheless he hazards certainly the finite to gain uncertainly the finite, without sinning against reason. The distance is not infinite between this certainty of what we risk and the uncertainty of gain; this is false. There is, in truth, an infinity between the certainty of gaining and the certainty of losing. But the uncertainty of gaining is proportioned to the certainty of what we hazard, according to the proportion of the chances of gain and loss; whence it comes that, if there are as many chances on one side as there are on the other, the game is playing even; and then the certainty of what we hazard is equal to the uncertainty of the gain: so far is it from being infinitely distant. And thus our proposition is of infinite force, when there is the finite to hazard in a play where the chances of gain and loss are equal, and the infinite to gain. This is demonstrative; and if men are capable of any truths, this is one of them.

I confess it, I admit it. But, still are there no means of seeing the trick of the game?—Yes, the Scripture, and the rest, etc.

Yes; but my hands are tied and my mouth is dumb: I am forced to wager, and I am not at liberty: I am not unfettered and so constituted that I cannot believe. What will you have me do then?

It is true. But learn, at least, your inability to believe, since reason brings you to it, and yet you cannot believe; try then to convince yourself, not by the augmentation of proofs of the existence of God, but by the diminution of your own passions. You would have recourse to faith, but you know not the way: you wish to be cured of infidelity, and you ask for the remedy: learn it from those who have been bound like yourself, and who would wager now all their goods; these know the road that you wish to follow, and are cured of a disease that you wish to be cured of. Follow their course, then, from its beginning; it consisted in doing all things as if they believed in them, in using holy water, in having masses said, etc. Naturally this will make you believe and stupefy you at the same time.— But this is what I fear.—And why? what have you to lose?

But to show you that this leads to it, this will diminish the passions, which are your great obstacles, etc. Now, what harm will come to you in taking this course? You would be faithful, virtuous, humble, grateful, beneficent, a sincere friend, truthful. Truly, you would not be given up to infectious pleasures, to false glory, or false joys; but would you not have other pleasures?

I say to you that you will gain by it in this life; and that at each step you take in this direction, you will see so much of the certainty of gain, and so much of the nothingness of what you hazard, that you will acknowledge in the end that you have wagered for something certain, infinite, for which you have given nothing.

Oh! this discourse transports me, delights me, etc. If this discourse pleases you and appears to you strong, know that it is made by a man who has put himself on his knees, before and after, to pray that Being, who is infinite and without parts, and to whom he entirely submits himself, that he would also subject you to himself for your good and his glory; and that thus power accords with this weakness.

Those who hope for salvation are happy in that, but they have a counter-poise in the fear of hell.—Who has the most reason to fear hell, he who is ignorant that there is a hell, and who is certain of damnation, if there is one; or he who is surely persuaded that there is a hell, and has hope of being saved, if there is!

I would very soon abandon these pleasures, they say, if I had faith. And I answer: You would very soon have faith, if you had abandoned these pleasures. Now, it is for you to begin. If I could, I would give you faith. I cannot do it; and, consequently I cannot prove the truth of what you say. But you may easily quit your pleasures, and experience whether what I say is true.

Whoever, having but a week to live, shall not find the way is to believe that all this is but a stroke of chance. . . . Now if the passions do not hold us, a week and a hundred years are the same.

Philip Jacob Spener (1635–1705)

Philip Jacob Spener was born in Alsace and was educated at Strassburg, Basel, Geneva, and Tubingen. He served pastorates first at Strassburg (1663–66), and then at Frankfurt (1666–86). While he was serving in Frankfurt, Spener developed a program of semiweekly meetings, known as *collegia pietatis* (Lat., "schools of piety"), for the education and edification of the laity. These meetings gave Pietism its name, as well as its reformatory model. In 1675 Spener published his most significant spiritual work, *Pia Desideria* (Lat., "heartfelt desires"), which delineated his program for bringing renewal to the Lutheran Church. The text of his six "Proposals to Correct Conditions in the Church," which constituted the core of *Pia Desideria*, is carried below. The innovation of the *collegia pietatis* and the publication of *Pia Desideria* established Philip Jacob Spener as the founder of German Pietism.

Spener's reformatory program, as it was embodied in his *collegia pietatis* and *Pia Desideria*, caused so much controversy that he was forced to resign his position in Frankfurt in 1686. He accepted a call to serve as a chaplain to the court of Elector John George III, of Saxony, but after three years in that position his fervent preaching and reformatory posture forced Spener to seek another position. In 1689 he accepted a call to serve in Berlin, where he had his most productive years of ministry.

Spener's spirituality stressed conversion, inner renewal, and religious experience at a time when doctrinaire theological distinctions seemed to dominate the religious landscape. His work sought to wed religious experience and practical piety. He stressed lay education and developed various means, such as *collegia pietatis*, prayer meetings, Bible study groups, and Sunday Schools, to promote lay spirituality. He also denounced the "worldly" habits of contemporary Christians, such as dancing, theater-going, card playing and the like, which Spener felt diverted their attention from the more important task of cultivating Christian character.

PROPOSALS TO CORRECT CONDITIONS IN THE CHURCH[41]

Thought should be given to a more extensive use of the Word of God among us. We know that by nature we have no good in us. If there is to be any good in us, it must be brought about by God. To this end the Word of God is the powerful means, since faith must be rekindled through the gospel, and the law provides the rules for good works and many wonderful impulses to attain them. The more at home the Word of God is among us, the more we shall bring about faith and its fruits. . . .

It should therefore be considered whether the church would not be well advised to introduce the people to Scripture in still other ways than through the customary sermons on the appointed lessons.

This might be done, first of all, by diligent reading of the Holy Scriptures, especially of the New Testament. It would be not difficult for every housefather to keep a Bible, or at least a New Testament, handy and read from it every day or, if he cannot read, to have someone else read. . . .

Then a second thing would be desirable in order to encourage people to read privately, namely, that where the practice can be introduced the books of the Bible be read one after another, at specified times in the public service, without further comment (unless one wished to add brief summaries). This would be intended for the edification of all, but especially of those who cannot read at all, or cannot read easily or well, or of those who do not own a copy of the Bible.

For a third thing it would perhaps not be inexpedient (and I set this down for further and more mature reflection) to reintroduce the ancient and apostolic kind of church meetings. In addition to our customary services with preaching, other assemblies would also be held in the manner in which Paul describes them in I Corinthians 14:26–40. One person would not rise to preach (although this practice would be continued at other times), but others who have been blessed with gifts and knowledge would also speak and present their pious opinions on the proposed subject to the judgment of the rest, doing all this in such a way as to avoid disorder and strife. . . .

Not a little benefit is to be hoped for from such an arrangement. Preachers would learn to know the members of their own congregations and their weakness or growth in doctrine and piety, and a bond of confidence would be established between preachers and people which would serve the best interests of both. At the same time the people would have a splendid opportunity to exercise their diligence with respect to the Word of God and modestly to ask their questions (which they do not always have the courage to discuss with their minister in private) and get answers to them. In a short time they would experience personal growth and would also become capable of giving better religious instruction to their children and servants at home. In the absence of such exercises, sermons

---

[41]Reprinted from Philip Jacob Spener, *Pia Desideria,* translated by Theodore Tappert. Copyright (c) 1964, by Fortress Press. Used by kind premission of Augsburg Fortress Press. Pages 87–116.

which are delivered in continually flowing speech are not always fully and adequately comprehended because there is no time for reflection in between or because, when one does stop to reflect, much of what follows is missed (which does not happen in a discussion). On the other hand, private reading of the Bible or reading in the household, where nobody is present who may from time to time help point out the meaning and purpose of each verse, cannot provide the reader with a sufficient explanation of all that he would like to know. What is lacking in both of these instances (in public preaching and private reading) would be supplied by the proposed exercises. It would not be a great burden either to the preachers or to the people, and much would be done to fulfill the admonition of Paul in Colossians 3:16, "Let the word of Christ dwell in you richly, as you teach and admonish one another in all wisdom, and as you sing psalms and hymns and spiritual songs." In fact, such songs may be used in the proposed meetings for the praise of God and the inspiration of the participants.

This much is certain: the diligent use of the Word of God, which consists not only of listening to sermons but also of reading, reforming something, whether this occurs in the proposed fashion or in some appropriate way. The Word of God remains the seed from which all that is good in us must grow. If we succeed in getting the people to seek eagerly and diligently in the book of life for their joy, their spiritual life will be wonderfully strengthened and they will become altogether different people.

Our frequently mentioned Dr. Luther would suggest another means, which is altogether compatible with the first. This second proposal *is the establishment and diligent exercise of the spiritual priesthood.* Nobody can read Luther's writings with some care without observing how earnestly the sainted man advocated this spiritual priesthood, according to which not only ministers but all Christians are made priests by their Savior, are anointed by the Holy Spirit, and are dedicated to perform spiritual-priestly acts. . . . This presumptuous monopoly of the clergy, alongside the aforementioned prohibition of Bible reading, is one of the principal means by which papal Rome established its power over poor Christians and still preserves it wherever it has opportunity. The papacy could suffer no greater injury than having Luther point out that all Christians have been called to exercise spiritual functions (although not called to the *public* exercise of them, which requires appointment by a congregation with equal right) and that they are not only permitted but, if they wish to be Christians, are obligated to undertake them.

Every Christian is bound not only to offer himself and what he has, his prayer, thanksgiving, good works, alms, etc. but also industriously to study in the Word of the Lord, with the grace that is given him to teach others, especially those under his own roof, to chastise, exhort, convert, and edify them, to observe their life, pray for all, and insofar as possible be concerned about their salvation. If this is first pointed out to the people, they will take better care of themselves and apply themselves to whatever pertains to their own edification and that of their fellow men. . . . No damage will be done to the ministry by a proper use of this priesthood. In fact, one of the principal reasons why the ministry cannot accomplish all that it ought is that it is too weak without the help of the universal priesthood. . . .

Connected with these two proposals is a third: the people must have impressed upon them and must accustom themselves to believing that *it is by no means enough to have knowledge of the Christian faith, for Christianity consists rather of practice.* Our dear Savior repeatedly enjoined love as the real mark of His disciples[42] . . . . Indeed, love is the whole life of the man who has faith and who through his faith is saved, and his fulfillment of the laws of God consists of love.

If we can therefore awaken a fervent love among our Christians, first toward one another and then toward all men (for these two, brotherly affection and general love, must supplement each other according to 2 Peter 1:7), and put this love into practice, practically all that we desire will be accomplished. For all the commandments are summed up in love (Rom. 13:9). . . .

Related to this is a fourth proposal: *We must beware how we conduct ourselves in religious controversies* with unbelievers and heretics. We must first take pains to strengthen and confirm ourselves, our friends, and other fellow believers in the known truth and to protect them with great care from every kind of seduction. Then we must remind ourselves of our duty toward the erring. . . .

I therefore hold (1) that not all disputation is useful and good. . . . Just as all disputing is not praiseworthy and useful, so (2) proper disputation is not the only means of maintaining the truth but requires other means alongside it. . . . If the glory of God is to be properly advanced, disputation must be directed toward the goal of converting opponents and apply the truth which has been defended to a holy obedience and a due gratitude toward God. Such a *convictio intellectus* or conviction of truth is far from being faith. Faith requires more. The intention must be there to add whatever is necessary to convert the erring and remove whatever is a hindrance to him. Above all, there must be a desire, in promoting God's glory, to apply to ourselves and to all others what we hold to be true, and in this light to serve God. . . .

Since ministers must bear the greatest burden in all these things which pertain to a reform of the church, and since their shortcomings do correspondingly great harm, it is of the utmost importance that the office of the ministry be occupied by men who, above all, are themselves true Christians and, then, have the divine wisdom to guide others carefully on the way of the Lord. It is therefore important, indeed necessary, for the reform of the church that only such persons be called who may be suited, and that nothing at all except the glory of God be kept in view during the whole procedure of calling. This would mean that all carnal schemes involving favor, friendship, gifts, and similarly unseemly things would be set aside. Not the least among the reasons for the defect in the church are the mistakes which occur in the calling of ministers, but we shall not elaborate on this here.

---

[42]John 13:34–35, 15:12; 1 John 3:10,18, 4:7–8,11–13,21.

However, if such suitable persons are to be called to the ministry they must be available, and hence they must be trained in *our schools and universities*. . . . [S]tudents should have unceasingly have it impressed upon them that holy life is not of less consequence than diligence and study, indeed that study without piety is worthless. . . .

Just because theology is a practical discipline and does not consist only of knowledge, study alone is not enough, nor is the mere accumulation and imparting of information. Accordingly thought should be given to ways of instituting all kinds of exercises through which students may become accustomed to and experienced in those things which belong to practice and to their edification. It would be desirable if such materials were earnestly treated in certain lectures, especially if the rules of conduct which we have from our dear Savior and his apostles were impressed upon students. It would also be desirable if students were given concrete suggestions on how to institute pious meditations, how to know themselves better through self-examination, how to resist the lusts of the flesh, how to hold their desires in check and die unto the world, . . . how to observe growth in goodness or where there is still lack, and how they themselves may do what they must teach others to do. Studying alone will not accomplish this. Our dear Luther expressed this opinion (Jena ed., II, 57): "A man becomes a theologian not by comprehending, reading, or speculating but by living and indeed dying and being damned." . . .

In addition to these exercises, which are intended to develop the Christian life of the students, it would also be useful if the teachers made provision for practice in those things with which the students will have to deal when they are in the ministry. For example, there should be practice at times in instructing the ignorant, in comforting the sick, and especially in preaching, where it should be pointed out to students that everything in their sermons should have edification as the *goal*. I therefore add this as a sixth proposal whereby the Christian church may be helped to a better condition: that *sermons* be achieved in the hearers to the greatest possible degree.

There are probably few places in our church in which there is such want that not enough sermons are preached. But many godly persons find that not a little is wanting in many sermons. There are preachers who fill most of their sermons with things that give the impression that the preachers are learned men, although the hearers understand nothing of this. . . . Many preachers are more concerned to have an outline that is artful and yet sufficiently concealed, and to have all the parts handled precisely according to the rules of oratory and suitably embellished, than they are concerned that the materials be chosen and by God's grace be developed in such a way that hearers may profit from the sermon in life and death. This ought not to be so. The pulpit is not the place for an ostentatious display of one's skill. It is rather the place to preach the Word of the Lord plainly but powerfully. Preaching should be the divine means to save the people, and so it is proper that everything be directed to this end. Ordinary people, who make up the largest part of a congregation, are always to be kept in view more than the few learned people. . . .

Jeanne Bouvier de la Mothe Guyon (1648–1717)

Jeanne Guyon was born at Montargis, near Orleans. Her early education in convents enhanced her interest in mysticism and personal religious experience. In 1664 she was given in marriage, through prior arrangement, to a wealthy, invalid man who was twenty-two years her senior. Although her marriage was not a happy one, Madame Guyon remained faithful to her husband and sought personal fulfillment by seeking a deep, inward relationship with Jesus Christ. She had a remarkable conversion experience, in 1668, which was described in her spiritual autobiography: ". . . Thou, O Divine Love, manifested Thy favor [to me]. The desire I had to please Thee, the tears I shed, the manifold pains I underwent, the labors I sustained, and the little fruit I reaped from them, moved Thee with compassion. This was the state of my soul when Thy goodness, surpassing all my vileness and infidelities, and abounding in proportion to my wretchedness, granted me in a moment, what all my own efforts could never procure. Beholding me rowing with laborious toil, the breath of Thy Divine operations turned in my favor, and carried me full sail over this sea of affliction."[43] After this experience Madame Guyon withdrew from the fashionable life pursued by the French nobility and gave herself wholeheartedly to Christ and the pursuit of Christian Spirituality.

When her husband died, in 1676, she resolved not to remarry and to devote her life to Christ. As Madame Guyon made known to others what she learned of Christian Spirituality, her fame as a spiritual director spread rapidly. Her direction took more tangible form through the publication of her *Short and Easy Method of Prayer* (1685). The work was widely read and appreciated, in part because of its ability to communicate and popularize spiritual disciplines among laity. But the work also bore enough similarity to that of Molinos[44] to bring Madame Guyon under suspicion of heresy. In 1688 those suspicions brought about her imprisonment, and during that period she became acquainted with Cardinal Fenelon, a person upon whom Madame Guyon exerted much positive influence. She recanted any errors in her publication and was subsequently released.

As Boussuet, Bishop of Meaux, began attacking François Fenelon, Archbishop of Cambrai, over the issue of quietism, the works of Madame Guyon again became the focus of unfavorable attention.[45] She was imprisoned in the Bastille from 1698–1702, and her *Short and Easy Method of Prayer* was banned by the Roman Catholic Church (1699), perhaps in part because of the popularity it had among Protestants. Its popularity continued to increase well into the eighteenth century.[46]

---

[43]Madame Guyon, *Autobiography*, Pt. I, p. 312 from the Christian Classics Etherial Library, http://ccel.wheaton.edu. Scanned by Harry Plantinga.

[44]A Spanish theologian and mystic, 1640–97. Molinos's principal work, *Guida spirituale* (1675), was condemned by the papal bull *Coelestis Pastor* in 1687.

[45]Elfrieda DuBois, "Fenelon and Quietism," in Wainwright, Jones, and Yarnold, *Study of Spirituality*, pp. 408–15, offers an excellent overview of the connection of Madame Guyon with François Fenelon, and quietism.

[46]She was a favorite of John Wesley and the Methodists, for example. Her *Autobiography* appears in abridged form in Wesley's famous *Christian Library*.

The remarkable life of Madame Guyon has been preserved in her own words through her *Spiritual Torments, an Autobiography* (1683).

Despite various limitations in her work, Madame Guyon's *Short and Easy Method of Prayer* popularized spiritual disciplines—which had previously been the purview of the officially "religious"—among the laity. Her spirituality was Christocentric in its focus, and stressed the abandonment of self to the Lord, Jesus Christ. Madame Guyon's stress upon prayer of the heart, simplicity, and inward holiness as the authentic regulator of outer life has received ready response all across the Christian tradition.

DEEP INWARD RELATIONSHIP WITH JESUS CHRIST[47]

As you pick up this book, you may feel that you simply are not one of those people capable of a deep experience with Jesus Christ. Most Christians do not feel that *they* have been called to a deep, inward relationship to their Lord. But we have all been called to the depths of Christ, just as surely as we have been called to salvation. When I speak of this "deep, inward relationship to Jesus Christ," what do I mean? Actually, it is very simple. It is only the turning and yielding of your heart to the Lord. It is the expression of love within your heart for Him. . . .

Once the Lord spoke and said, "I counsel you to buy from me gold tried in the fire that you may be rich" [Rev 3:18]. Dear reader, there is gold available to you. This gold is much more easily obtained than you could ever imagine. It is available to *you*. The purpose of this book is to launch you into this exploration and into this discovery.

I give you an invitation: if you are thirsty, come to the living waters. Do not waste your precious time digging wells that have no water in them (Jn 7:37; Jer 2:13). If you are starving and can find nothing to satisfy your hunger, then come. Come, and you will be filled. You who are poor, come. You who are afflicted, come. You who are weighed down with your load of wretchedness and your load of pain, come. You *will* be comforted! You who are sick, and need a physician, come. Don't hesitate because you have diseases. Come to your Lord and show Him all your diseases, and they will be healed! Come!

Dear child of God, your Father has His arms of love open wide to you. Throw yourself into His arms. You who have strayed and wandered away as sheep, return to your Shepherd. You who are sinners, come to your Savior.

I especially address those of you who are very simple and you who are uneducated, even you who cannot read and write. You may think you are the one person *most* incapable of this abiding experience of Christ, this farthest from a deep experience with the Lord; but, in fact, the Lord has *especially* chosen you! You are the one *most* suited to know Him well. So let no one feel left out. Jesus Christ has called us all.

---

[47]Reprinted from Jeanne Guyon, *Experiencing the Depths of Jesus Christ* (formerly entitled: *Short and Very Easy Method of Prayer*) (Gardiner, Me: Christian Books Publishing House, 1975), pp. 1–5.

Oh, I suppose there is one group who *is* left out! Do not come if you have no heart. You see, before you come, there is one thing you must do: You must first give your heart to the Lord. "But I do not know how to give my heart to the Lord." Well, in this little book you will learn what it means to give your heart to the Lord and how to make that gift to Him. . . . How then will you come to the Lord to know Him in such a deep way? Prayer is the key. But I have in mind a certain kind of prayer. It is a kind of prayer that is very simple and yet holds the key to perfection and goodness—things found only in God Himself. The type of prayer that I have in mind will deliver you from enslavement to every sin. It is a prayer that will release to you every Godly virtue.

You see, the only way to be perfect is to walk in the presence of God. The only way you can live in His presence in uninterrupted fellowship is by means of prayer, but a very special kind of prayer. It is a prayer that leads you into the presence of God and keeps you there at all times; a prayer that can be experienced under any conditions, any place, and any time. Is there really such a prayer? Does such an experience with Christ truly exist? Yes, there is such a prayer! A prayer that does not interfere with your outward activities or your daily routine. There is a kind of prayer that can be practiced by kings, by priests, by soldiers, by laborers, by children, by women, and even by the sick.

May I hasten to say that the kind of prayer I am speaking of is not a prayer that comes from your mind. It is a prayer that begins in the heart. It does not come from your understanding or your thoughts. Prayer offered to the Lord from your mind simply would not be adequate. Why? Because your mind is very limited. The mind can pay attention to only one thing at a time. Prayer that comes out of the heart is not interrupted by thinking! I will go so far as to say that nothing can interrupt this prayer, *the prayer of simplicity.*

Oh yes, there is *one* thing. Selfish desires can cause this prayer to cease. But even here there is encouragement, for once you have enjoyed your Lord and tasted the sweetness of His love, you will find that even your selfish desires no longer hold any power. You will find it impossible to have pleasure in anything except Him. . . .

By this "prayer of simplicity," this *experiencing* of Christ deep within, you may live by God Himself with less difficulty and with less interruption than you now live by the air which you take into you. If this is true, then I ask, wouldn't it be a sin not to pray? Yes, it would be a sin. But once you have learned how to seek Jesus Christ and how to lay hold of Him, you will find the way so easy that you will no longer neglect this relationship to your Lord. Let us go on, therefore, and learn this simple way to pray.

TWO WAYS TO COME TO THE LORD[48]

I would like to address you as though you were a beginner in Christ, one seeking to know Him. In so doing, let me suggest two ways for you to come to the

---

[48]Ibid., pp. 7–14.

Lord. I will call the first way "praying the Scripture;" the second way I will call "beholding the Lord" or "waiting in His presence."

"Praying the Scripture" is a unique way of dealing with the Scripture; it involves both reading and prayer. Here is how you should begin. Turn to the Scripture; choose some passage that is simple and fairly practical. Next, come to the Lord. Come quietly and humbly. There, before Him, read a small portion of the passage of Scripture you have opened to. Be careful as you read. Take in fully, gently and carefully what you are reading. Taste it and digest it as you read.

In the past it may have been your habit, while reading, to move very quickly from one verse of Scripture to another until you had read the whole passage. Perhaps you were seeking to find the main point of the passage. But in coming to the Lord by means of "praying the Scripture," you do not read quickly; you read very slowly. You do not move from one passage to another, not until you have *sensed* the very heart of what you have read. You may then want to take that portion of Scripture that has touched you and turn it into prayer. After you have sensed something of the passage and after you know that the essence of that portion has been extracted and all the deeper sense of it is gone, then, very slowly, gently, and in a calm manner begin to read the next portion of the passage. You will be surprised to find that when your time with the Lord has ended, you will have read very little, probably no more than half a page.

"Praying the Scripture" is not judged by *how much* you read but by the *way* in which you read. If you read quickly, it will benefit you little. You will be like a bee that merely skims the surface of a flower. Instead, in this new way of reading with prayer, you must become as the bee who penetrates into the *depths* of the flower. You plunge deeply within to remove its deepest nectar. Of course, there is a kind of reading in the Scripture for scholarship and for study—but not here. That studious kind of reading will not help you when it comes to matters that are *divine*! To receive any deep, inward profit from the Scripture, you must read as I have described. Plunge into the very depths of the words you read until revelation, like a sweet aroma, breaks out upon you. I am quite sure that if you will follow this course, little by little you will come to experience a very rich prayer that flows from your inward being.

Let us move now to the second kind of prayer, which I mentioned earlier. The second kind of prayer, which I described as "beholding the Lord" or "waiting on the Lord," *also* makes use of the Scripture but it is not actually a time of reading. . . .

What of this second path? In "beholding the Lord," you come to the Lord in a totally different way. Perhaps at this point I need to share with you the greatest difficulty you will have in waiting upon the Lord. It has to do with your mind. The mind has a very strong tendency to stray away from the Lord. Therefore, as you come before the Lord to sit in His presence, beholding Him, make use of the Scripture *to quiet your mind*. The way to do this is really quite simple. First, read a passage of Scripture. Once you sense the Lord's presence, the content of what you have read is no longer important. The Scripture has served its purpose; it has quieted your mind; it has brought you to Him.

So that you can see this more clearly, let me describe the way in which you come to the Lord by the simple act of beholding Him and waiting upon Him. You begin by setting aside a time to be with the Lord. When you do come to Him, come quietly. Turn your heart to the presence of God. How is this done? This, too, is quite simple. You turn to Him by *faith*. By faith you believe you have come into the presence of God. Next, while you are before the Lord, begin to read the same portion of Scripture. As you read, *pause*. The pause should be quite gentle. You have paused so that you may set your mind on the Spirit. You have set your mind *inwardly*—on Christ. (You should always remember that you are not doing this to gain some understanding of what you have read; rather, you are reading in order to turn your mind from outward things to the deep parts of your being. You are not there to learn or to read, but you are there to experience the presence of your Lord!)

While you are before the Lord, hold your heart in His presence. How? This you also do by faith. Yes, by faith you can hold your heart in the Lord's presence. Now, waiting before Him, turn all your attention toward your spirit. Do not allow your mind to wander. If your mind begins to wander, just turn your attention back again to the inward parts of your being. You will be free from wandering—free from any outward distractions—and you will be brought near to God. (The Lord is found *only* within your spirit, in the recesses of your being, in the Holy of Holies; this is where He dwells. The Lord once promised to come and make His home within you (Jn. 14:23). He promised to there meet those who worship Him and who do His will. The Lord *will* meet you in your spirit. It was St. Augustine who once said that he had lost much time in the beginning of his Christian experience by trying to find the Lord outwardly rather than by turning inwardly).

Once your heart has been turned inwardly to the Lord, you will have an impression of His presence. You will be able to notice His presence more acutely because your outer senses have now become very calm and quiet. Your attention is no longer on outward things or on the surface thoughts of your mind; instead, sweetly and silently, your mind becomes occupied with what you have read and by that touch of His presence. Oh, it is not that you will think about what you have read, but you will *feed* upon what you have read. Out of a love for the Lord you exert your will to hold your mind quiet before Him. When you have come to this state, you must allow your mind to rest.

How shall I describe what to do next? In this very peaceful state, *swallow* what you have tasted. At first this may seem difficult, but perhaps I can show you just how simple it is. Have you not, at times, enjoyed the flavor of a very tasty food? But unless you were willing to swallow the food, you received no nourishment. It is the same with your soul. In this quiet, peaceful, and simple state, simply take in what is there as nourishment.

What about distractions? Let us say your mind begins to wander. Once you have been deeply touched by the Lord's Spirit and are distracted, be diligent to bring your wandering mind back to the Lord. This is the easiest way in the world to overcome external distractions. When you mind has wandered, don't try to deal with it by changing what you are thinking. You see, if you pay attention to what you are thinking, you will only irritate your mind and stir it up more. Instead, *withdraw* from your mind! Keep turning within to the Lord's presence. By doing this you will win the war with your wandering mind and yet never directly engage in the battle!

Before we close this chapter, I would like to bring up one or two more points. Let us talk about divine revelation. In the past, your reading habit may have been to wander from one subject to another. But the best way to *understand* the mysteries that are hidden in the revelation of God *and* to *enjoy* them fully is to let them be imprinted deeply in your heart. How? You may do this by dwelling on that revelation just as long as it gives you a sense of the Lord. Do not be quick to go from one thought to another. Stay with what *the Lord* has revealed to you; stay there just as long as a sense of the Lord is also there. . . .

Be assured that as your soul becomes more accustomed to withdrawing to inward things, this process will become much easier. There are two reasons that you will find it easier each time to bring your mind under subjection to the Lord. One is that the mind, after much practice, will form a new habit of turning deep within. The second is that you have a gracious Lord! The Lord's chief desire is to reveal Himself to you and, in order for Him to do that, He gives you abundant grace. The Lord gives you the experiences of enjoying His presence. He touches you, and His touch is so delightful that, more than ever, you are drawn inwardly to Him.

THE PRAYER OF SIMPLICITY[49]

You now have some acquaintance with *praying the Scripture* and *beholding the Lord* or *waiting in His presence*. Let us assume that you have practiced these two ways of coming to the Lord. Let us say that you have passed through the awkward stage of this and have come into real experience. Now let us move on to consider a deeper level of experience with the Lord; that is, a deeper level of prayer. Some have described this second level as an experience of "faith and stillness." Others have referred to it as the "prayer of simplicity." I prefer the latter name.

Let us say you have grown accustomed to praying the Scripture and to waiting quietly in the sense of the Lord's presence, that these have made themselves part of your life. If this is so, you have found that it is now much easier to come to the Lord and to know His presence. But I would like to remind you once more that what was written previously was written *to those who are just beginning to know Christ.* . . .

You might think that I would now encourage you to continue on in this very successful path. Instead, I am going to encourage you to change your course just a little. In so doing, once more you are going to come to a point that might have some discouragement in it. Starting out on a new path to explore the Lord always means encountering some difficulties at the outset! Therefore, I would encourage you to have a believing heart from this point on. You *must not* be discouraged. There *will* be a little difficulty along the way as you seek to go into a deeper re-

---

[49]Ibid., pp. 21–23.

lationship with the Lord. Now with these words behind us, let us look at this new level of prayer.

First of all, come into the Lord's presence by faith. As you are there before Him, keep turning inward to your spirit until your mind is collected and you are perfectly still before Him. Now, when all your attention is finally turned within and your mind is set on the Lord, simply remain quiet before Him for a little while. Perhaps you will begin to enjoy a sense of the Lord's presence. If that is the case, *do not try to think* of anything. Do not try to *say* anything. Do not try to *do* anything! As long as the sense of the Lord's presence continues, *just remain there*. Remain before Him exactly as you are.

The awareness of His presence will eventually begin to decrease. When this happens, utter some words of love to the Lord or simply call on His name. Do this quietly and gently with a believing heart. In so doing, you will once again be brought back to the sweetness of His presence! You will discover that you once more return to that sweet place of utter enjoyment that you have just experienced! Once the sweetness of His presence has returned to its fullest, *again be still before Him. You should not seek to move as long as He is near.* What is the point? The point is this: There is a fire within you and it ebbs and grows. That fire, when it ebbs, must be gently fanned, but *only* gently. Just as soon as that fire begins to burn, again *cease all* your efforts. Otherwise, you might put out the flame. This, then, is the second level of prayer—a second level in experiencing Jesus Christ. . . .

ABANDONMENT[50]

. . . At this point, there must enter into your heart whole new attitudes toward your entire life. If you are to branch out beyond just a time of prayer each day, other parts of your life—and even your whole viewpoint of life—will have to be altered. This new attitude must come for a very special reason—so that you may go on deeper, still deeper, into another level with your Lord. To do this, you must have a fresh attitude toward yourself as well as toward the Lord; it is an attitude that must go much deeper than any you have known previously. To do this, I must introduce a new word to you. The word is *abandonment*.

To penetrate deeper in the experience of Jesus Christ, it is required that you begin to abandon your whole existence, giving it up to God. Let us take the daily occurrences of life as an illustration. You must utterly believe that the circumstances of your life, that is, every minute of your life, as well as the whole course of your life—anything, yes, *everything* that happens—have all come to you by His will and by His permission. You must utterly believe that everything that has happened to you is from God and is exactly what you need.

. . . You can begin by accepting every time of prayer, whether it be a glorious time with Him or a time when your mind wanders, as being exactly what He

---

[50]Ibid., pp. 31–35.

desired for you. Then learn to broaden this perspective until it encompasses *every* second of your life! Such an outlook towards your circumstances and such a look of faith towards your Lord will make you *content* with *everything*. Once you believe this, you will then begin to take everything that comes into your life as being from the hand of God, not from the hand of man.

Do you truly, sincerely desire to give yourself up to God? Then I must next remind you that once you have made the donation, you cannot take the gift back again. Once the gift has been presented, it no longer belongs to the giver. This little book is written to tell you how to experience the depths of Jesus Christ, but knowing the depths of Jesus Christ is not just a method. It is a life-long attitude. It is a matter of being enveloped by God and possessed by Him.

We have spoken of abandonment. Abandonment is a matter of the greatest importance if you are to make progress in knowing your Lord. Abandonment is, in fact, *the key* to the *inner court*—the key to the fathomless depths. Abandonment is the key to the inward spiritual life. The believer who knows how to abandon himself to the Lord will soon become perfect. Let us say you reach this state of abandonment. Once you have reached this state, you must continue, steadfast and immovable. Otherwise, to arrive there and remain only briefly is of little value. It is one thing to reach this state; it is another thing to remain there. Be careful; do not listen to the voice of your natural reasoning. You can expect just such reasoning to well up within you. Nonetheless, you must believe that *you can* abandon yourself utterly to the Lord for all your lifetime and that He will give you the grace to remain there! You must trust God, "hoping against hope" (Rom. 4:18). Great faith produces great abandonment.

What is abandonment? If we can understand what it is, perhaps we can better lay hold of it. Abandonment is casting off all your cares. Abandonment is dropping all your needs. This includes *spiritual* needs. Let me repeat that, for it is not easily grasped. Abandonment is laying aside, forever, *all* of your spiritual needs. All Christians *have* spiritual needs; but the believer who has abandoned himself to the Lord no longer indulges in the luxury of being aware of spiritual needs. Rather, he gives himself over completely to the disposal of God. Do you realize that all Christians have been exhorted to abandonment? The Lord Himself has said, "Take no thought for tomorrow, for your heavenly Father knows that you have need of all these things" (Mt. 6:32, 34). Again the Scripture says, "In all your ways acknowledge Him, and He will direct your paths" (Prov. 3:6). "Commit your works unto the Lord and your thoughts shall be established" (Prov. 16:3). . . .

True abandonment must cover two complete worlds, two complete realms. There must be an abandonment in your life concerning all *outward*, practical things. Secondly, there must also be an abandonment of all *inward*, spiritual things. You must come to the Lord and there engage in giving up *all* your concerns. All your concerns go into the hand of God. You forget yourself, and from that moment on you think *only of Him*. By continuing to do this over a long period of time, your heart will remain *unattached*; your heart will be free and at peace!

How do you practice abandonment? You practice it daily, hourly, and by the moment. Abandonment is practiced by *continually* losing your own will in the will of God; by plunging your will into the depths of *His* will, there to be lost forever! And how do you begin? You must begin by refusing every personal desire that comes to you just as soon as it arises—no matter how good that personal desire is, and no matter how helpful it might appear! Abandonment must reach a point where you stand in complete indifference to yourself. You can be sure that out of such a disposition a wonderful result will come.

The result of this attitude will, in fact, bring you to the most wonderful point imaginable. It is the point where your will breaks free of you completely and becomes free to be joined to the will of God! You will desire only what He desires, that is, what He *has desired* for all eternity. Become abandoned by simply resigning yourself to what the Lord wants, in all things, no matter what they are, where they come from, or how they affect your life.

What is abandonment? It is forgetting your past; it is leaving the future in His hands; it is devoting the present fully and completely to your Lord. Abandonment is being satisfied with the present moment, no matter what that moment contains. You are satisfied because you know that whatever that moment has, it contains—in that instant—God's eternal plan for you. You will always know that that moment is the absolute and total *declaration* of His will for your life. . . .

Do you wish to go into the depths of Jesus Christ? If you wish to enter into this deeper state of knowing the Lord, you must seek to know not only a deeper prayer but also abandonment in all realms of your life. This means branching out until your new relationship includes living 24 hours a day utterly abandoned to Him. Begin to surrender yourself to be led by God and to be dealt with by Him. Do so right now. Surrender yourself to allow Him to do with you exactly as He pleases—both in your *inward* life of experiencing Him and also in your *outward* life of accepting all circumstances as from Him.

Brother Lawrence (1611–91)

Nicholas Herman was born in Herimesnil, Lorraine. At the age of eighteen he became a soldier, and he served with the army of his native land during the Thirty Years War. Service in this "religious war" left Nicholas scarred in body and soul, and memories of the atrocities he witnessed haunted him to the degree that he resolved to dedicate his life to serving Christ.

After a brief and discouraging career as a footman in the service of the treasurer to the King of France, Herman followed the example of his uncle and became a Carmelite friar. After living an eremitical way of life, he realized that he was better suited for the spiritual life of a religious community; in 1640 he applied for admission as a lay brother at a monastery of the Discalaced Carmelites in Paris. He was admitted and given the name Brother Lawrence of the Resurrection; he made his profession in 1642.

Brother Lawrence's ministry was performed amidst menial tasks, such as working for years in the kitchen. His spirituality was characterized by an ability to experience and encounter God in mundane tasks and common things. He had learned, in the words of the title of his famous work, *The Practice of the Presence of God* (1642). The book, which comprises four conversations, sixteen letters, and a series of spiritual maxims, describes sanctification as the process of doing for God's sake what we commonly do for our own sake. Brother Lawrence taught that one could cultivate an abiding sense of the presence of God through prayer, conversation with God, and a habitual calling of God to mind.

THE PRESENCE OF GOD[51]

1. The presence of God is the applying of our spirit to God, or a realization of the presence of God, which can be brought about either by the imagination or by understanding.

2. I know a person who for forty years has practiced the presence of God intellectually but gives it several other names; sometimes he calls it a simple act or a clear and distinct knowledge of God; at other times an indistinct vision or a loving gaze, a sense of God; still other times he calls it a waiting on God, a silent conversation with God, trust in God, the life and peace of the soul; finally this person told me that all of these expressions for the presence of God, which has come to be natural with him, are only synonyms that express the same thing in this way:

3. By force of habit and by frequently calling his mind to the presence of God, he has developed such a habit that as soon as he is free from his external affairs, and even often while he is deeply immersed in them, the very heart of his soul, with no effort on his part, is raised up above all things and stays suspended and held there in God as in its center and its place of rest; nearly always, experiencing his soul in this state, and backed up by faith, satisfied him; and it is this that he calls the actual presence of God, which includes all the other kinds of presence of God and much more as well so that he lives now as if only God and himself were in the world, conversing always with God, asking Him for what he needs and continually rejoicing with Him in a thousand and one ways.

4. Nevertheless, it should be pointed out that this conversation with God is held in the deepest recesses and the very center of the soul; it is there that the soul talks with God heart to heart, and always in a most sublime peace in which the soul rejoices in God; everything that takes place outside is no more to the soul than as a fire of straw which burns itself out as it gives light, and these exterior affairs seldom, or very slightly, disturb its interior peace.

---

[51]Reprinted from John Delaney, trans., *The Practice of the Presence of God, by Brother Lawrence of the Resurrection*. Copyright (c) 1977 by John Delaney. Used with the kind permission of Doubleday, a division of Bantam Doubleday Dell Publishing Group, Inc. Pages 107–9.

5. But to return to our consideration of the presence of God, I tell you that this sweet and loving gaze of God insensibly kindles a divine fire in the soul which is set ablaze so ardently with the love of God that one is obliged to perform exterior acts to moderate it.

6. We would be very surprised if we knew what the soul sometimes says to God, who seems to be so pleased with these conversations that He allows anything to the soul provided that it wishes to be always with Him and in His heart; and as if he feared that it would return to human things, He takes care to provide it with all its desires so well that it often finds within itself a most delectable and most appetizing banquet though it has done nothing at all to obtain it except by consenting to it.

7. The presence of God, is, then, the life and nourishment of the soul which can acquire it by our Lord's grace by these means:

WAYS OF ACQUIRING THE PRESENCE OF GOD[52]

1. The first way is a great purity of life.

2. The second is a great faithfulness to the practice of His presence and an interior gaze on God which should always be quiet, humble and loving without succumbing to any difficulties or disquietude.

3. It is necessary to take particular care to begin, if only for a moment, your exterior actions with this interior gaze and that you do the same while you are doing them and when you have finished them. Since it is necessary to devote much time and effort to acquiring this habit you must not be discouraged when you fail since the habit is formed only with difficulty; but once you have acquired it, you will experience great joy.

   Is it not right that the heart which is the seat of life and which governs the other parts of the body should be the first and the last to love and adore God, should be the beginning and the ending of our activities, spiritual and corporal, and in general through all life's works? And it is the heart which can affect this little interior gaze which, as I have already said, can be brought about when done spontaneously and without study.

4. It would be pertinent for those who undertake this practice to make up interiorly short ejaculations such as: "My God, I am all yours," "God of love, I love You with all my heart," "Lord, make me according to Your heart," and any such words that love may beget on the spur of the moment. But they must be careful that the mind does not wander and return again to worldly things; they

---

[52]Ibid., pp. 109–10. Used by permission of Doubleday, a division of Bantam Doubleday Dell Publishing Group, Inc.

should stay close to God alone so that the mind, urged and impelled by the will, is forced to stay with God.

5. This presence of God, though a bit painful in the beginning, if practiced faithfully, works secretly in the soul and produces marvelous effects and draws down to it in abundance the graces of the Lord and leads it insensibly to the simple grace, that loving sight of God everywhere present, which is the most holy, the most solid, the easiest, the most efficacious manner of prayer.

6. Notice, if you please, that to attain this state you must take for granted the mortifications of the senses since it is impossible for a soul still attached to worldly pleasures to be completely joined to this divine presence since to be with God requires complete rejection of worldly things.

THE BENEFITS OF THE PRESENCE OF GOD[53]

1. The first benefit the soul receives from the presence of God is that faith becomes more alive and more active in every occasion of our life, particularly in our times of need, since it readily obtains grace for us in our temptations and in our unavoidable dealings with our fellow men; for the soul, accustomed by this exercise to rely on faith, by a simple act of recollection sees and feels God present, calls on Him freely and efficaciously, and obtains what it needs. You could say that doing this enables the soul to approach the state of the Blessed; the more it advances, the more alive its faith becomes, and finally it becomes so penetrating that the soul can almost say: "I no longer believe, since I see and I experience."

2. The practice of the presence of God strengthens us in our hope; our hope grows in proportion to our knowledge; to the extent that our faith by this holy practice penetrates the mysteries of the divinity, to that extent does it discover in God a beauty that surpasses infinitely not only that of the bodies we see on earth but that of the most perfect souls and that of the angels; and so our hope grows and is strengthened, encouraged and sustained by the grandeur of this good which it desires to enjoy and that in some way it savors.

3. It inspires in the will a contempt of worldly things and inflames it with the fire of divine love which, coming from God, is a consuming fire that reduces to ashes whatever is opposed to it; and this soul thus inflamed can live only in the presence of its God, a presence which produces in the heart a holy ardor, a sacred eagerness and a fervent desire to see this God, loved, known, served and adored by all creatures.

---

[53]Ibid., pp. 111–12. Used by permission of Doubleday, a division of Bantam Doubleday Dell Publishing Group, Inc.

4. By the presence of God and by this interior gaze, the soul comes to know God in such a way that it passes almost all its life in making continual acts of love, adoration, contrition, trust, actions of grace, offering, petition and of all the most excellent virtues; and sometimes it even becomes one endless act because the soul is always engaged in staying in this divine presence. . . .

John (1703–91) and Charles (1707–88) Wesley

John and Charles Wesley were two of the three sons and seventeen children born in the Anglican manse of Epworth, England. Their parents, Samuel and Susanna Annesly Wesley, embraced the Church of England with the special sort of fervor that belongs to converts. Susanna came from a long line of Puritan Divines, and the spirituality the Wesleys imbibed under her supervision was a rich blend of Anglican "means" and Puritan "methods."

This synthesis was further enhanced as John and Charles went "up to Oxford." John was admitted at Lincoln College (1720) and Charles at Christ Church (1726). Drawing on the resources of the Bible, Anglicanism, the ancient church, and their own experiments with spiritual disciplines and social service, the "Oxford Holy Club" that formed around the Wesley brothers (1726–35) became the laboratory in which Methodist spirituality developed. Classics of Christian devotion, like Bishop Taylor's *Holy Living and Holy Dying*, Thomas a' Kempis's *The Christian Pattern* (*Imitation of Christ*), and William Law's *A Serious Call to a Devout and Holy Life* (1729), were especially formative for the Wesleys' development of their practical spirituality.

After brief service as Anglican missionaries to the Georgia colony, both Wesley brothers experienced conversions in May of 1738. While significant inquiry has been made into the theological significance of those events, it is clear that the Wesleys viewed their conversions as authentic turning points in their spiritual pilgrimage, and found in them an inner authentication of the Christian doctrines and practices they had affirmed and embraced from early childhood.[54] Their various ministries turned the Wesleys into mass evangelists; within months of their conversions, John and Charles Wesley found themselves barred from preaching in Anglican churches. Undaunted, they took their message to the streets and marketplaces of England, where they met unchurched masses. Those who responded to Wesleyan evangelism were urged to supplement their participation in the Church of England with membership in a local Methodist "society." As members of the society, they joined a "class" and promised to adhere to the practices that the Wesleys prescribed for them via their various "Rules," and "Minutes." It was the formative spiritual prac-

---

[54]Charles Yrigoyen, ed., *Celebrating the 250th Anniversary of Aldergate* (Madison, N.J.: General Commission on Archives and History, The United Methodist Church, 1988); and Randy Maddox, ed., *Aldersgate Reconsidered* (Nashville, Tenn.: Abingdon Press, 1990).

tices of the Methodist society and class meetings that distinguished one as a Methodist.

The Wesley brothers established a "partnership" that lasted more than fifty years. John was the organizational force behind the Methodist movement, Charles became its poet-laureate. John's genius for organization imbued the movement with the "methods" of spiritual formation learned at Epworth and Oxford. Charles's 9,000 hymns and sacred poems gave Methodist spirituality a congregational voice, and became a catechism for the unlettered.[55]

In the selections that follow, John Wesley's famous "heart-warming" experience is recounted in his own words. Charles Wesley's hymnological interpretation of the event sets it in the appropriate theological context. It echoes the first-person religious language found in John's journal, and reverberates with the exuberance of personal experience. The role of religious experience in the Wesleyan tradition was ably expressed in John Wesley's sermon based on the biblical text: "The Spirit of God witnesses to my spirit that I am a child of God." The most distinctive element of Wesleyan spirituality (and perhaps also the most divisive) is their understanding of sanctification as Christian Perfection. John Wesley's *Plain Account of Christian Perfection* (1777) was the standard treatment of this aspect; it was an autobiographical account that chronicled the brothers' recognition of Christian Perfection as that doctrine that epitomized vital Christian faith. The treatise also had the apologetic task of demonstrating that the Wesleyan doctrine was in accord with classical (especially Greek) Christianity, and that the brothers had not altered their perspective on this emphasis from the very beginning of their ministry together. Central to the Wesleyan approach to sanctification was their willingness to define sin "as a willful transgression of a known law of God." Sin, understood as an acknowledged and willful transgression can (perhaps) be overcome in this life; but that does not imply that a Christian is free from ignorance, error, mistakes, and temptations.

"I FELT MY HEART STRANGELY WARMED"[56]

In my return to England [from Georgia], January, 1738, being in imminent danger of death, and very uneasy on that account, I was strongly convinced that the cause of that uneasiness was unbelief; and that the gaining a true, living faith was the "one thing needful" for me. But still I fixed not this faith on its right object: I meant only faith in God, not faith in or through Christ. Again, I knew not that I was wholly void of this faith; but only thought, I had not enough of it. So that when Peter Böhler, whom God prepared for me as soon as I came to London, affirmed of true faith in Christ . . . that it had those two fruits inseparably attending it, "Dominion over sin, and constant Peace from a sense of forgiveness," I was

---

[55] John R. Tyson, ed., *Charles Wesley: A Reader* (New York: Oxford University Press, 1989), pp. 20–35.
[56] Reprinted from Thomas Jackson, ed., *The Works of John Wesley*, 14 vols. (London: The Wesleyan Methodist Conference, 1872, various reprints), Vol. I, pp. 101–4.

quite amazed and looked upon it as a new Gospel. If this was so, it was clear I had not faith. . . .

When I met Peter Böhler again, he consented to put the dispute upon the issue which I desired, namely, Scripture and experience. I first consulted the Scripture. But when I set aside the glosses of men, and simply considered the words of God, comparing them together, endeavouring to illustrate the obscure by the plainer passages; I found they all made against me, and was forced to retreat to my last hold: "that experience would never agree with the *literal interpretation* of those scriptures. Nor could I therefore allow it to be true, till I found some living witness of it." . . . [T]he next day he came again with three others, all of whom testified, of their own personal experience, that a true living faith in Christ is inseparable from a sense of pardon for all past, and freedom from all present, sins. They added with one mouth, that this faith was the gift, the free gift of God; and that he would surely bestow it upon every soul who earnestly and perseveringly sought it. I was now thoroughly convinced; and, by the grace of God, I resolved to seek it unto the end, 1. By absolutely renouncing all dependence, in whole or in part, upon *my own* works or righteousness; on which I had really grounded my hope of salvation, though I knew it not, from my youth up. 2. By adding to the constant use of all the other means of grace, continual prayer for this very thing, justifying, saving faith, a full reliance on the blood of Christ shed for *me*; a trust in Him, as my *Christ*, as *my* sole justification, sanctification, and redemption. . . .

In the evening [of Wednesday, May 24] I went very unwillingly to a society in Aldersgate-Street, where one was reading Luther's preface to the *Epistle to the Romans*. About a quarter before nine, while he was describing the change which God works in the heart through faith in Christ, I felt my heart strangely warmed. I felt that I did trust in Christ, Christ alone for salvation; and an assurance was given me, that He had taken away *my* sins, even *mine*, and saved *me* from the law of sin and death. . . .

After my return home, I was much buffeted with temptations; but cried out, and they fled away. They returned again and again. I as often lifted up my eyes, and He "sent me help from His holy place" [Ps 20:2]. And herein I found the difference between this and my former state chiefly consisted. I was striving, yea, fighting with all my might under the law, as well as under grace. But then I was sometimes, if not often, conquered; now, I was always conqueror. . . .

FREE GRACE[57]

Charles Wesley's journal entry for May 23, 1738, reported: "At nine I began an hymn upon my conversion, but was persuaded to break off, for fear of pride. Mr.

---

[57]George Osborn, ed., *Poetical Works of John and Charles Wesley*, 13 vols. (London: The Wesleyan Methodist Conference, 1868–72), Vol. I, pp. 105–6. First published in Wesley's *Hymns and Sacred Poems* (1739), this hymn is carried in an altered form in many modern hymnals.

Bray coming, encouraged me to proceed in spite of Satan. I prayed Christ to stand by me and finished the hymn."[58] And the next evening, ". . . Towards ten, my brother was brought in triumph by a troop of our friends, and declared, 'I believe.' We sang the hymn with great joy. . . ."[59] Several hymns vie for the ascription of "Wesley's conversion hymn"[60]: one of them, "Free Grace," captures the wonderment that accompanies the experience of God's grace. The focus is Christological; it stresses the incarnation and death of Christ. The hymn is framed in doxological, first-person language, and takes on the tone of an autobiographical confession.

1.   And can it be, that I should gain
            An interest in the Saviour's blood?
      Died He for me?—who caused His pain!
            For me?—who Him to death pursued.
      Amazing love! how can it be
      That Thou, my God, shouldst die for me?

2.   'Tis mystery all! th' Immortal dies!
            Who can explore His strange design?
      In vain the first-born seraph tries
            To sound the depths of Love Divine.
      'Tis mercy all! Let earth adore;
      Let angel minds inquire no more.

3.   He left His Father's throne above,
      (So free, so infinite His grace!)
      Emptied Himself of all but love,
      And bled for *Adam's* helpless race;
      'Tis mercy all, immense and free!
      For, O my God! it found out me!

4.   Long my imprison'd spirit lay,
      Fast bound in sin and nature's night:
      Thine eye diffused a quickening ray;
            I woke; the dungeon flamed with light;
      My chains fell off, my heart was free,
      I rose, went forth, and follow'd Thee.

5.   Still the small inward voice I hear,
            That whispers all my sins forgiven;
      Still the atoning blood is near,

---

[58]Thomas Jackson, ed., The Journal of the Rev. Charles Wesley, M.A., 2 vols. (London: John Mason, 1849; reprinted by Baker Book House, 1980), Vol. I, p. 94.
[59]Ibid., p. 95.
[60]Neil Dixon, "The Wesleys' Conversion Hymn," *Proceedings of the Wesley Historical Society*, Vol. 37, (Feb. 1967), pp. 43–47; Peter Grant, "The Wesleys' Conversion Hymn," *Proceedings of the Wesley Historical Society*, Vol. 35 (Sept. 1966), pp. 161–64.

That quench'd the wrath of hostile Heaven;
I feel the life His wounds impart;
I feel my Saviour in my heart.

6.   No condemnation now I dread,
        Jesus, and all in Him is mine:
    Alive in Him, my Living Head,
    And clothed in righteousness Divine,
    Bold I approach th' eternal throne,
    And claim the crown, through Christ, my own.

THE WITNESS OF THE SPIRIT[61]

"The Spirit itself beareth witness with our spirit, that we are the children of God" (Rom. 8:16). None who believe the Scriptures to be the word of God, can doubt the importance of such a truth as this;—a truth revealeth therein, not once only, not obscurely, not incidently; but frequently, and in that express terms; but solemnly and of set purpose, as denoting one of the peculiar privileges of the children of God.

And it is the more necessary to explain and defend this truth, because there is a danger on the right hand and on the left. If we deny it, there is a danger lest our religion degenerate into mere formality; lest, "having the form of godliness," we neglect, if not "deny, the power of it" [2 Tim 3:5]. If we allow it, but do not understand what we allow, we are liable to run into all the wildness of enthusiasm. It is therefore needful, in the highest degree, to guard those who fear God from both these dangers, by a scriptural and rational illustration and confirmation of this momentous truth. . . .

It more nearly concerns the Methodists, so called, clearly to understand, explain, and defend this doctrine; because it is one grand part of the testimony which God has given them to bear to all mankind. It is by His peculiar blessing upon them in searching the Scriptures, confirmed by the experience of His children, that this great evangelical truth has been recovered, which had been for many years well nigh lost and forgotten. . . .

I observed many years ago, "It is hard to find words in the language of men, to explain the deep things of God. Indeed there are none that will adequately express what the Spirit of God works in His children. But perhaps one might say, (desiring any who are taught of God, to correct, soften, or strengthen the expression), by the testimony of the Spirit, I mean, an inward impression on the soul, whereby the Spirit of God immediately and directly witnesses to my spirit, that I am a child of God; that Jesus Christ hath loved me, and given Himself for me; that all my sins are blotted out, and I, even I, am reconciled to God.

---

[61]Reprinted from Jackson, ed., *Works of John Wesley*, Vol. V, pp. 123–34, "The Witness of the Spirit, Discourse II."

After twenty years further consideration, I see no cause to retract any part of this. Neither do I conceive how any of these expressions may be altered, so as to make them more intelligible. I can only add, that if any of the children of God will point out any other expressions, which are more clear, or more agreeable to the word of God, I will readily lay these aside.

Meanwhile let it be observed, I do not mean hereby, that the Spirit of God testifies this by any outward voice; no, nor always by an inward voice, although he may do this sometimes. Neither do I suppose, that He always applies to the heart (though He often may) one or more texts of Scripture. But He so works upon the soul by His immediate influence, and by a strong, though inexplicable operation, that the stormy wind and troubled waves subside, and there is a sweet calm; the heart resting as in the arms of Jesus, and the sinner being clearly satisfied that God is reconciled, that all his "iniquities are forgiven, and his sins covered" [Ps 85:2].

Now what is the matter of dispute concerning this? Not whether there be a witness or testimony of the Spirit. Not whether the Spirit does testify with our spirit, that we are the children of God. None can deny this, without flatly contradicting the Scriptures, and charging a lie upon God of truth. Therefore, that there is a testimony of the Spirit is acknowledged by all parties.

. . . But an abundance of objections have been made to this: the chief of which it may be well to consider. It is objected . . . "Experience is not sufficient to prove a doctrine which is not founded on Scripture." This is undoubtedly true; and it is an important truth; but it does not affect the present question; for it has been shown, that this doctrine is founded on Scripture: Therefore experience is properly alleged to confirm it. . . .

NATURE, DESIGN, AND GENERAL RULES OF THE UNITED SOCIETIES[62]

1. In the later end of the year 1739, eight or ten persons came to me in London, who appeared to be deeply convinced of sin, and earnestly groaning for redemption. They desired . . . that I would spend some time with them in prayer, and advise them how to flee from the wrath to come; which they saw continually hanging over their heads. That we might have more time for this great work, I appointed a day when they might all come together every week, namely, on Thursday, in the evening. To these . . . I gave those advices, from time to time, which I judged most needful for them; and we always concluded our meeting with prayer suited to their several necessities.

2. This was the rise of the United Society, first in London, and then in other places. Such a society is no other than "a company of men having the form and seek-

---

[62]Ibid., Vol. VIII, pp. 269–71.

ing the power of godliness, united in order to pray together, to receive the word of exhortation, and to watch over one another in love, that they may help each other work out their salvation."

3. That it may the more easily be discerned, whether they are indeed working out their own salvation, each society is divided into smaller companies, called *classes*, according to their respective places of abode. There are about twelve persons in every class; one of whom is styled *the Leader*. It is his business, (i) to see each person in his class once a week at least, in order to inquire how their souls prosper; to advise, reprove, comfort, or exhort, as occasion may require; to receive what they are willing to give toward the relief of the poor. (ii) To meet the Minister and the Stewards of the society once a week; in order to inform the Minister of any that are sick, or of any that walk disorderly, and will not be reproved; to pay to the Stewards what they have received of their several classes in the week preceding; and to show their account of what each person has contributed.

4. There is one only condition previously required in those who desire admission into these societies—a desire "to flee from the wrath to come, to be saved from their sins" [Mt 3:7]. But, wherever this is really fixed in the soul, it will be shown by its fruits. It is therefore expected of all who continue therein, that they should continue to evidence their desire of salvation,

First, by doing no harm, by avoiding evil in every kind; especially that which is most generally practiced: Such is, the taking of the name of God in vain; the profaning the day of the Lord, either by doing ordinary work thereon, or by buying or selling; drunkenness, buying or selling spirituous liquors, or drinking them, unless in cases of extreme necessity; fighting, quarreling, brawling; brother going to law with brother; returning evil for evil, or railing for railing; . . . the giving or taking things on usury, that is, unlawful interest; uncharitable or unprofitable conversation, particularly speaking evil of Magistrates or of Ministers; doing to others as we would not that they should do unto us; doing what we know is not for the glory of God, as the "putting on of gold or costly apparel;" the taking such diversions as cannot be used in the name of the Lord Jesus; the singing those songs or reading those books, which do not tend to the knowledge or love of God; softness, and needless self-indulgence; laying up treasures upon earth; borrowing without a probability of paying; or taking up goods without a probability of paying for them.

5. It is expected of all who continue in these societies, that they should continue to evidence their desire for salvation,

Secondly, doing good, by being, in every kind, merciful after their power; as they have opportunity, doing good of every possible sort, and as is possible, to all men;—to their bodies, of the ability which God giveth, by giving food to the hungry, by clothing the naked, by visiting or helping them that are sick, or in prison;—to their souls, by instructing, reproving, or exhorting all they have any intercourse with. . . . By doing good especially to them that are of the household of faith, or groaning to be; employing them preferably to others, buying one of another; helping each other in business; and so much the more, because the world will love its own, and them only: By all possible diligence and frugality, that the gospel be not blamed: By running with patience the race that is set before them, "denying themselves, and taking up their cross daily" [Lk 9:23]; "submitting to bear the reproach of Christ, to be as filth and offscouring of the world" [1 Cor 4:13]; and looking that men should "say all manner of evil of them falsely for the Lord's sake" [Mt 5:11].

6. It is expected of all who desire to continue in these societies that they should continue to evidence their desire of salvation. *Thirdly,* by attending upon all the ordinances of God. Such are, the public worship of God; the ministry of the word, either read or expounded; the supper of the Lord; family and private prayer; searching the Scriptures; and fasting, or abstinence.

7. These are the General Rules of our societies; all which we are taught of God to observe, even in His written Word, the only rule, and the sufficient rule, both of our faith and practice. And all these, we know, His Spirit writes upon every truly awakened heart. If there be any among us who observe them not, who habitually break any of them, let it be made known unto them who watch over that soul as they that must give an account. We will admonish him of the error of his ways; we will bear with him for a season; but then if he repent not, he hath no place among us. We have delivered our souls. [signed] John Wesley, Charles Wesley
May 1, 1743

THE MEANS OF GRACE[63]

I. *The Instituted [Means of Grace] Are,*

1. *Prayer*; private, family, [and] public; consisting of deprecation, petition, intercession, and thanksgiving. Do you use each of these? Do you use private prayer every morning and evening? If you can, at five in the evening; and the hour before or after morning preaching? . . . Do you ask everywhere "Have you family prayer?" Do you retire at five o'clock?

---

[63]Reprinted from Wesley's "Large Minutes" of 1746. Cf. Jackson, ed., *Works of John Wesley*, Vol. VIII, pp. 322–24.

2. *Searching the Scriptures* by, (i) reading; constantly, some part of [them] every day; regularly, all the Bible in order; carefully with the *Notes*[64]; seriously with prayer before and after; fruitfully, immediately practicing what you learn there? (ii) meditating: at set times? by any rule? (iii) hearing: Every morning? carefully; with prayer before, and after; immediately putting into practice? Have you a New Testament always about you?

3. *The Lord's Supper*: Do you use this at every opportunity? with solemn prayer before; with earnest and deliberate self devotion?

4. *Fasting*: How do you fast every Friday?

5. *Christian Conference*: Are you convinced how important and how difficult it is to "order your conversation right" [Ps 50:23]? Is it "always in grace seasoned with salt? meet to minister grace to the hearers" [Col 4:6]? Do not you converse too long at a time? Is not an hour commonly enough? Would it not be well always to have a determinate end in view; and to pray before and after it?

II. *Prudential Means* as we may use either as common Christians, as Methodists, as Preachers, or as Assistants. . . . These means may be used without fruit; but there are some means which cannot; namely, watching, denying ourselves, taking up our cross, exercise of the presence of God.

1. Do you steadily watch against the world, the devil, yourselves, your besetting sin?

2. Do you deny yourself every useless pleasure of sense, imagination, honour? Are you temperate in all things, for instance in food: Do you use only that kind and that degree which is best both for your body and soul? Do you see the necessity of this?

3. Do you eat no flesh suppers? no late suppers?

4. Do you eat no more at each meal than is necessary? Are you not heavy or drowsy after dinner?

5. Do you use only that kind and that degree of drink which is best both for your body and your soul?

6. Do you drink water? Why not? Did you ever? Why did you leave it off? If not for health, when will you begin again?

7. How often do you drink wine or ale? every day? Do you want [e.g., "need"] it?

8. Wherein do you "take up your cross daily" [Lk 9:23]? Do you cheerfully bear your cross (whatever is grievous to nature) as a gift from God, and labour to profit thereby?

9. Do you endeavour to set God always before you; to see His eye continu-

---

[64]John Wesley, *Notes Upon the Old and New Testaments*, 4 vols. (Bristol: William Pine, 1765; reprinted by Schmul: Salem, Ohio, 1975).

ally fixed upon you? Never can you use these means but a blessing will ensue. And the more you use them, the more will you grow in grace.

CHRISTIAN PERFECTION[65]

15. . . . Perhaps the general prejudice against Christian Perfection may chiefly arise from a misapprehension of the nature of it. We willingly allow, and continually declare, there is no such perfection in this life, as implies either a dispensation from doing good, and attending all the ordinances of God, or a freedom from ignorance, mistake, temptation, and a thousand infirmities necessarily connected with flesh and blood. . . .

But whom then do you mean by "one that is perfect?" We mean one in whom is "the mind which was in Christ" [Phil 2:5], and who so "walketh as Christ also walked;" a man "that hath clean hands and a pure heart" [Ps 24:4], or that is "cleansed from all filthiness of flesh and spirit" [2 Cor 7]; one in whom is "no occasion of stumbling" [1 Jn 1:2], and who, accordingly, "does not commit sin" [1 Jn 2:1]. To declare this a little more particularly: We understand by that scriptural expression, "a perfect man," one in whom God hath fulfilled His faithful word, "From all your filthiness and from all your idols I will cleanse you: I will also save you from all your uncleanness" [Ezek 36:25]. We understand hereby, one whom God hath "sanctified throughout in body, soul, and spirit;" one who "walketh in the light as He is in the light, in whom is no darkness at all; the blood of Jesus Christ His Son having cleansed him from all sin."

This man can now testify to all mankind, "I am crucified with Christ: Nevertheless I live; yet not I, but Christ liveth in me" [Gal 2:20]. He is "holy as God who called" him "is holy," both in heart and "in all manner of conversation." He "loveth the Lord his God with all his heart," and serveth Him "with all his strength." He "loveth his neighbor," every man, "as himself;" yea, "as Christ loveth us;" them, in particular that "despitefully use him and persecute him, because they know not the Son, neither the Father." Indeed his soul is all love, filled with "bowels of mercies, kindness, meekness, gentleness, longsuffering" [Col 3:12]. And his life agreeth thereto, full of "the work of faith, the patience of hope, the labour of love" [1 Thes 1:3]. "And whatsoever" he "doeth either in word or deed," he "doeth it in the name," in the love and power "of the Lord Jesus." In a word, he doeth "the will of God on earth, as it is done in heaven."

This it is to be a perfect man, to be "sanctified throughout;" even "to have a heart so all-flaming with the love of God," (to use Archbishop Usher's words), "as continually to offer up every thought, word, and work, as a spir-

---

[65]Reprinted from John Wesley's *Plain Account of Christian Perfection*, in Jackson, ed., *Works of John Wesley*, Vol. VIII, pp. 366–449.

itual sacrifice, acceptable to God through Christ" [1 Pet 2:5]. In every thought of our hearts, in every word of our tongues, in every work of our hands, to "show forth His praise, who hath called us out of darkness into His marvelous light" [1 Pet 2:9]. O that both we, and all who seek the Lord Jesus in sincerity, may thus "be made perfect in one!" This is the doctrine which we preached from the beginning, and which we preach at this day. . . .

19. At the Conference in the year 1759, perceiving some danger that a diversity of sentiments should insensibly steal in among us, we again largely considered this doctrine; and soon after I published "Thoughts on Christian Perfection". . . .

Question: What is Christian Perfection? *Answer*: The loving God with all our heart, mind, soul, and strength. This implies, that no wrong temper, none contrary to love, remains in the soul; and that all the thoughts, words, and actions, are governed by pure love.

Q. Do you affirm, that this perfection excludes all infirmities, ignorance, and mistake? *A.* I continually affirm the contrary, and always have done so.

Q. But how can every thought, word, and work, be governed by pure love, and the man be subject at the same time to ignorance and mistake? *A.* I see no contradiction here: "A man may be filled with pure love, and still be liable to mistake." Indeed I do not expect to be freed from actual mistakes, till this mortal puts on immortality. I believe this to be a natural consequence of the soul's dwelling in flesh and blood. For we cannot now think at all, but by the meditation of those bodily organs which have suffered equally with the rest of our frame. And hence we cannot avoid sometimes thinking wrong, till this corruptible shall have put on incorruption. But we may carry this further yet. A mistake in judgment may possibly occasion a mistake in practice. . . . Yet, where every word and action springs from love, such a mistake is not properly a sin. However, it cannot bear the rigour of God's justice, but needs the atoning blood. . . .

Q. But still, if they live without sin, does not this exclude the necessity of a Mediator? At least, is it not plain that they stand no longer in need of Christ in his priestly office? *A.* Far from it. None feel their need of Christ like these; none so entirely depend upon Him. For Christ does not give life to the soul separate from, but in and with, Himself. Hence His words are equally true of all men, in whatsoever state of grace they are; "As the branch cannot bear fruit of itself, except it abide in the vine; no more can ye, except ye abide in me: Without" (or separate from) "me ye can do nothing."

In every state we need Christ in the following respects. (1) Whatever grace we receive, it is a free gift from Him. (2) We receive it as His purchase, merely in consideration of the price He paid. (3) We have this grace, not only from Christ, but in Him. For our perfection is not like that of a tree, which flourishes by the sap derived from its own root, but, as was said before, like that of a branch which, united to the vine, bears fruit; but, severed from it, is dried up and withered. (4) All our blessings, temporal, spiritual, and eternal, depend on His intercession for us, which is one branch of His priestly office, whereof therefore we have always equal need. (5) The best of men still need Christ in His priestly office, to atone for their omissions, their short-comings, (as some improperly speak,) their mistakes in judgment and practice, and their defects of various kinds. For these are all deviations from the perfect law, and consequently need an atonement. Yet that they are not properly sins, we apprehend may appear from the words of St. Paul, "He that loveth, hath fulfilled the law; for love is the fulfilling of the law" (Rom. 13:10). Now, mistakes, and whatever infirmities necessarily flow from the corruptible state of the body, are noway contrary to love; nor therefore, in the Scripture sense, sin.

To explain myself a little further on this head: (1) Not only sin, properly so called, (that is, a voluntary transgression of a known law), but sin, improperly so called, (that is, an involuntary transgression of a divine law, known or unknown), needs the atoning blood [of Christ]. (2) I believe there is not such perfection in this life as excluded these involuntary transgressions which I apprehend to be naturally consequent on the ignorance and mistakes inseparable from mortality. (3) Therefore *sinless perfection* is a phrase I never use, lest I should seem to contradict myself. (4) I believe, a person filled with the love of God is still liable to these involuntary transgressions. (5) Such transgressions you may call sins, if you please: I do not, for the reasons above-mentioned. . . .

Q. But how can a liableness to mistake consist with perfect love? Is not a person who is perfected in love every moment under its influence? And can any mistake flow from pure love? A. I answer, (1) Many mistakes may consist with pure love; (2) Some may accidently flow from it: I mean, love itself may incline us to mistake. The pure love of our neighbor, springing from the love of God, thinketh no evil, believeth and hopeth all things. Now, this very temper, unsuspicious, ready to believe and hope the best of all men, may occasion our thinking some men to better than they really are. Here then is a manifest mistake, accidently flowing from pure love. . . .

WRESTLING JACOB[66]

This was one of Charles Wesley's most popular hymns. Using the imagery of the Jacob narrative (Gen 32), Wesley turned the patriarch's struggle for an angel's "blessing" into an account of the Christian's struggle for Christian Perfection. When John Wesley announced his brother's recent death at the 1788 Methodist annual conference he recalled: "Dr. [Isaac] Watts did not scruple to say, that 'that single poem, *Wrestling Jacob*, was worth all the verses he himself had written.'"[67] The hymn epit-

---

[66]Osborn, ed. *Poetical Works*, Vol. II, pp. 173–76. The hymn was first published in Wesley's *Hymns and Sacred Poems* (1742 edition), and was subsequently reprinted several times and included in the standard Methodist hymnbook, *A Collection of Hymns for the Use of the People Called Methodists* (1780).
[67]Jackson, ed., *Works of John Wesley*, Vol. XIII, p. 514.

omizes Charles Wesley's poetical hermeneutic and illustrates the interconnection between the Wesleyan hymns and Methodist spirituality.[68]

1.   Come, O Thou Traveller unknown,
      Whom still I hold but cannot see,
    My company before is gone,
      And I am left with Thee;
    With Thee all night I mean to stay,
    And wrestle till the break of day.

2.   I need not tell Thee who I am,
      My misery or sin declare,
    Thyself hast call'd me by my name,
      Look on Thy hands, and read it there;
    But who, I ask Thee, and tell me now.

3.   In vain Thou strugglest to get free,
      I never will unloose my hold;
    Art thou the Man that died for me?
      The secret of Thy love unfold;
    Wrestling I will not let Thee go
    Till I Thy name, Thy nature know.

4.   Wilt Thou not yet to me reveal
      Thy new, unutterable name?
    Tell me, I still beseech Thee, tell;
      To know it now resolved I am;
    Wrestling I will not let Thee go
    Till I Thy name, Thy nature know.

5.   'Tis all in vain to hold Thy tongue,
      Or touch the hollow of my thigh,
    Though every sinew be unstrung,
      Out of my arms Thou shalt not fly,
    Wrestling I will not let Thee go
    Till I Thy name, Thy nature know.

6.   What though my shrinking flesh complain,
      And murmur to contend so long,
    I rise superior to my pain,
      When I am weak then I am strong;
    And when my all of strength shall fall,
    I shall with the God-man prevail.

7.   My strength is gone, my nature dies,
      I sink beneath Thy weighty hand,

---

[68]Cf. John R. Tyson, "The Transfiguration of Scripture: Charles Wesley's Poetical Hermeneutic," *The Asbury Theological Journal*, Vol. 47 (No. 2, Fall 1992), pp. 17–41.

Faint to revive, and fall to rise,
　I fall, and yet by faith I stand,
I stand, and will not let Thee go,
Till I Thy name, Thy nature know.

8.　Yield to me now; for I am weak,
　　But confident in self-despair;
　Speak to my heart, in blessings speak,
　　Be conquer'd by my instant prayer;
　Speak, or Thou never hence shall move,
　And tell me if Thy name is Love.

9.　'Tis Love! 'tis Love! Thou diedst for me,
　　I hear Thy whisper in my heart;
　The morning breaks, the shadows flee;
　　Pure UNIVERSAL LOVE Thou art;
　To me, to all Thy bowels move[69];
　Thy nature, and Thy name is Love.

10.　My prayer hath power with God; the grace
　　Unspeakable I now receive,
　Through faith I see Thee face to face;
　　I see Thee face to face, and live;
　In vain I have not wept and strove;
　Thy nature and Thy name is Love.

11.　I know Thee, Saviour, who Thou art,
　　Jesus, the feeble sinner's Friend;
　Jesus, the feeble sinner's Friend;
　　But stay, and love me to the end;
　Thy mercies never shall remove;
　Thy nature, and Thy name is Love.

12.　The Sun of Righteousness on me
　　Hath rose with healing in His wings;
　Wither'd my nature's strength, from Thee
　　My soul its life and succour brings;
　My help is all laid up above;
　Thy nature, and Thy name is Love.

13.　Contended now upon my thigh
　　I halt, till life's short journey end;
　All helplessness, all weakness, I
　　On Thee alone for strength depend,
　Nor have I power from Thee to move;
　Thy nature, and Thy name is Love.

---

[69] As in Song of Solomon 5:4 (King James Version).

14.   Lame as I am, I take the prey,
         Hell, earth, and sin with ease o'ercome;
      I leap for joy, pursue my way,
         And as a bounding hart fly home,
      Through all eternity to prove,
      Thy nature, and Thy name is Love.

Jonathan Edwards (1703–58)

Sometimes called "America's first theologian," Jonathan Edwads was born in East Windsor, Connecticut. He was educated at Yale and graduated in 1720, before he had reached the age of seventeen. It was about that same time that Edwards experienced his "new apprehension of Christ." After a brief pastorate in New York City and two years as a tutor at Yale, he was ordained as a Congregational minister and assisted his grandfather, Solomon Stoddard, in the pastorate of Northampton, Massachusetts. In 1727 Stoddard died and Edwards served as senior pastor until 1750. His ministry at Northampton was a productive time for Edwards; through his fiery sermons, he became one of the driving forces behind the First Great Awakening (1734–44), and his *Sinners in the Hands of an Angry God* (1741) epitomized the preaching of the period. His *Treatise on Religious Affections* (1746) was also linked to the First Great Awakening, since it studied the effects that conversion should have upon the inner state of Christians.

In 1750, after twenty-three years of ministry, Jonathan Edwards was ousted from the Northampton pastorate because of a controversy that developed about church membership. From 1751–58 he served as pastor of the Stockbridge, (Mass.) Congregational Church, and as a missionary to the Housatonic Indians. During this period Edwards wrote several of his most philosophical and theological works, including *Freedom of the Will* (1751), *The Nature of Virtue* (1755), and *Original Sin* (1758). In 1758 he accepted a call to the presidency of Princeton College, only to die of smallpox (which he received through a preventive inoculation) five weeks after his inauguration.

Edwards was an authentic son of the Puritans and their Calvinistic theology. He is remembered as a powerful preacher of conversion and an ardent cultivater of the effects of conversion in a person's spiritual life.

A NEW APPREHENSION OF CHRIST[70]

   . . . The first instance that I remember of that sort of inward, sweet delight in God and divine things that I have lived much in since, was on reading those

---

[70]Reprinted from Jonathan Edwards, *The Works of President Edwards in Four Volumes: A Reprint of the Worcester Edition.* (New York: Leavitt, Trow, and Co., 1844), Vol. I, pp. 9, 11–12, 19, 26. The account of his conversion is reconstructed by fitting selections from his diary, "Resolutions" and "Account of His Conversion," into a chronological order.

words, 1 Tim. i. 17, "Now unto the King eternal, immortal, invisible, the only wise God, be honor and glory forever and ever, Amen." As I read the words, there came into my soul, and was as it were diffused through it, a sense of the glory of the Divine Being; a new sense, quite different from any thing I ever experienced before. Never any words of Scripture seemed to me as these words did. I thought with myself, how excellent a Being that was, and how happy I should be, if I might enjoy that God, and be rapt up to Him in heaven, and be as it were swallowed up in Him forever! I kept saying, and as it were singing over these words of Scripture to myself; and went to pray to God that I might enjoy Him, and prayed in a manner quite different from what I used to do; with a new sort of affection. But it never came into my thought, that there was any thing spiritual or of a saving nature, in this.

From about that time, I began to have a new kind of apprehensions and ideas of Christ, and the work of redemption, and the glorious way of salvation by Him. An inward, sweet sense of these things, at times, came into my heart; and my soul was led away in pleasant views and contemplations of them. And my mind was greatly engaged to spend my time in reading and meditating on Christ, on the beauty and excellency of His person, and the lovely way of salvation by free grace in Him. I found no books so delightful to me, as those that treated of these subjects. . . .

My sense of divine things seemed gradually to increase, until I went to preach at New York, which was about a year and a half after they began; and while I was there, I felt them, very sensibly, in a much higher degree than I had done before. My longings after God and holiness were much increased. Pure and humble, holy and heavenly Christianity, appeared exceeding amiable to me. I felt a burning desire to be in every thing a complete Christian; and conformed to the blessed image of Christ; and that I might live, in all things, according to the pure, sweet and blessed rules of the gospel. I had an eager thirsting after progress in these things; which put me upon pursuing and pressing after them. It was my continual strife day and night, and constant inquiry, how I should *be* more holy, and *live* more holily, and more becoming a child of God, and a disciple of Christ. I now sought an increase of grace and holiness, and a holy life, with much more earnestness than ever I sought grace before I had it. I used to be continually examining myself, and studying and contriving for likely ways and means, how I should live holily, with far greater diligence and earnestness, than ever I pursued any thing in my life; but yet with too great a dependence on my own strength; which afterwards proved a great damage to me. My experience had not then taught me, as it has done since, my extreme feebleness and impotence, every manner of way; and the bottomless depths of secret corruption and deceit there was in my heart. However, I went on with my eager pursuit after more holiness, and conformity to Christ. . . .

Saturday, Jan. 12 [1723], in the morning. I have this day solemnly renewed my baptismal covenant and self-dedication, which I renewed when I was received into the communion of the church. I have been before God; and have given myself, all that I am and have, to God, so that I am not in any respect my own: I can claim no right in myself, no right in this understanding, this will, these affections that are in me; neither have I any right to this body, or any of its members: no right to this tongue, these hands, nor feet; no right to these senses, these eyes, these ears, this smell or taste. I have given myself clear away, and have not retained any thing as my own. I have been to God this morning, and told Him that I gave myself *wholly* to Him. I have given every power to Him; so that for the future, I will challenge or claim no right in myself, in any respect. I have expressly promised Him, and do now promise Almighty God, that by His grace I will not. I have this morning told Him, that I did take Him for my whole portion and felicity, looking on nothing else as any part of my happiness, nor acting as if it were; and his law for the constant rule of my obedience; and would fight with all my might against the world, the flesh, and the devil, to the end of my life. And did believe in Jesus Christ, and receive Him as a Prince and a Saviour; and would adhere to the faith and obedience of the gospel, how hazardous and difficult soever the profession and practice of it may be. That I did receive the blessed Spirit as my teacher, sanctifier, and holy comforter; and cherish all His motions to enlighten, purify, confirm, comfort, and assist me. This I have done. And I pray God, for the sake of Christ, to look upon it as a self-dedication; and to receive me now as entirely His own, and deal with me in all respects as such; whether He afflicts me or prospers me, or whatever He pleases to do with me, who am His. Now, henceforth I am not to act in any respect as my own. I shall act as my own, if I ever make use of any of my powers to any thing that is not to the glory of God, or do not make the glorifying of Him my whole and entire business . . . . This day made the 42d and 43d Resolutions.[71]

. . . Though it seems to me, in some respects, I was a far better Christian, for two or three years after my first conversion, than I am now; and lived in a more constant delight and pleasure; yet, of late years, I have had a more full and constant sense of the absolute sovereignty of God, and a delight in that sovereignty; and have had more of a sense of the glory of Christ, as a Mediator revealed in the gospel. On one Saturday night, in particular, I had such a discovery of the excellency of the gospel above all other doctrines that I could not but say to myself, "this is my chosen light, my chosen doctrine;" and of Christ, "this is my chosen Prophet." It appeared sweet, beyond all expression to follow Christ, and to be taught, and enlightened, and instructed by Him; to learn of Him, and to live to Him. Another Saturday night (January, 1739) I had such a sense, how sweet and blessed a thing it was to walk in the way of duty; to do that which was right and meet to be done, and agreeable to the holy mind of God; that it caused me to break forth into a kind of loud weeping, which held me some time, so that I was forced to shut myself up, and fasten the doors. I could not but, as it were, cry out, "How happy are they which do that which is right in the sight of God! They are blessed indeed, they are the happy ones!" I had, at the same time, a very affect-

---

[71]Edwards wrote: "42. Resolved, frequently to renew the dedication of myself to God, which was made at my baptism; which I solemnly renewed, when I was received into the communion of the church; and which I have solemnly ratified this twelfth day of January, 1723. 43. Resolved, never to act as if I were any way my own, but entirely and altogether God's."

ing sense, how meet and suitable it was that God should govern the world, and order all things according to His own pleasure; and I rejoiced in it, that God reigned, and that His will was done.

RELIGIOUS AFFECTIONS:[72]

. . .[T]he proposition or doctrine, that I would raise from these words[73] [1 Pet 1:8], is this Doctrine. *True religion, in great part, consists in holy affections.* We see that the apostle, in observing and remarking the operations and exercises of religion in the Christian he wrote to, wherein their religion appeared to be true and of the right kind, when it had its greatest trial of what sort it was, being tried by persecution as gold is tried in the fire, and when their religion not only proved true, but was most pure, and cleansed from its dross and mixtures of that which was not true, and when religion appeared in them most in its genuine excellency and native beauty, and was found to praise, and honor and glory; he singles out the religious affections of *love* and *joy*, that were then in exercise in them: these are the exercises of religion he takes notice of, wherein their religion did thus appear true and pure, and in its proper glory.

Here I would: (1) Show what is intended by the affections. (2) Observe some things which make it evident, that a great part of religion lies in the affections.

It may be inquired, what the affections of the mind are? I answer: The affections are no other than the more vigorous and sensible exercises of the inclination and will of the soul. God has endued the soul with two faculties: one that is by which it is capable of perception and speculation, or by which it discerns, views, and judges of things; which is called the understanding.

The other faculty is that by which the soul does not merely perceive and view things, but is in some way inclined to respect the things it views or considers; either is inclined *to* them, or is disinclined and averse *from* them; or is the faculty by which the soul does not behold things, as an indifferent unaffected spectator, but either as liking or disliking, pleased or displeased, approving or rejecting. This faculty is called by various names; it is sometimes called the *inclination*; and, as it has respect to the actions that are determined and governed by it, [it] is called the *will*: and the mind, with regard to the exercises of this faculty, is often called the *heart*.

The exercises of this faculty are of two sorts; either those by which the soul is carried out towards things that are in view, in approving of them, being pleased with them, and inclined to them; or those in which the soul opposes the things that are in view, in disapproving of them, and in being displeased with them, averse from them, and rejecting them.

---

[72]Reprinted from Edwards, *The Works of President Edwards,*. Vol. III, pp. 2–7, with omissions.
[73]1 Peter 1:8, "Whom having not seen, ye love; in whom, though now ye see him not, yet believing, ye rejoice with joy unspeakable, and full of glory."

And the exercises of the inclination and will of the soul are various in their kinds, so they are much more various in their degrees. . . . [F]rom whence it comes to pass, that the mind, with regard to the exercises of this faculty, perhaps in all nations and ages, is called the *heart*. And, it is to be noted, that they are these more vigorous and sensible exercises of this faculty that are called the *affections*. The will, and the affections of the soul, are not two faculties; the affections are not essentially distinct from the will, nor do they differ from the mere actings of the will, and inclinations of the soul, but only in the liveliness and sensibleness of exercise. . . .

As all the exercises of the inclination and will, are either in approving and liking, or disapproving and rejecting; so the affections are of two sorts; they are those by which the soul is carried out to what is in view, cleaving to it, or seeking it; or those by which it is averse from it, and opposes it. Of the former sort are love, hope, joy, gratitude, complacence. Of the latter kind are hatred, fear, anger, grief, and such like . . . . And there are some affections wherein there is a composition of each of the aforementioned kinds of acting of the will; as in the affection of *pity*, there is something of the former kind, towards the person suffering, and something of the latter towards what he [or she] suffers. And so in zeal, there is in it high approbation of some person or thing, together with vigorous opposition to what is conceived to be contrary to it.

II. What has been said of the nature of the affections makes this evident, and it may be sufficient, without adding anything further, to put this matter out of doubt; for who will deny that true religion consists in a great measure, in vigorous and lively actings of the inclinations and will of the soul, or in the fervent exercises of the heart? . . .

If we be not good earnest in religion, and our wills and inclinations be not strongly exercised, we are nothing. The things of religion are so great, that there can be no suitableness in the exercises of our hearts, to their nature and importance, unless they be lively and powerful. In nothing is vigor in the actings of our inclinations so requisite, as in religion; and in nothing is luke-warmness so odious. True religion is evermore a powerful thing; and the power of it appears, in the first place in the inward exercises of it in the heart, where is the principal and original seat of it. Hence true religion is called the *power of godliness*, in distinction from the external appearances of it, that are the *form* of it, 2 Tim. 3:5, "Having a form of godliness, but denying the power of it." The Spirit of God, in those that have sound and solid religion, is a spirit of powerful holy affection; and therefore, God is said "to have given the Spirit of power, and of love, and of a sound mind," 2 Tim. 1:7. And such, when they receive the Spirit of God, in his sanctifying and saving influences are said to be "baptized with the Holy Ghost, and with fire;" by reason of the power and fervor of those exercises the Spirit of God excites in their hearts, whereby their heart, when grace is in exercise, may be said to "burn within them;" as is said of the disciples, Luke 24:32. . . .

The Author of the human nature has not only given affections to men, but has made them very much the spring of men's actions. As the affections do not only necessarily belong to the human nature, but are a very great part of it; so (inasmuch as by regenerations persons are renewed in the whole man, and sanctified throughout) holy affections do not only necessarily belong to true religion, but are a very great part of it. And as true religion is of a practical nature, and God hath so constituted the human nature, that the affections are very much the spring of men's actions, this also shows, that true religion must consist very much in the affections.

Such is man's nature, that he is very inactive, any otherwise than he is influenced by some affection, either love, or hatred, desire, hope, fear, or some other. These affections we see to be the springs that set men agoing, in all the affairs of life, and engage them in all their pursuits: these are the things that put men forward, and carry them along, in all their worldly business; and especially are men excited and animated by these, in all affairs wherein they are earnestly engaged, and which they pursue with vigor. We see the world of mankind to be exceedingly busy and active; and the affections of men are the springs of the motion: take away all love and hatred, al hope and fear, all anger, zeal, and affectionate desire, and the world would be, in a great measure motionless and dead; there would be no such things as activity amongst mankind, or any earnest pursuit whatsoever. It is affection that engages the covetous man, and him that is greedy of worldly profits, in his pursuits; and it is by the affections, that the ambitious man is put forward in his pursuit of worldly glory; and it is the affections also that actuate the voluptuous man, in his pursuit of pleasure and sensual delights: the world continues, from age to age, in a continual commotion and agitation, in a pursuit of these things; but take away all affection, and the spring of all this motion would be gone, and the motion itself would cease. And as in worldly things, worldly affections are very much the spring of men's motion and action; so in religious matters, the spring of their actions is very much religious affection: he that has doctrinal knowledge and speculation only, without affection, never is engaged in the business of religion.

. . . I am bold to assert, that there never was an considerable change wrought in the mind or conversation of any person, by anything of a religious nature, that ever he [or she] read, heard, or saw, that had not his [or her] affections moved. Never was a natural man engaged earnestly to seek his salvation; never were any such brought to cry after wisdom, and lift up their voice for understanding, and to wrestle with God in prayer for mercy; and never was one humbled, and brought to the foot of God, from any thing that ever he [or she] heard or imagined of his [or her] own unworthiness and deserving of God's displeasure; nor was ever one induced to fly for refuge unto Christ, while his heart remained unaffected. Nor was there ever a saint awakened out of a cold, lifeless frame, or recovered from a declining state in religion, and brought back from a lamentable departure from God, without having his [or her] heart affected. And in a word, there never was any thing considerable brought to pass in the heart of any man living, by the things of religion, that had not his heart deeply affected by those things. The holy Scriptures do everywhere place religion very much in the affection; such as fear, hope, love, hatred, desire, joy, sorrow, gratitude, compassion, and zeal. . . .

Hannah More (1745–1833)

Hannah More was the daughter of a middle-class school teacher, born in Stapelton (near Bristol), England. She was educated in the school operated by her father and sisters; by the time she was twenty she had also become a teacher in the same school. More began writing verse and drama at a very early age. By 1762 she had completed her first published work, a pastoral drama, *The Search for Happiness.*

In the early 1770s she relocated to London to pursue her interest in writing drama and became involved in the social life of the intellectual salons of the "blue stockings," where she met and conversed with David Garrick and other literary lights of the period.[74] Garrick's death, in 1779, seemed to mark a turning point in the life of Hannah More. She renounced the stage and returned to her native region, taking up residence in Cowslip Green (near Bristol). She soon became associated with the Clapham Sect, a reforming group of Evangelical Christians, and turned her attention almost exclusively toward religious and reformatory topics. Among her associates were William Cowper, John Newton, and William Wilberforce. More became the chief propagandist of the Clapham Sect. She wrote hundreds of pamphlets advocating the abolition of slavery, the equality of women, and the improvement of English social conditions. More was influential in the development of the Sunday School movement, and was one of the most popular religious writers of her period.

Among her significant religious works were *Practical Piety* (1811), *Christian Morals* (1812), *Character and Practical Writings of St. Paul* (1815), and *Reflections on Prayer* (1819). The subtitle of *Practical Piety, The Influence of the Religion of the Heart on the Conduct of Life*, describes well the thrust of her work. Hannah More stressed that Christianity is "an internal principle" that bears very practical fruit in the conduct of human life. Her work is clearly shaped by its intellectual context since More attacked the premises of Deism, and also defended the doctrine of original sin and other elements of classical Christianity.

AN INTERNAL PRINCIPLE[75]

Christianity bears all the marks of a divine original. It came down from heaven, and its gracious purpose is to carry us up thither. Its author is God. It was foretold from the beginning by prophecies, which grew clearer and brighter as they approached the period of their accomplishment. It was confirmed by miracles, which continued till the religion they illustrated was established. It was ratified by the blood of its Author. Its doctrines are pure, sublime, consistent. Its precepts

---

[74]Bonnie S. Anderson and Judith P. Zinsser, *A History of Their Own: Women in Europe from Prehistory to the Present*, Vol. II (New York: Harper & Row, 1988), p. 125.
[75]Reprinted from Hannah More, *Practical Piety: or the Influence of the Religion of the Heart on the Conduct of Life* (New York: The American Tract Society, 1811), pp. 11–17.

just and holy. Its worship is spiritual. Its service reasonable, and rendered practicable by the offers of Divine aid to human weaknesses. It is sanctioned by the promise of eternal happiness to the faithful, and the threat of everlasting misery to the disobedient. It had no collusion with power, for power sought to crush it. It should not be in any league with the world, for it set out by declaring itself the enemy of the world;—it reprobated its maxims, it showed the vanity of its glories, the danger of its riches, the emptiness of its pleasures.

Christianity, though the most perfect rule of life that ever was devised, is far from being barely a rule of life. . . .   This religion does not consist in an external conformity to practices which, though right in themselves, may be adopted from human motives, and to answer secular purposes. It is not a religion of forms, and modes, and decencies. It is being transformed into the image of God. It is being like-minded with Christ. It is considering Him as our sanctification, as well as our redemption. It is endeavoring to live to Him here, that we may live with Him hereafter. It is desiring earnestly to surrender our will to His, our heart to the conduct of His Spirit, our life to the guidance of His Word.

The change in the human heart, which the Scriptures declare to be necessary, they represent to be not so much an old principle improved, as a new one created; not educed out of the former character, but implanted in the new one. This change is there expressed in great varieties of language, and under different figures of speech. Its being so frequently described, or figuratively intimated, in almost every part of the volume of inspiration, entitles the doctrine itself to our reverence, and ought to shield from obloquy the obnoxious terms in which it is sometimes conveyed.

The sacred writings frequently point out the analogy between natural and spiritual things. The same Spirit, which in the creation of the world moved upon the face of the waters, operates on the human character to produce a new heart and a new life. By this operation the affects and faculties of the man receive a new impulse—his dark understanding is illuminated, his rebellious will is subdued, his irregular desires are rectified; his judgment is informed, his imagination is chastised, his inclinations are sanctified; his hopes and fears are directed to their true and adequate end. Heaven becomes the object of his hopes, an eternal separation from God the object of his fears. His love of the world is transmuted into the love of God. The lower faculties are pressed into the new service. The senses have a higher direction. The whole internal frame and constitution receive a nobler bent; the intents and purposes of the mind, a sublimer aim; his aspirations, a loftier flight; his vacillating desires find a fixed object; his vagrant purposes a settled home; his disappointed heart a certain refuge. That heart, no longer the worshipper of the world, is struggling to become its conqueror. Our blessed Redeemer, in overcoming the world, bequeathed us His command to overcome it also; but as he did not give the command without the example, so He did not give the example without the offer of a power to obey the command.

Genuine religion demands not merely an external profession of our allegiance to God, but an inward devotedness of ourselves to His service. It is not a recognition, but a dedication. It puts the Christian into a new state of things, a new condition of being. It raises him above the world, while he lives in it. It dispenses the illusions of sense, by opening his eyes to realities in the place of those shadows which he has been pursuing. It presents this world as a scene whose original beauty sin has darkened and disordered; man as a helpless and dependent creature; Jesus Christ as the repairer of all the evil which sin has caused, and as our restorer to holiness and happiness.—Any religion short of this, any at least which has not this for its end and object, is not that religion which the Gospel has presented to us, which our Redeemer came down on earth to teach us by His precepts, to illustrate by his example, to confirm by His death, and to consummate by His resurrection. . . .

The mistake of many in religion appears to be, that they do not begin with the beginning. They do not lay their foundation in the persuasion that man is by nature in a state of alienation from God. They consider him rather as an imperfect than as a fallen creature. They allow that he requires to be improved, but deny that he requires a thorough renovation of heart. But genuine Christianity can never be grafted on any other stock than the apostasy of man. The design to reinstate beings who have not fallen, to propose a restoration without a previous loss, a cure where there was no radical disease, is altogether an incongruity which would seem too palpable to require confutation, did we not so frequently see the doctrine of redemption maintained by those who deny that man was in a state to require such redemption. But would Christ have been sent "to preach deliverance to the captives," if there had been no captivity? And "the opening of the prison, to them that were bound," had men been in no bondage?

We are aware that many consider the doctrine in question as a bold charge against our Creator; but may we not venture to ask, "Is it not a bolder charge against God's goodness to presume that He made beings originally wicked, and against God's veracity to believe, that having made such beings, he pronounced them 'good?' Is not that doctrine more reasonable which is expressed or implied in every part of Scripture, that the moral corruption of our first parent has been entailed on his whole posterity? That from this corruption they are no more exempt than from natural death?"

We must not, however, think falsely of our nature: we must humble, but not degrade it. Our original brightness is obscured, but not extinguished. If we consider ourselves in our natural state, our estimation cannot be too low; when we reflect at what a price we have been bought, we can hardly over-rate ourselves in the view of immortality. . . .

The religion which is the object of these pages to recommend, has been sometimes misunderstood, and not seldom misrepresented. It has been described as an unproductive theory, and ridiculed as a fanciful extravagance. For the sake of distinction it is here called *the religion of the heart. There* it subsists as the fountain of spiritual life; *thence* it sends forth, as from the central seat of its existence, supplies of life and warmth through the whole frame; there is the soul of virtue, there is the vital principle which animates the whole being of a Christian. . . .

PRAYER[76]

Prayer is the application of want to Him who only can relieve it, the voice of sin to Him who alone can pardon it. It is the urgency of poverty, the prostration of humility, the fervency of penitence, the confidence of trust. It is not eloquence, but earnestness; not the definition of helplessness, but the feeling of it; not figures of speech, but compunction of soul. It is the "Lord, save us, we perish," of drowning Peter [Mt 8:15]; the cry of faith to the ear of mercy.

Adoration is the noblest employment of created beings; confession, the natural language of guilty creatures; gratitude, the spontaneous expression of pardoned sinners. Prayer is desire; it is not a mere conception of the mind, nor a mere effort of the intellect, nor an act of the memory; but an elevation of the soul towards its Maker; a pressing sense of our own ignorance and infirmity; a consciousness of the perfection of God, of His readiness to hear, of His power to help, of His willingness to save. It is not an emotion produced in the senses, nor an effect wrought by the imagination; but a determination of the will, an effusion of the heart.

Prayer is the guide to self-knowledge, by prompting us to look after our sins in order to pray against them; a motive to vigilance, by teaching us to guard against those sins which, through self-examination, we have been enabled to detect.

Prayer is an act both of the understanding and of the heart. The understanding must apply itself to the knowledge of the Divine perfections, or the heart will not be led to the adoration of them. It would not be a *reasonable* service, if the mind was excluded. It must be rational worship, or the human worshipper would not bring to the service the distinguishing faculty of his nature, which is reason. It must be spiritual worship, or it would want ["lack"] the distinctive quality to make it acceptable to Him who is a Spirit, and Who has declared that He will be worshipped "in spirit and in truth." Prayer is right in itself as the most powerful means of resisting sin and advancing in holiness. It is above all right, as every thing is which has the authority of Scripture, the command of God, and the example of Christ. . . .

It is a hackneyed objection to the use of prayer, that it is offending to the omniscience of God to suppose He requires information of our wants. But no objection can be more futile. We do not pray to inform God of our wants, but to express our sense of the wants which He already knows. As He has not so much made His promises to our necessities as to our requests, it is reasonable that our requests should be made before we can hope that our necessities will be relieved. God does not promise to those who want, that they shall "have," but to those who "ask;" nor to those who need, that they shall "find," but to those who "seek." So far, therefore, from his previous knowledge of our wants being a ground of

---

[76]Ibid., pp. 83–87.

objection to prayer, it is in fact, the true ground itself for our application. Were He not Knowledge itself, our information would be of as little use as our application would be were He not Goodness itself.

We cannot attain a just notion of prayer while we remain ignorant of our own nature, of the nature of God as revealed in Scripture, of our relation to Him, and dependence on Him. If, therefore, we do not live in the daily study of the Holy Scriptures, we shall want the highest motives to this duty and the best helps for performing it; if we do, the cogency of these motives, and the inestimable value of these helps, will render argument unnecessary, and exhortations superfluous.

One cause, therefore, of the dullness of many Christians in prayer, is their slight acquaintance with the sacred volume. They hear it periodically, they read it occasionally, they are contented to know it historically, to consider it superficially; but they do not endeavor to get their minds imbued with its spirit. If they store their memory with its facts, they do not impress their hearts with its truths. They do not regard it as the nutriment on which their spiritual life and growth depend. They do not pray over it; they do not consider all its doctrines as of practical application; they do not cultivate that spiritual discernment which alone can enable them judiciously to appropriate its promises and its denunciations to their own actual case. They do not apply it as an unerring line to ascertain their own rectitude or obliquity.

In our retirements we too often fritter away our precious moments—moments rescued from the world—in trivial, sometimes, it is to be feared, in corrupt thoughts. But if we must give the reins to our imagination, let us sent this excursive faculty to range among great and noble objects. Let it stretch forward, under the sanction of faith and the anticipation of prophecy, to the accomplishment of those glorious promises and tremendous threatenings which will soon be realized in the eternal world. These are topics which, under the safe and sober guidance of Scripture, will fix its largest speculations and sustain its loftiest flights. The same Scripture, while it expands and elevates the mind, will keep it subject to the domination of truth; while, at the same time, it will teach it that its boldest excursions must fall infinitely short of the astonishing realities of a future state. . . .

Charles Finney (1792–1875)

Charles Finney was born in Warren, Connecticut. At the age of two he moved with his parents to Oneida County, New York. He attended high school and taught school in New Jersey from 1808 to 1816. He subsequently returned to New York because of his mother's illness, and in 1818 became an apprentice in a law practice in Adams, New York. Quotations in Finney's law books pointed him to the Bible; he soon purchased a copy of the holy book and became involved in a local church.

In 1821, Finney experienced a dramatic conversion, with his conversion; came a profound sense of a call to preach the gospel. In 1824 he was ordained to ministry in the Presbyterian Church; during that same spring he was employed by the Female Mission Society of the Western District to served as a missionary to the settlers of rural western New York. This ministry marked the beginning of Charles Finney's revivalist efforts as he evangelized villages throughout Jefferson and St. Lawrence counties. By 1825 his work spread to the larger cities of the same region, including Troy, Utica, Rome, and Auburn. It was during this service that Finney began developing his so-called "new measures" for revivalism.

In 1827, at a meeting of the leading eastern evangelists held at New Lebanon, Charles Finney emerged as the consolidator and leader of the revivalist cause. From 1827 to 1832 his evangelistic efforts were centered in major eastern cities, including New York City, Philadelphia, Boston, and Rochester. In 1832 a serious bout with cholera left him in such weakened physical condition that he had to curtail his incessant travels, and he served a series of significant pastorates. In 1835 he accepted a call to serve as Professor of Theology at Oberlin College; he subsequently served as president from 1851 to 1866.

Finney's theological perspective is sometimes called "New School Calvinism." He affirmed the guiding providence of God as an overarching influence in human life; but, like the Arminians, he also affirmed the necessity of humans making an uncohersed response to God's grace. His theology of sanctification was closely akin to the Wesleyan-holiness tradition, but with an increased emphasis upon the gifts and ministry of the Holy Spirit. A significant aspect of Finney's revivalist effort was his desire to see individual conversions bear fruit through social reformation. Hence, he was an ardent abolitionist, a champion of the poor, of temperance, of simplicity, and of women's rights. These values were enshrined in the programs and benevolent societies associated with Oberlin College.

Among Charles Finney's significant works were *Lectures of Revivals of Religion* (1835), *Lectures on Systematic Theology* (1846), and his *Memoirs* (1876). His theology stressed the role of the human will in responding to God, and hence his approach to faith and holy living emphasized the choices and responses to God's grace that Christians make in their spiritual pilgrimage. Finney's persuasive preaching, which looked for a conviction of the will and mind of the hearer, was directly linked to his understanding of the role the human will plays in conversion and Christian Perfection.

CONVERSION TO CHRIST[77]

On a Sabbath evening in the autumn of 1821, I made up my mind that I would settle the question of my soul's salvation at once, that if it were possible I would make my peace with God. But as I was very busy in the affairs of the office, I knew that without great firmness of purpose, I should never effectually attend to the subject. I therefore, then and there resolved, as far as possible, to avoid all

---

[77]Reprinted from Charles Finney, *The Memoirs of Rev. Charles Finney* (New York: A.S. Barnes & Company, 1870), pp. 12–19.

business, and everything that would divert my attention of my soul. I carried this resolution into execution as sternly and thoroughly as I could. I was, however, obliged to be a good deal in the office. But as the providences of God would have it, I was not much occupied either on Monday or Tuesday; and had opportunity to read my Bible and engage in prayer most of the time.

But I was very proud without knowing it. I had supposed that I had not much regard for the opinions of others, whether they thought this or that in regard to myself; and I had in fact been quite singular in attending prayer meetings, and in the degree of attention that I had paid to religion, while in Adams. In this respect I had been so singular as to lead the church at times to think I must be an anxious inquirer. But I found, when I came to fact the question, that I was very unwilling to have any one know that I was seeking the salvation of my soul. When I prayed I would only whisper my prayer, after having stopped the key-hole to the door, lest some one should discover that I was engaged in prayer. Before that time I had my Bible lying on the table with the law-books; and it never had occurred to me to be ashamed of being found reading it, any more than I should be ashamed of being found reading my other books.

But after I had addressed myself in earnest to the subject of my own salvation, I kept my Bible, as much as I could, out of sight. If I was reading it when anybody came in, I would throw my law-books upon it, to create the impression that I had not had it in my hand. Instead of being outspoken and willing to talk with anybody and everybody on the subject as before, I found myself unwilling to converse with anybody. I did not want to see my minister, because I did not want to let him know how I felt, and I had no confidence that he would understand my case, and give me the direction that I needed. For the same reasons I avoided conversation with the elders of the church, or with any of the Christian people. I was ashamed to let them know how I felt, on the one hand; and on the other, I was afraid they would misdirect me. I felt myself shut up to the Bible.

During Monday and Tuesday my conviction increased; but still it seemed as if my heart grew harder. . . .

Tuesday night I had become very nervous; and in the night a strange feeling came over me as if I was about to die. I knew that if I did I should sink down to hell; but I quieted myself as best I could until morning. At an early hour I started for the office. But just before I arrived at the office, something seemed to confront me with questions like these: indeed, it seemed as if the inquiry was within myself, as if an inward voice said to me, "What are you waiting for? Did you not promise to give your heart to God? And what are you trying to do? Are you endeavoring to work out a righteousness of your own?"

Just as this point the whole question of Gospel salvation opened to my mind in a manner most marvelous to me at the time. I think I then saw, as clearly as I ever have in my life, the reality and fullness of the atonement of Christ. I saw that His work was a finished work; and that instead of having, or needing, any righteousness of my own to recommend me to God, I had to submit myself to the righteousness of God through Christ. Gospel salvation seemed to me to be an offer of something to be accepted; and that it was full and complete; and that all that was necessary on my part, was to get my own consent to give up my sins, and accept Christ. Salvation, it seemed to me, instead of being a thing to be wrought out, by my own works, was a thing to be found entirely in the Lord Jesus Christ, who presented Himself before me as my God and my Savior.

Without being distinctly aware of it, I had stopped in the street right where the inward voice seemed to arrest me. How long I remained in that position I cannot say. But after this distinct revelation had stood for some little time before my mind, the question seemed to be put, "Will you accept it now, to-day?" I replied, "Yes, I will accept it to-day, or I will die in the attempt."

North of the village, and over a hill, lay a piece of woods, in which I was in the almost daily habit of walking, more or less, when it was pleasant weather. It was now October, and the time was past for my frequent walks there. Nevertheless, instead of going to the office, I turned and bent my course toward the woods, feeling that I must be alone, and away from all human eyes and ears, so that I could pour out my prayer to God.

But still my pride must show itself. As I went over the hill, it occurred to me that some one might see me and suppose that I was going away to pray. Yet probably there was not a person on earth that would have suspected such a thing, had he seen me going. But so great was my pride, and so much was I possessed with the fear of man, that I recollect that I skulked along under the fence, till I got so far out of sight that no one from the village could see me. I then penetrated into the woods, I should think, a quarter of a mile, went over the other side of the hill, and found a place where some large trees had fallen across each other, leaving an open place between. There I saw I could make a kind of closet. I crept into this place and knelt down for prayer. As I turned to go up into the woods, I recollect to have said, "I will give my heart to God, or I never will come down from there." I recollect repeating this as I went up—"I will give my heart to God before I ever come down again."

But when I attempted to pray I found that my heart would not pray. I had supposed that if I could only be where I could speak aloud, without being overheard, I could pray freely. But lo! when I came to try, I was dumb; that is, I had nothing to say to God; or at least I could say but a few words, and those without heart. In attempting to pray I would hear a rustling in the leaves, as I thought, and would stop and look up to see if somebody were not coming. This I did several times.

Finally I found myself verging fast to despair. I said to myself, "I cannot pray. My heart is dead to God, and will not pray." I then reproached myself for having promised to give my heart to God before I left the woods. When I came to try, I found I could not give my heart to God. My inward soul hung back and there was no going out of my heart to God. I began to feel deeply that it was too late; that it must be that I was given up of God and was past hope.

The thought was pressing me of the rashness of my promise, that I would give my heart to God that day or die in the attempt. It seemed to me as if that was binding upon my soul; and yet I was going to break my vow. A great sinking and discouragement came over me, and I felt almost too weak to stand upon my knees.

Just at this moment I again thought I heard some one approach me, and I opened my eyes to see whether it were so. But right there the revelation of my pride of heart, as the great difficulty that stood in the way, was distinctly shown to me. An overwhelming sense of my wickedness in being ashamed to have a human being see me on my knees before God, took such a powerful possession of me, that I cried at the top of my voice, and exclaimed that I would not leave that place if all the men on earth and all the devils in hell surrounded me. "What!" I said, "such a degraded sinner as I am, on my knees confessing my sins to the great and holy God; and ashamed to have any human being, and a sinner like myself, find me on my knees endeavoring to make my peace with my offended God!" The sin appeared awful, infinite. It broke me down before the Lord.

Just at that point this passage of Scripture seemed to drop into my mind with a flood of light: "Then shall ye go and pray unto me, and I will hearken unto you. Then shall ye seek me and find me, when ye shall search for me with all your heart." I instantly seized hold of this with my heart. I had intellectually believed the Bible before; but never had the truth been in my mind that faith was a voluntary trust instead of an intellectual state. I was conscious as I was of my existence, of trusting at that moment in God's veracity. Somehow I knew that that was a passage of Scripture, though I do not think I had ever read it. I knew that it was God's word, and God's voice, as it were, that spoke to me. I cried to Him, "Lord, I take thee at thy word. Now thou knowest that I do search for thee with all my heart, and that I have come here to pray to thee; and thou hast promised to hear me."

That seemed to settle the question that I could then, that day, perform my vow. The Spirit seemed to lay stress upon that idea in the text, "When you search for me with all your heart." The question of when, that is of the present time, seemed to fall heavily into my heart. I told the Lord that I should take Him at His word; that He could not lie; and that therefore I was sure that He heard my prayer, and that He would be found of me. . . .

I continued thus to pray, and to receive and appropriate promises for a long time, I know not how long. I prayed till my mind became so full that, before I was aware of it, I was on my feet and tripping up the ascent toward the road. The question of my being converted, had not so much as arisen to my thought; but as I went up, brushing through the leaves and bushes, I recollect saying with great emphasis, "If I am ever converted, I will preach the Gospel."

I soon reached the road that led to the village, and began to reflect upon what had passed; and I found that my mind had become most wonderfully quiet and peaceful. I said to myself. "What is this? I must have grieved the Holy Ghost entirely away. I have lost all my conviction. I have not a particle of concern about my soul; and it must be that the Spirit has left me." "Why!" thought I, "I never was so far from being concerned about my own salvation in my life." . . .

Just before evening the thought took possession of my mind, that as soon as I was left alone in the new office, I would try to pray again—that I was not going to abandon the subject of religion and give it up, at any rate; and therefore, although I no longer had any concern about my soul, still I would continue to pray.

By evening we got the books and furniture adjusted; and I made up, in an open fire-place, a good fire, hoping to spend the evening alone. Just at dark Squire W—, seeing that everything was adjusted, bade me good-night and went to his home. I had accompanied him to the door; and as I closed the door and turned around, my heart seemed to be liquid within me. All my feelings seemed to rise and flow out; and the utterance of my heart was, "I want to pour my whole soul out to God." The rising of my soul was so great that I rushed into the room back of the front office to pray.

There was no fire, and no light, in the room; nevertheless it appeared to me as if it were perfectly light. As I went in and shut the door after me, it seemed as if I met the Lord Jesus Christ face to face. It did not occur to me then, nor did it for some time afterward, that it was wholly a mental state. On the contrary it seemed to me that I saw him as I would see any other man. He said nothing, but looked at me in such a manner as to break me right down at His feet. I have always since regarded this as a most remarkable state of mind; for it seemed to me a reality, that he stood before me, and I fell down at His feet and poured out my soul to Him. I wept aloud like a child, and made such confessions as I could with my choked utterance. It seemed to me that I bathed His feet with my tears; and yet I had no distinct impression that I touched Him, that I recollect.

I must have continued in this state for a good while; but my mind was too much absorbed with the interview to recollect anything that I said. But I know, as soon as my mind became calm enough to break off from the interview, I returned to the front office, and found that the fire that I had made of large wood was nearly burnt out. But as I turned and was about to take a seat by the fire, I received a mighty baptism of the Holy Ghost. Without any expectation of it, without ever having the thought in my mind that there was any such thing for me, without any recollection that I had ever heard the thing mentioned by any person in the world, the Holy Spirit descended upon me in a manner that seemed to go through me, body and soul. I could feel the impression, like a wave of electricity, going through and through me. Indeed it seemed to come in waves and waves of liquid love; for I could not express it in any other way. It seemed like the very breath of God. I can recollect distinctly that it seemed to fan me, like immense wings.

No words can express the wonderful love that was shed abroad in my heart. I wept aloud with joy and love; and I do not know but I should say, I literally bellowed out the unutterable gushings of my heart. These waves came over me, and over me, and over me, one after the other, until I recollect I cried out, "I shall die if these waves continue to pass over me." I said, "Lord, I cannot bear any more;" yet I had no fear of death.

How long I continued in this state, with this baptism continuing to roll over me and go through me, I do not know. But I know it was late in the evening when a member of my choir—for I was the leader of the choir—came into the office to see me. He was a member of the church. He found me in this state of loud weeping, and said to me, "Mr. Finney, what ails you?" I could make him no answer for some time. He then said, "Are you in pain?" I gathered myself up as best I could, and replied, "No, but so happy that I cannot live." . . .

WHAT IS A REVIVAL?[78]

It is the renewal of the first love of Christians, resulting in the awakening and conversion of sinners to God. In the popular sense, a revival of religion in a community is the arousing, quickening, and reclaiming of the more or less backslidden church and the more or less general awakening of all classes, and insuring attention to the claims of God.

It presupposes that the church is sunk down in a backslidden state, and a revival consists in the return of a church from her backslidings, and in the conversion of sinners.

1. A revival always includes conviction of sin on the part of the church. Backslidden professors cannot wake up and begin right away in the services of God, without deep searchings of heart. The fountains of sin need to be broken up. In a true revival, Christians are always brought under such convictions; they see their sins in such a light, that often they find it impossible to maintain a hope of their acceptance with God. It does not always go to that extent; but there are always, in a genuine revival, deep convictions of sin, and often cases of abandoning all hope.

2. Backslidden Christians will be brought to repentance. A revival is nothing else than a new beginning of obedience to God. Just as in the case of a converted sinner, the first step is a deep repentance, a breaking down of heart, a getting down into the dust before God, with deep humility, and forsaking sin.

3. Christians will have their faith renewed. While they are in their backslidden state they are blind to the state of sinners. Their hearts are as hard as marble. The truths of the Bible only appear like a dream. They admit it to be all true; their consciences and their judgment assent to it; but their faith does not see it standing out in bold relief, in all the burning realities of eternity. But when they enter into a revival, they no longer see men as trees walking, but they see things in that strong light which will renew the love of God in their hearts. This will lead them to labor zealously to bring others to Him. They will feel grieved that others do not love God, when they love Him so much. And they will set themselves feelingly to persuade their neighbors to give Him their hearts. So their love to men will be renewed. They will be filled with a tender and burning love for souls. They will have a longing desire for the salvation of the whole world. They will be in agony for individuals whom they want to have saved—their friends, relations, enemies. They will not only be urging them to give their hearts to God, but they will carry them to God in the arms of faith, and with strong crying and tears beseech God to have mercy on them, and save their souls from endless burnings.

---

[78]Reprinted from Charles G. Finney, *Lectures on Revivals of Religion* (New York: Fleming H. Revell, 1815, reprint 1868), pp. 14–16.

4. A revival breaks the power of the world and of sin over Christians. It brings them to such vantage ground that they get a fresh impulse towards heaven. They have a new foretaste of heaven, and new desires after union after God; and the charm of the world is broken and the power of sin overcome.

5. When the churches are thus awakened and reformed, the reformation and salvation of sinners will follow, going through the same stages of conviction, repentance, and reformation. Their hearts will be broken down and changed. Very often the most abandoned profligates are among the subjects. Harlots, and drunkards, and infidels, and all sorts of abandoned characters, are awakened and converted. The worst among human beings are softened, and reclaimed, and made to appear as lovely specimens of the beauty of holiness. . . .

HINDRANCES TO REVIVALS[79]

. . . 19. Revivals are hindered when ministers and *churches take wrong ground in regard to any question involving human rights*. Take the subject of **SLAVERY** for instance. The time was when the subject was not before the public mind. . . . [D]oubtless, many slave dealers and slave holders in our own country have been converted, notwithstanding their participation in this abomination, because the sinfulness of it was apparent to their minds. So ministers and churches, to a great extent throughout the land, have held their peace, and borne no testimony against this abominable abomination, existing in the church and in the nation. But recently, the subject has come up for discussion, and the providence of God has brought it distinctly before the eyes of all men. Light is now shed upon this subject, as it has been upon the cause of temperance. Facts are exhibited, and principles established, and light thrown in upon the minds of men, and this monster is dragged from his horrid den, and exhibited before the church, and it is demanded of them, **"IS THIS SIN?"** Their testimony *must* be given on this subject. They are God's witnesses. They are sworn to tell "the truth, the whole truth, and nothing but the truth." It is impossible that their testimony should not be given, on one side or the other. Their silence can no longer be accounted for upon the principle of ignorance, and that they have never had their attention turned to the subject. Consequently, the silence of Christians upon the subject is virtually saying *that they do not* consider slavery as a sin. The truth is, it is a subject upon which they cannot be silent without guilt. The time has come, in the providence of God, when every southern breeze is loaded down with the cries of lamentation, mourning and woe. Two millions of degraded heathen in our own land stretch their hands, all shackled and bleeding, and send forth to the church of God the agonizing cry for help. And shall the church, in her efforts to reclaim and save the world, deafen her ears to this voice of agony and despair? God forbid. The church

---

[79]Ibid., pp. 272–73.

cannot turn away from this question. It is a question for the church and for the nation to decide, and God will push it to a decision.

It is vain for the churches to resist it for fear of distinction, contention, and strife. It is in vain to account it an act of *piety* to turn away the ear from hearing this cry of distress.

The church must testify, and testify "the truth, the whole truth, and nothing but the truth," on this subject, or she is perjured, and the Spirit of God departs from her. She is under oath to testify, and ministers and churches who do not pronounce it sin bear false testimony for God. It is doubtless true that one of the reasons for the low state of religion at the present time is that many churches have taken the wrong side on the subject of slavery, have suffered prejudice to prevail over principle, and have feared to call this abomination by its true name.

Phoebe Worral Palmer (1807–84)

Phoebe Worral, a Methodist lay woman, revivalist, feminist, and social reformer, was born in New York City. She married Walter C. Palmer, a physician, when she was nineteen. In 1835 she became active in the "Tuesday Meeting for the Promotion of Holiness," which met in the home of her sister, Sarah Worral Langford. Palmer gradually assumed leadership of the group and developed a popular approach to communicating the Wesleyan conception of Christian Perfection or Entire Sanctification. Her approach was based on the phraseology of Matthew 23:19, which stated: "the altar sanctifies the gift." Utter consecration to God, and a willingness to keep oneself upon "the altar," was the foundation upon which she built her version of the Wesleyan distinctive. Her exposition of Christian Perfection was presented in *The Way to Holiness* (1845). A similar perspective was brought to a wide range of practical issues through Palmer's editorship of the magazine *Guide to Holiness* (1864–74).

Phoebe Palmer founded Hedding Church in the slums, and in 1850 she established the Five Points Mission—upon the site of New York's "Old Brewery—which became the model for Protestant attempts at social reform in an urban context. She championed women's rights and equality in ministry through her writings and through her actions. Palmer conducted more than 300 evangelistic crusades, and her efforts provided an important link between Finney's clergy-dominated, smaller revivals, and the subsequent lay-oriented, mass urban meetings conducted by Dwight L. Moody.

IS THERE A SHORTER WAY TO HOLINESS?[80]

"I have always thought," said one of the children of Zion to the other, as in love they journeyed onward in the way cast up for the ransomed of the Lord to walk

---

[80]Reprinted from Phoebe Palmer, *The Way of Holiness with Notes By the Way: Being a Narrative of Religious Experience Resulting from a Determination to Be a Bible Christian* (New York: G. Lane & C.B. Tippett, 1845), pp. 17–22.

in; "I have thought," said he, "whether there is not a shorter way of getting into this way of holiness than some of our . . . brethren apprehend?"[81] "Yes," said the sister addressed, who was a member of the denomination alluded to; "Yes, brother, THERE IS A SHORTER WAY! O! I am sure this long waiting and struggling with the powers of darkness is not necessary. There is a shorter way." And then, with a solemn feeling of responsibility, and with a realizing conviction of the truth uttered, she added, "But, brother, there is but one way."

Days and even weeks elapsed, and yet the question, with solemn bearing, rested upon the mind of that sister. She thought of the affirmative given in answer to the inquiry of the brother—examined yet more closely the Scriptural foundation upon which the truth of the affirmation rested—and the result of the investigation tended to add still greater confirmation to the belief, that many sincere disciples of Jesus . . . consume much time in endeavoring to get into this way, which might . . . be employed in making progress in it, and testifying, from experimental knowledge, of its blessedness.

How many, whom Infinite Love would long since have brought into this state, instead of seeking to be brought into the possession of the blessing at once, are seeking a preparation for the reception of it! They feel that their *convictions* are not deep enough to warrant an approach to the throne of grace, with the confident expectation of receiving the blessing *now*. Just at this point some may have been lingering months and years. Thus did the sister, who so confidently affirmed "there is a shorter way." And here, dear child of Jesus, permit the writer to tell you just how that sister found the "shorter way."

On looking at the requirements of the word of God, she beheld the command, "Be ye holy" [1 Pet 1:16]. She then began to say in her heart, "Whatever my former deficiencies may have been, God requires that I should *now* be holy. Whether *convicted*, or otherwise, *duty is plain*. God requires *present* holiness." On coming to this point, she at once apprehended a simple truth before unthought of, i.e. *Knowledge* is *conviction*. She well knew that, for a long time, she had been assured that God required holiness. But she had never dreamed this knowledge a sufficient plea to take to God—and because of present need, to ask a present bestowment of the gift.

Convinced that in this respect she had mistaken the path, she now, with renewed energy, began to make use of the knowledge already received, and to discern a "shorter way."

Another difficulty by which her course had been delayed she found to be here. She had been accustomed to look at the blessing of holiness as such a high attainment, that her general habit of soul inclined her to think it almost beyond her reach. This erroneous impression rather influenced her to rest the matter thus:—"I will let every high state of grace, in name, alone, and seek only to be *fully conformed to the will of God, as recorded in his written word*. My chief endeavors shall be centered in the aim to be an humble *Bible Christian*. By the grace of God, all my energies shall be directed to this one point. With this single aim, I will journey onward, even though my faith may be tried to the uttermost by those

---

[81]This probably refers to "Methodist brethren."

manifestations being withheld, which have previously been regarded as essential for the establishment of faith."

On arriving at this point, she was enabled to gain yet clearer insight into the simplicity of the way. And it was by this process. After having taken the Bible as the rule of life . . . she found that no one declaration spoke more appealingly to her understanding than this: "Ye are not your own, ye are bought with a price, therefore glorify God in your body and spirit which are his" [1 Cor 6:20]. By this she perceived the duty of *entire consecration* in a stronger light, and as more sacredly binding, than ever before. Here she saw God as her Redeemer, claiming, by virtue of the great price paid for the redemption of body, soul, and spirit, the *present and entire service* of all these redeemed powers.

By this she saw that if she lived constantly in the entire surrender of all that had been thus dearly purchased unto God, she was but an unprofitable servant; and that, if less than all was rendered, she was worse than unprofitable, inasmuch as she would be guilty of keeping back part of that price which had been purchased unto God . . . should she not at once resolve on living in the *entire* consecration of all her redeemed powers to God.

Deeply conscious of past unfaithfulness, she now determined that the time past should suffice; and with a humility of spirit, induced by a consciousness of not having lived in the performance of such a "reasonable service" [Rom 12:1], she was enabled, through grace, to resolve, with firmness of purpose, that entire devotion of heart and life to God should be the absorbing subject of the succeeding pilgrimage of life.

THE WAY OF RESTORATION[82]

. . . God, in his infinite love, has provided a way by which lost, guilty men may be redeemed, justified, cleansed, and saved, with the power of an endless life. Provision has thus been made for the restoration of man, by availing himself of which, in the way designated in the Scriptures, he may regain that which was lost in Adam—even the image of God re-enstamped upon the soul.

To bring about this restoration, the Father so loved the world that he gave his only-begotten Son, who from eternity had dwelt in his bosom. At the appointed time, Christ, the anointed of God, was revealed, and, as our example, lived a life of disinterested devotion to the interests of mankind; and, as the Lamb slain from the foundation of the world,[83] laid himself upon the altar; "tasted death for every man" [Heb 2:9], and "bore the sins of the whole world in his own body" [1 Pet 2:24]. As an assurance of the amplitude of his grace, and that he is no respecter of persons, he hath said, "And I, if I be lifted up, will draw all men unto me" [Jn 12:32]. "The Spirit of truth which proceedeth from the Father, he shall testify of me" [Jn 15:26]. The Spirit, true to its appointed office, reproves of sin,

---

[82]Reprinted from Palmer, *Way of Holiness*, sec. IX, pp. 60–71.
[83]An allusion to Revelations 13:8.

righteousness, and judgment. And now the entire voice of divine revelation proclaims "*all* things ready" [Mt 22:4]! The Spirit and the Bride say, "Come" [Rev 22:17]!

The altar, thus provided by the conjoint testimony of the Father, Son, and Holy Spirit, is Christ. His sacrificial death and sufferings are the sinner's plea; the immutable promises of the Lord Jehovah the ground of claim. If true to the Spirit's operations on the heart, men as workers together with God, confess their sins, the faithfulness and justice of God stand pledged not only to *forgive*, but also to *cleanse from all unrighteousness*.

By the resolve to be a "Bible Christian," this traveler in the "way of holiness" placed herself in the way to receive the direct teachings of the Spirit, and in the *one* and the only *way* for the attainment of the salvation promised in the gospel of Christ, inasmuch as it is written, "He became the author of eternal salvation to all them that *obey him*" [Heb 5:9]. And by the determination to consecrate all upon the altar of sacrifice to God, with the resolve to "enter into the bonds of an everlasting covenant to be wholly the Lord's for time and eternity," and then acting in conformity with this decision, *actually laying all upon the altar.* . . .

It was thus, by "laying all upon the altar," she . . . laid herself under the most sacred obligation to *believe* that the sacrifice became "holy and acceptable," and virtually the *Lord's property*, even by virtue of the sanctity of the *altar* upon which it was laid, and continued "holy and acceptable," so long as kept inviolably upon this hallowed altar. At an early stage of her experience in the "way of holiness," the Holy Spirit powerfully opened to her understanding the following passage, as corroborative of this view of the subject: Rom. xii.1, "I beseech you, therefore, brethren, by the mercies of God that ye present your bodies a living sacrifice holy, acceptable unto God, which is your reasonable service."

From these important considerations she perceived that it was indeed by the Spirit's teachings she had been led to "enter into the bonds of an everlasting covenant to be wholly the Lord's," inasmuch as by the removal of this offering from off this *hallowing* altar, she should *cease to be holy*, as it is "the altar that sanctifieth the gift" [Mt 23:19]. In this light she also saw why it is, that *all* is so imperatively required, inasmuch as it is the Redeemer who makes the demand for the "living sacrifice," having purchased *all*, body, soul, and spirit, unto himself. And she wondered not that an offering *consciously* not entire—known by the offerer to be *less* than *all*—is not acceptable, inasmuch as God has pronounced such offerings unacceptable.[84] . . . And that such a one *could not believe* while still halting between the world and an *entire surrender*, she thought fully explained by the words of the Savior, "How can ye believe who receive honor one of another, and seek not that honor which cometh from God only" [Jn 5:44]? . . .

It was on coming to *this altar* she was enabled to realize *how* it is that the devotions of the believer, while resting here, are "unto God a sweet savor of Christ" [2 Cor 2:15], inasmuch as no service can be "holy, acceptable" unto God, unless

---

[84]Malachi 1:8,13,14 was cited in the text as an example.

presented through this medium. . . . And thus, as has been related, she found the "*shorter*, the *one*, and the *only way*," of which it is said, "The redeemed of the Lord shall walk there" [Is 35:10], by surrendering all to the Redeemer, and venturing, *believingly*, the entire being upon *Jesus*! Resting here, she proved, experimentally, the truth of his declaration, "I am the way" [Jn 14:6], and was enabled to realize continually the purifying virtue of his atoning blood, and to testify that it was not in vain he had "offered himself up that he might sanctify the people with his own blood" [Heb 13:12].

And though she apprehended that nothing but the blood of Jesus could *sanctify* and *cleanse* from sin, yet she was also scripturally assured that it was needful for the recipient of this grace, as a worker together with God, to place himself believingly *upon* "the altar that sanctifieth the gift" [Mt 23:19], ere he could prove the efficacy of the all-cleansing blood. Gracious intentions, and strong desires, she was convinced, are not sufficient to bring about this important result; corresponding *action* is also necessary; the offering must be *brought* and believingly *laid upon the altar*, ere the acceptance of it *can* be realized. In this crucifixion of nature, the Spirit helpeth our infirmities, and worketh mightily to *will*—but *man must act*. . . .

She also found one act of faith not sufficient to insure a continuance in the "way of holiness," but that a *continuous* act was requisite. "As ye have received Christ Jesus the Lord, so walk ye in him" [Col 2:6], was an admonition greatly blessed to her soul. Assured that there was no other way of retaining this state of grace but by the exercise of the same resoluteness of character, presenting *all* and *keeping* all upon the hallowed altar, and also in the exercise of the same faith, she was enabled, through the teachings of the Spirit, "to walk by the same rule, and mind the same thing" [Phil 3:16], and for years continued an onward walk in the "way of holiness."

Being thus impelled by a divine constraint to test every progressive step by the powerful persuasive, "Thus it is written," she became increasingly confident in her rejoicings, "that her faith did not stand in the wisdom of men, but in the power of God" [1 Cor 2:5], and instead of being "vacillating in her experience," as had been so painfully suggested by the tempter, she was enabled daily to become more firmly rooted and grounded in the faith, abounding therein with thanksgiving. . . .

Søren Kierkegaard (1813–55)

Søren Kierkegaard was born and spent most of his life in Copenhagen, Denmark. He was the seventh son of a wealthy wool merchant. He took degrees in philosophy and theology but did not seek ordination. Kierkegaard's ill health gave his thought a somewhat morbid and introspective cast. Among his chief contributions to Christian spirituality was his stress on the decisions and risks of individual faith over and against the established religion of the Danish National Lutheran Church. His stress upon the life and faith of the individual made Kierkegaard seem to be a forerunner of Christian existentialism. He wrote a number of "edifying discourses" that sought to incite vital Christian faith. The most famous of these, *Purity of Heart Is to Will One Thing*, challenged individuals to will "the Good," and thereby to strip themselves of self-interest and the other hindrances to purity of heart. It was designed as a series of meditations to prepare a person for confession.

PURITY OF HEART[85]

So let us . . . speak about this sentence: **PURITY OF HEART IS TO WILL ONE THING** as we base our meditation on the Apostle James's words in his Epistle, Chapter 4, verse 8: *"Draw nigh to God and he will draw nigh to you. Cleanse your hands, ye sinners; and purify your hearts ye double-minded."* For only the pure in heart can see God, and therefore, draw nigh to Him; and only by God's drawing nigh to them can they maintain this purity. And he who in truth wills only one thing can will only the Good, and he who only wills one thing when he wills the Good can only will the Good in truth.

Let us speak of this, but let us first put out of our minds the occasion of the office of Confession in order to come to an agreement of an understanding of this verse, and on what the apostolic word of admonition "purify your hearts ye double-minded" is condemning, namely *doublemindedness. . . .*

I. If it is to be possible, that a man can will only one thing, then he must will the good. To will only one thing: but will this not inevitably become a long-drawn-out talk? If one should consider this matter properly must he not first consider, one by one, each goal in life that a man could conceivably set up for himself, mentioning separately all of the many things that a man might will? And not only this; since each of these considerations readily becomes too abstract in character, is he not obliged as the next step to attempt to will, one after the other, each of these goals in order to find out what is the single thing he is to will, if it is a matter of willing only one thing? Yes, if someone should begin in this fashion, then he would never come to an end. Or more accurately, how could he ever arrive at the end since at the outset he took the wrong way and then continued to go on further and further along this false way? It is only when the wanderer turns around and goes back. For as the Good is only a single thing, so all ways lead to the Good, even the false ones: when the repentant one follows the same way back. Oh, Thou the unfathomable trust-worthiness of the Good! Wherever a man may be in the world, whichever road he travels, when he wills one thing, he is on a road that leads him to Thee! Here such a far flung enumeration would only work harm. Instead of wasting many moments on naming the vast multitude of goals or squandering life's costly years in personal experiments upon them, can the talk do as life ought to do—with a commendable brevity stick to the point?

---

[85]Excerpts from Søren Kierkegaard, *Purity of Heart Is to Will One Thing*, translated by Douglas V. Steere. English translation copyright 1938, by Harper & Brothers, renewed (c) 1966 by Douglas V. Steere. Reprinted by permission of HarperCollins Publishers, Inc. Pages 53–67, 218–19.

In a certain sense nothing can be spoken of so briefly as the Good, when it is well described. For the Good without condition and without qualification, without preface and without compromise is, absolutely the only thing that a man may and should will, and is only one thing. Oh, blessed brevity, oh, blessed simplicity, that seizes swiftly what cleverness, tired out in the service of vanity, may grasp but slowly! That which a simple soul, in the happy impulse of a pious heart, feels no need of understanding in an elaborate way, since he simply seizes the Good immediately, is grasped by the clever one only at the cost of much time and much grief. The way this one thing is willed is not such that: one man wills one thing but that which he wills is not the Good; another wills one thing nor is what he wills the Good; a third wills one thing and what he wills *is* the Good. No, it is not done in that way. The person who wills one thing that is not the Good, he does not truly will one thing. It is a delusion, an illusion, a deception, a self-deception that he wills only one thing. For in his innermost being he is, he is bound to be, double-minded. Therefore the Apostle says, "Purify your hearts ye double-minded," that is, purify your hearts, in truth will only one thing, for therein is the heart's purity.

And again it is of this same purity of heart that the Apostle is speaking when he says, "If someone lacks wisdom, then let him pray . . . but in faith, not like a double-minded man" (James 1:5, 6, 8). For purity of heart is the very wisdom that is acquired through prayer. A man of prayer does not pore over learned books for he is the wise man "whose eyes are opened"—when he kneels down (Numbers 24:16).

In a word, then, there is a man whose mind remains piously ignorant of the multitude of things, for the Good is one thing. The more difficult part of the talk is directed to the man whose mind in its double-mindedness has made the doubtful acquaintance of the multitude of things, and of knowledge. If it is certain that a man in truth wills one thing, then he wills the Good, for this alone can be willed in this manner. But both of these assertions speak of identical things, or they speak of different things. The one assertion plainly designates the name of the Good, declaring it to be that one thing. The other assertion cunningly conceals this name. It appears almost as if it spoke of something else. But just on that account it forces its way, searchingly, into a man's innermost being. And no matter how much he may protest, or defy, or boast that he wills only one thing, it searches him through and through in order to show the double-mindedness in him if the one thing he wills is not the Good.

For in truth there was a man on earth who seemed to will only one thing. It was unnecessary for him to insist upon it. Even if he had been silent about it, there were witnesses enough against him who testified how inhumanly he steeled his mind, how nothing touched him, neither tenderness, nor innocence, nor misery; how his blinded soul had eyes for nothing, and how the senses in him had only eyes for the one thing that he willed. And yet it was certainly a delusion, a terrible delusion, that he willed one thing. For pleasure and honor and riches and power and all that this world has to offer only appear to be one thing. It is not, nor does it remain one thing, while everything else is in change or while himself is in change. It is not in all circumstances the same. On the contrary, it is subject to continual alteration. Hence even if this man named but one thing whether it be pleasure, or honor or riches, actually he did not will one thing. Neither can he be said to will one thing when that one thing which he wills is not in itself one: is in itself a multitude of things, a dispersion, the toy of changeableness, and the prey of corruption! In the time of pleasure see how he longed for one gratification after another. Variety was his watchword. Is variety, then, to will one thing that shall ever remain the same? On the contrary, it is to will one thing that must never be the same. It is to will a multitude of things. And a person who wills in this fashion is not only double-minded but is at odds with himself. For such a man wills first one thing and then immediately wills the opposite, because the oneness of pleasure is a snare and a delusion. It is the diversity of pleasures that he wills. So when the man of whom we are speaking had gratified himself up to the point of disgust, he became weary and sated. Even if he still desired one thing—what was it that he desired? He desired new pleasures; his enfeebled soul raged so that no ingenuity was sufficient to discover something new—something new! It was change he cried out for as pleasure served him, change! change! And it was change that he cried out for as he came to pleasure's limit, as his servants were worn out—change! change!

Now it is to be understood that there are also changes in life that can prove to a man whether he wills one thing. There is the change of the perishable nature when the sensual man must step aside, when dancing and the tumult of the whirling senses are over, when all becomes soberly quiet. That is the change of death. If, for once, the perishable nature should seem to forget to close in, if it should seem as if the sensual one had succeeded in slipping by: death does not forget. The sensual one will not slip past death, who has dominion over what belongs to the earth and who will change into nothing the one thing which the sensual person desires.

And last of all, there is the change of eternity, which changes all. Then only the Good remains and it remains the blessed possession of the man that has willed only one thing. But that rich man whom no misery could touch, that rich man who even in eternity to his own damnation must continue to will one thing, ask him now whether he really wills one thing. So, too, with honor and riches and power. For in the time of strength as he aspired to honor, did he really discover some limit, or was that not simply the striver's restless passion to climb higher and higher? Did he find some rest amid his sleeplessness in which he sought to capture honor and to hold it fast? Did he find some refreshment in the cold fire of his passion? And if he really won honor's highest prize, then is earthly honor in itself one thing? Or in its diversity when the thousands and thousands braid the wreath, is honor to be likened to the gorgeous carpet of the field—created by a single hand? No, like worldly contempt, worldly honor is a whirlpool, a play of confused forces, an illusory moment in the flux of opinions. It is a sense-deception, as when a swarm of insects at a distance seem to the eye like one body; a sense-deception, as when the noise of the many at a distance seems to the ear like a single voice. . . .

To will one thing, therefore, cannot mean to will that which only appears to be one thing. The fact is that the worldly goal is not one thing in its essence because it is unreal. Its so-called unity is actually nothing but emptiness which is hidden beneath the manyness. In the short-lived moment of delusion the worldly goal is therefore a multitude of things, and thus not one thing. So far is it from a state of being and remaining one thing, that in the next moment it changes itself into its opposite. Carried to its extreme limit, what is pleasure other than disgust? What is earthly honor at its dizzy pinnacle other than contempt for existence? What are riches, the highest superabundance of riches, other than poverty? For no matter how much all the earth's gold hidden in covetousness may amount to, is it not infinitely less than the smallest mite hidden in the contentment of the poor! What is worldly omnipotence other than dependence? What slave in chains is as unfree as a tyrant! No, the worldly goal is not one thing. Diverse as it is, in life it is changed into its opposite, in death into nothing, in eternity into damnation: for the one who has willed this goal. Only the Good is one thing in its essence and the same in each of its expressions. Take love as an illustration. The one who truly loves does not love once and for all. Nor does he use a part of his love, and then again another part. For to change it into small coins is not to use it rightly. No, he loves with all his love. It is away as a whole, and yet he keeps it intact as a whole, in his heart. Wonderful riches! When the miser has gathered all the world's gold in sordidness—then he has become poor. When the lover gives away his whole love, he keeps it entire—in the purity of the heart. Shall a man in truth will one thing, then this one thing that he wills must be such that it remains unaltered in all changes, so that by willing it he can win immutability. If it changes continually, then he himself becomes changeable, double-minded, and unstable. And this continual change is nothing else than impurity. . . .

In truth to will one thing, then, can only mean to will the Good, because every other object is not a unity; and the will that only wills that object, therefore, must become double-minded. For as the coveted object is, so becomes the coveter. Or would it be possible that a man by willing the evil could will one thing, provided that it was possible for a man so to harden himself as to will nothing but the evil? Is not this evil, like evil persons, in disagreement with itself, divided against itself? Take one such man, separate him from society, shut him up in solitary confinement. Is he not at odds with himself there, just as a poor union between persons of his sort is an association that is ridden with dissension? But a good man, even if he lived in an out-of-the-way corner of the world and never saw any human being, would be at one with himself and at one with all about him because he wills one thing. Each one who in truth would will one thing must be led to will the Good, by willing one thing that is not in its deepest sense the Good although it may be something quite innocent; and then, little by little, he is changed really in truth to will one thing by willing the Good. Love, from time to time, has in this way helped a man along the right path. Faithfully he only willed one thing, his love. For it, he would live and die. For it, he would sacrifice all and in it alone he would have his eternal reward. Yet the act of being in love is still not in the deepest sense the Good. But it may possibly become for him a helpful educator, who will finally lead him by the possession of his beloved one or perhaps by her loss, in truth to will one thing and to will the Good. In this fashion a man is educated by many means; and true love is also an education toward the Good. . . .

Father in Heaven! What is a man without Thee! What is all that he knows, vast accumulation though it be, but a chipped fragment if he does not know Thee! What is all his striving, could it even encompass that world, but a half-finished work if he does not know Thee: Thee the One, who art one thing and who art all! So may Thou give to the intellect, wisdom to comprehend that one thing; to the heart, sincerity to receive this understanding; to the will, purity that wills only one thing. In prosperity may Thou grant perseverance to will one thing; amid distractions, collectedness to will one thing; in suffering, patience to will one thing. Oh, Thou that giveth both the beginning and the completion, may Thou early, at the dawn of day, give to the young man the resolution to will one thing. As the day wanes, may Thou give to the old man a renewed remembrance of his first resolution. that the first may be like the last, the last like the first, in possession of a life that has willed only one thing. Alas, but this has indeed not come to pass. Something has come in between. The separation of sin lies in between. Each day, and day after day something is being placed in between: delay, blockage, interruption, delusion, corruption. So in this time of repentance may Thou give the courage once again to will one thing. True, it is an interruption of our daily tasks; we do lay down our work as though it were a day of rest, when the penitent (and it is only in a time of repentance that the heavey-laden worker may be quiet in the confession of sin) is alone before Thee in self-accusation. This is indeed an interruption. But it is an interruption that searches back into its very beginnings that it might bind up anew that which sin has separated, that in its grief it might atone for lost time, that in its anxiety it might bring to completion that which lies before it. Oh, Thou that givest both the beginning and the completion, give Thou victory in the day of need so that what neither a man's burning wish nor his determined resolution may attain to, may be granted unto him in the sorrowing of repentance: to will only one thing.

Horace Bushnell (1802–76)

Horace Bushnell was born in Bantam, Connecticut, and graduated from Yale College in 1827. After studying law, also at Yale, from 1829 to 1831, he was converted to Christian faith during a revival in 1831. In response to that experience he entered Yale Divinity School; graduating with the B.D. in 1833, he was ordained to the ministry of the Congregational Church and took up the pastorate of North Church in Hartford, Connecticut. He served there till 1859.

Bushnell's *Christian Nurture* (1847) was, in part, a reaction to the prevalent revivalist model of salvation. It championed, instead, an approach to Christian life that stressed the nurture and gradual growth of a child into Christian faith. He put the proposition in this way: "The child is to grow up a Christian and never know himself as being otherwise." Bushnell's approach brought renewed stress upon the church as a nurturing, formative community and offered a theological rationale equipping ministries like the Sunday-school movement.

WHAT CHRISTIAN NURTURE IS[86]

There is then some kind of nurture which is of the Lord, deriving a quality and a power from Him, and communicating the same. Being instituted by Him, it will of necessity have a method and a character peculiar of itself, or rather to Him. It will be the Lord's way of education, having aims appropriate to Him, and, if realized in its full intent, terminating in results impossible to be reached by any merely human method. . . .

In ordinary cases, the better and more instructional way of handling this subject, would be to go directly into the practical methods of parental discipline, and show by what modes of government and instruction we may hope to realize the best results. But unhappily the public mind is preoccupied extensively by a view of the whole subject, which I must regard as a theoretical mistake, and one which will involve, as long as it continues, practical results systematically injurious. This mistaken view is necessary, if possible to remove. And accordingly what I have to say will take the form of an argument on the question thus put in issue; though I design to gather round the subject, as I proceed, as much of practical instruction as the mode of argument will suffer. Assuming then the question above stated, What is the true idea of Christian education?—I answer in the following proposition, which it will be the aim of my argument to establish, viz: *That the child is to grow up a Christian, and never know himself as being otherwise.*

In other words, the aim, effort, and expectation should be, not, as is commonly assumed, that the child is to grow up in sin, to be converted after he comes to a mature age; but that he is to open on the world as one that is spiritually renewed, not remembering the time when he went through a technical experience, but seeming rather to have loved what is good from his earliest years. I do not affirm that every child may, in fact and without exception, be so trained that he certainly will grow up a Christian. . . .

There is then, as the subject appears to us—

1. No absurdity in supposing that children are to grow up in Christ. On the other hand, if there is no absurdity, there is a very clear moral incongruity in setting up a contrary supposition, to be the aim of a system of Christian education. There could not be a worse or more baleful implication given to a child, than that he is to reject God and all holy principle, till he has come to a mature age. What authority have you from the Scriptures to tell your child, or, by any sign, to show him that you do not expect him truly to love and obey God, till after he has spent whole years in hatred and wrong? What authority to make him feel that he is the most unprivileged of all human beings, capable of sin, but incapable of repentance; old enough to resist all good, but too young to receive any good whatsoever? It is reasonable to suppose that you have some express authority for a lesson so manifestly cruel and hurtful, else you would shudder

---

[86]Reprinted from Horace Bushnell, *Christian Nurture* (New York: Charles Scribner, 1865), pp. 9–33, with omissions.

to give it. I ask you for the chapter and verse, out of which it is derived. Meantime, wherein would it be less incongruous for you to teach your child that he is to lie and steal, and go the whole round of the vices, and then, after he comes to mature age, reform his conduct by the rules of virtue? . . .

But my child is a sinner, you will say; and how can I expect him to begin a right life, until God gives him a new heart? This is the common way of speaking, and I state the objection in its own philosophy, that it may recognize itself. Who then has told you that a child can not have the new heart of which you speak? Whence do you learn that if you live the life of Christ, before him and with him, the law of the Spirit of Life may not be such as to include and quicken him also? And why should it be thought incredible that there should be some really good principle awakened in the mind of a child? For this is all that is implied in a Christian state. The Christian is one who has simply *begun* to love what is good for its own sake, and why should it be thought impossible for a child to have this love begotten in him? Take any scheme of depravity you please, there is yet nothing in it to forbid the possibility that a child should be led, in his first moral act, to cleave unto what is good and right, any more than in the first of his twentieth year. He is, in that case, only a child converted to good, leading a mixed life as all Christians do. The good in him goes into combat with the evil, and holds a qualified sovereignty. And why may not this internal conflict of goodness cover the whole life from its dawn, as well as any part of it? And what more appropriate to the doctrine of spiritual influence itself, than to believe that as the Spirit of Jehovah fills all the worlds of matter, and holds a presence of power and government in all objects, so all human souls, the infantile as well as the adult, have a nurture of the Spirit appropriate to their age and their wants? What opinion is more essentially monstrous, in fact, than that which regards the Holy Spirit as having no agency in the immature souls of children who are growing up, helpless and unconscious, into the perils of time?

2. It is to be expected that Christian education will radically differ from that which is not Christian. Now, it is the very character and mark of all unchristian education, that it brings up the child for future conversion. No effort is made, save to form a habit of outward virtue, and, if God please to convert the family to something higher and better, after they come to the age of maturity, it is well. Is then Christian education, or the nurture of the Lord, no way different from this? Or is it rather to be supposed that it will have a higher aim and a more sacred character?

And since it is the distinction of Christian parents, that they are themselves in the nurture of the Lord, since Christ and the Divine Love, communicated through him, are become the food of their life, what, will they so naturally seek as to have their children partakers with them, heirs together with them, in the grace of life? I am well aware of the common impression that Christian education is sufficiently distinguished by the endeavor of Christian parents to teach their children the lessons of Scripture history, and the doctrines or dogmas of Scripture theology. But if they are given to understand, at the same time, that these lessons can be expected to produce no fruit till they are come to a mature age—that they are to grow up still in the same character as other children do, who have no such instruction—what is this but to enforce the practical rejection of all the lessons taught them? And which, in truth, is better for them, to grow up in sin under Scripture light, with a heart hardened by so many religious lessons; or to grow up in sin, unvexed and unannoyed by the wearisome drill of lectures that only discourage all practical benefit? Which is better, to be piously brought up in sin, or to be allowed quietly to vegetate in it? . . .

Such facts . . . suggest the possibility also that Christian piety should begin in other and milder forms of exercise, than those which commonly distinguish the conversion of adults; that Christ himself, by that renewing Spirit who can sanctify from the womb, should be practically infused into the childish mind; in other words, that the house, having a domestic Spirit of grace dwelling in it, should become the church of childhood, the table and hearth a holy rite, and life an element of saving power. Something is wanted that is better than teaching, something that transcends mere effort and will-work—the loveliness of a good life, the repose of faith, the confidence of righteous expectation, the sacred and cheerful liberty of the Spirit—all glowing about the young soul, as a warm and genial nurture, and forming in it, by methods that are silent and imperceptible, a spirit of duty and religious obedience to God. This only is Christian nurture, the nurture of the Lord. . . .

4. Assuming the corruption of human nature, when should we think it wisest to undertake or expect a remedy? When evil is young and pliant to good, or when it is confirmed by years of sinful habit? And when, in fact, is the human heart found to be so ductile to the motives of religion, as in the simple, ingenuous age of childhood? How easy is it then, as compared with the stubbornness of adult years, to make all wrong seem odious, all good lovely and desirable. If not discouraged by some ill-temper which bruises all the gentle sensibilities, or repelled by some technical view of religious character which puts it beyond his age, how ready is the child to be taken by good, as it were beforehand, and yield his ductile nature to the truth and Spirit of God, and to a fixed prejudice against all that God forbids.

He can not understand, of course, in the earliest stage of childhood, the philosophy of religion as a renovated experience, and that is not the form of the first lessons he is to receive. He is not to be told that he must have a new heart and exercise faith in Christ's atonement. We are to understand, that a right spirit may be virtually exercised in children, when, as yet, it is not intellectually received, or as a form of doctrine. Thus, if they are put upon an effort to be good, connecting the fact that God desires it and will help them in the endeavor, that is all which, in a very early age, they can receive, and that includes everything—repentance, love, duty, dependence, faith. Nay, the operative truth necessary to a new life, may possibly be communicated through and from the parent, being revealed in his looks, manners, and ways of life, before they are of an age to understand the teaching of words; for the Christian scheme, the gospel, is really wrapped up in the life of every Christian parent, and beams out from him [or her] as a living epistle, before it escapes from the lips, or is taught in words. And the Spirit of truth may as well make this living truth effectual, as the preaching of the gospel itself.

Never is it too early for good to be communicated. Infancy and childhood are the ages most pliant to good. And who can think it necessary that the plastic nature of childhood must first be hardened into stone, and stiffened into enmity towards God and all duty, before it can become a candidate for Christian character! There could not be a more unnecessary mistake, and it is as unnatural and pernicious, I fear, as it is unnecessary. . . .

5. It is implied in all our religious philosophy, that if a child ever does anything in a right spirit, ever loves anything because it is good and right, it involves the dawn of a new life. This we can not deny or doubt, without bringing in question our whole scheme of doctrine. Is it then incredible that some really good feeling should be called into exercise in a child? . . .

Nor is there any age, which offers itself to God's truth and love, and to that Quickening Spirit whence all good proceeds, with so much of ductile feeling and susceptibilities so tender. The child is under parental authority too for the very purpose, it would seem, of having the otherwise abstract principle of all duty impersonated in his parents, and thus brought home to his practical embrace; so that, learning to obey his [or her] parents in the Lord, because it is right, he may thus receive, before he can receive it intellectually, the principle of all piety and holy obedience. And when he is brought to exercise a spirit of true and loving submission to the good law of his parents, what will you see, many times, but a look of childish joy, and a happy sweetness of manner, and a ready delight in authority, as like to all the demonstrations of Christian experience, as anything childish can be to what is mature?

6. Children have been so trained as never to remember the time when they began to be religious. Baxter was, at one time, greatly troubled concerning himself, because he could recollect no time when there was a gracious change in his character. But he discovered, at length, that "education is as properly a means of grace as preaching," and thus found the sweeter comfort in his love to God, that he learned to love him too early. The European churches, generally, regard Christian piety more a habit of life, formed under the training of childhood, and less as a marked spiritual change in experience. . . .

And this is the very idea of Christian education, that it begins with nurture or cultivation. And the intention is that the Christian life and spirit of the parents, which are in and by the Spirit of God, shall flow into the mind of the child, to blend with his incipient and half-formed exercises; that they shall thus beget their own good within him [or her]—their thoughts, opinions, faith, and love, which are to become a little more, and yet a little more, his [or her] own separate exercise, but still the same in character. The contrary assumption, that virtue must be the product of separate and absolutely independent choice, is pure assumption. As regards the measure of personal merit and demerit, it is doubtless true that every subject of God is to be responsible only for what is his own. But virtue still is rather a *state* of being than an act or series of acts; and, if we look at the causes which induce or prepare such a state, the will of the person himself may have a part among these causes more or less important, and it works no absurdity to suppose that one may be even prepared to such a state, by causes prior to his own will; so that, when he sets off to act for himself, his struggle and duty may be rather to sustain and perfect the state begun, than to produce a new one. Certain it is that we are never, at any age, so independent as to be wholly out of the reach of organic laws which affect our character.

All society is organic—the church, the state, the school, the family; and there is a spirit in each of these organisms, peculiar to itself, and more or less hostile, more or less favorable to religious character, and to some extent, at least, sovereign over the individual man. A very great share of the power in what is called a revival of religion, is organic power; nor is it any the less divine on that account. The child is only more within the power of organic laws than we all are. We possess only a mixed individuality all our life long. A pure, separate, individual man, living *wholly* within, and from himself, is a mere fiction. No such person ever existed, or ever can. I need not say that this view of an organic connection of character subsisting between parent and child, lays a basis for notions of Christian education, far different from those which now prevail, under the cover of a merely fictitious and mischievous individualism.

Perhaps it may be necessary to add, that, in the strong language I have used concerning the organic connection of character between the parent and child, it is not designed to assert a power in the parent to renew the child, or that the child can be renewed by any agency of the Spirit less immediate, than that which renews the parent himself. When a germ is formed on the stem of any plant, the formative instinct of the plant may be said in one view to produce it; but the same solar heat which quickens the plant, must quicken also the germ, and sustain the internal action of growth, by a common presence in both. So, if there be an organic power of character in the parent, such as that of which I have spoken, it is not a complete power in itself, but only such a power as demands the realizing presence of the Spirit of God, both in the parent and the child, to give it effect. As Paul said, "I have begotten you through the gospel," so may we say of the parent, who, having a living gospel enveloped in his life, brings it into organic connection with the soul of childhood. But the declaration excludes the necessity of a divine influence, not more in one case than in the other. . . .

Therese of Lisieux (1873–97)

Marie François Therese Martin was born in Alençon, France. She was the youngest of nine children born to Louis and Zelie; four of their children died in infancy. The Martins were devout Roman Catholics; both parents had aspired to the religious life when they were young. Therese's mother died when she was four years old, and her father, a watchmaker, relocated the family to Lisieux.

Therese had a strong, personal devotion to Jesus Christ and to the Virgin Mary from her earliest recollections. She followed three of her sisters into the Carmelite Order in search of the purity of the love of Jesus. Her brief but very significant pilgrimage is amply examined in her spiritual autobiography, *The Story of a Soul* (1899). A very humble person, she wrote her autobiography only under the direct order of her prioress. Although she saw nothing remarkable in her own life, others recognized the depth of her spirituality and pressed Therese to write the account of her life; it was completed shortly before her untimely death.

Among her contributions to Christian Spirituality was St. Therese's "little way." Her's was a spirituality of the ordinary; by God's grace she was able to see, learn, and experience extraordinary things through her everyday surroundings. Even the smallest tasks can become vessels for God's love. Equally significant was her willingness to envision the entire enterprise of Christian Spirituality as a pursuit of selfless love. She was declared to be a saint in 1925.

THE LITTLE FLOWER[87]

I am going to entrust the story of my soul to you, my darling Mother [her prioress and older sister], to you who are doubly my mother. When you asked me to do this, I felt it might be too great a distraction and might make me too concerned about myself, but afterwards Jesus made me realize that I should please Him by unquestioning obedience. Besides, it involves me in only one thing: to start extolling now the mercies of the Lord—which I shall go on doing throughout eternity. . . .

I had wondered for a long time why God had preferences and why all souls did not receive an equal amount of grace. I was astonished to see how He showered extraordinary favours on saints who had sinned against Him, saints such as St. Paul and St. Augustine. He forced them, as it were, to accept His graces. I was just as astonished when I read the lives of saints to see that Our Lord cherished certain favoured souls from the cradle to the grave and never allowed any kind of obstacle to check their flight towards Him. He bestowed such favours on them that they were unable to tarnish the spotless splendour of their baptismal robe. I also wondered why such vast numbers of poor savages died before they had even heard the name of God.

Jesus saw fit to enlighten me about this mystery. He set the book of nature before me and I saw that all the flowers He has created are lovely. The splendour of the rose and the whiteness of the lily do not rob the little violet of its scent nor the daisy of its simple charm. I realized that if every tiny flower wanted to be a rose, spring would lose its loveliness and there would be no wild flowers to make the meadows gay.

---

[87]Reprinted from John Bevers, trans., *The Autobiography of St. Therese of Lisieux: The Story of a Soul.* Copyright (c) 1957 by Doubleday. Used by permission of Doubleday, a division of Bantam Doubleday Dell Publishing Group, Inc. Pages 19–21.

It is just the same in the world of souls—which is the garden of Jesus. He has created the great saints who are like the lilies and the roses, but He has also created much lesser saints and they must be content to be the daisies or the violets which rejoice His eyes whenever He glances down. Perfection consists in doing His will, in being that which He wants us to be.

I also understood that God's love shows itself just as well in the simplest soul which puts up no resistance to His grace as it does in the loftiest soul. Indeed, as it is love's nature to humble itself, if all souls were like those of the holy doctors who have illumined the Church with the light of their doctrine, it seems that God would not have stooped low enough by entering their hearts. But God has created the baby who knows nothing and can utter only feeble cries. He has created the poor savage with no guide but natural law, and it is to their hearts that He deigns to stoop. They are His wild flowers whose homeliness delights Him. By stooping down to them, He manifests His infinite grandeur. The sun shines equally both on cedars and on every tiny flower. In just the same way God looks after every soul as if it had no equal. All is planned for the good of every soul, exactly as the seasons are so arranged that the humblest daisy blossoms at the appointed time. . . .

I have now reached a stage in my life when I can glance back at the past, for my soul has matured in a crucible of inner and external trials. Now, like a flower braced by a storm, I can raise my head and see that the words of the Psalmist have been fulfilled in me: "The Lord is my shepherd; how can I lack anything? He gives me a resting place where there is green pasture, leads me out to the cool water's brink, refreshed and content. . . . dark be the valley about my path, but I fear none while he is with me." For me, the Lord has always been "pitying and gracious, patient and rich in mercy." So, Mother, it is with joy that I shall sing to you of His mercies. As it is for you alone that I am going to write the story of the Little Flower gathered by Jesus, I shall speak quite freely, without worrying about style or all the digressions I'm sure to make. A mother always understands her child even though it can lisp only a few words. So I am sure you will understand me, as it was you who fashioned my soul and offered it to Jesus.

I believe that if a little flower could speak, it would tell very simply and fully all that God had done for it. It would not say that it was ungraceful and had no scent, that the sun had spoilt its freshness, or that a storm had snapped its stem—not when it knew the exact opposite was true.

The flower who is now going to tell her story rejoices at having to relate all the kindnesses freely done her by Jesus. She is well aware that there was nothing about her to attract His attention, and that it is His mercy alone which has created whatever there is of good in her. It was He who ensured that she began to grow in a most pure and holy soil, and it was He who saw to it that eight fair white lilies came before her. His love made Him want to keep His little flower safe from the tainted breezes of the world, and so she had scarcely begun to unfold her petals before he transplanted her on to the mountain Carmel. . . .

I CHOOSE ALL[88]

. . . One day [my sister] Leonie, no doubt thinking she was too old to play with dolls, came to us both with a basket filled with their clothes, ribbons, and other odds and ends. Her own doll was on top. She said: "Here you are, darlings. Take what you want." Celine took a little bundle of silk braid. I thought for a moment, then stretched out my hand and declared: "I choose everything," and, without more ado, I carried off the lot. Everyone thought this was quite fair.

This episode sums up the whole of my life. Much later, when I understood what perfection was, I realized that to become a saint one must suffer a great deal, always seek what is best, and forget oneself. I understood that there were many kinds of sanctity and that each soul was free to respond to the approaches of Our Lord and to do little or much for Him—in other words, to make a choice among the sacrifices He demands. Then, just as when I was a child, I cried: "My God, I choose all. I do not want to be a saint by halves. I am not afraid to suffer for You. I fear only one thing—that I should keep my own will. So take it, for I choose all that You will." . . .

I AM THIRSTY[89]

. . . One Sunday when I was looking at a picture of Our Lord on the Cross, I saw the Blood coming from one of His hands, and I felt terribly sad to think that It was falling to the earth and that no one was rushing forward to catch It. I determined to stay continually at the foot of the Cross and receive It. I knew that I should then have to spread It among other souls. The cry of Jesus on the Cross— "I am thirsty"—rang continually in my heart and set me burning with a new, intense longing. I wanted to quench the thirst of my Well-Beloved and I myself was consumed with a thirst for souls. I was concerned not with the souls of priests but with those of great sinners which I wanted to snatch from the flames of hell.

God showed me He was pleased with these longings of mine. I'd heard of a criminal who had just been condemned to death for some frightful murders. It seemed that he would die without repenting. I was determined at all costs to save him from hell. I used every means I could. I knew that by myself I could do nothing, so I offered God the infinite merits of Our Lord and the treasures of the Church. I was quite certain that my prayers would be answered, but to give me courage to go on praying for sinners I said to God: "I am sure You will forgive this wretched Pranzini. I shall believe You have done so even if he does not con-

---

[88]Ibid. Used by permission of Doubleday, a division of Bantam Doubleday Dell Publishing Group, Inc. Page 26.

[89]Ibid. Used by permission of Doubleday, a division of Bantam Doubleday Dell Publishing Group, Inc. Pages 63–64.

fess or give any other sign of repentance, for I have complete faith in the infinite mercy of Jesus. But I ask You for just one sign of his repentance to encourage me."

This prayer was answered. Daddy never allowed us to read any newspapers, but I thought I was justified in looking at the stories about Pranzini. On the day after his execution I eagerly opened *La Croix* and I had to rush away to hide my tears at what I read. Pranzini had mounted the scaffold without confessing and was ready to thrust his head beneath the guillotine's blade when he suddenly turned, seized the crucifix offered him by the priest, and thrice kissed the Sacred Wounds.

I had been given my sign, and it was typical of the graces Jesus has given me to make me eager to pray for sinners. It was at the sight of the Precious Blood from the Wounds of Jesus that my thirst for souls had been born. I wanted to let them drink of this Immaculate Blood to cleanse them of their sins and the lips of my "first child" had pressed against the Sacred Wounds! What a wonderful reply to my prayers! After this striking favour my longing for souls grew every day. I seemed to hear Jesus say to me what He said to the Samaritan Woman: "Give me to drink." It was a real exchange of love: I gave souls the Blood of Jesus and offered Him these purified souls that His thirst might be quenched. The more I gave Him to drink, the more the thirst of my own poor soul increased, and He gave me this burning thirst to show His love for me. . . .

SMALL GOOD DEEDS[90]

. . . I'll return to the lessons Our Lord gave me. One evening, after Compline, I looked in vain for my lamp on the shelves where they were kept. As it was the Lent Silence, I couldn't ask for it. I thought—rightly—that a sister had taken it in mistake for hers. So, because of this mistake, I had to spend a whole hour in darkness and it was an evening when I'd planned to do a lot of work. But for the interior light of grace I should certainly have been very sorry for myself. As it was, instead of feeling upset, I rejoiced and thought that true poverty meant being without essentials, not only of pleasant things. And in the darkness of my cell my soul was flooded with divine light.

During this period I was seized with a passion for the ugliest and most inconvenient things. For instance, I was delighted when a pretty little jug in my cell was replaced by a big chipped one. I also tried hard not to make excuses. This was very difficult, especially where our novice mistress was concerned, for I wanted to hide nothing from her.

My first victory was not a big one, but it cost me a great deal. A small vase, which someone had left lying behind a window, was found broken. Our novice mistress thought I was guilty of leaving it lying about. She was cross, told me I was thoroughly untidy, and ordered me to be more careful in the future. With-

[90]Ibid. Used by permission of Doubleday, a division of Bantam Doubleday Dell Publishing Group, Inc. Pages 98–99.

out a word, I kissed the ground and promised not to be untidy again. As I've said, these trifles cost me a lot because I was so lacking in virtue, and I had to remember that all would be revealed on the Day of Judgment.

Above all, I tried to do my small good deeds in secret. I loved folding up the mantles forgotten by the sisters and seized every possible opportunity of helping them. I was also attracted towards penance, but I was not allowed to satisfy my longing. The only mortification granted me was to master my self-love, and that did me far more good than any bodily penance. . . .

MY VOCATION[91]

O my Beloved! This grace [through a dream of the Venerable Mother Anne of Jesus] was only the prelude of the greater ones You wished to shower on me. Let me recall them to You, and forgive me if I talk nonsense in trying to tell You again about those hopes and desires of mine which are almost limitless . . . forgive me and heal my soul by granting it what it wants. It should be enough for me, Jesus, to be Your spouse, to be a Carmelite and, by union with You, to be a mother of souls. Yet I long for other vocations: I want to be a warrior, a priest, an apostle, a doctor of the Church, a martyr. . . . I would like to perform the most heroic deeds. I feel I have the courage of a Crusader. I should like to die on the battlefield in defence of the Church.

If only I were a priest! How lovingly, Jesus, would I hold You in my hands when my words had brought You down from heaven and how lovingly would I give You to the faithful. Yet though I long to be a priest, I admire and envy the humility of St. Francis of Assisi and feel that I should imitate him and refuse the sublime dignity of the priesthood. How can I reconcile these desires?

Like the prophets and the doctors of the Church, I should like to enlighten souls. I should like to wander through the world, preaching Your Name and raising Your glorious Cross in pagan lands. But it would not be enough to have only one field of mission work. I should not be satisfied unless I preached the Gospel in every quarter of the globe and even in the most remote islands. Nor should I be content to be a missionary for only a few years. I should like to have been one from the creation of the world and to continue as one till the end of time. But, above all, I long to be a martyr. From my childhood I have dreamt of martyrdom, and it is a dream which has grown more and more real in my little cell in Carmel. But I don't want to suffer just one torment. I should have to suffer them all to be satisfied. Like you, my adorable Jesus, I want to be scourged and crucified. I want to be flayed like St. Bartholomew. Like St. John, I want to be flung into boiling oil. Like St. Ignatius of Antioch, I long to be ground by the teeth of wild beasts, ground into a bread worthy of God. With St. Agnes and St. Cecilia, I want to offer my neck to the sword of the executioner and like Joan of Arc, murmur the

---

[91]Ibid. Used by permission of Doubleday, a division of Bantam Doubleday Dell Publishing Group, Inc. Pages 153–59.

name of Jesus at the stake. My heart leaps when I think of the unheard tortures Christians will suffer in the reign of anti-Christ. I want to endure them all. My Jesus, fling open that book of life in which are set down the deeds of every saint. I want to perform them all for You!

Now what can You say to all my silliness? Is there anywhere in the world a tinier, weaker soul than mine? Yet just because I am so weak, You have granted my little, childish desires and now You will grant those desires of mine which are far vaster than the universe. These desires caused me a real martyrdom, and so one day I opened the epistles of St. Paul to try to find some cure for my sufferings. And in chapters twelve and thirteen of the First Epistle to the Corinthians I read that we cannot all be apostles, prophets, and doctors, that the Church is made up of different members, and that the eye cannot also be the hand. This answer was clear enough, but it did not satisfy me and brought me no peace. But as St. John of the Cross says, "descending into the depths of my own nothingness, I was raised so high that I reached my goal." I went on reading and came to: "Be zealous for the better gifts. And I show unto you a yet more excellent way." The apostle explains how even all the most perfect gifts are nothing without love and that charity is the most excellent way of going safely to God. I had found peace at last.

I thought of the Mystical Body of the Church, but I could not recognize myself in any of its members listed by St. Paul—or, rather, I wanted to recognize myself in them all. Charity gave me the key to *my vocation*. I realized that if the Church was a body made up of different members, she would not be without the greatest and most essential of them all. I realized that love includes all vocations, that love is all things, and that, because it is eternal, it embraces every time and place.

Swept by an ecstatic joy, I cried: "Jesus, my love! At last I have found my vocation. My vocation is love! I have found my place in the bosom of the Church and it is You, Lord, who has given it me. In the heart of the Church, who is my Mother, *I will be love*. So I shall be everything and so my dreams will be fulfilled!" Why do I speak of "ecstatic joy"? It's the wrong phrase to use. Instead, I should speak of peace, that calm, tranquil peace which the helmsman feels as he sees the beacon which guides him into harbour. How brightly this beacon of love burns! And I know how to reach it and how to make its flames my own.

I am only a weak and helpless child, yet it is my very weakness which has made me daring enough to offer myself to You, Jesus, as the victim of Your love. Long ago only pure and spotless victims were accepted by Almighty God. The divine justice could be satisfied only by immaculate victims, but the law of love has replaced that of fear, and love has chosen me as victim—feeble and imperfect creature that I am. Is the choice of me worthy of love? Yes, it is, because in order for love to be fully satisfied it must descend to nothingness and transform that nothingness to living fire. I know, Lord, that "love is repaid by love alone." And so I have sought and I have found the way to ease my heart—by giving You love for love. . . .

Jesus, I love you, and I love the Church my Mother. I remember that "the smallest act of love is more to her than every other work put together." But is my heart really full of this pure love? Are my limitless desires a dream, a piece of foolishness? If they are, tell me, for You know I want the truth. If my desires are rash, take them away, for they are a most terrible martyrdom. Yet I confess that even if I never enter these high realms to which my soul aspires, I shall have known more sweetness in my martyrdom and in my folly than I shall ever know in the midst of eternal joy. That is, unless by a miracle You wiped from my memory the hopes I had while on earth. Jesus, my Jesus, if this longing for love is so wonderful, what will it be like to actually possess and enjoy it forever? How can a soul as imperfect as mine hope for love in all its fullness? Why do You keep these boundless longings for great souls, those eagles which soar to the heights? I, alas, am only a poor little unfledged bird. I am not an eagle. All I have are the eyes and the heart of one, for in spite of my littleness I dare gaze at the Sun of love and long to fly towards it. I want to fly and imitate the eagles, but all I can do is flap my tiny wings. They are too weak to lift me. What shall I do? Die of grief at being so helpless. Oh no! I shan't even let it trouble me. With cheerful confidence I shall stay gazing at the Sun until I die. Nothing will frighten me, neither wind nor rain. If thick clouds hide the Sun and if it seems that nothing exists beyond the night of this life—well, then, that will be a moment of *perfect joy*, a moment to feel complete trust and stay very still, secure in the knowledge that my adorable Sun still shines behind the clouds.

O God, I do understand Your love for me, but, as You know, I very often let myself be turned aside from the only thing I care about. I stay away from You and soil my half-formed wings in the dirty puddles of the world. Then "I cry like a young swallow" and my cry tells You all and, in Your infinite mercy, You remember that You did "not come to call the just, but sinners." Yet if You refuse to heed the plaintive cries of Your feeble creature, if You remain hidden, I shall just stay wet and numb with cold and again rejoice in my deserved suffering. O my beloved Sun, I delight in feeling small and helpless in Your presence and my heart is at peace. . . . I know that all the eagles of heaven pity me, protect me, defend me, and drive off the vultures—the demons—who would destroy me. I have no fear of these vultures. I am not fated to become their prey, but that of the divine Eagle.

O eternal Word, my Saviour, You are the Eagle I love and the One who fascinates me. You swept down to this land of exile and suffered and died so that You could bear away every soul and plunge them into the heart of the Blessed Trinity, that inextinguishable furnace of love. You re-entered the splendours of heaven, yet stayed in our vale of tears hidden under the appearance of a white Host so that You can feed me with Your own substance. O Jesus, do not be angry if I tell You that Your love is a mad love . . . and how can You expect my heart, when confronted with this folly, not to soar up to You? How can there be any limit to my trust?

I know that for You the saints have also been foolish. Because they were eagles they have done great deeds. I am too small to do anything great, and so my folly is to hope that Your love will accept me as its victim; my folly is to rely on the angels and the saints so that I may fly to You, my adored Eagle, with Your own wings. For as long as You wish, I will stay with my eyes on You. I want to be *fascinated* by Your gaze. I want to be the prey of Your love. I hope that one day

You will swoop down on me, carry me off to the furnace of love, and plunge me into its burning depths so that I can be its ecstatic victim for all eternity.

O Jesus, if only I could tell all *little souls* of Your immeasurable condescension. I feel that if You found a soul feebler than mine—though that's impossible— You would delight in heaping even greater favours on it if it abandoned itself with supreme confidence to Your infinite mercy.

But why do I want to tell the secrets of Your love, my Beloved? You alone have taught me them and surely You can reveal them to others. I know You can and I implore You to: *I beseech You to cast Your divine glance upon a vast number of little souls. I beg You to choose in this world a multitude of little victims worthy of Your LOVE!!!*

Walter Rauschenbusch (1861–1918)

Walter Rauschenbusch was born in Rochester, New York, and was educated there as well as in Germany. After graduating from Rochester Theological Seminary (1886), he pastored a German-speaking Baptist Church on the edge of "Hell's Kitchen" in New York City. In his eleven years in Hell's Kitchen Rauschenbusch encountered the debilitating effects of poverty, unemployment, disease, and crime, and this experience profoundly shaped his theology.

After brief studies in Germany, during which he encountered the social theology of Albrecht Ritschl, Rauschenbusch began his teaching career at Rochester Seminary (1897). His recognition of the social crisis produced by industrialization and waves of immigration was fused with his theological emphasis (drawn in part from Ritschl) upon the kingdom of God "as the progressive transformation of all human affairs by the thought and spirit of Christ" to produce the "social gospel." His book, *Christianity and the Social Crisis* (1907), epitomized the perspective that stressed that Christianity was a social (as opposed to an individualistic or private) religion, that was inherently concerned with social reform. His later work, *Christianizing the Social Order* (1912), offered a program for progressive, democratic social reform that incarnated the Kingdom of God. Rauschenbush's *A Theology for the Social Gospel* (1917) provided a systematic theology for the movement. Among his influential popular works was *For God and the People: Prayers for the Social Awakening* (1910), which evidences Rauschenbush's interconnection of the Social Gospel and Christian Spirituality.

THE SOCIAL MEANING OF THE LORD'S PRAYER[92]

The Lord's Prayer is recognized as the purest expression of the mind of Jesus. It crystallizes his thoughts. It conveys the atmosphere of his childlike trust in the Father. It gives proof of the transparent clearness of peace of his soul.

---

[92]Reprinted from Walter Rauschenbusch, *For God and the People: Prayers of the Social Awakening* (Norwood, Mass: Plimpton Press, 1910), pp. 15–23.

It first took shape as a protest against the wordy flattery with which men tried to wheedle their gods. He demanded simplicity and sincerity in all expressions of religion, and offered this as an example of the straightforwardness with which men might deal with their Father. Hence the brevity and conciseness of it . . . [Mt 6:7–13] . . .

The Lord's Prayer is so familiar to us that few have stopped to understand it. The general tragedy of misunderstanding which has followed Jesus throughout the centuries has frustrated the purpose of his model prayer also. He gave it to stop vain repetitions, and it has been turned into a contrivance for incessant repetition.

The churches have employed it for their ecclesiastical ritual. Yet it is not ecclesiastical. There is no hint in it of the church, the ministry, the doctrines of theology, or the sacraments—though the Latin Vulgate has turned the petition for the daily bread into a prayer for the "super-substantial" bread of the sacrament.

It has also been used for the devotions of the personal religious life. It is, indeed, profoundly personal. But its deepest significance for the individual is revealed only when he dedicates his personality to the vaster purposes of the kingdom of God, and approaches all his personal problems from that point of view. Then he enters both into the real meaning of the Lord's Prayer, and into the spirit of the Lord himself.

The Lord's Prayer is part of the heritage of social Christianity which has been appropriated by men who have had little sympathy with its social spirit. It belongs to the equipment of the soldiers of the kingdom of God. I wish to claim it here as the great charter of all social prayers.

When he bade us say, "Our Father," Jesus spoke from that consciousness of human solidarity which was a matter of course in all his thinking. He compels us to clasp hands in spirit with all our brothers and thus to approach the Father together. This rules out all selfish isolation in religion. Before God no man stands alone. Before the All-seeing he is surrounded by the spiritual throng of all to whom he stands related near and far, all whom he loves and hates, whom he serves or oppresses, whom he wrongs or saves. We are one with our fellow-men in all our needs. We are one in our sin and our salvation. To recognize that oneness is the first step toward praying the Lord's Prayer aright. That recognition is also the foundation of social Christianity.

The three petitions with which the prayer begins express the great desire which was fundamental in the heart and mind of Jesus: "Hallowed be thy name. Thy kingdom come. Thy will be done, as in heaven, so on earth." Together they express his yearning faith in the possibility of a reign of God on earth in which his name shall be hallowed and his will be done. They look forward to the ultimate perfection of the common life of humanity on this earth, and pray for the divine revolution which is to bring that about.

There is no request here that we be saved from earthliness and go to heaven which has been the great object of churchly religion. We pray here that heaven may be duplicated on earth through the moral and spiritual transformation of humanity, both in its personal units and its corporate life. No form of religion has ever interpreted this prayer aright which did not have a loving understanding for the plain daily relations of men, and a living faith in their possible spiritual nobility.

And no man has outgrown the crude selfishness of religious immaturity who has not followed Jesus in setting this desire for the social salvation of mankind ahead of all personal desires. The desire for the kingdom of God precedes and outranks everything else in religion, and forms the tacit presupposition of all our wishes for ourselves. In fact, no one has a clear right to ask for bread for his body or strength for his soul, unless he has identified his will with this all-embracing purpose of God, and intends to use the vitality of body and soul in the attainment of that end.

With that understanding we can say that the remaining petitions deal with personal needs.

Among these the prayer for the daily bread takes first place. Jesus was never as "spiritual" as some of his later followers. He never forgot nor belittled the elemental need of men for bread. The fundamental place which he gives to this petition is a recognition of the economic basis of life.

But he lets us pray only for the bread that is needful, and for that only when it becomes needful. The conception of what is needful will expand as human life develops. But this prayer can never be used to cover luxuries that deliberate, nor accumulations of property that can never be used but are sure to curse the soul of the holder with the diverse diseases of mammonism.

In this petition, too, Jesus compels us to stand together. We have to ask in common for our daily bread. We sit at the common table in God's great house, and the supply of each depends on the security of all. The more society is socialized, the clearer does that fact become, and the more just and humane its organization becomes, the more will that recognition be at the bottom of all our institutions. As we stand thus in common, looking up to God for our bread, everyone of us ought to feel the sin and shame of it if he habitually takes more than his fair share and leaves others hungry that he may surfeit. It is inhuman, irreligious, and indecent.

The remaining petitions deal with the spiritual needs. Looking backward, we see that our lives have been full of sin and failure, and we realize the need of forgiveness. Looking forward, we tremble at the temptations that await us and pray for deliverance from evil.

In these prayers for the inner life, where the soul seems to confront God alone, we should expect to find only individualistic religion. But even here the social note sounds clearly.

This prayer will not permit us to ask for God's forgiveness without making us affirm that we have forgiven our brothers and are on a basis of brotherly love with all men: "Forgive us our debts, as we also have forgiven our debtors." We shall have to be socially right if we want to be religiously right. Jesus will not suffer us to be pious toward God and merciless toward men.

In the prayer, "Lead us not into temptation," we feel the human trembling of fear. Experience has taught us our frailty. Every man can see certain contingencies just a step ahead of him and knows that his moral capacity for resistance would collapse hopelessly if he were placed in these situations. Therefore Jesus gives voice to our inarticulate plea to God not to bring us into such situations.

But such situations are created largely by the social life about us. If the society in which we move is rank with sexual looseness, or full of the suggestiveness and solicitations of alcoholism; if our business life is such that we have to lie and cheat and be cruel in order to live and prosper; if our political organization offers an ambitious man the alternative of betraying the public good or of being thwarted and crippled in all his efforts, then the temptations are created in which men go under, and society frustrates the prayer we utter to God. No church can interpret this petition intelligently which closes its mind to the debasing or invigorating influence of the spiritual environment furnished by society. No man can utter this petition without conscious or unconscious hypocrisy [of one] who is helping to create the temptations in which others are sure to fall.

The words "Deliver us from the evil one" have in them the ring of battle. They bring to mind the incessant grapple between God and the permanent and malignant powers of evil in humanity. To the men of the first century that meant Satan and his host of evil spirits who ruled in the oppressive, extortionate, and idolatrous powers of Rome. Today the original spirit of that prayer will probably be best understood by those who are pitted against the terrible powers of organized covetousness and institutionalized oppression.

Thus the Lord's Prayer is the great prayer of social Christianity. It is charged with what we call "social consciousness." It assumes the social solidarity of men as a matter of course. It recognizes the social basis of all moral and religious life even in the most intimate personal relations to God.

It is not the property of those whose chief religious aim is to pass through an evil world in safety, leaving the world's evil unshaken. Its dominating thought is the moral and religious transformation of mankind in all its social relations. It was left us by Jesus, the great initiator of the Christian revolution; and it is the rightful property of those who follow his banner in the conquest of the world.

CHAPTER 5

Contemporary Spirituality

As the nineteenth century gave way to the twentieth there was growing disaffection with some of the central emphases of the earlier generation. Several foundational tensions—like the debate that emerged between theological traditionalists and modernists—continued and became more severe and more divisive. Other foundational themes, like the nineteenth century's optimism about human nature and human capacity for good, would almost immediately be called into question.

The reformist mood of the earlier age, which stressed the need for Christian unity and concerted action in order to make an impact on an increasingly irreligious world, remained powerful and took theological expression in Protestantism's renewed emphasis upon the church and ecumenism. It was for this reason that the period was justifiably hailed as "the Age of the church."[1] In the face of the horrors of World War I and continued social deterioration, however, many of the earlier ideological foundations—like the inevitability of progress, and the goodness of humanity—seemed irrelevant. Indeed, Walter Rauschenbusch acknowledged that in his earlier work he "adopted an 'optimism not warranted by the facts.'"[2] Karl Barth's so-called "theology of crisis" was born in the pastor's study as Barth sought to fill the theological vacuum created by the apparent irrelevance of some of the central tenants of nineteenth-century liberalism.

Spirituality of the era was shaped by the continuing secularization of modern society. In some instances, like the work of Evelyn Underhill, Christian Spirituality quarried the resources of the past to find fresh and relevant models of Christian mys-

---

[1]Jaroslav Pelikan, *The Christian Tradition*, Vol. 5: *Christian Doctrine and Modern Culture* (Chicago: University of Chicago Press, 1989), "The Sobornost of the Body of Christ," pp. 282–337.
[2]Ibid., p. 324 quoting Walter Rauschenbush's *Conception of Missions*, pp. 270–71.

ticism. For others, like Simone Weil, the path toward spirituality lay not so much in mysticism as in a worldly asceticism that was based in the challenges of life in the world. A second world war, in less than three decades, gave voice to a religious existentialism that expressed the pessimism and uncertainty of contemporary Christians (especially for Europeans). Where a nineteenth-century spirituality advocated optimism and concerted action on behalf of God, the war-ravaged twentieth century found itself waiting, somewhat uncertainly, for a manifestation of the Divine. Advances in the social sciences and psychology made it seem necessary for religious expression to stand in dialogue with those emerging areas of investigation. In this context Pierre Teihard de Chardin pioneered a synthesis of spiritual and scientific insights to produce a religious understanding of the world and its processes. Others, like A.W. Tozer spoke of human life as a sacrament; the "sacrament of living."

The horrors of the Holocaust, poverty, and oppression brought the question of human suffering forcefully to the forefront of theological reflection near the midpoint of the century. For some, like the martyred Dietrich Bonhoeffer, the magnitude of the horror impelled an assault against the citadel of evil. Others, like Mother Teresa, sought resolution of this profound problem by finding a sanctifying side to suffering. In a similar fashion, Howard Thurman found Jesus most profoundly present among the disinherited. Nonviolent protest against oppression became the spiritual tool of Martin Luther King and Desmond Tutu.

The technological advances developed in the latter half of the century made the world an increasingly smaller place. Communication, information, and contact across national, cultural, and linguistic barriers became increasingly common and rapid. The recognition that the task of Christian Spirituality was to be carried out in the midst of a global community was one of the new thresholds of the second half of the century. Figures as diverse as Martin Luther King (who studied Gandhi's nonviolent philosophy) and Thomas Merton (who studied the Zen masters) looked eastward and found formative influences for their life and thought. New spiritualities were born in nonwestern social contexts and problems, like that of Gustavo Gutierrez in Latin America and Mother Teresa in the slums of Calcutta. Gutierrez echoed the poignant question of the psalmist, "How shall we sing the Lord's songs in a foreign land?" In a similar way diverse cultural contexts shaped Christian Spirituality in more direct and overt ways than in previous ages. Hence, it became necessary and appropriate to explore the distinctive contribution of the African American experience to the development of Christian Spirituality—as does the work of James Cone—or the feminist perspective as represented in the work of Rosemary Reuther.

These contemporary spiritualities take their own context as the appropriate beginning point for envisioning the nature and task of Christian Spirituality. Alongside the contextual approaches emerged more traditional ones (like those of Evelyn Underhill, C. S. Lewis, and Richard Foster), which looked back to classical Christian themes and practices for resources with which to embrace a new future. And, as Karl Rahner described in the "Spirituality of the Future," this meeting of the past and the future forms the basis for a new and vital Christian Spirituality.

Rudolf Otto (1869–1937)

Rudolf Otto was born at Peine in Hanover, Germany. He was educated in philosophy and theology at Erlangen and Göttingen. Otto taught at Göttingen, Breslau, and Marburg (1907–37). His interests were rather diverse, and he published works on Christ, on Indian religious thought and its relation to Christianity, as well as on theological topics. His chief contribution to Christian Spirituality, however, was Otto's stress on one's experience of "otherness" of God—which he described as both a fascinating and overpowering feeling. This emphasis took expression in his chief work *The Idea of the Holy* (1917). Equally important was Otto's willingness to counter the rationalism of his age with a profound emphasis on the validity of religious feelings and experience.

THE NON-RATIONAL ELEMENT IN RELIGION[3]

It is essential to every theistic conception of God, and most of all to the Christian, that it designates and precisely characterizes Deity by the attributes Spirit, Reason, Purpose, Good Will, Supreme Power, Unity, Selfhood. The nature of God is thus thought of by analogy with our human nature of reason and personality; only, whereas in ourselves we are aware of this as qualified by restriction and limitation, as applied to God the attributes we use are "completed," i.e. thought as absolute and unqualified. Now all these attributes constitute clear and definite *concepts*: they can be grasped by the intellect; they can be analyzed by thought; they even admit of definition. An object that can thus be thought conceptually may be termed rational. The nature of deity described in the attributes above mentioned is, then, a rational nature; and a religion which recognizes and maintains such a view of God is in so far a "rational" religion. Only on such terms is Belief possible in contrast to mere *feeling*. And of Christianity at least it is false that "feeling is all, the name but sound and smoke,"[4]—where "name" stands for conception or thought. Rather we count this the very mark and criterion of a religion's high rank and superior value—that it should have no lack of *conceptions* of God; that it should admit knowledge—the knowledge that comes by faith—of the transcendent in terms of conceptual thought, and whether those already mentioned or others which continue and develop them. Christianity not only possesses such conceptions but possesses them in unique clarity and abundance, and this is, though not the sole or even the chief, yet a very real sign of its superiority over religions of other forms and at other levels. . . .

---

[3]Reprinted from Rufolf Otto, *The Idea of the Holy,* translated by John W. Harvey (2nd ed. 1950) by permission of Oxford University Press. Pages 1–4.
[4]From Goethe, *Faust.*

But, when this is granted, we have to be on our guard against an error which would lead to a wrong and one-sided interpretation of religion. This is the view that the essence of deity can be given completely and exhaustively in such "rational" attributions as have been referred to above and in others like them. It is not an unnatural misconception. We are prompted to it by the traditional language of edification, with its characteristic phraseology and ideas; by the learned treatment of religious themes in sermon and theological instruction; and further even by our Holy Scriptures themselves. In all these cases the "rational" element occupies the foreground, and often nothing else seems to be present at all. But this is after all to be expected. All language, in so far as it consists of words, purports to convey ideas or concepts;—that is what language means;—and the more clearly and unequivocally it does so, the better the language. And hence expositions of religious truth in language inevitably tend to stress the "rational" attributes of God. . . .

Here . . . we come up against the contrast between Rationalism and profounder religion, and with this contrast and its signs we shall be repeatedly concerned in what follows. We have here in fact the first and most distinctive mark of Rationalism, with which all the rest are bound up. It is not that which is commonly asserted, that Rationalism is the denial, and its opposite the affirmation, of the miraculous. That is manifestly a wrong or at least a very superficial distinction. . . . The difference between Rationalism and its opposite is to be found elsewhere. It resolves itself rather into a peculiar difference of *quality* in the mental attitude and emotional content of the religious life itself. All depends upon this: in our idea of God is the non-rational overborne, even perhaps wholly excluded, by the rational? Or conversely, does the non-rational itself preponderate over the rational? Looking at the matter thus, we see that the common dictum, that Orthodoxy itself has been the mother of Rationalism, is in some measure well founded. It is not simply that Orthodoxy was preoccupied with doctrine and the framing of dogma, for these have been no less a concern of the wildest mystics. It is rather that Orthodoxy found in the construction of dogma and doctrine no way to do justice to the non-rational aspect of its subject. So far from keeping the non-rational element in religion alive in the heart of the religious experience, orthodox Christianity manifestly failed to recognize its value, and by this failure gave to the idea of God a one-sidedly intellectualistic and rationalistic interpretation.

This bias to rationalism still prevails, not only in theology but in the science of comparative religion in general, and from top to bottom of it. The modern students of mythology, and those who pursue research into the religion of "primitive man" and attempt to reconstruct the "bases" or "sources" of religion, are all victims to it. . . . And so it is salutary that we should be incited to notice that Religion is not exclusively contained and exhaustively comprised in any series of "rational" assertions; and it is well worth while to attempt to bring the relation of the different "moments" of religion to one another clearly before the mind, so that its nature may become more manifest. This attempt we are not to make with respect to the quite distinctive category of the holy or sacred.

THE NUMINOUS[5]

"Holiness"—"the holy"—is a category of interpretation and valuation peculiar to the sphere of religion. It is, indeed, applied by transference to another sphere—that of Ethics—but it is not itself derived from this. While it is complex, it contains a quite specific element or "moment," which sets it apart from "the Rational" in the meaning we gave to that word above, and which remains inexpressible—an *arraton* (Grk.) or *ineffable*—in the sense that it completely eludes apprehension in terms of concepts. The same thing is true (to take a quite different region of experience) of the category of the beautiful.

Now these statements would be untrue from the outset if "the holy" were merely what is meant by the word, not only in common parlance, but in philosophical, and generally even in theological usage. The fact is we have come to use the words *holy, sacred* (Ger. *helig*) in an entirely derivative sense, quite different from that which they originally bore. We generally take "holy" as meaning "completely good"; it is the absolute moral attribute, denoting the consummation of moral goodness. . . . But this common usage of the term is inaccurate. It is true that all this moral significance is contained in the word "holy," but it includes in addition—as even we cannot but feel—a clear overplus of meaning, and this it is now our task to isolate. Nor is this merely a later or acquired meaning; rather, "holy," or at least the equivalent words in Latin and Greek, in Semitic and other ancient languages, denoted first and foremost *only* this overplus; if the ethical element was present at all, at any rate it was not original and never constituted the whole meaning of the word. Any one who uses it today does undoubtedly always feel "the morally good" to be implied in "holy"; and accordingly in our inquiry into that element which is separate and peculiar to the idea of the holy it will be useful, at least for the temporary purpose of the investigation, to invent a special term to stand for "the holy" *minus* its "rational" aspect altogether. . . .

Accordingly, it is worth while . . . to find a word to stand for this element in isolation, this "extra" in the meaning of "holy" above and beyond the meaning of goodness. By means of a special term we shall the better be able, first, to keep the meaning clearly apart and distinct, and second, to apprehend and classify connectedly whatever subordinate forms or stages of development it may show. For this purpose I adopt a word coined from the Latin *numen. Omen* has given us *ominous*, and there is no reason why from *numen* we should not similarly form a word *"numinous."* I shall speak then of a unique "numinous" category of value and of a definitely "numinous" state of mind, which is always found wherever the category is applied. This mental state is perfectly *sui generis* and irreducible to any other; and therefore, like every absolutely primary and elementary datum, while it admits of being discussed, it cannot be strictly defined. There is only one way to help another to an understanding of it. He must be guided and led on by consideration and discussion of the matter through the ways of his own mind, until

---

[5]Reprinted from Otto, *Idea of the Holy*, by permission of Oxford University Press. Pages 5–7.

he reach the point at which "the numinous" in him perforce begins to stir, to start into life and into consciousness. We can co-operate in this process by bringing before his notice all that can be found in other regions of the mind, already known and familiar, to resemble, or again to afford some special contrast to, the particular experience we wish to elucidate. Then we must add: "This X of ours is not precisely *this* experience, but akin to this one and the opposite of that other. Cannot you realize for yourself what it is?" In other words our X cannot, strictly speaking, be taught, it can only be evoked, awakened in the mind; as everything that comes "of the spirit" must be awakened.

Evelyn Underhill (1875–1941)

Evelyn Underhill (Mrs. Stuart Moore) was an only child of a comfortable, nonreligious British family. Her father, (Sir) Arthur, was a distinguished barrister; her mother, Alice Lucy, was the daughter of Moses Ironmonger, Justice of the Peace of Wolverhampton.

Underhill was a part of a larger movement of spiritual pilgrims that emerged out of the devastation of World War I; among her contemporaries were Dean Inge, Olive Wyon, Hywel Hughes, Charles Williams, and Baron Friedrich von Hugel.[6] Von Hugel was particularly influential for her, and under his guidance she professed Christian faith and took steps to join the Roman Catholic Church. She stopped short of that association, however, in 1907 when Pope Pius X issued his decree (*Lamentabili*) against "modernism" in the church. Feeling that her intellectual freedom might be compromised, Evelyn Underhill joined the Church of England instead.

Besides serving as a spiritual counselor and leader of religious retreats, Evelyn Underhill authored several significant works including *Mysticism* (1911) and *Worship* (1936). Her sympathetic reading of the classical works of Christian Spirituality gave Underhill's work a tone that was both scholarly and warmly personal. Her *Mysticism* remains a standard work for understanding and interpreting the movement.

THE CHARACTERISTICS OF MYSTICISM[7]

. . . Now returning to our original undertaking, that of defining if we can the characteristics of true mysticism, I think that we have already reached a point at which William James's celebrated "four marks" of the mystic state, Ineffability, Noetic Quality, Transiency, and Passivity, will fail to satisfy us. In their place I propose

---

[6]Hugh T. Kerr and John M. Mulder, eds., *Conversions* (Grand Rapids, Mich.: W. B. Eerdmans, 1983), pp. 184–85.
[7]Reprinted from Evelyn Underhill, *Mysticism: A Study in the Nature and Development of Man's Spiritual Consciousness* (New York: E.P. Dutton, 1911; reprinted 1961), pp. 80–82.

to set out, illustrate and, I hope, justify four other rules or notes which may be applied as tests to any given case which claims to take rank amongst the mystics.

1. True mysticism is active and practical, not passive and theoretical. It is an organic life-process, a something which the whole self does; not something as to which its intellect holds an opinion.

2. Its aims are wholly transcendental and spiritual. It is in no way concerned with adding to, exploring, re-arranging, or improving anything in the visible universe. The mystic brushes aside that universe, even in its supernormal manifestations. Though he does not, as his enemies declare, neglect his duty to the many, his heart is always set upon the changeless One.

3. This One is for the mystic, not merely the Reality of all that is, but also a living and personal Object of Love; never an object of exploration. It draws his whole being homeward, but always under the guidance of the heart.

4. Living union with this One—which is the term of his adventure—is a definite state or form of enhanced life. It is obtained either from an intellectual realization of its delights, nor from the most acute emotional longings. Though these must be present, they are not enough. It is arrived at by an arduous psychological and spiritual process—the so-called Mystic Way—entailing the complete remaking of character and the liberation of a new, or rather latent, form of consciousness; which imposes on the self the condition which is sometimes inaccurately called "ecstasy," but is better named the Unitive State.

Mysticism, then, is not an opinion: it is not a philosophy. . . . On the one hand it is not merely the power of contemplating Eternity: on the other it is not to be identified with any kind of religious queerness. It is the name of that organic process which involves the perfect consummation of the Love of God: the achievement here and now of the immortal heritage of man. Or, if you like it better—for this means exactly the same thing—it is the art of establishing his conscious relation with the Absolute.

The movement of the mystic consciousness towards this consummation, is not merely the sudden admission to an overwhelming vision of Truth: though such dazzling glimpses may from time to time be vouchsafed to the soul. It is rather an ordered movement towards ever higher levels of reality, ever closer identification with the Infinite. "The mystic experience," says Recejac, "ends with the words, 'I live, yet not I, but God in me.' This feeling of identification, which is the term of mystical activity, has a very important significance. In its early stages the mystic conscienceness feels the Absolute in opposition to the Self . . . as mystic activity goes on it tends to abolish this opposition. . . . When it has reached its term the consciousness finds itself possessed by the sense of a Being at one and the same time greater than the Self and identical with it: great enough to be God, intimate enough to be me." This is that mystic union which is the only possible fulfillment of mystic love. . . .

PHASES OF THE MYSTICAL LIFE[8]

The first thing we notice about this composite portrait is that the typical mystic seems to move towards his goal through a series of strongly marked oscillations between "states of pleasure" and "states of pain." The existence and succession of these states—sometimes broken and confused, sometimes crisply defined—can be traced, to a greater or less degree, in almost every case of which we possess anything like a detailed record. . . . The soul, as it treds the ascending spiral of its road towards reality, experiences alternately the sunshine and the shade. These experiences are "constants" of the transcendental life. "The Spiritual States of the Soul are all Eternal," said Blake, with the true mystical genius for psychology.

The complete series of these states—and it must not be forgotten that few individuals present them all in perfection, whilst in many instances several are blurred or appear to be completely suppressed—will be, I think, most conveniently arranged under five heads. . . . The groups, however, must be looked upon throughout as diagrammatic, and only as answering loosely and generally to experiences which seldom present themselves in so rigid and unmixed a form. These experiences, largely conditioned as they are by surroundings and by temperament, exhibit all the variety and spontaneity which are characteristic of life in its highest manifestations: and, like biological specimens, they lose something of their essential reality in being prepared for scientific investigation. Taken all together, they constitute phases in a single process of growth; involving the movement of consciousness from lower to higher levels of reality, the steady remaking of character in accordance with the "independent spiritual world." But as the study of physical life is made easier for us by an artificial division into infancy, adolescence, maturity, and old age, so a discreet indulgence of the human passion for map-making will increase our chances of understanding the nature of the Mystic Way. Here, then, is the classification under which we shall study the phases of the mystical life.

1. The awakening of the Self to consciousness of Divine Reality. This experience, usually abrupt and well-marked, is accompanied by intense feelings of joy and exaltation.

2. The Self, aware for the first time of Divine Beauty, realizes by contrast its own finiteness and imperfection, the manifold illusions in which it is immersed, the immense distance which separates it from the One. Its attempts to eliminate by discipline and mortification all that stands in the way of its progress towards union with God constitute *Purgation*: a state of pain and effort.

---

[8]Ibid., pp. 168–70.

3. When by Purgation the Self has become detached from the "things of sense," and acquired those virtues which are the "ornaments of the spiritual marriage," its joyful consciousness of the Transcendent Order returns in an enhanced form. Like the prisoners in Plato's "Cave of Illusion," it has awakened to knowledge of Reality, has struggled up the harsh and difficult path to the mouth of the cave. Now it looks upon the sun. This is *Illumination*: a state which includes in itself many of the stages of contemplation, . . . visions and adventures of the soul described by St. Teresa and other mystical writers. . . . Illumination is the "contemplative state" *par excellence*. It forms, with the two preceding states, the "first mystic life." Many mystics never go beyond it; and, on the other hand, many seers and artists not usually classed amongst them, have shared, to some extent, the experiences of the illumined state. Illumination brings a certain apprehension of the Absolute, a sense of the Divine Presence: but not true union with it. It is a state of happiness.

4. In the development of the great and strenuous seekers after God, this is followed—or sometimes intermittently accompanied—by the most terrible of all the experiences of the Mystic Way: the final and complete purification of the Self, which is called by some contemplatives the "mystic pain" or "mystic death," by others the Purification of the Spirit or *Dark Night of the Soul*. The consciousness which had, in Illumination, sunned itself in the sense of the Divine Presence, now suffers under an equally intense sense of the Divine Absence: learning to dissociate the personal satisfaction of mystical vision from the reality of mystical life. As in Purgation the senses were cleansed and humbled, and the energies and interests of the Self were concentrated upon transcendental things: so now the purifying process is extended to the very center of I-hood, the will. The human instinct for personal happiness must be killed. This is the "spiritual crucifixion" so often described by the mystics: the great desolation in which the soul seems abandoned by the Divine. The Self now surrenders itself, its individuality, and its will, completely. It desires nothing, asks nothing, is utterly passive, and is thus prepared for

5. *Union*: the true goal of the mystic quest. In this state the Absolute Life is not merely perceived and enjoyed by the Self, as in Illumination: but is *one* with it. This is the end towards which all the previous oscillations of consciousness have tended. It is a state of equilibrium, of purely spiritual life; characterized by peaceful joy, by enhanced powers, by intense certitude. To call this state, as some authorities do, by the name Ecstacy, is inaccurate and confusing: since the term Ecstacy has long been used both by psychologists and ascetic writers to define that short and rapturous trance—a state with well-marked physical and psychical accompaniments—in which the contemplative, losing all consciousness of the phenomenal world, is caught up to a brief and immediate enjoyment of the Divine Vision. Ecstasies of this kind are often experienced by the mystic in Illumination, or even on his first conversion. They cannot therefore be regarded as exclusively characteristic of the Unitive Way. . . . Union must be looked upon as the true goal of mystical growth; that permanent establishment of life upon transcendent levels of reality, of which ecstasies give

a foretaste to the soul. Intense forms of it, described by individual mystics, under symbols such as those of Mystical Marriage, Deification, or Divine Fecundity, all prove on examination to be aspects of this same experience. . . .

Karl Barth (1886–1968)

Karl Barth was born in Basel, Switzerland, where his roots sank deep into the heritage of the Reformed (Calvinistic) Church; both of his grandfathers, his father, and his older brother were ministers of the Reformed Church. His own appetite for theology was first whetted during studies for his confirmation, at the age of sixteen. During that event Barth posed himself the personal challenge to know and understand the confessions of his church; indeed he was determined to "understand them from within."

After being educated at Berne, Berlin, Tübingen, and Marburg—where he studied with the famous liberal theologian Wilhelm Hermann—Barth entered the ministry of the Reformed Church and accepted a call to serve the Church of Geneva in late 1909. He moved to the Safenwil in 1911. The destruction and disillusionment that came with World War I caused Barth to question the validity of the liberal optimism he had imbibed during his university studies. This crisis forced him back to familiar foundations, the Bible, and Calvin, as well as the emerging theology of Søren Kierkegaard; out of this synthesis came a new theological alignment that was based on the Reformed tradition and modern theological methods. Barth called this formulation a "crisis theology"; others termed it neoorthodoxy because of its combination of new (neo) and classical (orthodox) theological themes and methods.

Barth's Romerbrief (1919) signaled the beginning of Barth's crisis theology. It took expression in the Barmen Declaration that he penned against the rising Nazism in the German church, and most supremely in Barth's multivolume systematic theology Church Dogmatics—which was arguably the most fresh and comprehensive theological system since that of Thomas Aquinas. His chief contribution to Christian Spirituality is seen in his willingness to reshape and apply classical Christian themes and disciplines to fit the needs of the contemporary age.

THE PROBLEM OF PRAYER[9]

. . . Here we are, then, we Christians, looked upon as believers, as obedient servants, and as such faced with a new problem: that of prayer. Is it really a new problem? beyond faith and obedience? So it would seem. Calvin says that prayer deals with our life and our relation to the exigencies of this world. The question is as follows: I, who am a Christian, can I really live according to the word of the

---

[9]Reprinted from Karl Barth, Prayer. Used by permission of Westminster John Knox Press and by permission of Society for Promoting Christian Knowledge. Pages 29–32.

gospel and of the law, according to my faith and in obedience? Shall I be able to live thus in the midst of the necessities of my existence?—Yes, according to the gospel it is possible in the holiness of obedience to live that which is given us to live, that which we must live. In order to do this, we must listen to what is told us about prayer and ask God himself to come to our aid, to instruct us, to give us the possibility of walking in this path. Such a quest must be made in order that we may live. Prayer is this quest. . . .

On the one hand, there is our inward life, that of weak and wily human beings. On the other hand, there is our outward life in this world, with all its enigmas and difficulties. There is also the judgment of God, who encounters us and says to us at every moment, "This is not enough." I may even reach the point of asking myself, "Underneath it all, am I a Christian? My faith being small and my obedience slight, of what meaning are these words: 'I believe, I obey'?" Deep is the abyss. The core of our being is put to question at the very moment we believe and obey as well as we can. In this situation (which is the same for every Christian) prayer means going toward God, asking him to give us what we lack—strength, courage, serenity, prudence—asking him to teach us how to obey the law and accomplish the commandments, and then that God may instruct us how to continue in believing and believing yet more, and that he may renew our faith. . . .

Prayer means that we address ourselves to God, who has already spoken to us in the gospel and in the law. We find ourselves face to face with him when we are tormented by the imperfection of our obedience and the discontinuity of our faith. Because of God we are in distress. God alone is able to heal us of it. In order to ask him to do so, we pray. . . . Thus for the Reformers everything was reduced to this question: How is it possible for me to have an encounter with God? I have heard his word, I wish sincerely to listen to it, and yet here I am in my insufficiency. The Reformers were not unaware of other difficulties, but they knew that such hindrances are all implicit in the following reality: I stand before God with my desires, my thoughts, my misery; I must live with him, for to live means nothing other than to live with God. Here I am, caught between the exigencies of life, both small and great, and the necessity of prayer. The Reformers tell us the first thing is to pray.

PRAYER AS A GIFT OF GOD[10]

Prayer is a grace, an offer of God. . . . Let us approach the subject from the given fact that God answers. God is not deaf, but listens; more than that, he acts. God does not act in the same way whether we pray or not. Prayer exerts an influence upon God's action, even upon his existence. This is what the word "answer" means. . . . How does God answer us? . . . We cannot better understand God's answer than by keeping in mind this thought: Jesus Christ is our brother, we be-

---

[10]Ibid. Used by permission of Westminster John Press, 1985; and SPCK. Pages 33–38.

long to him; he is the head of the body of which we are the members; and at the same time he is the Son of God, of God himself. It is he who has been given to us as mediator and advocate before God. We are not separated from God, and more important still, God is not separated from us. We may be without God, but God is not without humankind. This we must know, and this is what matters. Facing the godless, there is God, who is never without us, because humanity—all of us—is the presence of God. If God knows humanity, if he sees us and judges us, it is always through the person of Jesus Christ, his own Son, who has been obedient and is the object of his delight. By Jesus Christ, humanity is in the presence of God. God looks at Christ, and it is through him that he looks at us. We have, therefore, a representative before God.

Calvin even says that we pray through the mouth of Jesus Christ, who speaks for us because of what he has been, because of what he has suffered in obedience and faithfulness to his Father. And we ourselves pray as though with his mouth, inasmuch as he gives us access and audience, and intercedes for us. Thus, fundamentally, our prayer is already made even before we formulate it. When we pray, we can only return to that prayer which was uttered in the person of Jesus Christ and which is constantly repeated because God is not without humankind.

God is the Father of Jesus Christ, and that very man Jesus Christ has prayed, and he is praying still. Such is the foundation of our prayer in Jesus Christ. It is as if God himself has pledged to answer our request because all our prayers are summed up in Jesus Christ; God cannot fail to answer, since it is Jesus Christ who prays.

The fact that God yields to human petitions, that he alters his intentions and follows the bent of our prayers, is not a sign of weakness. In his own majesty and in the splendor of his might, he has willed and yet wills it so. He desires to be the God who has been made flesh in Jesus Christ. Therein lies his glory, his omnipotence. He does not then impair himself by yielding to our prayer; on the contrary, it is in so doing that he shows his greatness.

If God himself wishes to enter into fellowship with humankind and be close to us as a father is to his child, he does not thereby weaken his might. God cannot be greater than he is in Jesus Christ. If God answers our prayer, it is not then only because he listens to us and increases our faith . . . but because he is God: Father, Son, and Holy Spirit, God whose word has been made flesh. . . .

Furthermore, God, since he is our God, causes our prayer to proceed from his grace. Wherever there is the grace of God, human beings pray. God works in us, for we know not how to pray as we ought. It is the Spirit of God that incites us and enables us to pray in a fitting manner. We are not skilled to judge whether we are worthy or capable of praying, or whether we have sufficient zeal to pray. Grace in itself is the answer to this question. When we are comforted by the grace of God, we begin to pray with or without words.

God also points out a way that will lead us to prayer. Prayer is neither an arbitrary act nor a step to be taken blindly. When we pray, we cannot venture according to whim in this or that direction, with just any sort of request. For God commands us to follow him and to take the place that he has assigned to us. It is a matter ruled by God, not by our own initiative.

How shall we pray? It was not by chance that Jesus gave us a formulary in the Lord's Prayer to instruct all human beings how to pray aright. God himself teaches us how we are to pray, for we have so many things to ask! And we think that what we desire is always so important! Besides, it is necessary for us to believe this. But in order that our act may become true prayer, we must accept the offer that God tenders us. We cannot pray by ourselves, and if we have deceptions in prayer, we must accept God's showing us the way of true prayer. He therefore starts us, with all our needs and problems, on a certain path by which we can bring everything to him; but we must take that path. . . .

Because he is our God in Jesus Christ, God himself compels us to take in his presence an attitude that at first sight appears to be rash and bold. He obliges us to meet him with a certain audacity: "Thou has made us promises, thou hast commanded us to pray; and here I am, coming, not with pious ideas or because I like to pray (perhaps I do not like to pray), and I say to thee what thou has commanded me to say, 'Help me in the necessities of my life.' Thou must do so; I am here." Luther is right: the position of one at prayer requires utter humility as well as an attitude of boldness. There is a good kind of humility; it consists in accepting, through liberty, this place that we have in Jesus vis-à-vis God. If we are sure of our attitude, and if we do not come to God merely on account of our good intentions, then this liberty is self-evident. Thus God's will in our favor and his mercy in Jesus Christ are decisive elements in the matter now at hand. . . . [O]ur sure foundation rests on the fact that, because of Jesus Christ, God can answer our prayer in spite of our unworthiness.

PRAYER AS A HUMAN ACT[11]

According to the foregoing considerations, prayer is an altogether simple act by which we accept and use the divine offer; an act in which we obey this command of the majestic grace that identifies itself with the will of God. To obey grace—to give thanks—means that prayer is also an act on the part of human beings, who know themselves to be sinners and call upon the grace of God. We find ourselves confronted by the gospel, the law, and the weakness of our faith, even if we are not conscious of it. We experience at once a certain sadness and a certain joy. But we have not yet understood that we are sinners or that we do not perfectly realize obedience. We do not yet know that we are under a veil. It must be removed. When we pray, our human condition is unveiled to us, and we know then that we are in this distress and also in that hope. It is God who places us in this situation; but at the same time he comes to our aid. Prayer is thus our human response when we understand our distress and know that help will come.

It is not permissible to consider prayer as a good work to be done, as a pious, nice, and pretty duty to be performed. Prayer cannot be for us a means of

---

[11]Ibid., Used by permission of Westminster John Knox Press, and SPCK. Pages 38–41.

creating something, of making a gift to God and to ourselves; we are in the position of persons who can only receive, who are obliged to speak now to God, since they have no one else whom they can address. Luther has said that we must all be destitute, for we are faced by a great void and have everything to receive and learn from God.

Prayer as a human act cannot be a gossiping, a series of phrases or mumblings. . . . rayer must be an act of affection; it is more than a question of using the lips, for God asks the allegiance of our hearts. If the heart is not in it, if it is only a form which is carried out more or less correctly, what is it then? Nothing! All prayers offered solely by the lips are not only superfluous, but they are also displeasing to God; they are not only useless, but they are offensive to God. . . .

We are not free to pray or not to pray, or to pray only when we feel so inclined, for prayer is not an act that comes naturally to us. It is a grace, and we can expect this grace only through the Holy Spirit. This grace is there, with God and his word in Jesus Christ. If we say yes to all that, if we receive what God gives, then everything is done, everything is settled, not on account of our good pleasure, but by the freedom we have in obeying him.

Above all, let us not begin by believing that humankind is passive, that we are in a sort of *fariente* ["do nothing"], in an armchair, and that we can say, "The Holy Spirit will pray for me." Never! Humankind is impelled to pray. We must do it. Prayer is an act, as well as a supplication to the Lord that he put us in this frame of mind which is agreeable to him. This is one of the facets of the problem of grace and liberty: we work but at the same time we very well know that God wills to fulfill our work; we are in this human liberty which is not crushed by the liberty of God; we allow the Holy Spirit to act, and yet, during this time, our mind and our heart do not sleep. Such is prayer when viewed as a human act.

Our participation in the work of God is the action that consists in giving our allegiance to this work. It is a great thing to preach, to believe, and to fulfill our small obedience to God's commandments. But in all these forms of obedience and faith it is prayer that puts us in rapport with God and permits us to collaborate with him. God wishes us to live with him, and we on our side reply, "Yes, Father, I wish to live with thee." And then he says, "Pray, call me: I am listening to you. I shall live and reign with you." . . .

A PASTORAL PRAYER[12]

O Sovereign God, it is through your inconceivable greatness that we are able to call upon you; Lord, *our* God, *our* Creator, *our* Parent, *our* Savior. In that greatness you know and love us all, you desire to be known and loved by us all, you see and guide our paths, and we all may come before you and go to be with you.

And now we pour out before you all our cares, that you may care for us; our

---

[12]Ibid., Used by permission of Westminster John Knox Press, and SPCK. Pages 90–93.

hopes and wishes, that they may be granted not according to our will but according to *your* will; our sins, that you may forgive them; our whole life in these times, that you may bring us to the resurrection of all humanity and to eternal life. We remember before you all who are in this house, and also all the men and women in prison throughout the world. Be with the members of our families at home, with all who are poor, sick, hard beset, or sorrowing. Enlighten the thoughts and rule the actions of those who in our land and in all lands are responsible for law, order, and peace. Let it be done, through Jesus Christ, our Lord. Amen.

Dietrich Bonhoeffer (1906–45)

Dietrich Bonhoeffer was born in Breslau, Germany. His father was a prominent physician, who became a professor at the University of Berlin. Dietrich studied theology at Tübingen and Berlin, as well as at Union Theological Seminary in New York. He studied under Karl Barth, who was a significant influence in his theological development, but he gradually moved away from Barth's emphasis upon revelation to develop what Bonhoeffer believed was a more Christocentric approach. He pastored congregations in Barcelona and London, as well as in Germany; from 1930 to 1936 he taught at the University of Berlin.

The rise of Nazism in Germany was a second formative influence on Dietrich Bonhoeffer's life and spirituality. In 1934 Bonhoeffer, Karl Barth, and others urged German Christians to stand apart from the state Lutheran Church because it supported the Nazi regime. The Barmen Declaration grew out of these efforts; it established the Confessing Church movement in Germany, and placed its authors in grave danger. In 1935, as the official Lutheran seminaries fell into line with Nazi ideology, Bonhoeffer founded a seminary for the Confessing Church in rural Finkenwalde. The seminary was subsequently moved several times and eventually forced underground by pressure from the Nazis, but it operated (in some fashion) until 1939, when Bonhoeffer left Germany to join the faculty of Union Theological Seminary in New York. He arrived in New York on June 12, and within two weeks he felt compelled to return to Germany; he could not live safely in exile while the Confessing Church faced Nazi persecution.

Although it was not known at that time, with the closing of the seminary Bonhoeffer joined his brother-in-law and several high-ranking military leaders in a plot to assassinate Hitler and overthrow his government. Dietrich's role in the plot was to use his position as a courier for the German military Intelligence Service and his international contacts to work for the resistance. After two attempts against Hitler's life failed, the conspiracy was uncovered and the paper trail led to Dietrich Bonhoeffer (and many others). In 1943 he was imprisoned in Tegal prison (Berlin). As the war ground to a close Bonhoeffer and his fellow conspirators were moved from prison to prison to avoid liberation by allied troops. After almost two years of imprisonment Bonhoeffer was hanged by the Gestapo just one month before the end of the war.

Bonhoeffer's location in history and the trials he faced caused him to reflect insightfully upon the meaning of being a Christian in the midst of severe crises. His most influential work, *The Cost of Discipleship* (1937), challenged the prevailing churchly notions of faith, grace, and discipleship by mounting a clarion call for a costly discipleship of radical obedience to Jesus Christ.

COSTLY GRACE[13]

Cheap grace is the deadly enemy of our Church. We are fighting today for costly grace. Cheap grace means grace sold on the market like cheapjack's wares. The sacraments, the forgiveness of sin, and the consolations of religion are thrown away at cut prices. Grace is represented as the Church's inexhaustible treasury, from which she showers blessings with generous hands, without asking questions or fixing limits. Grace without price; grace without cost! The essence of grace, we suppose, is that the account has been paid in advance; and, because it has been paid, everything can be had for nothing. Since the cost was infinite, the possibilities of using and spending it are infinite. What would grace be if it were not cheap?

Cheap grace means grace as a doctrine, a principle, a system. It means forgiveness of sins proclaimed as a general truth, the love of God taught as the Christian "conception" of God. An intellectual assent to that idea is held to be of itself sufficient to secure remission of sins. The Church which holds the correct doctrine of grace has, it is supposed, *ipso facto* a part in that grace. In such a Church the world finds a cheap covering for its sins; no contribution is required, still less any real desire to be delivered from sin. Cheap grace therefore amounts to a denial of the living Word of God, in fact, a denial of the Incarnation of the Word of God.

Cheap grace means the justification of sin without the justification of the sinner. Grace alone does everything, they say, and so everything can remain as it was before. . . . Instead of following Christ, let the Christian enjoy the consolations of his grace! That is what we mean by cheap grace, the grace which amounts to the justification of sin without the justification of the repentant sinner who departs from sin and from whom sin departs. Cheap grace is not the kind of forgiveness of sin which frees us from the toils of sin. Cheap grace is the grace we bestow on ourselves.

Cheap grace is the preaching of forgiveness without requiring repentance, baptism without church discipline, Communion without confession, absolution without personal confession. Cheap grace is grace without discipleship, grace without the cross, grace without Jesus Christ, living and incarnate.

Costly grace is the treasure hidden in the field; for the sake of it a man will gladly go and sell all that he has. It is the pearl of great price to buy which the

---

[13]Reprinted with the permission of Simon & Schuster from *The Cost of Discipleship* by Dietrich Bonhoeffer, translated by R. H. Fuller with some revision by Irmgard Booth. Copyright (c) 1959 by SCM Press, Ltd. Pages 45–48. Reprinted with the permission of SCM Press.

merchant will sell all his good. It is the kingly rule of Christ, for whose sake a man will pluck out the eye which causes him to stumble, it is the call of Jesus Christ at which the disciple leaves his nets and follows him.

Costly grace is the gospel which must be *sought* again and again, the gift which must be *asked* for, the door at which a man must *knock*. Such grace is *costly* because it calls us to follow, and it is *grace* because it calls us to follow *Jesus Christ*. It is costly because it costs a man his life, and it is grace because it gives a man the only true life. It is costly because it condemns sin, and grace because it justifies the sinner. Above all, it is *costly* because it cost God the life of his Son: "Ye were bought at a price," and what has cost God much cannot be cheap for us. Above all, it is *grace* because God did not reckon his Son too dear a price to pay for our life, but delivered him up for us. Costly grace is the Incarnation of God.

Costly grace is the sanctuary of God; it has to be protected from the world, and not thrown to the dogs. It is therefore the living word, the Word of God, which he speaks as it pleases him. Costly grace confronts us as a gracious call to follow Jesus, it comes as a word of forgiveness to the broken spirit and the contrite heart. Grace is costly because it compels a man to submit to the yoke of Christ and follow him; it is grace because Jesus says: "My yoke is easy and my burden is light."

THE CALL TO DISCIPLESHIP[14]

The call goes forth, and is at once followed by the response of obedience. The response of the disciples is an act of obedience, not a confession of faith in Jesus. . . . And what does the text [Mk 2:14] inform us about the content of discipleship? Follow me, run along behind me! That is all. To follow in his steps is something which is void of all content. It gives us no intelligible programme for a way of life, no goal or ideal to strive after. It is not a cause which human calculation might deem worthy of our devotion, even the devotion of ourselves. What happens? At the call, Levi leaves all that he has—but not because he thinks that he might be doing something worth while, but simply for the sake of the call. Otherwise he cannot follow in the steps of Jesus. This act on Levi's part has not the slightest value in itself, it is quite devoid of significance and unworthy of consideration. The disciple simply burns his boats and goes ahead. He is called out, and has to forsake his old life in order that he may "exist" in the strictest sense of the word. The old life is left behind, and completely surrendered. The disciple is dragged out of his relative security into a life of absolute insecurity (that is, in truth, into the absolute security and safety of the fellowship of Jesus), from a life which is observable and calculable (it is, in fact, quite incalculable) into a life where everything is unobservable and fortuitous (that is, into one which is necessary and calculable), out of the realm of finite (which is in truth the infinite) into the

---

[14]Ibid., pp. 61–64. Reprinted with permission of Simon & Schuster and of SCM Press.

realm of infinite possibilities (which is the one liberating reality). Again it is no universal law. Rather is it the exact opposite of all legality. It is nothing else than bondage to Jesus Christ alone, completely breaking through every programme, every ideal, every set of laws. No other significance is possible, since Jesus is the only significance. Beside Jesus nothing has any significance. He alone matters.

When we are called to follow Christ, we are summoned to an exclusive attachment to his person. The grace of his call bursts all the bonds of legalism. It is a gracious call, a gracious commandment. It transcends the difference between the law and the gospel. Christ calls, the disciple follows: that is grace and commandment in one. "I will walk at liberty, for I seek thy commandments" (Ps 119:45).

Discipleship means adherence to Christ, and, because Christ is the object of that adherence, it must take the form of discipleship. An abstract Christology, a doctrinal system, a general religious knowledge on the subject of grace or on the forgiveness of sins, render discipleship superfluous, and in fact they positively exclude any idea of discipleship whatever, and are essentially inimical to the whole conception of following Christ. With an abstract idea it is possible to enter into a relation of formal knowledge, to become enthusiastic about it, and perhaps even to put it into practice; but it can never be followed in personal obedience. Christianity without the living Christ is inevitably Christianity without discipleship, and Christianity without discipleship is always Christianity without Christ. It remains an abstract idea, a myth which has a place for the Fatherhood of God, but omits Christ as the living Son. And a Christianity of that kind is nothing more or less than the end of discipleship. . . . Discipleship without Jesus Christ is a way of our own choosing. It may be the ideal way. It may even lead to martyrdom. but it is devoid of all promise. Jesus will certainly reject it.

DISCIPLESHIP AND THE CROSS[15]

. . . "If any man would come after me, let him deny himself." . . . Self-denial is never just a series of isolated acts of mortification or asceticism. It is not suicide, for there is an element of self-will even in that. To deny oneself is to be aware only of Christ and no more of self, to see only him who goes before and no more the road which is too hard for us. Once more, all that self-denial can say is: "He leads the way, keep close to him."

". . . and take up his cross." Jesus has graciously prepared the way for this word by speaking first of self-denial. Only when we have become completely oblivious of self are we ready to bear the cross for his sake. If in the end we know only him, if we have ceased to notice the pain of our own cross, we are indeed looking only unto him. If Jesus had not so graciously prepared us for this word, we should have found it unbearable. But by preparing us for it he has enabled

---

[15]Ibid., pp. 97–101. Reprinted with permission of Simon & Schuster and of SCM Press.

us to receive even a word as hard as this as a word of grace. It comes to us in the joy of discipleship and confirms us in it. . . .

The cross is laid on every Christian. The first Christ-suffering which every man must experience is the call to abandon the attachments of this world. It is that dying of the old man which is the result of his encounter with Christ. As we embark upon discipleship we surrender ourselves to Christ in union with his death—we give over our lives to death. Thus it begins; the cross is not the terrible end to an otherwise god-fearing and happy life, but it meets us at the beginning of our communion with Christ. When Christ calls a man, he bids him come and die. It may be a death like that of the first disciples who had to leave home and work to follow him, or it may be a death like Luther's, who had to leave the monastery and go out into the world. But it is the same death every time—death in Jesus Christ, the death of the old man at his call. Jesus' summons to the rich young man was calling him to die, because only the man who is dead to his own will can follow Christ. In fact every command of Jesus is a call to die, with all our affections and lusts. But we do not want to die, and therefore Jesus Christ and his call are necessarily our death as well as our life. The call to discipleship, the baptism in the name of Jesus Christ means both death and life. The call of Christ, his baptism, sets the Christian in the middle of the daily arena against sin and the devil. Every day he encounters new temptations, and every day he must suffer anew for Jesus Christ's sake. The wounds and scars he receives in the fray are living tokens of this participation in the cross of his Lord. But there is another kind of suffering and shame which the Christian is not spared. While it is true that only the sufferings of Christ are a means of atonement, yet since he has suffered for and borne the sins of the whole world and shares with his disciples the fruits of his passion, the Christian also has to undergo temptation, he too has to bear the sins of others; he too must bear their shame and be driven like a scapegoat from the gate of the city. But he would certainly break down under this burden, but for the support of him who bore the sins of all. The passion of Christ strengthens him to overcome the sins of others by forgiving them. . . .

Suffering, then, is the badge of true discipleship. The disciple is not above his master. Following Christ means *passio passiva*, suffering because we have to suffer. That is why Luther reckoned suffering among the marks of the true Church, and one of the memoranda drawn up in preparation for the Augsburg Confession similarly defines the Church as the community of those "who are persecuted and martyred for the gospel's sake." If we refuse to take up our cross and submit to suffering and rejection at the hands of men, we forfeit our fellowship with Christ and have ceased to follow him. But if we lose our lives in his service and carry our cross, we shall find our lives again in the fellowship of the cross with Christ. The opposite of discipleship is to be ashamed of Christ and his cross and all the offence which the cross brings in its train.

Discipleship means allegiance to the suffering Christ, and it is therefore not at all surprising that Christians should be called upon to suffer. In fact it is a joy and a token of his grace. The acts of the early Christian martyrs are full of evidence which shows how Christ transfigures for his own the hour of their mortal agony by granting them the unspeakable assurance of his presence. In the hour of the cruellest torture they bear for his sake, they are made partakers in the perfect joy and bliss of fellowship with him. To bear the cross proves to be the only way of triumphing over suffering. This is true for all who follow Christ, because it was true for him. . . .

Simone Weil (1909–43)

Simone Weil was born in Paris, in an agnostic, Jewish home. She was educated in philosophy and began teaching the subject in 1931. In 1934 she left teaching and took a job in the Renault auto works in order to better understand the plight of the workers and to identify with their situation. She became deeply involved in leftist political activities. In 1938 she had a mystical experience in which "Christ came down and took me."

In June 1941 she met J. M. Perrin, O.P. and through him the Catholic writer Gustave Thibon. Their friendship shaped her spirituality. In May 1942 she fled France ahead of the anti-Semitic persecutions of the Vichy French government (which cooperated with the Nazis). She eventually settled in London, in November 1942, where she worked on behalf of the French government-in-exile. As conditions worsened in France, Simone Weil became ill in England; she refused food and treatment that would elevate her above the conditions of her countrymen during the Nazi occupation. Because of these acts of self-denial, Weil died on August 29, 1943.

Simone Weil's spirituality was often expressed in letters and meditations that she wrote to her friend Fr. Perrin. These have been collected into her principal work, *Waiting for God*. Of particular significance is the way in which she intertwined the themes of love for God, suffering, and self-denial. She was an unconventional Christian, who distrusted traditional ways of expressing and experiencing God's love. Simone was an "implicit Christian" who found God's love in "implicit expressions" like love of neighbors, friends, religious ceremonies, and the beauty of the world. She believed these forms of the implicit love of God prepare the soul for the explicit love of God which comes through direct encounter.

SPIRITUAL AUTOBIOGRAPHY[16]

. . . Before leaving I want to speak to you again, it may be the last time perhaps, for over there I shall probably send you only my news from time to time just so as to have yours.

---

[16]Reprinted by permission of the Putnam Publishing Group from *Waiting for God*, by Simone Weil. Copyright (c) 1951 by G.P. Putnam's Sons; renewed (c) 1979 by G.P. Putnam's Sons. Letter IV, pp. 61–69; The letter is directed to "Dear Father," Father Perrin, and dated "From Marseilles, about May 15."

I told you that I owed you an enormous debt. I want to try to tell you exactly what it consists of. I think that if you could really understand what my spiritual state is you would not be at all sorry that you did not lead me to baptism. But I do not know if it is possible for you to understand this.

You neither brought me the Christian inspiration nor did you bring me to Christ; for when I met you there was no longer any need; it had been done without the intervention of any human being. If it had been otherwise, if I had not already been won, not only implicitly but consciously, you would have given me nothing, because I should have received nothing from you. My friendship for you would have been a reason for me to refuse your message, for I should have been afraid of the possibilities of error and illusion which human influence in the divine order is likely to involve.

I may say that never at any moment in my life have I "sought for God." For this reason, which is probably too subjective, I do not like this expression and it strikes me as false. As soon as I reached adolescence, I saw the problem of God as a problem the data of which could not be obtained here below, and I decided that the only way of being sure not to reach a wrong solution, which seemed to me the greatest possible evil, was to leave it alone. So I left it alone. I neither affirmed nor denied anything. It seemed to me useless to solve the problem, for I thought that, being in this world, our business was to adopt the best attitude with regard to the problems of this world, and that such an attitude did not depend upon the solution of the problem of God.

This held good as far as I was concerned at any rate, for I never hesitated in my choice of an attitude; I always adopted the Christian attitude as the only possible one. I might say that I was born, I grew up, and I always remained within the Christian inspiration. While the very name of God had no part in my thoughts, with regard to the problems of this world and this life I shared the Christian conception in an explicit and rigorous manner, with the most specific notions it involves. Some of these notions have been part of my outlook for as far back as I can remember. With others I know the time and manner of their coming and the form under which they imposed themselves upon me. . . .

At fourteen I fell into one of those fits of bottomless despair that come with adolescence, and I seriously thought of dying because of the mediocrity of my natural faculties. The exceptional gifts of my brother, who had a childhood and youth comparable to those of Pascal,[17] brought my own inferiority home to me. I did not mind having no visible successes, but what did grieve me was the idea of being excluded from that transcendent kingdom to which only the truly great have access and wherein truth abides. I preferred to die rather than live without that truth. After months of inward darkness, I suddenly had the everlasting conviction that any human being, even though practically devoid of natural faculties, can penetrate to the kingdom of truth reserved for genius, if only he longs

---

[17]Blaise Pascal (1623–62), a brilliant French philosopher, mathematician, spiritual writer; as a youth he had a serious accident that turned his thoughts toward Christian faith. Excepts from one of his most famous religious work, *Pensees* ("Thoughts"), are presented on pp. 294–301.

for truth and perpetually concentrates all his attention upon its attainment. He thus becomes a genius too, even though for lack of talent his genius cannot be visible from the outside. Later on, when the strain of headaches caused the feeble faculties I possess to be invaded by a paralysis, which I was quick to imagine as probably incurable, the same conviction led me to persevere for ten years in an effort of concentrated attention that was practically unsupported by any hope of results.

Under the name of truth I also included beauty, virtue, and every kind of goodness, so that for me it was a question of a conception of the relationship between grace and desire. The conviction that had come to me was that when one hungers for bread one does not receive stones. But at that time I had not read the Gospel.

Just as I was certain that desire has in itself an efficacy in the realm of spiritual goodness whatever its form, I thought it was also possible that it might not be effective in any other realm.

As for the spirit of poverty, I do not remember any moment when it was not in me, although only to that unhappily small extent compatible with my imperfection. I fell in love with Saint Francis of Assisi[18] as soon as I came to know about him. I always believed and hoped that one day Fate would force upon me the condition of a vagabond and a beggar which he embraced freely. Actually I felt the same way about prison.

From my earliest childhood I always had also the Christian idea of love for one's neighbor, to which I gave the name of justice—a name it bears in many passages of the Gospel and which is so beautiful. You know that on this point I have failed seriously several times.

The duty of acceptance in all that concerns the will of God, whatever it may be, was impressed upon my mind as the first and most necessary of all duties from the time when I found it set down in Marcus Aurelius[19] under the form of the *amor fati* ["love of fate"] of the Stoics. I saw it as a duty we cannot fail in without dishonoring ourselves.

The idea of purity, with all that this word can imply for a Christian, took possession of me at the age of sixteen, after a period of several months during which I had been going through the emotional unrest natural in adolescence. This idea came to me when I was contemplating a mountain landscape and little by little it was imposed upon me in an irresistible manner.

Of course I knew quite well that my conception of life was Christian. This is why it never occurred to me that I could enter the Christian community. I had the idea that I was born inside. But to add dogma to this conception of life, without being forced to do so by indisputable evidence, would have seemed to me like a lack of honesty. I should even have thought I was lacking in honesty had

---

[18]Francis of Assisi (1182–1226) founder of the Franciscan order, understood himself as one married to "sister poverty." Cf. pp. 163–66 for selections from his works.

[19]Marcus Aurelius Antoninus (121–80), Stoic philosopher and Roman emperor, authored a notable collection of *Meditations*.

I considered the question of the truth of dogma as a problem for myself or even had I simply desired to reach a conclusion on this subject. I have an extremely severe standard for intellectual honesty, so severe that I never met anyone who did not seem to fall short of it in more than one respect; and I am always afraid of failing in it myself. . . .

After my year in the factory, before going back to teaching, I had been taken by my parents to Portugal, and while there I left them to go alone to a little village. I was, as it were, in pieces, soul and body. That contact with affliction had killed my youth. Until then I had not had any experience of affliction, unless we count my own, which, as it was my own, seemed to me, to have little importance, and which moreover was only a partial affliction, being biological and not social. I knew quite well that there was a great deal of affliction in the world, I was obsessed with the idea, but I had not had prolonged and first-hand experience of it. As I worked in the factory, indistinguishable to all eyes, including my own, from the anonymous mass, the affliction of others entered into my flesh and my soul. Nothing separated me from it, for I had really forgotten my past and I looked forward to no future, finding it difficult to imagine the possibility of surviving all the fatigue. What I went through there marked me in so lasting a manner that still today when any human being, whoever he may be and in whatever circumstances, speaks to me without brutality, I cannot help having the impression that there must be a mistake and that unfortunately the mistake will in all probability disappear. There I received forever the mark of a slave, like the branding of the red-hot iron the Romans put on the foreheads of their most despised slaves. Since then I have always regarded myself as a slave.

In this state of mind then, and in a wretched condition physically, I entered the little Portuguese village, which, alas, was very wretched too, on the very day of the festival of its patron saint. I was alone. It was the evening and there was a full moon over the sea. The wives of the fishermen were, in procession, making a tour of all the ships, carrying candles and singing what must certainly be very ancient hymns of a heart-rending sadness. Nothing can give any idea of it. I have never heard anything so poignant unless it were the song of the boatsmen on the Volga. There the conviction was suddenly borne in upon me that Christianity is pre-eminently the religion of slaves, that slaves cannot help belonging to it, and I among others. . . .

In 1938 I spent ten days at Solesmes, from Palm Sunday to Easter Tuesday, following all the liturgical services. I was suffering from splitting headaches, each sound hurt me like a blow; by an extreme effort of concentration I was able to rise above this wretched flesh, to leave it to suffer by itself, heaped up in a corner, and to find a pure and perfect joy in the unimaginable beauty of the chanting and the words. This experience enabled me by analogy to get a better understanding of the possibility of loving Divine love in the midst of affliction. It goes without saying that in the course of these services the thought of the Passion of Christ entered into my being once and for all.

There was a young English Catholic there from whom I gained my first idea of the supernatural power of the sacraments because of the truly angelic radiance with which he seemed to be clothed after going to communion. Chance—for I always prefer saying chance rather than Providence—made him a messenger to me. For he told me of the existence of those English poets of the seventeenth century who are named metaphysical. In reading them later on, I discovered the poem of which I read you what is unfortunately a very inadequate translation. It is called "Love."[20] I learned it by heart. Often, at the culminating point of a violent headache, I make myself say it over, concentrating all my attention upon it and clinging with all my soul to the tenderness it enshrines. I used to think I was merely reciting it as a beautiful poem, but without my knowing it the recitation had the virtue of a prayer. It was during one of these recitations, as I told you, Christ Himself came down and took possession of me. . . . Moreover, in this sudden possession of me by Christ, neither my senses nor my imagination had any part; I only felt in the midst of my sufferings the presence of a love, like that which one can read in the smile of a beloved face. . . . Yet I still half refused, not [because of] my love but my intelligence. For it seemed to me certain, and I still think so today, that one can never wrestle with God if one does so out of pure regard for the truth. Christ likes us to prefer truth to Him because, before being Christ, He is truth. If one turns aside from Him to go toward the truth, one will not go far before falling into His arms. . . .

IMPLICIT AND EXPLICIT LOVE[21]

Even the most narrow-minded of Christians[22] would not dare to affirm that compassion, love of the beauty of the world, love of religious practices, and friendship belonged exclusively to those centuries and countries that recognized the Church. These forms of love are rarely found in their purity, but it would even be difficult to say that they were met with more frequently in those centuries and countries than others. To think that love in any of these forms can exist anywhere where Christ is absent is to belittle him so grievously that it amounts to an outrage. It is impious and almost sacrilegious.

These kinds of love are supernatural, and in a sense they are absurd. They are the height of folly. So long as the soul has not had direct contact with the very person of God, they cannot be supported by any knowledge based either on experience or reason. They cannot therefore rest upon any certainty, unless the word is used in a metaphorical sense to indicate the opposite of hesitation. In consequence it is better that they should not be associated with any belief. This is more honest intellectually, and it safeguards our love's purity more effectively. On this account it is more fitting. In what concerns divine things, belief is not fitting. Only certainty will do. Anything less than certainty is unworthy of God.

---

[20]This poem is by George Herbert (1593–1633), an English poet and clergyman. It can be found on pp. 277–78.

[21]Reprinted by permission of the Putnam Publishing Group from *Waiting for God*. Pages 208–215.

[22]Ms. Weil wrote "Catholics," but it seems appropriate to broaden her term to include all Christians—given the thrust of her argument.

During the period of preparation these indirect loves constitute an upward movement of the soul, a turning of the eyes, not without some effort, toward higher things. After God has come in person, not only to visit the soul as he does for a long time beforehand, but to possess it and to transport its center near to His very heart, it is otherwise. The chicken has cracked its shell; it is outside the egg of the world. These first loves continue; they are more intense than before, but they are different. He who has passed through this adventure has a deeper love than ever for those who suffer affliction and for those who help him in his own, for his friends, for religious practices, and for the beauty of the world. But his love in all these forms has become a movement of God Himself, a ray merged in the light of God. That at least is what we may suppose. . . .

We all know that there is no true good here below, that everything that appears to be good in this world is finite, limited, wears out, and once worn out, leaves necessity exposed in all its nakedness. Every human being has probably had some lucid moments in his [or her] life when he has definitely [to?] acknowledge to himself that there is not final good here below. But as soon as we have seen this truth we cover it up with lies. Many people even take pleasure in proclaiming it, seeking a morbid joy in their sadness, without ever having been able to bear facing it for a second. Men feel that there is a mortal danger in facing this truth squarely for any length of time. That is true. Such knowledge strikes more surely than a sword; it inflicts a death more frightening than that of the body. After a time it kills everything within us that constitutes our ego. In order to bear it we have to love truth more than life itself. Those who do this turn away from the fleeting things of time with all their souls, to use the expression of Plato. . . .

It does not rest with the soul to believe in the reality of God if God does not reveal this reality. In trying to do so it either labels something else with the name of God, and that is idolatry, or else its belief in God remains abstract and verbal. Such a belief prevails wherever religious dogma is taken for granted, as is the case with those centuries and countries in which it never enters anyone's head to question it. The state of nonbelief is then what Saint John of the Cross calls a night. The belief is verbal and does not penetrate the soul. At a time like the present, incredulity may be equivalent to the dark night of Saint John of the Cross if the unbeliever loves God, if he is like the child who does not know whether there is bread anywhere, but who cries out because he is hungry.

When we are eating bread and even when we have eaten it, we know that it is real. We can nevertheless raise doubts about the reality of the bread. Philosophers raise doubts about the reality of the world of the senses. Such doubts are however purely verbal; they leave the certainty intact and actually serve only to make it more obvious to a well-balanced mind. In the same way he to whom God has revealed His reality can raise doubts about this reality without any harm. They are purely verbal doubts, a form of exercise to keep his intelligence in good health. What amounts to criminal treason, even before such a revelation and much more afterward, is to question the fact that God is the only thing worthy of love. That is a turning away of our eyes, for love is the soul's looking. It means that we have stopped for an instant to wait and to listen. . . .

He . . . whose soul has seen, heard, and touched for itself, he will recognize

God as the reality inspiring all indirect loves, the reality of which they are as it were the reflections. God is pure beauty. This is incomprehensible, for beauty, by its very essence, has to do with the senses. To speak of an imperceptible beauty must seem [to be] a misuse of language to anyone who has any sense of exactitude: and with reason. Beauty is always a miracle. But the miracle is raised to the second degree when the soul receives an impression of beauty which, while it is beyond all sense perception, is no abstraction, but real and direct as the impression caused by a song at the moment it reaches our ears. Everything happens as though, by miraculous favor, our very senses themselves had been made aware that silence is not the absence of sounds, but something infinitely more real than sounds, and the center of a harmony more perfect than anything which a combination of sounds can produce. Furthermore there are degrees of silence. There is a silence in the beauty of the universe which is like a noise when compared with the silence of God.

God is, moreover, our real neighbor. The term of person can only be rightly applied to God, and this is also true of the term impersonal. God is He who bends over us, afflicted as we are, and reduced to the state of being nothing but a fragment of inert and bleeding flesh. Yet at the same time He is in some sort the victim of misfortune as well, the victim who appears to us as an inanimate body, incapable of thought, this nameless victim of whom nothing is known. The inanimate body is this created universe. The love we owe to God, this love that would be our crowning perfection if we were able to attain to it, is the divine model both of gratitude and compassion.

God is also the perfect friend. So that there should be between Him and us, bridging the infinite distance, something in the way of equality, He has chosen to place an absolute quality in His creatures, the absolute liberty of consent, which leaves us free to follow or swerve from the God-ward direction He has communicated to our souls. He has also extended our possibilities of error and falsehood so as to leave us the faculty of exercising a spurious rule in imagination, not only over the universe and the human race, but also over God Himself, in so far as we do not know how to use His name aright. He has given us this faculty of infinite illusion so that we should have the power to renounce it out of love.

In fact, contact with God is the true sacrament. We can, however, be almost certain that those whose love of God has caused the disappearance of pure loves belonging to our life here below are no true friends of God.

Our neighbor, our friends, religious ceremonies, and the beauty of the world do not fall to the level of unrealities after the soul has had direct contact with God. On the contrary, it is only then that these things become real. Previously they were half dreams. Previously they had no reality.

A(iden). W(ilson). Tozer (1897–1963)

A. W. Tozer was born and raised on a farm in Newburg, Pennsylvania. One biographer considered this "an invaluable asset," which "paid regular dividends in grass-roots common sense, graphic illustrations, and parables for tongue and pen."[23] In 1912 the family moved to Akron, Ohio, where Tozer joined his father, brother, and sister Essie at work in the Goodrich plant. The move provided employment, as well as the opportunity to attend church regularly, and in 1915—before his eighteenth birthday—A. W. Tozer experienced a transforming conversion. Almost immediately he began attending, and subsequently leading, prayer meetings. He engaged in street preaching and other forms of Christian witness. Although his education was meager, only through grammar school, Tozer became an insatiable reader of the Bible and Christian classics. Although he was a self-educated man, he was extraordinarily well read; among his favorite religious resources, in addition to Scripture, were the Church Fathers and mystics.

Ordained to the ministry of the Christian and Missionary Alliance in 1920, he served churches in West Virgina, Ohio, and Indiana, before pastoring the prominent Southside Alliance Church of Chicago for more than thirty years (1928–1959). From 1959 until his death, A.W. Tozer was minister of preaching at Avenue Road (C & MA) Church in Toronto. He was twice elected vice president of his denomination, and served as editor of its periodical, *The Alliance Witness,* for thirteen years. Tozer was a prolific writer, and was author of more than thirty popular books on Christian Spirituality and Christian living. His spirituality was profoundly shaped by Tozer's own location in Evangelical Protestantism, but his immersion in the texts of classical Christian Spirituality brought a breadth to his work that allowed it to speak across traditional ecclesiological boundaries. In many ways, Tozer seemed to be a twentieth-century Brother Lawrence, utterly intent to see God at work in the "regular" though profound aspects of Christian living. His most representative work was *The Pursuit of God* (1949); among his significant contributions to Christian Spirituality were *Keys to the Deeper Life* (1957), *The Knowledge of the Holy* (1961), and *The Christian Book of Mystical Verse* (1963).

THE SACRAMENT OF LIVING[24]

One of the greatest hindrances to internal peace which the Christian encounters is the common habit of dividing our lives into two areas—the sacred and the secular. As these areas are conceived to exist apart from each other and to be morally and spiritually incompatible, and as we are compelled by the necessities of living to be always crossing back and forth from the one to the other, our inner lives tend to break up so that we live a divided instead of a unified life.

Our trouble springs from the fact that we who follow Christ inhabit at once two worlds—the spiritual and the natural. As children of Adam we live our lives on earth subject to the limitations of the flesh and the weaknesses and ills to which human nature is heir. Merely to live among men requires of us years of hard toil

---

[23]David J. Fant, *A. W. Tozer: A Twentieth Century Prophet* (Harrisburg, Pa.: Christian Publications, 1964), p. 11.
[24]A. W. Tozer, *The Pursuit of God* (Camp Hill, Pa.: Christian Publications, reprint 1982, pp. 117–28.

and much care and attention to the things of this world. In sharp contrast to this is our life in the Spirit. There we enjoy another and higher kind of life—we are children of God; we possess heavenly status and enjoy intimate fellowship with Christ.

This tends to divide our total life into two departments. We come unconsciously to recognize two sets of actions. The first are performed with a feeling of satisfaction and a firm assurance that they are pleasing to God. These are the sacred acts and they are usually thought to be prayer, Bible reading, hymn singing, church attendance and such other acts as spring directly from faith. They may be known by the fact that they have no direct relation to this world, and would have no meaning whatever except as faith shows us another world, "an house not made with hands, eternal in the heavens" (2 Cor. 5:1).

Over against these sacred acts are the secular ones. They include all the ordinary activities of life which we share with the sons and daughters of Adam: eating, sleeping, working, looking after the needs of the body and performing our dull and prosaic duties here on earth. These we often do reluctantly and with many misgivings, often apologizing to God for what we consider a waste of time and strength. The upshot of this is that we are uneasy most of the time. We go about our common tasks with a feeling of deep frustration, telling ourselves pensively that there's a better day coming when we shall slough off this earthly shell and be bothered no more with the affairs of this world.

This is the old sacred-secular antithesis. Most Christians are caught in its trap. They cannot get a satisfactory adjustment between the claims of the two worlds. They try to walk the tight rope between two kingdoms and they find no peace in either. Their strength is reduced, their outlook confused and their joy taken from them.

I believe this state of affairs to be wholly unnecessary. We have gotten ourselves on the horns of a dilemma, true enough, but the dilemma is not real. It is a creature of misunderstanding. The sacred-secular antithesis has no foundation in the New Testament. Without doubt, a more perfect understanding of Christian truth will deliver us from it.

The Lord Jesus Christ Himself is our perfect example, and He knew no divided life. In the Presence of His Father He lived on earth without strain from babyhood to His death on the cross. God accepted the offering of His total life, and made no distinction between act and act. "I do always the things that please him," was His brief summary of His own life as it related to the Father (Jn. 8:29). As He moved among men He was poised and restful. What pressure and suffering He endured grew out of His position as the world's sin bearer; they were never the result of moral uncertainty or spiritual maladjustment.

Paul's exhortation to "do all to the glory of God" is more than pious idealism. It is an integral part of the sacred revelation and is to be accepted as the very Word of Truth. It opens before us the possibility of making every act of our lives contribute to the glory of God. Lest we should be too timid to include everything, Paul mentions specifically eating and drinking. This humble privilege we share with the beasts that perish. If these lowly animal acts can be so performed as to honor God, then it becomes difficult to conceive of one that cannot. . . .

Perversion, misuse and abuse of our human powers should give us cause enough to be ashamed. Bodily acts done in sin and contrary to nature can never honor God. Wherever the human will introduces moral evil we have no longer our innocent and harmless powers as God made them; we have instead an abused and twisted thing which can never bring glory to its Creator.

Let us, however, assume that perversion and abuse are not present. Let us think of a Christian believer in whose life, the twin wonders have been wrought. He is now living according to the will of God as he understands it from the written Word. Of such a one it may be said that every act of his life is or can be as truly sacred as prayer or baptism or the Lord's Supper. To say this is not to bring all acts down to one dead level; it is rather to lift every act up into a living kingdom and turn the whole life into a sacrament.

If a sacrament is an external expression of an inward grace, then we need not hesitate to accept the above thesis. By one act of consecration of our total selves to God we can make every subsequent act express that consecration. We need no more be ashamed of our body—the fleshly servant that carries us through life—than Jesus was of the humble beast upon which He rode into Jerusalem. "The Lord hath need of him" may well apply to our mortal bodies. If Christ dwells in us, we may bear about the Lord of glory as the little beast did of old and give occasion to the multitude to cry, "Hosanna in the highest."

That we *see* this truth is not enough. If we would escape from the toils of the sacred-secular dilemma, the truth must "run in our blood" and condition the complexion of our thoughts. We must practice living to the glory of God, actually and determinedly. By meditation upon this truth, by talking it over with God often in our prayers, by recalling it to our minds frequently as we move about among men, a sense of its wondrous meaning will take hold of us. The old painful duality will go down before a restful unity of life. The knowledge that we are all God's, that He has received all and rejected nothing, will unify our inner lives and make everything sacred to us.

This is not quite all. Long-held habits do not die easily. It will take intelligent thought and a great deal of reverent prayer to escape completely from the sacred-secular psychology. For instance, it may be difficult for the average Christian to get hold of the idea that his daily labors can be performed as acts of worship acceptable to God by Jesus Christ. The old antithesis will crop up in the back of his head sometimes to disturb his peace of mind. Nor will that old serpent, the devil, take all this lying down. He will be there in the cab or at the desk or in the field to remind the Christian that he is giving the better part of his day to the things of this world and allotting to his religious duties only a trifling portion of his time. And unless great care is taken, this will create confusion and bring discouragement and heaviness of heart.

We can meet this successfully only by the exercise of an aggressive faith. We must offer all our acts to God and believe that He accepts them. Then hold firmly to that position and keep insisting that every act of every hour of the day and night be included in the transaction. Keep reminding God in our times of private prayer that we mean every act for His glory; then supplement those times by a thousand thought-prayers as we go about the job of living. Let us practice the fine art of making every work a priestly ministration. Let us believe that God is in all our simple deeds and learn to find Him there. . . .

In order that I may be understood and not be misunderstood I would throw into relief the practical implications of the teaching for which I have been arguing, i.e. the sacramental quality of everyday life. Over against its positive meanings, I should like to point out a few things it does not mean.

It does not mean, for instance, that everything we do is of equal importance with everything else we do or may do. One act of a good man's life may differ widely from another in importance. Paul's sewing of tents was not equal to his writing of an Epistle to the Romans, but both were accepted of God and both were true acts of worship. Certainly it is more important to lead a soul to Christ than to plant a garden, but the planting of the garden *can* be as holy an act as the winning of a soul.

Again, it does not mean that every man is as useful as every other man. Gifts differ in the body of Christ. A Billy Bray is not to be compared with a Luther or a Wesley for sheer usefulness to the church and to the world; but the service of the less gifted brother is as pure as that of the more gifted, and God accepts both with equal pleasure.

The "layman" need never think of his humbler task as being inferior to that of his minister. Let every man abide in the calling wherein he is called and his work will be as sacred as the work of the ministry. It is not what a man does that determines whether his work is sacred or secular, it is why he does it. The motive is everything. Let a man sanctify the Lord God in his heart and he can thereafter do no common act. All he does is good and acceptable to God through Jesus Christ. For such a man, living itself will be sacramental and the whole world a sanctuary. His entire life will be a priestly ministration. As he performs his never-so-simple task, he will hear the voice of the seraphim saying, "Holy, Holy, Holy, is the Lord of hosts: the whole earth is full of his glory."

[Prayer] *Lord, I would trust Thee completely; I would be altogether Thine; I would exalt Thee above all. I desire that I may feel no sense of possessing anything outside of Thee. I want constantly to be aware of Thy overshadowing presence and to hear Thy speaking voice. I long to live in restful sincerity of heart. I want to live so fully in the Spirit that all my thoughts may be as sweet incense ascending to Thee and every act of my life may be an act of worship. Therefore I pray in the words of Thy great servant of old, "I beseech Thee so for to cleanse the intent of mine heart with the unspeakable gift of Thy grace, that I may perfectly love Thee and worthily praise Thee." And all this I confidently believe Thou wilt grant me through the merits of Jesus Christ Thy Son. Amen.*

Howard Thurman (1900–81)

Howard Thurman was born in Daytona Beach, Florida, and grew up in poverty and segregation. His father died when he was seven, and—as he recalled in his book *Jesus and the Disinherited* (1949)—"I was cared for by my grandmother, who was born a slave . . . she could neither read nor write. Two or three times a week I read the Bible aloud to her". His grandmother's recollection of "the master's minister" using the text: "Slaves, be obedient to those that are your masters . . . as unto Christ," set Howard Thurman to the task of severing the connection too often drawn between Christianity and oppression of African Americans. Thurman's quest for a freeing and empowering gospel became a central focus in his ministry and many publications.

After attending public elementary school in Daytona Beach, Thurman entered Florida Baptist Academy (Jacksonville). He graduated from Howard University (1923), and Colgate-Rochester Divinity School (1926). After a brief pastorate in Oberlin, Ohio, Thurman moved his family to Atlanta, in 1926, because of his wife Katie's failing health; he became Professor of Theology at Morehouse College, and preacher at Spelman College. His wife died in 1930, leaving Howard with a baby daughter (Olive Katharine). After a year of sabbatical and reflection, funded by a Charles Fisher Kent Fellowship, Thurman returned to Morehouse and Spelman colleges. In 1932 he accepted a call to Howard University, in Washington, D.C. Thurman took a leave of absence from Howard in 1935 to participate in a "Pilgrimage of Friendship," sponsored by the World Student Christian Fellowship, to India, Burma, and Ceylon. During that pilgrimage he met Mohandas Gandhi and other spiritual leaders who criticized Christianity for fostering segregation. In *Jesus and the Disinherited* Thurman recalled these conversations as being formative for his own spiritual development.

In 1953, after a series of influential and innovative pastorates, Howard Thurman was appointed Dean of the Chapel and professor of spiritual resources at the School of Theology, Boston University. He was the first African American to become a full-time member of the faculty of Boston University. Among his significant publications were the aforementioned *Jesus and the Disinherited* (1949), *Deep Is the Hunger* (1951), *Meditations of the Heart* (1953), and his autobiography *With Head and Heart* (1979).

JESUS AND THE DISINHERITED[25]

. . . I can count on the fingers of one hand the number of times that I have heard a sermon on the meaning of religion, of Christianity, to the man who stands with his back against the wall. It is urgent that my meaning be crystal clear. The masses of men live with their backs constantly against the wall. They are the poor, the disinherited, the dispossessed. What does our religion say to them? The issue is not what it counsels them to do for others whose need may be greater, but what religion offers to meet their own needs. The search for an answer to this question is perhaps the most important religious quest of modern life. . . .

We begin with the simple historical fact that Jesus was a Jew. The miracle of the Jewish people is almost as breath-taking as the miracle of Jesus. Is there some-

---

[25]Reprinted from Howard Thurman, *Jesus and the Disinherited*. Copyright (c) 1976 Howard Thurman. Used with the kind permission of the Howard Thurman Educational Trust. Pages 13–35.

thing unique, some special increment of vitality in the womb of the people out of whose loins he came, that made of him a logical flowering of a long development of racial experience, ethical in quality and Godlike in tone? It is for Jesus to be understood outside of the sense of community which Israel held with God. This does not take anything away from him; rather does it heighten the challenge which his life presents, for such reflection reveals him as the product of the constant working of the creative mind of God upon the life, thought, and character of a race of men. Here is one who was so conditioned and organized within himself that he became a perfect instrument for the embodiment of a set of ideals—ideals of such dramatic potency that they were capable of changing the calendar, rechanneling the thought of the world, and placing a new sense of the rhythm of life in a weary, nerve-snapped civilization. . . .

The second important fact for our consideration is that Jesus was a poor Jew. There is recorded in Luke the account of the dedication of Jesus at the temple: "And when the days of her purification according to the law of Moses were accomplished, they brought him . . . to the Lord . . . to offer a sacrifice according to that which is said in the law of the Lord, a pair of turtledoves, or two young pigeons" [Lk 2:22–24]. When we examine the regulation in Leviticus [12:2–8], an interesting fact is revealed: "And when the days of her purifying are fulfilled, for a son . . . she shall bring a lamb of the first year for a burnt offering, and a young pigeon, or a turtledove, for a sin offering . . . . And if she be not able to bring a lamb, then she shall bring two turtle [dove]s, or two young pigeons; the one for a burnt offering and the other for a sin offering." It is clear from the text that the mother of Jesus was one whose means were not sufficient for a lamb, and who was compelled, therefore, to use doves or young pigeons.

The economic predicament with which he was identified in birth placed him initially with the great mass of men on earth. The masses of the people are poor. If we dare take the position that in Jesus there was at work some radical destiny, it would be safe to say that in his poverty he was more truly Son of man than he would have been if the incident of family or birth had made him a rich son of Israel. It is not a point to be labored, for again and again men have transcended circumstance of birth and training; but it is an observation not without merit.

The third fact is that Jesus was a member of a minority group in the midst of a larger dominant and controlling group. In 63 B.C. Palestine fell into the hands of the Romans. After this date the gruesome details of loss of status were etched, line by line, in the sensitive soul of Israel, dramatized ever by an increasing desecration of the Holy Land. To be sure, there was Herod, an Israelite, who ruled from 37 to 4 B.C.; but in some ways he was completely apostate. Taxes of all kinds increased, and out of these funds, extracted from the vitals of the people, temples in honor of Emperor Augustus were built within the boundaries of the holy soil. It was a sad and desolate time for the people. Herod became the symbol of shame and humiliation for all of Israel. . . .

There is one overmastering problem that the socially and politically disinherited always face: Under what terms is survival possible? In the case of the Jewish people in the Greco-Roman world the problem was even more acute than under ordinary circumstances, because it had to do not only with physical survival in terms of life and limb but also with the actual survival of a culture and a faith. Judaism was a culture, a civilization, and a religion—a total world view in which there was no provision for any form of thoroughgoing dualism. The crucial problem of Judaism was to exist as an isolated, autonomous, cultural, religious, and political unit in the midst of the hostile Hellenic world. If there had been sharp lines distinguishing the culture from the religion, or the religion from political autonomy, a compromise could have been worked out. Because the Jews thought that a basic compromise was possible, they sought political annexation to Syria which would bring them under Roman rule directly and thereby guarantee them, within the framework of Roman policy, religious and cultural autonomy. But this merely aggravated the already tense nationalistic feeling and made a direct, all-out attack against Roman authority inevitable.

In the midst of this psychological climate Jesus began his teaching and his ministry. His words were directed to the House of Israel, a minority within the Greco-Roman world, smarting under the loss of status, freedom, and autonomy, haunted by the dream of the restoration of a lost glory and a former greatness. His message focused on the urgency of a radical change in the inner attitude of the people. He recognized fully that out of the heart are the issues of life and that no external force, however great and overwhelming, can at long last destroy a people if it does not first win the victory of the spirit against them. "To revile because one has been reviled—this is the real evil because it is the evil of the soul itself." Jesus saw this with almighty clarity. Again and again he came back to the inner life of the individual. With increasing insight and startling accuracy he placed his finger on the "inward center" as the crucial arena where the issues would determine the destiny of his people. . . .

The striking similarity between the social position of Jesus in Palestine and that of the vast majority of American Negroes is obvious to anyone who tarries long over the facts. We are dealing here with conditions that produce essentially the same psychology. There is meant no further comparison. It is the similarity of a social climate at the point of a denial of full citizenship which creates the problem for creative survival. For the most part, Negroes assume that there are no basic citizenship rights, no fundamental protection, guaranteed to them by the state, because their status as citizens has never been clearly defined. There has been for them little protection from the dominant controllers of society and even less protection from the unrestrained elements within their own group.

The result has been a tendency to be their own protectors, to bulwark themselves against careless and deliberate aggression. The Negro has felt, with some justification, that the peace officer of the community provides no defense against the offending or offensive white man; and for an entirely different set of reasons the peace officer gives no protection against the offending Negro. Thus the Negro feels that he must be prepared, at a moment's notice, to protect his own life and take the consequence therefore. Such a predicament has made it natural for some of them to use weapons as a defense and to have recourse to premeditated or precipitate violence.

Living in a climate of deep insecurity, Jesus, faced with so narrow a margin of civil guarantees, had to find some other basis upon which to establish a sense of well-being. He knew that the goals of religion as he understood them could never be worked out within the then-established order. Deep from within that order he projected a dream, the logic of which would give to all the needful security. There would be room for all, and no man would be a threat to his brother. "The kingdom of God is within" [Lk 17:21]. "The Spirit of the Lord is upon me, because he hath anointed me to preach the gospel to the poor."[26]

The basic principles of his way of life cut straight through to the despair of his fellows and found it groundless. By inference he says, "You must abandon your fear of each other and fear only God. You must not indulge in any deception and dishonesty, even to save your lives. Your words must be Yea—Nay; anything else is evil. Hatred is destructive to hated and hater alike. Love your enemy, that you may be children of your Father who is in heaven."

C(live). S(taples). Lewis (1898–1963)

C. S. Lewis was born in Belfast, in a conservative Christian home. As he accumulated degrees and acclaim on his way to a post as Professor of Medieval and Renaissance Literature at Cambridge University, Lewis drifted into agnosticism. Lewis's return to Christian faith (see below) was chronicled in his autobiography, *Surprised by Joy*. Joy was a significant element in his spiritual life and works, most notably in the fantasies like *Chronicles of Narnia*, or his science fiction *Space Trilogy*. The most famous product of his sanctified imagination was *The Screwtape Letters*. Constructed as a series of instructional memos from a senior official in "the Kingdom Below" to a fledgling tempter on how to disrupt the spirituality of a new convert, the *Letters* give practical, spiritual instruction by way of indirection.

A layman and communicant in the Church of England, C. S. Lewis was widely known as a commonsense Christian apologist and author of works like *Mere Christianity*. Lewis brought this same vigorous, commonsense approach to Christian Spirituality through works like *Letters to Malcolm: Chiefly on Prayer* (1964).

SURPRISED BY JOY[27]

The odd thing was that before God closed in on me, I was in fact offered what now appears a moment of wholly free choice. In a sense, I was going up Headington Hill on the top of a bus. Without words and (I think) almost without im-

---

[26]Luke 4:18 = Isaiah 61:1,2.
[27]Excerpts from C. S. Lewis, *Surprised by Joy: The Shape of My Early Life*. Copyright (c) 1955 by C.S. Lewis PTE Ltd., renewed 1984 by Arthur Owen Barfield. Reprinted by permission of Harcourt, Brace, & Company, and Harper Collins, U.K. Pages 224–38.

ages, a fact about myself was somehow presented to me. I became aware that I was holding something at bay, or shutting something out. Or, if you like, that I was wearing some stiff clothing, like corsets, or even a suit of armor, as if I were a lobster. I felt myself being, there and then, given a free choice. I could open the door or keep it shut; I could unbuckle the armor or keep it on. Neither choice was presented as a duty; no threat or promise was attached to either, though I knew that to open the door or to take off the corset meant the incalculable. The choice appeared to be momentous but it was also strangely unemotional. I was moved by no desires or fears. In a sense I was not moved by anything. I chose to open, to unbuckle, to loosen the rein. I say, "I chose," yet it did not really seem possible to do the opposite. On the other hand, I was aware of no motives. You could argue that I was not a free agent, but I am more inclined to think that this came nearer to being a perfectly free act than most that I have ever done. Necessity may not be the opposite of freedom, and perhaps a person is most free when, instead of producing motive, he could only say, "I am what I do." Then came the repercussion on the imaginative level. I felt as if I were a man of snow at long last beginning to melt. The melting was starting in my back—drip-drip and presently trickle-trickle. I rather disliked the feeling. . . .

Remember, I had always wanted, above all things, not to be "interfered with." I had wanted (mad wish) "to call my soul my own." I had been far more anxious to avoid suffering than to achieve delight. I had always aimed at limited liabilities. The supernatural itself had been to me, first, an illicit dram, and then, as by a drunkard's reaction, nauseous. Even my recent attempt to live my philosophy had secretly (I now knew) been hedged round by all sorts of reservations. I had pretty well known that my ideal of virtue would never be allowed to lead me into anything intolerably painful; I would be "reasonable." But now what had been an ideal became a command; and what might not be expected of one? Doubtless, by definition, God was Reason itself. But would He also be "reasonable" in that other, more comfortable, sense? Not the slightest assurance on that score was offered me. Total surrender, the absolute leap in the dark, were demanded. The reality with which no treaty can be made was upon me. The demand was not even "All or nothing." I think that stage had been passed, on the bus top when I unbuckled my armor and the snowman started to melt. Now, the demand was simply "All."

You must picture me alone in that room in Magdalene [College], night after night, feeling, whenever my mind lifted even for a second from my work, the steady, unrelenting approach of Him whom I so earnestly desired not to meet. That which I greatly feared had at last come upon me. In the Trinity Term of 1929 I gave in, and admitted that God was God, and knelt and prayed: perhaps, that night, the most dejected and reluctant convert in all England. I did not then see what is now the most shining and obvious thing; the Divine humility which will accept a convert even on such terms. The Prodigal Son [Lk 15] at least walked home on his own feet. But who can duly adore that Love which will open the high gates to a prodigal who is brought in kicking, struggling, resentful, and darting his eyes in every direction for a chance of escape? The words *compelle intrare*, compel them to come in, have been so abused by wicked men that we shudder at them; but properly understood, they plumb the depth of the Divine mercy. The hardness of God is kinder than the softness of men, and His compulsion is our liberation.

It must be understood that the conversion . . . was only to Theism, pure and simple, not to Christianity. I knew nothing yet about the Incarnation. The God to whom I surrendered was sheerly nonhuman. . . . As I drew near the conclusion, I felt a resistance almost as strong as my previous resistance to Theism. As strong, but shorter-lived, for I understood it better. Every step I had taken from the Absolute to "Spirit" and from "Spirit" to "God," had been a step toward the more imminent, to the more compulsive. At each step one had less chance "to call one's soul one's own." To accept the Incarnation was a further step in the same direction. It brings God nearer, or near in a new way. And this, I found, was something I had not wanted. But to recognize the ground for my evasion was of course to recognize both its shame and its futility. I know very well when, but hardly how, the final step was taken. I was driven to Whipsnade one sunny morning. When we set out I did not believe that Jesus Christ is the Son of God, and when we reached the zoo I did. Yet I had not exactly spent the journey in thought. Nor in great emotion. "Emotion" is perhaps the last word we can apply to some of the most important events. It was more like when a person, after a long sleep, still lying motionless in bed, becomes aware that he is now awake. And it was, like that moment on top of the bus, ambiguous. Freedom or necessity? Or do they differ at their maximum? At that maximum a person is what he [or she] does; there is nothing of him left over or outside the act. As for what we commonly call Will, and what we commonly call Emotion, I fancy these usually talk too loud, protest too much, to be quite believed, and we have a secret suspicion that the great passion or the iron resolution is partly a put-up job. . . .

But what, in conclusion, of Joy? for that, after all, is what the story has mainly been about. To tell you the truth, the subject has lost nearly all interest for me since I became a Christian. I cannot, indeed, complain, like Wordsworth, that the visionary gleam has passed away. I believe (if the thing were at all worth recording) that the old stab, the bitter-sweet, has come to me as often and as sharply since my conversion as at any time of my life whatever. But I now know that the experience, considered as a state of my own mind, had never had the kind of importance I once gave it. It was valuable only as a pointer to something other and outer. While that other was in doubt, the pointer naturally loomed large in my thoughts. When we are lost in the woods and the sight of a signpost is a great matter. He who first sees it cries "Look!" The whole party gathers round and stares. But when we have found the road and are passing signposts every few miles, we shall not stop and stare. They will encourage us and we will be grateful to the authority that set them up. But we shall not stop and stare, or not much; not on this road, though their pillars are of silver and their lettering of gold. "We would be at Jerusalem." . . .

A LETTER FROM UNCLE SCREWTAPE[28]

My Dear Wormwood,

The amateurish suggestions in your last letter warn me that it is high time for me to write you fully on the painful subject of prayer. You might have spared the comment that my advice about his prayers for his mother "proved singularly unfortunate." That is not the sort of thing that a nephew should write to his uncle—nor a junior tempter to the under-secretary of a department. It also reveals an unpleasant desire to shift responsibility; you must learn to pay for your own blunders.

The best thing, where it is possible, is to keep the patient from the serious intention of praying altogether. When the patient is an adult recently re-converted to the Enemy's party, like your man, this is best done by encouraging him to re-member, or to think he remembers, the parrot-like nature of his prayers in child-hood. In reaction against that, he may be persuaded to aim at something entirely spontaneous, inward, informal, and unregularised; and what this will actually mean to a beginner will be an effort to produce in himself a vaguely devotional *mood* in which real concentration of will and intelligence have no part. One of their poets, Coleridge, has recorded that he did not pray "with moving lips and bended knees" but merely "composed his spirit to love" and indulged "a sense of supplication." That is exactly the sort of prayer we want; and since it bears a superficial resemblance to the prayer of silence as practiced by those who are very far advanced in the Enemy's service, clever and lazy patients can be taken in by it for quite a long time. At the very least, they can be persuaded that the bodily position makes no difference to their prayers; for they constantly forget, what you must always remember, that they are animals and that whatever their bodies do affects their souls. It is funny how mortals always picture us putting things into their minds; in reality our best work is done by keeping things out.

If this fails, you must fall back on a subtler misdirection of his intention. Whenever they are attending to the Enemy Himself we are defeated, but there are ways of preventing them from doing so. The simplest is to turn their gaze from Him towards themselves. Keep them watching their own minds and trying to produce *feelings* there by the action of their own wills. When they meant to ask Him for charity, let them, instead, start trying to manufacture charitable feelings for themselves and not notice this is what they are doing. When they meant to pray for courage, let them really be trying to feel brave. When they say they are praying for forgiveness, let them be trying to feel forgiven. Teach them to esti-mate the value of each prayer by their success in producing the desired feeling; and never let them suspect how much success or failure of that kind depends on whether they are well or ill, fresh or tired, at the moment.

But of course the Enemy will not meantime be idle. Wherever there is prayer, there is danger of His own immediate action. He is cynically indifferent to the

---

[28]Reprinted from C. S. Lewis, The Screwtape Letters (New York: Macmillian Publishing Company, rev. ed. 1982), pp. 19–23. Used by kind permission of HarperCollins Publisher, Ltd.

dignity of His position, and ours, as pure spirits, and to human animals on their knees He pours out self-knowledge in a quite shameless fashion. But even if He defeats your first attempt at misdirection, we have a subtler weapon. The humans do not start from that direct perception of Him which we, unhappily, cannot avoid. They have never known that ghastly luminosity, that stabbing and searing glare which makes the background of permanent pain to our lives. If you look into your patient's mind when he is praying, you will not find *that*. If you examine the object to which he is attending, you will find that it is a composite object containing many quite ridiculous ingredients. There will be images derived from pictures of the Enemy as He appeared during the discreditable episode known as the Incarnation: there will be vaguer—perhaps quite savage and puerile—images associated with the other two Persons. There will even be some of his own reverence (and of bodily sensations accompanying it) objectified and attributed to the object revered. I have known cases where what the patient called his "God" was actually *located*—up and to the left at the corner of the bedroom ceiling, or inside his own head, or in a crucifix on the wall. But whatever the nature of the composite object, you must keep him praying to *it*—to the thing that he has made, not to the Person who has made him. You may even encourage him to attach great importance to the correction and improvement of his composite object, and to keeping it steadily before his imagination during the whole prayer. For if he ever comes to make the distinction, if ever he consciously directs his prayers "Not to what I think thou are but to what thou knowest thyself to be," our situation is, for the moment, desperate. Once all his thoughts and images have been flung aside or, if retained, retained with a full recognition of their merely subjective nature, and the man trusts himself to the completely real, external, invisible Presence, there with him in the room and never knowable by him as he is known by it—why, then it is that the incalculable may occur. In avoiding this situation— this real nakedness of the soul in prayer—you will be helped by the fact that the humans themselves do not desire it as much as they suppose. There's such a thing as getting more than they bargained for! Your affectionate uncle, Screwtape.

Karl Rahner (1904–84)

Karl Rahner was born in Freiburg im Breisgau, Germany, a middle child of seven born to a college professor and a "courageous" (his term) mother.[29] The family was devoutly Roman Catholic, and Rahner followed his older brother Hugo into the Jesuit priesthood, in 1922. A devout, insightful, and ecumenical scholar, he devoted fifty-two years to the priesthood and forty-five years to theological inquiry and teaching. He taught theology at Innsbruck, Munich, and Munster. Rahner was one of the most published and noteworthy scholars of the contemporary period.

---

[29]Harvey D. Egan, ed., *An Anthology of Christian Mysticism* (Collegeville, Min.: The Liturgical Press, 1991), p. 598.

His spirituality, like that of his Protestant contemporary Karl Barth, was Christocentric in focus. Rahner understood mysticism as a fundamental aspect of the incarnation; Jesus Christ is the incarnation of God's mystical word, and Christ takes flesh again in human devotion to the Word and human self-giving. This means that religious experience is essential both to authentic human nature and to Christian living. Paralleling his incarnational focus was what commentators have termed Rahner's "Ignatian mysticism of the joy of the world."[30] God is to be found in all things, however mundane and ordinary, and all things find their true meaning in God.

Among his monumental works were the twenty volumes of *Theological Investigations* (1961ff), as well as *Encyclopedia of Theology* (1975) and *Foundations of Christian Faith* (1978). A volume particularly germane to Karl Rahner's approach to Christian Spirituality is his *The Practice of the Faith: A Handbook of Contemporary Spirituality* (1992).

SPIRITUALITY OF THE FUTURE[31]

For a Catholic the *first* thing to be said about a future spirituality is quite obviously that, despite all change coming or to come, it is and will remain albeit in a mysterious identity, the old spirituality of the Church's history up to the present time. Consequently the spirituality of the future will be one related to the living God, who has revealed himself in the history of humanity, who has established himself in his most intimate reality—even as basic ground, as innermost dynamism and final end—at the very heart of the world and the humanity created by him.

Christian spirituality of the future also will be about the God of Abraham, Isaac, and Jacob, the God and Father of Jesus Christ. This spirituality can never and may never degenerate into a mere humanism of a horizontal type. It will always be a spirituality of adoration of the incomprehensible God in spirit and in truth. This spirituality will always be related to Jesus Christ, the Crucified and Risen, as to the ultimate, victorious and irreversible self-promise of God, historically manifested to the world; it will be a discipleship of Jesus and will receive from him and from the concreteness of his life a norm, an internal structural principle, that can no longer disintegrate into a theoretical morality; it will always be an acceptance of the death of Jesus who, without any reassurance and yet absolutely openly, allowed himself in his death to fall into the abyss of God's incomprehensibility and incalculable decrees, in faith, hope and love, so that in this way and no other we attain to the infinite truth, freedom and salvation of God. . . .

The spirituality of the future will be a spirituality of the Sermon on the Mount and of the evangelical counsels, continually involved in renewing its protest

---

[30]*Ibid.*, p. 600.

[31]Karl Rahner, *The Practice of Faith: A Handbook of Contemporary Spirituality* (New York: Crossroad, 1992), pp. 18–26, with omissions. Used by kind permission of Crossroad Press. Also from Karl Rahner, *The Practice of Faith* (SCM Press, 1992), with the kind permission of SCM Press.

against the idols of wealth, pleasure, and power. The spirituality of the future will be a spirituality of hope, awaiting an absolute future, enabling man to be grimly realistic and continually to break down the illusion that he could himself, by his own power and shrewdness, produce in this world and in its continuing history the eternal kingdom of truth and freedom. The spirituality of the future will always preserve the memory of the past history of piety, will regard as stupid, inhuman and unChristian the view that man's piety is continually making a fresh start—unhistorically—at zero and consists in nothing but wild revolutions.

This future spirituality therefore will learn over and over again positively and negatively from the Church's past. . . . The spirituality of the future will preserve the history of the Church's piety and will continually discover afresh that what is apparently old and past can offer the true future to our present time. That was the *first* thing to be said about the spirituality of the future. This first statement of course does not exclude but includes the possibility that many individual forms and shapes of the piety of the past in their concreteness are no more than what has been and the Church must have the sober courage forthrightly to abandon them.

A *second* thing can certainly be predicted of the spirituality of the future: compared to the spirituality of former times, it will certainly have to concentrate very clearly on what is most essential to Christian piety. . . . The spirituality of the future will be concentrated on the ultimate data of revelation: that God is, that we can speak to him, that his ineffable comprehensibility is itself the very heart of our existence and consequently of our spirituality; that we can live and die with Jesus and properly with him alone in an ultimate freedom from all powers and authorities; that his incomprehensible cross is set up above our life and that this scandal reveals the true, liberating and beatifying significance of our life. These and similar things were not lacking of course even in the spirituality of former times, but they will make their impact more clearly, more forcefully and with a certain exclusiveness on the future spirituality of a bleaker age. Why should not this be so, if man and the Church actively realize that they are not masters of their history, but must so shape their spirituality that it is adapted to the historical situation imposed on us and not made by us and consequently should be credible even for non-Christians. Even this statement is of course burdened with all the reservations that are involved in the unforeseeability of the future.

There is a *third* point to be made. The spirituality of the future will not be supported or at any rate will be much less supported by a sociologically Christian homogeneity of its situation; it will have to live much more clearly than hitherto out of a solitary, immediate experience of God and his Spirit in the individual. . . .

In such a situation the lonely responsibility of the individual in his or her decision of faith is necessary and required in a way much more radical than it was in former times. That is why the modern spirituality of the Christian involves courage for solitary decision contrary to public opinion, the lonely courage analogous to that of the martyrs of the first century of Christianity, the courage for a spiritual decision of faith, drawing its strength from itself and not needing to be supported by public agreement, particularly since even the Church's public opinion does not so much sustain the individual in his or her decision of faith, but is itself sustained by the latter. Such a solitary courage, however, can exist only if it lives out of a wholly personal experience of God and his Spirit.

It has already been pointed out that the Christian of the future will be a mystic or he or she will not exist at all. If by mysticism we mean, not singular parapsychological phenomena, but a genuine experience of God emerging from the very heart of our existence, this statement is very true and its truth and importance will become still clearer in the spirituality of the future. . . .

We may now attempt to describe a *fourth* characteristic of the spirituality of the future which is part of a singular dialectical unity with the third, the solitary experience of God on the part of the individual. What we mean is the fraternal fellowship in which the same all-sustaining experience of the Spirit becomes possible : fraternal community as a real and essential element of the spirituality of tomorrow. . . .

Where was there a communal experience of the Spirit, clearly conceived, desired and experienced in a general way—as it evidently was at the Church's first Pentecost—that was not presumably an accidental local gathering of a number of individualistic mystics, but an experience of the Spirit on the part of a community as such? Such a "collective experience" cannot and of course is not meant to take away from the individual Christian his radical decision for faith coming from his solitary experience of God nor to spare him this, since human individuality and solidarity are not factors to be balanced against each other nor can they replace each other. But this is not to say that an experience of the Spirit in a small community is as such *a priori* inconceivable, even though we older clerics at least never or scarcely ever experienced anything of this kind and still less attempted to practice it. Why should it not happen? Why should not younger people and clergy now and even more in the future have easier access to such a communal experience of the Spirit? Why should not—as part of the spirituality of the future—phenomena like joint consultation among Christians, genuinely human communication in truly human and not merely external technical dimensions, events in group dynamics, etc. be embraced, exalted and sanctified by a communal experience of the Spirit of God and thus become a truly fraternal fellowship in the Holy Spirit? . . .

In conclusion, a *fifth* element of the spirituality of the future may be mentioned here: it will have a new ecclesial aspect. Regarded abstractly and in principle, this ecclesial character of Catholic spirituality is in itself something that must be taken for granted at all times, since we are talking about a spirituality rooted in a common faith and always to be sacramentally realized. But there is no need to deny or conceal the fact that this ecclesial aspect of a Catholic spirituality in the future will take a form somewhat different from that to which we were accustomed, especially in the last century and a half of . . . the Church. At least once in this period the Church was the object of an almost fanatical love, regarded as our natural home, sustaining and sheltering us in our spirituality, where whatever we needed was available as a matter of course and had only to be willingly and joyfully appropriated. The Church supported us, it did not need to be supported by us.

Today all this is different. . . . What we now see is the poor Church of sinners, the tent of the pilgrim people of God, pitched in the desert and shaken by all the storms of history, the Church laboriously seeking its way into the future, groping and suffering many internal afflictions, striving over and over again to make sure of its faith; we are aware of a Church of internal tensions and conflicts, we feel burdened in the Church both by the reactionary callousness of the institutional factor and by the reckless modernism that threatens to squander the sacred heritage of faith and to destroy the memory of its historical experience. The Church can be an oppressive burden for the individual's spirituality by doctrinalism, legalism and ritualism, to which true spirituality, if it really is authentic and genuine, can have no positive relationship. But none of this can dispense the spirituality of the individual from having an ecclesial character, least of all at a time when solidarity and sociability in the secular field are obviously bound in the future to increase and cannot decline. Why then could not the spirituality of the future take the form of a superior, duplicate naivety, marked by wisdom and patience, which has an ecclesial character because of the fact and in the very fact that it bears and endures as a matter of course the misery and inadequacy of the Church? . . .

This kind of attachment to the Church must be a part of the spirituality of the future. Otherwise it is elitist arrogance and a form of unbelief, failing to grasp the fact that the holy Word of God has come into the flesh of the world and sanctifies this world by taking on himself the sin of the world and also of the Church. The ecclesial aspect of the spirituality of the future will be less triumphalist than formerly. But attachment to the Church will also in the future be an absolutely necessary criterion for genuine spirituality: patience with the Church's form of a servant in the future also is an indispensable way into God's freedom, since by not following this way, we shall eventually get no further than our own arbitrary opinions and the uncertainties of our own life selfishly caught up in itself. . . .

Thomas Merton (1915–68)

Thomas Merton was born in Midi, in France. His father was from New Zealand and his mother was an American; both were artists. Merton had an unhappy childhood, his mother dying when he was six years old and his father dying a decade later. But he was well educated, in France and in America, in art and literature; he excelled at both. After teaching literature briefly, Merton experienced a dramatic conversion (see below) to Christianity (1938) and to the Roman Catholic faith. Merton's spiritual autobiography is well documented in his best-selling book, *The Seven Story Mountain* (1948). He entered the Trappist (O.C.S.O.) abbey of Our Lady of Gethsemani in Kentucky in 1941.

Until his untimely and accidental death, in Bangkok, Thailand, Thomas Merton was (arguably) *the* popular voice of the contemplative tradition in the contemporary world. His many popular writings included journals, such as *The Sign of Jonas* (1953); devotional pieces, like *Bread in the Wilderness* (1953) and *New Seeds*

of Contemplation (1962); poems, like Emblems in a Season of Fury (1963) and Selected Poems (1959); and essays, like Raids on the Unspeakable (1966). Merton
maintained a robust social consciousness and was an outspoken critic of oppression, injustice, and the nuclear arms race. His many writings transformed the popular conception of monasticism and revitalized interest in Christian contemplation.
As Brother Patric Hart (O.C.S.O.) wrote of Merton: "All his writings can be summed
up as a proclamation of God's mercy in his life, the story of the ultimate triumph
of grace in the heart of a monk."[32] A growing and irenic spirit, Merton's spirituality moved well beyond the bounds of his abbey as he explored the depth and breadth
of the Christian tradition, as well as Eastern religious contemplation. This later inquiry was represented in works like Merton's Mystics and Zen Masters (1967) and
Zen and the Birds of Appetite (1968).[33]

The significance of Merton's spirituality, for our purposes, is found in his definition of contemplation and the contemplative life as being integral to the life and
experience of every Christian. Indeed, religious contemplation, described as the apprehension of God, is fundamental to understanding one's self and life in the world.
Merton's approach to contemplation broke down the walls that separated contemporary Christians from the contemplative life, and by locating contemplation at the
heart of Christian existence Merton popularized and revitalized it for an entire generation of Christians.

TO BEGIN THE CLIMB[34]

As November began, my mind was taken up with this one thought: of getting
baptized and entering at last into the supernatural life of the Church. In spite of
all my studying and all my reading and all my talking, I was still infinitely poor
and wretched in my appreciation of what was about to take place within me. I
was about to set foot on the shore at the foot of the high, seven circled mountain
of a Purgatory steeper and more arduous than I was able to imagine, and I was
not at all aware of the climbing I was about to have to do.

The essential thing was to begin the climb. Baptism was that beginning, and
a most generous one, on the part of God. For, although I was baptized condi-
tionally, I hope that His mercy swallowed up all the guilt and temporal punishment of my twenty-three black years of sin in the waters of the font, and allowed
me a new start. But my human nature, my weakness, and the cast of my evil
habits still remained to be fought and overcome.

---

[32]Lawrence S. Cunningham, ed., Thomas Merton: Spiritual Master—the Essential Writings (New York:
Paulist Press, 1992), "Foreword," p. 3.

[33]Lawrence S. Cunningham, ed., in Thomas Merton: Spiritual Master offers a reliable sampling of Merton's diverse literary corpus.

[34]Excerpts from Thomas Merton, The Seven Story Mountain. Copyright 1948 by Harcourt Brace & Company, renewed 1976 by the Trustees of the Merton Legacy Trust. Reprinted by permission of the
publisher, and by permission of Curtis Brown, Ltd. Pages 221–225.

Towards the end of the first week in November, Father Moore told me I would be baptized on the sixteenth. I walked out of the rectory that evening happier and more contented than I had ever been in my life. I looked at a calendar to see what saint had that day for a feast, and it was marked for St. Gertrude.

It was only in the last days before being liberated from my slavery to death, that I had the grace to feel something of my own weakness and helplessness. It was not a very vivid light that was given to me on the subject: but I was really aware, at last, of what a poor and miserable thing I was. On the night of the fifteenth of November, the eve of my Baptism and First Communion, I lay in my bed awake and timorous for fear that something might go wrong the next day. And to humiliate me still further, as I lay there, fear came over me that I might not be able to keep the eucharistic fast. It only meant going from midnight to ten o'clock without drinking any water or taking any food, yet all of a sudden this little act of self-denial which amounts to no more, in reality, than a sort of an abstract token of good-will, grew in my imagination until it seemed to be utterly beyond my strength—as if I were about to go without food and drink for ten days, instead of ten hours. I had enough sense left to realize that this was one of those curious psychological reactions with which our nature, not without help from the devil, tries to confuse us and avoid what reason and our will demand of it, and so I forgot about it all and went to sleep.

In the morning, when I got up, having forgotten to ask Father Moore if washing your teeth was against the eucharistic fast or not, I did not wash them, and, facing a similar problem about cigarettes, I resisted the temptation to smoke. I went downstairs and out into the street to go to my happy execution and rebirth.

The sky was bright and cold. The river glittered like steel. There was a clean wind in the street. It was one of those fall days full of life and triumph, made for great beginnings, and yet I was not altogether exalted: for there were still in my mind these vague, half animal apprehensions about the externals of what was to happen in the church—would my mouth be so dry that I could not swallow the [Eucharistic] Host? If that happened, what would I do? I did not know. . . .

The whole thing was very simple. First of all, I knelt at the altar of Our Lady where Father Moore received my abjuration of heresy and schism. Then we went to the baptistery, in a little dark corner by the main door. I stood at the threshold.

"*Quid Petis ab ecclesia Dei?*" asked Father Moore.
"*Fidem!*"
"*Fides quid tibi praestat?*"
"*Vitam aeternam.*"

Then the young priest began to pray in Latin, looking earnestly and calmly at the page of the *Rituale* through the lenses of his glasses. And I, who was asking for eternal life, stood and watched him, catching a word of the Latin here and there. He turned to me: "*Abrenuntias Satanae?*"

In a triple vow I renounced Satan and his pomps and his works. "Dost thou believe in God the Father almighty, Creator of heaven and earth?" "*Credo!*" "Dost thou believe in Jesus Christ His only Son, Who was born, and suffered?" "*Credo!*" "Dost thou believe in the Holy Spirit, in the Holy Catholic Church, the Communion of saints, the remission of sins, the resurrection of the body and eternal life?" "*Credo!*"

What mountains were falling from my shoulders! What scales of dark night were peeling off my intellect, to let in the inward vision of God and His truth! But I was absorbed in the liturgy, and waiting for the next ceremony. It had been one of the things that had rather frightened me—or rather, which frightened the legion that had been living in me for twenty-three years.

Now the priest blew into my face. He said: "*Ex ab eo, spiritus immunde*: Depart from him, thou impure spirit, and give place to the Holy Spirit, the Paraclete."

It was the exorcism. I did not see them leaving, but there must have been more than seven of them. I had never been able to count them. Would they ever come back? Would that terrible threat of Christ be fulfilled, that threat about the man whose house was clean and garnished, only to be reoccupied by the first devil and many others worse than himself?

The priest, and Christ in him—for it was Christ that was doing these things through his visible ministry, in the Sacrament of my purification—breathed again into my face. "Thomas, receive the good Spirit through this breathing, and receive the Blessing of God. Peace be with thee."

Then he began again to pray, and sign me with Crosses, and presently came the salt which he put on my tongue—the salt of wisdom, that I might have the savor of divine things, and finally he poured the water on my head, and named me Thomas, "if thou be not already baptized."

After that, I went into the confessional, where one of the other assistants was waiting for me. I knelt in the shadows. Through the dark, close-meshed wire of the grille between us, I saw Father McGough, his head bowed, and resting on his hand, inclining his ear towards me. "Poor man," I thought. He seemed very young and he had always looked so innocent to me that I wondered how he was going to identify and understand the things I was about to tell him.

But one by one, that is, species by species, as best I could, I tore out all those sins by their roots, like teeth. Some of them were hard, but I did it quickly, doing the best I could to approximate the number of times all these things had happened—there was no counting them, only guessing.

I did not have any time to feel how relieved I was when I came stumbling out, as I had to go down to the front of the church where Father Moore would see me and come out to begin his—and my—Mass. But ever since that day, I have loved confessionals.

Now he was at the altar, in his white vestments, opening the book. I was kneeling right at the altar rail. The bright sanctuary was all mine. I could hear the murmur of the priest's voice, and the responses of the server, and it did not matter that I had no one to look at, so that I could tell when to stand up and kneel down again, for I was still not very sure of these ordinary ceremonies. But when the little bells were rung I knew what was happening. And I saw the raised Host— the silence and simplicity with which Christ once again triumphed, raised up, drawing all things to Himself—drawing me to Himself.

Presently the priest's voice was louder, saying the *Pater Noster*. Then, soon, the server was running through the *Confiteor* in a rapid murmur. That was for me. Father Moore turned around and made a big cross in absolution, and held up the little Host. "Behold the Lamb of God: behold Him Who taketh away the sins of the world."

And my First Communion began to come towards me, down the steps. I was the only one at the altar rail. Heaven was entirely mine—that Heaven in which sharing makes no division or diminution. But this solitariness was a kind of reminder of singleness with which this Christ, hidden in the small Host, was giving Himself for me, and to me, and, with Himself, the entire Godhead and Trinity—a great new increase of the power and grasp of their indwelling that had begun only a few minutes before the font.

I left the altar rail and went back to the pew . . . and I hid my face in my hands.

In the Temple of God that I had just become, the One Eternal and Pure Sacrifice was offered up to the God dwelling in me; the sacrifice of God to God, and me sacrificed together with God, incorporated in His Incarnation. Christ born in me, a new Bethlehem, and sacrificed in me, His new Calvary, and risen in me: offering me to the Father, in Himself, asking the Father, my Father and His, to receive me into His infinite and special love—not the love He has for all things that exist—for mere existence is a token of God's love, but the love of those creatures who are drawn to Him in and with the power of His own love for Himself.

For now I had entered into the everlasting movement of that gravitation which is the very life and spirit of God: God's own gravitation towards the depths of His own infinite nature, His goodness without end. And God, that center Who is everywhere, and whose circumference is nowhere, finding me, through incorporation with Christ, incorporated into this immense and tremendous gravitational movement which is love, which is the Holy Spirit, loved me.

And He called out to me from His own immense depths.

WHAT IS CONTEMPLATION?[35]

Contemplation is the highest expression of man's intellectual and spiritual life. It is that life itself, fully awake, fully active, fully aware that it is alive. It is spiritual wonder. It is spontaneous awe at the sacredness of life, of being. It is gratitude for life, for awareness and for being. It is a vivid realization of the fact that life and being in us proceed from an invisible, transcendent and infinitely abundant Source. Contemplation is, above all, awareness of the reality of that Source. It *knows* the Source, obscurely, inexplicably, but with a certitude that goes both beyond reason and beyond simple faith. For contemplation is a kind of spiritual vision to which both reason and faith aspire, by their very nature, because without

---

[35]Reprinted from Thoms Merton, *New Seeds of Contemplation*. Copyright (c) 1972 by the Abbey of Gethsemani, Inc. Reprinted by permission of New Directions Publishing Corp. Pages 1–6.

it they must always remain incomplete. Yet contemplation is no vision because it sees "without seeing" and knows "without knowing." It is a more profound depth of faith, a knowledge too deep to be grasped in images, in words or even in clear concepts. It can be suggested by words, by symbols, but in the very moment of trying to indicate what it knows the contemplative mind takes back what it has said, and denies what it has affirmed. For in contemplation we know by "unknowing." Or, better, we know *beyond* all knowing or "unknowing."

Poetry, music and art have something in common with the contemplative experience. But contemplation is beyond aesthetic intuition, beyond art, beyond poetry. Indeed, it is also beyond philosophy, beyond speculative theology. It resumes, transcends and fulfills them all, and yet at the same time it seems, in a certain way, to supersede and to deny them all. Contemplation is always beyond our own knowledge, beyond our own light, beyond system, beyond explanations, beyond discourse, beyond dialogue, beyond our own self. To enter into the realm of contemplation one must in a certain sense die: but this death is in fact the entrance into a higher life. It is a death for the sake of life, which leaves behind all that we can know or treasure as life, as thought, as experience, as joy, as being.

And so contemplation seems to supersede and to discard every other form of intuition and experience—whether in art, in philosophy, in theology, in liturgy or in ordinary levels of love and of belief. This rejection is of course only apparent. Contemplation is and must be compatible with all these things, for it is their highest fulfillment. But in the actual experience of contemplation all other experiences are momentarily lost. They "die" to be born again on a higher level of life.

In other words, then, contemplation reaches out to the knowledge and even to the experience of the transcendent and inexpressible God. It knows God by seeming to touch Him. Or rather it knows Him as if it had been invisibly touched by Him. . . . Touched by Him Who has no hands, but Who is pure Reality and the source of all that is real! Hence contemplation is a sudden gift of awareness, an awakening to the Real within all that is real. A vivid awareness of infinite Being at the roots of our own limited being. An awareness of our contingent reality as received, as a present from God, as a free gift of love. This is the existential contact of which we speak when we use the metaphor of being "touched by God."

Contemplation is also the response to a call: a call from Him Who has no voice, and yet Who speaks in everything that is, and Who, most of all, speaks in the depths of our own being: for we ourselves are words of His. But we are words that are meant to respond to Him, to answer to Him, to echo Him, and even in some way to contain Him and signify Him. Contemplation is this echo. It is a deep resonance in the inmost center of our spirit in which our very life loses its separate voice and re-sounds with the majesty and the mercy of the Hidden and Living One. He answers Himself in us and this answer is divine life, divine creativity, making all things new. We ourselves become His echo and His answer. It is as if in creating us God asked a question, and in awakening us to contemplation He answered the question, so that the contemplative is at the same time, question and answer.

The life of contemplation implies two levels of awareness; first, awareness of the question, and second, awareness of the answer. Though these are two distinct and enormously different levels, yet they are in fact an awareness of the same thing. The question is, itself, the answer. And we ourselves are both. But we cannot know this until we have moved into the second kind of awareness. We awaken, not to find an answer absolutely distinct from the question, but to realize that the question is its own answer. And all is summed up in one awareness—not a proposition, but an experience: "I AM."

The contemplation of which I speak here is not philosophical. It is not the static awareness of metaphysical essences apprehended as spiritual objects, unchanging and eternal. It is not the contemplation of abstract ideas. It is the religious apprehension of God, through my life in God, or through "sonship" as the New Testament says. "For whoever are led by the Spirit of God, they are sons of God. . . . The Spirit Himself gives testimony to our own spirit that we are sons of God." "To as many as received Him He gave the power to become sons of God. . . ." And so the contemplation of which I speak is a religious and transcendent gift. It is not something to which we can attain alone, by intellectual effort, by perfecting our natural powers. It is not a kind of self-hypnosis, resulting from concentration on our own inner spiritual being. It is not the fruit of our own efforts. It is the gift of God Who, in His mercy, completes the hidden and mysterious work of creation in us by enlightening our minds and hearts, by awakening in us the awareness that we are words spoken in His One Word, and that Creating Spirit (*Creator Spiritus*) dwells in us, and we in Him. That we are "in Christ" and that Christ lives in us. That the natural life in us has been completed, elevated, transformed and fulfilled in Christ by the Holy Spirit. Contemplation is the awareness and realization, even in some sense *experience*, of what each Christian obscurely believes: "It is now no longer I that live but Christ lives in me."

Hence contemplation is more than a consideration of abstract truths about God, more even than affective meditation on the things we believe. It is awakening, enlightenment and the amazing intuitive grasp by which love gains certitude of God's creative and dynamic intervention in our daily life. Hence contemplation does not simply "find" a clear idea of God and confine Him within the limits of that idea, and hold Him there as a prisoner to Whom it can always return. On the contrary, contemplation is carried away by Him into His own realm, His own mystery and His own freedom. It is a pure and a virginal knowledge, poor in concepts, poorer still in reasoning, but able, by its very poverty and purity, to follow the Word "wherever He may go."

THE WOMAN CLOTHED WITH THE SUN[36]

. . . Mary alone, of all the saints, is, in everything, incomparable. She has the sanctity of them all and yet resembles none of them. And still we can talk of being like her. This likeness to her is not only something to desire—it is one human

---

[36]Ibid., pp. 169–72. Reprinted by kind permission of New Directions Publishing Corp.

quality most worthy of our desire: but the reason for that is that she, of all creatures, most perfectly recovered the likeness to God that God willed to find, in varying degrees, in us all.

It is necessary, no doubt, to talk about her privileges as if they were something that could be made comprehensible in human language and could be measured by some human standard. It is most fitting to talk about her as a Queen and to act as if you knew what it meant to say she has a throne above all the angels. But this should not make anyone forget that her highest privilege is her poverty and her greatest glory is that she is most hidden, and the source of all her power is that she is as nothing in the presence of Christ, of God.

This is often forgotten by Catholics themselves, and therefore it is not surprising that those who are not Catholic often have a completely wrong conception of Catholic devotion to the Mother of God. They imagine, and sometimes we can understand their reasons for doing so, that Catholics treat the Blessed Virgin as an almost divine being in her own right, as if she had some glory, some power, some majesty of her own that placed her on a level with Christ Himself. They regard the Assumption of Mary into heaven as a kind of apotheosis and her Queenship as a strict divinization. Hence her place in the Redemption would seem to be equal to that of her Son. But this is all completely contrary to the true mind of the Catholic Church. It forgets that Mary's chief glory is in her nothingness, in the fact of being the *"Handmaid* of the Lord," as one who in becoming the Mother of God acted simply in loving submission to His command, in the pure obedience of faith. She is blessed not because of some mythical pseudo-divine prerogative, but in all her human and womanly limitations as *one who has believed*. It is the faith and fidelity of this humble handmaid, "full of grace," that enables her to be the perfect instrument of God, and nothing else but His instrument. The work that was done in her was purely the work of God. "He that is mighty hath done great things in me." The glory of Mary is purely and simply the glory of God in her, and she, like anyone else, can say that she has nothing that she has not received from Him through Christ.

As a matter of fact, this is precisely her greatest glory: that having nothing of her own, retaining nothing of a "self" that could glory in anything for her own sake, she placed no obstacle to the mercy of God and in no way resisted His love and His will. Hence she received *more* from Him than any other saint. He was able to accomplish His will perfectly in her, and His liberty was in no way hindered or turned from its purpose by the presence of an egotistical self in Mary. She was and is in the highest sense a person precisely because, being "immaculate," she was free from every taint of selfishness that might obscure God's light in her being. She was then a freedom that obeyed Him perfectly and in this obedience found the fulfillment of perfect love.

The genuine significance of Catholic devotion to Mary is to be seen in the light of the Incarnation itself. The Church cannot separate the Son and the Mother. Because the Church conceives of the Incarnation as God's descent into flesh and into time, and His great gift of Himself to His creatures, she also believes that the one who was closest to Him in this great mystery was the one who participated most perfectly in the gift. When a room is heated by an open fire, surely there is nothing strange in the fact that those who stand closest to the fireplace are the ones who are warmest. And when God comes into the world through the instrumentality of one of His servants, then there is nothing surprising about the fact that His chosen instrument should have the greatest and most intimate share in the divine gift.

Mary, who was empty of all egoism, free from all sin, was as pure as the glass of a very clean window that has no other function than to admit the light of the sun. If we rejoice in that light, we implicitly praise the cleanness of the window. And of course it might be argued that in such a case we might well forget the window altogether. This is true. And yet the Son of God, in emptying Himself of His majestic power, having become a child, abandoning Himself in complete dependence to the loving care of a human Mother, in a certain sense draws our attention once again to her. The Light has wished to remind us of the window, because He is grateful to her and because He has an infinitely tender and personal love for her. If He asks us to share this love, it is certainly a great grace and a privilege, and one of the most important aspects of this privilege is that it enables us to some extent to appreciate the mystery of God's great love and respect for His creatures. . . .

Martin Luther King, Jr. (1929–68)

A Baptist minister and the son of a Baptist minister, King emerged as leader of the Southern Christian Leadership Conference, and de facto leader of the civil rights movement. Martin Luther King was a powerful preacher and social activist; his philosophy of nonviolent social change had its basis in the gospel. His faith gave him the "strength to love" in the midst of strife and oppression. A skillful preacher, King earned the B.D. at Crosier Theological Seminary (Philadelphia), and the Ph.D. at Boston University in 1955. He was awarded the Nobel Peace Prize, in 1964, because of his prodigious efforts on behalf of nonviolent social change. Dr. King was assassinated on April 4, 1968, in Memphis, Tennessee, while he was leading demonstrations on behalf of the underpaid city sanitation workers. Martin Luther King's life and works left a profound legacy of the power of Christian love to transform people and society.

A CUP OF COFFEE WITH GOD[37]

As I come to the conclusion of my message, I would wish you to permit a personal experience. The first twenty-four years of my life were years packed with

---

[37]From Martin Luther King, Jr., *Strength to Love* (Philadelphia: Fortress Press, 1981, rev., pp. 113–14. Copyright 1963 by Martin Luther King, Jr. Copyright renewed 1991 by Coretta Scott King. Reprinted by arrangement with The Heirs to the Estate of Martin Luther King, Jr., c/o Writers House, Inc. as agent for the proprietor.

fulfillment. I had no basic problems or burdens, Because of concerned and loving parents who provided for my every need, I sallied through high school, college, theological school, and graduate school without interruption. It was not until I became a part of the leadership of the Montgomery bus protest that I was actually confronted with the trials of life. Almost immediately after the protest had been undertaken, we began to receive threatening telephone calls and letters in our home. Sporadic in the beginning, they increased day after day. At first I took them in my stride, feeling they were the work of a few hotheads who would become discouraged after they discovered that we would not fight back. But as the weeks passed by, I realized that many of the threats were in earnest. I felt myself faltering and growing in fear.

After a particularly strenuous day, I settled in bed at a late hour. My wife had already fallen asleep and I was about to doze off when the telephone rang. An angry voice said: "Listen nigger, we've taken all we want from you. Before next week you"ll be sorry you ever came to Montgomery." I hung up, but I could not sleep. It seemed that all of my fears had come down on me at once. I had reached the saturation point.

I got out of bed and began to walk the floor. Finally, I went to the kitchen and heated a pot of coffee. I was ready to give up. I tried to think of a way to move out of the picture without appearing to be a coward. In this state of exhaustion, when my courage seemed almost gone, I determined to take my problem to God. My head in my hands, I bowed over the kitchen table and prayed aloud. The words I spoke to God that midnight are still vivid in my memory. "I am here taking a stand for what I believe is right. But now I am afraid. The people are looking to me for leadership, and if I stand before them without strength and courage, they too will falter. I am at the end of my powers, I have nothing left. I've come to the point where I can't face it alone."

At that moment I experienced the presence of the Divine as I had never before experienced Him. It seemed as though I could hear the quiet assurance of an inner voice, saying, "Stand up for righteousness, stand up for truth. God will be at your side forever." Almost at once my fears began to pass from me. My uncertainty disappeared. I was ready to face anything. The outer situation remained the same, but God had given me inner calm.

Three nights later, our home was bombed. Strangely enough, I accepted the word of the bombing calmly. My experience with God had given me new strength and trust. I knew now that God is able to give us the interior resources to face the storms and problems of life.

Let this affirmation be our ringing cry. It will give us courage to face the uncertainties of the future. It will give our tired feet new strength as we continue our forward stride toward the city of freedom. When our days become dreary with low-hovering clouds and our nights become darker than a thousand midnights. let us remember that there is a great benign Power in the universe whose name is God, and He is able to make a way out of no way, and transform dark yesterdays into bright tomorrows. This is our hope for becoming better men. This is our mandate for seeking to make a better world.

LOVING YOUR ENEMIES[38]

"Ye have heard that it hath been said, Thou shalt love thy neighbor, and hate thine enemy. But I say unto you, Love your enemies, bless them that curse you, do good to them that hate you, and pray for them which despitefully use you, and persecute you; that ye may be children of your Father which is in heaven" [Mt 5:43–45].

Probably no admonition of Jesus has been more difficult to follow than the command to "love your enemies." Some people have sincerely felt that its actual practice is not possible. It is easy, they say, to love those who love you, but how can one love those who openly and insidiously seek to defeat you? Others, like the philosopher Nietzsche, contend that Jesus" exhortation to love one's enemies is testimony to the fact that the Christian ethic is designed for the weak and cowardly, and not for the strong and courageous. Jesus, they say, was an impractical idealist.

In spite of these insistent questions and persistent objections, this command of Jesus challenges us with new urgency. Upheaval after upheaval has reminded us that modern humanity is traveling along a road called hate, in a journey that will bring us to destruction and damnation. Far from being the pious injunction of a Utopian dreamer, the command to love one's enemy is an absolute necessity for our survival. Love even for enemies is the key to the solution of the problems of our world. Jesus is not an impractical idealist; He is the practical realist.

I am certain that Jesus understood the difficulty inherent in the act of loving one's enemy. He never joined the ranks of those who talk glibly about the easiness of the moral life. He realized that every genuine expression of love grows out of a consistent and total surrender to God. So when Jesus said "Love your enemy," He was not unmindful of its stringent qualities. Yet He meant every word of it. Our responsibility as Christians is to discover the meaning of this command and seek passionately to live it out in our daily lives.

Let us be practical and ask the question, *How do we love our enemies?* First, we must develop and maintain the capacity to forgive. He who is devoid of the power to forgive is devoid of the power to love. It is impossible even to begin the act of loving one's enemies without the prior acceptance of the necessity, over and over again, of forgiving those who inflict evil and injury upon us. It is also necessary to realize that the forgiving act must always be initiated by the person who has been wronged, the victim of some great hurt, the recipient of some tortuous injustice, the absorber of some terrible act of oppression. The wrongdoer may request forgiveness. He may come to himself like the prodigal son [Lk 15:11ff], move up some dusty road, his heart palpitating with the desire for forgiveness. But only the injured neighbor, the loving father back home, can really pour out the warm waters of forgiveness.

Forgiveness does not mean ignoring what has been done or putting a false label on an evil act. It means, rather, that the evil act no longer remains as a bar-

---

[38]Ibid., pp. 49–57. Reprinted by arrangement with the Heirs to the Estate of Martin Luther King, Jr. c/o Writers House, Inc. as agent for the proprietor.

rier to the relationship. Forgiveness is a catalyst creating the atmosphere necessary for a fresh start and a new beginning. It is the lifting of a burden or the cancelling of a debt. The words, "I will forgive you, but I'll never forget what you've done," never explain the real nature of forgiveness. Certainly one can never forget, if that means erasing it totally from his mind. But when we forgive, we forget in the sense that the evil deed is no longer a mental block impeding a new relationship. Likewise, we can never say, "I will forgive you, but I won't have anything further to do with you." Forgiveness means reconciliation, a coming together again. Without this, no one can love his enemies. The degree to which we are able to forgive determines the degree to which we are able to love our enemies.

Second, we must recognize that the evil deed of the enemy-neighbor, the thing that hurts, never quite expresses all that he is. An element of goodness may be found even in our worst enemy. Each of us is something of a schizophrenic personality, tragically divided against ourselves. A persistent civil war rages within all of our lives. Something within us causes us to lament with Ovid, the Latin poet, "I see and approve the better things, but follow worse," or to agree with Plato that human personality is like a charioteer having two headstrong horses, each wanting to go in a different direction, or to repeat with the Apostle Paul, "The good that I would I do not; but the evil which I would not, that I do" [Rom 7:19].

This simply means that there is some good in the worst of us and some evil in the best of us. When we discover this, we are less prone to hate our enemies. When we look beneath the surface, beneath the impulsive evil deed, we see within our enemy-neighbor a measure of goodness and know that the viciousness and evilness of his acts are not quite representative of all that he is. We see him in a new light. We recognize that his hate grows out of fear, pride, ignorance, prejudice, and misunderstanding, but in spite of this, we know God's image is ineffably etched in his being. Then we love our enemies by realizing that they are not totally bad and that they are not beyond the reach of God's redemptive love.

Third, we must not seek to defeat or humiliate the enemy but to win his friendship and understanding. At times we are able to humiliate our worst enemy. Inevitably, his weak moments come and we are able to thrust in his side the spear of defeat. But this we must not do. Every word and deed must contribute to an understanding with the enemy and release those vast reservoirs of goodwill which have been blocked by impenetrable walls of hate.

The meaning of love is not to be confused with some sentimental outpouring. Love is something much deeper than emotional bosh. Perhaps the Greek language can clear our confusion at this point. In the Greek New Testament are three words for love. The word *eros* is a sort of aesthetic or romantic love. In the Platonic dialogues *eros* is a yearning of the soul for the realm of the divine. The second word is *philia*, a reciprocal love and the intimate affection and friendship between friends. We love those whom we like, and we love because we are loved. The third word is *agape*, understanding and creative, redemptive goodwill for all men. An overflowing love which seeks nothing in return, *agape* is the love of God operating in the human heart. At this level, we love people not because we like them, nor because their ways appeal to us, nor even because they possess some type of divine spark; we love every person because God loves him or her. At this level, we love the person who does an evil deed, although we hate the evil that he does.

Now we can see what Jesus meant when he said, "Love your enemies." We should be happy that He did not say, "Like your enemies." It is almost impossible to like some people. "Like" is a sentimental and affectionate word. How can we be affectionate toward a person whose avowed aim is to crush our very being and place innumerable stumbling blocks in our path? How can we like a person who is threatening our children and bombing our homes? That is impossible. But Jesus recognized that *love* is greater than *like*. When Jesus bids us to love our enemies, He is speaking neither of *eros* nor *philia*; He is speaking of *agape*, understanding and creative, redemptive goodwill for all people. Only by following this way and responding with this type of love are we able to be children of our Father who is in heaven.

Let us move now from the practical *how* to the theoretical *why*: *Why should we love our enemies?* The first reason is fairly obvious. Returning hate for hate multiplies hate, adding deeper darkness to a night already devoid of stars. Darkness cannot drive out darkness; only light can do that. Hate cannot drive out hate; only love can do that. Hate multiplies hate, violence multiplies violence, and toughness multiplies toughness in a descending spiral of destruction. So when Jesus says "Love your enemies," He is setting forth a profound and ultimately inescapable admonition. Have we not come to such an impasse in the modern world that we must love our enemies—or else? The chain reaction of evil—hate begetting hate, wars producing more wars—must be broken, or we shall be plunged into the dark abyss of annihilation.

Another reason why we must love our enemies is that hate scars the soul and distorts the personality. Mindful that hate is an evil and dangerous force, we too often think of what it does to the person hated. This is understandable, for hate brings irreparable damage to its victims. We have seen its ugly consequences in the ignominious deaths brought to six million Jews by a hate-obsessed madman named Hitler, in the unspeakable violence inflicted upon Negroes by bloodthirsty mobs and injustices perpetrated against millions of God's children by unconscionable oppressors.

But there is another side which we must never overlook. Hate is just as injurious to the person who hates. Like an unchecked cancer, hate corrodes the personality and eats away its vital unity. Hate destroys a person's sense of values and his objectivity. It causes him to describe the beautiful as ugly and the ugly as beautiful, and to confuse the true with the false and the false with the true. . . . Modern psychology recognizes what Jesus taught centuries ago: hate divides the personality and love in an amazing and inexorable way unites it.

A third reason why we should love our enemies is that love is the only force capable of transforming an enemy into a friend. We never get rid of an enemy by meeting hate with hate; we get rid of an enemy by getting rid of enmity. By its very nature, hate destroys and tears down; by its very nature, love creates and builds up. Love transforms with redemptive power. . . .

We must hasten to say that these are not the ultimate reasons why we should love our enemies. An even more basic reason why we are commanded to love is expressed explicitly in Jesus' words, "Love your enemies . . . *that ye may be children of your Father which is in heaven.*" We are called to this difficult task in order to realize a unique relationship with God. We are potential sons and daughters of God. Through love that potential becomes actuality. We must love our enemies, because only by loving them can we know God and experience the beauty of His holiness.

The relevance of what I have said to the crisis in race relations should be readily apparent. There will be no permanent solution to the race problem until oppressed people develop the capacity to love their enemies. The darkness of racial prejudice will be displaced only by the light of forgiving love. For more than three centuries American Negroes have been battered by the iron rod of oppression, frustrated by day and bewildered by night by unbearable injustice, and burdened with the ugly weight of discrimination. Forced to live with these shameful conditions, we are tempted to become bitter and to retaliate with a corresponding hate. But if this happens the new order we seek will be little more than a duplicate of the old order. We must in strength and humility meet hate with love.

Of course, this is not *practical.* Life is a matter of getting even, of hitting back, of dog eat dog. Am I saying that Jesus commands us to love those who hurt and oppress us? Do I sound like most preachers—idealistic and impractical? Maybe in some distant Utopia, you say, that idea will work, but not in the hard, cold world in which we live. My friends, we have followed the so-called practical way for too long a time now, and it has led inexorably to deeper confusion and chaos. Time is cluttered with the wreckage of communities which have surrendered to hatred and violence. For the salvation of our nation and the salvation of mankind, we must follow another way. This does not mean that we abandon our righteous efforts. With every ounce of our energy we must continue to rid this nation of the incubus of segregation. But we shall not in the process relinquish our privilege and our obligation to love. While abhorring segregation, we shall love the segregationist. This is the only way to create the beloved community.

To our most bitter opponents we say: "We shall match your capacity to inflict suffering by our capacity to endure suffering. We shall meet your physical force with soul force. Do to us what you will, and we shall continue to love you. We cannot in all good conscience obey your unjust laws, because noncooperation with evil is as much a moral obligation as is cooperation with good. Throw us in jail, and we shall still love you. Send your hooded perpetrators of violence into our community at the midnight hour and beat us and leave us half dead, and we shall still love you. But be assured that we will wear you down by our capacity to suffer. One day we shall win freedom, but not only for ourselves. We shall so appeal to your heart and conscience that we shall win *you* in the process, and our victory will be a double victory."

Love is the most durable power in the world. This creative force, so beautifully exemplified in the life of our Christ, is the most potent instrument available in mankind's quest for peace and security. . . . Jesus is eternally right. History is replete with the bleached bones of nations that refused to listen to Him. May we in the twentieth century hear and follow His words—before it is too late. May we solemnly realize that we shall never be true sons [and daughters] of our heavenly Father until we love our enemies and pray for those who persecute us.

James H. Cone (1938–)

James Cone was born in Fordyce and raised in Bearden, Arkansas. The experiences of segregation, and racism, as well as the resources of the African American church were prominent factors in his spiritual formation. He graduated from Philander Smith College (B.A. 1958), and Garrett Theological Seminary (B.D. 1961). He did graduate work in systematic theology at Northwestern University, earning the M.A. in 1961 and the Ph.D. in 1965. Cone is a member of the African Methodist Episcopal Church.

After academic appointments at Philander Smith College (1964–66) and Adrian College (1966–69), James Cone joined the faculty of Union Theological Seminary, New York. He is widely considered the originator and one of the chief exponents of Black Theology. His contribution to Christian Spirituality is most directly seen in Cone's ability to formulate theological responses to racism and the African American experience that are rooted in the religious resources of the black church. He stresses that liberation of the oppressed is inherent in the gospel of Jesus Christ, and that experiences of oppression and liberation are constituent factors of black worship and the African American experience. Among Cone's influential works are *Black Theology and Black Power* (1969), *A Black Theology of Liberation* (1970), *Spirituals and the Blues* (1972), *God of the Oppressed* (1975), *My Soul Looks Back* (1982), and *Martin & Malcolm & America: A Dream or Nightmare* (1993).

A LIBERATING EXPERIENCE[39]

Martin Luther King, Jr.'s assassination (April 4, 1968) marked a turning point in the political consciousness of many black Americans regarding nonviolence as a method for social change and as an expression of Christian love. Because of King's commitment to nonviolence and thus rejection of Black Power, many blacks were cautious in their public acceptance of Black Power in that it implied a rejection of Martin King. But after he was killed by white violence, Black Power seemed not only a logical but a necessary choice for the black community.

Although I had already embraced Black Power before King's murder, that event intensified my conviction and made me more determined to write an extended essay equating Black Power with the Christian gospel. By the summer of

---

[39]James H. Cone, *My Soul Looks Back*. (Maryknoll, N.Y.: Orbis Books, 1986), pp. 46–63 with omissions. Copyright (c) by James H. Cone. Used by kind permission of Orbis Books.

that year, I had so much anger pent up in me that I had to let it out or be destroyed by it. The cause of my anger was not merely my reaction to the murder of Martin King. Neither was it due simply to the death of Malcolm X or the killing of so many blacks in the cities. My anger stretched back to the slave ships, the auction block, and the lynchings. But even more important were my personal encounters with racism in Bearden, Little Rock, Evanston, and Adrian. Because of these experiences, I promised myself that I would never again make a political or theological compromise with racism. Racism is a deadly disease that must be resisted by any means necessary. Never again would I ever expect white racists to do right in relation to the black community. A moral or theological appeal based on white definition of morality or theology will always serve as a detriment to our attainment of black freedom. The only option we blacks have is to fight in every way possible, so that we can begin to create a definition of freedom based on our own history and culture. We must not expect white people to give us freedom. Freedom is not a gift, but a responsibility, and thus must be taken against the will of those who hold us in bondage.

The writing of *Black Theology and Black Power* that summer was a therapeutic and a liberating experience for me. It is an understatement to say that I did not attempt to write a "balanced" and "objective" view regarding black-white relations in theology, church, and society. I knew whose side I was on and I was not going to allow my training in white "academic scholarship" to camouflage my feelings. With a Ph.D. degree, I had already demonstrated that I knew how to play the academic game. Furthermore, since the academic game in theology and other disciplines had little to do with black people's self-determination, why should I let the ethos of the white seminary or university control the content and the form of my writing?

When it became clear to me that my intellectual consciousness should be defined and controlled by black history and culture and not by standards set in white seminaries and universities, I could feel in the depth of my being a liberation that began to manifest itself in the energy and passion of my writing. Writing for the first time became as natural as talking and preaching. Of course, they were not identical, but writing was no longer an alien experience. It became a joyful experience, a creation of a perspective on life that I could objectify and analyze in the ecstasy of my engagement with the black experience.

In addition to being therapeutic and liberating, the writing of *Black Theology and Black Power* was also a conversion experience. It was like experiencing the death of white theology and being born again into the theology of the black experience. A foretaste of this rebirth occurred in my writing of "Christianity and Black Power." But its full manifestation did not happen until the writing of my first book on black theology. I now realized why it was so difficult for me to make the connection between the black experience and theology. As long as theology was exclusively defined by whites, the connection could never be made because of their racism. Racists do not define theology in a way that challenges their racism. To expect white theologians to voluntarily make theology relevant to black people's struggle for justice would be like expecting Pharaoh in Egypt to voluntarily liberate Israelites from slavery. It is the victims and those who identify with them who must make the connection between their struggle and the gospel.

Furthermore when the victims of injustice make the connection between their struggle and the gospel of Jesus, their oppressors always deny that such a connection exists. As I was writing my first book on black theology, I knew that the majority of white theologians and preachers would either ignore it or denounce it as unchristian and not real theology. But the anticipation of negative comments from white theologians and preachers gave me more energy and intensified my passion to state the case for black theology and against white theology. As far as I was concerned, the white church and its theology represented the antichrist and needed to be exposed for what they were. Indeed I felt "called" by God's Holy Spirit to be an agent of this exposure.

Of course, I would be less than honest if I failed to acknowledge the intellectual and religious pride involved in my newly discovered theological calling. It is always difficult to distinguish one's own interests and desires from what one designates as the Holy Spirit. That is why it is important to develop criteria for distinguishing between human work that comes from God and human activity that is motivated exclusively by human pride. In my case, I felt that despite the presence of my own interest, the reality of God's presence in black people's struggle for justice could hardly be denied by any committed Christian. If this assumption is true, what then is the relationship between my training as a theologian and the black struggle for freedom? For what reason had God allowed a poor black boy from Bearden [Ark.] to become a professional systematic theologian? As I struggled with these questions and the ambiguity involved in my vocation, I could not escape the overwhelming conviction that God's Spirit was calling me to do what I could for the enhancement of justice in the world, especially on behalf of my people. It seemed obvious to me that the best contribution I could make was to uncover the hypocrisy of the white church and its theology. I had been studying and teaching white theology for more than ten years and had achieved the highest professional degree possible. Not many blacks had my technical training in theology, and no one, not even white theologians, could question my academic credentials. I felt that God must have been preparing me for this vocation, that is, the task of leveling the most devastating black critique possible against the white church and its theology.

As I wrote, I kept thinking about my slave grandparents in Arkansas, Alabama, and Mississippi, and of the silence of white theologians about their struggle to survive the whip and the pistol. I also thought about the auction block and the Underground Railroad, and what both meant for the realities of slavery and black people's struggle to liberate themselves in an extreme situation of oppression. While I had not lived during the time of legal slavery, its impact upon black life was still visibly present in the contemporary economic, social, and political structures of the United States. Lynching is the most dramatic manifestation of the legacy of black slavery. Aside from the memory of the Bearden whites' threat to lynch my father, I also thought about the approximately five thousand documented lynchings in the last half of the nineteenth and the first half of the twentieth centuries, and the support that these demonic acts received from white churches. The more I thought about the oppression of black people and the conspicuous silence of white churches and their theologians, the more determined I became to expose their true character as being demonic and thus unchristian.

I could not avoid thinking of my mother and father, who were still living in Bearden at the time, and their struggle to create a humane and Christian environment for their children. Lucy and Charlie Cone had worked hard and endured much white dehumanization in Bearden so that I could have a sense of worth and self-confidence, thereby enabling me to become a teacher and writer of Christian theology. Therefore I had to say something that would represent the truth of their lives. If I did not do that, then I did not even deserve to be a theologian.

Also dominant on my mind was the fact that none of the major theological interpreters of Europe and North America used the experience of the black poor as a source of doing theology. That is why I could study for years at Garrett-Northwestern and not be required to even read a book on racism or any aspect of the black experience. The one occasion on which I ventured to raise the issue created such chaos that the class had to be dismissed. That kind of experience makes a person bitter and also determined to find ways to render an appropriate judgment upon all who participated in it or identified with it. I knew that most of my former white classmates, professors, and administrators of Garrett would not like what I was writing. But that only pleased me, for I could not forget their attitudes of superiority as white professors and administrators gave all the scholarships and fellowships to white students, as if other blacks and I were too dumb to get one.

It is not possible to endure humiliating experiences like that and not be angry about it. The thing that made me so angry was the knowledge that what had happened to me had happened to many black students at Garrett and also routinely happened at other seminaries at that time. (Unfortunately such things still occur today.) With my own and other black students' humiliating experience on my mind, every time I made a cogent theological point, I smiled and said to myself: "This is for Garrett, and what white professors and students did to black students." Whatever else I wanted to achieve, one chief concern was to expose the racism at Garrett in particular and in the white churches and seminaries in general. When one part of me began to say that maybe I was being a little too hard and perhaps unfair regarding white churches and their theology, there was a stronger side of me that recalled how inhumane white people had been toward black people. The extent of white brutality against my people had been so great that there was no way I could possibly overstate the case for black liberation. White churches and their theology had been so wicked that my little book would not even make a dent in revealing the extent of their evil. My book would be like a fly on a horse's back, annoying perhaps, but with not even a chance of destroying the beast. Why then should I tone down the truth of my claim? Why should I allow a few white exceptions to camouflage the enormity of white people's brutality against black people? . . .

When a person writes about something that matters to him or her existentially, and in which his or her identity is at stake, then the energy for it comes easily and naturally. The writing is no longer being done for someone else but for oneself as a requirement for survival. One writes because one has to write and there is no other option. It is like the call to preach or to testify. The spirit of another invades one's being and compels one to tell the truth. That was something of what I felt in writing *Black Theology and Black Power*. . . .

THE HOLY SPIRIT AND BLACK WORSHIP[40]

Since the appearance of Black Theology in the late 1960's, much has been said and written about the theme of liberation in black religion. The names of Henry Highland Garnet, David Walker, Daniel Payne, and Henry McNeil Turner have been widely quoted in black theological circles, because they related the Christian gospel to the politics of black liberation. For the same reason, such spirituals as "Go Down Moses," "O Freedom," and "Steal Away" are often quoted in contemporary black theological discourse. Black theologians are concerned to show the liberating character of black Christianity in our struggle for social and political justice. But in our effort to show that the gospel is political, we black theologians have sometimes been in danger of reducing black religion to politics and black worship to a political strategy session, thereby distorting the essence of black religion. . . . Hopefully I will be able to clarify the connection between the experience of holiness in worship and the struggle for political justice in the larger society.

Black worship is essentially a spiritual experience of the truth of black life. The experience is spiritual because the people encounter the presence of the divine Spirit in their midst. Black worship is truthful because the Spirit's presence authenticates their experience of freedom by empowering them with courage and strength to bear witness in their present existence, what they know is coming in God's own eschatological future.

> Have I got a witness?
> Certainly Lord!
> Have I got a witness?
> Certainly Lord!
> Certainly, certainly, certainly Lord.

This call and response is an essential element of the black worship style. Black worship is a community happening wherein the people experience the truth of their lives as lived together in the struggle of freedom and held together by God's Spirit. There is no understanding of black worship apart from the presence of the Spirit who descends upon the gathered community, lighting a spiritual fire in

---

[40]Excerpted from James H. Cone, *Speaking the Truth: Ecumenism, Liberation, and Black Theology* (Grand Rapids, Mich.: Wm. B. Eerdmans, 1986), pp. 17–22. Copyright (c) 1986 by Wm. B. Eerdmans. Used by kind permission of the publisher.

their hearts. The divine Spirit is not a metaphysical entity but rather the power of Jesus, who breaks into the lives of the people giving them a new song to sing as confirmation of God's presence with them in historical struggle. It is the presence of the divine Spirit that accounts for the intensity in which black people engage in worship. There is no understanding of black worship apart from the rhythm of the song and sermon, the passion of prayer and testimony, the ecstasy of the shout and conversion as the people project their humanity in the togetherness of the Spirit.

The black church congregation is an eschatological community that lives as if the end of time were already at hand. The difference between the earliest Christian community as an eschatological congregation and the black church community is this: the post-resurrection community expected a complete cosmic transformation in Jesus' immediate return because the end of time was at hand. The eschatological significance of the black community is found in the people believing that the Spirit of Jesus is coming to visit them in the worship service each time two or three are gathered in his name and to bestow upon them a new vision of their future humanity. This eschatological revolution is not so much a cosmic change as it is a change in the people's identity, wherein they are no longer named by the world but named by the Spirit of Jesus. Roberta Flack expresses the significance of this eschatological change in the people's identity in her singing of "I told Jesus it would be all right if he changed my name. He told me that the world will turn away from you, child, if I changed your name." This change in identity affects not only one's relationship with the world but also with one's immediate family. "He told me that your father and mother won't know you, child, if I changed your name." Because the reality of the Spirit's liberating and sanctifying presence is so overwhelming on the believer's identity, the believer can still say with assurance: "I told Jesus it would be all right if he changed my name."

The Holy Spirit's presence with the people is a liberating experience. Black people who have been humiliated and oppressed by the structures of white society six days of the week gather together each Sunday morning in order to experience another definition of their humanity. The transition from Saturday to Sunday is not just a chronological change from the seventh to the first day of the week. It is rather a rupture in time, a *kairos*-event which produces a radical transformation in the people's identity. The janitor becomes the chairperson of the Deacon Board; the maid becomes president of the Stewardess Board Number 1. Everybody becomes Mr. and Mrs. or Brother and Sister. The last becomes first, making a radical change in the perception of one's self and one's calling in the society. Every person becomes somebody, and one can see the people's recognition of their newfound identity by the way they walk and talk and "carry themselves." They walk with a rhythm of an assurance that they know where they are going, and they talk as if they know the truth about which they speak. It is this experience of being radically transformed by the power of the Spirit which defines the primary style of black worship. This transformation is found not only in the titles of Deacons, Stewardesses, Trustees, and Ushers, but also in the excitement of the entire congregation at worship. To be at the end of time where one has been given a new name requires a passionate response commensurate with the felt power of the Spirit in one's heart.

In the act of worship itself, the experience of liberation becomes a constituent of the community's being. In this context, liberation is not exclusively a political event but also an eschatological happening. It is the power of God's Spirit invading the lives of the people, "building" them up where they are torn down and "proppin'" them up on every leanin' side." When a song is sung right and the sermon is delivered in response to the Spirit, the people experience the eschatological presence of God in their midst. Liberation is no longer a future event, but a present happening in the worship itself. That is why it is hard to sit still in a black worship service. For the people claim that "if you don't put anything into the service, you sure won't get anything out of it." Black worship demands involvement. Sometimes a sister does not plan to participate too passionately, but before she knows what is happening "a little fire starts to burning and a little prayer-wheel starts to turning in her heart." In response to the Spirit and its liberating presence, she begins to move to the Spirit's power. How and when she moves depends upon the way the Spirit touches her soul and engages her in the dynamics of the community at worship. She may acknowledge the Spirit's presence with a song.

> Every time I feel the spirit
> Moving in my heart I will pray.
> Every time I feel the spirit
> Moving in my heart I will pray.
>
> Upon the mountain my Lord spoke.
> Out of His mouth came fire and smoke.
> In the valley on my knees,
> Asked my Lord, Have mercy please.
>
> Every time I feel the spirit
> Moving in my heart I will pray. . . .

However, song is only one possible response to the Spirit's presence. God's Spirit also may cause a person to preach, pray, or testify. "I believe I will testify for what the Lord has done for me" is an often-heard response in the black church. But more of the presence of the Spirit elicits what W. E. B. DuBois called the "Frenzy" and what the people call the "shout," which refers not to sound but to bodily movement. "When the Lord gets ready," the people claim, "you've got to move"— that is, to "stand up and let the world know that you are not ashamed to be known as a child of God."

There is no authentic black worship service apart from the presence of the Spirit, God's power to be with and for the people. It is not unusual for the people to express their solidarity with John on the island of Patmos and to say with him: "I was in the Spirit on the Lord's day" (Rev. 1:10, KJV). Like John, black people believe that to be in the Spirit is to experience the power of another presence in their midst. The Spirit is God's guarantee that the little ones are never, no not ever, left alone in their struggle for freedom. God's Spirit is God's way of being with the people, enabling them to shout for joy when the people have no obvious reason in their lives to warrant happiness. The Spirit sometimes makes you run and clap your hands; at other times, you want just to sit still and perhaps pat your feet, wave your hands, and hum the melody of a song: "Ain't no harm to praise the Lord."

It is difficult for an outsider to understand what is going on in a black worship service. To know what is happening in this eschatological event, one cannot approach this experience as a detached observer in the role of a sociologist of religion or as a psychologist, looking for an explanation not found in the life-experiences of the people. One must come as a participant in black reality, willing to be transformed by one's encounter with the Spirit. If one is willing to let the Spirit have her way, being open to what God has in store for him, then he will probably understand what the people mean when they sing:

> Glory, glory hallelujah
> Since I laid my burdens down,
> Glory, glory, hallelujah,
> Since I laid my burdens down.

> I'm going home to live with Jesus,
> Since I laid my burdens down.
> I'm going home to live with Jesus,
> Since I laid my burdens down.

It is the people's response to the presence of the Spirit that creates the unique style of black worship. The style of black worship is a constituent of its content, and both elements point to the theme of liberation. Unlike whites, who often drive a wedge between content and style in worship (as in their secular-sacred distinction), blacks believe that a sermon's content is inseparable from the way in which it is proclaimed. Blacks are deeply concerned about *how* things are said in prayer and testimony and their effect upon those who hear them. The way I say "I love the Lord, he heard my cry" cannot be separated from my intended meaning as derived from my existential and historical setting. For example, if I am one who has just escaped from slavery, and my affirmation is motivated by that event, I will express my faith-claim with the passion and ecstasy of one who was once lost and now found. There will be no detachment in my proclamation of freedom. Only those who do not know bondage existentially can speak of liberation "objectively." Only those who have not been in the "valley of death" can sing the songs of Zion as if they are uninvolved. Black worship is derived from the meeting with the Lord in the struggle to be free. If one has not met the Spirit of God in the struggle for freedom, there can be no joy and no reason to sing with ecstatic passion "I am so glad that trouble don't last always."

Mother Teresa (1910–97)

Mother Teresa, of Calcutta, was one of the most highly respected contemporary Christian women. She was internationally known for her work among the victims of poverty and neglect in the slums of Calcutta, India. In 1979 she received the Noble Peace Prize in recognition of her humanitarian work. Born Agnes Bojaxhiu, in Skopje, Macedonia, she joined the Institute of the Blessed Virgin Mary in 1928. Within six weeks she had begun her service in India, first as a teacher and then as a nurse who lived in the slums to give care and solace to the poor.

In 1950 Mother Teresa founded the Order of the Missionaries of Charity, a congregation of women dedicated to serving the poor; at the present time more than 3,000 nuns are affiliated with the Order. Mother Teresa's deep understanding of the inner connection of Christian love and Christian service permeates her spiritual writings, and is most poignantly expressed in her ability to see Christ personified in the faces and the needs of the poor, the sick, the suffering and the outcast.

ON SUFFERING[41]

Suffering is increasing in the world today. People are hungry for something beautiful, for something greater than people round about can give. There is great hunger for God in the world today. Everywhere there is much suffering, but there is also great hunger for God and love for each other.

There is hunger for ordinary bread, and there is hunger for love, for kindness, for thoughtfulness; and this is the great poverty that makes people suffer so much.

Suffering in itself is nothing; but suffering shared with Christ's passion is a wonderful gift. Man's most beautiful gift is that he can share in the passion of Christ. Yes, a gift and a sign of His love; because this is how His Father proved that He loved the world—by giving His Son to die for us.

And so in Christ it was proved that the greatest gift is love: because suffering was how he paid for sin. Without Him we could do nothing. And it is at the altar that we meet our suffering poor. And in Him that we see that suffering can become a means to greater love and greater generosity.

Without our suffering, our work would just be social work, very good and helpful, but not the work of Jesus Christ, not part of the Redemption. Jesus wanted to help by sharing our life, our loneliness, our agony, our death. Only by being one with us has He redeemed us.

We are asked to do the same; all the desolation of the poor people, not only their material poverty, but their spiritual destitution, must be redeemed. And we

---

[41]Excerpts from Mother Teresa, *A Gift for God: Prayers and Meditations*. Copyright (c) 1975 by Mother Teresa Missionaries of Charity. Reprinted by permission of HarperCollins Publishers, Inc. Pages 19–25.

must share it, for only by being one with them can we redeem them by bringing God into their lives and bringing them to God.

If sometimes our poor people have had to die of starvation, it is not because God didn't care for them, but because you and I didn't give, were not instruments of love in the hands of God, to give them that bread, to give them that clothing; because we did not recognize Him, when once more Christ came in distressing disguise—in the hungry man, in the lonely man, in the homeless child, and seeking for shelter.

God has identified Himself with the hungry, the sick, the naked, the homeless; hunger, not only for bread, but for love, for care, to be somebody to someone; nakedness, not of clothing only, but nakedness of that compassion that very few people give to the unknown; homeless, not only just for shelter made of stone, but that homelessness that comes from having no one to call your own.

IMITATION OF CHRIST[42]

. . . Because we cannot see Christ we cannot express our love to Him; but our neighbors we can always see, and we can do for them what, if we saw Him, we would like to do for Christ.

Today, the same Christ is in people who are unwanted, unemployed, uncared for, hungry, naked, and homeless. They seem useless to the state and to society; nobody has time for them. It is you and I as Christians, worthy of the love of Christ if our love is true, who must find them, and help them; they are there for the finding.

Christians stand as the light for the others . . . for the people in the world. If we are Christians then we must be Christlike.

If you will learn this art of being thoughtful, you will become more and more Christlike, for His heart was meek and He always thought of others. Thoughtfulness is the beginning of sanctity. Our vocation, to be beautiful, must be full of thought for others. Jesus went about doing good. Our Lady in Cana only thought of the needs of others and made their needs known to Jesus.

To be a true Christian means the true acceptance of Christ, and the becoming of another Christ one to another. To love as we are loved, as Christ has loved us from the Cross, we have to love each other and give to others.

When Christ said: "I was hungry and you fed me" [Mt 25:35], He didn't mean only the hunger for bread and for food; He also meant the hunger to be loved. Jesus himself experienced this loneliness. He came amongst His own and His own received Him not [Jn 1:11], and it hurt Him then and it has kept on hurting Him. The same hunger, the same loneliness, the same having no one to be accepted by and to be loved and wanted by. Every human being in that case resembles Christ in his loneliness; and that is the hardest part, that's real hunger.

---

[42]Ibid., p. 27–31. Reprinted by permission of HarperCollins Publishers, Inc.

CO-WORKERS OF CHRIST[43]

As each Sister is to become a Co-Worker of Christ in the slums, each ought to understand what God and the Missionaries of Charity expect from her. Let Christ radiate and live His life in her and through her in the slums. Let the poor, seeing her, be drawn to Christ and invite Him to enter their homes and their lives. Let the sick and suffering find in her a real angel of comfort and consolation. Let the little ones of the streets cling to her because she reminds them of Him, the friend of the little ones.

Our lives are wove in Jesus in the Eucharist, and the faith and the love that come from the Eucharist enable us to see Him in the distressing disguise of the poor, and so there is but one love of Jesus, as there is but one person in the poor—Jesus. We take vows of chastity to love Christ with undivided love; to be able to love Him with undivided love we take a vow of poverty that frees us from all material possessions, and with that freedom we can love Him with undivided love, and from this vow of undivided love we surrender ourselves totally to Him in the person who takes His place. So our vow of obedience is another way of giving, of being loved. And the fourth vow that we take is to give wholehearted free service to the poorest of the poor. By this vow, we bind ourselves to be one of them, to depend solely on divine providence, to have nothing, yet possess all things in possessing Christ.

Make sure that you let God's work in your souls by accepting whatever He gives you, and giving Him whatever He takes from you. True holiness consists in doing God's will with a smile. . . .

Co-Workers should give love in action. Our works of love are nothing but works of peace. Let us do them with greater love and efficiency, each in his or her own work, in daily life, at home, with one's neighbor.

Keep giving Jesus to your people, not by words, but by your example, by your being in love with Jesus, by radiating His holiness and spreading His fragrance of love everywhere you go. Just keep the joy of Jesus as your strength. Be happy and at peace. Accept whatever He gives—and give whatever He takes with a big smile. You belong to Him. Tell Him: "I am yours, and if you cut me to pieces, every single piece will be only all yours." Let Jesus be the victim and the priest in you.

Actually we are touching Christ's body in the poor. In the poor it is the hungry Christ that we are feeding, it is the naked Christ that we are clothing, it is to the homeless Christ that we are giving shelter. It is not just hunger for bread or the need of the naked for clothes or of the homeless for a house made of bricks. Even the rich are hungry for love, being cared for, for being wanted, for having someone to call their own.

We ourselves feel that what we are doing is just a drop in the ocean. But if that drop was not in the ocean, I think the ocean would be less because of that

---

[43]Ibid., pp. 33–45, 74. Reprinted by permission of HarperCollins Publishers, Inc.

missing drop. I do not agree with the big way of doing things. To us what matters is an individual. To get to love the person we must come in close contact with him. If we wait till we get the numbers, then we will be lost in the numbers. And we will never be able to show that love and respect for the person. I believe in person to person; every person is Christ for me, and since there is only one Jesus, that person is the one person in the world at that moment.

Let us try more and more to make every Sister, Brother, and Co-Worker grow into the likeness of Christ, to allow Him to live His live of compassion and humanity in the world of today. Your love for Christ must be great. Keep the light of Christ always burning in your heart, for He alone is the Way to walk. He is the Life to live. He is the Love to love.

We must become holy, not because we want to feel holy, but because Christ must be able to live His life fully in us. We are to be all love, all faith, all purity, for the sake of the poor we serve. And once we have learned to seek God and His will, our contacts with the poor will become the means of great sanctity to ourselves and to others.

ON LOVING GOD[44]

"Thou shalt love the Lord thy God with thy whole heart, with thy whole soul, and with thy whole mind" [Mt 22:37]. This is the commandment of the great God, and He cannot command the impossible. Love is a fruit in season at all times, and within reach of every hand. Anyone may gather it and no limit is set. Everyone can reach this love through meditation, spirit of prayer, and sacrifice, by an intense inner life.

There is no limit, because God is love and love is God, and so you are really in love with God. And then, God's love is infinite. But part is to love and to give until it hurts. And that's why it's not how much you do, but how much love you put into the action. How much love we put into our presents. That's why people—maybe they are very rich people—who have not got a capacity to give and to receive love are the poorest of the poor. And I think this is what our Sisters have got—the spreading of joy that you see in many religious people who have given themselves without reserve to God.

We need to find God, and He cannot be found in noise and restlessness. God is the friend of silence. See how nature—trees, flowers, grass—grows in silence; see the stars, the moon, and the sun, how they move in silence. Is not our mission to give God to the poor in the slums? Not a dead God, but a living, loving God. The more we receive in silent prayer, the more we can give in our active life. We need silence to be able to touch souls. The essential thing is not what we say, but what God says to us and through us. All our words will be useless un-

---

[44]Ibid., pp. 67–70. Reprinted by permission of Harper-Collins Publishers, Inc.

less they come from within; words that do not give the light of Christ increase the darkness.

To show great love for God and our neighbor we need not do great things. It is how much love we put in the doing that makes our offering Something Beautiful for God.

Our progress in holiness depends on God and ourselves—God's grace and on our will to be holy. We must have a real living determination to reach holiness. "I will be a saint" means I will despoil myself of all that is not God; I will strip my heart of all created things; I will live in poverty and detachment; I will renounce my will, my inclinations, my whims and fancies, and make myself a willing slave to the will of God.

PRAYERS[45]

Dearest Lord, may I see You today and every day in the person of your sick, and whilst nursing them, minister unto you. Though You hide yourself behind the unattractive disguise of the irritable, the exacting, the unreasonable, may I still recognize you, and say: "Jesus, my patient, how sweet it is to serve You."

Lord, help us to see in Your crucifixion and resurrection an example of how to endure and seemingly to die in the agony and conflict of daily life, so that we may live more fully and creatively. You accepted patiently and humbly the rebuffs of human life, as well as the tortures of your crucifixion and passion. Help us to accept the pains and conflicts that come to us each day as opportunities to grow as people and become more like You. Enable us to go through them patiently and bravely, trusting that You will support us. Make us realize that it is only by frequent deaths of ourselves and our self-centered desires that we can come to live more fully; for it is only by dying with You that we can rise with You.

JOY[46]

Joy is prayer, joy is strength; joy is love; joy is a net of love by which you can catch souls. God loves a cheerful giver. She gives most who gives with joy. The best way to show our gratitude to God and the people is to accept everything with joy. A joyful heart is the inevitable result of a heart burning with love. Never let anything so fill you with sorrow as to make you forget the joy of the Christ risen.

We all long for heaven where God is, but we have it in our power to be in

[45]Ibid., pp. 71–76. Reprinted by permission of HarperCollins Publishers, Inc.
[46]Ibid., pp. 77–78. Reprinted by permission of HarperCollins Publishers, Inc.

heaven with Him right now—to be happy with Him at this very moment. But being happy with Him now means:

> loving as He loves,
>
> helping as He helps,
>
> giving as He gives,
>
> serving as He serves,
>
> rescuing as He rescues,
>
> being with Him for all the twenty-four hours,
>
> touching Him in His distressing disguise.

Richard Foster (1942–)

Richard Foster was born in Albuquerque, New Mexico. A member of the Society of Friends, he attended George Fox College, where he earned the B.A. in 1964. In 1980 he earned his doctoral degree in pastoral theology from Fuller Theological seminary. After serving numerous significant pastorates, Foster became a Special Lecturer and Writer in Residence at Friends University, Wichita, Kansas.

Foster's contribution to contemporary Christian Spirituality stems from his ministry of speaking and writing. He is a staunch proponent of practical spiritual disciplines as means for spiritual growth and renewal. To this end, he established *Renovaré*, a renewal movement based in Wichita, and he lectures all across North America. Among Foster's significant publications are *The Freedom of Simplicity* (1981), *Celebration of Discipline: The Path to Spiritual Growth* (1988, 2nd ed.), *Meditative Prayer* (1983), *The Challenge of the Disciplined Life* (1985), and *Study Guide to Money, Sex, and Power* (1985).

THE WAY OF DISCIPLINED GRACE[47]

Superficiality is the curse of our age. The doctrine of instant satisfaction is a primary spiritual problem. The desperate need today is not for a greater number of intelligent people, or gifted people, but for deep people. The classical Disciplines of the spiritual life call us to move beyond surface living into the depths. They invite us to explore the inner caverns of the spiritual realm. They urge us to be the answer to a hollow world. John Woolman counseled, "It is for thee to dwell deep, that thou mayest feel and understand the spirits of the people."

---

[47]Excerpts from Richard Foster, *Celebration of Discipline: The Path to Spiritual Growth.* Copyright (c) 1978 by Richard Foster. Reprinted by permission of HarperCollins Publisher, Inc., and Hoder and Staoughton Publisher, London. Pages 1–9.

We must not be led to believe that the Disciplines are for spiritual giants and hence beyond our reach, or for contemplatives who devote all their time to prayer and meditation. Far from it. God intends the Disciplines of the spiritual life to be for ordinary human beings; people who have jobs, who care for children, who must wash dishes and mow lawns. In fact, the Disciplines are best exercised in the midst of our normal daily activities. If they are to have any transforming effect, the effect must be found in the ordinary junctures of human life; in our relationships with our husband or wife, our brothers and sisters, our friends and neighbors.

Neither should we think of the Spiritual Disciplines as some dull drudgery aimed at exterminating laughter from the face of the earth. Joy is the keynote of all the Disciplines. The purpose of the Disciplines is liberation from the stifling slavery to self-interest and fear. When one's inner spirit is set free from all that holds it down, that can hardly be described as dull drudgery. Singing, dancing, even shouting characterize the Disciplines of the spiritual life. . . .

Those who have heard the distant call deep within and who desire to explore the world of the Spiritual Disciplines are immediately faced with two difficulties. The first is philosophic. The materialistic base of our age has become so pervasive that it has given people grave doubts about their ability to reach beyond the physical world. Many first-rate scientists have passed beyond such doubts, knowing that we cannot be confined to a space-time box. But the average person is influenced by popular science which is a generation behind the times and is prejudiced against the nonmaterial world. It is hard to overcome how saturated we are with the mentality of popular science. Meditation, for example, if allowed at all, is not thought of as contact with a real spiritual world but as psychological manipulation. Usually people will tolerate a brief dabbling in the "inward journey," but then it is time to get on with *real* business in the *real* world. We need the courage to move beyond the prejudice of our age and affirm with our best scientists that there exists more than the material world. In intellectual honesty, we should be willing to study and explore this other realm with all the rigor and determination we would give to any field of research.

The second difficulty is a practical one. We simply do not know how to go about exploring the inward life. That has not always been true. In the first century and earlier, it was not necessary to give instruction on how to "do" the Disciplines of the spiritual life. The Bible called people to such Disciplines as fasting, meditation, worship, and celebration and gave almost no instruction about how to do them. The reason for that is easy to see. Those Disciplines were so frequently practiced and such a part of the general culture that the "how to" was common knowledge. Fasting, for example, was so common that no one had to ask what to eat before a fast, or how to break a fast, or how to avoid dizziness while fasting— everyone already knew.

That is not true of our generation. Today there is an abysmal ignorance of the most simple and practical aspects of nearly all the classic Spiritual Disciplines. Hence any book written on the subject must take that need into account and provide practical instruction on the mechanics of the Disciplines. One word of caution, however, must be given at the outset; to know the mechanics does not mean that we are practicing the Discipline. The Spiritual Disciplines are an inward and spiritual reality and the inner attitude of the heart is far more crucial than the mechanics for coming into the reality of the spiritual life.

We are accustomed to thinking of sin as individual acts of disobedience to God. That is true enough as far as it goes, but Scripture goes much farther. In Romans the apostle Paul frequently referred to sin as a condition that plagues the human race (i.e. Rom. 3:9–18). Sin as a condition works its way out through the "bodily members"; that is, the ingrained habits of the body (Rom. 7:5ff). And there is no slavery that can compare to the slavery of ingrained habits of sin. . . .

Our ordinary method of dealing with ingrained sin is to launch a frontal attack. We rely on our willpower and determination. Whatever the issue for us may be—anger, bitterness, gluttony, pride, sexual lust, alcohol, fear—we determine never to do it again; we pray against it, fight against it, set our will against it. But it is all in vain, and we find ourselves once again morally bankrupt or, worse yet, so proud of our external righteousness that "whitened sepulchers" is a mild description of our condition. Heini Arnold in his excellent little book entitled *Freedom from Sinful Thoughts* writes, "We . . . want to make it quite clear that we cannot free and purify our own heart by exerting our own will."

In Colossians Paul listed some of the outward forms people use to control sin: "touch not, taste not, handle not." He then added that these things "have indeed a show of wisdom in *will worship*" (Col. 2:20–23, KJV). "Will worship"— what a telling phrase, and how descriptive of so much of our lives! The moment we feel we can succeed and attain victory over our sin by the strength of our will alone is the moment we are worshipping the will. Isn't it ironic that Paul looked at our most strenuous efforts in the spiritual walk and called it idolatry: "will worship?"

Willpower will never succeed in dealing with the deeply ingrained habits of sin. Emmet Fox writes, "As soon as you resist mentally any undesirable or unwanted circumstance, you thereby endow it with more power—power which it will use against you, and you will have depleted your own resources to that exact extent." Heini Arnold concludes, "As long as we think we can save ourselves by our own will power, we will only make the evil in us stronger than ever." This same truth has been experienced by all of the great writers of the devotional life from St. John of the Cross to Evelyn Underhill.

"Will worship" may be able to have an outward show of success for a time, but in the cracks and crevices of our lives, our deep inner condition will always be revealed. Jesus described that condition when He spoke of the outward show of righteousness of the Pharisees. "Out of the abundance of the heart the mouth speaks. . . . I tell you, on the day of judgment men will render account for every *careless word* they utter" (Mt. 12:34–36). By dint of will people can make a good showing for a time, but sooner or later there will come the unguarded moment when the "careless word" will slip out to reveal the true condition of the heart. If we are full of compassion, it will be revealed; if we are full of bitterness, that also will be manifested. . . .

When we despair of gaining inner transformation through human powers of will and determination, we are open to a wonderful new realization: inner righteousness is a gift from God to be graciously received. The needed change within us is God's work, not ours. The demand is for an inside job, and only God can work from the inside. We cannot attain or earn this righteousness of the kingdom of God; it is a price that is given. . . .

The moment we grasp this breathtaking insight we are in danger of an error in the opposite direction. We are tempted to believe there is nothing we can do. If all human strivings end in moral bankruptcy (and having tried it, we know it is so), and if righteousness is a gracious gift from God (as the Bible clearly states), then is it not logical to conclude that we must wait for God to come and transform us? Strangely enough, the answer is "no." The analysis is correct: human striving *is* insufficient and righteousness *is* a gift from God. It is the conclusion that is faulty, for happily there is something we can do. We do not need to be hung on the horns of the dilemma of either human works or idleness. God has given us the Disciplines of the spiritual life as a means of receiving His grace. The Disciplines allow us to place ourselves before God so that He can transform us.

The apostle Paul said, "he who sows to his own flesh will from the flesh reap corruption; but he who sows to the Spirit will from the Spirit reap eternal life" (Gal. 6:8). A farmer is helpless to grow grain; all he can do is provide the right conditions for the growing of grain. He puts the seed in the ground where the natural forces take over and up comes the grain. That is the way with the Spiritual Disciplines—they are a way of sowing to the Spirit. The Disciplines are God's way of getting us into the ground; they put us where He can work within us and transform us. By themselves the Spiritual Disciplines can do nothing; they can only get us to the place where something can be done. They are God's means of grace. The inner righteousness we seek is not something that is poured on our heads. God has ordained the Disciplines of the spiritual life as the means by which we are placed where He can bless us. In this regard it would be proper to speak of "the way of disciplined grace." It is "grace" because it is free; it is "disciplined" because there is something for us to do. In *The Cost of Discipleship* Dietrich Bonhoeffer made clear that grace is free, but it is not cheap. Once we clearly understand that God's grace is unearned and unearnable, and if we expect to grow, we must take up a consciously chosen course of action involving both individual and group life. That is the purpose of the Spiritual Disciplines. . . .

The Spiritual Disciplines are intended for our good. They are meant to bring the abundance of God into our lives. It is possible, however, to turn them into another set of soul-killing laws. Law-bound Disciplines breathe death.

Jesus taught that we must go beyond the righteousness of the scribes and the Pharisees (Mt. 5:20). Yet we need to see that their righteousness was no small thing. They were committed to following God in a way that many of us are not prepared to do. One factor, however, was always central to their righteousness: *externalism.* Their righteousness consisted in control over externals, often including the manipulation of others. The extent to which we have gone beyond the righteousness of the scribes and the Pharisees is seen in how much our lives demonstrate the internal work of God upon the heart. It will have external results, but the work will be internal. It is easy in our zeal for the Spiritual

Disciplines to turn them into the external righteousness of the scribes and the Pharisees.

When the Disciplines degenerate into law, they are used to manipulate and control people. We take explicit commands and use them to imprison others. The result of such deterioration of the Spiritual Disciplines is pride and fear. Pride takes over because we come to believe that we are the right kind of people. Fear takes over because the power of controlling other carries with it the anxiety of losing control, and the anxiety of being controlled by others. . . . As we enter the inner world of the Spiritual Disciplines, there will always be the danger of turning them into laws. But we are not left to our own human devices. Jesus Christ has promised to be our present Teacher and Guide. His voice is not hard to hear. His instruction is not hard to understand. If we are beginning to calcify what should always remain alive and growing, He will tell us. We can trust His teaching. If we are wandering off toward some wrong idea or unprofitable practice, He will guide us back. If we are willing to listen to the Heavenly Monitor, we will receive the instruction we need. . . .

Gustavo Gutierrez (1928–)

Gustavo Gutierrez was born in Peru, of Native American ancestry. As a young man he experienced the poverty and discrimination that is part of the life of many people in his region. Student activism gave way to religious activism as he entered seminary, eventually studying in France and Rome. Ordained a priest in 1959, Gutierrez teaches theology and social work at the Catholic Pontifical University in Lima.

Gutierrez's most famous book, *A Theology of Liberation* (1979), epitomizes the theological movement that seeks to read the transforming power of the gospel over against the context of poverty, oppression, and social change. A more recent work, *We Drink from Our Own Wells* (1984), explores the interconnection between poverty, oppression, and Christian Spirituality.

HOW SHALL WE SING TO THE LORD IN A FOREIGN LAND?[48]

There is no Christian life without "songs" to the Lord, without thanksgiving for God's love, and without prayer. But the songs are sung by persons living in particular historical situations, and these provide the framework within which they perceive God's presence and also God's absence (in the biblical sense of this term;

---

[48]Reprinted from Gustavo Gutierrez, *We Drink From Our Own Wells: the Spiritual Journey of a People*, translated by Matthew J. O'Connell. English translation copyright (c) 1984 by Orbis Books, Maryknoll, New York, and SCM Press, London. Pages 7–16. The question posed in the title of this section is a citation from Psalm 137:4. In most instances Gutierrez's footnotes have been omitted. Used by kind permission of Orbis Books and SCM Press.

see Jer. 7:1–7; Mat. 7:15–21). In our Latin American context we may well ask our-selves: How can we thank God for the gift of life when the reality around us is one of premature and unjustly inflicted death? How can we express joy at know-ing ourselves to be loved by the Father when we see the suffering of our broth-ers and sisters? How can we sing when the suffering of an entire people chokes the sound in our throats?

These questions are troublesome and far from superficial; they are not to be stilled by facile answers that underestimate the situation of injustice and mar-ginalization in which the vast majority of Latin Americans live. On the other hand, it is also evident that this reality does not silence the song or make inaudible the voice of the poor. This state of affairs amounts to a critical judgment on many as-pects of the spirituality that is still accepted in some Christian circles. At the same time, however, it represents a "favorable time" (2 Cor. 6:2), a *kairos*, a moment of heightened revelation both of God and of new paths on the journey of fidelity to the word of God. . . .

Serious questioners are today challenging the spirituality that until not too long ago was generally accepted in ecclesial circles. I want to single out two char-acteristics of that spirituality, along with the criticisms now raised against them.

1. Christian spirituality has long been presented as *geared to minorities*. It seems to be the peculiar possession of select and, to some extent, closed groups; it is linked for the most part to the existence of religious orders and congregations. Religious life, in the narrow sense of this term, encompassed a "state of per-fection"; it implicitly supposed, therefore, that there were other, imperfect states of Christian life. Religious life was marked by a full and structured quest for holiness; in the other states there were found, at best, only the less de-manding elements of this spirituality. The way proper to religious life sup-posed some kind of separation from the world and its everyday activities (one form of the well-known *fuga mundi*, "flight from the world"). The second way did not call for that kind of effort and could be traveled without fanfare in the midst of occupations that had little or nothing religious about them.

   The "spirituality of the laity" that accompanied the rise of the lay apos-tolic movement in the first decades of our century was a reaction against that perfect/imperfect outlook. It was a reaction at least against its more rigid as-pects, those that represented a narrowing and impoverishment of Christian life.[49] The counter-claim was provocative but inadequate, because the spiritu-ality of the laity was still—and could not help being—strongly characterized by important elements taken from the way of Christian perfection that had been canonized by the experience of monastic and religious life. . . .

   One thing is certain: any spirituality limited to minorities is today under heavy crossfire. It is challenged on the one side by the spiritual experience of

---

[49]Gutierrez points his readers to the pivotal work of Yves Congar in this regard. Cf. Congar's *Lay Peo-ple in the Church: A Study for a Theology of the Laity* (Westminster, Md.: Newman, 1957), ch. 9.

the dispossessed and marginalized—and those who side with them—in their commitment to the struggle for liberation. Out of this experience has come the inspiration for a popular and community quest of the Lord that is incompatible with elitist models. It is challenged, on the other side, by the questioning of those who live a life focused on concerns of the spiritual order and who are now beginning to realize that such a life is made possible for them, at least in part, by their freedom from material worries (food, lodging, health needs). These, of course, are concerns that fill the daily lives of the poor masses of the human race.

It is rather difficult to face up to the fact that the minorities to whom this spirituality is directed are also privileged minorities from the social, cultural, and to some extent, economic standpoint. In any case, we are dealing here with a matter that calls for radical treatment: a return to the sources, a salvaging of the values contained therein, and a rejection of the inertia and sense of established position that inevitably mark such a situation. Only thus is it possible to prevent the cancerous growth of aspects of spirituality that are legitimate in themselves.

2. A second characteristic of the spirituality in question, and one that is also being challenged today, is its *individualistic bent*. The spiritual journey has often been presented as a cultivation of individualistic values as a way to personal perfection. The relationship with God seemed to obscure the presence of others and encouraged individual Christians to be absorbed in their own interiority in order to understand and develop it better. For this reason the spiritual life was called *the interior life*, which many understood as a life lived exclusively within the individual. The important thing in it was the deployment of the virtues as potentialities that had to do with the individual and had little or no connection with the outside world. In this outlook the important thing is one's intention. It is this that gives value to human actions; the external effects of these actions are less important. Actions without any apparent human significance thus acquired spiritual and sanctifying value if done for important and legitimate motives.

When only a few authentic dimensions of Christian life are thus developed, the result may be a dangerous privatization of spirituality. As certain spiritual traditions moved away from their sources . . . they went astray—and in the process began to dry up—as increasingly shallow streams representing only an individualistic outlook. The community dimensions inherent in all Christian life became formalities; they were unable to alter the perspective that turned the journey to God into a purely individual venture. It is not surprising, then, that in such a context charity should be regarded as simply another Christian virtue to be cultivated. . . .

It seems to me that an important source of the "spirituality of evasion" . . . is the individualism of which I have been speaking. Individualism operates, in fact, as a filter that makes it possible to "spiritualize" and even volatilize what in the Bible are nuanced statements of a social and historical nature. For example, the poor/rich opposition (a social fact) is reduced to the humble/proud opposition (something within the individual). "Passage" through the individual interiorizes, and robs their historical bite, categories reflective of the objective realities in which individuals and peoples live and die, struggle and assert their faith. This kind of reduction has often taken place. It is a frequent occurrence in the interpretation of the Magnificat—that profoundly beautiful expression of the spirituality of the poor of Yahweh—when the exegete loses sight of its roots in the life and hopes of Mary's people and, in the final analysis, in the personal experience of the mother of Jesus herself [cf. Lk 1:46–56].

Individualism and spiritualism thus combine to impoverish and even distort the following of Jesus. An individualistic spirituality is incapable of offering guidance in this following to those who have embarked on a collective enterprise of liberation. Nor does it do justice to the different dimensions of the human person, including the so-called material aspects . . . .

A FAVORABLE TIME[50]

Our increasingly clear awareness of the harsh situation in Latin America and the sufferings of the poor must not make us over-look the fact that the harshness and sufferings are not what is truly new in the present age. What is new is not wretchedness and repression and premature death, for these, unfortunately, are ancient realities in these countries. What is new is that the people are beginning to grasp the causes of their situation of injustice and are seeking to release themselves from it. Likewise new and important is the role which faith in the God who liberates is playing in the process.

It can therefore be said without any fear of exaggeration that we are experiencing today an exceptional time in the history of Latin America and the life of the church. Of this situation we may say with Paul: "Now is the favorable time; this is the day of salvation" (2 Cor. 6:2). Such a vision of things does not make the journey of the poor less difficult nor does it gloss over the obstacles they encounter in their efforts to defend their most elementary rights. The demanding, cruel reality of wretchedness, exploitation, hostility, and death—our daily experience—will not allow us to forget it. There is question here, then, not of a facile optimism but rather of a deep trust in the historical power of the poor and, above all, a firm hope in the Lord.

These attitudes do not automatically ensure a better future; but as they draw nourishment from a present that is full of possibilities, they in turn nourish the present with promises. So true is this that if we do not respond to the demands of the present, because we do not know in advance whither we may be led, we

---

[50]Reprinted from Gutierrez, *We Drink From Our Own Wells* Used by kind permission of Orbis Books and SCM Press. Pages 20–25.

are simply refusing to hear the call of Jesus Christ. We are refusing to open to Him when He knocks on the door and invites us to sup with Him.

We are today experiencing a *time of solidarity* in Latin America. Throughout its length and breadth there is a growing movement of solidarity in defense of human rights and, in particular, the rights of the poor. . . . More than this, at the base level and the local level there has been a proliferation of groups and organizations dedicated to solidarity among and with the dispossessed. The ease with which the popular sectors move from the local scene to the Latin American scene is impressive. This is the first flowering at the continental level of what Jose" Maria Arguedas used to call "the fellowship of the wretched." The anonymous heroes involved in these efforts are countless, and the generosity poured out in them is beyond measure. . . .

The present is also *a time of prayer*. Anyone who is in contact with base-level ecclesial communities can attest that there is a great deal of intense and hope-filled prayer going on in Latin America today. . . . Nor am I speaking only of those great moments that are milestones in the journey of a people with its advances and retreats. At such moments the communities have given evidence of great creativity and depth in the matter of prayer. But when I speak of the wealth and intensity of prayer I have in mind also, and above all, the daily practice of humble prayer in numberless localities. No where in the Latin American church is more fervent and joyous prayer to be found amid daily suffering and struggle than in the Christian communities among the poor. It is our acts of gratitude and hope in the Lord that make us free (Gal. 5:1).

For many, then . . . a growing maturity in their solidary with the commitment to liberation has, by a dialectical process, brought with it a new emphasis on prayer as a fundamental dimension of Christian life. The result has been a mighty development of prayer in popular Christian groups. I know how difficult it is to measure such things, but daily experience, and even the result in writings (this among a people for whom oral expression is the dominant kind), are proof that prayer is widespread and creative.

It is, then, a time of solidarity and a time of prayer—but also, and in a sense synthesizing those two, a *time for martyrdom* as well. There are many who have devoted their lives, to the point of suffering death, in order to bear witness to the presence of the poor in the Latin American world and to the preferential love that God has for them. Nor has this bloodletting ceased as yet. . . .

What did the contemporaries of the early martyrs think about the events of their time? Perhaps the complexity of the factors in any historical situation, their own closeness to the events, and even their lack of personal courage prevented them from seeing the significance of occurrences that today seem so clearly to have been heroic testimonies to faith in the Lord. It is a fact that a consensus with regard to what is happening before our eyes is always more difficult to reach; this is because present events, unlike those of the past, are not situated in a world that we regard as idyllic and that we envelop in golden legends. Present events form part of our own universe and demand of the individual a personal decision, a rejection of every kind of complicity with executioners, a straightforward solidarity, an uncompromising denunciation of evil, a prayer of commitment.

But the poor are not fooled; they see the truth and speak out when others remain silent. They see in the surrender of these lives a profound and radical testimony of faith; they observe that in a continent where the powerful spread death in order to protect their privileges, such a testimony to God often brings the murder of the witness; and they draw nourishment from the hope that sustains these lives and these deaths. According to the very earliest Christian tradition the blood of martyrs gives life to the ecclesial community, the assembly of the disciples of Jesus Christ. This is what is happening today in Latin America. Fidelity unto death is a wellspring of life. It signals a new, demanding, and fruitful course in the following of Jesus.

The new way is, of course, not entirely new. The present-day Latin American experience of martyrdom bids us all turn back to one of the major sources of all spirituality: the blood-stained experience of the early Christian community, which was so weak in the face of the imperial power of that day.

I have spoken of questions and crises. These two terms, however, do not adequately cover the total reality of the following of Jesus in present-day Latin America; in fact, they are not even most representative of that following. They simply represent a road that must be traveled and a price that must be paid for the sake of what is fundamental; *the recognition of the time of salvation* in which these countries are now living. . . . The Latin American church is passing through an unparalleled period of its history. The concrete and efficacious commitment of so many Christians to the poorest and most disinherited, as well as the serious difficulties they encounter in their commitment to solidarity, are leaving a profound mark on the history of Latin America. . . . To some all this may smack of facile and naive optimism. True enough, the exhaustion produced by an unending situation of wretchedness; the tensions caused by the resistance men and women must engage in if they are to win out in their commitment to liberation; the depression felt at the abiding attitude of suspicion that greets every effort at effective solidarity with an exploited people; the resistance experienced within the people of God itself—these facts do not permit an easy optimism or allow us to forget the marginalization, the suffering, the deaths. At the same time, however, we must be aware of the change that has taken place. When all is said and done, despite— or thanks to—the immense price that is being paid, the present situation is nourishing new life, revealing new paths to be followed, and providing reason for profound joy.

The spendthrift generosity (sometimes accompanied by the giver's own blood . . .) that has been shown in Latin America in recent years is making its nations fruitful and is confronting the ecclesial community with a demanding, but at the same time, most promising moment in its history. In the faces and hands of the dispossessed the Lord is knocking, and knocking loudly, on the community's door. By feeding the hope of the poor (that is what Archbishop Romero accepted as his pastoral mission) the church will be accepting the banquet to which the Lord of the kingdom invites us. . . . Solidarity, prayer, and martyrdom add up to a time of salvation and judgment, a time of grace and a stern demand—a time above all, of hope.

Rosemary Radford Ruether (1936–)

Rosemary Ruether was born in St. Paul, Minnesota. Her father, Robert, an Anglican, died when she was twelve years old. "He remained," as Ruether later wrote, "a shadowy figure, who was away in the Second World War for much of my grade-school years and left again for Greece in 1947."[51] Much of Rosemary's early personal and religious formation came from her mother, Rebecca. "My own personality," Ruether intimated, "I see as much more directly a product of my mother's influence."[52] Her mother raised Rosemary Ruether in the Catholic faith. While avoiding the ethnic extremes, she gave her a profound sense of the depth and breadth of Catholicism. Ruether recalled: ". . . my impression of Catholicism was of something with deep historical roots, both profound and meaningful in content, not something trite or vulgar."[53]

Her educational process, beginning with Scripps College (A.B. 1958), and continuing at Claremont Graduate School (M.A. 1960, Ph.D. 1965), involved Ruether in the exploration of her Roman Catholic roots as well as a testing of their credibility from the standpoint of her own place in the world as a Christian and as a contemporary woman.

Dr. Ruether has taught at Howard University and Harvard University, and since 1976 has served as Georgia Harkness Professor of Applied Theology at Garrett Evangelical Divinity School. She is the author of many influential books and articles, including *The Radical Kingdom* (1970), *Liberation Theology* (1972), *New Woman/New Earth* (1975), *Mary, the Feminine Face of God* (1977), *Women of Spirit* (1979), (with Rosemary Keller) *Women and Religion in America* (1981), *Sexism and God-Talk* (1983), *Womanguides* (1985), and *Women-Church* (1986).

BECOMING A FEMINIST[54]

It is hard to trace my awakening to feminism . . . because it seems to me that I was implicitly always a feminist, if by being a feminist one means a woman who fights for her full realization and accepts no special barriers to her aspirations on the basis of sexual identity. Even as a small child I can remember an instinctive

---

[51]Rosemary Radford Ruether, *Disputed Questions on Being a Christian* (Nashville, Tenn.: Abingdon Press, 1982), p. 19.

[52]Ibid., p. 20.

[53]Ibid.

[54]Reprinted from Ruether, *Disputed Questions on Being a Christian*, pp. 109–26. Used by kind permission of Dr. Rosemary Radford Ruether.

rejection of efforts to define me in traditional female roles. I recall an incident that took place about the age of eight. I had baked a cake and presented it to the family. My older sister remarked somewhat complacently, "You will make some man a good wife someday." I said nothing, but remember experiencing an automatic feeling of anger and betrayal. In naming my accomplishment in terms of my ability to be someone's wife someday, my sister had thoughtlessly tried to deprive me of my own identity and future as a person. I felt an enormous sense of injustice and insult, without being able to name exactly the cause of my annoyance. . . .

Both my father's family and my mother's paternal relatives held very traditionalist, not to say chauvinist, notions about women's place and role. But these became largely inoperative for me by the absence of these male relatives during much of my early childhood. . . . Although my mother never directly challenged the dominant conceptions of woman's future destiny as wife and mother, she did little to reinforce them either. As a child we used to play a game about "what you are going to do when you grow up." She would mention all kinds of fantastic possibilities, such as "doctor, lawyer, merchant, or chief," but I never remember once her mentioning wife or mother. This means that in some ways she left me fairly unprepared for the realities of this role. But this also meant that, implicitly, she never gave me the idea that this should be my primary identity. . . .

In my local Catholic school, those in charge from the top administration down to the classroom teacher were female. There were no boys in our classrooms. Priests were rare and distant figures. Even the divine appeared to be immediately represented by a female, Mary. God and Christ were somewhere in the distance, like the priests, but Mary was the one you talked to if you wanted to pray. So, too, the local Carmelite convent where my mother went to daily Mass. Here was a female world of elderly patients and sprightly nuns. As a child I played in the apple tree of their great yard, got fed an occasional ice cream bar from their freezer, and taught some of the nuns to ride a bike. Once they even dressed me up in their habit and took my picture to send to the register of Catholic women's religious orders, because, as they said, they were all old and they wanted to advertise their order with the picture of someone who was young and pretty.

Although I occasionally glimpsed a narrower and more authoritarian side of nuns, most of my memory is of a cozy, female-run world where I felt myself a favored daughter. The recent radicalization of American nuns and their emancipation of their own communities into creative places of social and feminist advancement allows me to continue this positive association in my contemporary life.

In La Jolla [California], too, I lived in a world where men were distant and unavailable figures. The role models and means of on-going life lay in communities of women, widows, and daughters. When men appeared, back from some distant war or conflict, the women grew silent and respectful. A certain homage was paid to these almost godlike creatures. But one managed effectively on a day-to-day basis without them. Although there were undoubtedly a lot of male figures—priests, male relatives, teachers—who could have given me strong messages about my inferiority as a woman, I didn't encounter them until it was far to late for me to change my assumptions. . . .

These experiences contributed to two basic feelings that I sense had shaped my life long before I consciously reflected on it as a feminist. First, that, as a female, the world ought to be a trustworthy extension of a home that would continue to support and encourage my growth; and, second, that the occasional intrusions of male authority which said me nay lacked real credibility. The priest circling the altar in silken vestments and forbidding access to the altar to women; the mustachioed military relative who showed up filled with glory and stories from distant wars was an object of some awe and curiosity. But secretly, one suspected that their aura of superiority was fragile facade, a bombast concealing secret impotence. This impotence of male authority was an unspoken secret between women who carried on, in practice, without them. This perception was probably accentuated for me by the extent of my early segregation. But I suspect that it is actually far more widespread than has been admitted. For endless generations women have paid public deference to male authority while, privately, not really believing in it or counting on it.

Consequently, the occasional challenges to my belief in my unlimited horizons, which I encountered while growing up, I could dismiss rather easily. It was only when I married, at the age of twenty, that I experienced the first major and serious assault upon my well-being as a woman in the world. It astonishes me to think of how thoughtlessly I got married at the end of my junior year in college, a thoughtlessness that was part of the culture of the fifties. By the end of college, women were supposed to get married. . . .

Before our marriage, as we were walking together one day, something was said about home and family. Nothing had prepared me for any decisions on the subject, but almost instinctively and without premeditation, I blurted out that I had no intention of simply becoming a housewife, I intended to continue in school for my Ph.D. It was clear that Herc (my husband's nickname) was startled. He assumed that women simply quit and became mothers and housewives after marriage. Fortunately he adjusted immediately to this announcement in good grace and has been very supportive of my education and work ever since. . . .

The chief strains for us came in coping with the irrationality of the Catholic Church's position on contraception. It was evident to me from the beginning that I did not agree with the position and intended to practice child-planning. But the message of the church became positively menacing toward a young couple in that period of American Catholicism. From all sides I received messages that my salvation lay in passive acquiescence to God and biological destiny; that any effort to interfere with "nature" was the most heinous crime. Virtually no criticism of this position was culturally available in the world in which I moved at that time.

I was left to work out my own dissent, both what to do and what it signified. This meant that an enormous amount of energy in the first ten years of marriage went into simply defending myself against this assault, trying to juggle children, marriage, housework, teaching, and graduate work. This struggle has, at least, come out of the closet in the 1970's. Young people have some models and some plans about how to manage. In the late fifties and sixties it was a silent conflict, going on in uncounted households, among people who never communicated this struggle with one another or analyzed its causes. . . .

In the late sixties I began formal research on attitudes toward women in the Christian tradition. My classical and historical training was indispensable here. Since I already knew the sources and techniques for getting at the material, it was not difficult to document historic views toward women and sexuality. I have sometimes been asked where I found these sources, as though there were something mysterious about the vast panorama of material on sexism being gradually disclosed through feminist scholarship of the last decade. Of course, writings by women themselves or writings expressing alternative views to the dominant tradition have often been dropped out of the official tradition, and their remains have to be dug up through careful detective work. But the dominant male tradition about women is not hidden at all. It lies right on the surface of all the standard texts of Plato, Aristotle, Augustine, Aquinas, and the like and its message has been absorbed and taken-for-granted over the generations. It takes a new consciousness to go back and isolate this whole body of material as a problem rather than as normative tradition. The consciousness and methodology for criticism has had to be developed by feminist scholars on their own. No professor ever taught me to recognize it as an "issue." . . . .

Desmond Mpilo Tutu (1931–)

Desmond Tutu was born in Klerksdorp, Winterstrand, Transvaal, South Africa. His father was a teacher and his mother was a domestic worker. When he was twelve years old his family relocated to Johannesburg, where Tutu met the Anglican priest Father Trevor Huddelston. Huddlelston was a formative influence in Tutu's early life.

After graduating from Western High School, Tutu found himself unable to afford the tuition needed for medical school. He completed diploma studies at the Bantu Normal College, and earned a B.A. degree at the University of Johannesburg. Tutu embarked upon a career in education, but resigned his position in 1957 in protest over the passage of the Bantu Education Act (which was discriminatory toward African people). At the same time he joined Father Huddleston in an Anglican religious life; henceforth, Christian spirituality and social change would be inseparably linked in Tutu's life and ministry.

After studying theology at Saint Peter's Theological College in Johannesburg, Desmond Tutu was ordained a priest in 1961. He held several pastorates in South Africa prior to studying in England from 1962 to 1966, where he was also curate at Saint Alban's and Saint Mary's (London).

Returning to South Africa in 1967, Tutu continued to pastor significant churches and also began teaching at the Federal Theological Seminary, and at the National University. In 1975 he was named the Anglican Dean of Johannesburg. In 1976 Tutu was consecrated as the Bishop of Lesotho. He became the first black General Secretary of the South African Council of Churches, and under his leadership the SACC became a powerful, spiritual force for racial equality in South Africa.

Since 1986 Tutu has served as the Anglican Archbishop of Capetown. From the beginning of his ministry he was a leading opponent of apartheid (the legal system of racial segregation). His opposition to inequality was firmly rooted in Tutu's Christian faith; the universal character of the gospel of Jesus Christ and the dignity of humans as creatures created in the image of God were persistent themes with him. For the same reasons he also opposed armed resistance against the government, and urged a program of peaceful transition—very much like the one that actually brought an end to apartheid. Archbishop Tutu remains a leading spokesman for racial equality and human rights in South Africa and around the world. In token of his worldwide impact, Desmond Tutu was awarded the Noble Peace Prize in 1985, the Gold Medal for the Society for the Family of Man (1983), and the Martin Luther King Peace Award (1986).

BISHOP TUTU'S TESTIMONY[55]

We have no political axes to grind, and I think that should be stressed. The same gospel of Jesus Christ, which compels us to reject apartheid as totally unchristian, is the very gospel that constrains us to work for justice, for peace and reconciliation. God has given us a mandate to be ministers of His reconciliation.

We thank God that you and your government have come to recognize that the destiny of the peoples of South Africa cannot be decided by one group alone. We want to urge you, yet again, to negotiate for orderly change, by calling a National Convention, where our common future can be mapped out by the acknowledged leaders of every section of the South African population. To this end we believe fervently that the political prisoners in jail, in detention, in exile, must be permitted to attend such a convention. After all, your predecessor Mr. Vorster counselled Mr. Ian Smith to release black political prisoners, and sit around a conference table with them to try to hammer out a solution for their country. . . .

We believe that there can be no real peace in our beloved land until there is fundamental change. General Malan has said that the crisis in South Africa is 20% military and 80% political. You yourself have courageously declared that whites must be ready to adapt or die. This adapting, or change, has to go to the heart of

[55]Desmond Tutu, *Crying in the Wilderness: The Struggle for Justice in South Africa* (Grand Rapids, Mich.: Wm. B. Eerdmans, 1982), pp. 55–58. Used by kind permission of William B. Eerdmans Publishing Company and Cassell PLC, London. This address was given at a meeting of the South African Council of Churches (SACC) and the South African government. While many of Bishop Tutu's points were appreciated by the government, no formal support for them was forthcoming.

the matter—to the dismantling of apartheid. Please believe us when we say there is much goodwill left, although we have to add time and patience are running out. Hatred, bitterness and anger are growing, and unless something is done to demonstrate your intentions to bring about fundamental change, leading to power sharing, then we are afraid that the so-called ghastly alternative will be upon us. We recognize that this kind of fundamental change cannot happen overnight, and so we suggest that only four things need be done to give real hope that this change is going to happen. We can assure you that if we go along this road, you will gain most of South Africa and the world, while losing some of your party dissidents. These are the four points:

1. *Let the government commit themselves to a common citizenship in an undivided South Africa.* If this does not happen we will have to kiss goodbye to peaceful change.

2. *Please abolish the Pass Laws.* Nothing is more hateful in a hateful system for blacks than these laws. Let it be a phased process, because none of us want to have a chaotic country. But I wish God could give me the words that could describe the dramatic change that would occur in relationships in this country, if the real abolition of the Pass Laws were to happen.

3. *Please stop immediately all population removals and the uprooting of people.* It is in my view totally evil and has caused untold misery.

4. *Set up a uniform educational system.* We are glad to note that you have agreed to the calling up of a commission to look into this matter. We want to suggest, in relation to this, that all universities be declared open, and that the black universities be free to appoint blacks who have credibility in the black community. Otherwise we fear that the unrest in these institutions will continue.

If these four things were done, as starters, then we would be the first to declare out loud: please give the government a chance, they seem in our view to have embarked on the course of real change. I certainly would be one of the first to shout this out from the rooftops. For then, through that process, we would all have *real* security, not a security that depends on force for its upholding. What a wonderful country we can have when we all, black and white, walk out heads high to this glorious future together. Because we will have a non-racial society, a just society, where everyone, black and white, is a child of God, created in his image. And you, sir, will go down in history as a truly great man. If this does not happen now, urgently, then I fear we will have to say we have had it. But God is good, and God loves all of us, and God has filled this country with His Holy Spirit. Let us be open to that Holy Spirit and share our fears and anxieties. . . .

AN EASTER MESSAGE[56]

Nothing could have been deader than Jesus on the Cross on that first Good Friday. And the hopes of his disciples had appeared to die with his crucifixion. Nothing could have been deeper than the despair of his followers when they saw their Master hanging on the Cross like a common criminal. The darkness that covered the earth for three hours during that Friday symbolized the blackness of their despair.

And then Easter happened. Jesus rose from the dead. The incredible, the unexpected happened. Life triumphed over death, light over darkness, love over hatred, good over evil. That is what Easter means—hope prevails over despair. Jesus reigns as Lord of Lords and King of Kings. Oppression and injustice and suffering can't be the end of the human story. Freedom and justice, peace and reconciliation, are his will for all of us, black and white, in this land and throughout the world. Easter says to us that despite everything to the contrary, his will for us will prevail, love will prevail over hate, justice over injustice and oppression, peace over exploitation and bitterness. The Lord is risen. Alleluia.

THE CERTAINTY OF FREEDOM[57]

We often hear it said that people learn from history—not to repeat the mistakes of the past and to benefit from the experience of others. But a cynic, looking at our sorry record, declared: "We learn from history that we don't learn from history." There is much evidence to support that remark. We have a wonderful capacity for self-deception. When we are driving along our roads we see the wrecks that lie about our roadsides—cars that for one reason or another have come to grief. Almost always we tell ourselves that could not happen to me—it always happens to others, doesn't it?

I write in this vein to set the backdrop to my belief—that the liberation and freedom of the blacks in this land are inevitable. And the liberation of blacks involves the liberation of whites in our beloved country, because until blacks are free, the whites can never be really free. There is no such thing as separate freedom—freedom is indivisible. At the present time we see our white fellow South Africans investing much of their resources to protect their so-called separate freedoms and privileges. They have little time left to enjoy them as they check the burglar proofing, the alarm system, the gun under the pillow and the viciousness of the watchdog. These resources could be employed in more creative ways to improve the quality of life of the entire community. Our white fellow South Africans think that their security lies in possessing a formidable and so-

---

[56]Ibid., pp. 82–83. Used by kind permission of Wm. B. Eerdmans Publishing Company, and Cassell PLC, London.

[57]Ibid., pp. 87–89. Used by kind permission of Wm. B. Eerdmans Publishing Company, and Cassell PLC, London. Bishop Tutu wrote this article on November 8, 1978.

phisticated arsenal of weapons. But they must know in their hearts that the security of all of us consists in a population whose members, black and white, are reasonably contented because they share more equitably in the good things of life, which all, black and white, have co-operated to produce.

So why do I believe that black liberation is inevitable? Or to put it another way: "Why do I believe that real change, not just cosmetic change, is inevitable?" I believe this to be so because even the government thinks it must happen. Long ago, oh so long ago, we were told that South Africa was moving away from discrimination based on race. Nearly everybody is agreed that change is necessary. . . . But more fundamentally, I believe history teaches us a categorical lesson that once a people are determined to become free, then nothing in the world can stop them reaching their goal. In the eighteenth century, Great Britain enjoyed a hegemony that extended to what came to be called the New World. She ruled over the thirteen Colonies of North America, as their Mother Country. These Colonies began to chafe at the bit, to find their colonial status galling. They had heard a British Parliamentarian pleading the case for their independence, and proclaiming: "Taxation without representation is tyranny." When their appeals for self-determination appeared to fall on deaf ears, then the thirteen Colonies, these puny things, threw the gauntlet down to the intimidating British Empire. The struggle seemed wholly unequal, but in the end, the thirteen Colonies emerged victorious against formidable odds. Nobody would have thought that when they signed their Declaration of Independence on 4 July 1776, that the thirteen Colonies would emerge the victors, thereby laying the foundation for the present-day United States of America.

There are many other examples from history. France, through the French Revolution with its slogan of Liberty, Fraternity, and Equality, when the exploited, against all the odds, overturned an oppressive system. In modern times we have had the Civil Rights movement in the USA, and the emergence out of colonial bondage of the so-called Dark Continent. Then there was the extraordinary resistance of the peasant people of Vietnam, who frustrated the efforts first of France, and then, incredibly, of the most powerful nation of the world—the USA—who were made to bite the dust in this struggle for the right to self-determination of a small people. My last reference is from the history of the Afrikaners. They believed themselves to be victims of British exploitation and misunderstanding. And we know what happened. They triumphed so that today they are at the pinnacle of their power.

It seems, therefore, to be a universal law that when a people decide to become free, then absolutely nothing will eventually prevent them from reaching their goal. Why should it be thought that we blacks in South Africa will prove the exception to this rule?

For those among our people who feel despondent and hopeless, I want to assert that we shall be free. Do not despair of this. We shall be free because our cause is a just cause. We do not want to dominate others. We just want to have our humanity acknowledged. Our freedom is not in the gift of the white people. They cannot decide to give or to withhold it. Our freedom is an inalienable right bestowed on us by God. And the God whom we worship has always shown himself to be one who takes sides. He is a God who opposes evil and injustice and oppression. He is a God who sides with those who are oppressed because he is that kind of God, and not because the oppressed are morally better than their oppressors. And in setting at liberty the oppressed and exploited, he will also set free those who are enslaved by their human sinfulness. Let us rejoice. Let us lift up our heads and straighten our drooping shoulders. God cares and God will act decisively to bring justice, peace, and reconciliation in our land. We will walk, black and white together, into this new South Africa, where people will matter because they are persons of infinite value, created in the image of God, the liberator God.

General Index*

Abandonment, 307, **312–14**, 372, **384**,
Abraham, 12, 13, 103, 139, 294, 414
Abstinence, 46, 71, 224, 301, 324, 325, 326, 343.
   See also Prudentials, Temperance
Acceptance (a sense of), 348, 394, 403
Activist Piety, 14–15, **288–89**, 317, 318, 382. *See*
   also Mary and Martha, Service
Adam, 5, 6, 9, 10, 14, 67, 81, 90, 100, 147, 167,
   188, 252, 272, 273, 277, 321, 340, 352, 402,
   403
Affections (religious), 11, 69, 70, 71, 92, 96, 105,
   152, 184, 199, 252, **253–55**, 263, 266, 272, 333,
   335–38, **338–41**, **355–59**, 394
Affirmative theologies, 129–31
Affliction, 266, **279–80**, 285, 292, 306, 334, 398,
   400. *See also* Persecution, Tribulation
Africa, 60, 63, 73, 103, **457–62**
African-Americans, 45, 45n (hymnody), **349–50**,
   377, 406, **408–09**, **425–31**, **431–39**
Against Heresies, 8, 20n, 66
Agnes of Prague, St., **166–68**
Aldersgate experience (John Wesley's), 17,
   319–20
Alienation, 6, 9, 10, 91, 340
Allegory, 73, **74–76**, 141
Altar, 13, 138, 156, **275**, 288, 350, 352, 353, 354,
   419, 420, 421, 456
Ambrose of Milan, St., 39, 107–8
Anaesthesia, 73
Anabaptist tradition, 23, 35, 205, **222–30**
Anchorite(ss), 34, 25, 188. *See also* Hermits
"And Can It Be," 321
Anglican tradition, 17, 36, 39, 46, 48, 205,
   240–44, **274–82**, **286–92**, 318, 381, 454, 457,
   458
Anselm of Canterbury, St., 141, **142–48**, 149
Antichrist, **156–59**, 370
Antony, St. the Hermit, 4, 22, 34, **87–88**, 111,
   111n
Apatheia, 73, 262
Apologist(s), 58, 63, 66, 73, 86, 88, 293
Apostle(s), 55, 64, 65, 66, 68, 74, 117, 141, 150,
   218, 229, 238, 239, 240, 241, 260
Aquinas, Thomas St., 141, **172–77**, 177, 385, 457
"Arise, My Soul, Arise," 26
Aristotle, 141, 172, 173, 176, 457
Arius(ism), 86, 86n, 94
Arndt, Johann, 27, **270–74**
Athanasius of Alexanderia, 20, 22, 34, 39, **86–88**
Arnold, Heinri, 446

Ascetics(ism), 41, **73–74**, **113–20**, **124–28**, 141,
   182, 377. *See also* Mortification
Atone(ment), 26, **144–46**, 190, 200, 218, 243, 292,
   320, 321, 329, 344, 352, 354, 362, 394, 403
Augsburg Confession, 37, 39, 394
Augustine of Hippo, St., 6, 8, 10, 10n, 14, 30, 31,
   31n, 44, 87, **103–113**, 142, 176, 176n, 177,
   180, 182, 211, 213, 256, 298, 310, 365, 457
Augustinian spirituality, 3, 15, 149, 206, 211,
   217, 293
Augustus, Caesar, Emperor, 407
Aurelius, Marcus, Emperor, 66
Awe, (sense of), 18, 289, **378–81**, 414

Baptism, 22, 24, 30, 35, 41, 57, 58, 63n, 69, 136,
   223–24, **226**, 273, **276**, 332, 336, 365, 394, 396,
   404, 418, 419, 420
  of the Holy Ghost, **347**
Baptist church, 46, 372, 425
Barth, Karl, 14, 14n, 42, **385–90**, 390, 414
Bartholeme de las Casas, 205, **235–40**
Base communities, 36, 452
Basil the Great, St., 88, **91–94**
Baxter, Richard, 363
Beguines, 141, **168–72**, 177
Bellarmine, Robert, 3n
Benedict of Nursia, St., 4, 22, 34, 113, **124–28**
Benedictine spirituality, 141, 148, 149, 153, 172, 222
Bernard of Clairvaux, St., 7, 7n, 19, 25, 30, 141,
   148–53, 154, 211, 271, 288
Bible (Scripture), 8, 12, 19, 37, 45, 46, 47, 48,
   49–50, **50–51**, 53, 55, 69, 73, 76, 80, 88, 93,
   94, 95, 96, 99, 100, 102, 111, 113, 114, 118,
   120, 121, 122, 123, 125, 126, 127, 133, 141,
   152, 154, 159, 172, 196, 197, 210, 213, 214,
   220, 221, 227, 236, 243, 244, 249, 263, **278–79**,
   300, 302–03, 309, 311, 318, 320, 322, 323, 326,
   329, 333, 337, 339, 340, 341, 342, 344, 346,
   348, 351, 352, 353, 360, 361, 362, 379, 385,
   402, 403, 404, 406, 446, 447, 450
  interpretation of, **74–76**, 108, 141. *See also Lecto*
   Divina.
Biel, Gabriel, 15
Bishop, 55, 57, 87, 101, 121, 122, 123, 124, 128,
   135, 159, 162, 217, 230, 235, 458
Black Theology and Black Power, 431, 432, 435
Blake, William, 383
Blood of Christ, 26, 31, 32, 56, **68–69**, 144, 158,
   162, 187, 190, 208, 233, **242**, 279, 280, 320,
   321, 327, 354, 367, 368

---

*Page numbers indicated in **bold** refer to particularly pertinent materials in primary source documents.

Love (*continued*)
Four Degrees of, 7, **149–53**
gift of, 29, 34, 45
of God, 20, 24, 25, 26, 50, 51, 104, 105, 109,
   209, 266, 329, 339, 348, 382–83. *See also* God
God is Love, **179–80**, 206, **206–9**
Implicit and Explicit Love, **399–401**
Love Your Enemies, **427–31**
of neighbor, 10, 136, 186. *See also* Neighbor
perfection of, 34, 45, 74, 93, 127, 150, 152, 170.
   See also Perfection
Pure Love, 209–10
Three Rules of, **210–11**
Lust(s), 105, 108, 109, 126, 136, 150, 197, 278,
   305, 446
Luther, Martin, 4, 10, 10n, 15, 16, 17, 17n, 42, 50,
   205, **211–17**, 231, 271, 303, 305, 320, 388, 389,
   394, 405
Lutheran, 15, 24, 35, 37
spirituality, 3, 42, 46, 205, 212, 226, 270, 271, 390

Macquarrie, John, 39, 39n
Macrina, (the younger) St., **88–91**, 94
Malcolm X, 431, 432
Man (humanity), 5, 6, 10, 25, 30, 67, 104, 450,
   461. *See also* Human nature
Manicheanism, 103, 107
Manresa (Ignatius at), **248–50**
Marks of Christ (stigmata), 25, 26, 189, 198. *See
   also* Wounds
Marriage, **65–66**, 206, 456–57
spiritual marriage, 214, 255, **259–260**, **384–85**.
   See also Union, Unitive Dimension
Martyr(dom), 4, 24, 25, 33, 35, 41, 44, 53, **54–55**,
   60–63, 66, 73, 103, 153, 189, 201, **225–28**, 246,
   293, 369, 371, 377, 394, **352–53**, 390, 425
Mary (the Virgin), **38–40**, 40, 56, 65, 67, **81–86**,
   138, 139, **146**, 167, 191–92, 210, **226**, 247, 248,
   249, 251, 252, 292, 365, 419, **423–25**, 451, 455
and Christology, 38–40, 146, **423–25**
intercession of, 39, 226, **423–25**, 455
Queen of heaven, **146**, 424
theotokos, 39
Mary and Martha, **114–15**, **181–82**, **199–200**, 255,
   260–62. *See also* Activist piety, Service
Mass, 19, 20, 203, 207, 208, 248, 249, 300, 455.
   See also Communion, Eucharist, Lord's
   Supper
Maximus the confessor, 32, **132–36**
McBrien, Richard, 3n, 12n, 39, 41n, 128n
Means of grace, 5, 17, 23, 24, 46, 47, 48, 113–14,
   212, 230, 258, 259, 268, 283, 296, 301, **325–27**,
   444–48. *See also* Bible, Disciplines, Fasting,
   Mortification, Prayer, Sacraments
Mechthild of Magedeburg, **168–72**
Meditation, 11, 24, 34, 49, 127, 128, 143, 179, 198,
   212, 235, 250, 251, 264, 283, 284, 305, 333,
   355, 395, 404, 423, 442, 445
Mendicant tradition, 34, 140, 141
Memo on Christian Perfection, **284–86**
Mercy, 10, 16, 49, 104, 112, 127, 143, 144, 188,
   193, 242, 244, 257, 296, 298, 337, 341, 366,
   368, 411, 418
Merits, 10, 26, 243, 363, 367, 405
Methodist(ism), 17, 35, 43, 45, 270, 287, 306n,
   318–32, 350
Merton, Thomas, 49, 377, **417–25**
Meyerdroff, John, 21, 21n

Mind, **231–32**, **238–40**, 266, 272, 298, 308, 310,
   315, 316, 339, 342, 343, 344, 347, 356, 400.
   See also Reason
Missal, 48, 419
Monk(s), 34, 53, 101, **113–15**, **125–28**, 141, 148,
   217, 227, 282, 418
"Four Kinds of," **125–28**. *See also* Monasticism
Montanism, 63
Moody, Dwight L., 350
More, Hannah, 270, **338–42**
Mortification, 101, 113, 114, 135, 201, 208, 259,
   261, 262, 263, 369, 446
Moses, 18, 67, 94, 95, **97–99**, 119, 130, 139, 220,
   234, 407
Mother (God as), 18, **193–95**
Monasticism, 22, 33, 34, 35, 41, 87, **91–94**, 99,
   102, 113, **113–20**, **124–28**, 137, 141, 153, 211,
   217, 222, 394, 418, 449
Mortality (s), 104, 105, 152, 155, 278, 412. *See also*
   Death, Human Nature, Man (Humans)
Mystagogy, **132–36**
Mystery(ies), 18, 98, 153, 154, 157, 158, 159, 269,
   317, 133–135. *See also* Sacraments
Mystical Theology, **128–32**
Mystics (Mysticism), 6, 8, 15, 26, 38, 43, 44, 45,
   73, 128, 132, 140, 141–42, **177–82**, 205, 262,
   271, 282, 376–77, **381–85**, 402, **415–16**
characteristics of, **381–83**
phases of, **383–85**
Mysterium tremendum, 18, 19, 207

Nature, 5, 20, 21, 42, 137, 164, **165–66**, 269,
   365–66, 414
Negative theologies (*via negativa*), 129–32, 262
Neighbor, 10, 52, 79, 149, 150, 184, 186, 197, 210,
   216, 243, 244, 283, 284, 329, 348, 395, 400,
   401, 428, 441, 443
New birth, 271, 272–74
New Seeds of Contemplation, 417, **421–25**
Niebuhr, H. Richard, 33n, 41n
Nominalist(ism), 15, 205, 211, 218
Numinious (God as), **380–81**
Nun(s), 153, 455
Nurture (Christian), 270, **259–64**

Obedience, 23, 33, 34, 53, 67, 70, 126, 151, 161,
   163, 188, 207, 231, 235, 273, 334, 348, 353,
   362, 363, 365, **368–69**, 386, 387, 392, 393, 441
Obermann, Heiko, 15, 15n
Occam, William of, 15
Oden, Thomas, 37, 38, 38n
On First Principles (De Principis), 73
On Loving God, **149–53**
On Prayer, 73–80
On the Incarnation of the Word of God, 20
Origen of Alexanderia, 49, **73–80**, 94, 116n, 132,
   149
Otto, Rudolph, 18, 18n, **378–81**

Pachomius, 34
Palm Sunday, 23, 122, 164, 250, 398
Palmer, Pheobe Worral, **350–54**
Pardon, 14, 134, 136, 244, 320, 341
Parenting, **359–64**
Parousia (return of Christ), **44–45**, 65, 135, 200
Pascal, Blaise, 270, **292–301**, 396, 396n
Pacifism (nonviolence), 35, **60–63**, **224–25**, 227,
   377, 425, **427–29**, 431

Scripture Index